Best Editorial Cartoons of the Year

BRIAN DUFFY
Courtesy Des Moines Register

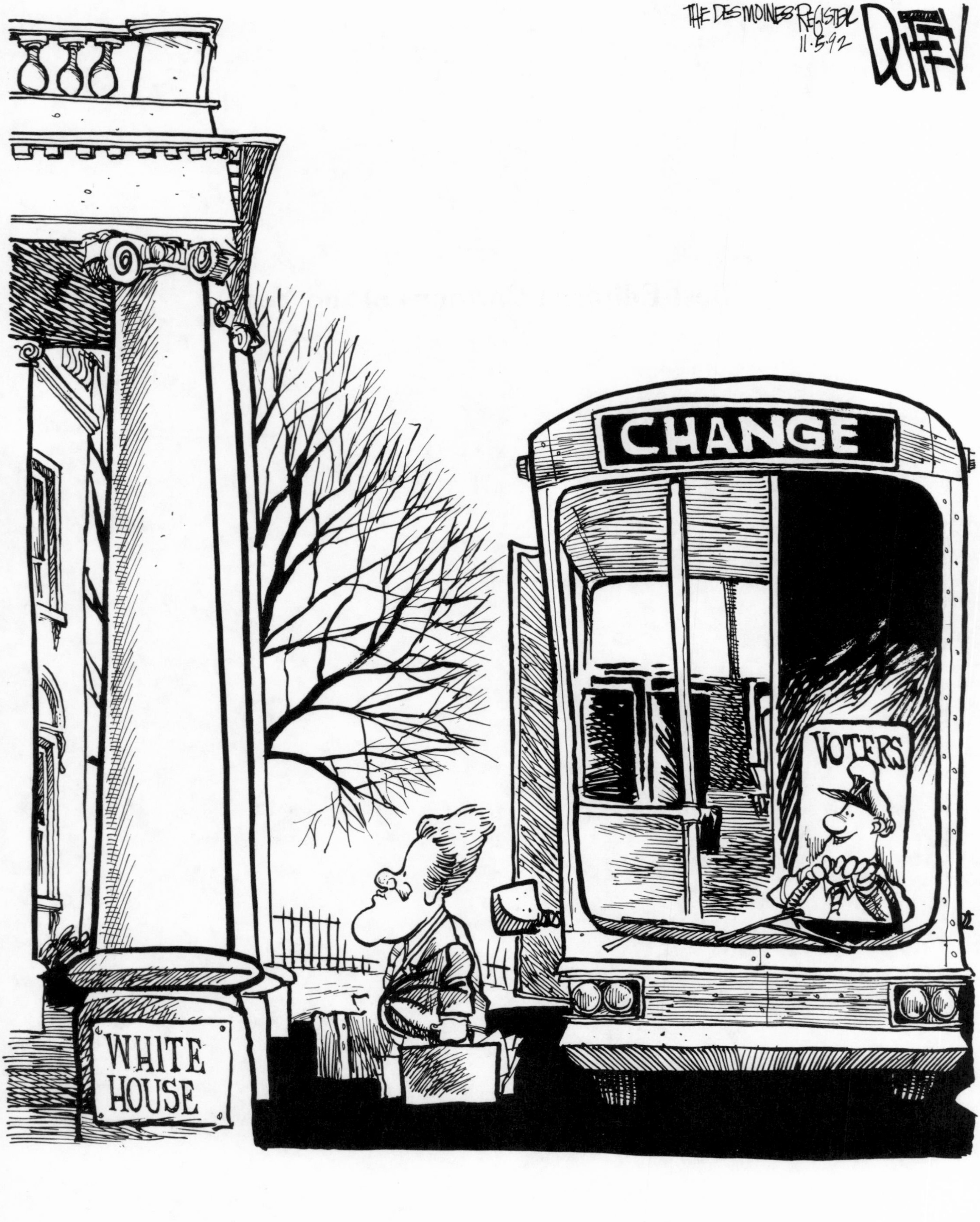
THE DES MOINES REGISTER
11-5-92
DUFFY
CHANGE
VOTERS
WHITE HOUSE

BEST EDITORIAL CARTOONS OF THE YEAR

1993 EDITION

Edited by
CHARLES BROOKS

PELICAN PUBLISHING COMPANY
Gretna 1993

The cartoons in this volume are reproduced with the expressed permission of
the individual cartoonists and their respective publications and/or syndicates.
Any unauthorized reproduction is strictly prohibited.

Library of Congress Serial Catalog Data

Best editorial cartoons. 1972-
    Gretna [La.] Pelican Pub. Co.
    v. 29 cm. annual-
"A pictorial history of the year."

    1. United States- Politics and government –
1969 – Caricatures and Cartoons – Periodicals.
E839.5.B45   320.9'7309240207   73-643645
ISSN 0091-2220   MARC-S

Manufactured in the United States of America
Published by Pelican Publishing Company, Inc.
1101 Monroe Street, Gretna, Louisiana 70053

Contents

Award-Winning Cartoons

1992 PULITZER PRIZE

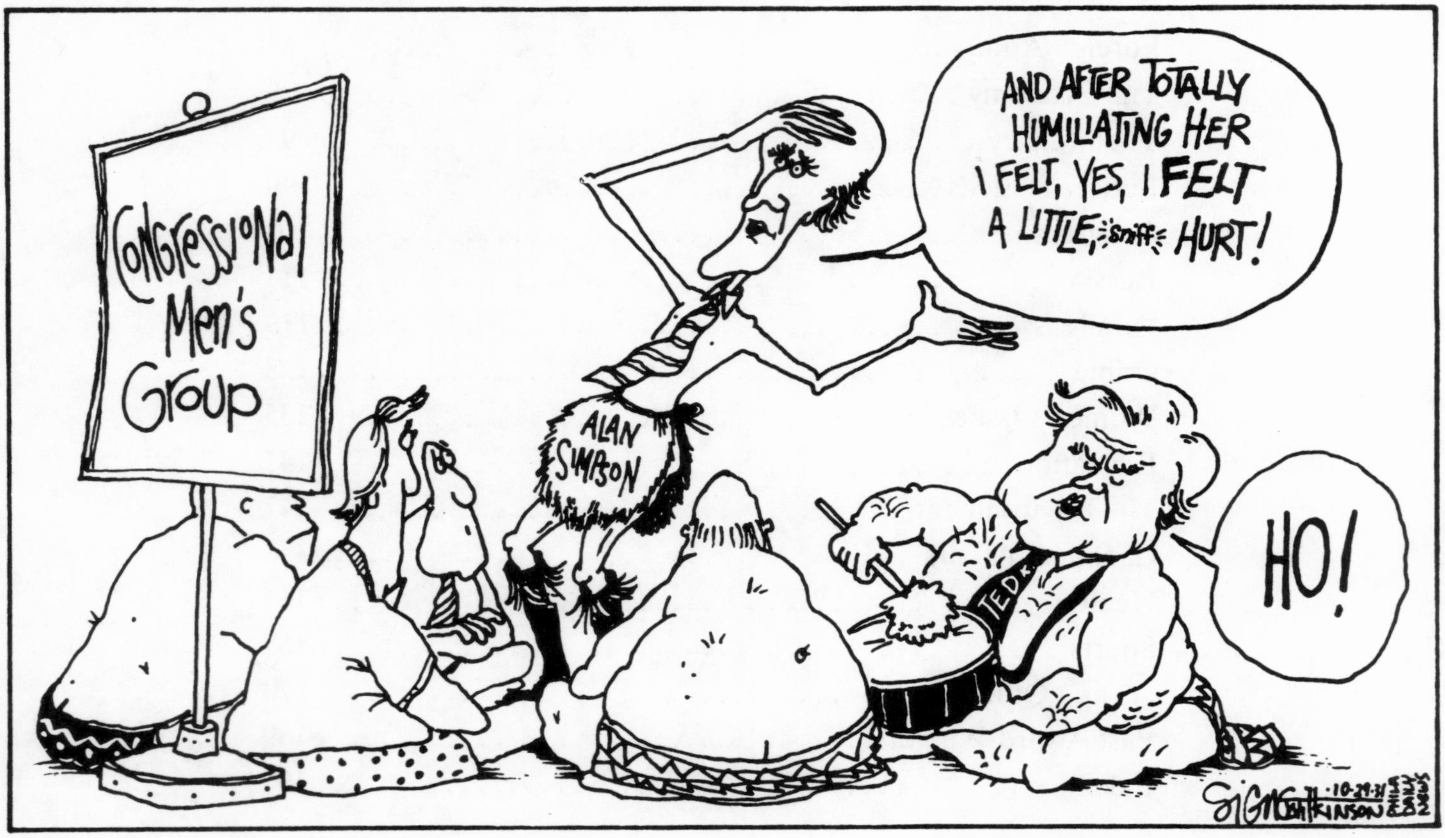
Congressional Men's Group
AND AFTER TOTALLY HUMILIATING HER I FELT, YES, I FELT A LITTLE, sniff HURT!
ALAN SIMPSON
HO!
TED

SIGNE WILKINSON
Editorial Cartoonist
Philadelphia Daily News

Native of Wichita Falls, Texas; studied at Philadelphia College of Art and Pennsylvania Academy of Fine Arts; began newspaper career as reporter for the *Daily Local News*, West Chester, Pa.; cartoonist for the *San Jose Mercury-News*; editorial cartoonist, *Philadelphia Daily News*, 1986 to present; first female editorial cartoonist to win the Pulitzer Prize.

1992 NATIONAL HEADLINERS CLUB AWARD

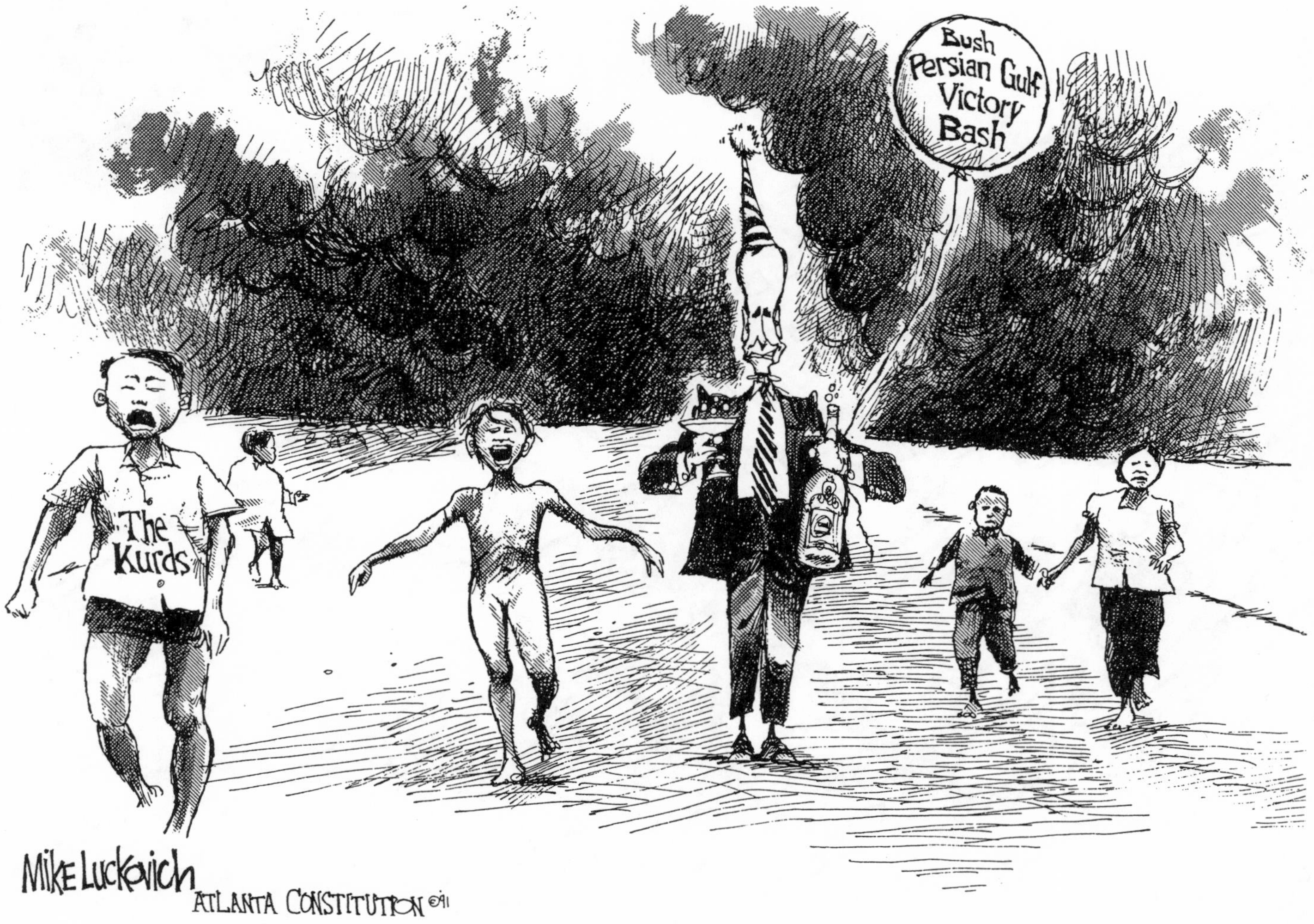
Bush Persian Gulf Victory Bash
The Kurds
MIKE LUCKOVICH
ATLANTA CONSTITUTION ©91

MIKE LUCKOVICH

Editorial Cartoonist
Atlanta Constitution

Born in 1960; editorial cartoonist, *Greenville News*, 1984-1985, the *New Orleans Times-Picayune*, 1985-1989, and the *Atlanta Constitution*, 1989 to the present; cartoons syndicated in 150 newspapers, winner of the Overseas Press Club Award, 1990.

1991 NATIONAL SOCIETY OF PROFESSIONAL JOURNALISTS AWARD
(Selected in 1992)

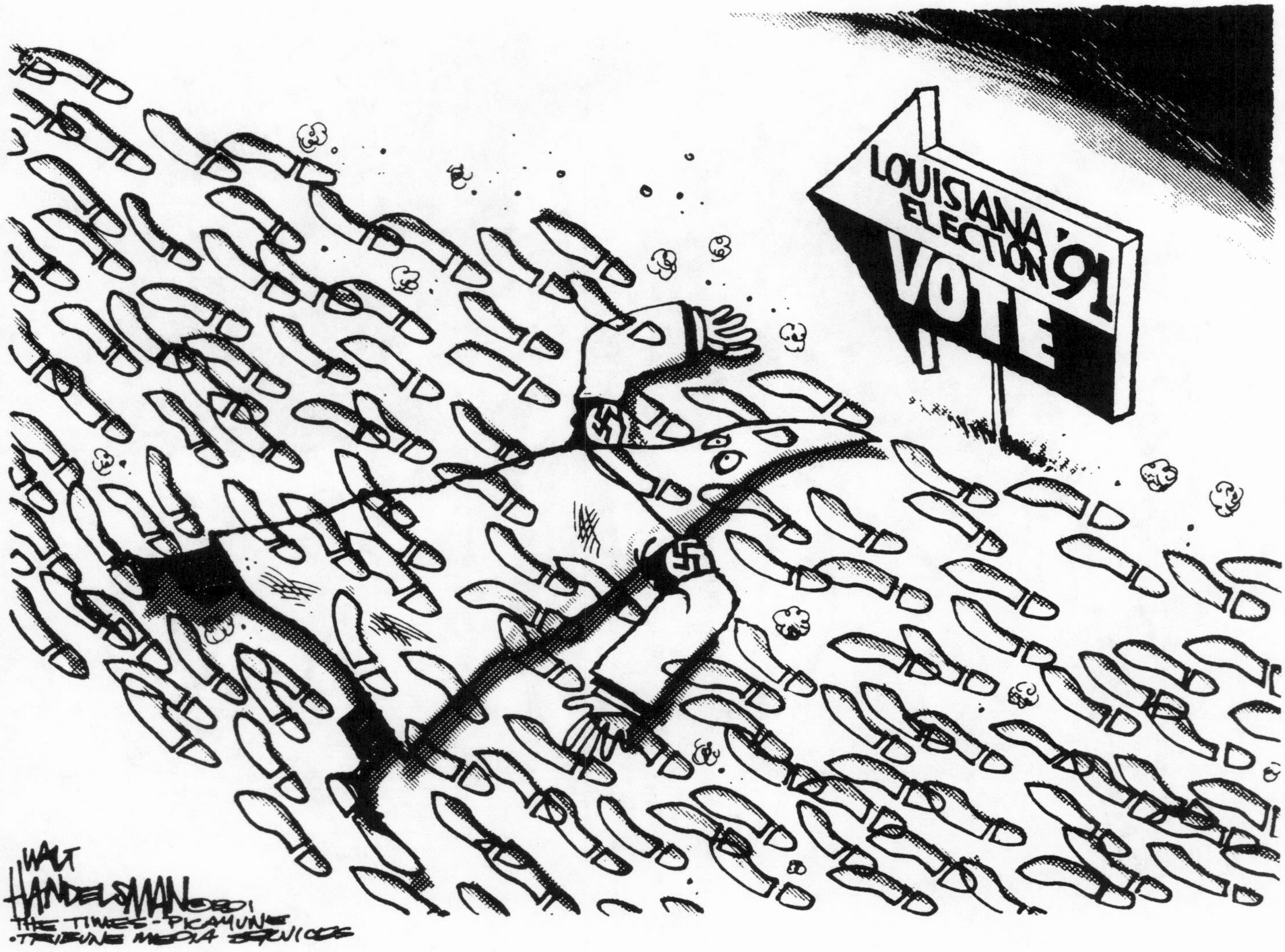
LOUISIANA ELECTION '91
VOTE
WALT HANDELSMAN ©'91
THE TIMES - PICAYUNE
• TRIBUNE MEDIA SERVICES

WALT HANDELSMAN
Editorial Cartoonist
New Orleans Times-Picayune

Born 1957; graduate of the University of Cincinnati; editorial cartoonist, the Pautuxent Publishing Corp., 1982-1985, the *Scranton Times*, 1985-1989, and the *New Orleans Times-Picayune*, 1989 to present; syndicated cartoons appear in more than eighty-five newspapers; winner of the National Headliners Club Award, 1989, and thirteen other awards for cartooning excellence.

1992 FISCHETTI AWARD

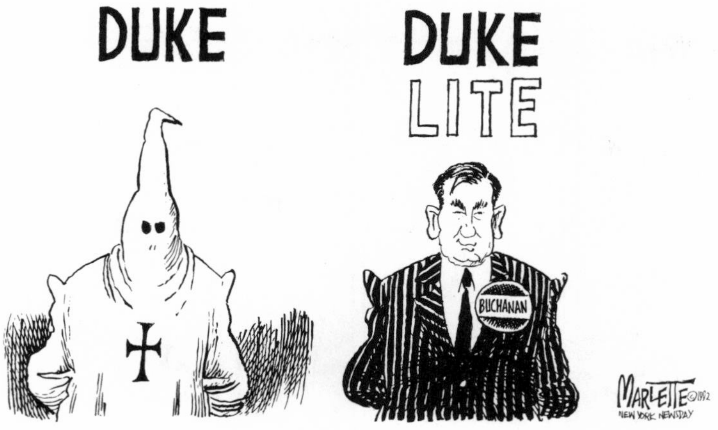
DUKE
DUKE
LITE
BUCHANAN
MARLETTE ©1992
NEW YORK NEWSDAY

DOUG MARLETTTE
Editorial Cartoonist
New York Newsday

Born in Greensboro, North Carolina, 1950; editorial cartoonist, the *Charlotte Observer*, 1972-1987, the *Atlanta Constitution*, 1987-1989, and the *New York Newsday*, 1989 to the present; draws syndicated comic strip "Kudzu"; recipient of the Nieman Fellowship; winner of the National Society of Professional Journalists Award for editorial cartooning, 1985, the National Headliners Club Award, 1988, and the Pulitzer Prize, 1988.

1992 REUBEN AWARD

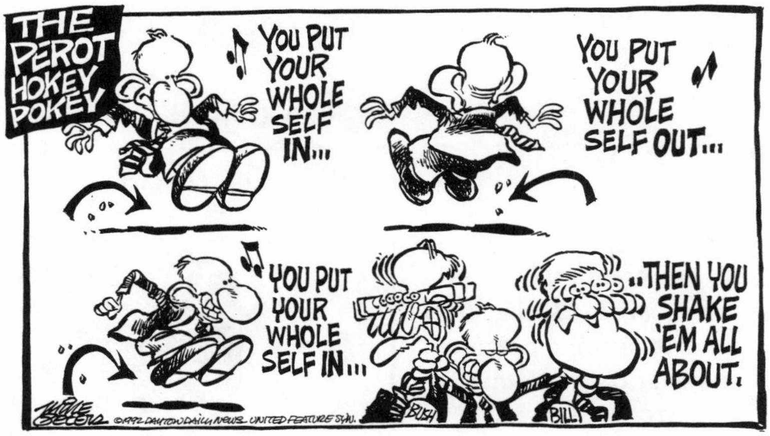
THE PEROT HOKEY POKEY
YOU PUT YOUR WHOLE SELF IN...
YOU PUT YOUR WHOLE SELF OUT...
YOU PUT YOUR WHOLE SELF IN...
..THEN YOU SHAKE 'EM ALL ABOUT.
BUSH
BILL

MIKE PETERS
Editorial Cartoonist
Dayton Daily News

Born in St. Louis, Missouri; graduate of Washington University, 1965; editorial cartoonist, the *Chicago Daily News*, 1965-1969, and the *Dayton Daily News*, 1969 to the present; winner of the Pulitzer Prize, 1981, the National Headliners Club Award, 1982 and 1987, and the National Society of Professional Journalists Award, 1985.

1992 MENCKEN AWARD

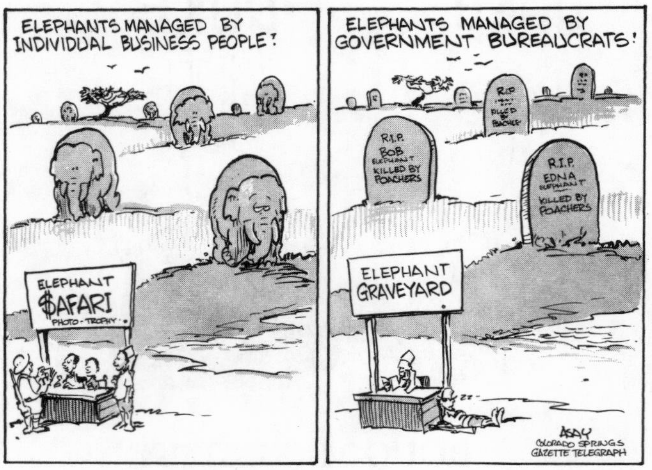
ELEPHANTS MANAGED BY INDIVIDUAL BUSINESS PEOPLE!
ELEPHANT $AFARI
PHOTO-TROPHY
ELEPHANTS MANAGED BY GOVERNMENT BUREAUCRATS!
R.I.P. BOB ELEPHANT KILLED BY POACHERS
R.I.P. EDNA ELEPHANT KILLED BY POACHERS
ELEPHANT GRAVEYARD
ASAY
COLORADO SPRINGS GAZETTE TELEGRAPH

CHUCK ASAY

Editorial Cartoonist

Colorado Springs Gazette Telegraph

Reared on a farm; teacher in public and Bureau of Indian Affairs schools; a fireman; free-lance artist; editorial cartoonist for the *Colorado Springs Gazette Telegraph*; previous winner of the Mencken Award, 1987; winner of the Best of the West Award, 1989.

1991 NATIONAL NEWSPAPER AWARD/CANADA

(Selected in 1992)

GUY BADEAUX

Editorial Cartoonist

Le Droit, Ottawa

Born in Montreal, 1949; editorial cartoonist, *Le Droit*, 1981 to the present; former president of the Association of Canadian Editorial Cartoonists; winner of the National Business Writing Award, 1986; author of three books.

"Bourassa clarifies his position"

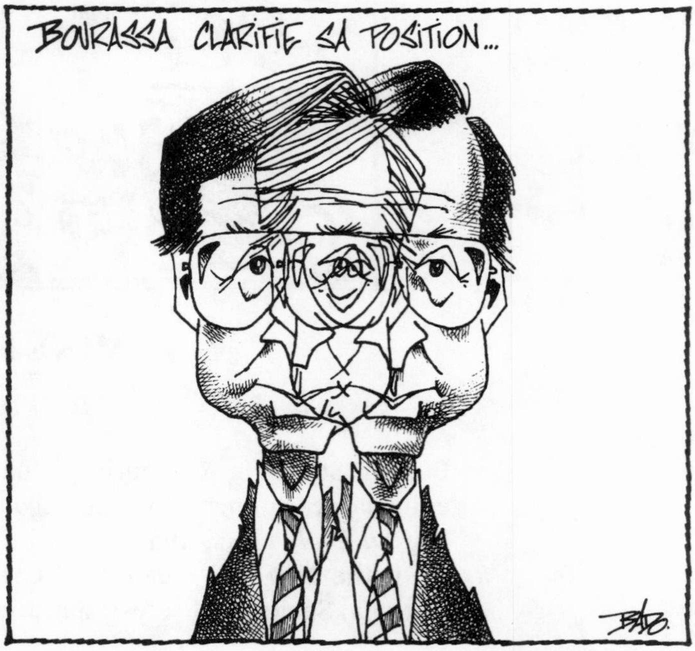
BOURASSA CLARIFIE SA POSITION...
BDO.

Best Editorial Cartoons of the Year

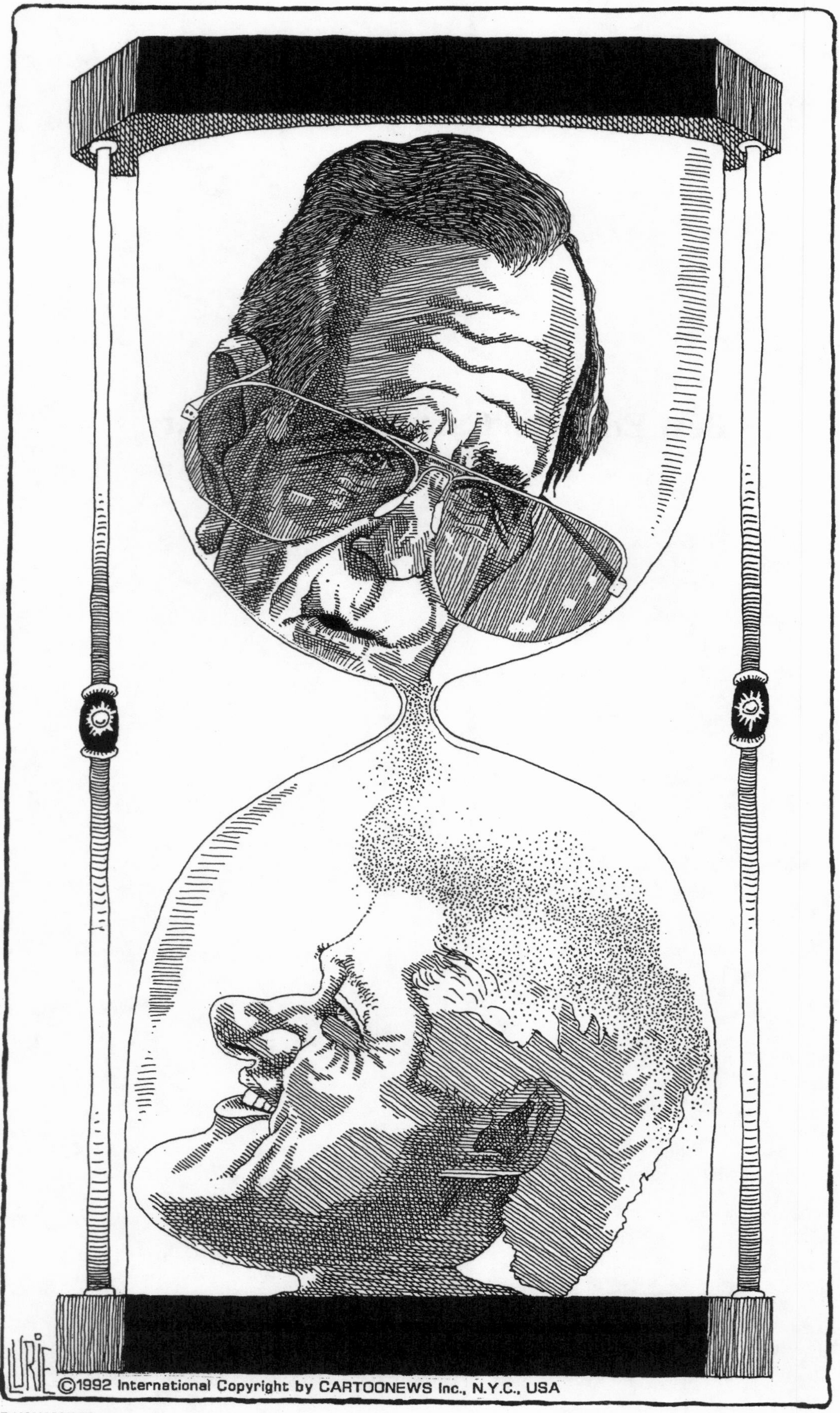
LURIE
©1992 International Copyright by CARTOONEWS Inc., N.Y.C., USA

RANAN LURIE
Courtesy Cartoonews International

1992 Campaign

The Democrats fielded six major candidates to challenge President George Bush in the 1992 campaign. There was much speculation about New York Gov. Mario Cuomo, but he eventually announced he would not be a candidate. After a heated intraparty fight, the nomination went to Arkansas Gov. Bill Clinton.

One of the major issues of the campaign was Clinton's personal character. Gennifer Flowers declared she had had a long-term affair with the Arkansas governor and played tapes of telephone conversations with him. Clinton did not exactly deny the charges but talked about how strong his marriage was. He did acknowledge having smoked marijuana, but explained, "I didn't inhale." Clinton was repeatedly questioned about avoiding the draft during the Vietnam War and his admitted demonstrations against the war while in England.

Continuing economic doldrums assured defeat for incumbent Bush, who also faced charges about the diversion of funds to the Contras and the building of Saddam Hussein's war machine.

Television commentator Pat Buchanan challenged Bush for the Republican nomination on the grounds that the president had deserted conservatives.

MICHAEL RAMIREZ
Courtesy Memphis Commercial Appeal

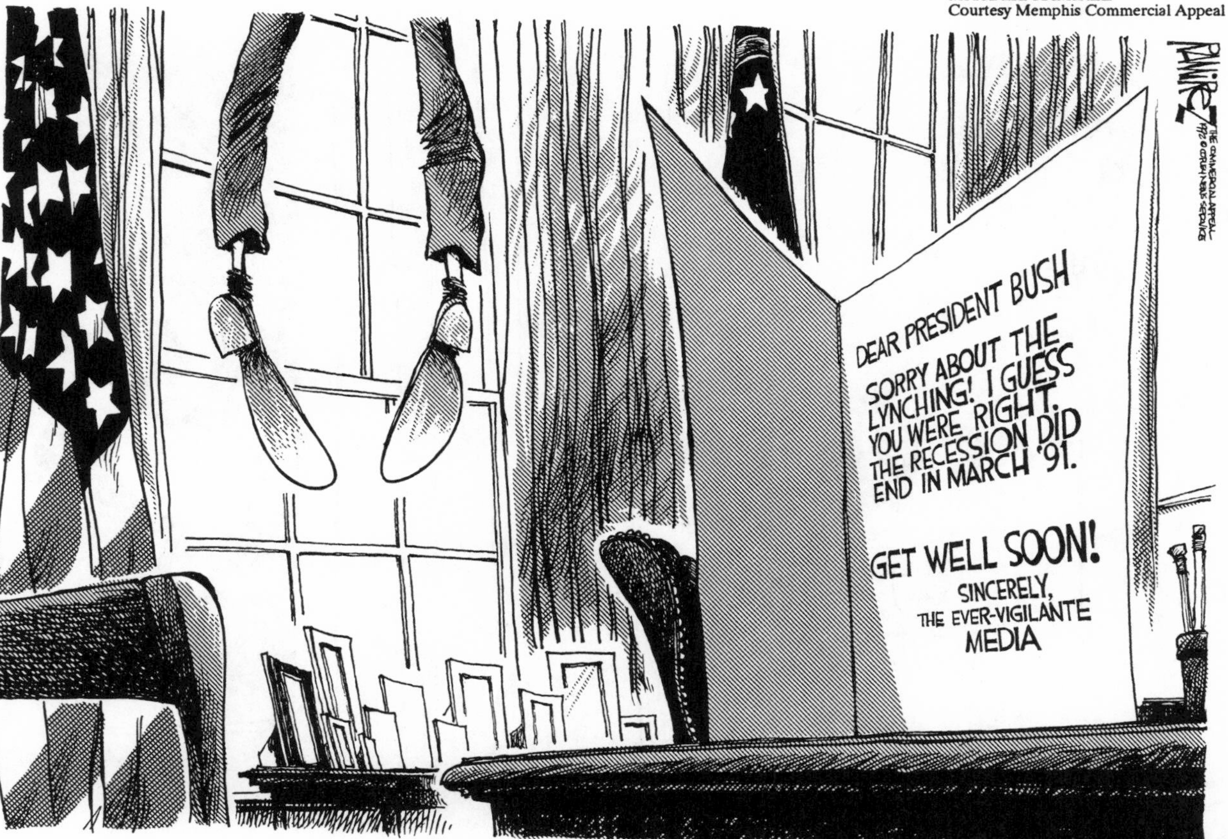
DEAR PRESIDENT BUSH
SORRY ABOUT THE LYNCHING! I GUESS YOU WERE RIGHT. THE RECESSION DID END IN MARCH '91.
GET WELL SOON!
SINCERELY, THE EVER-VIGILANTE MEDIA

WILLIAM COSTELLO
Courtesy NEA

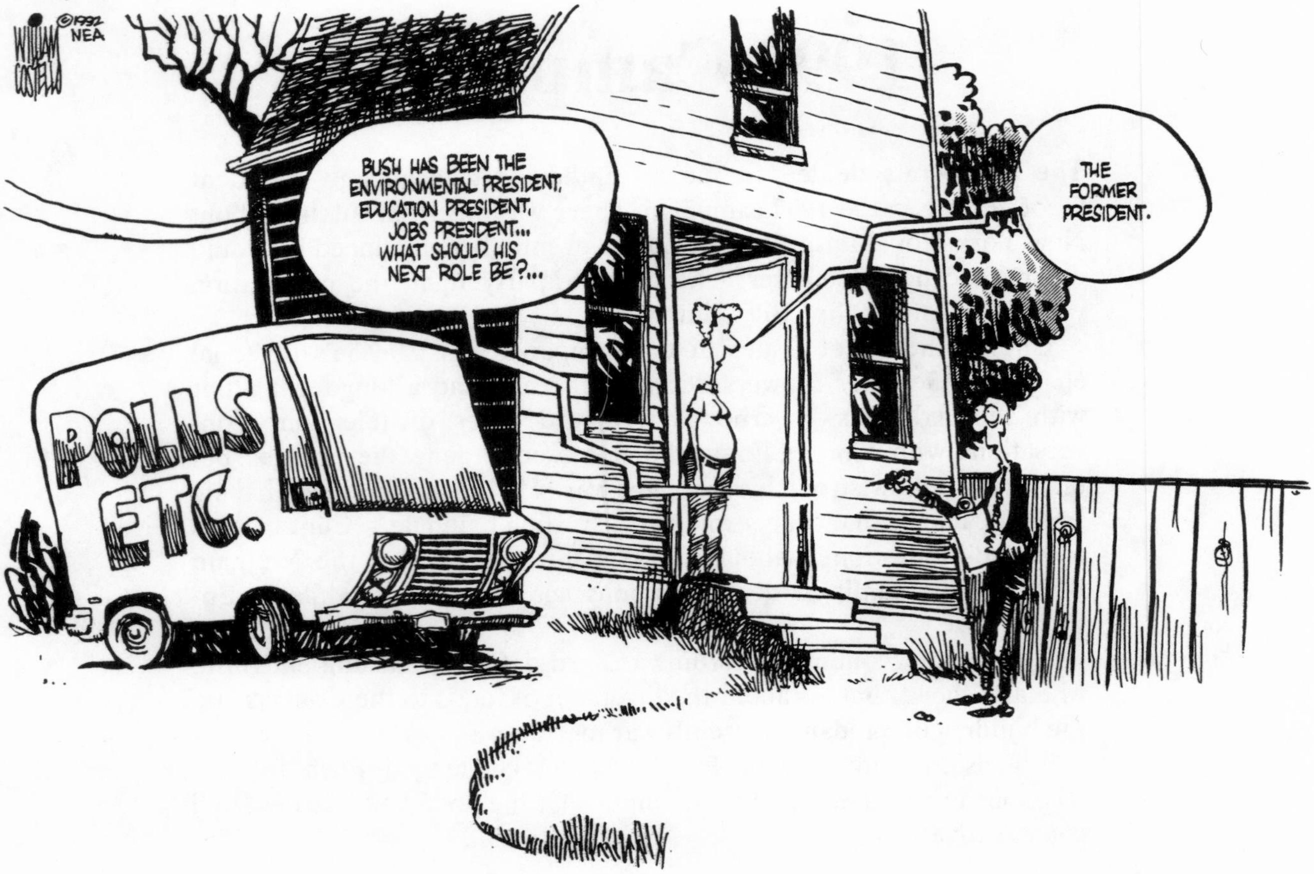
©1992 NEA
WILLIAM COSTELLO
BUSH HAS BEEN THE ENVIRONMENTAL PRESIDENT, EDUCATION PRESIDENT, JOBS PRESIDENT... WHAT SHOULD HIS NEXT ROLE BE?...
THE FORMER PRESIDENT.
POLLS ETC.

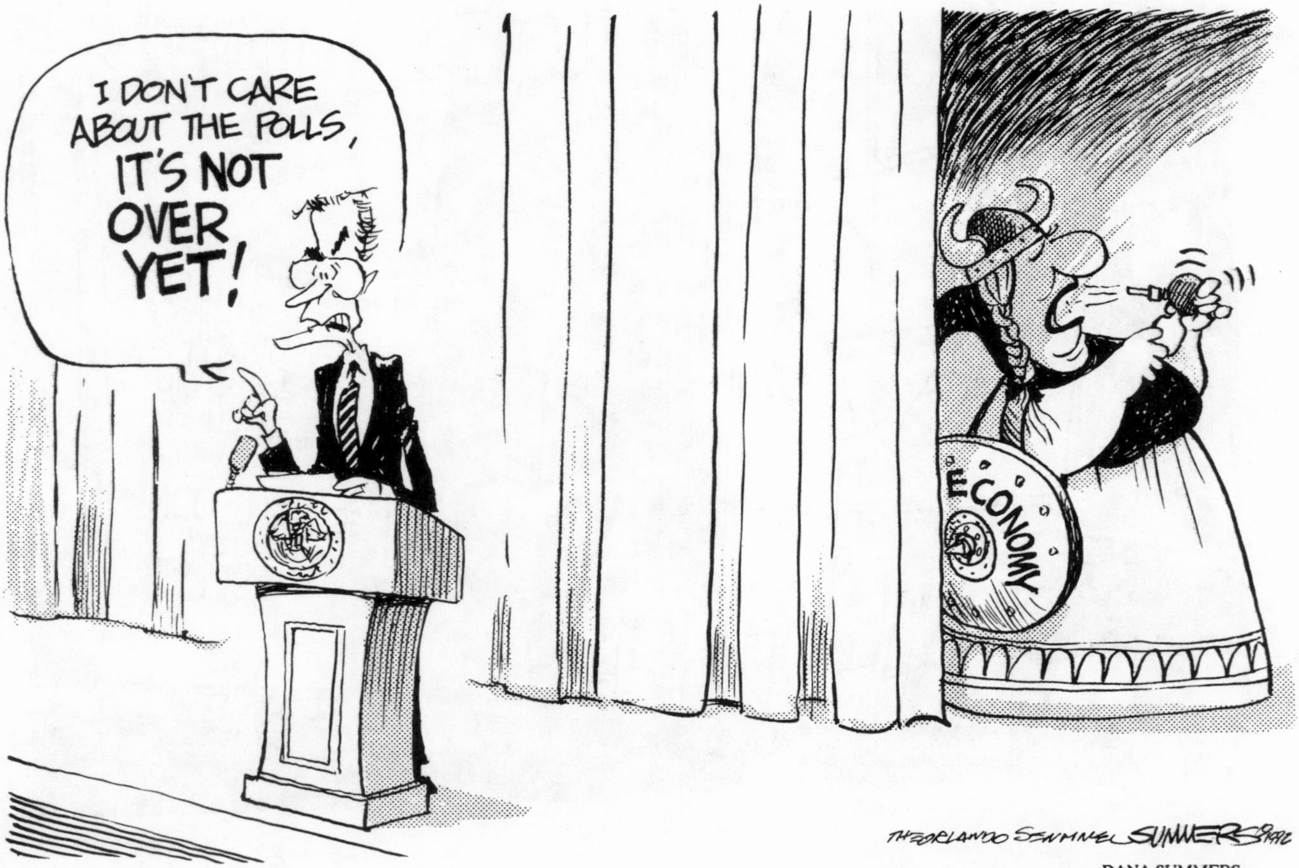
I DON'T CARE ABOUT THE POLLS, IT'S NOT OVER YET!
ECONOMY
THE ORLANDO SENTINEL SUMMERS ©1992

DANA SUMMERS
Courtesy Orlando Sentinel

MICHAEL RAMIREZ
Courtesy Memphis Commercial Appeal

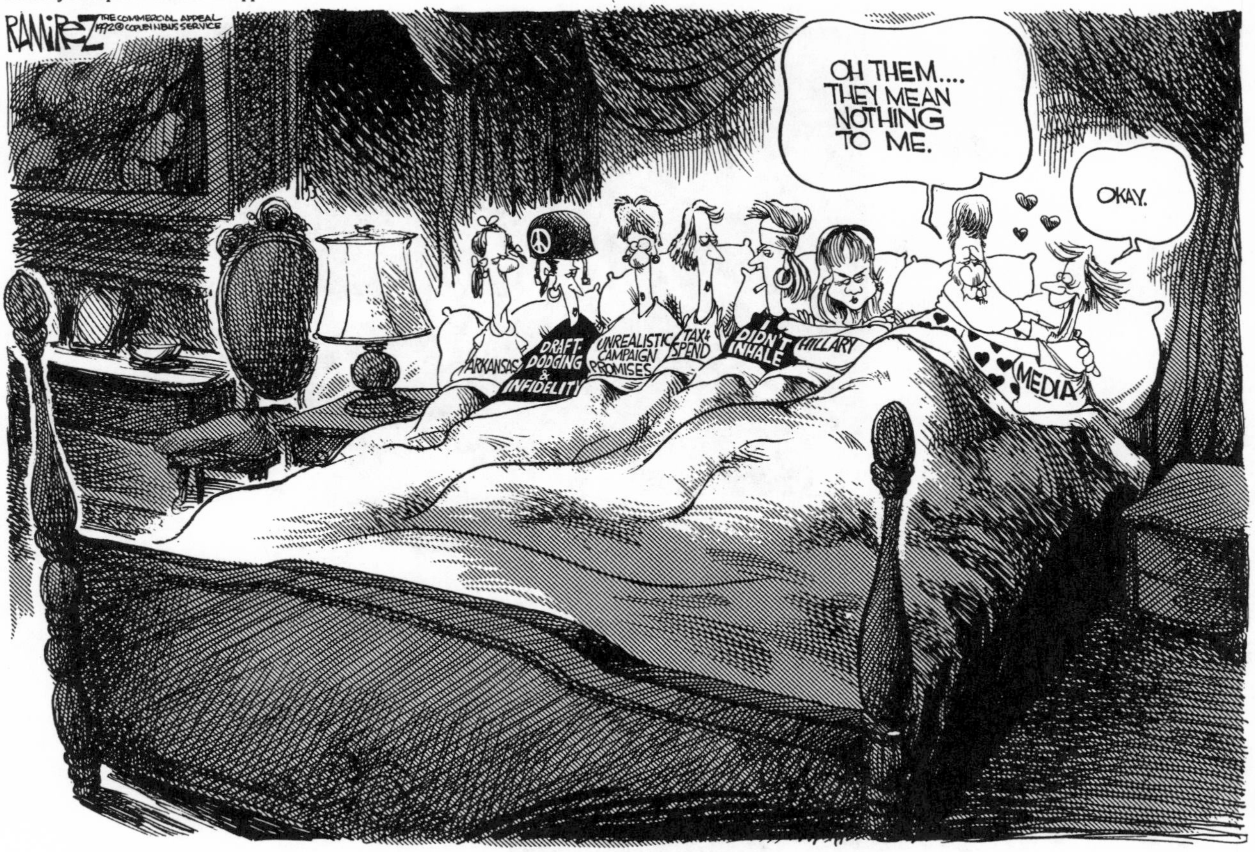
RAMIREZ THE COMMERCIAL APPEAL 1992 © COPLEY NEWS SERVICE
OH THEM.... THEY MEAN NOTHING TO ME.
OKAY.
ARKANSAS
DRAFT-DODGING & INFIDELITY
UNREALISTIC CAMPAIGN PROMISES
TAX & SPEND
I DIDN'T INHALE
HILLARY
MEDIA

DICK LOCHER
Courtesy Chicago Tribune

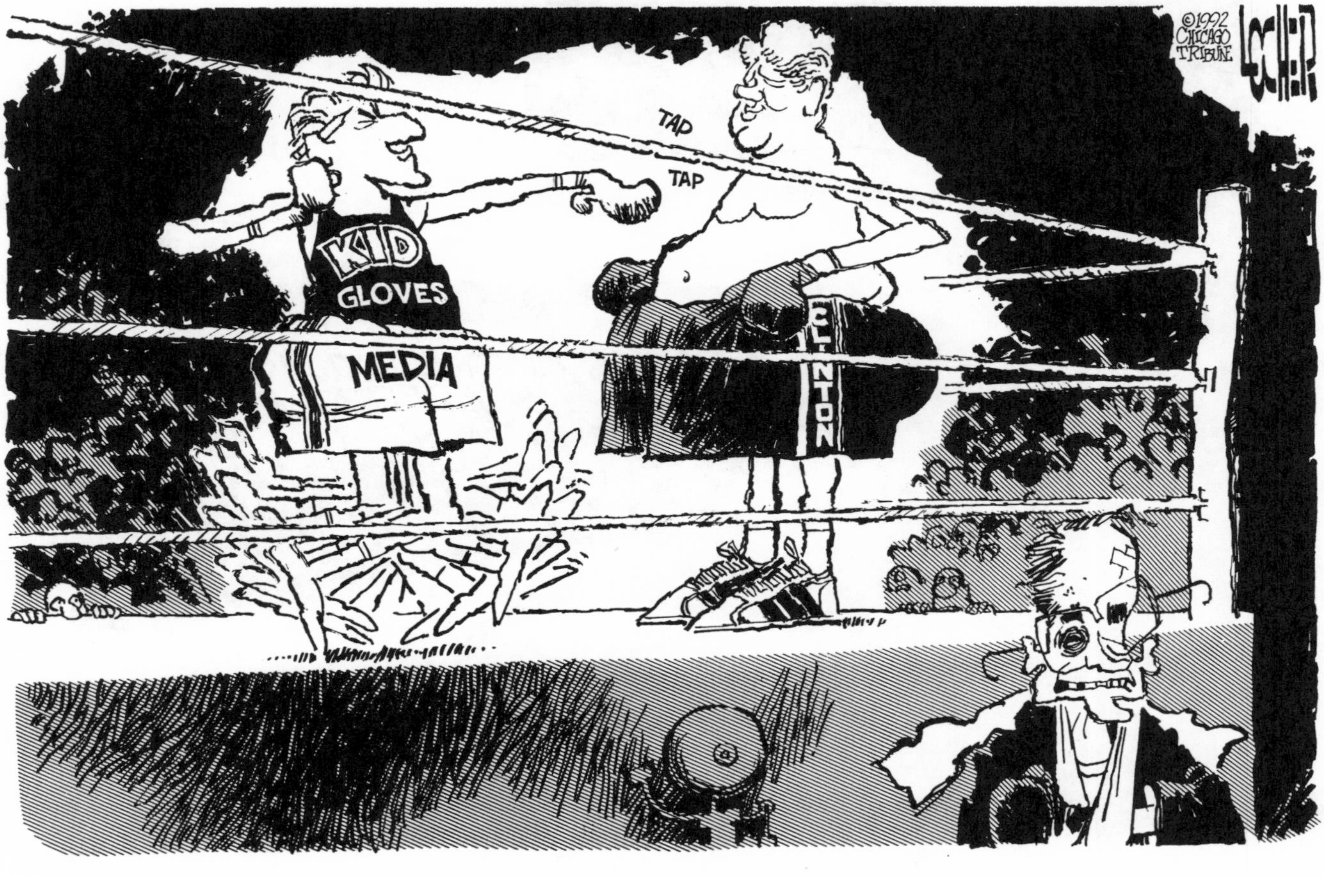
©1992 CHICAGO TRIBUNE LOCHER
TAP
TAP
KID GLOVES
MEDIA
CLINTON

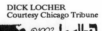

JOE MAJESKI
Courtesy The Times-Leader (Pa.)

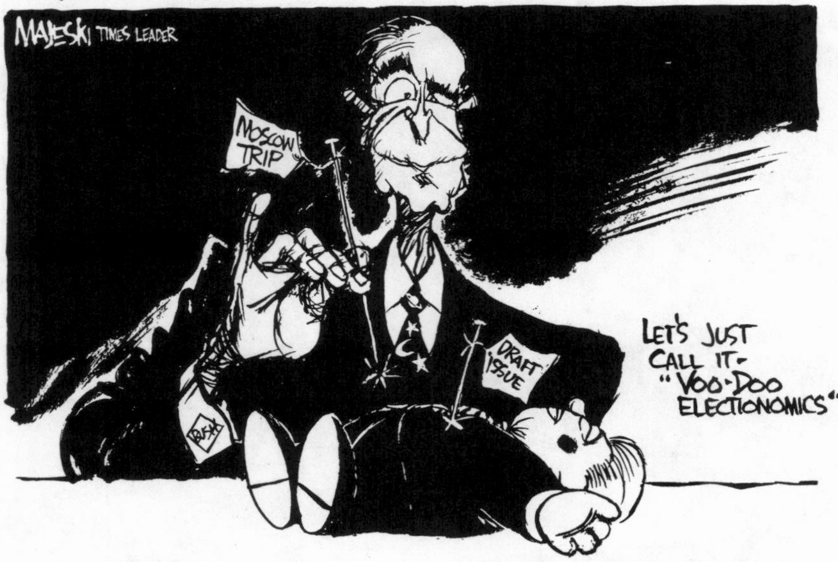
MAJESKI TIMES LEADER
MOSCOW TRIP
BUSH
DRAFT ISSUE
LET'S JUST CALL IT- "VOO-DOO ELECTIONOMICS"

DENNIS DRAUGHON
Courtesy Scranton Times

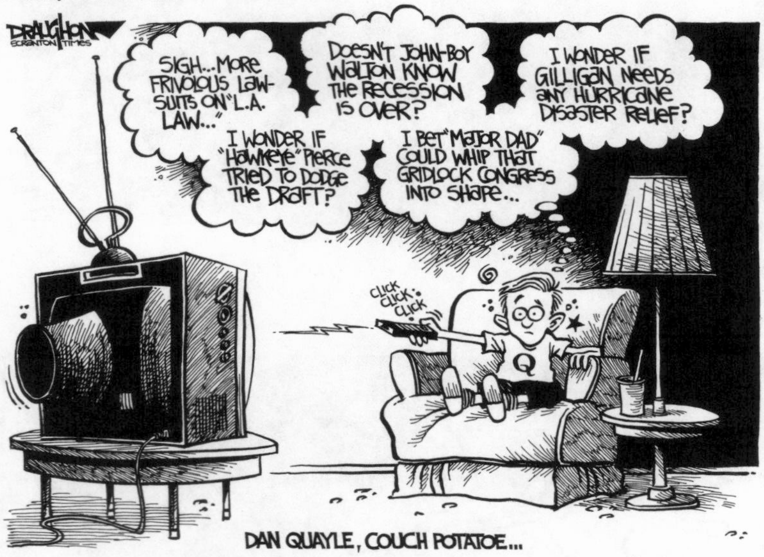
DRAUGHON SCRANTON TIMES
SIGH...MORE FRIVOLOUS LAW-SUITS ON "L.A. LAW..."
DOESN'T JOHN-BOY WALTON KNOW THE RECESSION IS OVER?
I WONDER IF GILLIGAN NEEDS ANY HURRICANE DISASTER RELIEF?
I WONDER IF "HAWKEYE" PIERCE TRIED TO DODGE THE DRAFT?
I BET "MAJOR DAD" COULD WHIP THAT GRIDLOCK CONGRESS INTO SHAPE...
CLICK CLICK CLICK
Q
DAN QUAYLE, COUCH POTATOE...

GARY MCCOY
Courtesy Suburban Journals

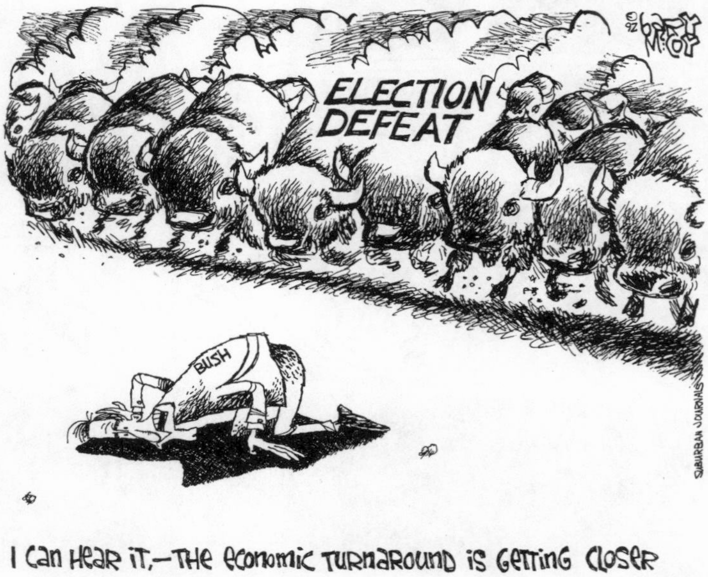
ELECTION DEFEAT
BUSH
SUBURBAN JOURNALS
I CAN HEAR IT,—THE ECONOMIC TURNAROUND IS GETTING CLOSER

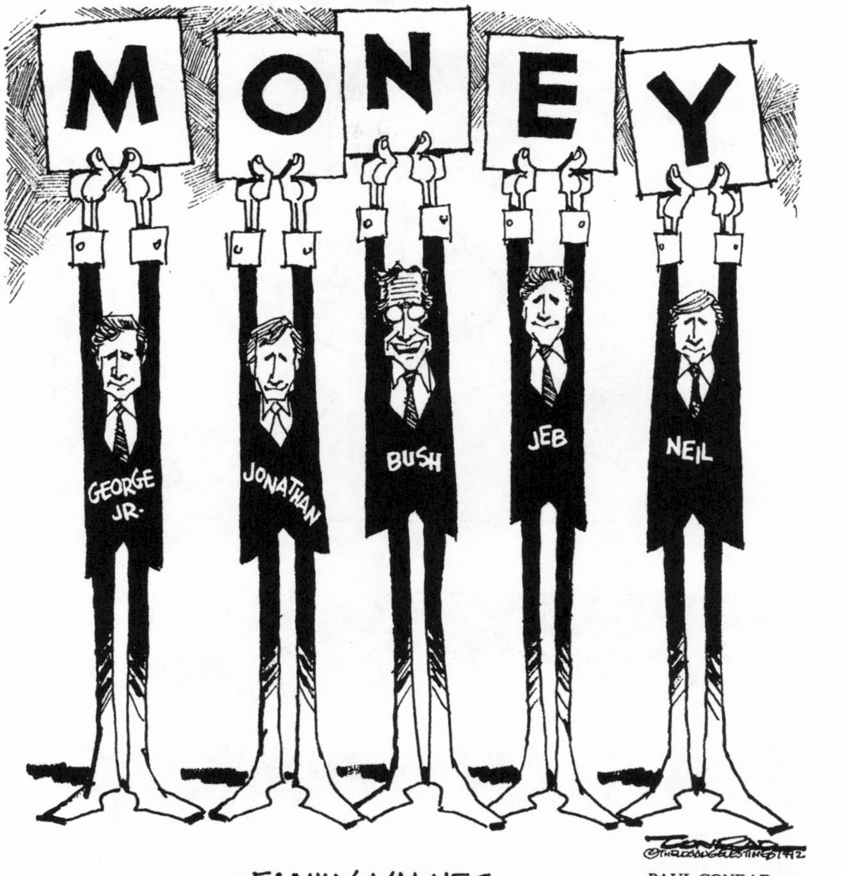
MONEY
GEORGE JR.
JONATHAN
BUSH
JEB
NEIL

FAMILY VALUES

PAUL CONRAD
Courtesy Los Angeles Times

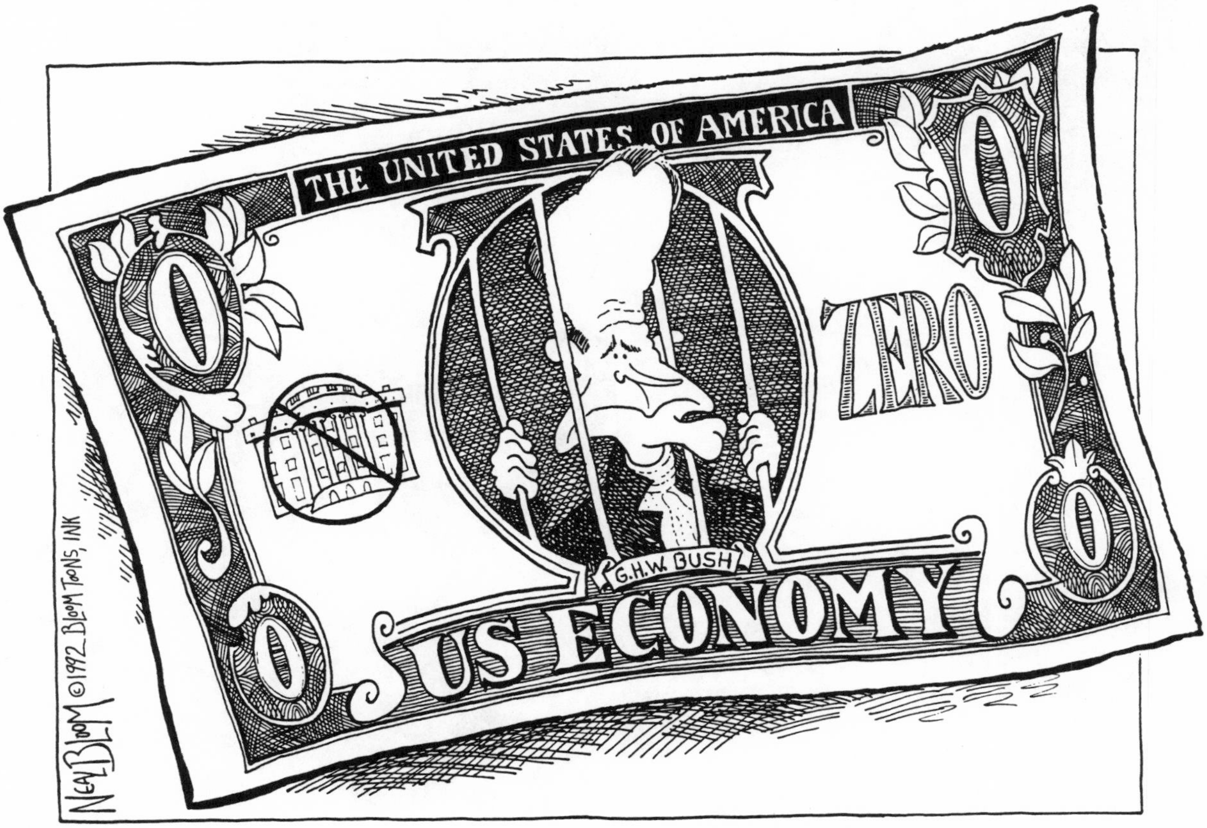
THE UNITED STATES OF AMERICA
ZERO
G.H.W. BUSH
US ECONOMY
NEAL BLOOM ©1992 BLOOM TOONS, INK

NEAL BLOOM
Courtesy Bloom Toons, INK

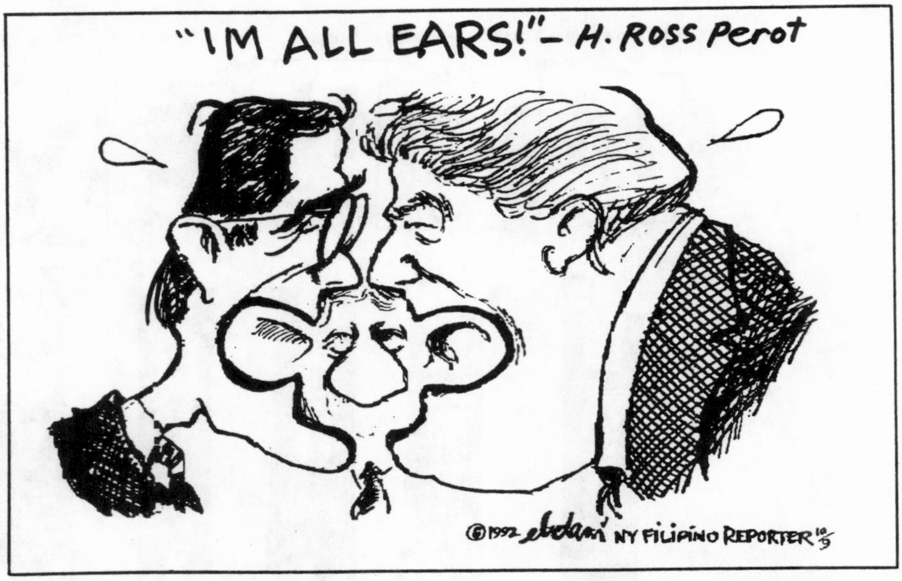
"I'M ALL EARS!" – H. Ross Perot
©1992 NY FILIPINO REPORTER

DANI AGUILA
Courtesy Filipino Reporter

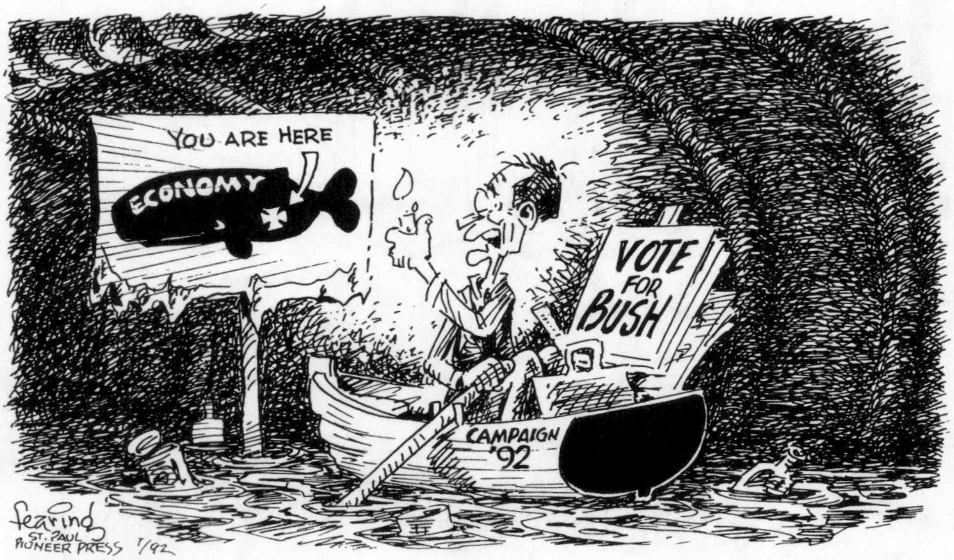
YOU ARE HERE
ECONOMY
VOTE FOR BUSH
CAMPAIGN '92
Fearing ST. PAUL PIONEER PRESS

JERRY FEARING
Courtesy St. Paul Pioneer Press-Dispatch

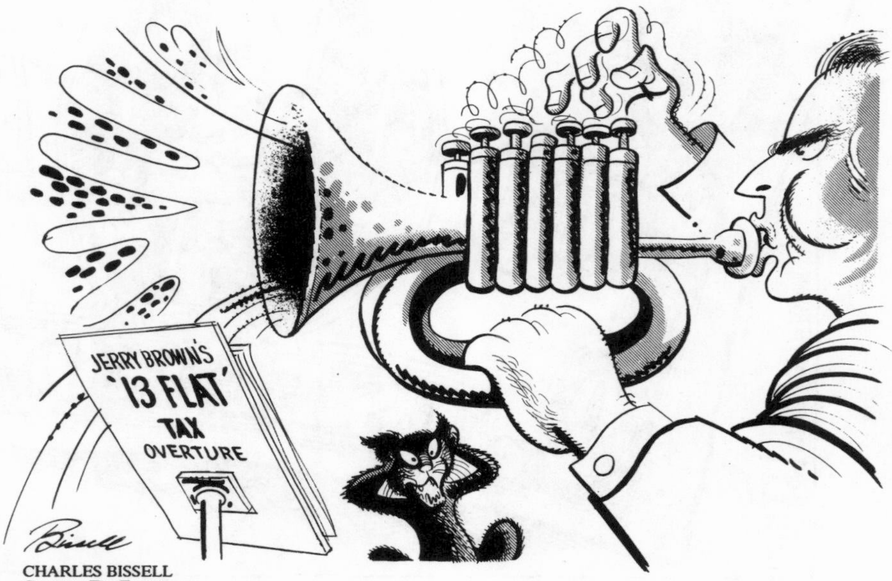
JERRY BROWN'S '13 FLAT' TAX OVERTURE
Bissell

CHARLES BISSELL
Courtesy The Tennessean

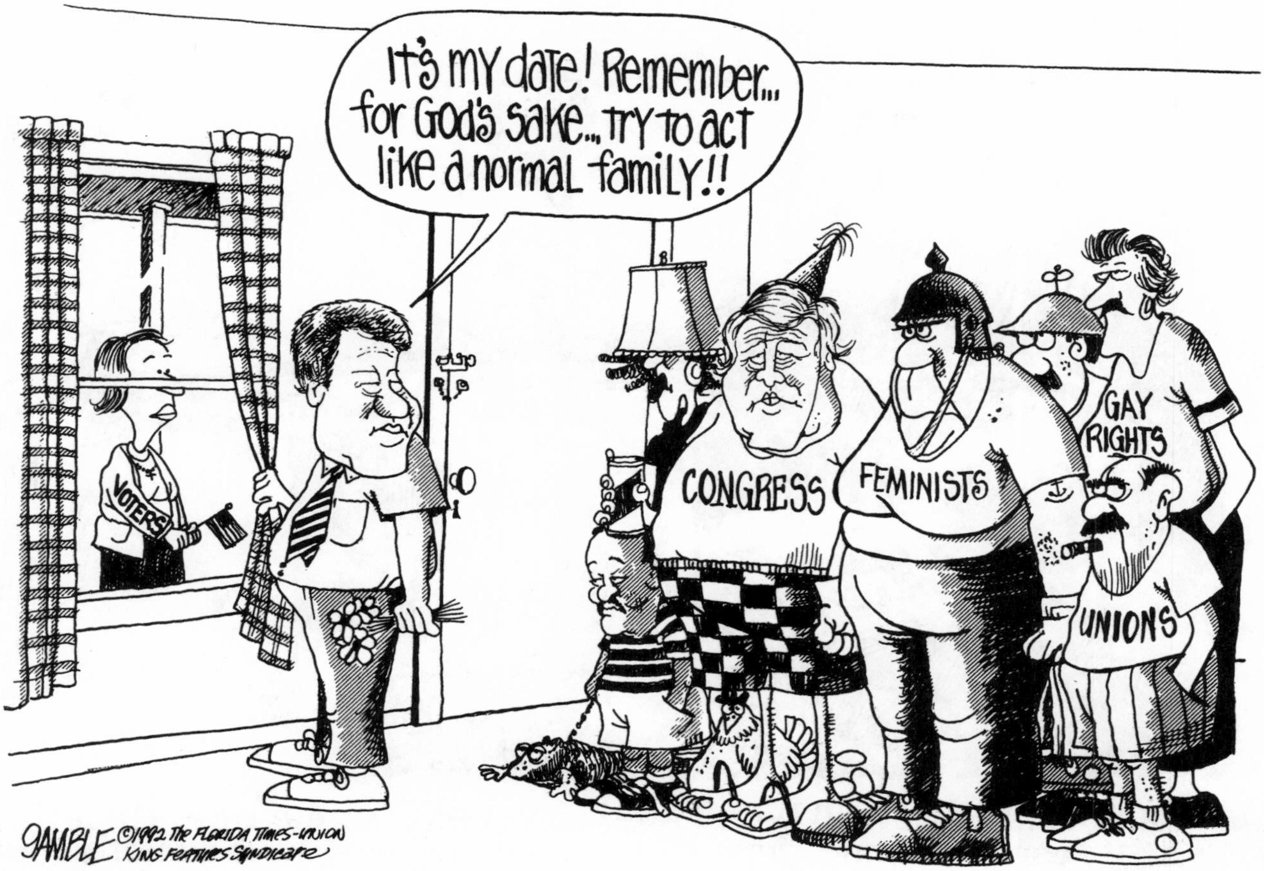
It's my date! Remember... for God's sake... try to act like a normal family!!
VOTERS
CONGRESS
FEMINISTS
GAY RIGHTS
UNIONS
GAMBLE ©1992 The Florida Times-Union King Features Syndicate

ED GAMBLE
Courtesy Florida Times-Union

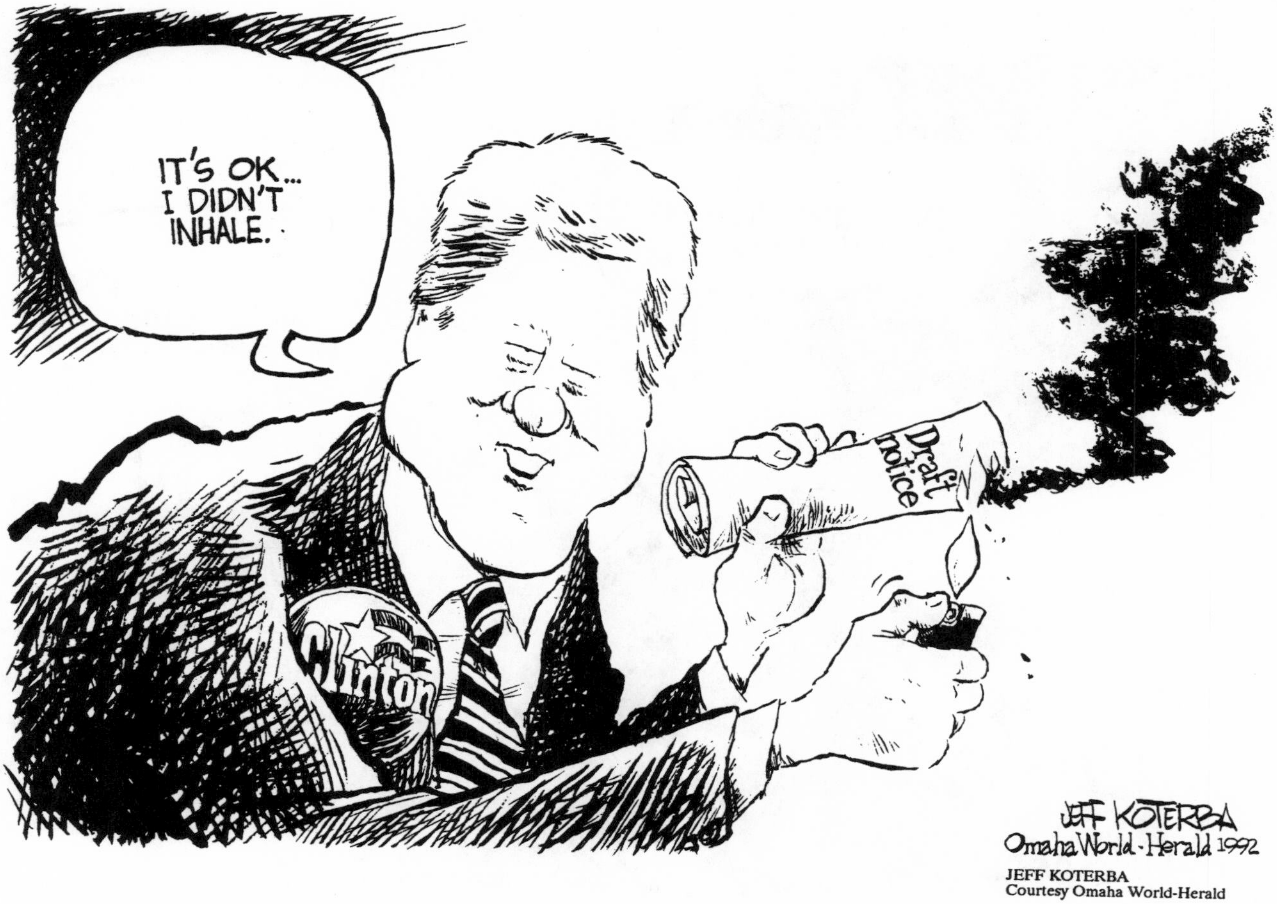
IT'S OK... I DIDN'T INHALE.
Draft notice
Clinton
JEFF KOTERBA
Omaha World-Herald 1992

JEFF KOTERBA
Courtesy Omaha World-Herald

JIMMY MARGULIES
Courtesy The Record (N.J.) copyright 1992
North America Syndicate

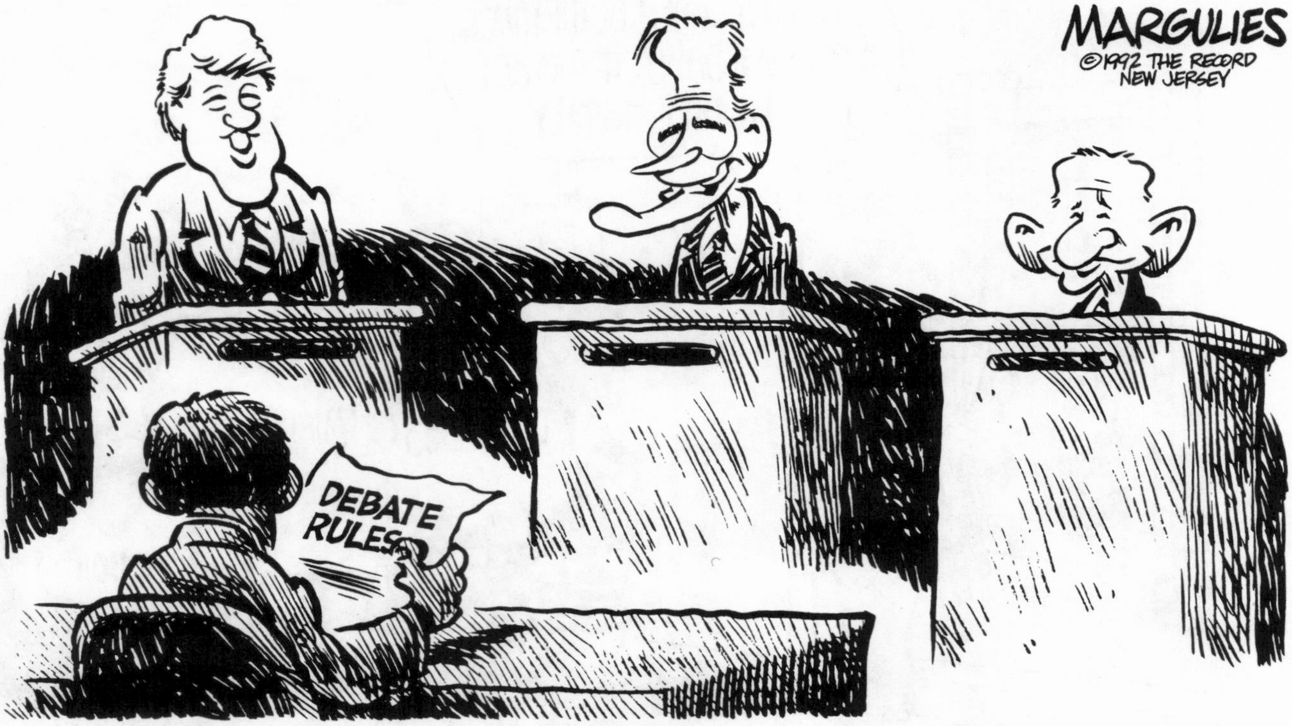
MARGULIES
©1992 THE RECORD
NEW JERSEY
DEBATE
RULES

"Each candidate will be allowed an opening sound-bite, then they may respond to questions with a memorable slogan or withering put-down, and finally have the chance for a closing zinger..."

MIKE LUCKOVICH
Courtesy Atlanta Constitution

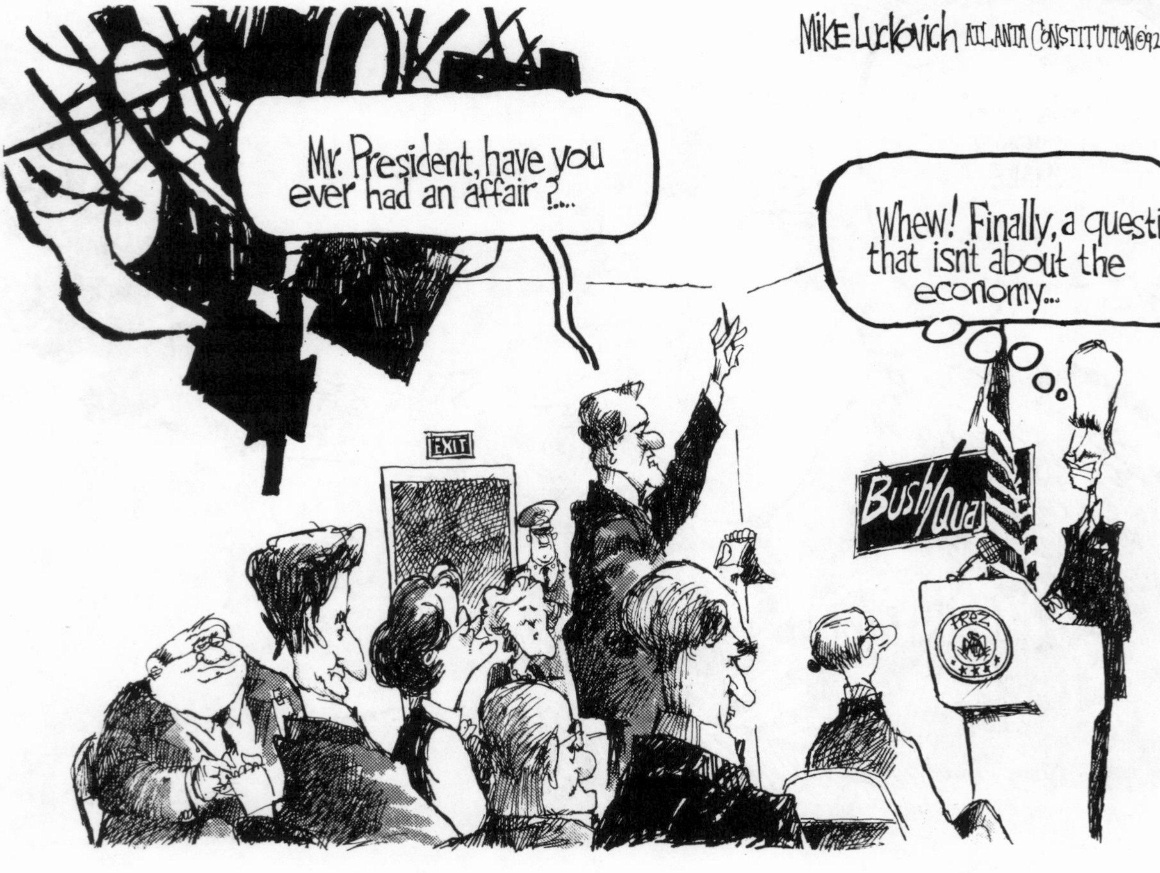
MIKE LUCKOVICH ATLANTA CONSTITUTION ©92
Mr. President, have you ever had an affair ?...
Whew! Finally, a question that isn't about the economy...
EXIT
Bush/Quay

DICK LOCHER
Courtesy Chicago Tribune

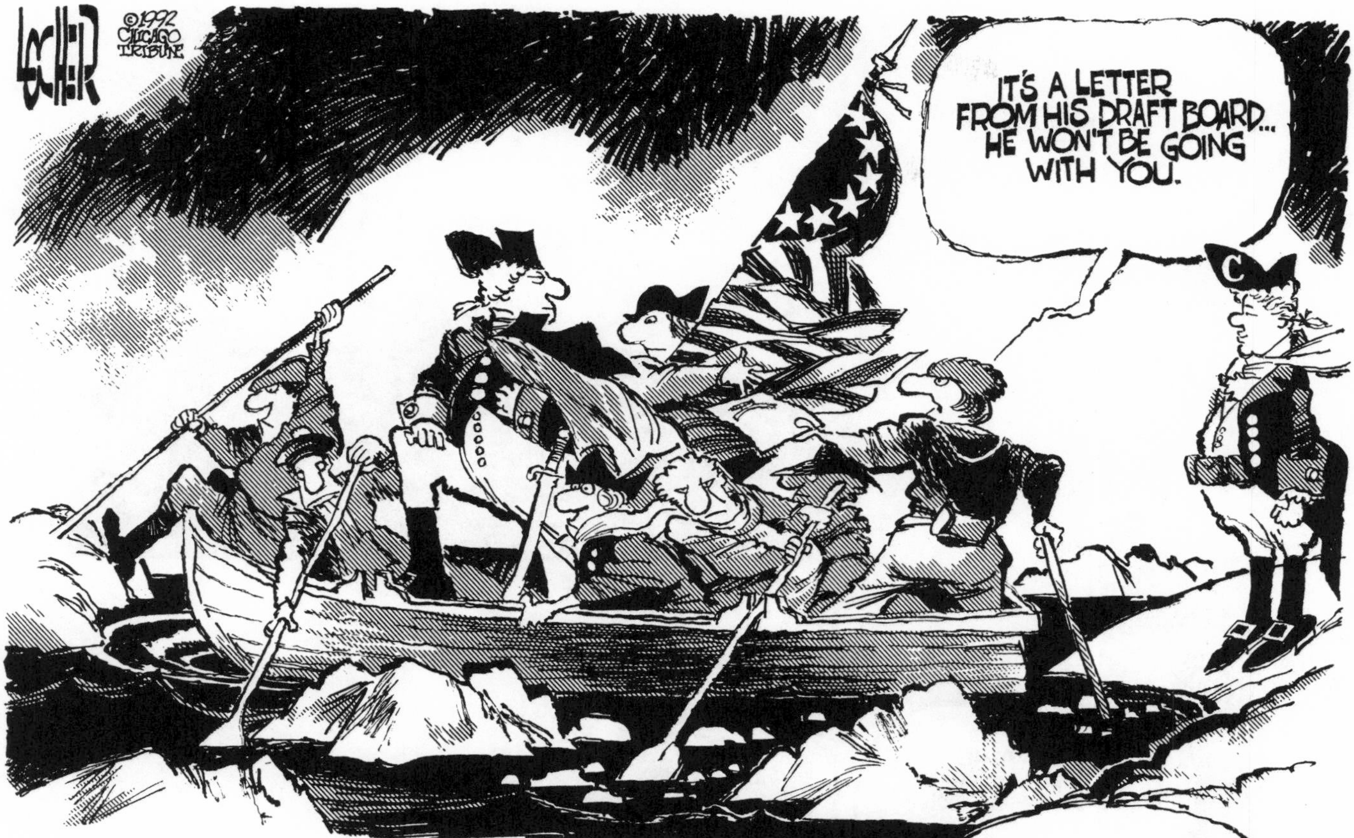

IT'S A LETTER FROM HIS DRAFT BOARD... HE WON'T BE GOING WITH YOU.
THE RICH

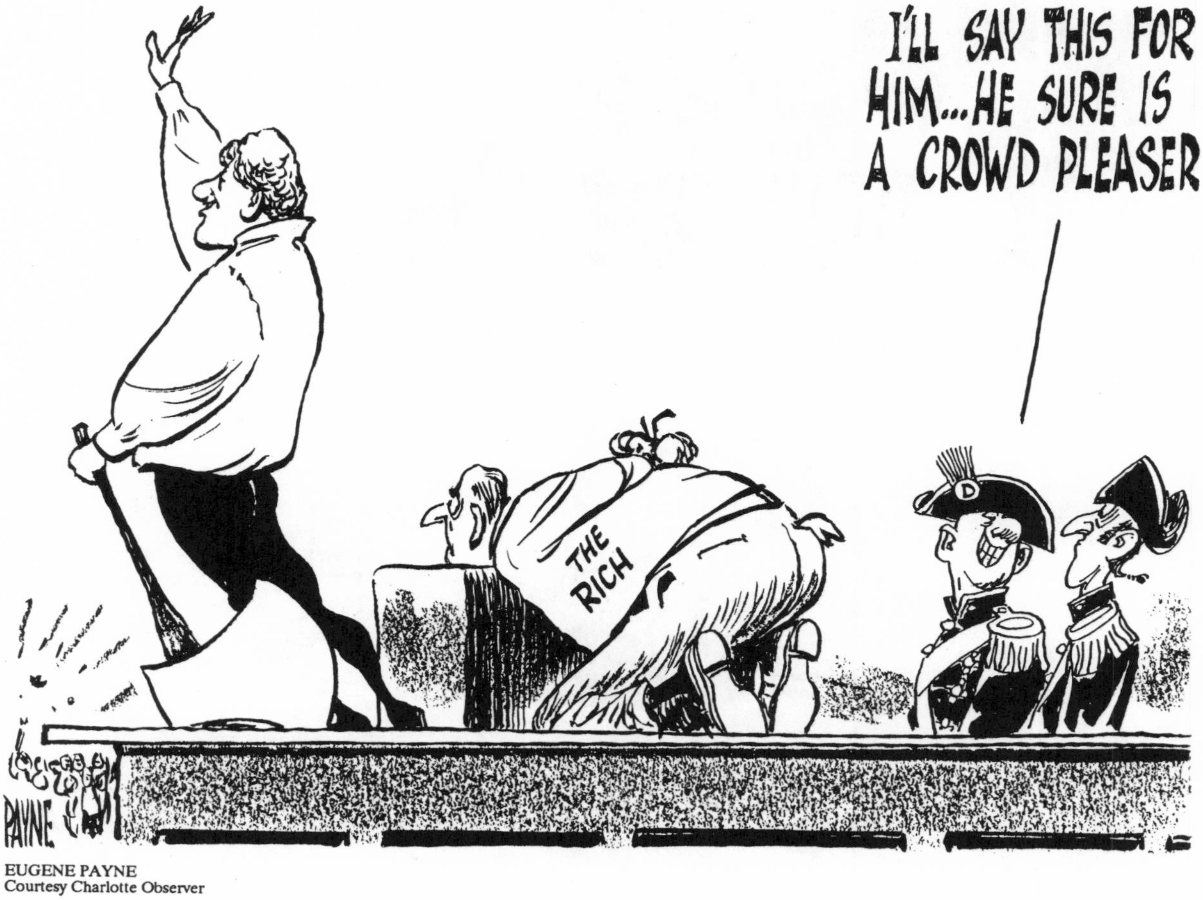

I'LL SAY THIS FOR HIM...HE SURE IS A CROWD PLEASER
THE RICH

EUGENE PAYNE
Courtesy Charlotte Observer

FRANK CAMMUSO
Courtesy Syracuse Herald-American

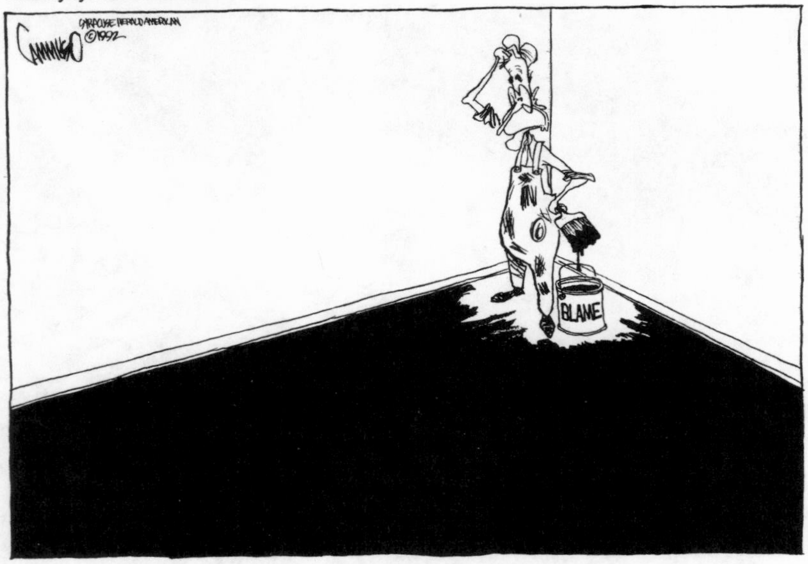
BLAME

ROB ROGERS
Courtesy Pittsburgh Press

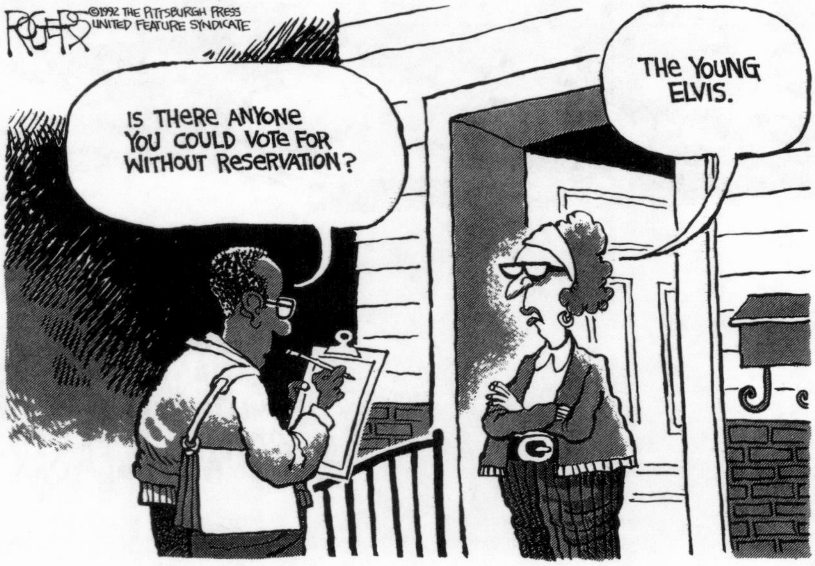
©1992 THE PITTSBURGH PRESS UNITED FEATURE SYNDICATE
IS THERE ANYONE YOU COULD VOTE FOR WITHOUT RESERVATION?
THE YOUNG ELVIS.

DAVE COVERLY
Courtesy Bloomington Herald-Times

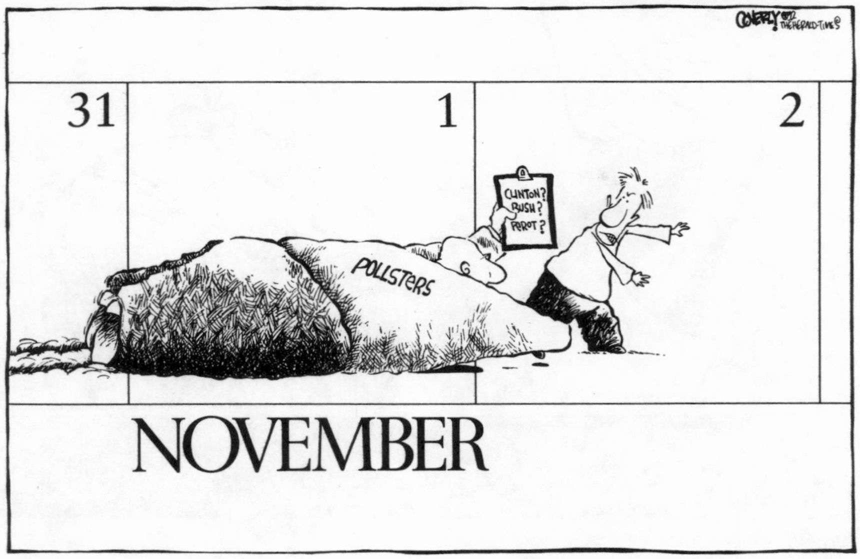
31
1
2
CLINTON? BUSH? PEROT?
POLLSTERS
NOVEMBER

BEN SARGENT
Courtesy Austin American Statesman

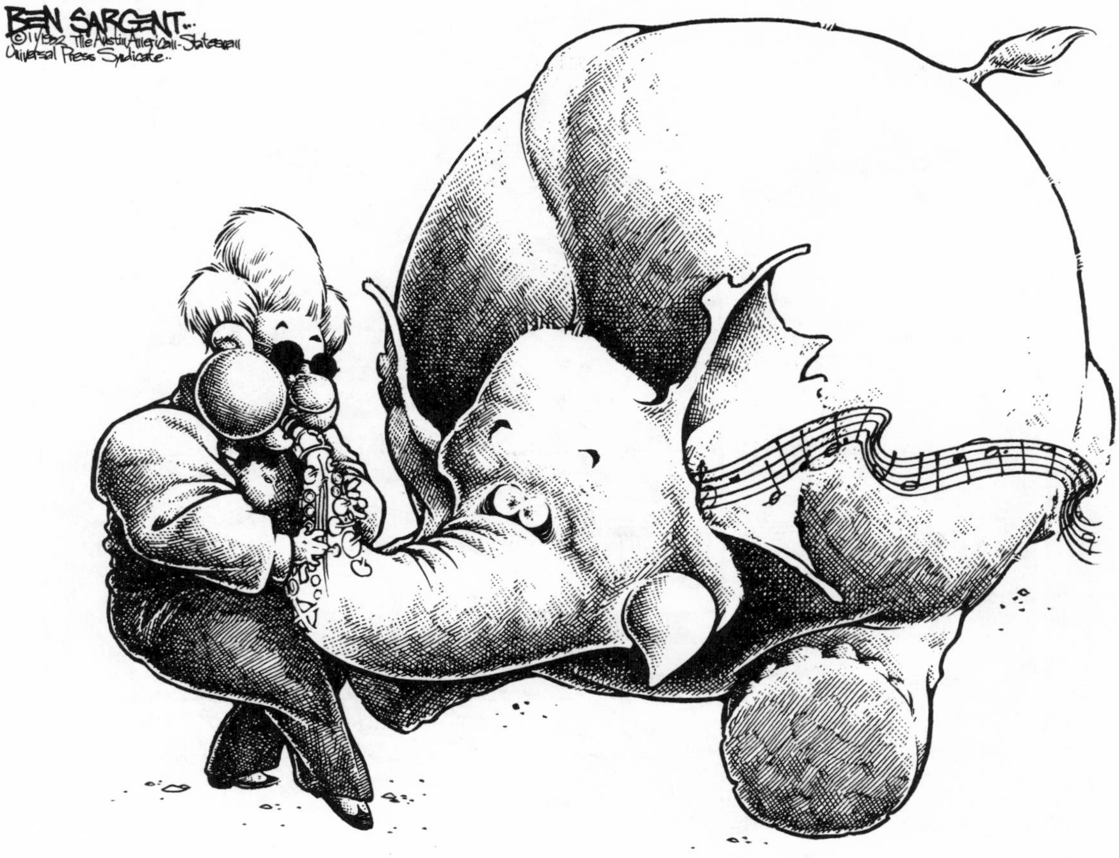
BEN SARGENT...
Universal Press Syndicate

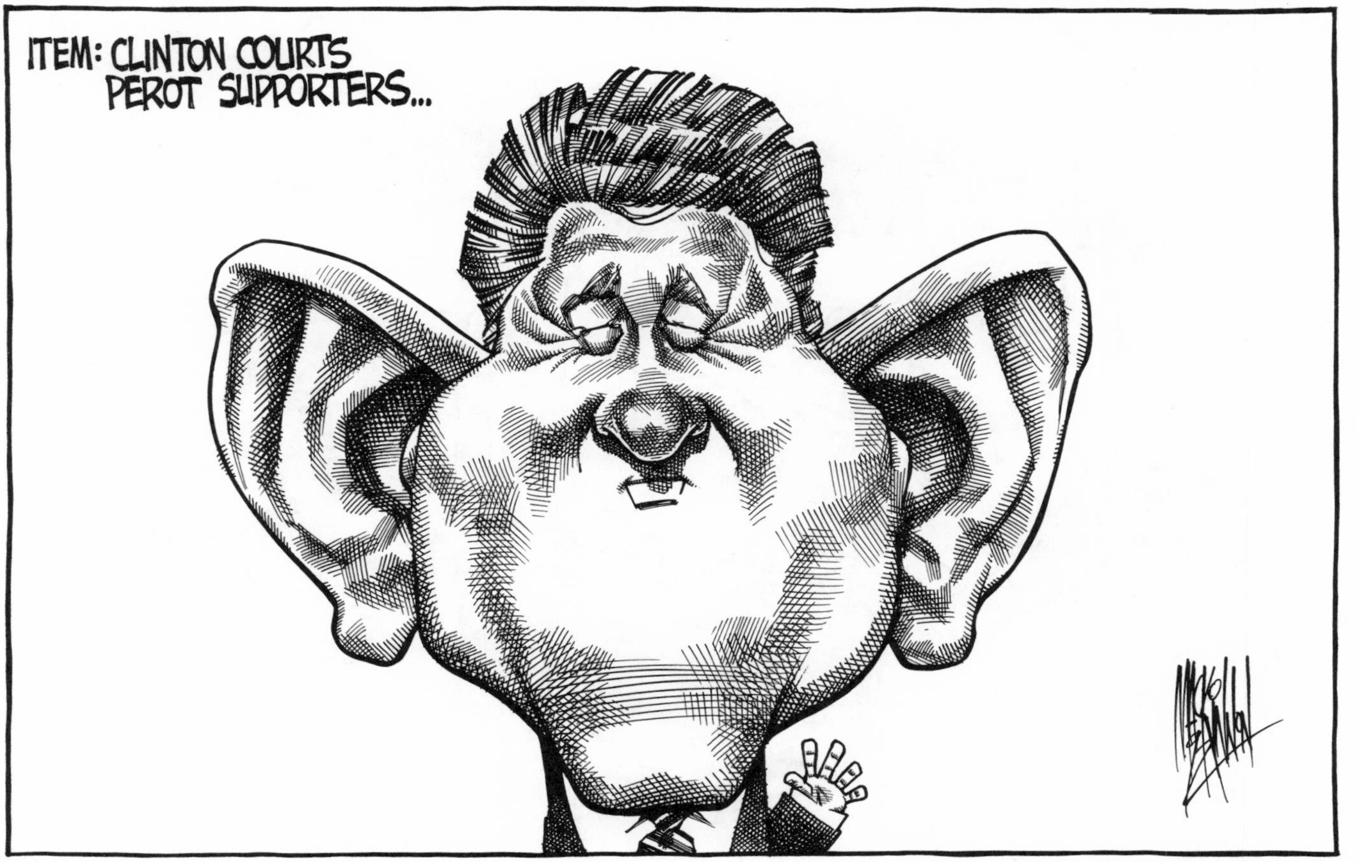
ITEM: CLINTON COURTS
PEROT SUPPORTERS...

BRUCE MACKINNON
Courtesy Halifax Chronicle-Herald

NEIL GRAHAME
Courtesy Spencer Newspapers

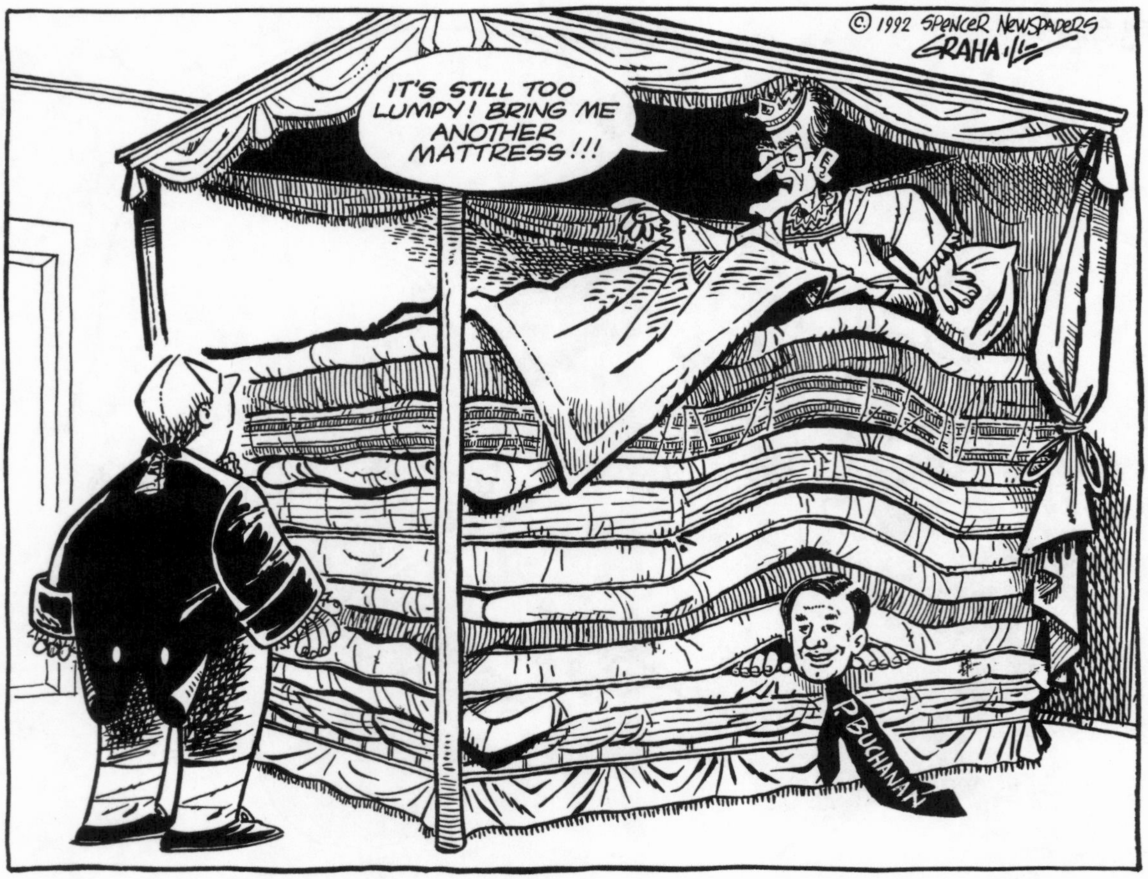
© 1992 SPENCER NEWSPAPERS
GRAHAME
IT'S STILL TOO LUMPY! BRING ME ANOTHER MATTRESS!!!
P. BUCHANAN

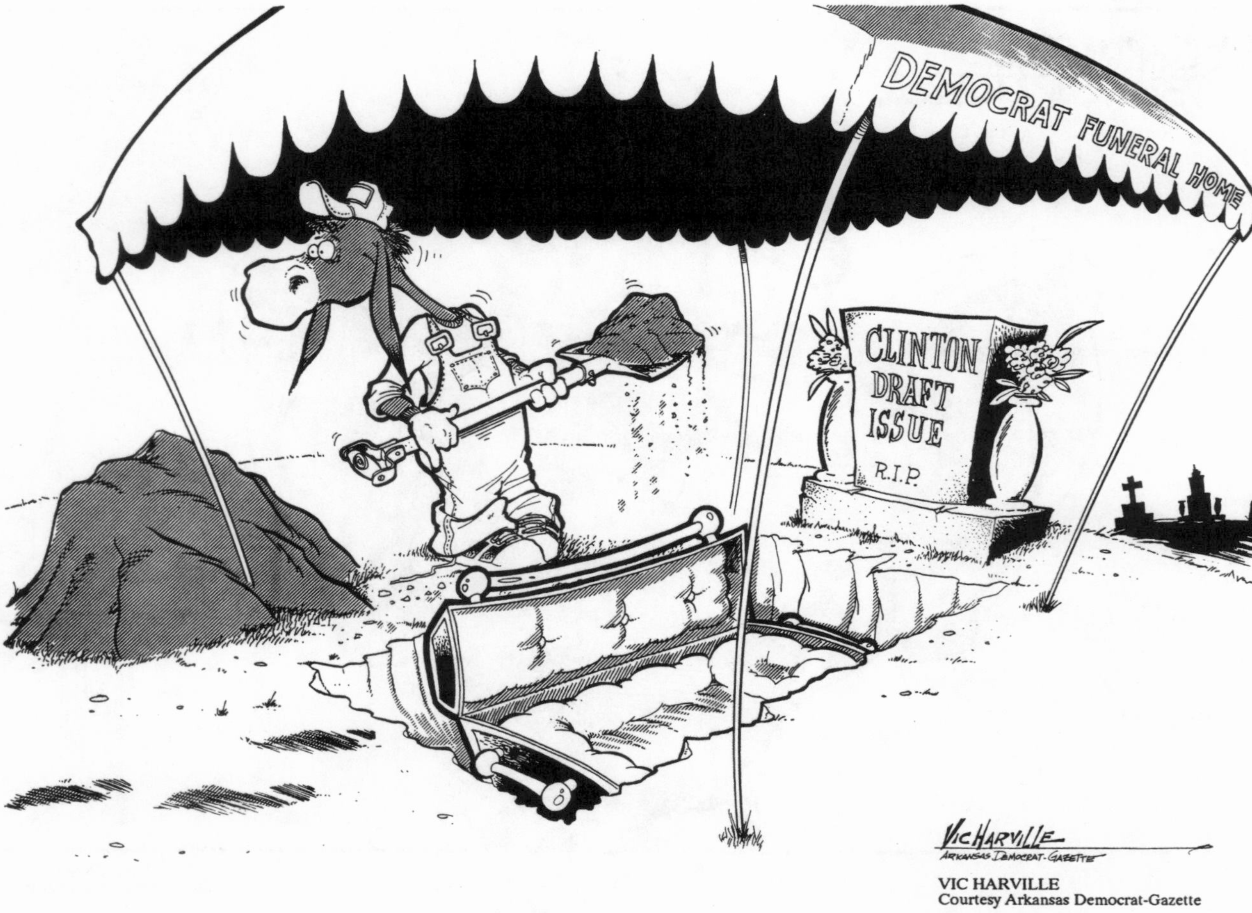
DEMOCRAT FUNERAL HOME
CLINTON DRAFT ISSUE
R.I.P.
VIC HARVILLE
ARKANSAS DEMOCRAT-GAZETTE

VIC HARVILLE
Courtesy Arkansas Democrat-Gazette

STEPHEN TEMPLETON
Courtesy National Forum/Associated Features

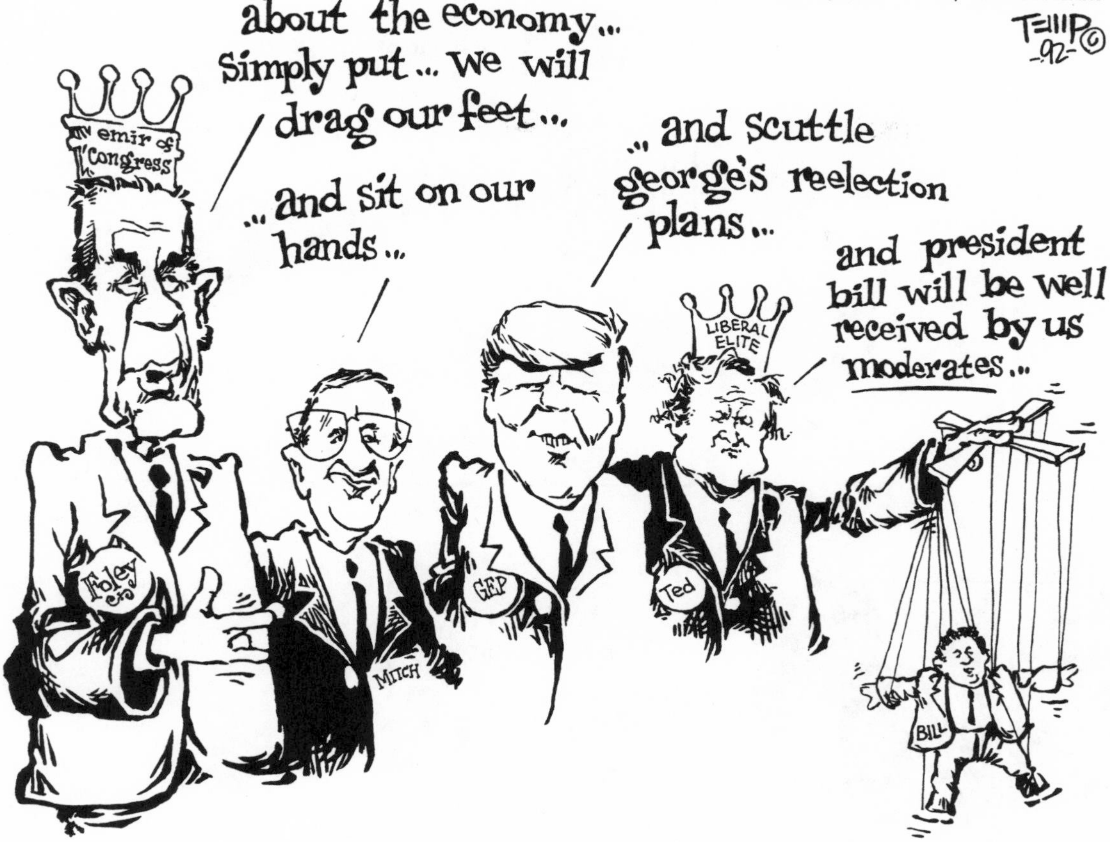
TEMP -92- ©
about the economy... Simply put... we will drag our feet...
... and sit on our hands...
... and scuttle george's reelection plans...
and president bill will be well received by us moderates...
emir of Congress
Foley
MITCH
GEP
LIBERAL ELITE
Ted
BILL

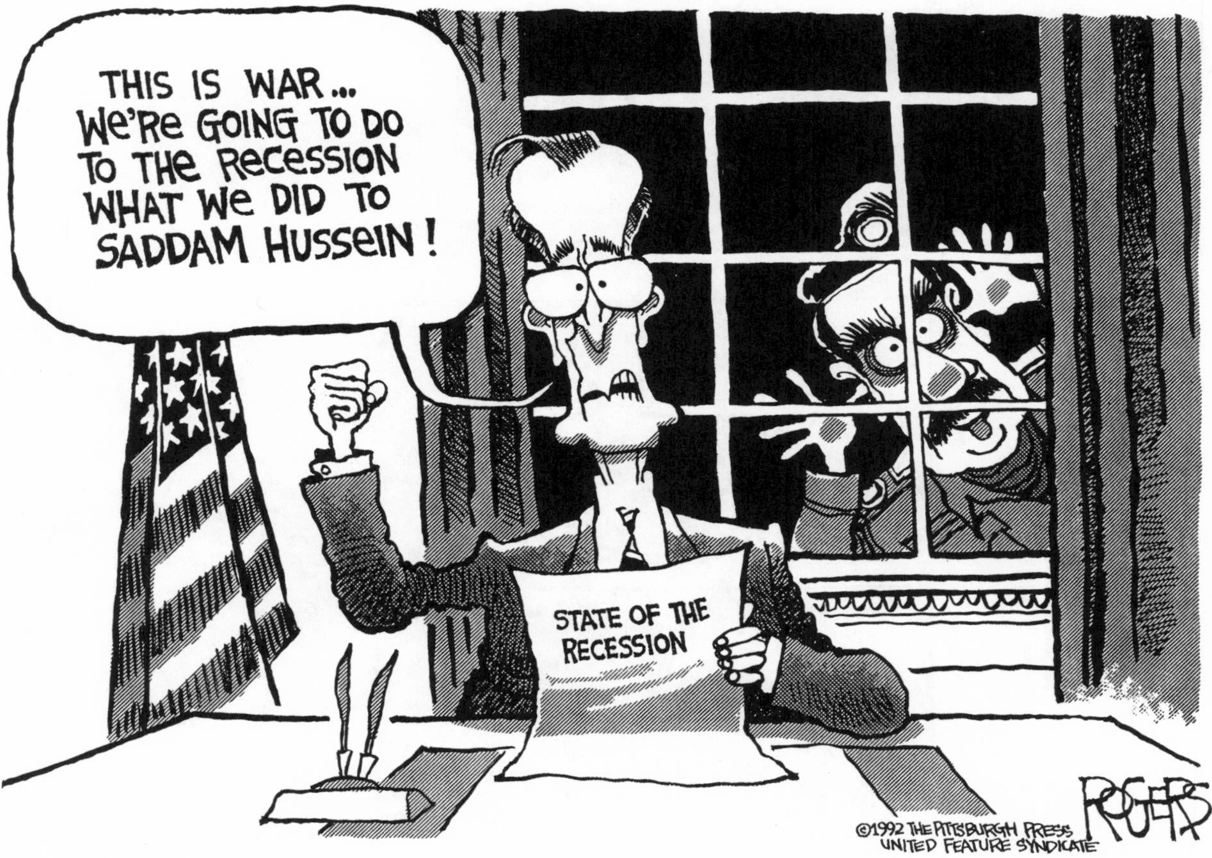
THIS IS WAR... WE'RE GOING TO DO TO THE RECESSION WHAT WE DID TO SADDAM HUSSEIN!
STATE OF THE RECESSION
©1992 THE PITTSBURGH PRESS UNITED FEATURE SYNDICATE
ROGERS

ROB ROGERS
Courtesy Pittsburgh Press

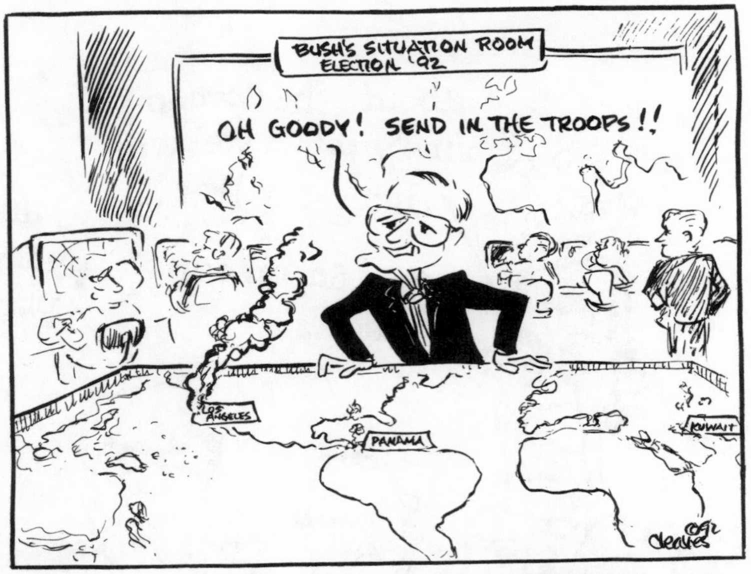
BUSH'S SITUATION ROOM
ELECTION '92
OH GOODY! SEND IN THE TROOPS!!
LOS ANGELES
PANAMA
KUWAIT
©92 Cleaves

ANN CLEAVES
Courtesy La Prensa (San Diego)

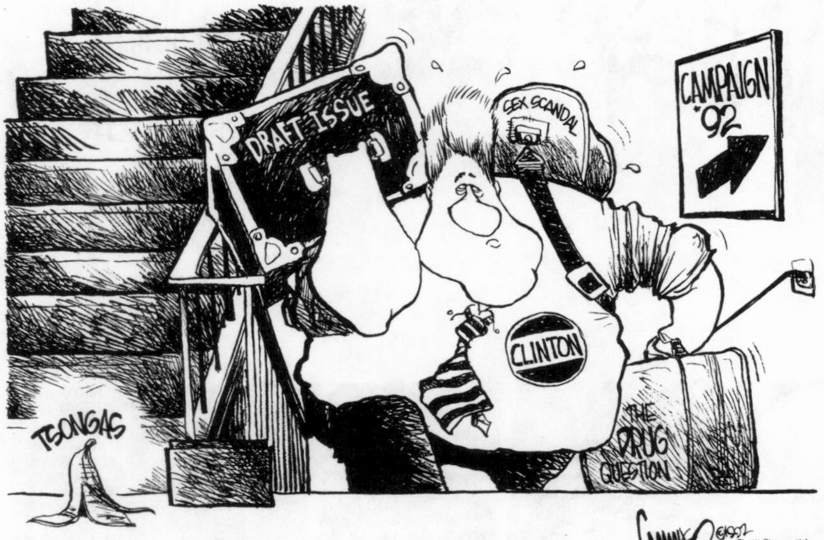
DRAFT ISSUE
SEX SCANDAL
CAMPAIGN '92
CLINTON
THE DRUG QUESTION
TSONGAS

FRANK CAMMUSO
Courtesy Syracuse Herald-Journal

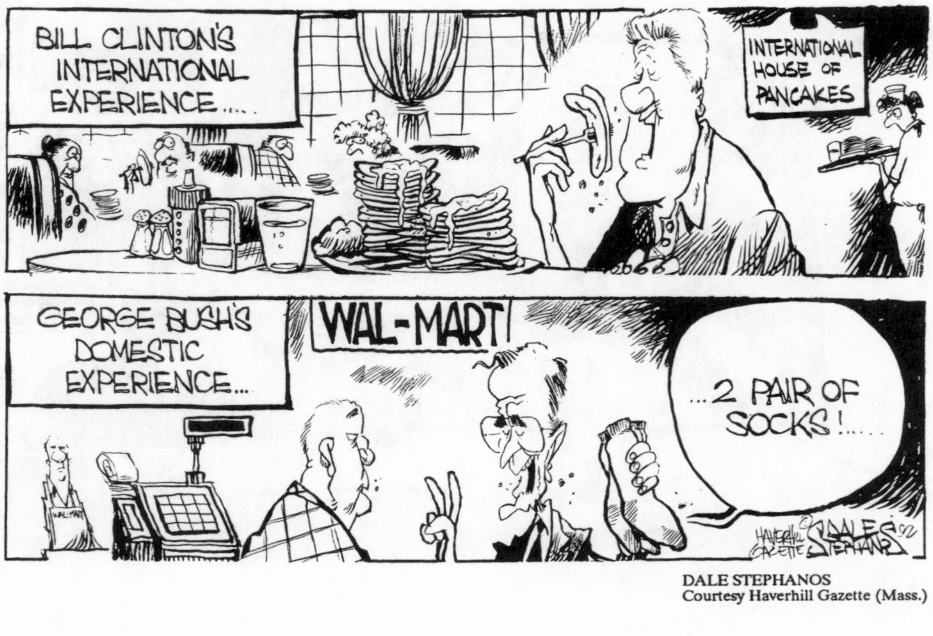
BILL CLINTON'S INTERNATIONAL EXPERIENCE....
INTERNATIONAL HOUSE OF PANCAKES
GEORGE BUSH'S DOMESTIC EXPERIENCE...
WAL-MART
...2 PAIR OF SOCKS!.....
HAVERHILL GAZETTE
DALE STEPHANOS '92

DALE STEPHANOS
Courtesy Haverhill Gazette (Mass.)

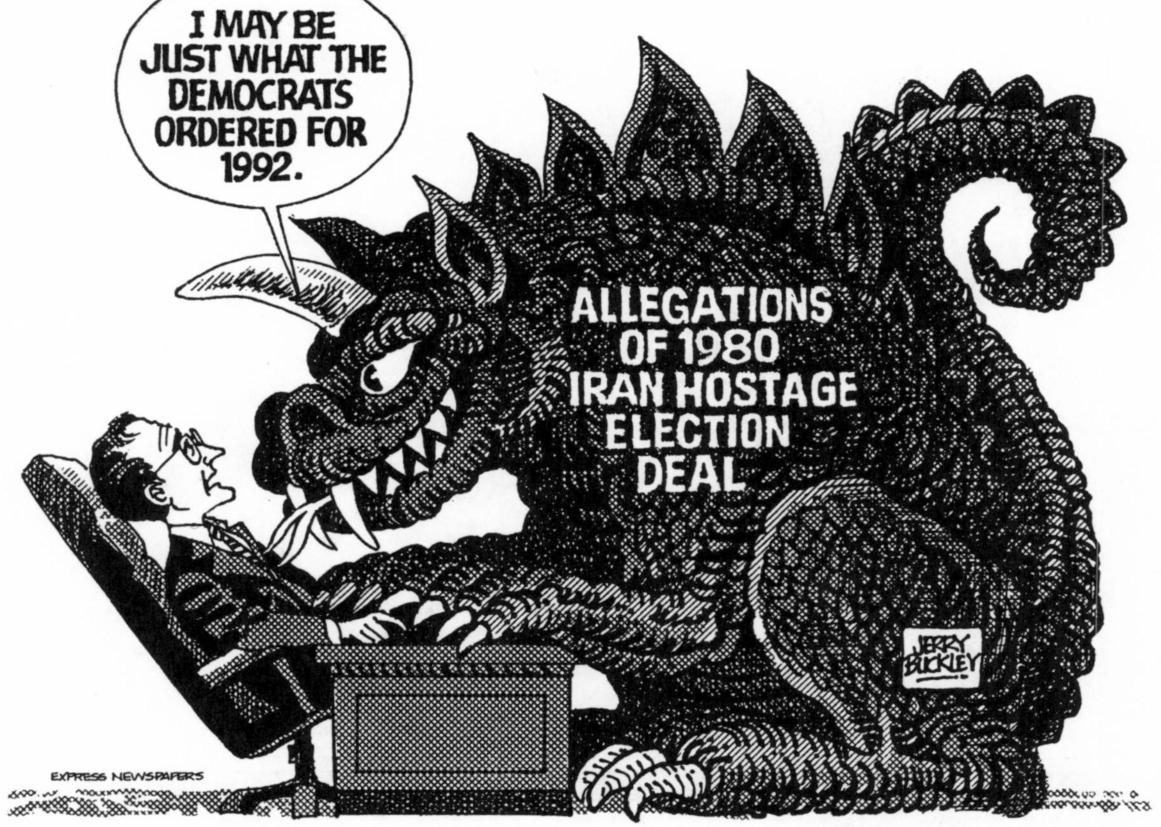
I MAY BE JUST WHAT THE DEMOCRATS ORDERED FOR 1992.
ALLEGATIONS OF 1980 IRAN HOSTAGE ELECTION DEAL
JERRY BUCKLEY
EXPRESS NEWSPAPERS

JERRY BUCKLEY
Courtesy Express Newspapers

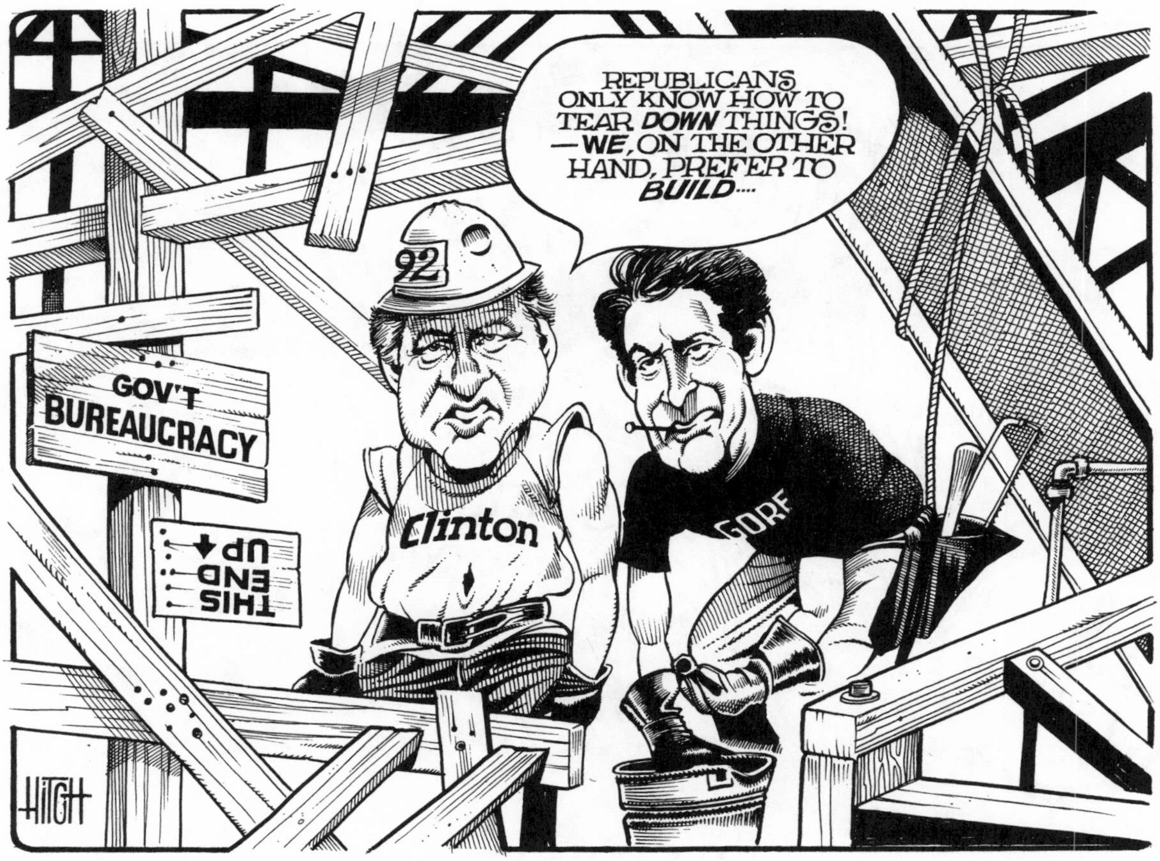
REPUBLICANS ONLY KNOW HOW TO TEAR *DOWN* THINGS! —*WE*, ON THE OTHER HAND, PREFER TO *BUILD*....
92
GOV'T BUREAUCRACY
THIS END UP
Clinton
GORE
HITCH

DAVID HITCH
Courtesy Worcester Telegram & Gazette

DAVE COVERLY
Courtesy Bloomington Herald-Times

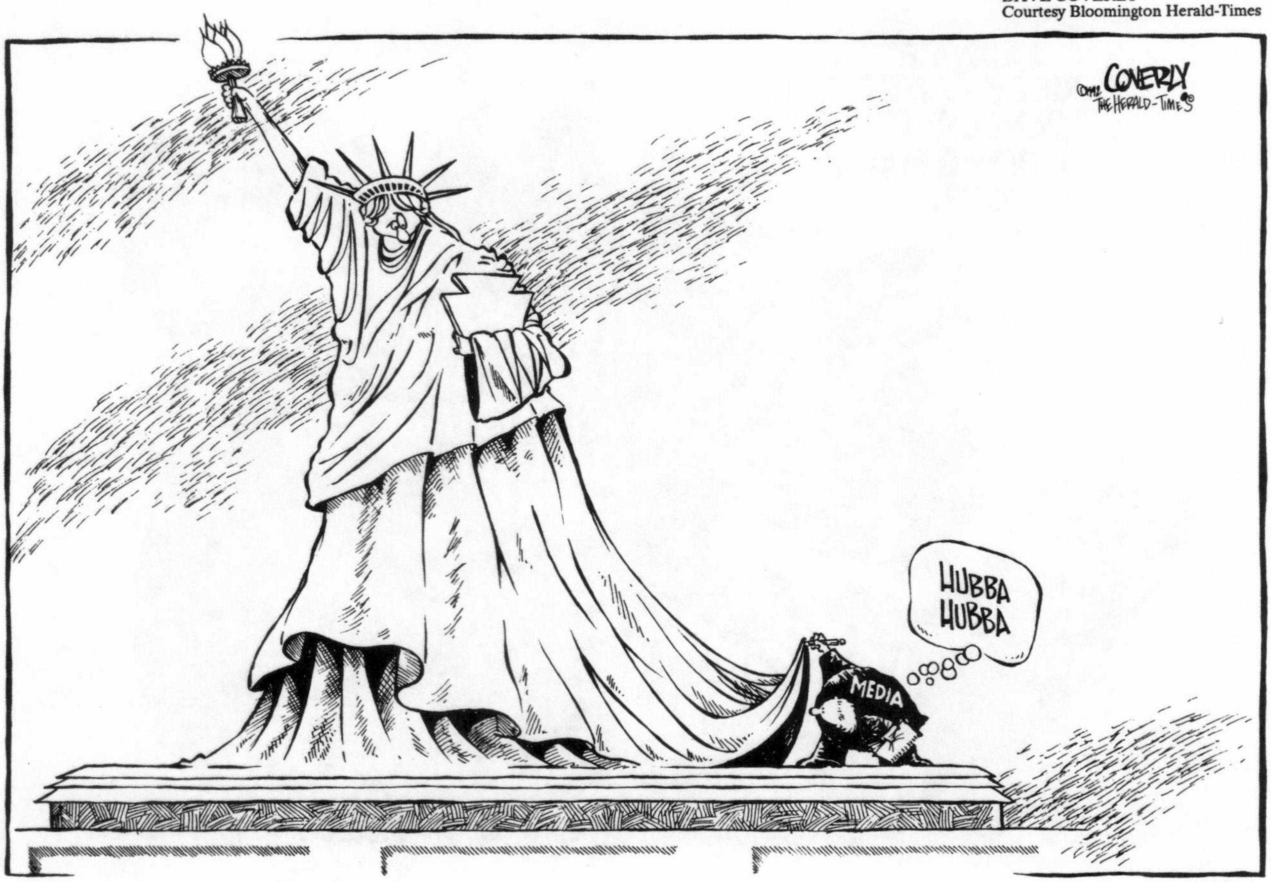
©1992 COVERLY THE HERALD-TIMES
HUBBA HUBBA
MEDIA

LEO ABBETT
Courtesy Boston Herald

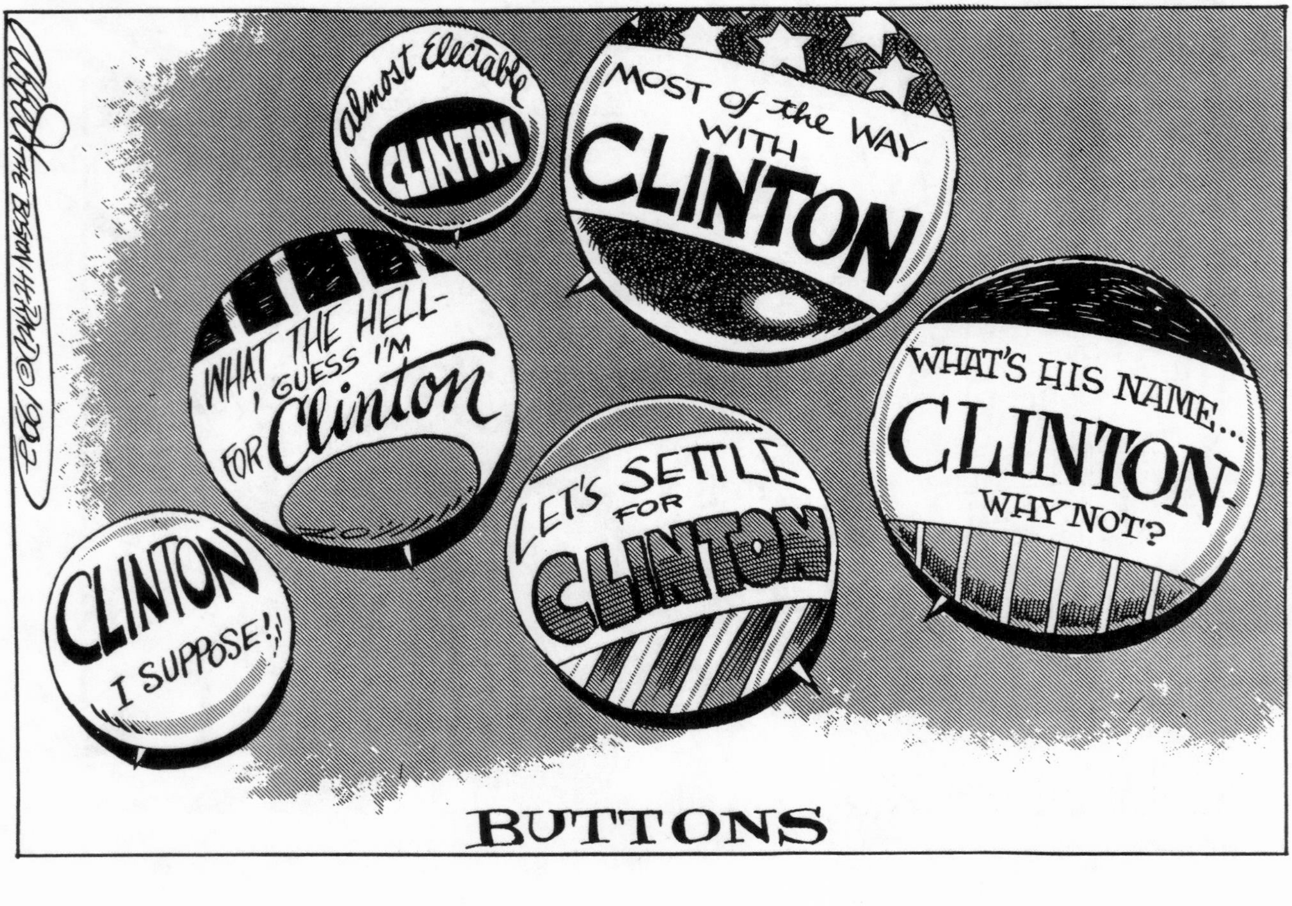
Almost Electable CLINTON
MOST of the WAY WITH CLINTON
WHAT THE HELL- I GUESS I'M FOR Clinton
WHAT'S HIS NAME... CLINTON- WHY NOT?
LET'S SETTLE FOR CLINTON
CLINTON I SUPPOSE!
BUTTONS

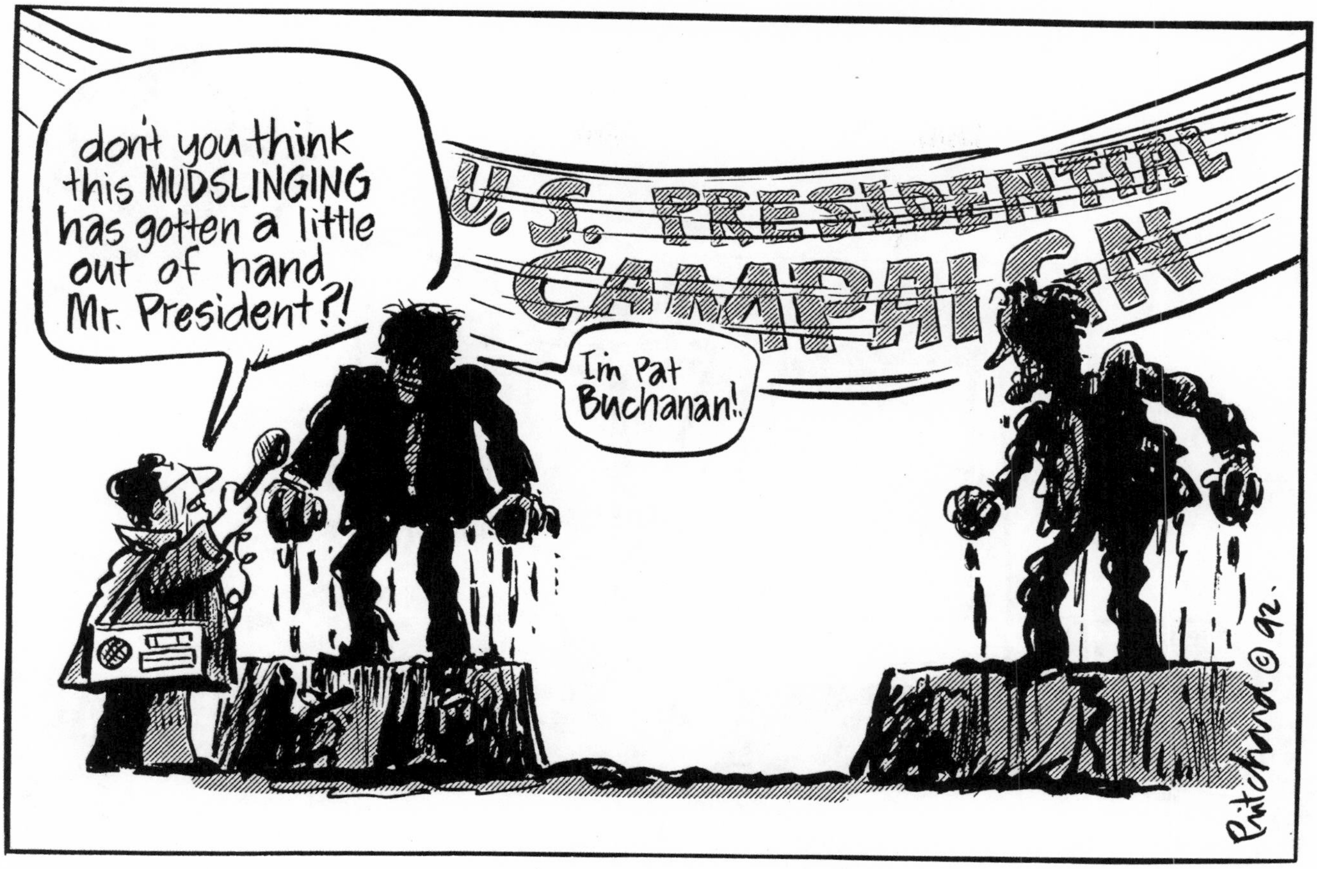
don't you think this MUDSLINGING has gotten a little out of hand Mr. President?!
U.S. PRESIDENTIAL CAMPAIGN
I'm Pat Buchanan!
Pritchard © 92.

DENNY PRITCHARD
Courtesy Ottawa Citizen

BEN SARGENT
Courtesy Austin American Statesman

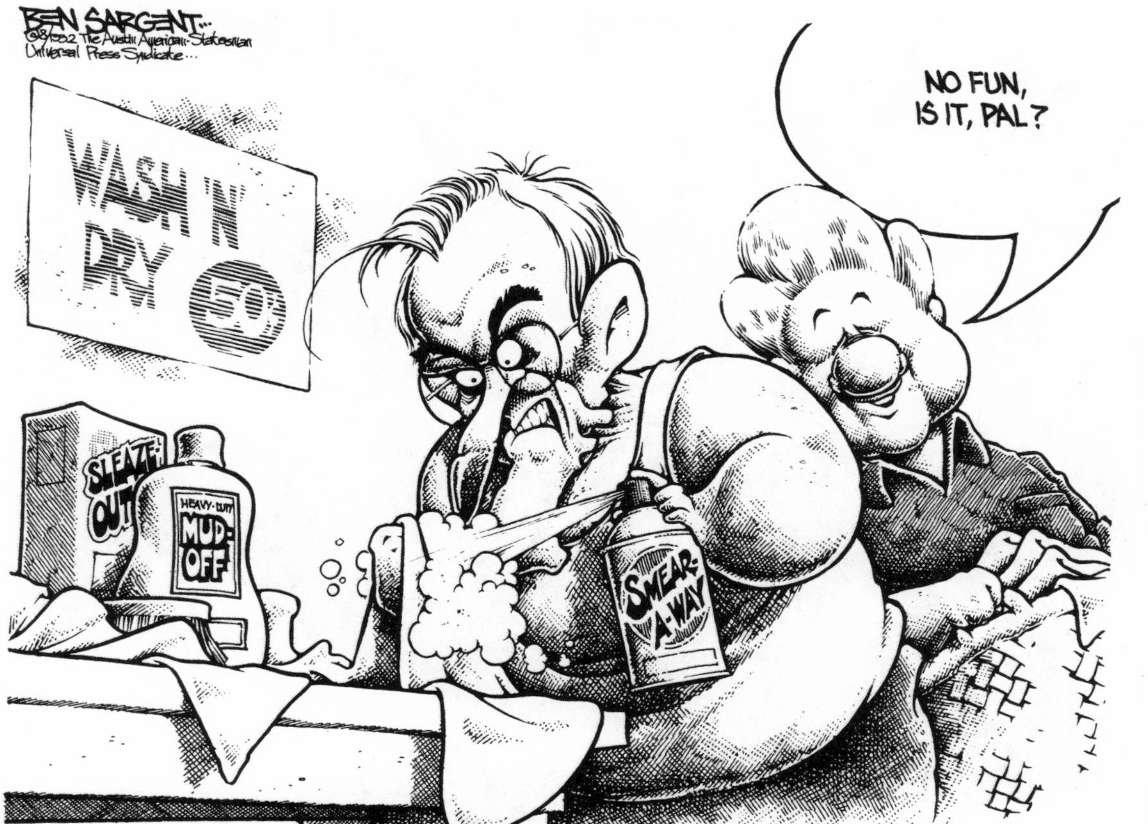
BEN SARGENT...
NO FUN, IS IT, PAL?
WASH 'N' DRY 50¢
SLEAZE-OUT
HEAVY-DUTY MUD-OFF
SMEAR-A-WAY

WILLIAM COSTELLO
Courtesy NEA

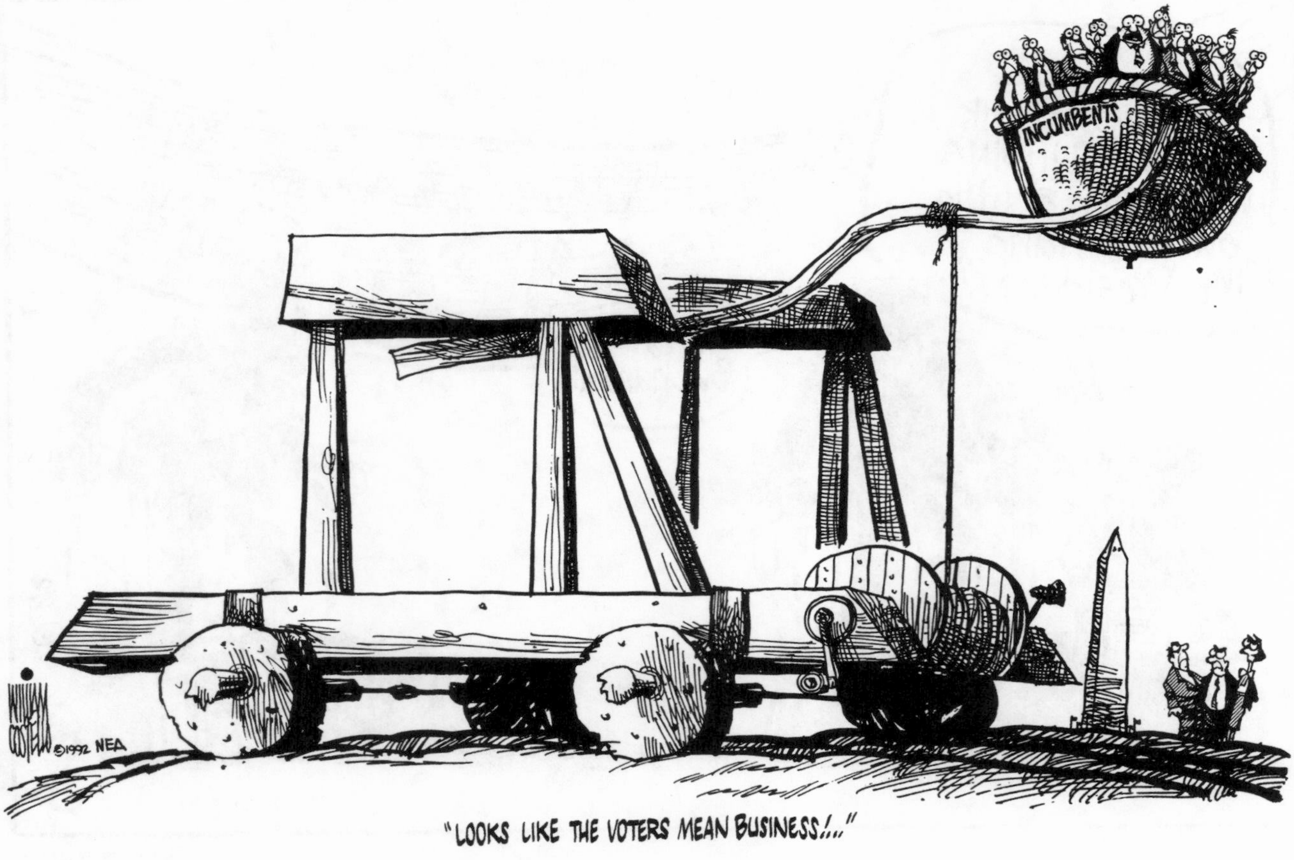
INCUMBENTS
WILLIAM COSTELLO ©1992 NEA
"LOOKS LIKE THE VOTERS MEAN BUSINESS!..."

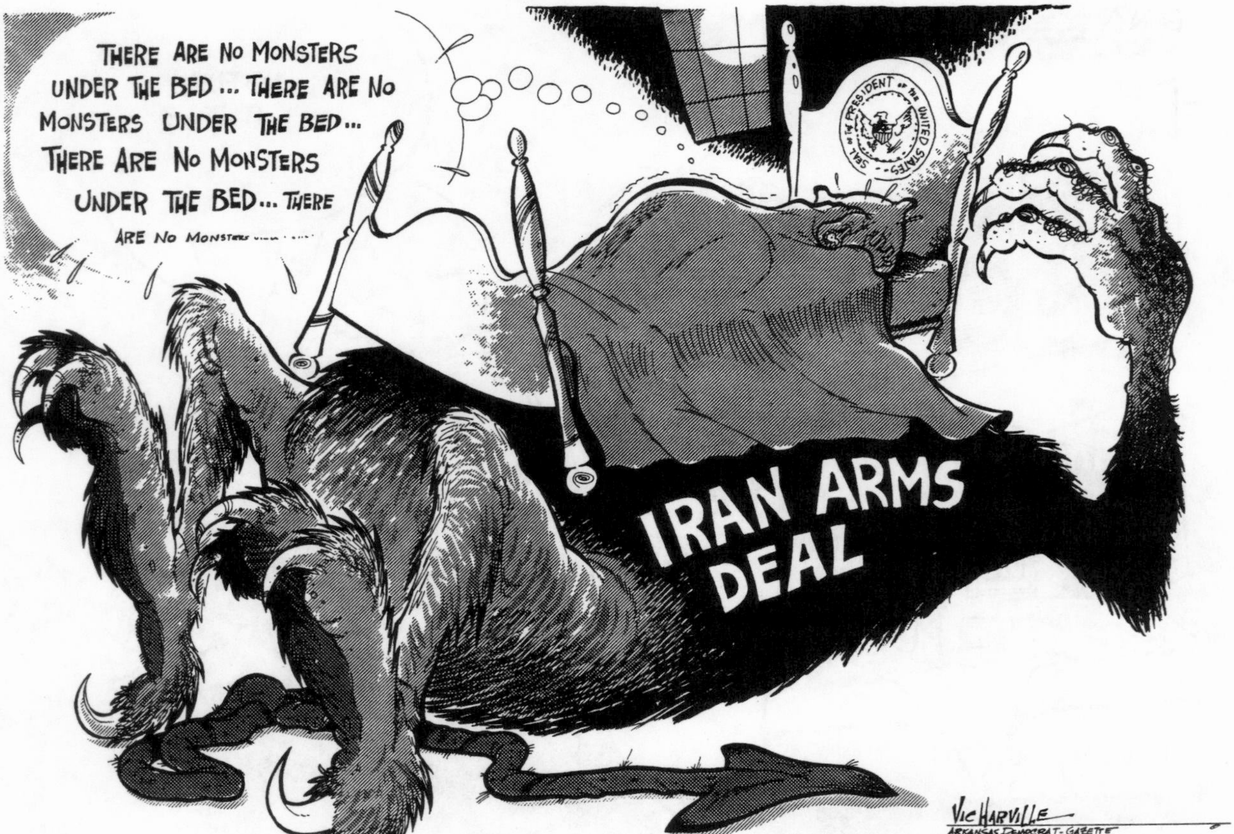
THERE ARE NO MONSTERS UNDER THE BED ... THERE ARE NO MONSTERS UNDER THE BED... THERE ARE NO MONSTERS UNDER THE BED... THERE ARE NO MONSTERS
SEAL OF THE PRESIDENT OF THE UNITED STATES
IRAN ARMS DEAL
VIC HARVILLE
ARKANSAS DEMOCRAT-GAZETTE

VIC HARVILLE
Courtesy Arkansas Democrat-Gazette

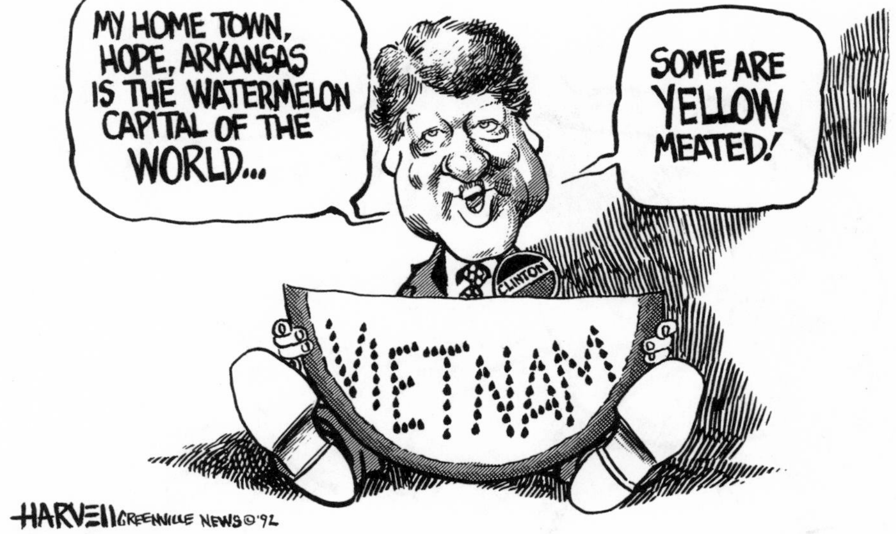
MY HOME TOWN, HOPE, ARKANSAS IS THE WATERMELON CAPITAL OF THE WORLD...
SOME ARE YELLOW MEATED!
CLINTON
VIETNAM
HARVELL GREENVILLE NEWS © '92

ROGER HARVELL
Courtesy Greenville News

JERRY LEFLER
Courtesy Ventura County Star-Free Press

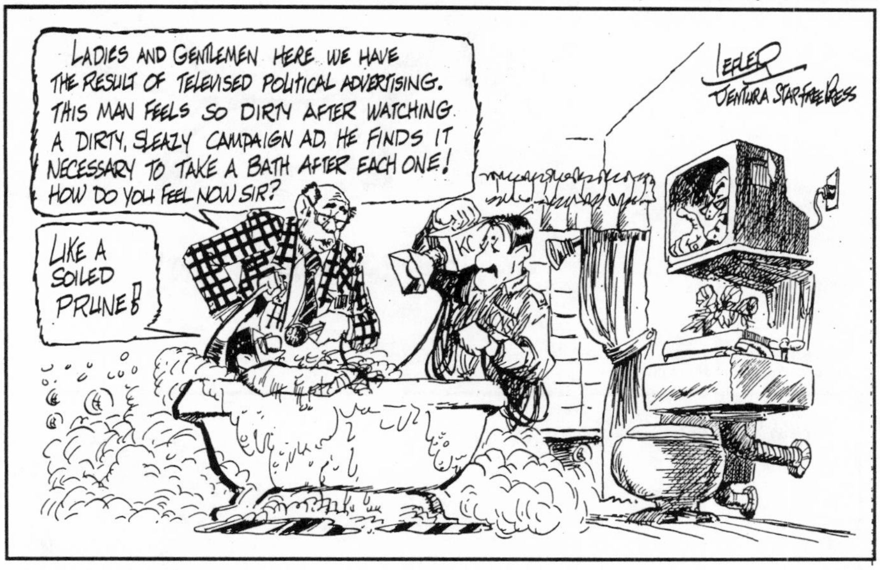
LADIES AND GENTLEMEN HERE WE HAVE THE RESULT OF TELEVISED POLITICAL ADVERTISING. THIS MAN FEELS SO DIRTY AFTER WATCHING A DIRTY, SLEAZY CAMPAIGN AD, HE FINDS IT NECESSARY TO TAKE A BATH AFTER EACH ONE! HOW DO YOU FEEL NOW SIR?
LIKE A SOILED PRUNE!!
LEFLER Ventura Star-Free Press

JOHN DEERING
Courtesy Arkansas Democrat-Gazette

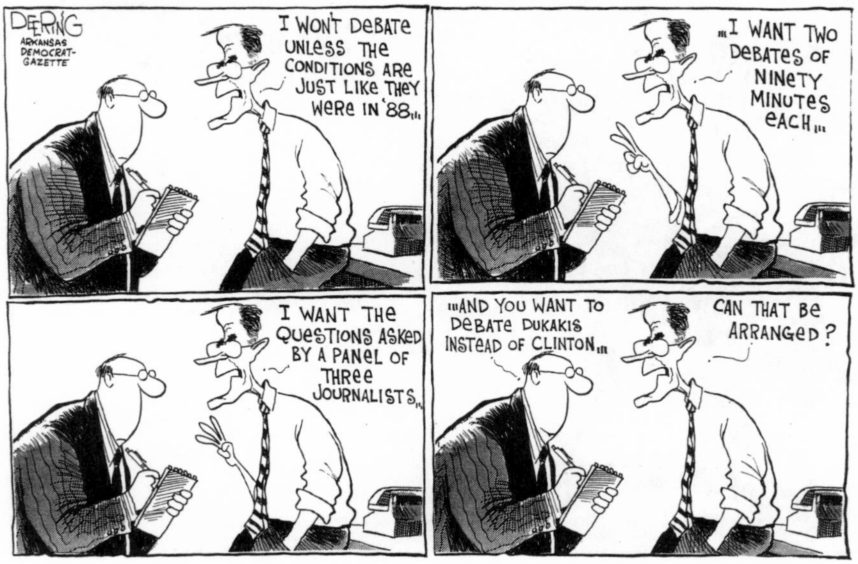
DEERING ARKANSAS DEMOCRAT-GAZETTE
I WON'T DEBATE UNLESS THE CONDITIONS ARE JUST LIKE THEY WERE IN '88...
...I WANT TWO DEBATES OF NINETY MINUTES EACH...
I WANT THE QUESTIONS ASKED BY A PANEL OF THREE JOURNALISTS...
...AND YOU WANT TO DEBATE DUKAKIS INSTEAD OF CLINTON...
CAN THAT BE ARRANGED?

DON LANDGREN, JR.
Courtesy Clinton Daily Item (Mass.)

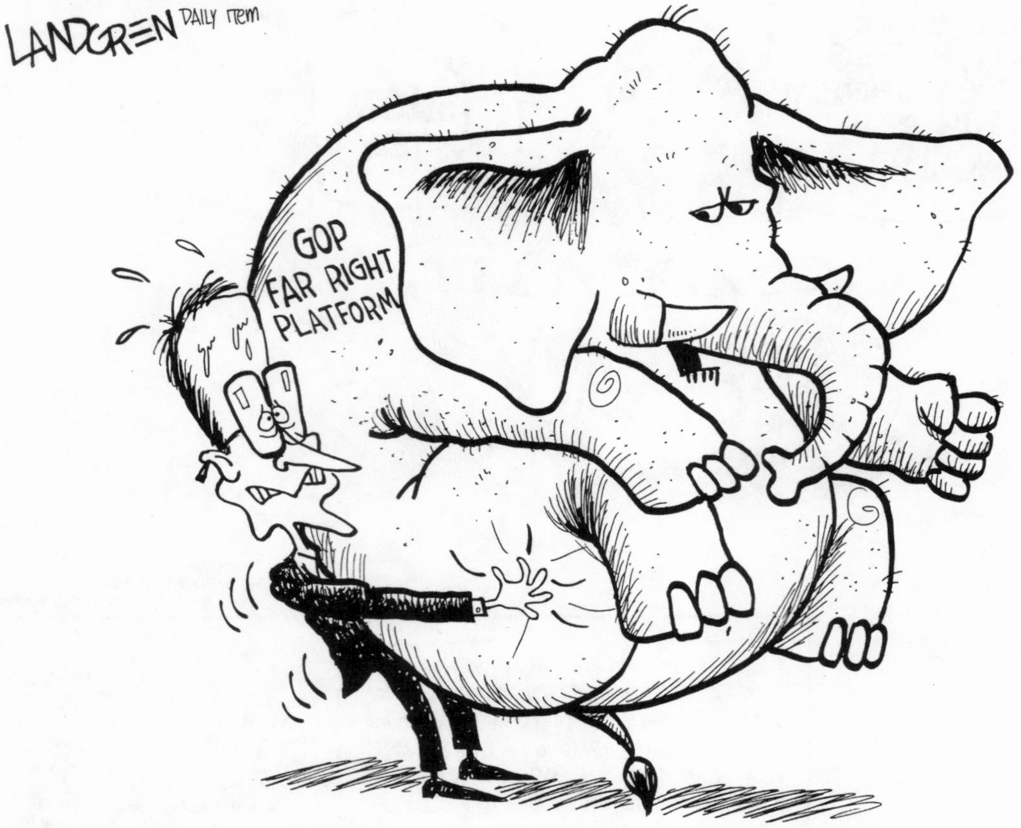
LANDGREN DAILY ITEM
GOP
FAR RIGHT
PLATFORM

"OK, GEORGE, NOW RUN!"

DICK WRIGHT
Courtesy Providence Journal-Bulletin

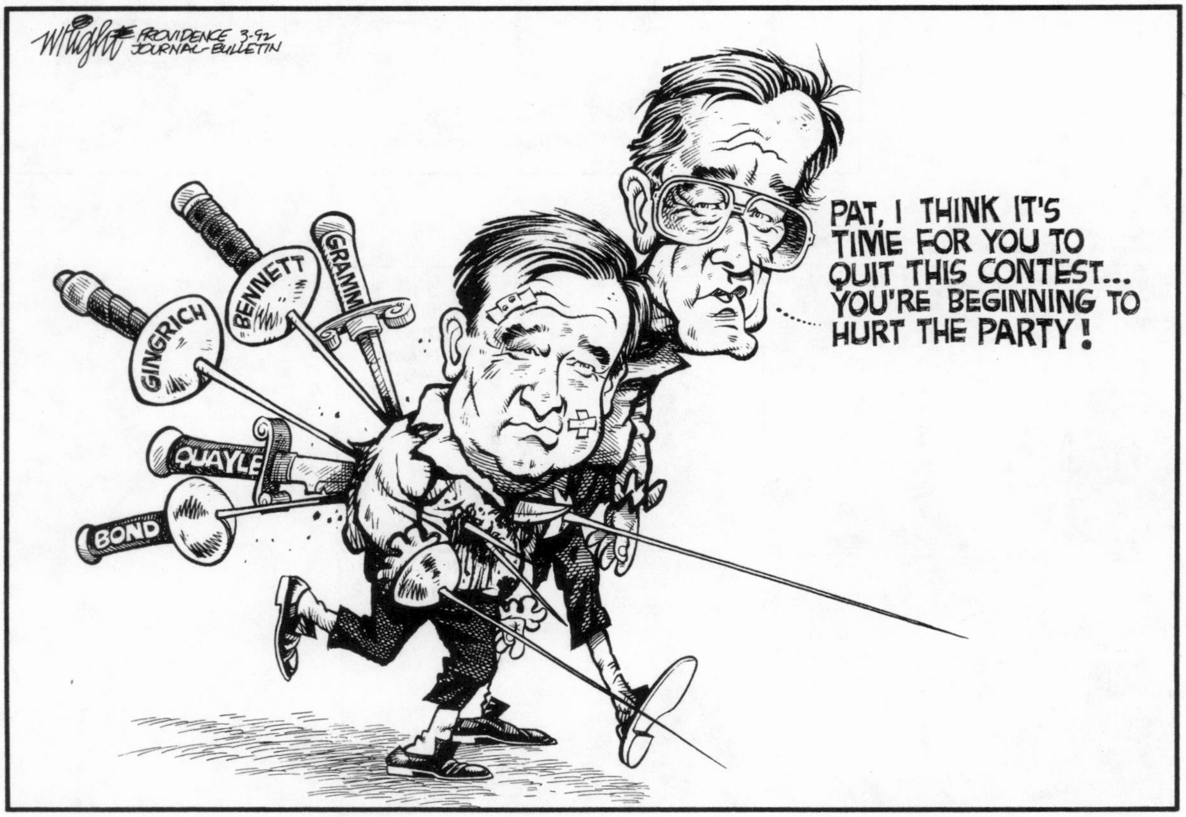
WRIGHT PROVIDENCE 3-92 JOURNAL-BULLETIN
PAT, I THINK IT'S TIME FOR YOU TO QUIT THIS CONTEST... YOU'RE BEGINNING TO HURT THE PARTY!
GINGRICH
BENNETT
GRAMM
QUAYLE
BOND

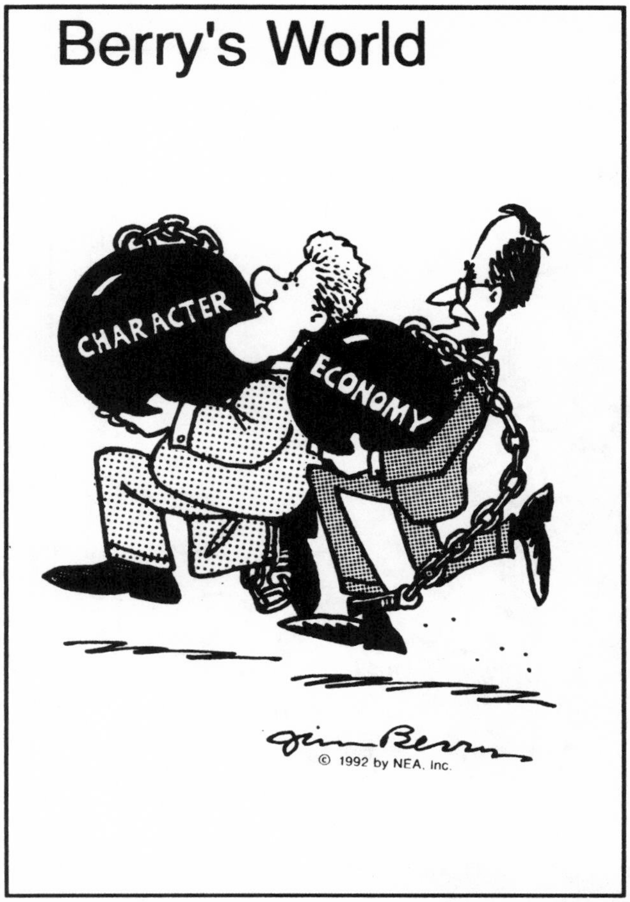
Berry's World
CHARACTER
ECONOMY
© 1992 by NEA, Inc.

JIM BERRY
Courtesy NEA

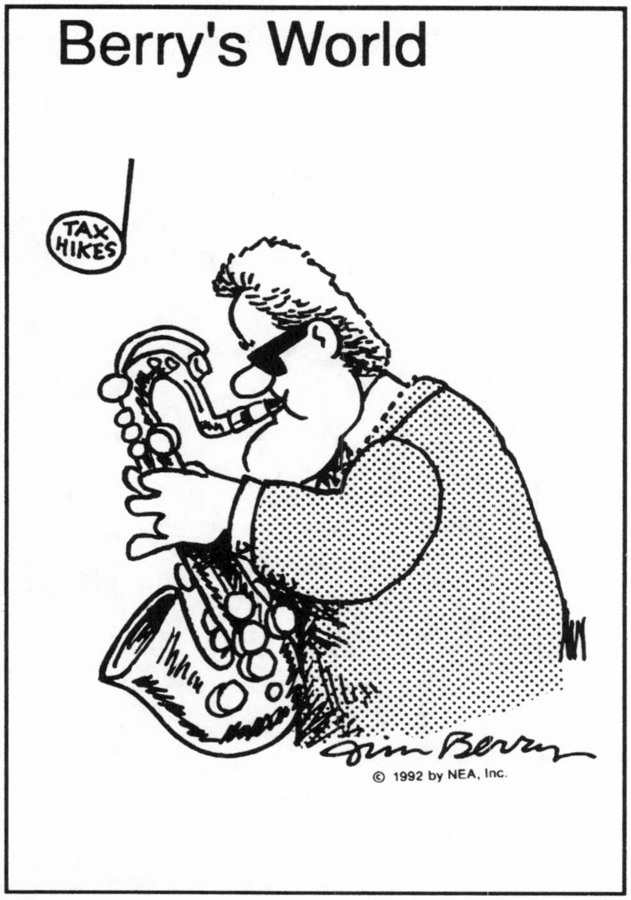
Berry's World
TAX HIKES
© 1992 by NEA, Inc.

JIM BERRY
Courtesy NEA

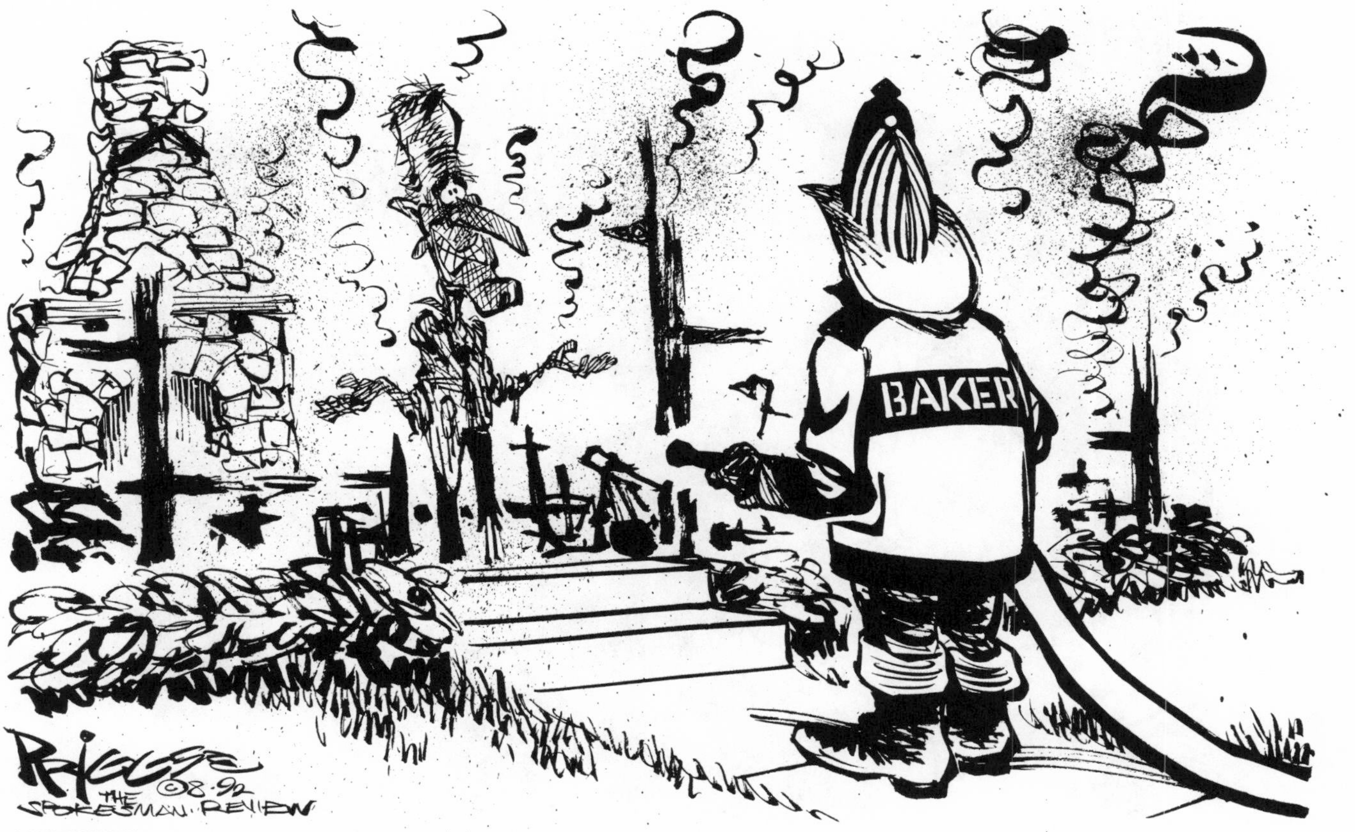
BAKER
PRIGGEE
©8·92
THE SPOKESMAN·REVIEW

MILT PRIGGEE
Courtesy Spokane Spokesman-Review

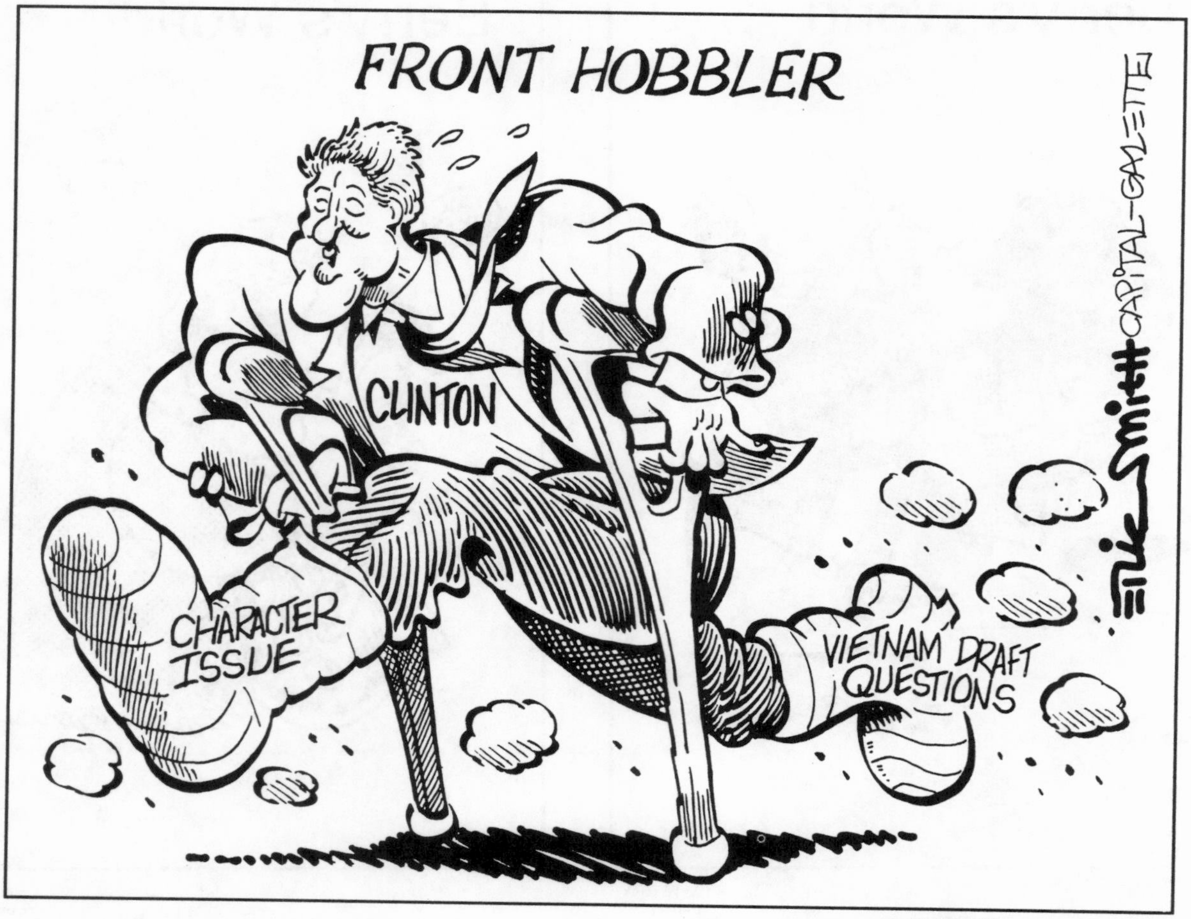
FRONT HOBBLER
CLINTON
CHARACTER ISSUE
VIETNAM DRAFT QUESTIONS
Eric Smith CAPITAL-GAZETTE

ERIC SMITH
Courtesy Capital Gazette Newspapers

JIM McCLOSKEY
Courtesy Staunton Daily News Leader

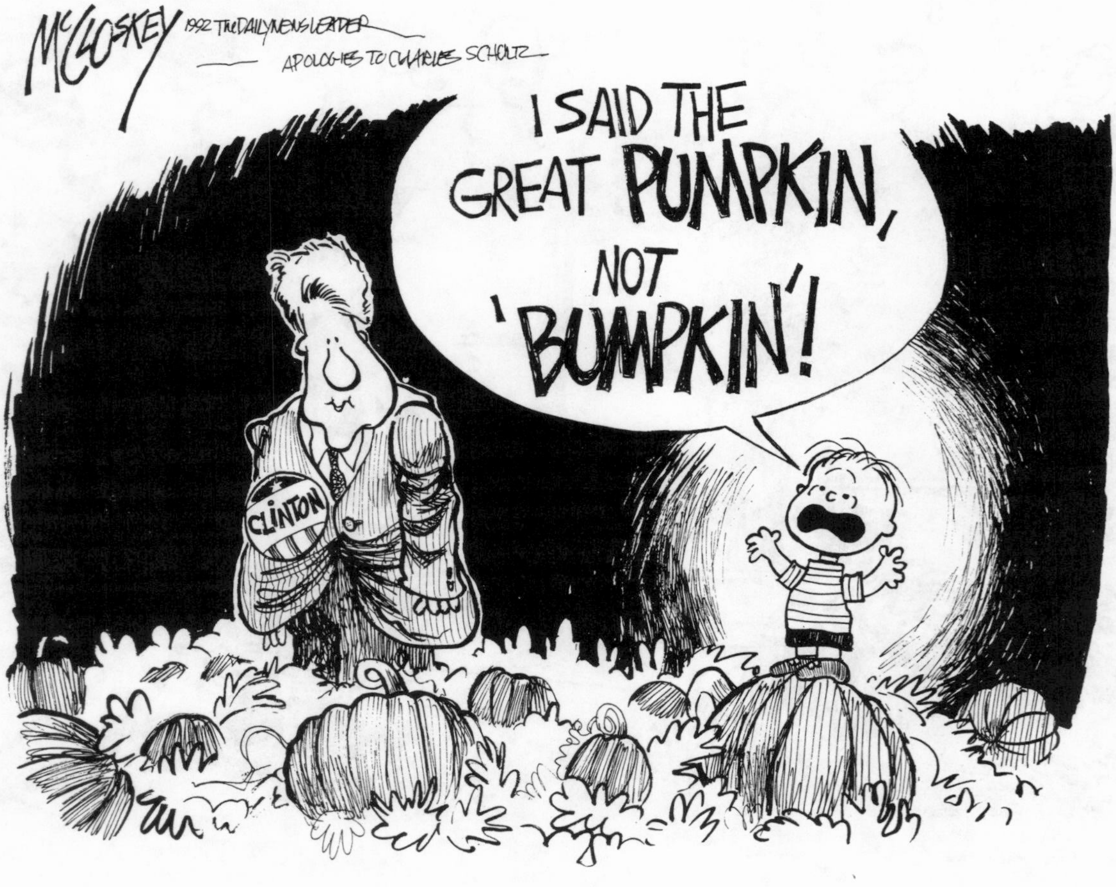
McCLOSKEY 1992 The Daily News Leader
APOLOGIES TO CHARLES SCHULTZ
I SAID THE GREAT PUMPKIN, NOT 'BUMPKIN'!
CLINTON

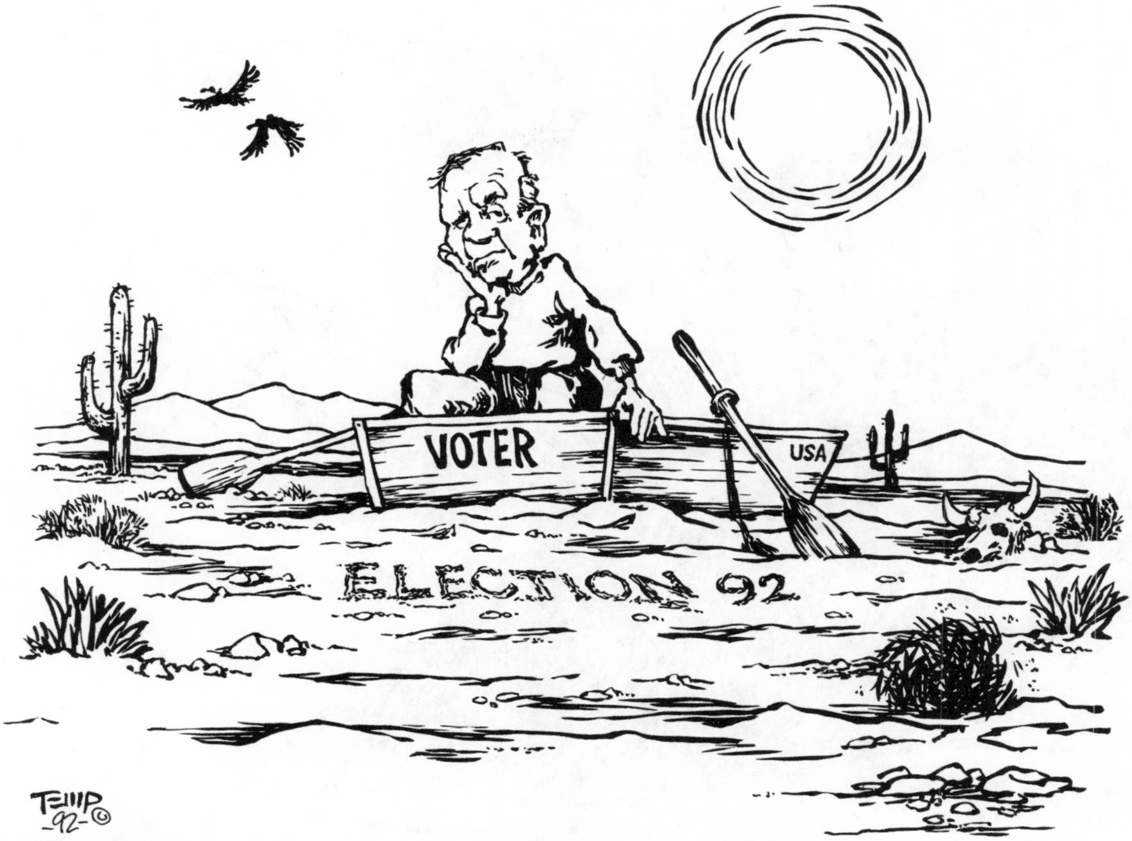

VOTER
USA
ELECTION 92
TEMP -92- ©

STEPHEN TEMPLETON
Courtesy National Forum/Associated Features

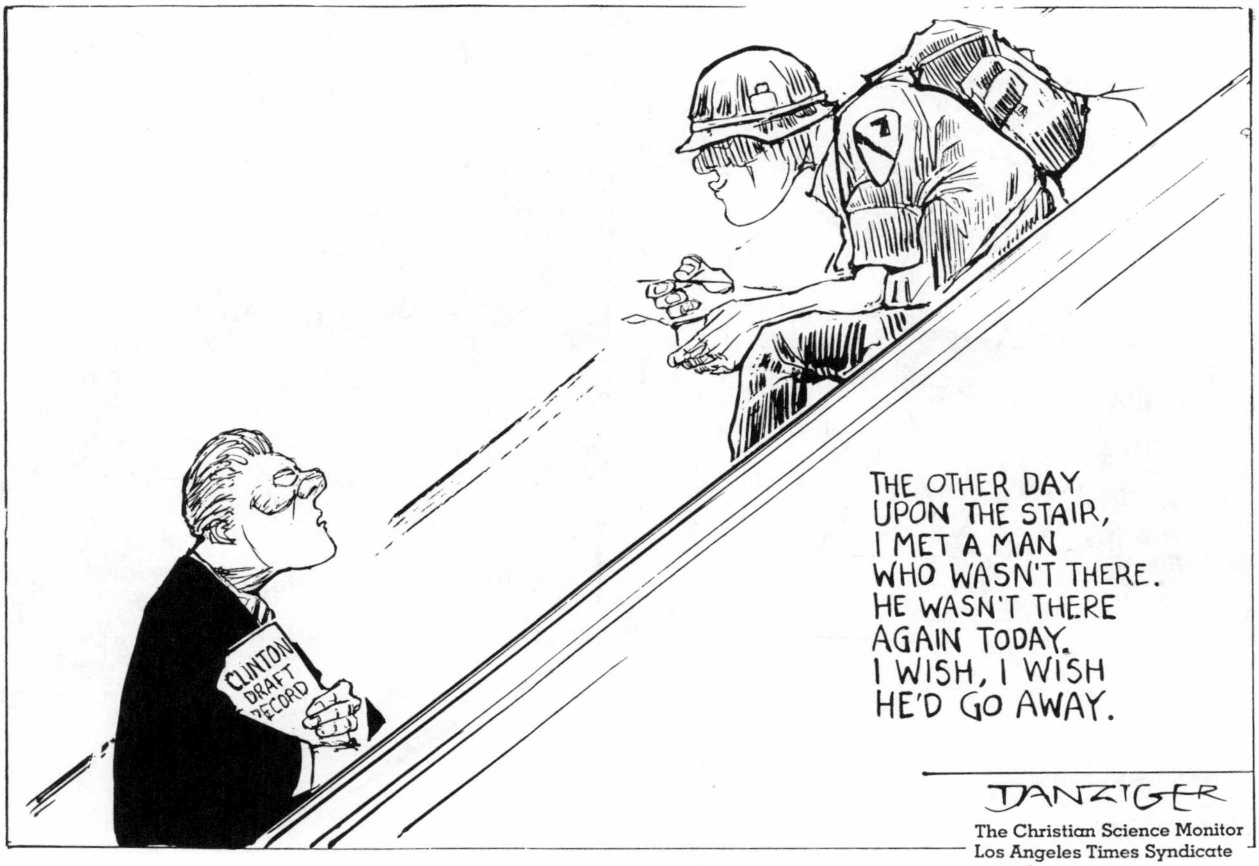

CLINTON DRAFT RECORD
THE OTHER DAY UPON THE STAIR, I MET A MAN WHO WASN'T THERE. HE WASN'T THERE AGAIN TODAY. I WISH, I WISH HE'D GO AWAY.
DANZIGER
The Christian Science Monitor
Los Angeles Times Syndicate

JEFF DANZIGER
Courtesy Christian Science Monitor

DAVID SWANN
Courtesy Huntsville Times (Ala.)

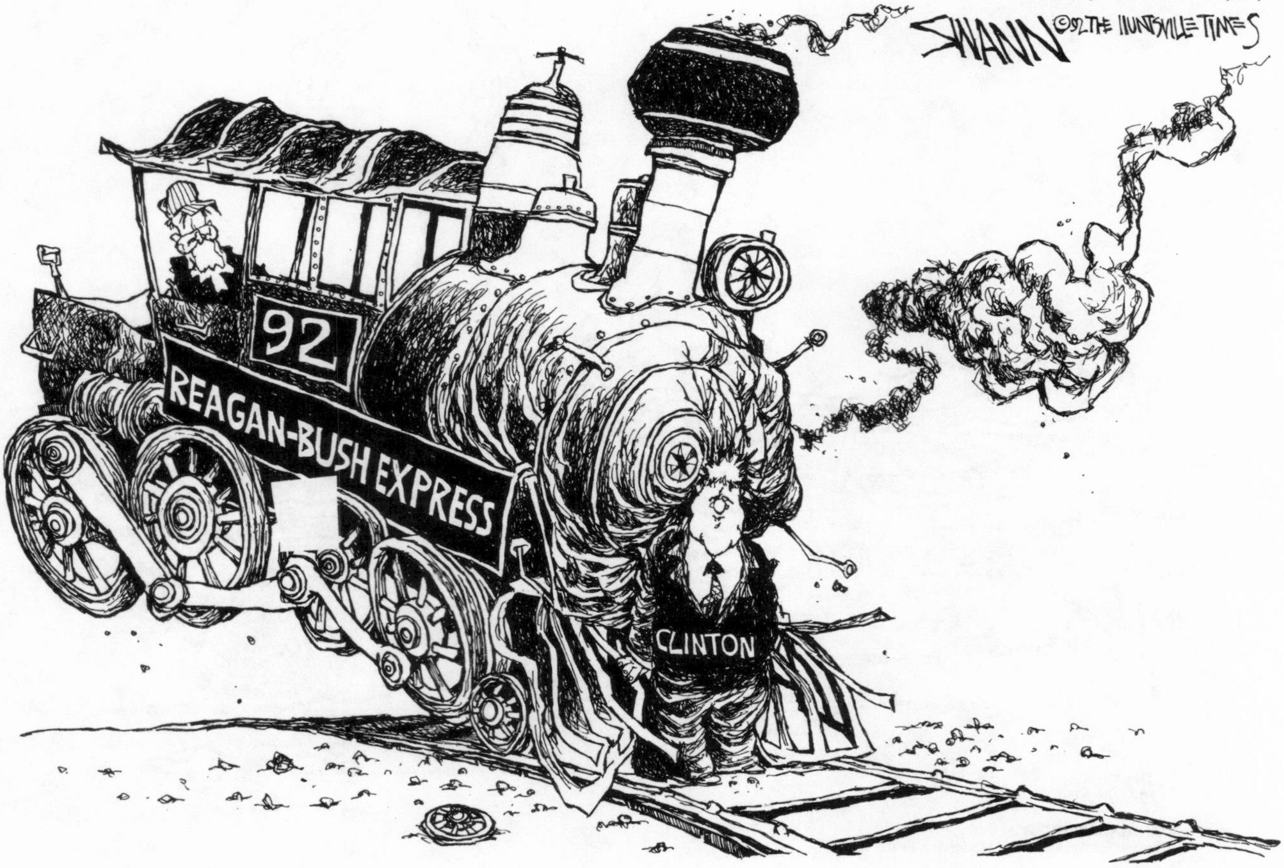
SWANN ©92 THE HUNTSVILLE TIMES
92
REAGAN-BUSH EXPRESS
CLINTON

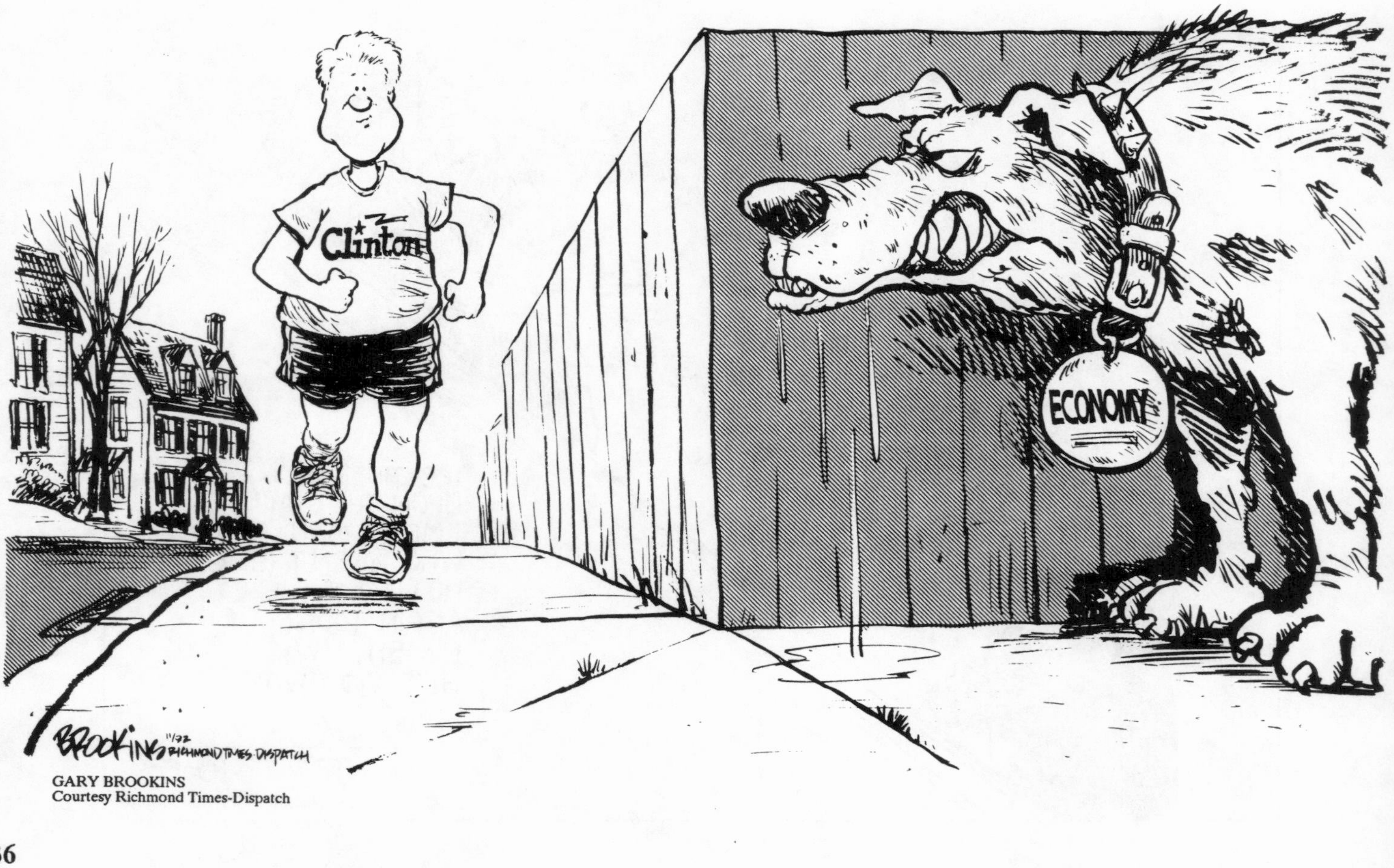
Clinton
ECONOMY
BROOKINS 11/92 RICHMOND TIMES DISPATCH

GARY BROOKINS
Courtesy Richmond Times-Dispatch

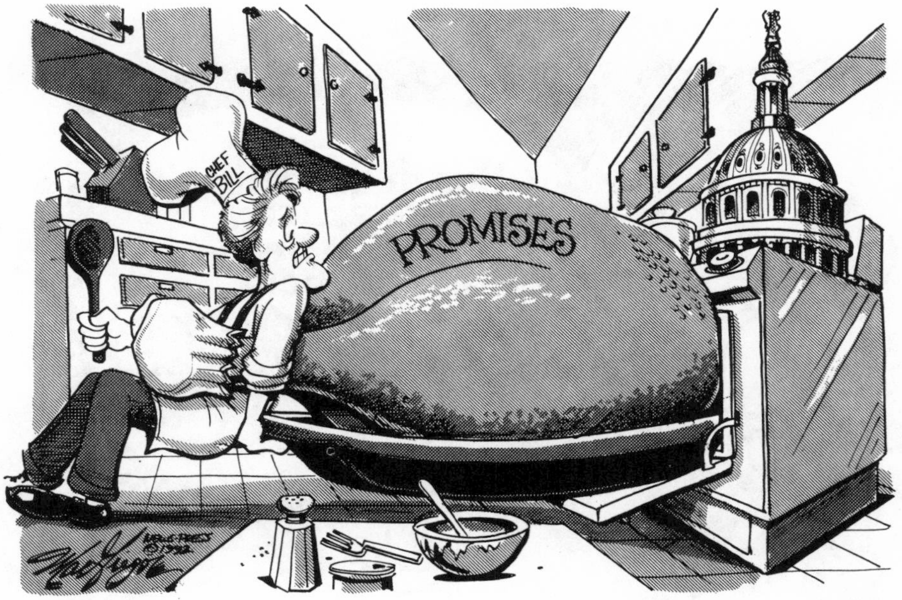
CHEF BILL
PROMISES

DOUG MACGREGOR
Courtesy Ft. Meyers News-Press

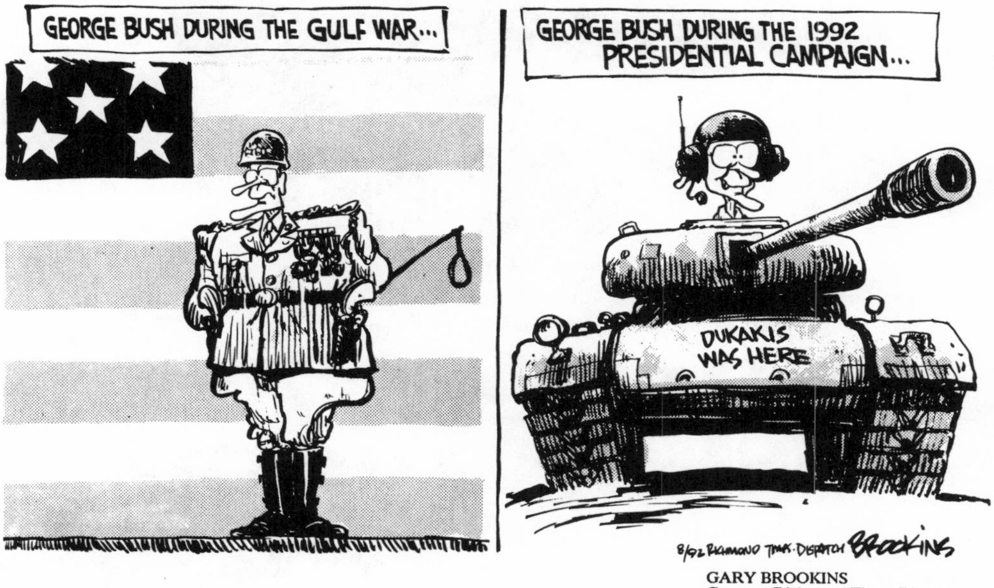
GEORGE BUSH DURING THE GULF WAR...
GEORGE BUSH DURING THE 1992 PRESIDENTIAL CAMPAIGN...
DUKAKIS WAS HERE
8/92 RICHMOND TIMES-DISPATCH BROOKINS

GARY BROOKINS
Courtesy Richmond Times-Dispatch

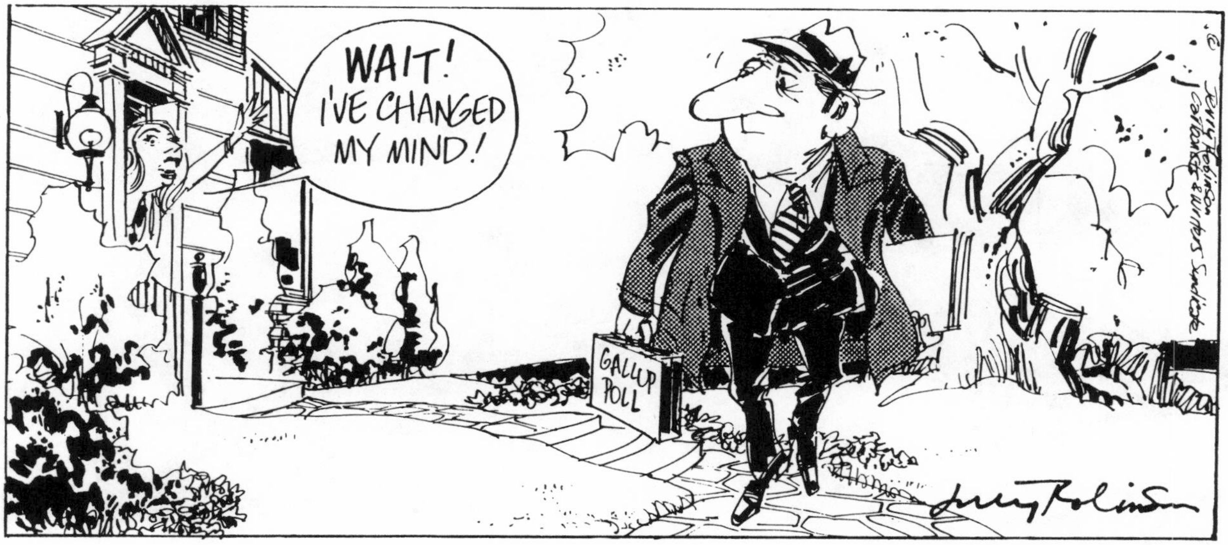
WAIT! I'VE CHANGED MY MIND!
GALLUP POLL
Jerry Robinson

JERRY ROBINSON
Courtesy Cartoonists & Writers Syndicate

JIMMY MARGULIES
Courtesy The Record (N.J.) copyright 1992
North America Syndicate

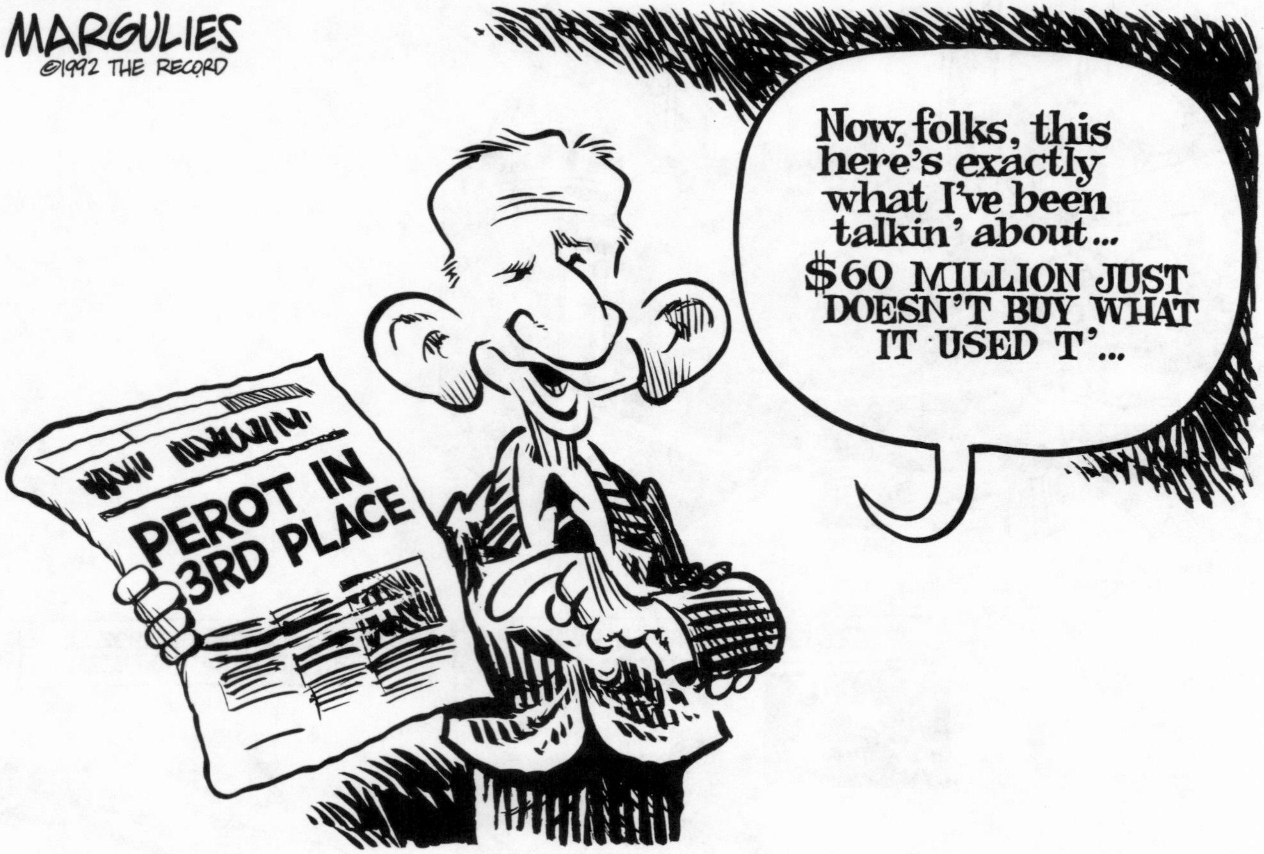
MARGULIES
©1992 THE RECORD
PEROT IN 3RD PLACE
Now, folks, this here's exactly what I've been talkin' about... $60 MILLION JUST DOESN'T BUY WHAT IT USED T'...

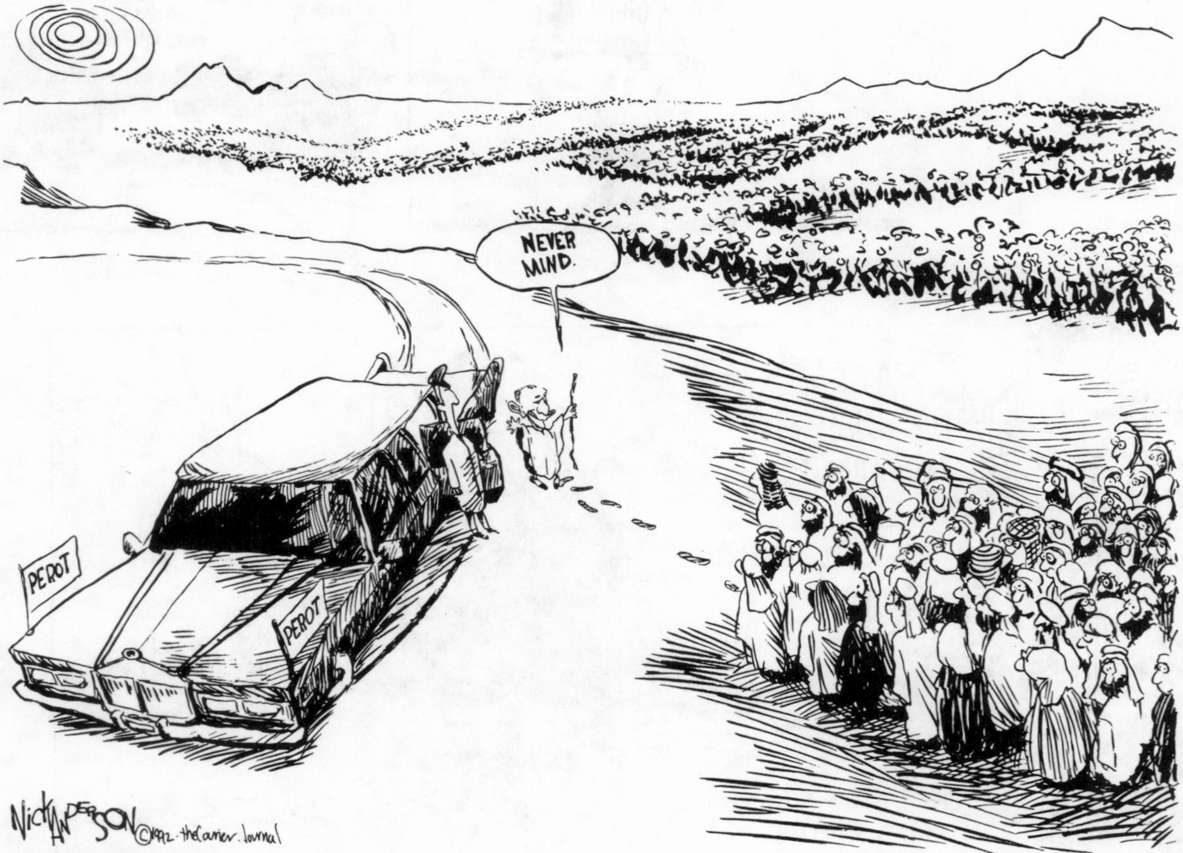
NEVER MIND.
PEROT
PEROT

NICK ANDERSON
Courtesy Louisville Courier Journal

Ross Perot

Early in the year, the country seemed to be heading for a dull election year of politics as usual. George Bush's popularity remained high after Desert Storm, and a second term appeared inevitable.

Then one night on Larry King's CNN television talk show, Ross Perot, a Texas billionaire computer magnate, casually mentioned that he would consider running for president if volunteers could get his name on all fifty state ballots. It was like a breath of fresh air to millions of Americans who were tired of political gridlock and politicians in general. Within weeks, a volunteer force obtained enough voter signatures to place his name on ballots in a majority of the states.

A surprised Perot plunged into the fray, appearing repeatedly on television talk shows and in thirty-minute commercials to explain his views, particularly on how to reduce the deficit. Then, he abruptly withdrew from the race.

Weeks later, he once again announced his candidacy, but was unable to reinspire his earlier supporters. Many of his volunteers already had begun campaigning for other candidates. He spent some $57 million of his own money and pulled 19 percent of the vote, the highest percentage for a third party candidate since Theodore Roosevelt.

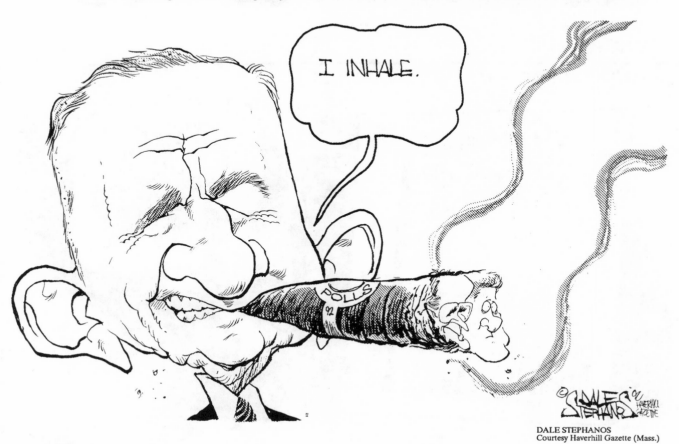

DALE STEPHANOS
Courtesy Haverhill Gazette (Mass.)

MALCOLM MAYES
Courtesy Edmonton Journal

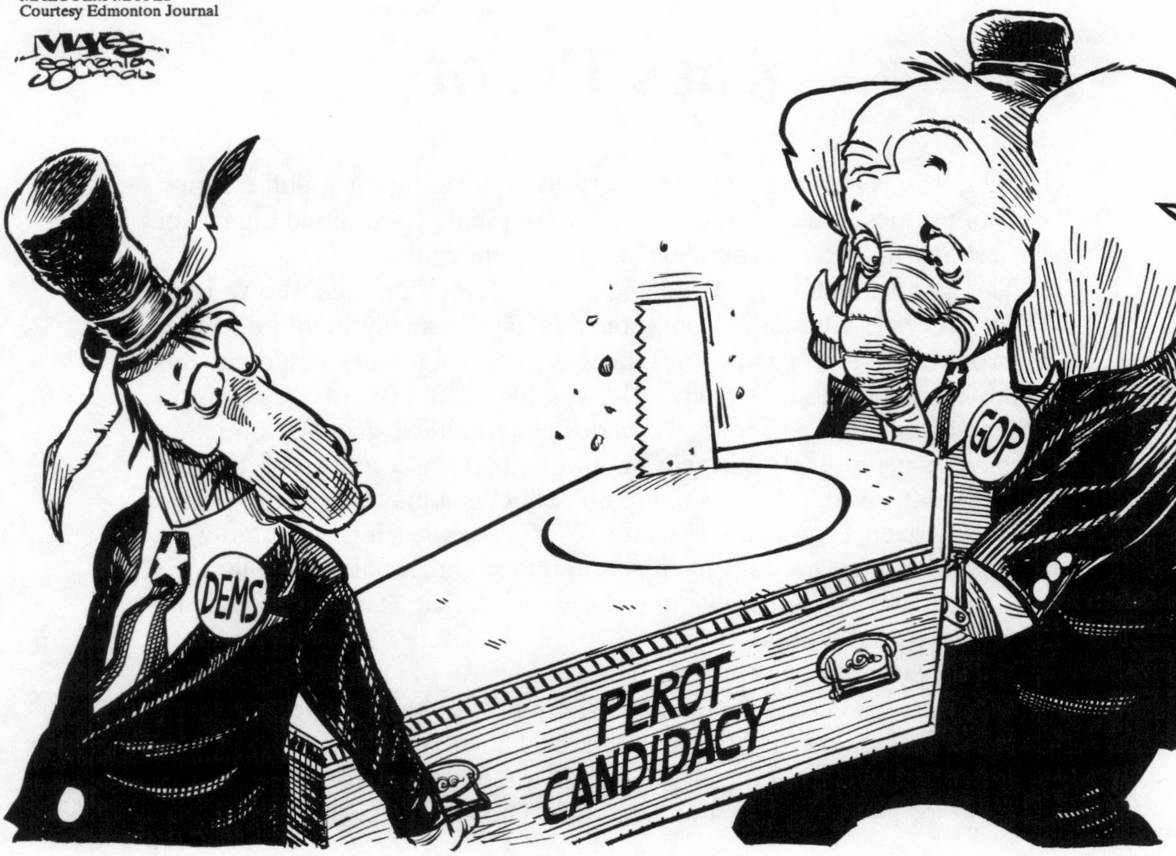
MAYES Edmonton Journal
DEMS
GOP
PEROT CANDIDACY

JIM BORGMAN
Courtesy Cincinnati Enquirer

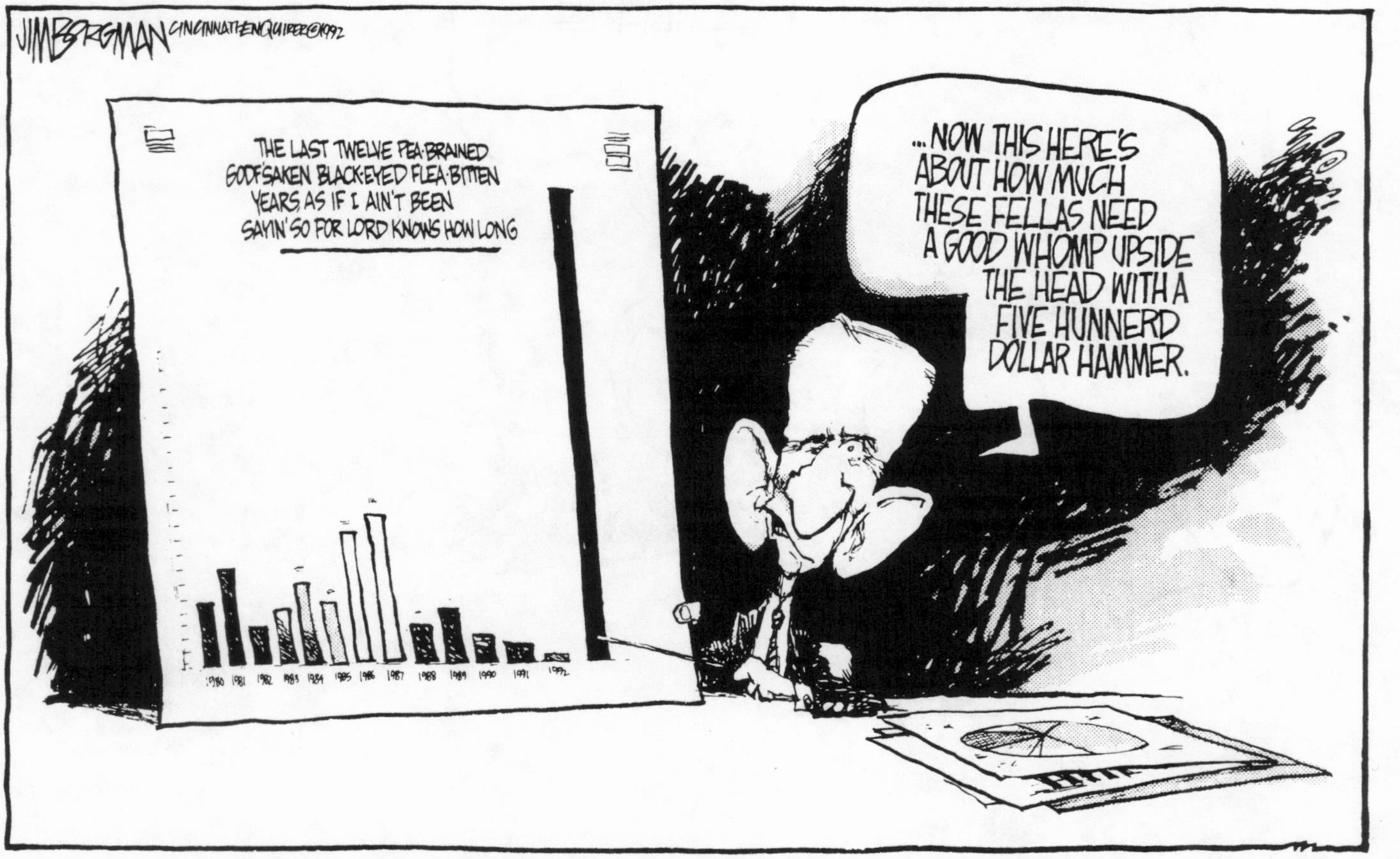
JIM BORGMAN CINCINNATI ENQUIRER ©1992
THE LAST TWELVE PEA-BRAINED GODFSAKEN BLACK-EYED FLEA-BITTEN YEARS AS IF I AIN'T BEEN SAYIN' SO FOR LORD KNOWS HOW LONG
1980 1981 1982 1983 1984 1985 1986 1987 1988 1989 1990 1991 1992
...NOW THIS HERE'S ABOUT HOW MUCH THESE FELLAS NEED A GOOD WHOMP UPSIDE THE HEAD WITH A FIVE HUNNERD DOLLAR HAMMER.

JEFF MACNELLY
Courtesy Chicago Tribune and
Tribune Media Services

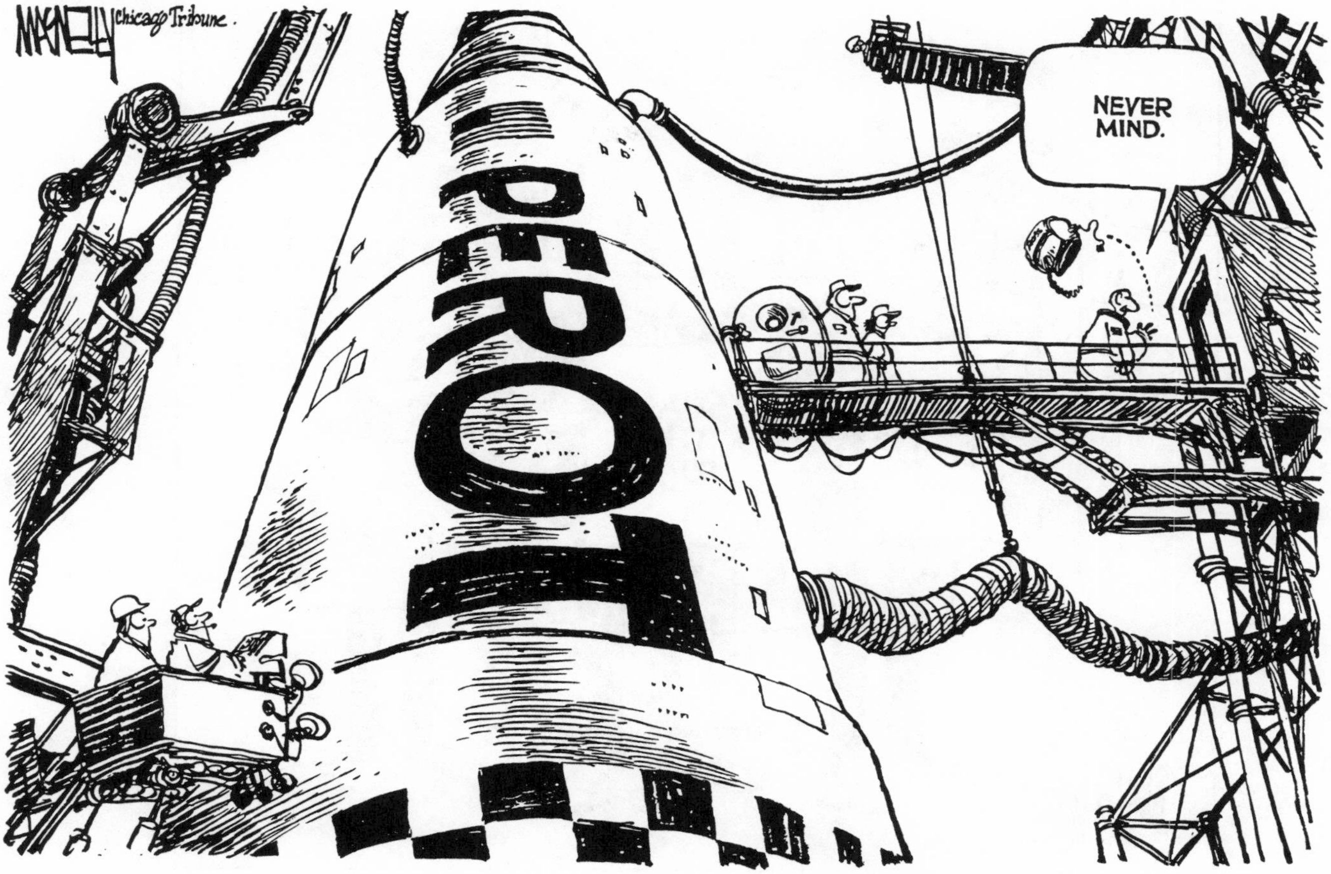
MACNELLY Chicago Tribune
PEROT
NEVER MIND.

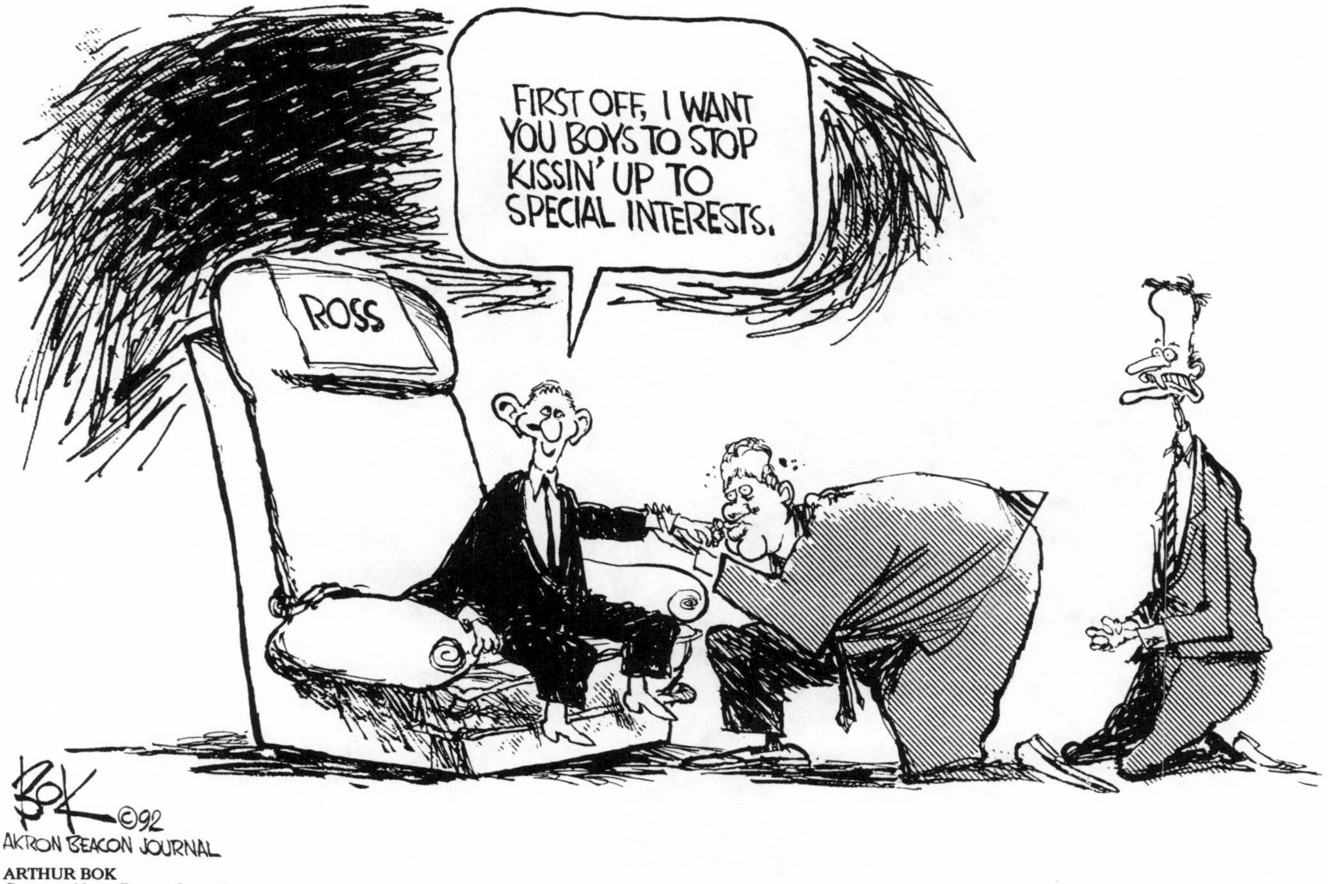
FIRST OFF, I WANT YOU BOYS TO STOP KISSIN' UP TO SPECIAL INTERESTS.
ROSS
BOK ©92 AKRON BEACON JOURNAL

ARTHUR BOK
Courtesy Akron Beacon Journal

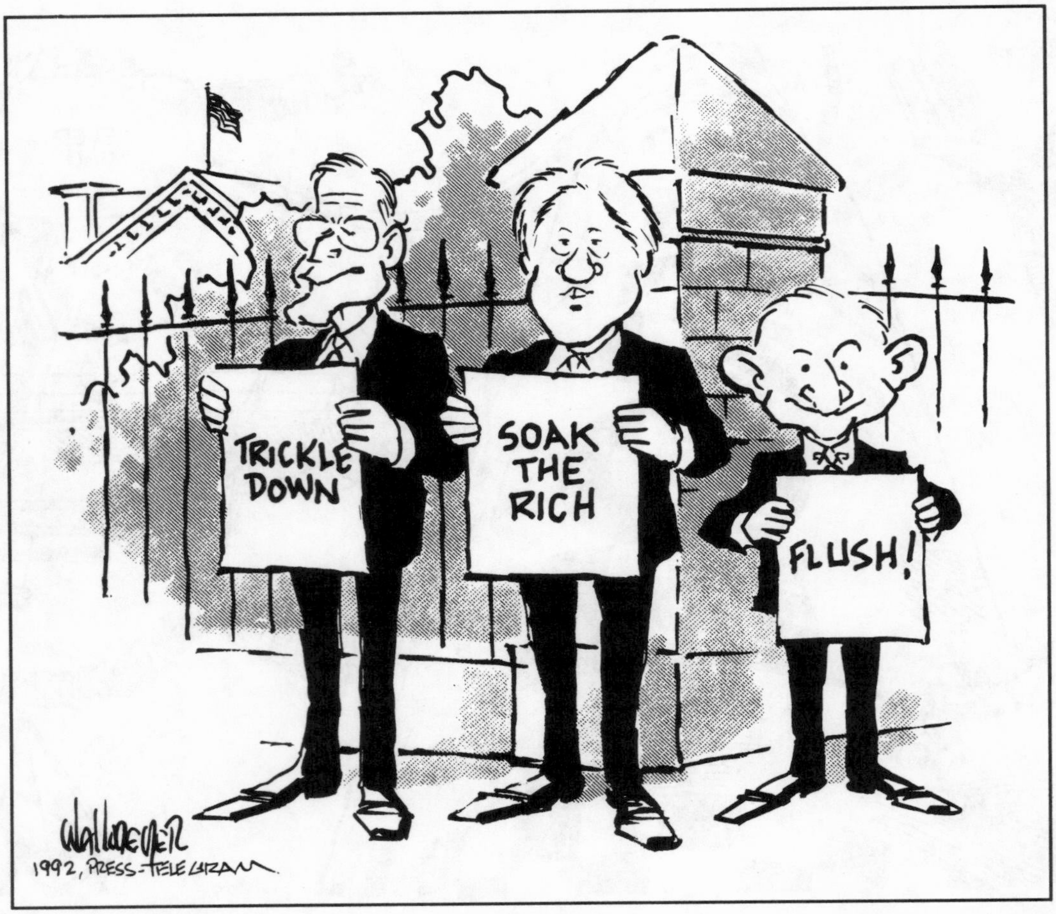
TRICKLE DOWN
SOAK THE RICH
FLUSH!
WALLMEYER
1992, PRESS-TELEGRAM

DICK WALLMEYER
Courtesy Long Beach Press-Telegram

MICHAEL RAMIREZ
Courtesy Memphis Commercial Appeal

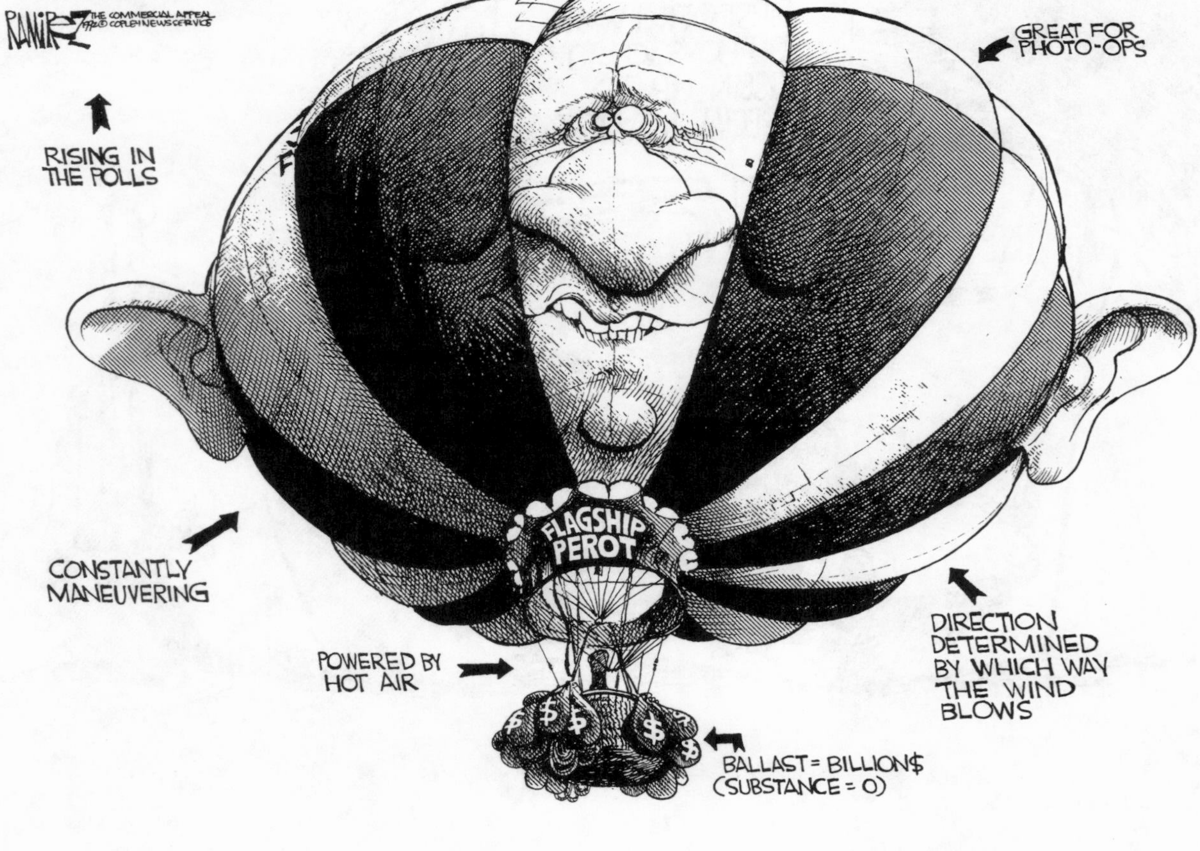
RAMIREZ
GREAT FOR PHOTO-OPS
RISING IN THE POLLS
FLAGSHIP PEROT
CONSTANTLY MANEUVERING
DIRECTION DETERMINED BY WHICH WAY THE WIND BLOWS
POWERED BY HOT AIR
BALLAST = BILLION$ (SUBSTANCE = 0)

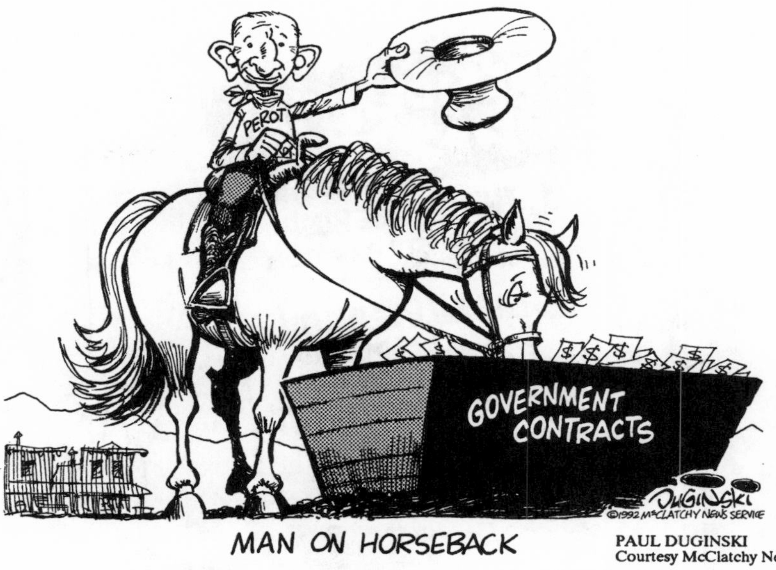
PEROT
GOVERNMENT CONTRACTS
DUGINSKI
©1992 McCLATCHY NEWS SERVICE
MAN ON HORSEBACK

PAUL DUGINSKI
Courtesy McClatchy News Service

V. CULLUM ROGERS
Courtesy Spectator Magazine

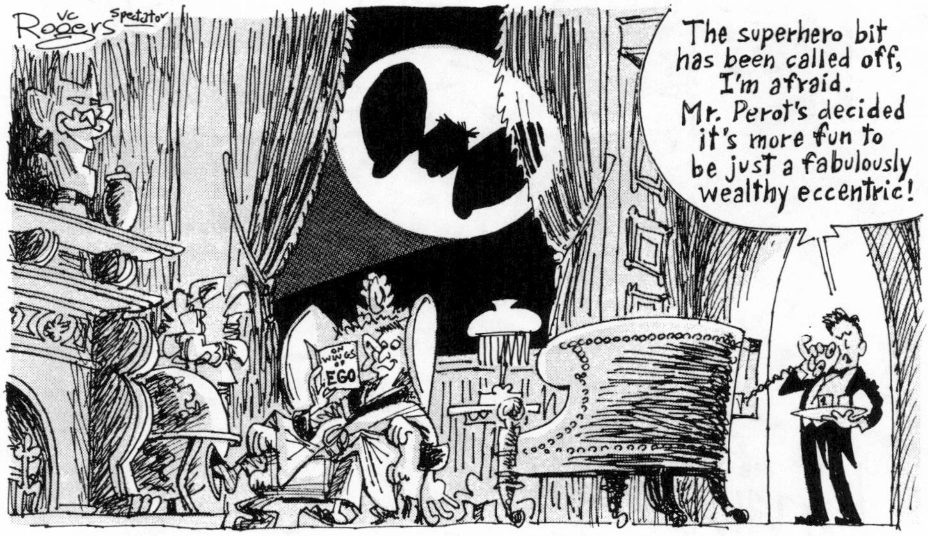
VC Rogers Spectator
The superhero bit has been called off, I'm afraid. Mr. Perot's decided it's more fun to be just a fabulously wealthy eccentric!
ON WINGS OF EGO

DOUGLAS REGALIA
Courtesy San Ramon Valley Times (Calif.)

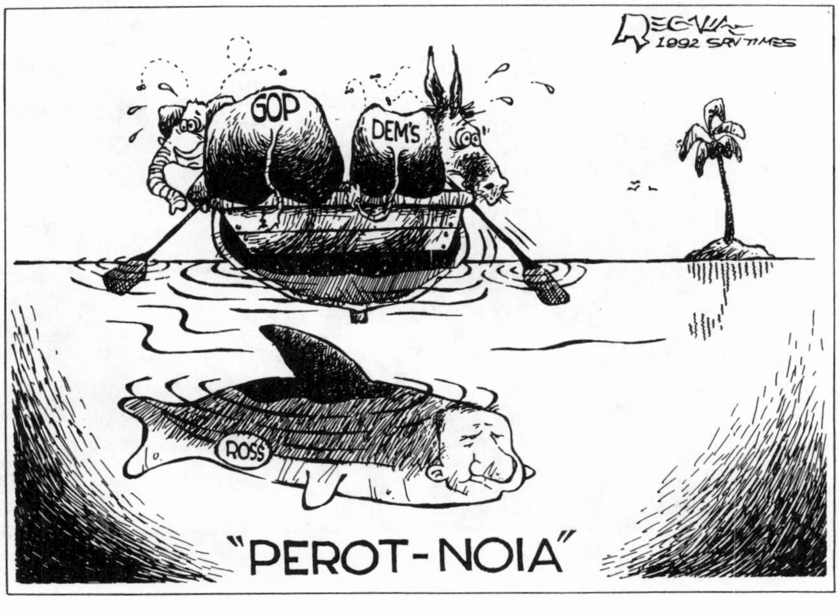
1992 SRV TIMES
GOP
DEM'S
ROSS
"PEROT-NOIA"

STEVE KELLEY
Courtesy San Diego Union

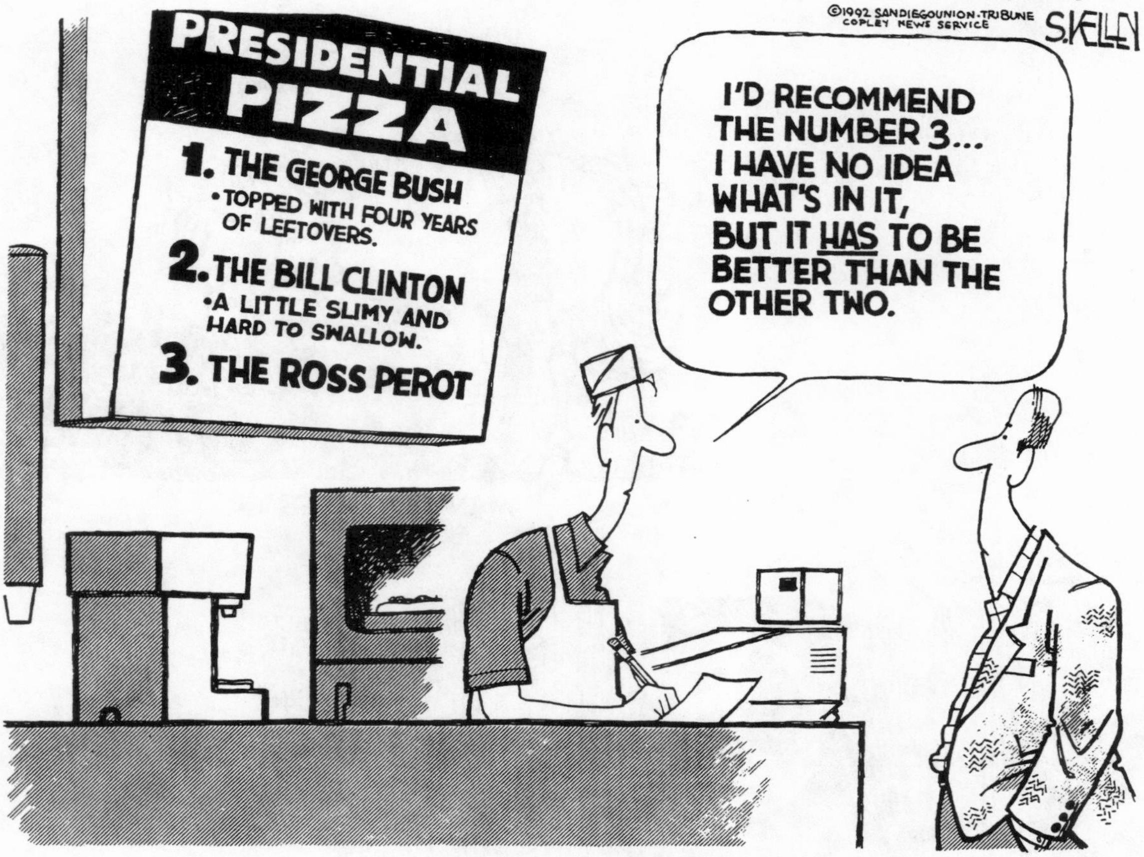

©1992 SANDIEGOUNION-TRIBUNE COPLEY NEWS SERVICE
S.KELLEY
PRESIDENTIAL PIZZA
1. THE GEORGE BUSH
•TOPPED WITH FOUR YEARS OF LEFTOVERS.
2. THE BILL CLINTON
•A LITTLE SLIMY AND HARD TO SWALLOW.
3. THE ROSS PEROT
I'D RECOMMEND THE NUMBER 3... I HAVE NO IDEA WHAT'S IN IT, BUT IT HAS TO BE BETTER THAN THE OTHER TWO.

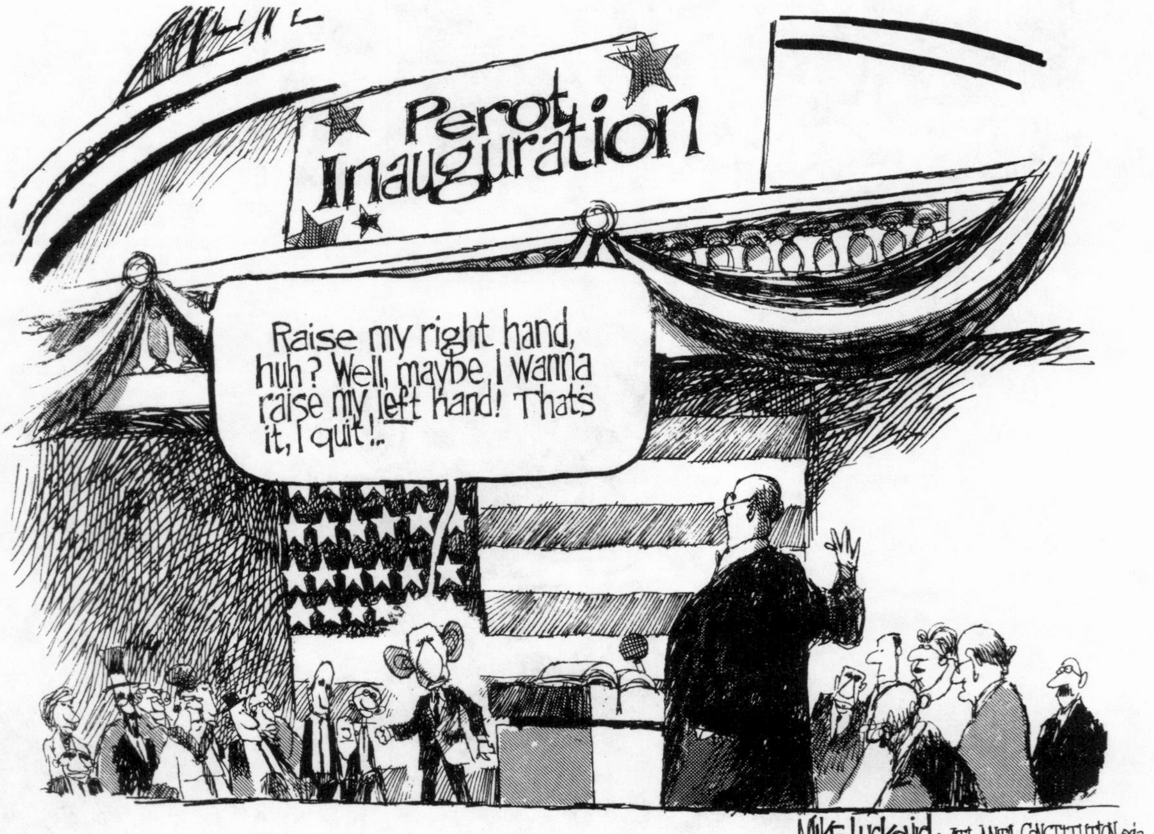

Perot Inauguration
Raise my right hand, huh? Well, maybe I wanna raise my left hand! That's it, I quit!..
MIKE Luckovich ATLANTA CONSTITUTION

MIKE LUCKOVICH
Courtesy Atlanta Constitution

STUART CARLSON
Courtesy Milwaukee Sentinel

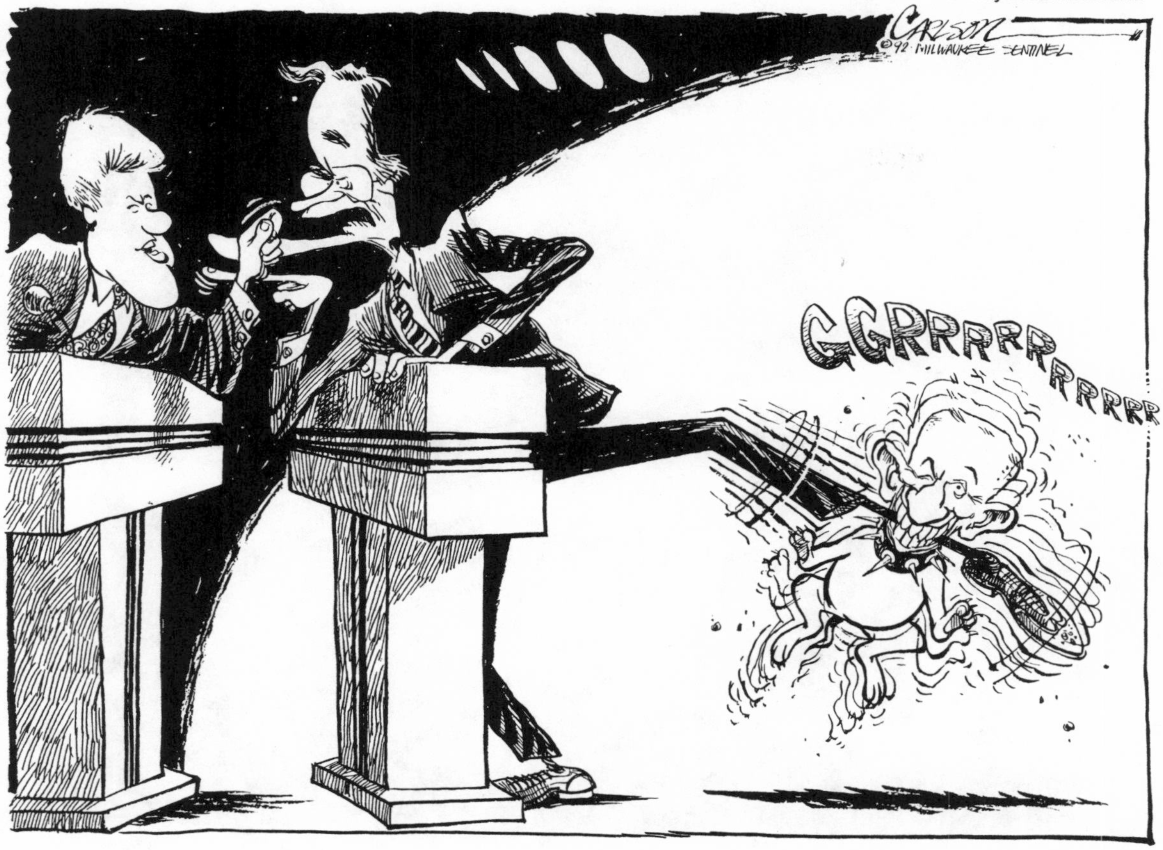
CARLSON
©'92 MILWAUKEE SENTINEL
GGRRRRRRRRRRRR

BOB GORRELL
Courtesy Richmond Times-Dispatch

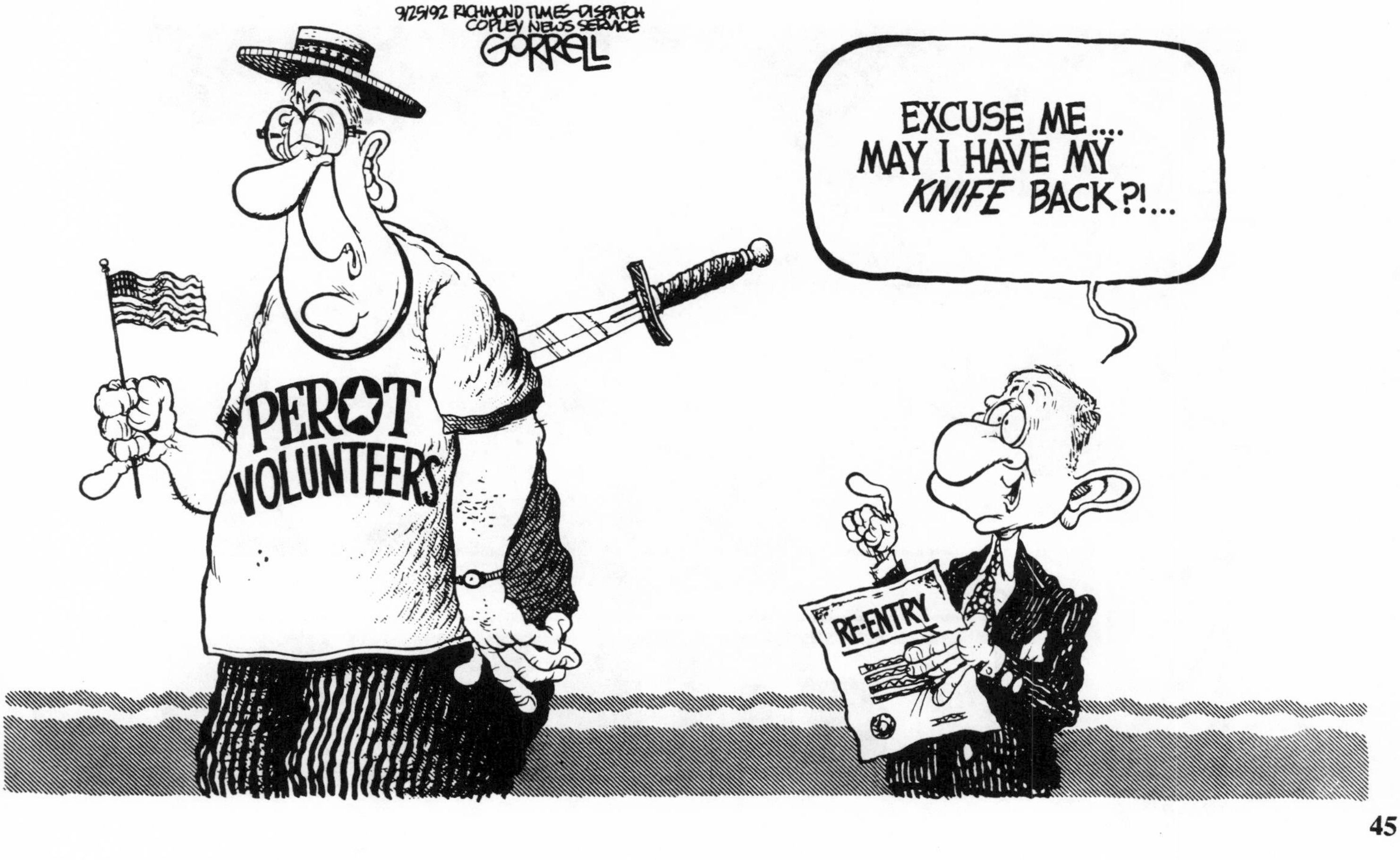
9/25/92 RICHMOND TIMES-DISPATCH
COPLEY NEWS SERVICE
GORRELL
EXCUSE ME.... MAY I HAVE MY *KNIFE* BACK?!...
PEROT VOLUNTEERS
RE-ENTRY

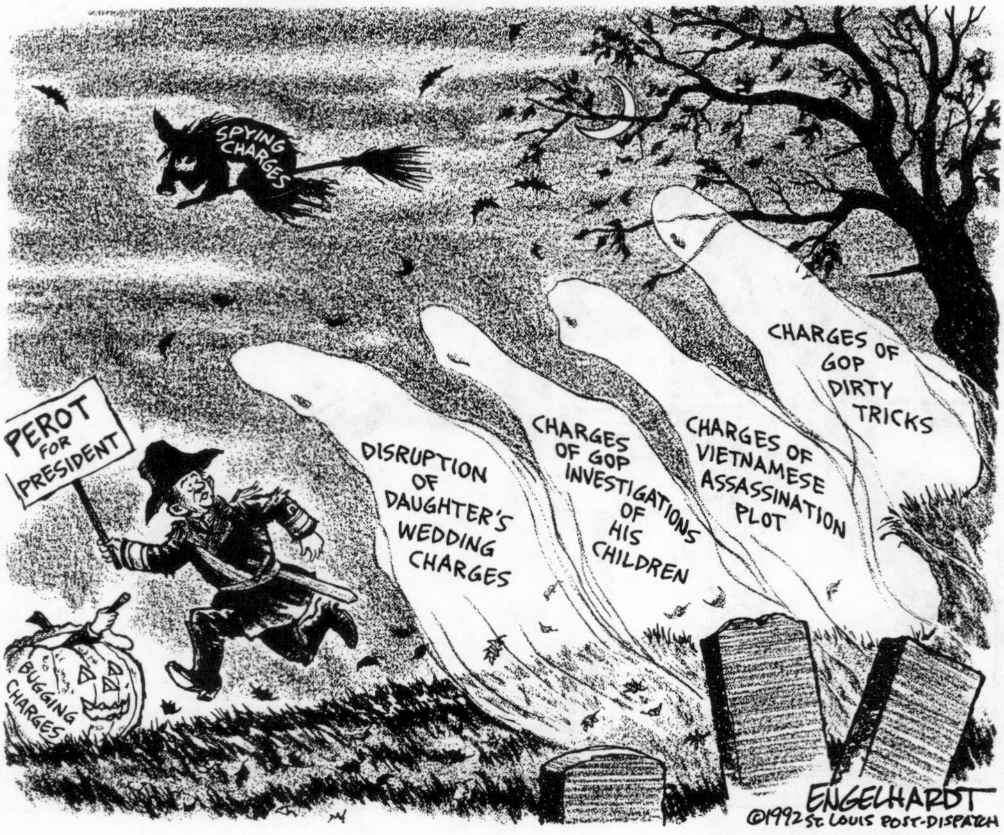
SPYING CHARGES
PEROT FOR PRESIDENT
BUGGING CHARGES
DISRUPTION OF DAUGHTER'S WEDDING CHARGES
CHARGES OF GOP INVESTIGATIONS OF HIS CHILDREN
CHARGES OF VIETNAMESE ASSASSINATION PLOT
CHARGES OF GOP DIRTY TRICKS
ENGELHARDT
©1992 St. Louis Post-Dispatch

TOM ENGELHARDT
Courtesy St. Louis Post-Dispatch

'Charge!'

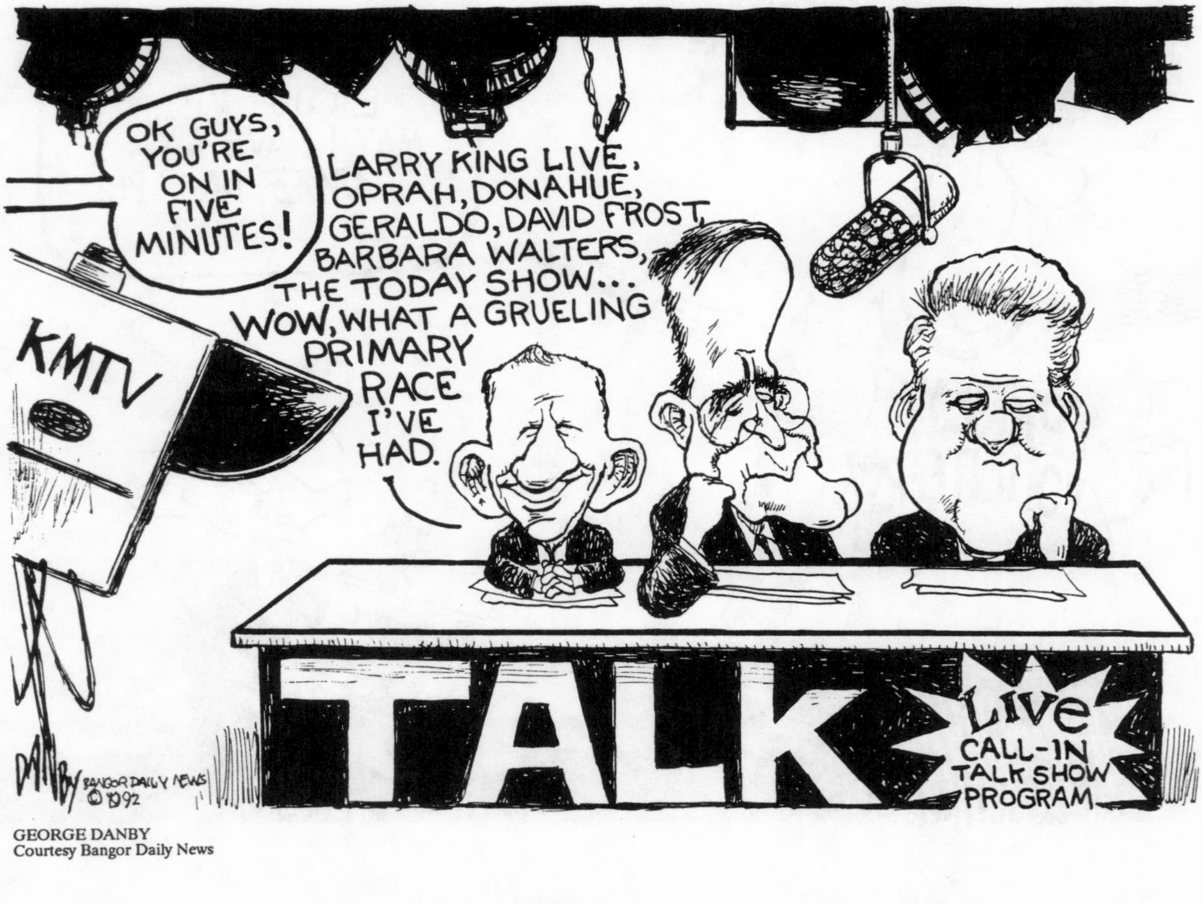
OK GUYS, YOU'RE ON IN FIVE MINUTES!
LARRY KING LIVE, OPRAH, DONAHUE, GERALDO, DAVID FROST, BARBARA WALTERS, THE TODAY SHOW... WOW, WHAT A GRUELING PRIMARY RACE I'VE HAD.
KMTV
TALK
Live CALL-IN TALK SHOW PROGRAM
DANBY
BANGOR DAILY NEWS ©1992

GEORGE DANBY
Courtesy Bangor Daily News

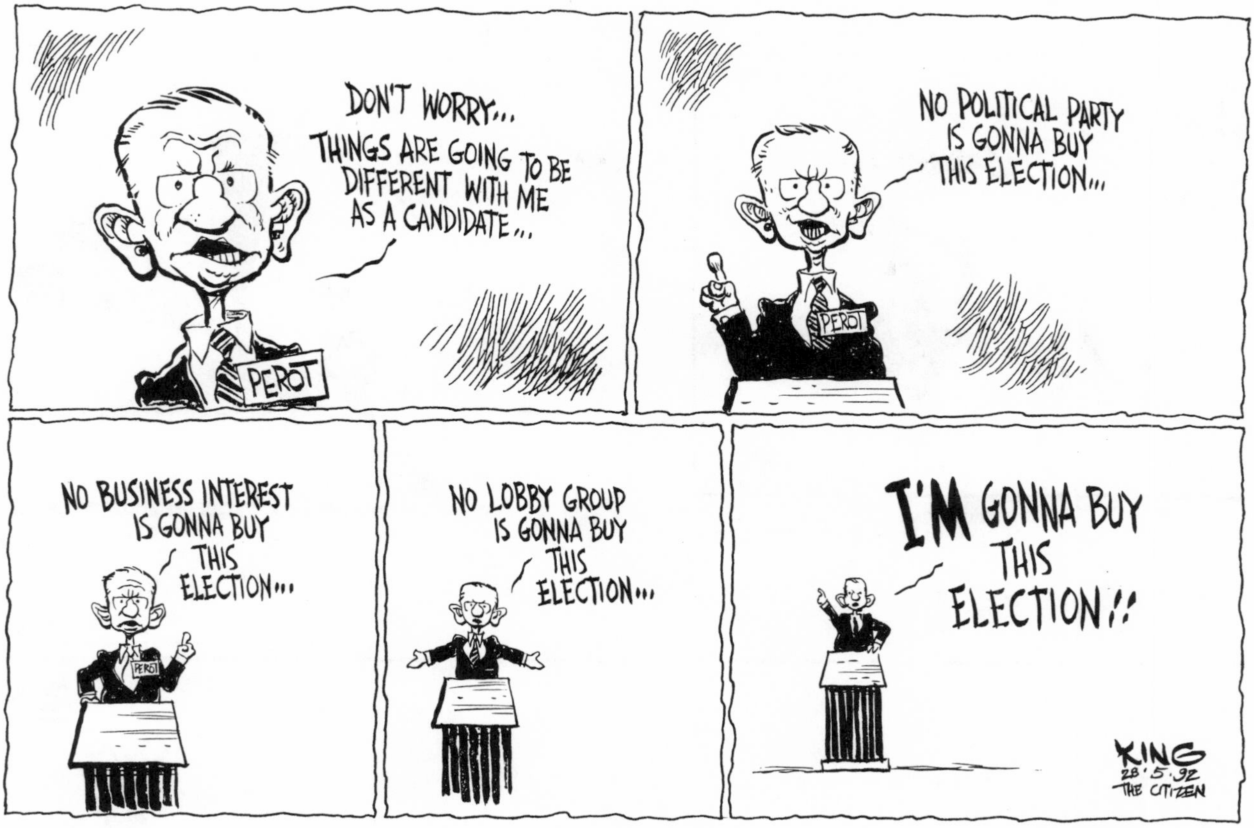
DON'T WORRY...
THINGS ARE GOING TO BE DIFFERENT WITH ME AS A CANDIDATE...
PEROT
NO POLITICAL PARTY IS GONNA BUY THIS ELECTION...
PEROT
NO BUSINESS INTEREST IS GONNA BUY THIS ELECTION...
PEROT
NO LOBBY GROUP IS GONNA BUY THIS ELECTION...
I'M GONNA BUY THIS ELECTION!!
KING 28·5·92 THE CITIZEN

ALAN KING
Courtesy Ottawa Citizen

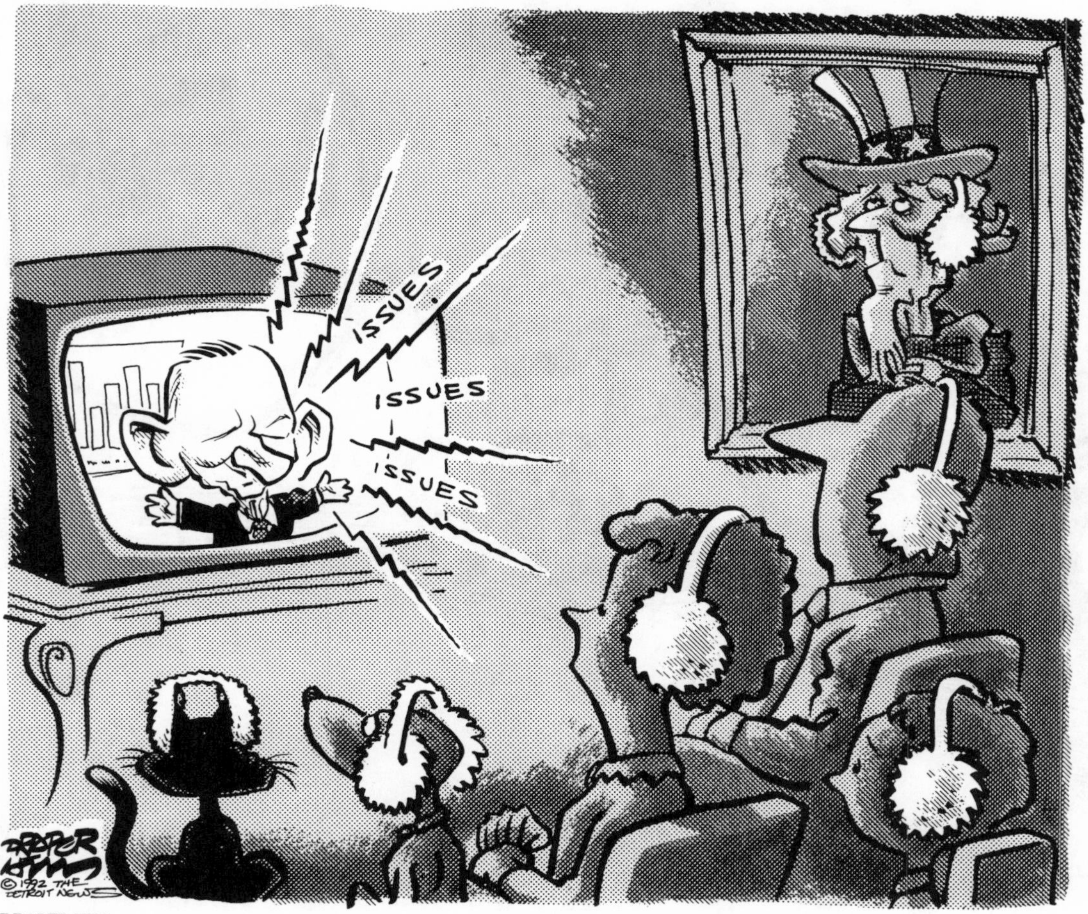
ISSUES
ISSUES
ISSUES

DRAPER HILL
Courtesy Detroit News

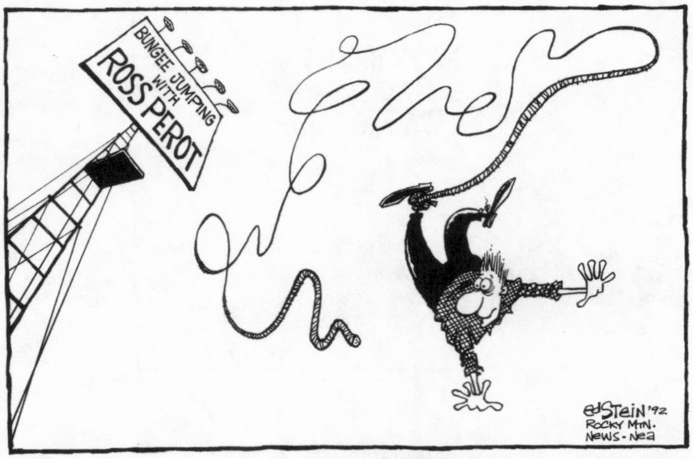
BUNGEE JUMPING WITH ROSS PEROT
EdStein '92 Rocky Mtn. News - NEA

ED STEIN
Courtesy Rocky Mountain News and NEA

ETTA HULME
Courtesy Ft. Worth Star-Telegram

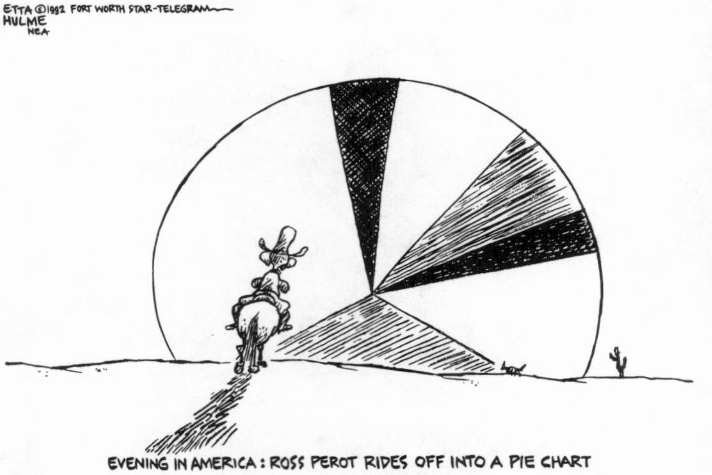
ETTA ©1992 FORT WORTH STAR-TELEGRAM
HULME
NEA

EVENING IN AMERICA : ROSS PEROT RIDES OFF INTO A PIE CHART

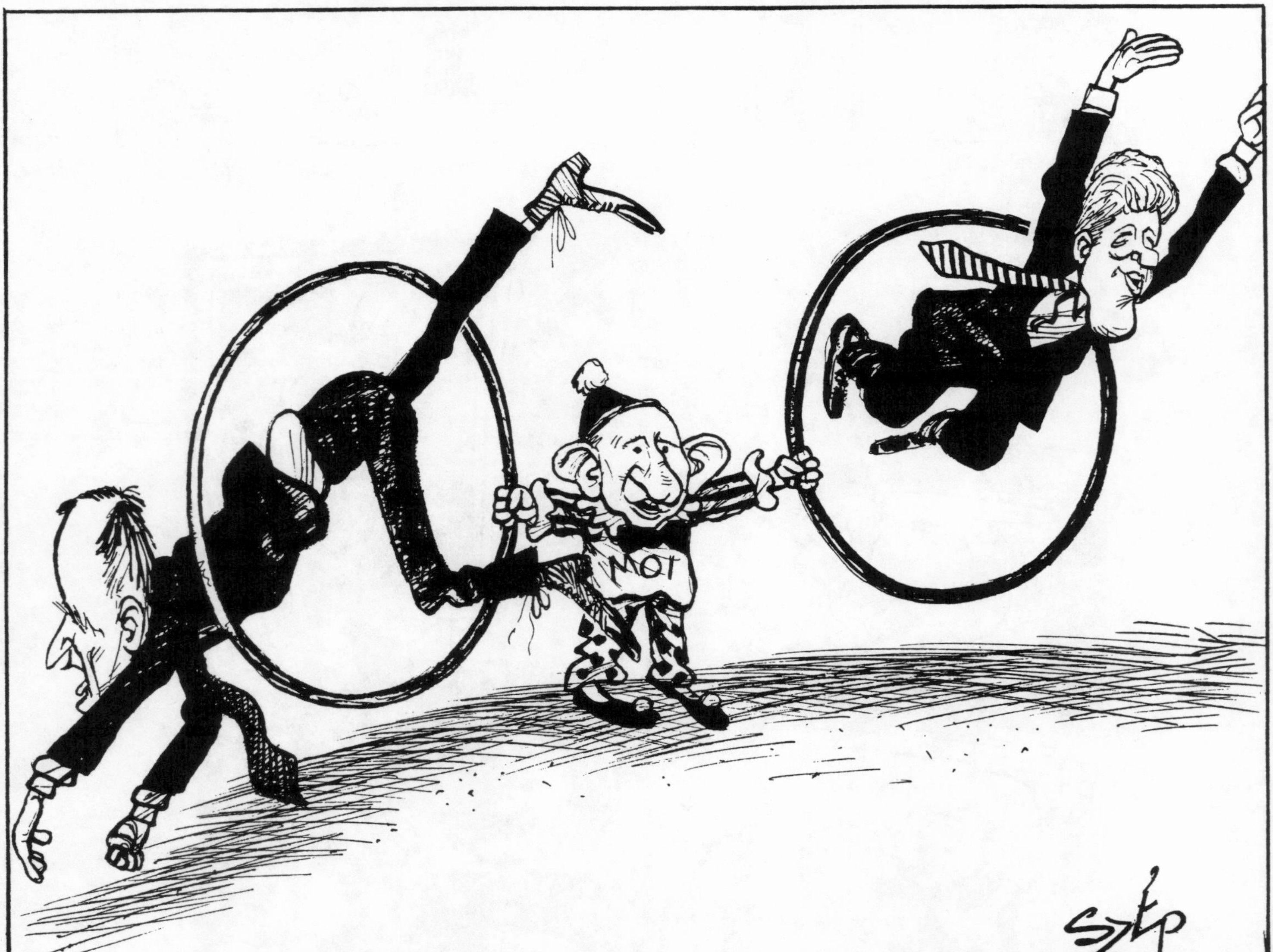
MOI
SZEP
THE BOSTON GLOBE

PAUL SZEP
Courtesy Boston Globe

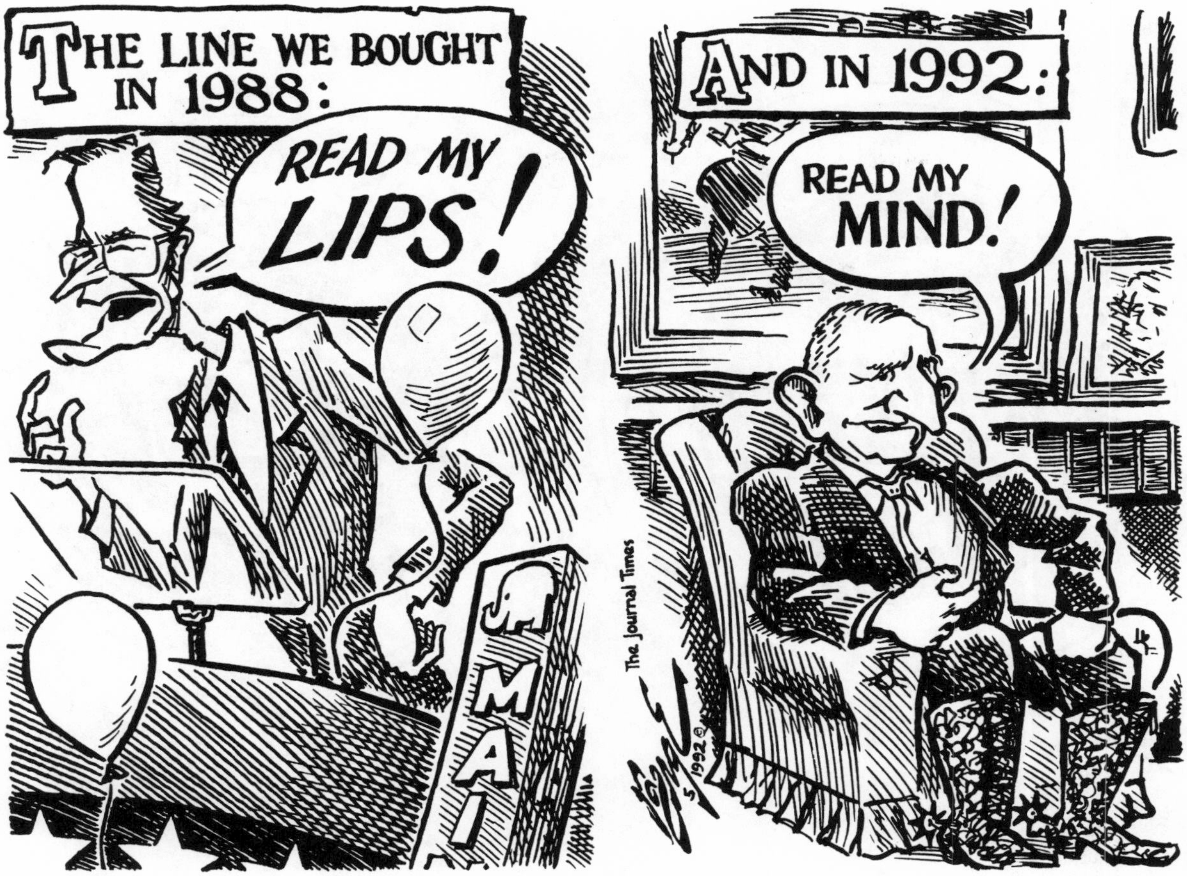
THE LINE WE BOUGHT IN 1988:
READ MY LIPS!
AND IN 1992:
READ MY MIND!
The Journal Times
1992 ©

PAUL BERGE
Courtesy Racine Journal Times

RANDY WICKS
Courtesy Valencia Signal (Calif.)

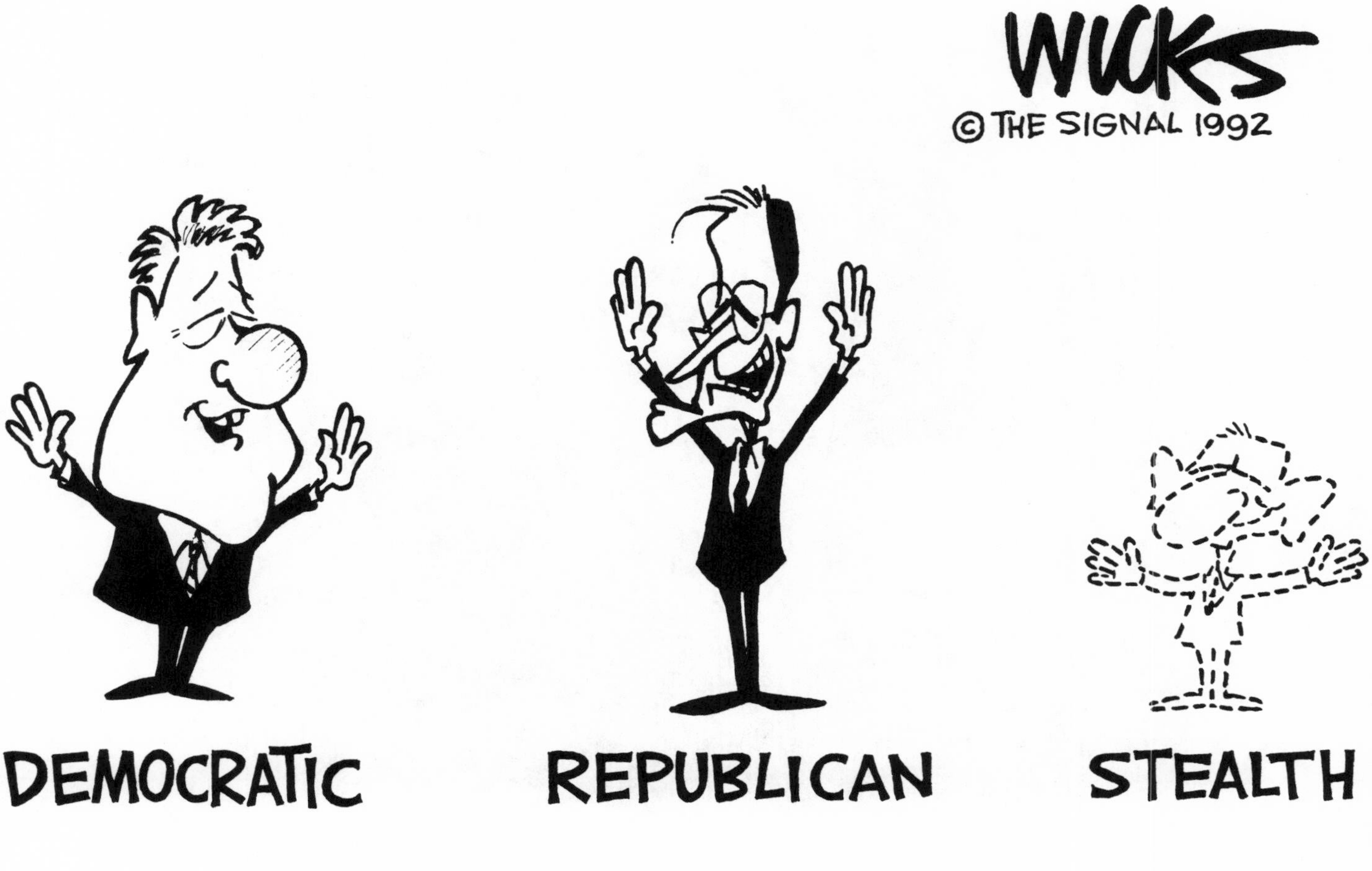
WICKS
© THE SIGNAL 1992
DEMOCRATIC
REPUBLICAN
STEALTH

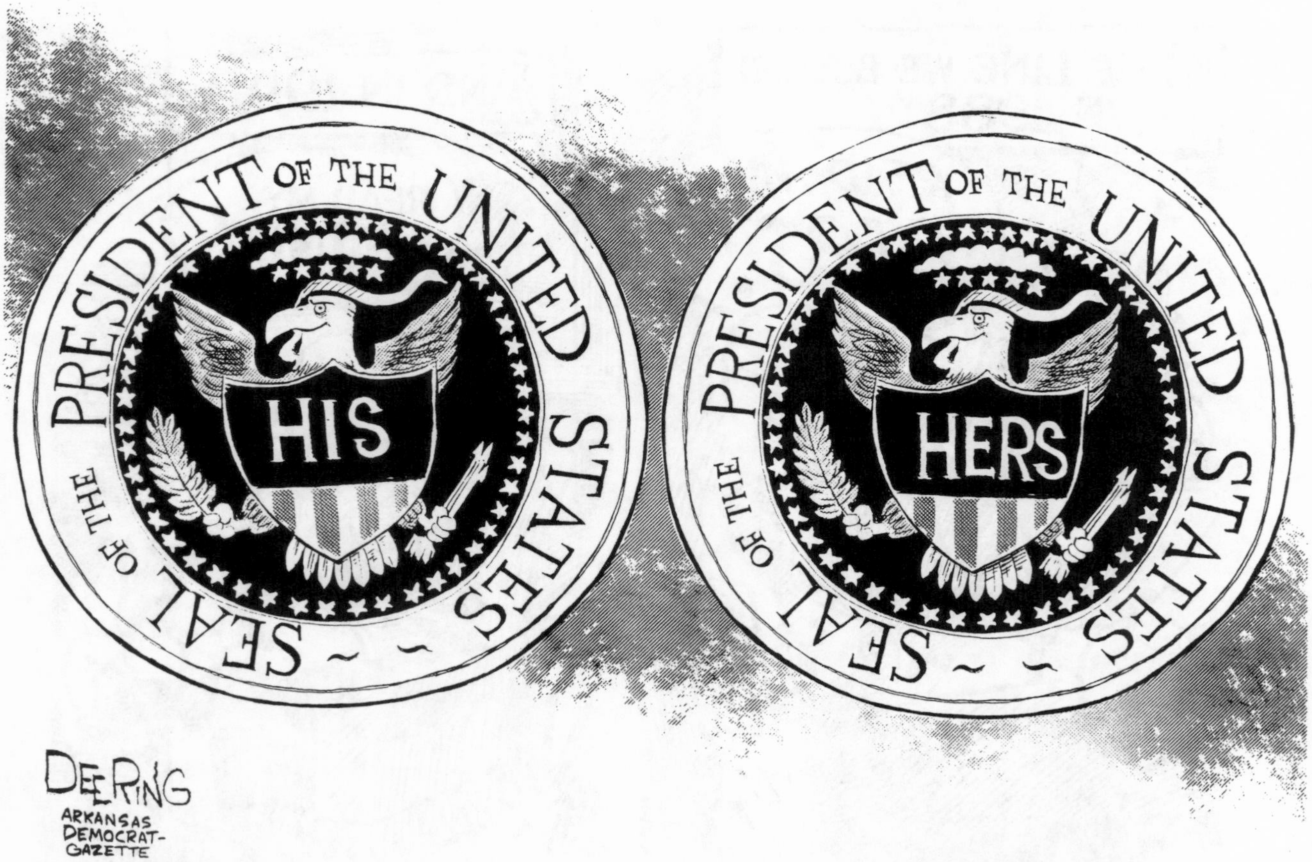
SEAL OF THE PRESIDENT OF THE UNITED STATES
HIS
SEAL OF THE PRESIDENT OF THE UNITED STATES
HERS
DEERING
ARKANSAS
DEMOCRAT-
GAZETTE

JOHN DEERING
Courtesy Arkansas Democrat-Gazette

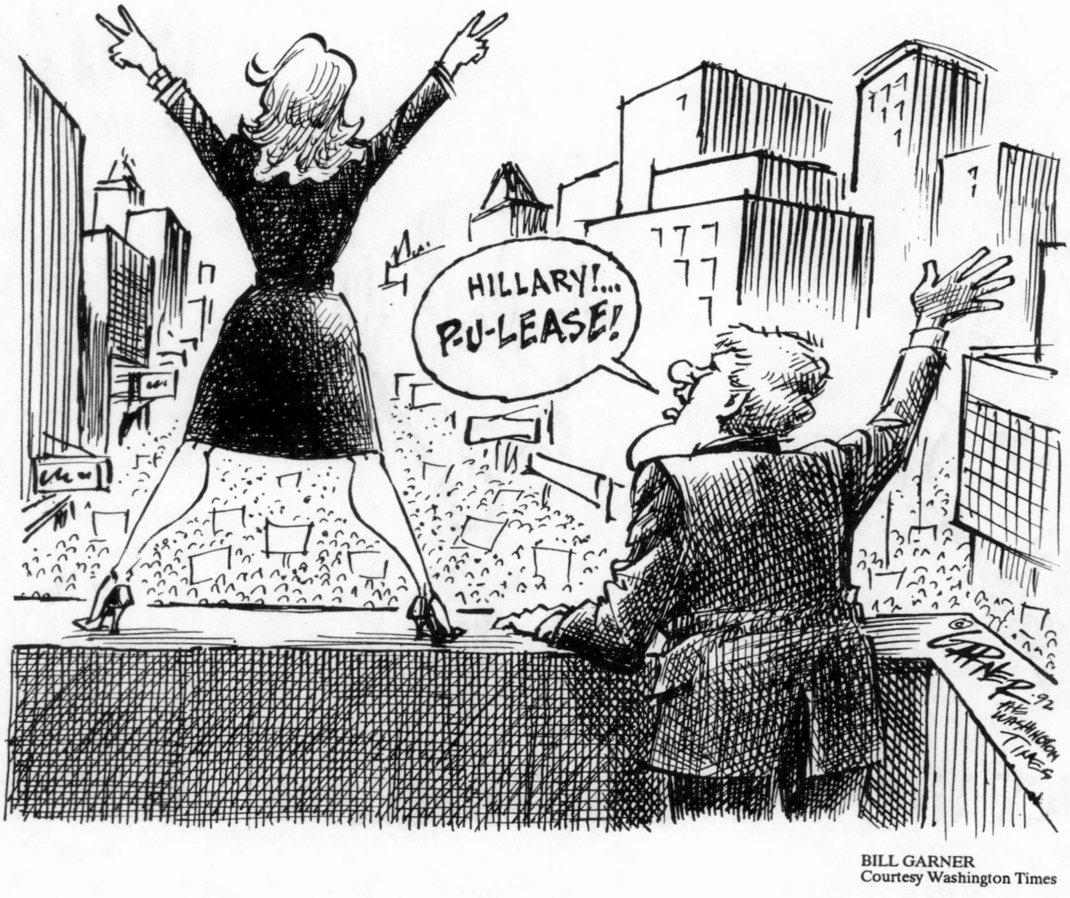
HILLARY!...
P-U-LEASE!
GARNER '92
THE WASHINGTON TIMES

BILL GARNER
Courtesy Washington Times

Politics

During his twelve years as governor of Arkansas, Bill Clinton frequently was accused of waffling and changing his mind. As president-elect, he immediately began to distance himself from promises made during the campaign concerning the deficit, gays in the military, Haitian refugees, and the economy. As a candidate, Clinton repeatedly vowed to sweep lobbyists out of Washington. As president, he appointed a goodly number of them to high positions.

In choosing his cabinet, he drew heavily on Carter retreads and like-minded liberals. It was not immediately clear what role his wife, Hillary, would play, but it was certain to be substantial. After all, the women's vote had put him in the White House.

Pat Buchanan, contending that the White House had forsaken conservatives, opposed George Bush in the party primary. But his candidacy never really caught fire with Republican voters.

After the election, the conservative wing of the GOP launched an effort to regain a major voice in the party. One of their champions was Rush Limbaugh, a talk-radio-television host, who had developed a huge nationwide following among Reagan conservatives.

MIKE PETERS
Courtesy Dayton Daily News

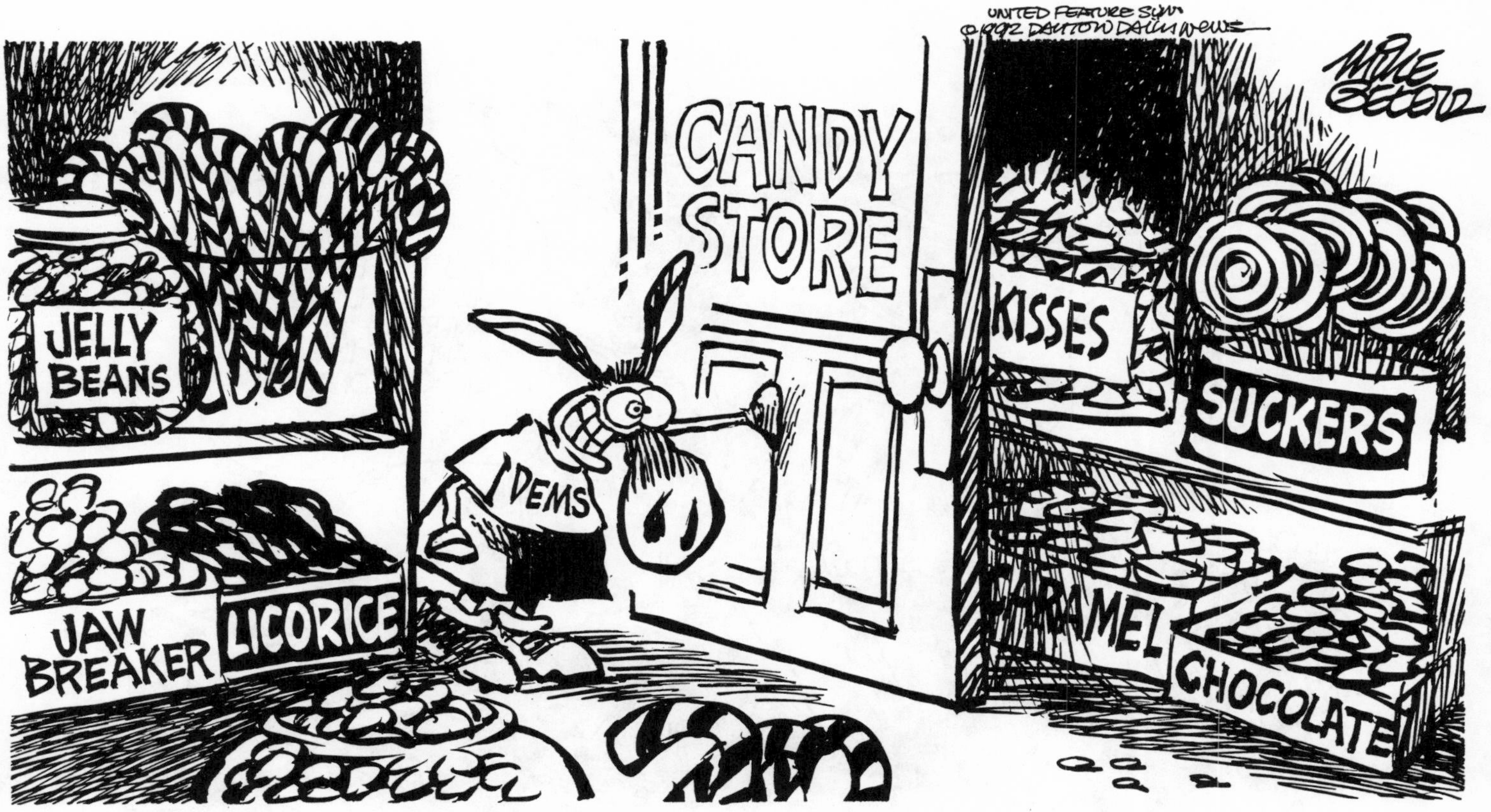

CANDY STORE
JELLY BEANS
JAW BREAKER
LICORICE
DEMS
KISSES
SUCKERS
CARAMEL
CHOCOLATE

RICHARD CROWSON
Courtesy Wichita Eagle

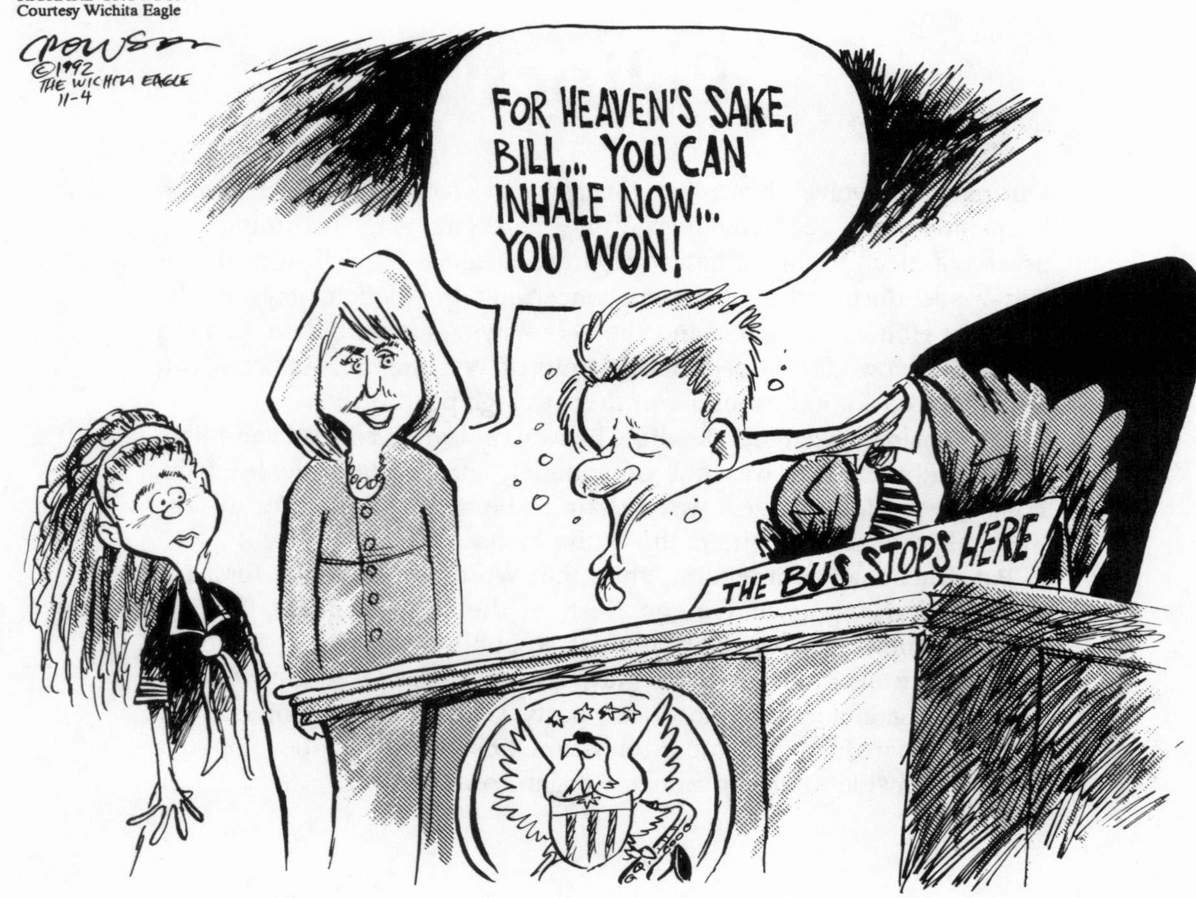
CROWSON ©1992 THE WICHITA EAGLE 11-4
FOR HEAVEN'S SAKE, BILL... YOU CAN INHALE NOW... YOU WON!
THE BUS STOPS HERE

MICHAEL RAMIREZ
Courtesy Memphis Commercial Appeal

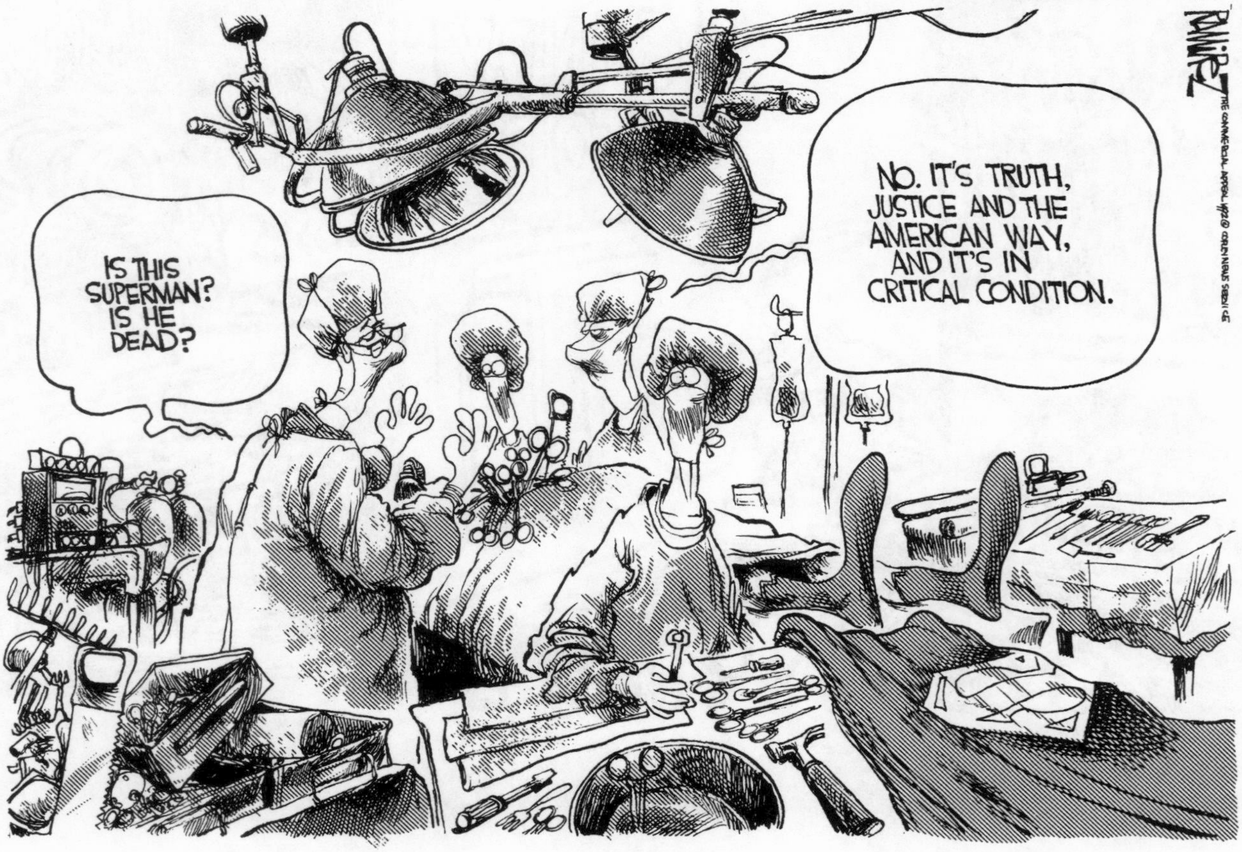
RAMIREZ
IS THIS SUPERMAN? IS HE DEAD?
NO. IT'S TRUTH, JUSTICE AND THE AMERICAN WAY, AND IT'S IN CRITICAL CONDITION.

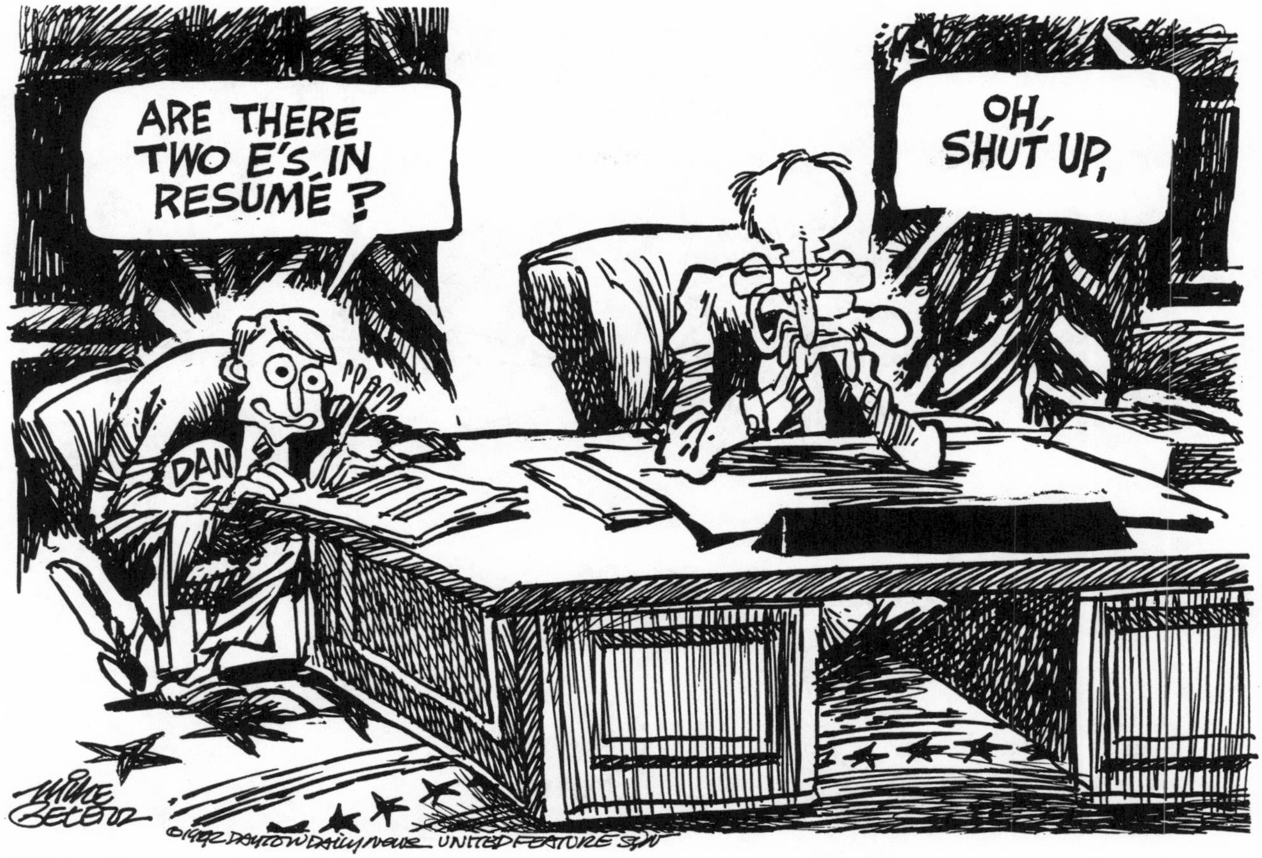
ARE THERE TWO E'S IN RESUMÉ?
OH, SHUT UP,
DAN
©1992 DAYTON DAILY NEWS UNITED FEATURE SYN

MIKE PETERS
Courtesy Dayton Daily News

DICK LOCHER
Courtesy Chicago Tribune

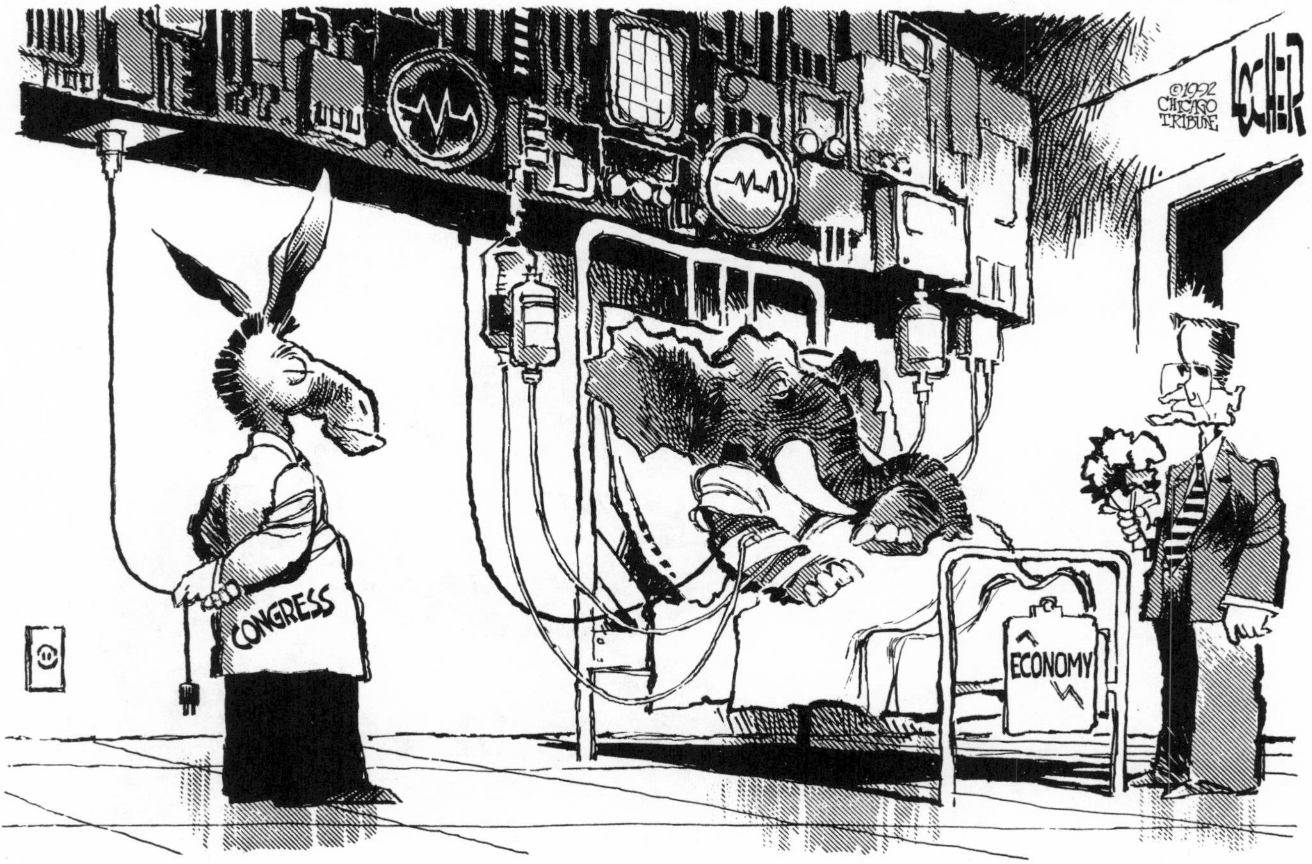
©1992 CHICAGO TRIBUNE
LOCHER
CONGRESS
ECONOMY

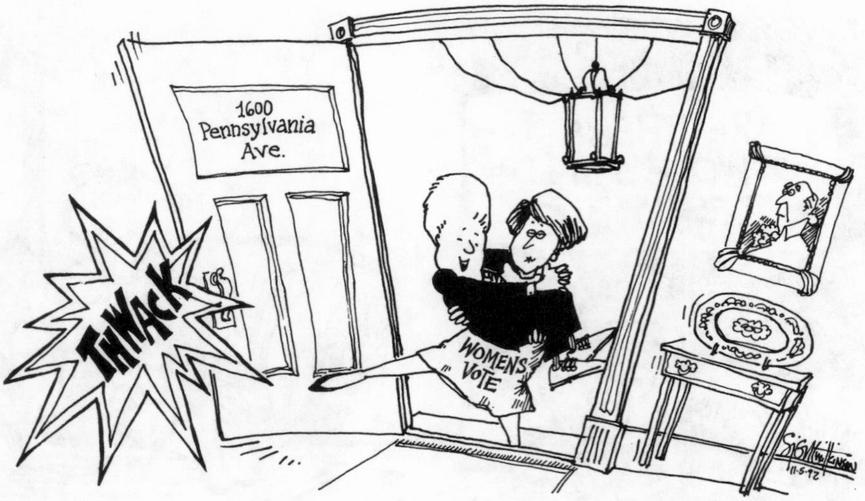
1600
Pennsylvania
Ave.
THWACK
WOMENS
VOTE

SIGNE WILKINSON
Courtesy Philadelphia Daily News

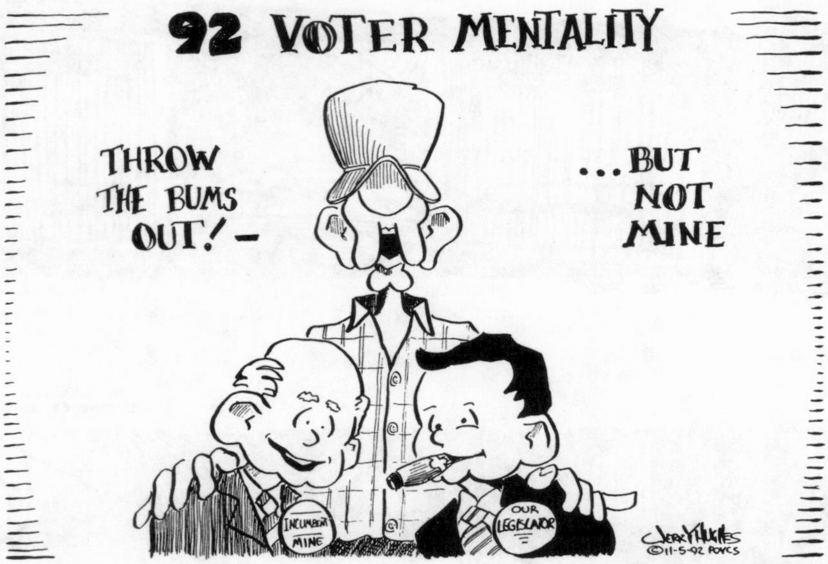
92 VOTER MENTALITY
THROW
THE BUMS
OUT! –
...BUT
NOT
MINE
INCUMBENT
MINE
OUR
LEGISLATOR

JERRY HUGHES
Courtesy Enterprise Ledger

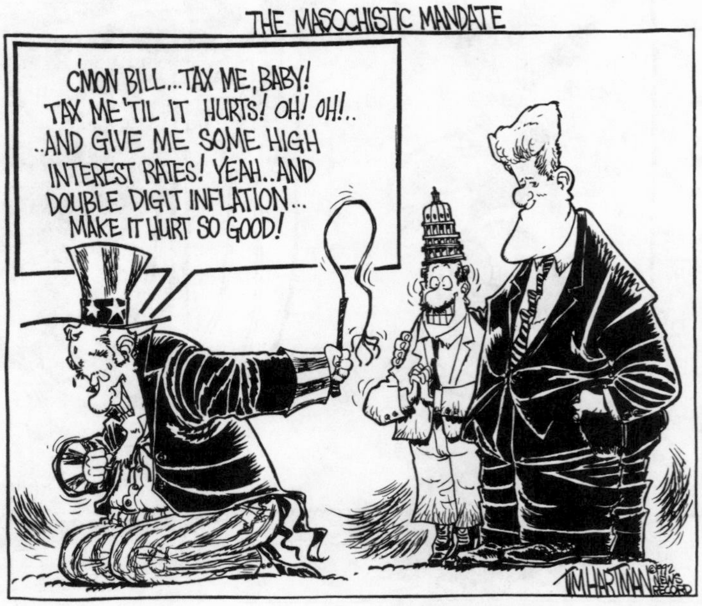
THE MASOCHISTIC MANDATE
C'MON BILL...TAX ME, BABY!
TAX ME 'TIL IT HURTS! OH! OH!..
..AND GIVE ME SOME HIGH
INTEREST RATES! YEAH..AND
DOUBLE DIGIT INFLATION...
MAKE IT HURT SO GOOD!

TIM HARTMAN
Courtesy North Hills News Record (Pa.)

GENE BASSET
Courtesy Atlanta Journal

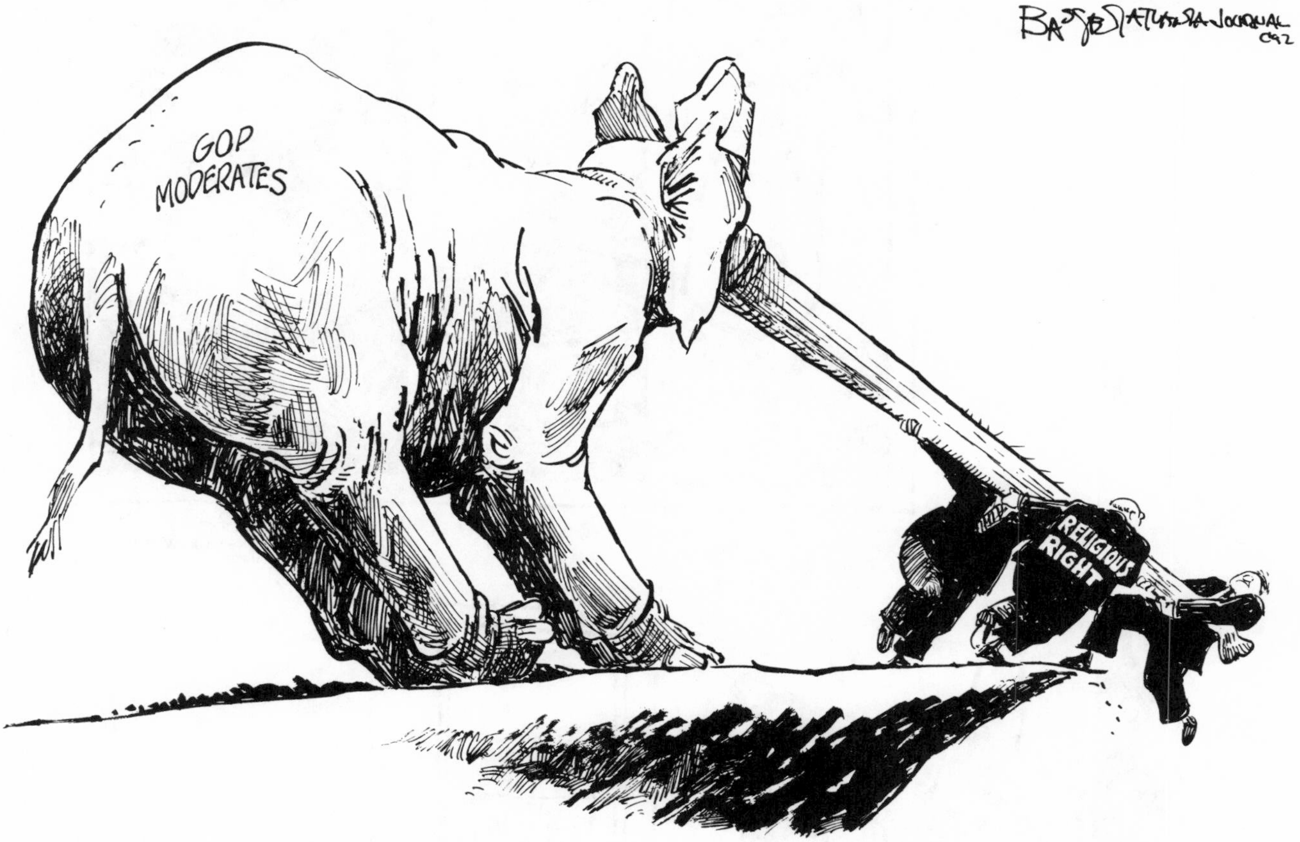

GOP MODERATES
RELIGIOUS RIGHT

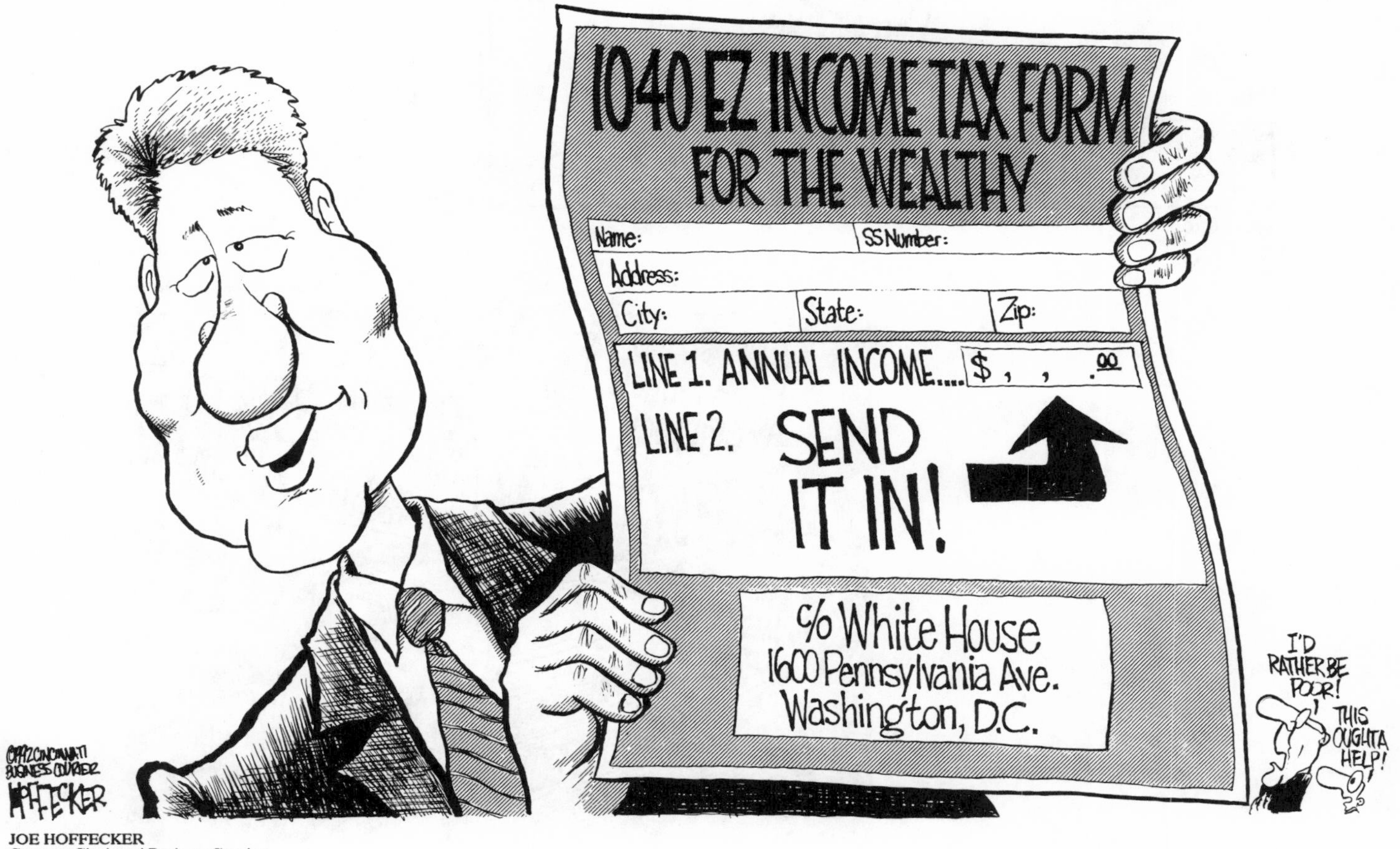

1040 EZ INCOME TAX FORM
FOR THE WEALTHY
Name:
SS Number:
Address:
City:
State:
Zip:
LINE 1. ANNUAL INCOME..... $, , .00
LINE 2. SEND IT IN!
c/o White House
1600 Pennsylvania Ave.
Washington, D.C.
I'D RATHER BE POOR!
THIS OUGHTA HELP!

JOE HOFFECKER
Courtesy Cincinnati Business Courier

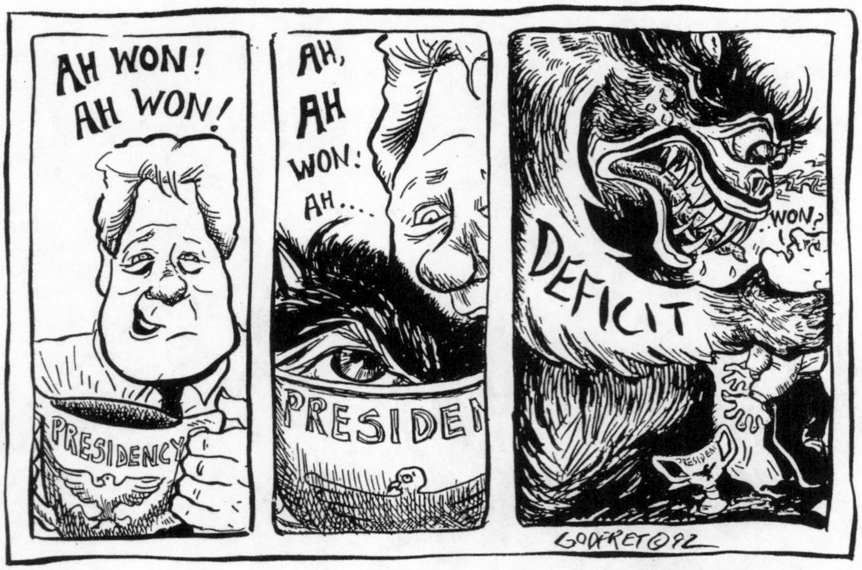
AH WON!
AH WON!
PRESIDENCY
AH,
AH
WON!
AH....
PRESIDEN
DEFICIT
WON?
GODFREY©92

LINDA GODFREY
Courtesy Janesville Gazette
and Walworth County Week (Wis.)

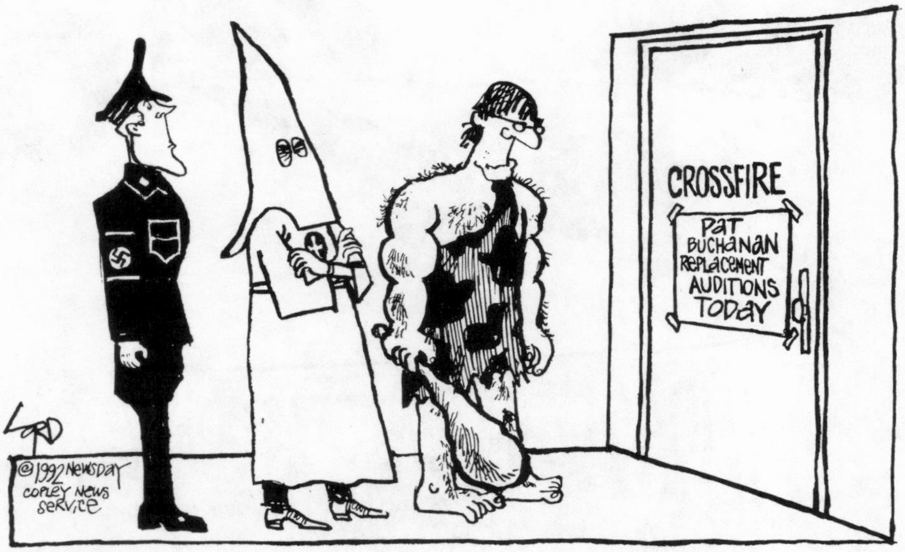
CROSSFIRE
Pat
Buchanan
Replacement
AUDITIONS
TODAY
LORD
©1992 NEWSDAY
COPLEY NEWS
SERVICE

M. G. LORD
Courtesy Newsday

JOHN TREVER
Courtesy Albuquerque Journal

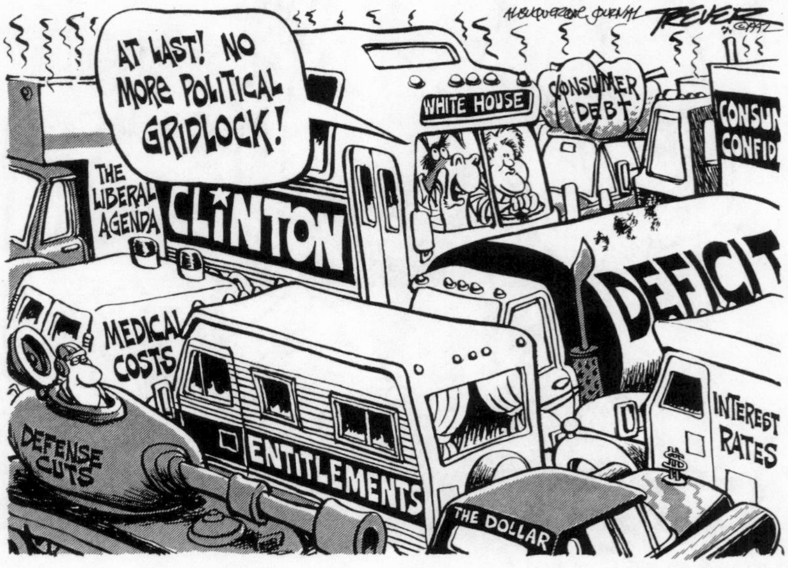
AT LAST! NO
MORE POLITICAL
GRIDLOCK!
WHITE HOUSE
CONSUMER
DEBT
THE
LIBERAL
AGENDA
CLINTON
DEFICIT
MEDICAL
COSTS
DEFENSE
CUTS
ENTITLEMENTS
INTEREST
RATES
THE DOLLAR
TREVER

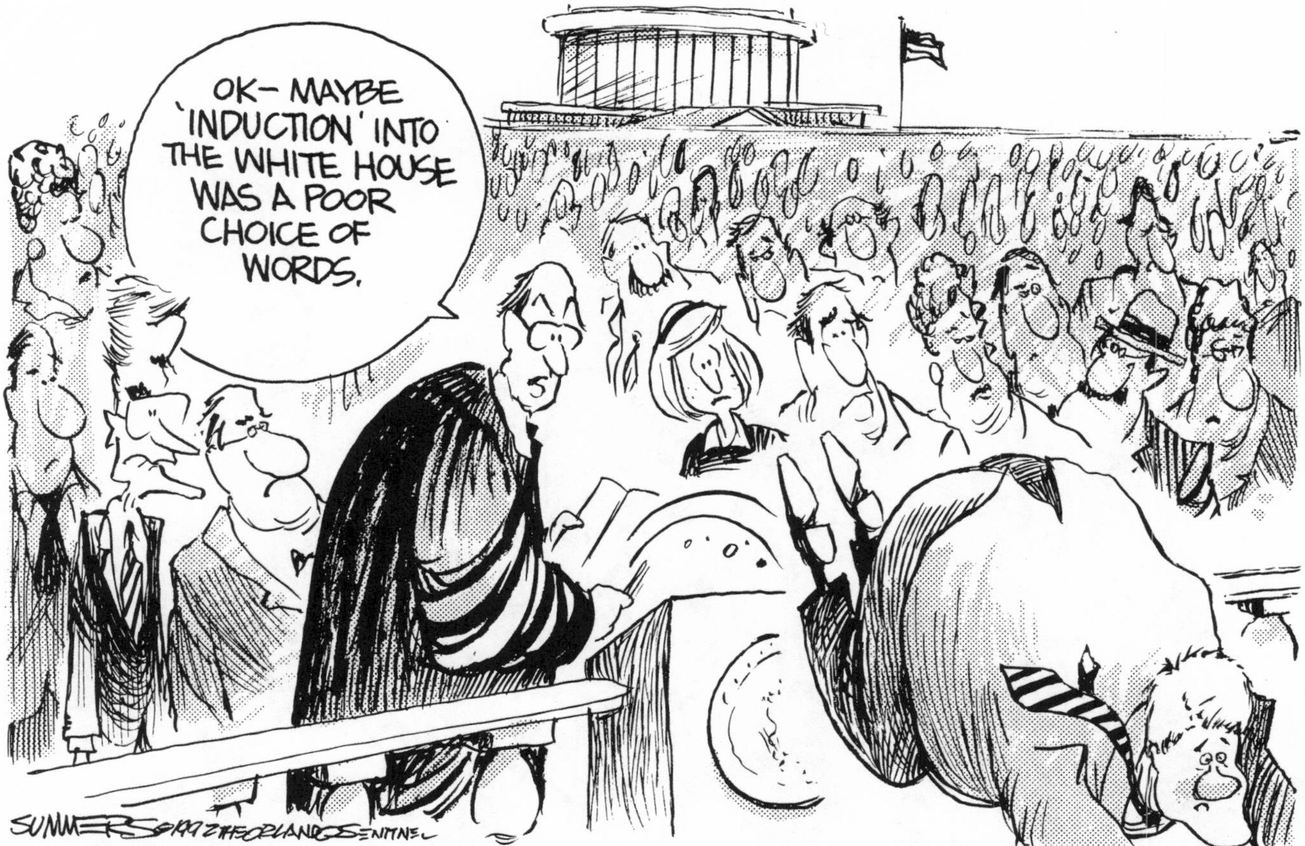
OK– MAYBE 'INDUCTION' INTO THE WHITE HOUSE WAS A POOR CHOICE OF WORDS.
SUMMERS ©1992 THE ORLANDO SENTINEL
DANA SUMMERS
Courtesy Orlando Sentinel

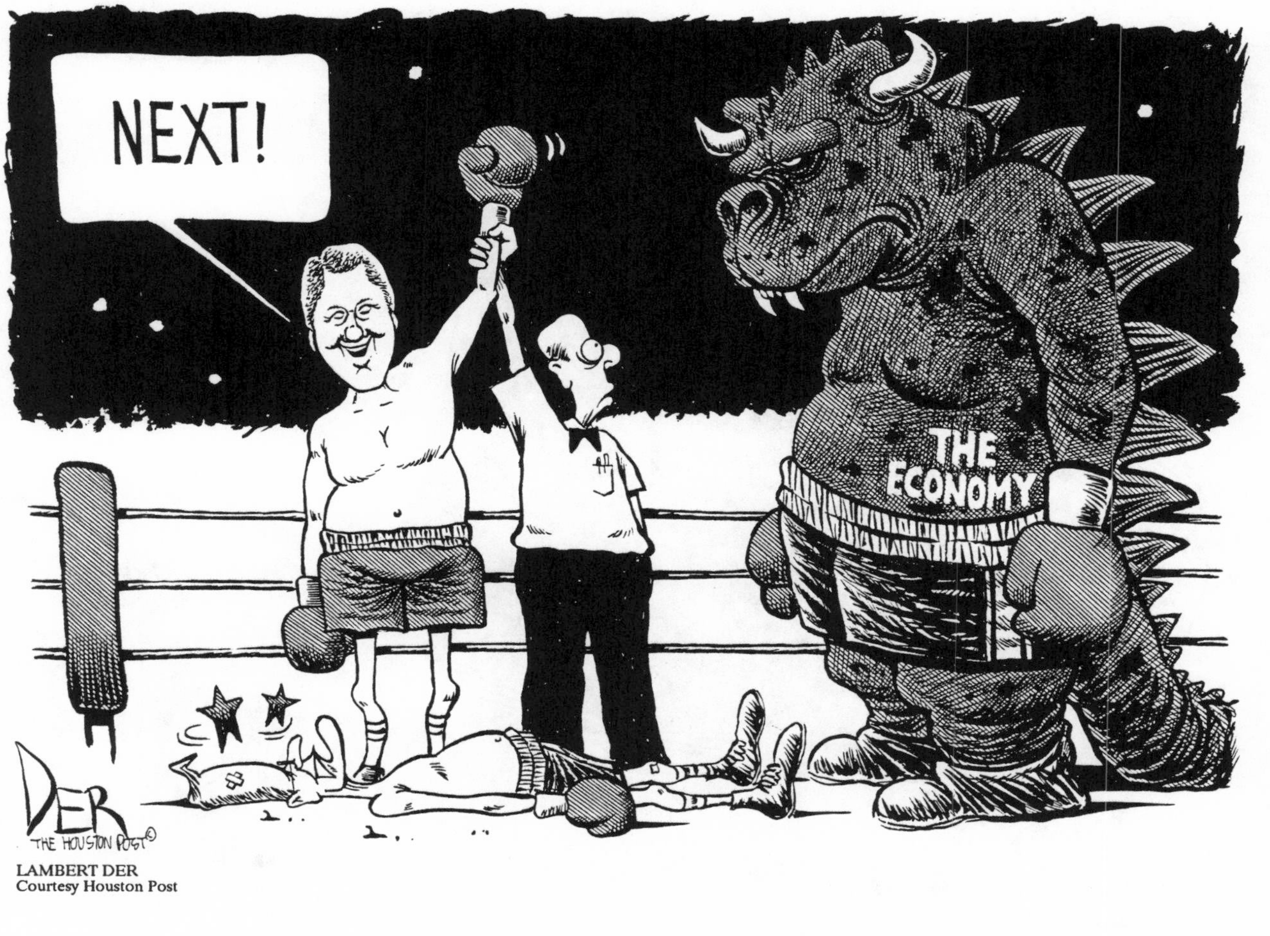
NEXT!
THE ECONOMY
DER
THE HOUSTON POST ©
LAMBERT DER
Courtesy Houston Post

WALT HANDELSMAN
Courtesy Times-Picayune (N.O.)

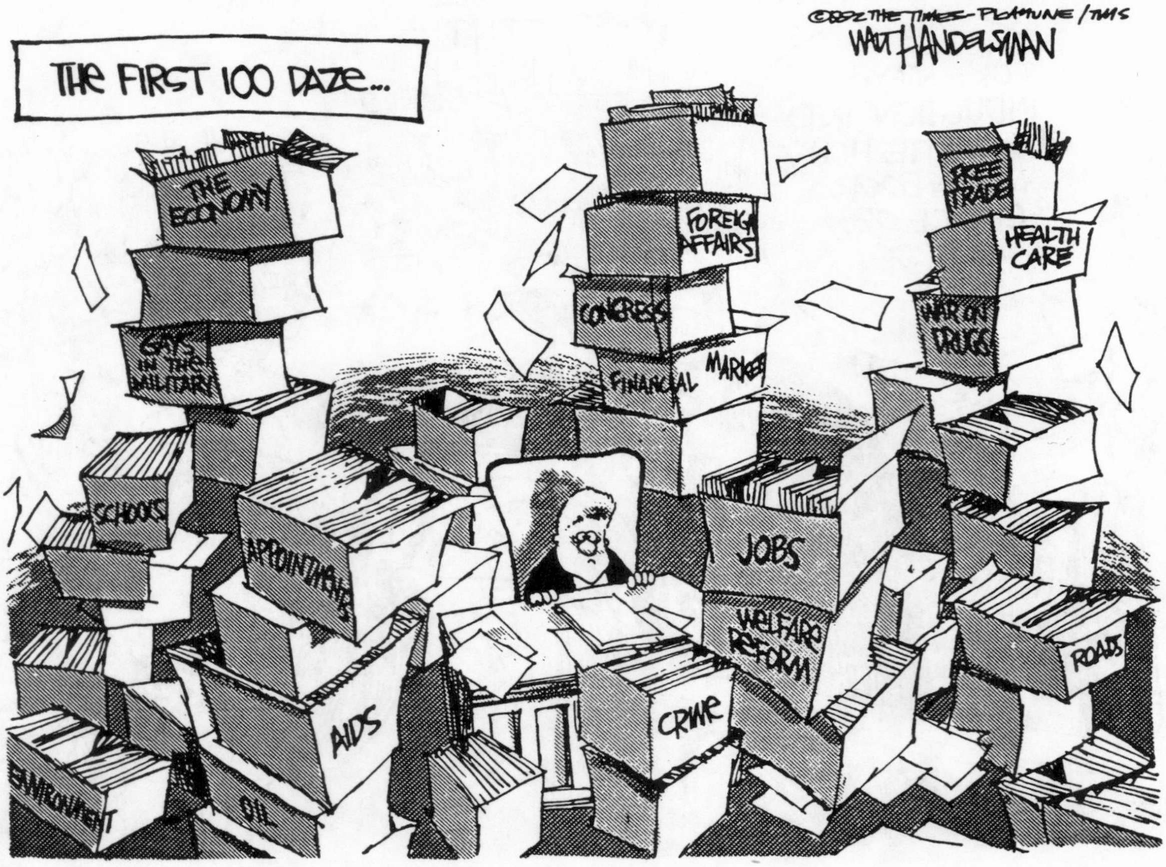
WALT HANDELSMAN
THE FIRST 100 DAZE...
THE ECONOMY
GAYS IN THE MILITARY
SCHOOLS
APPOINTMENTS
AIDS
ENVIRONMENT
OIL
FOREIG AFFAIRS
CONGRESS
FINANCIAL MARKET
JOBS
WELFARE REFORM
CRIME
FREE TRADE
HEALTH CARE
WAR ON DRUGS
ROADS

BOB DORNFRIED
Courtesy Greenwich News and Rothco

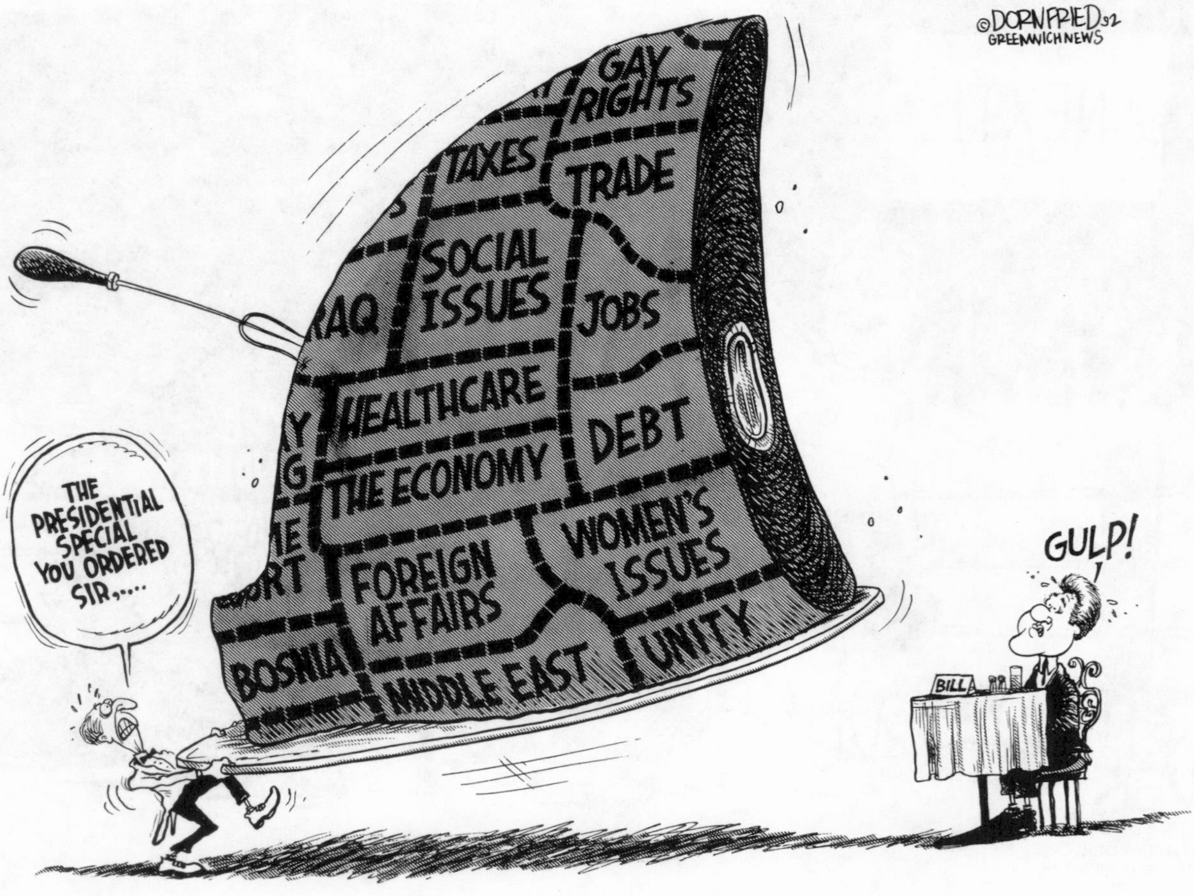
©DORNFRIED '92
GREENWICH NEWS
GAY RIGHTS
TAXES
TRADE
SOCIAL ISSUES
JOBS
HEALTHCARE
DEBT
THE ECONOMY
WOMEN'S ISSUES
FOREIGN AFFAIRS
BOSNIA
MIDDLE EAST
UNITY
THE PRESIDENTIAL SPECIAL YOU ORDERED SIR,....
GULP!
BILL

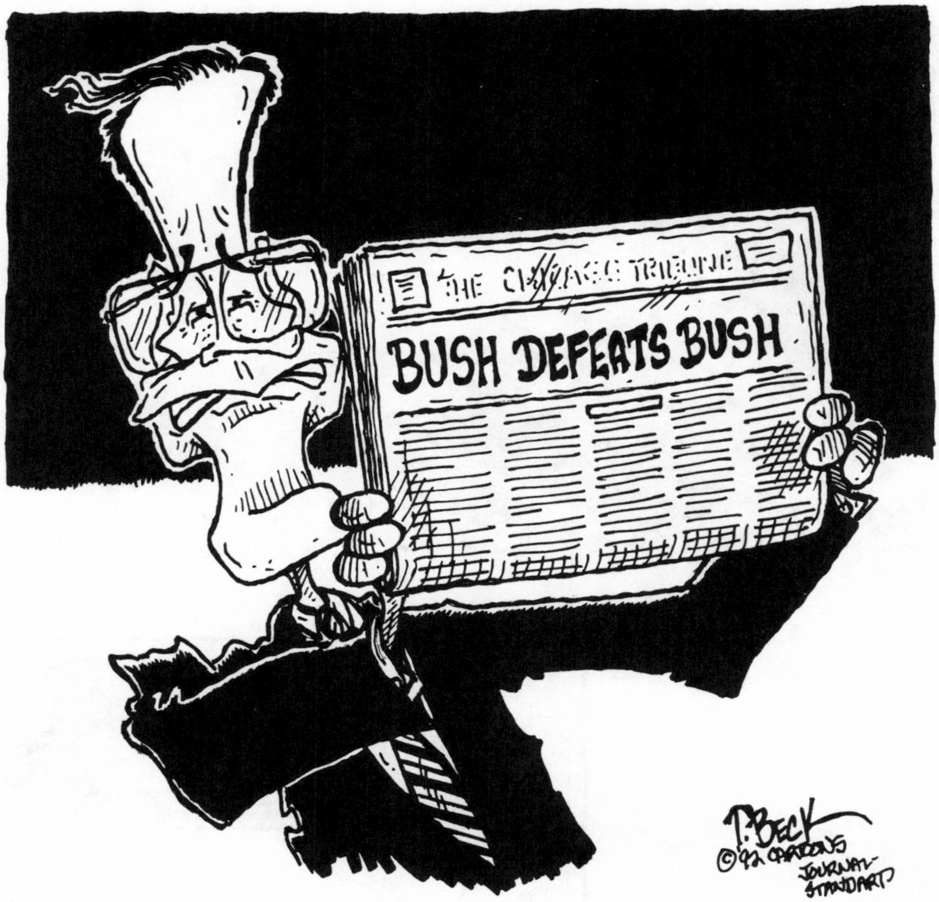
BUSH DEFEATS BUSH
T. BECK
©'92 CARTOONS JOURNAL-STANDARD

TOM BECK
Courtesy Journal-Standard (Ill.)

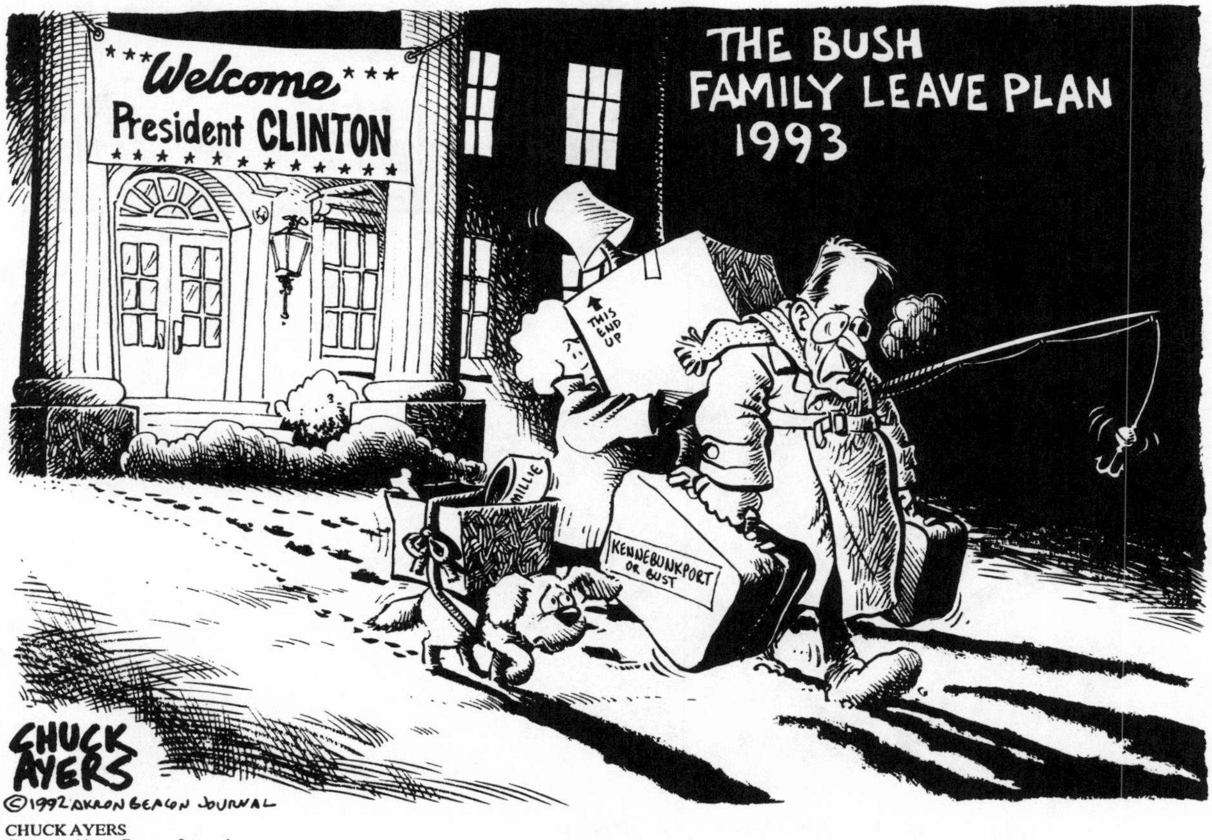
Welcome
President CLINTON
THE BUSH
FAMILY LEAVE PLAN
1993
THIS END UP
MILLIE
KENNEBUNKPORT OR BUST
CHUCK AYERS
©1992 AKRON BEACON JOURNAL

CHUCK AYERS
Courtesy Akron Beacon Journal

YOU CAN COME OUT NOW!
CLINTON
LIBERAL DEMOCRATS
PAYNE

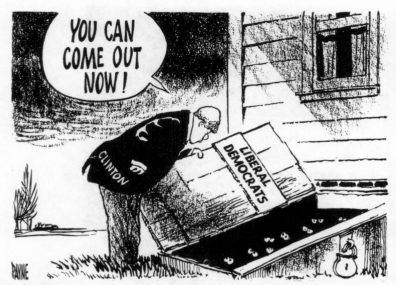

EUGENE PAYNE
Courtesy Charlotte Observer

Now remember to make a wish...
HAPPY BIRTHDAY
HAPPY BIRTHDAY
HAPPY BIRTHDAY
Bennett

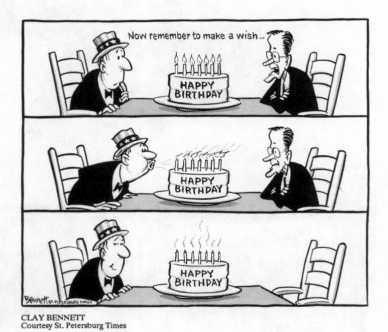

CLAY BENNETT
Courtesy St. Petersburg Times

J. R. SHINGLETON
Courtesy Waterbury Republican-American

WHERE IS THE POLITICAL APPOINTEE LINE?
YOU'RE IN IT!

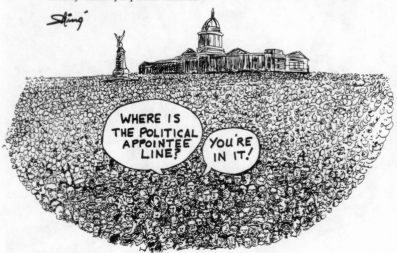

GRIDLOCK AT LITTLE ROCK

Foreign Affairs

After seventy-four years, strife-torn Czechoslovakia faded into history, becoming the new state of Slovakia and the Czech Republic. In Peru, the leader of the notorious Shining Path guerrilla movement was captured, but the twelve-year war that has taken some 25,000 lives continued.

In the Middle East, peace negotiations needed a decisive push at year's end. Apartheid in South Africa did not end peacefully as had been hoped, and signs indicated that a civil war in Natal province might be imminent. A severe famine in the African nation of Somalia that had claimed 300,000 lives prompted President Bush to send U.S. troops in December. Two years of civil strife had prevented food shipments from getting to the hungry and starving.

DICK WALLMEYER
Courtesy Long Beach Press-Telegram

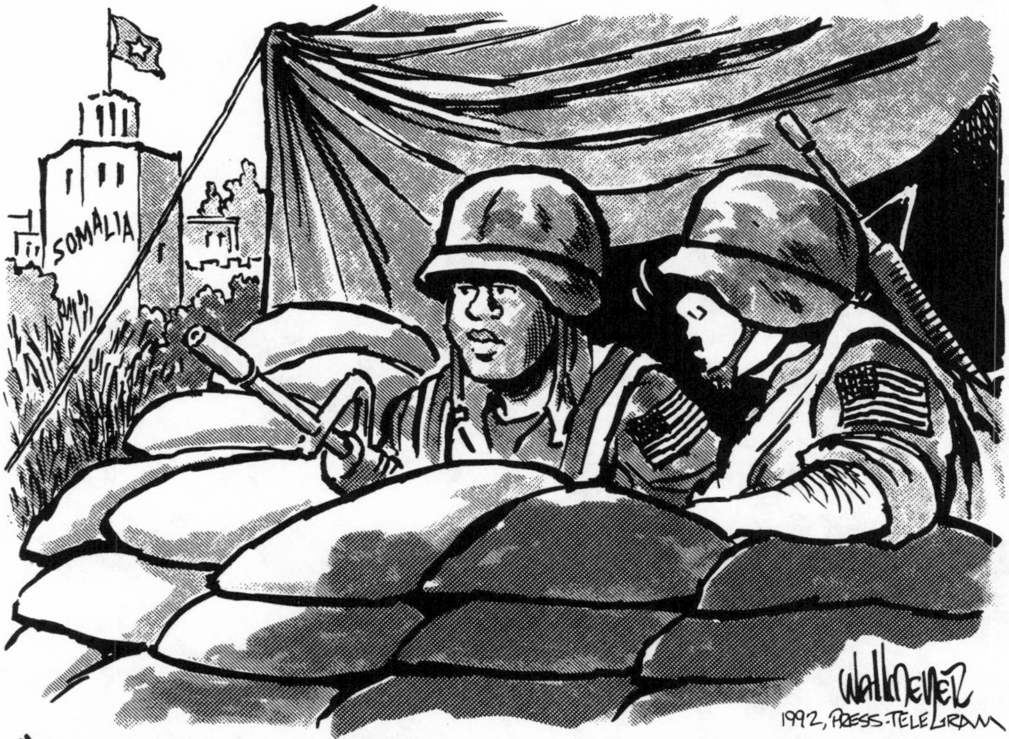
SOMALIA
WALLMEYER
1992, PRESS-TELEGRAM

"DRUGS, STREET GANGS WITH AUTOMATIC WEAPONS... REMINDS ME OF BACK HOME."

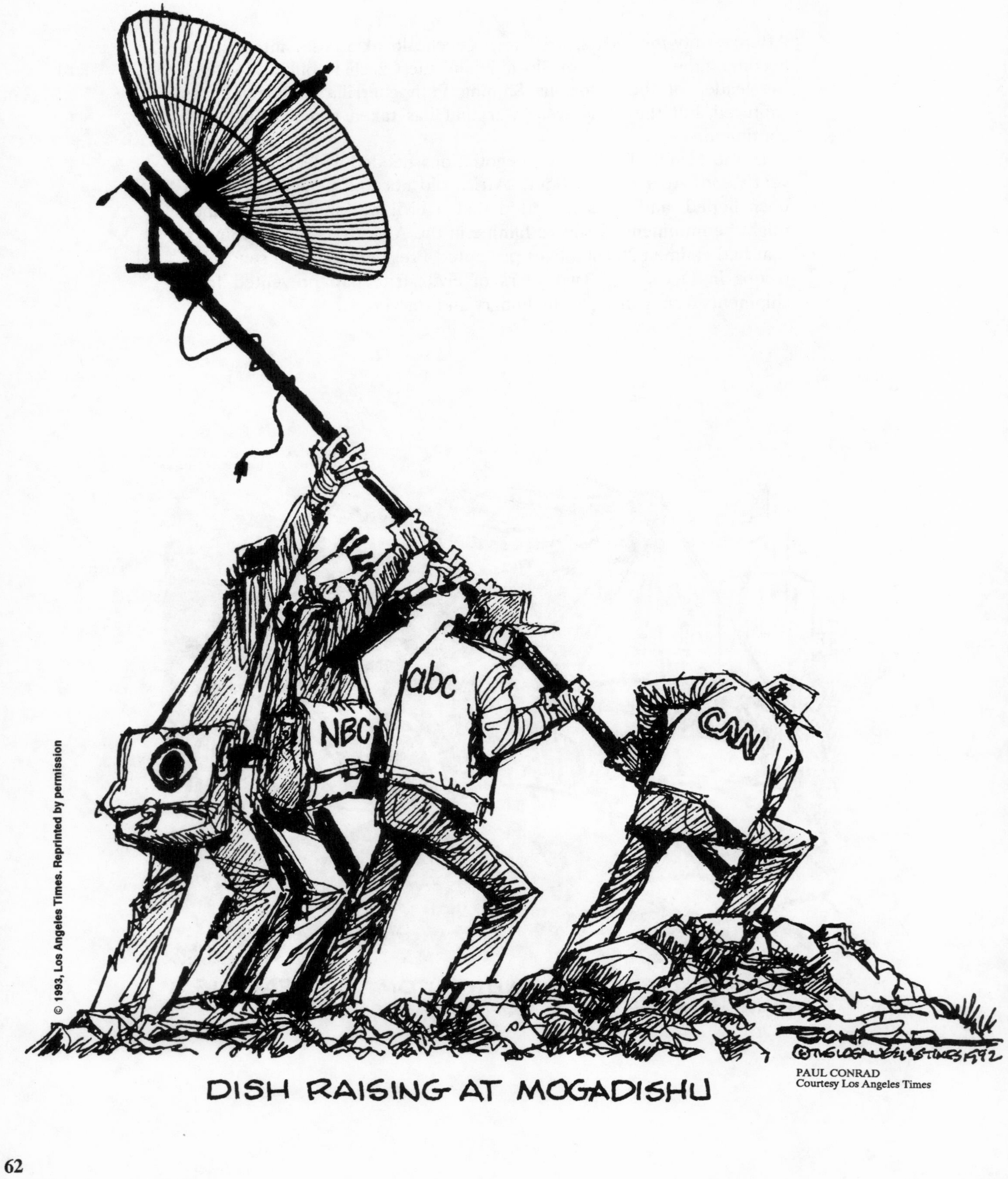
abc
NBC
CNN

DISH RAISING AT MOGADISHU

PAUL CONRAD
Courtesy Los Angeles Times

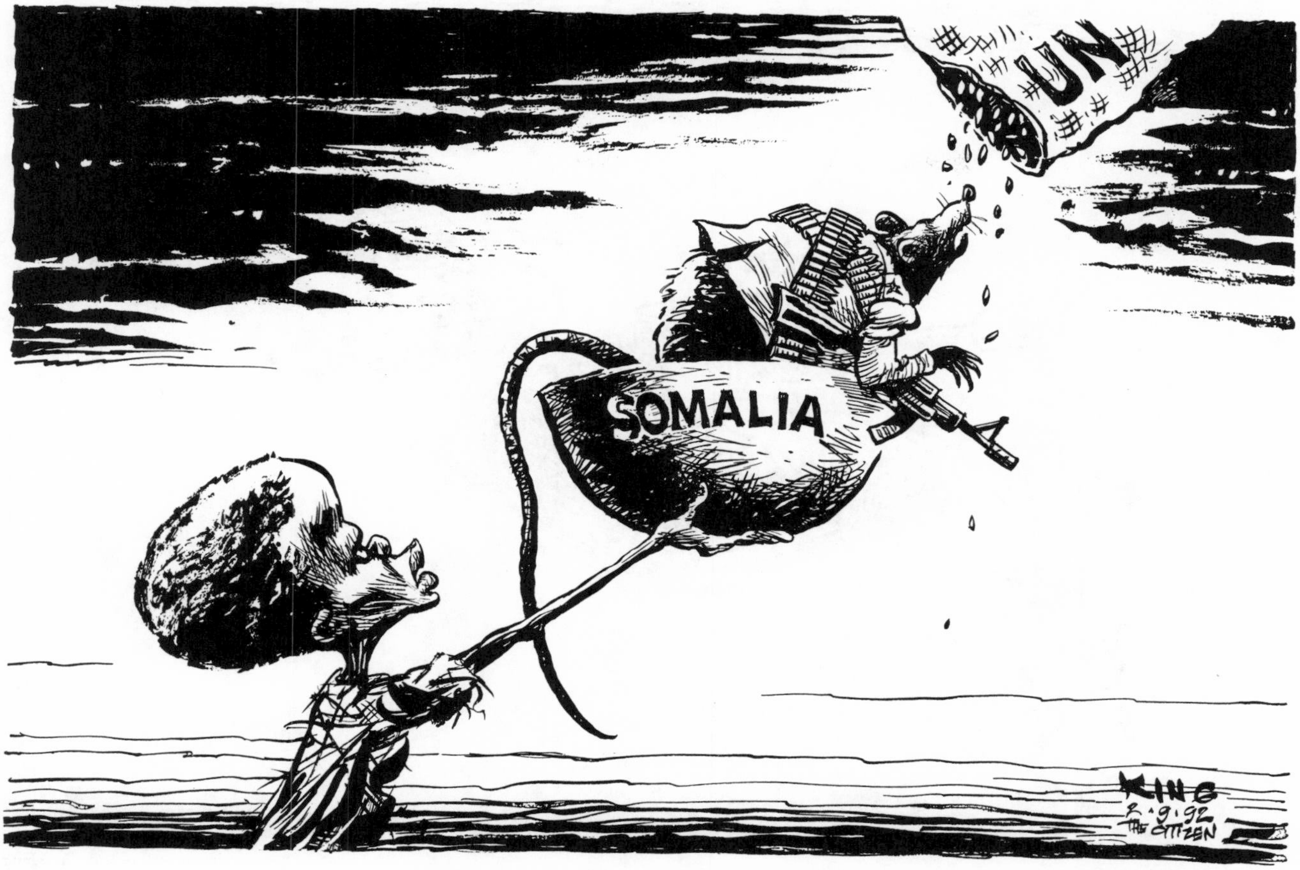
UN
SOMALIA
KING
2·9·92
THE CITIZEN

ALAN KING
Courtesy Ottawa Citizen

DAVID HORSEY
Courtesy Seattle Post-Intelligencer

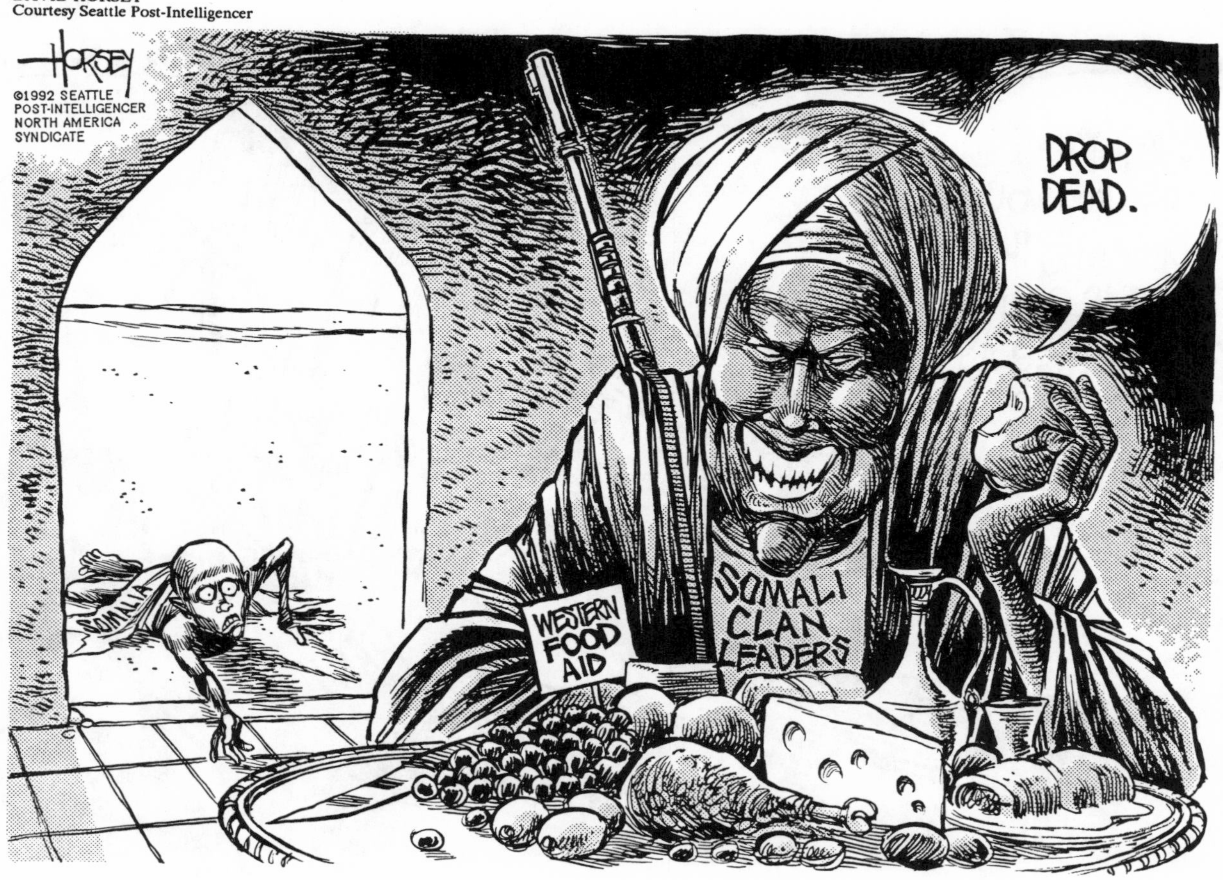
HORSEY
©1992 SEATTLE
POST-INTELLIGENCER
NORTH AMERICA
SYNDICATE
DROP DEAD.
SOMALIA
WESTERN FOOD AID
SOMALI CLAN LEADERS

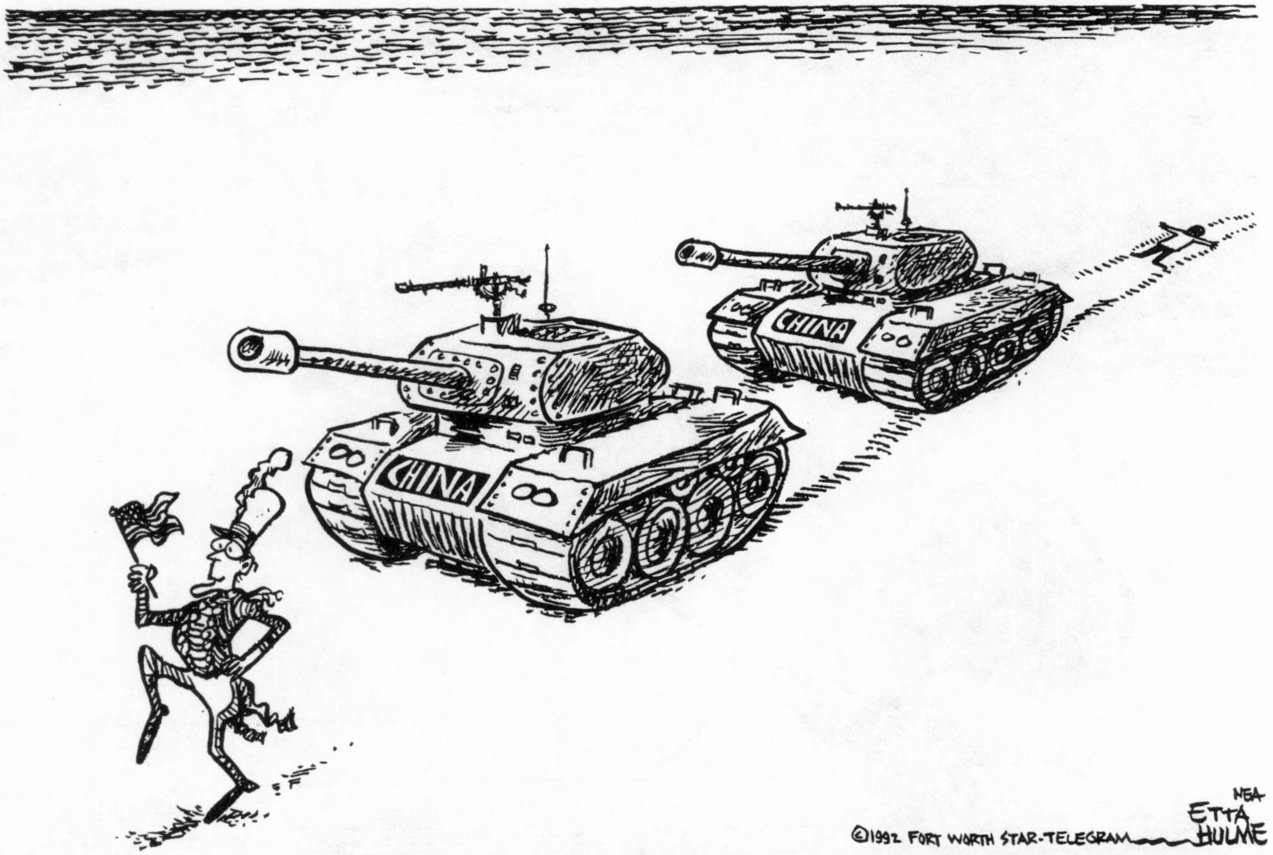

CHINA
CHINA
©1992 FORT WORTH STAR-TELEGRAM
NEA
ETTA HULME

ETTA HULME
Courtesy Ft. Worth Star-Telegram

MIKE KEEFE
Courtesy Denver Post

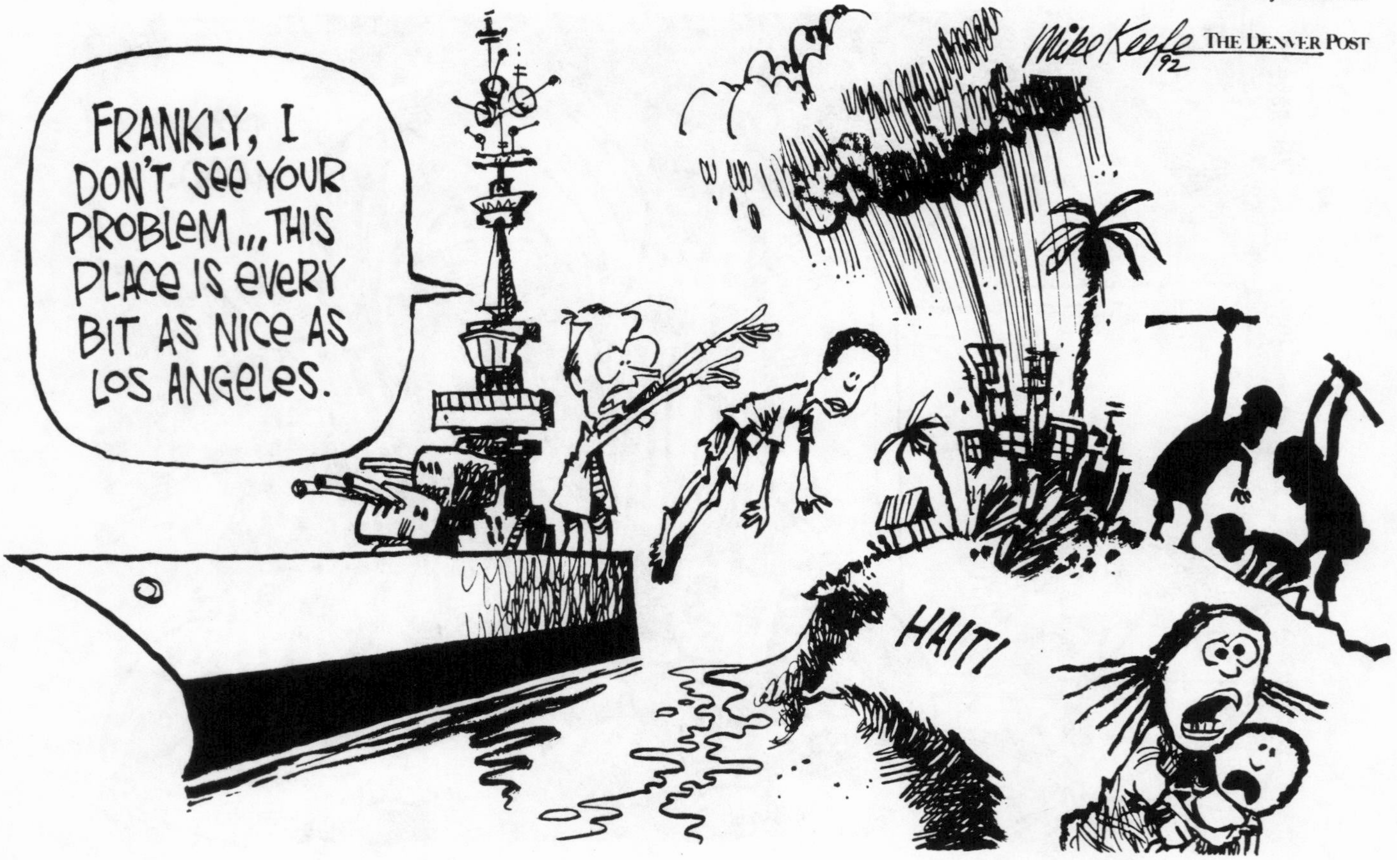

Mike Keefe 92
THE DENVER POST
FRANKLY, I DON'T SEE YOUR PROBLEM... THIS PLACE IS EVERY BIT AS NICE AS LOS ANGELES.
HAITI

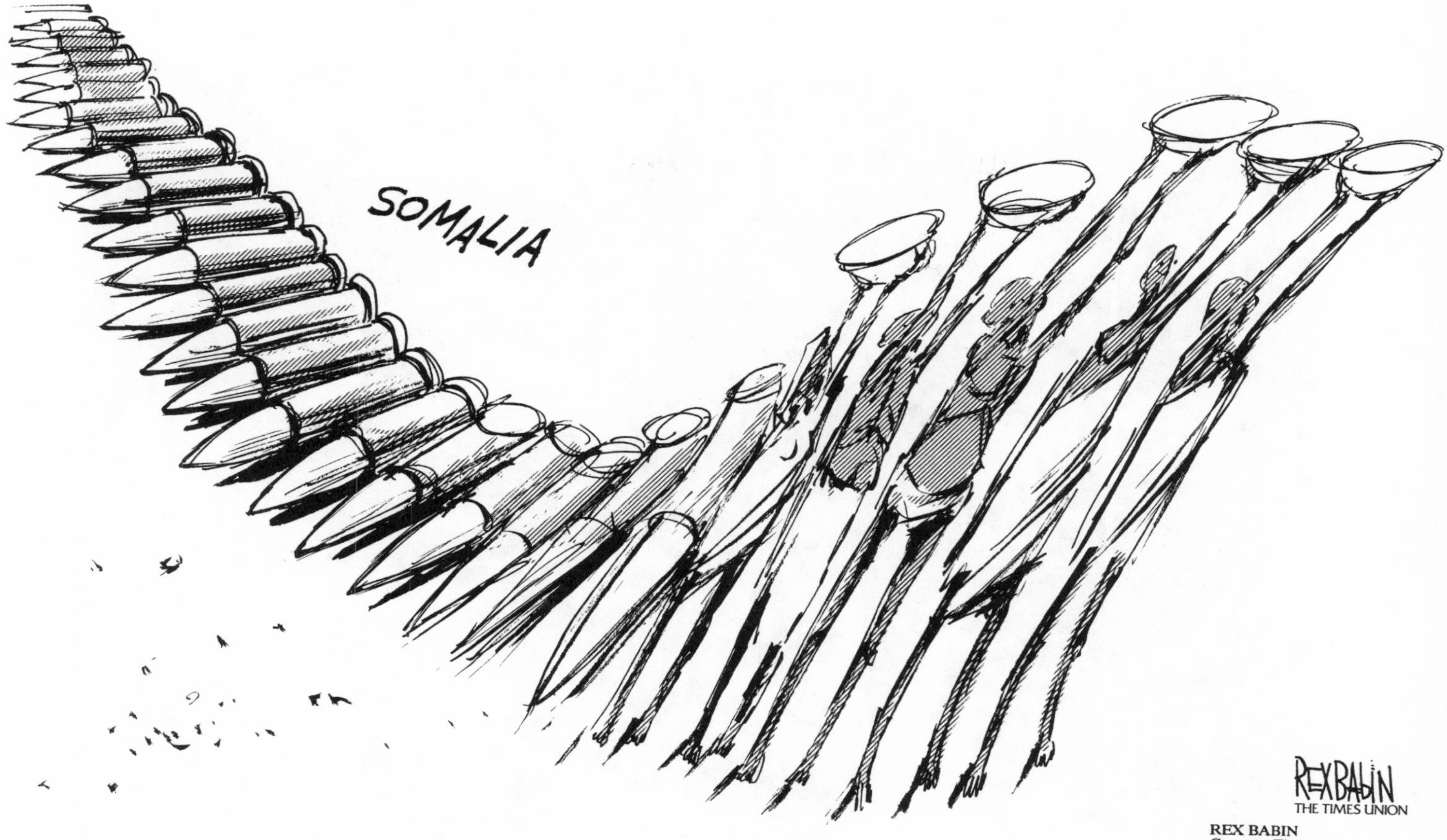
SOMALIA
REXBABIN
THE TIMES UNION

REX BABIN
Courtesy Times Union (N.Y.)

CHUCK AYERS
Courtesy Akron Beacon Journal

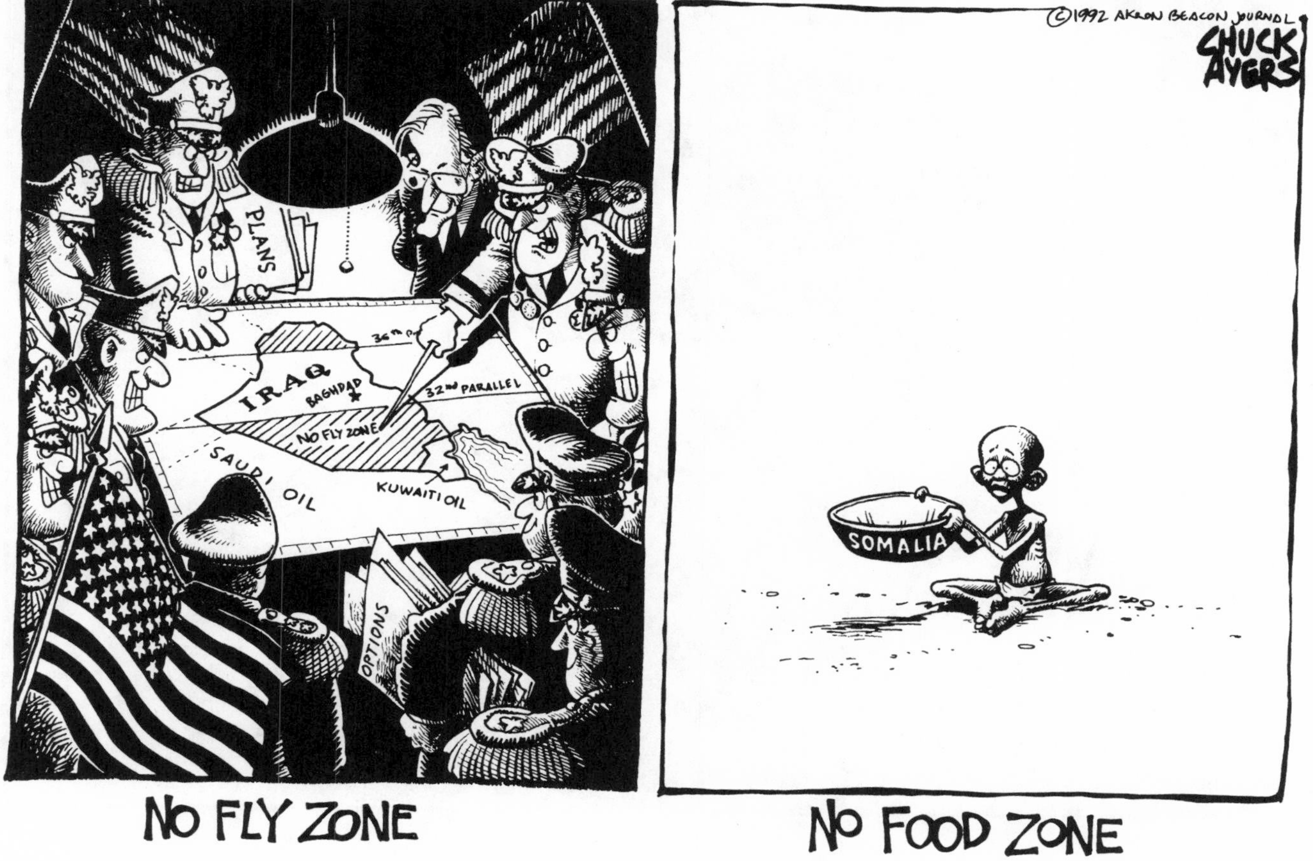
©1992 AKRON BEACON JOURNAL
CHUCK AYERS
PLANS
IRAQ
BAGHDAD
32nd PARALLEL
NO FLY ZONE
SAUDI OIL
KUWAITI OIL
OPTIONS
SOMALIA
NO FLY ZONE
NO FOOD ZONE

FRED CURATOLO
Courtesy Edmonton Sun

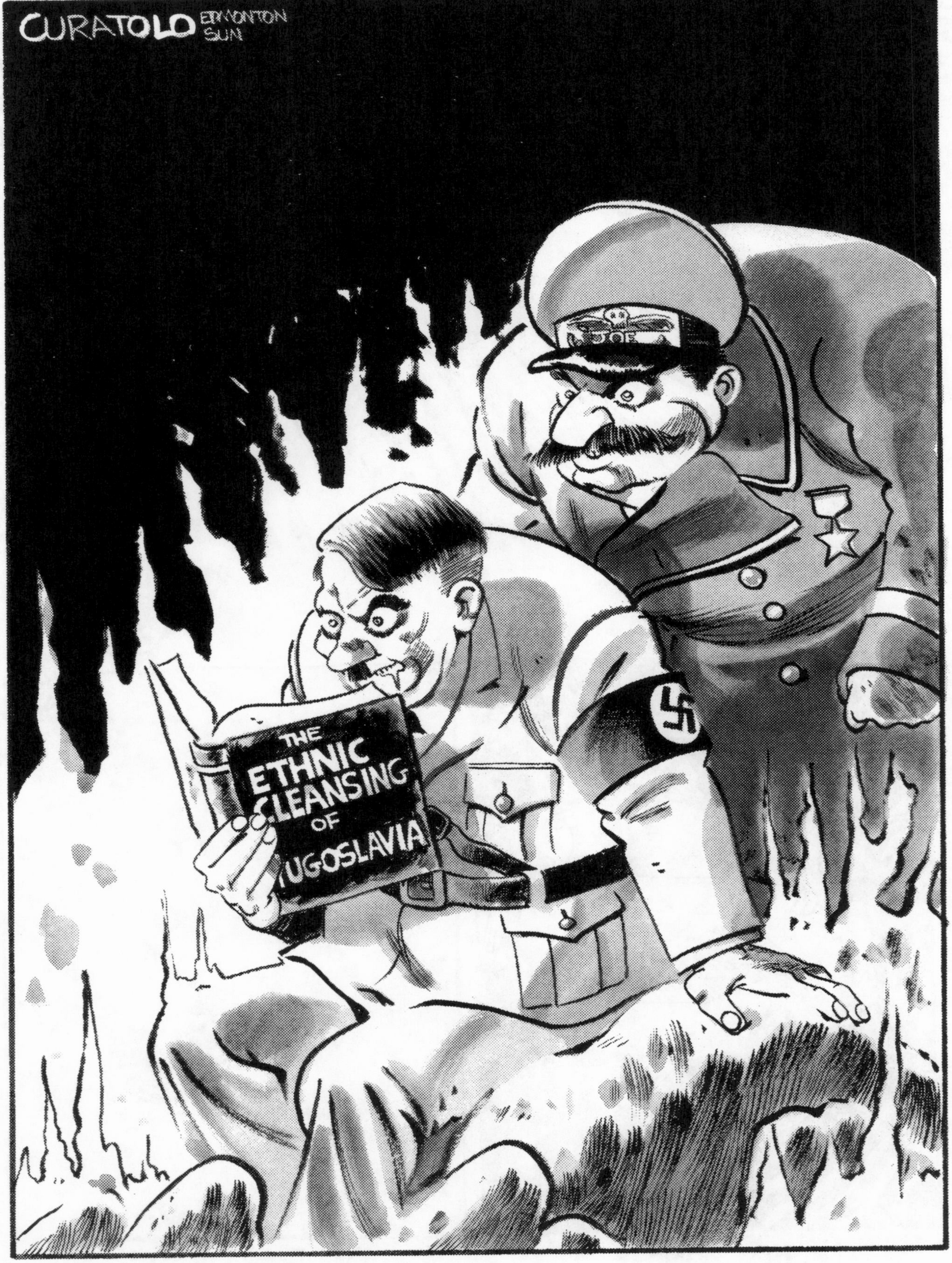
CURATOLO EDMONTON SUN
JOE
THE ETHNIC CLEANSING OF YUGOSLAVIA

SON OF FRANKENSTEIN
NAZI HOLOCAUST
SERBIAN "ETHNIC CLEANSING"

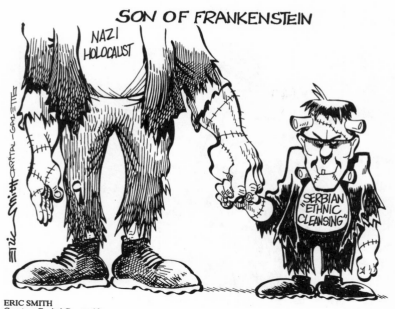

ERIC SMITH
Courtesy Capital Gazette Newspapers

ROMAN GENN
Courtesy Easy Reader

BOSNIA
U.N.

THE HORN OF AFRICA
6.92

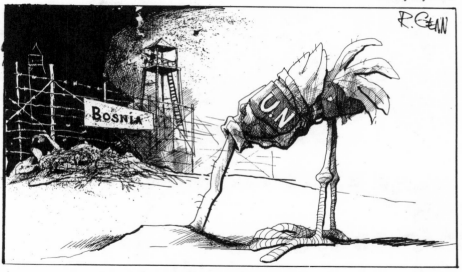

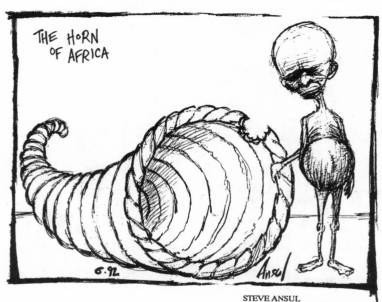

STEVE ANSUL
Courtesy Wilmington News Journal

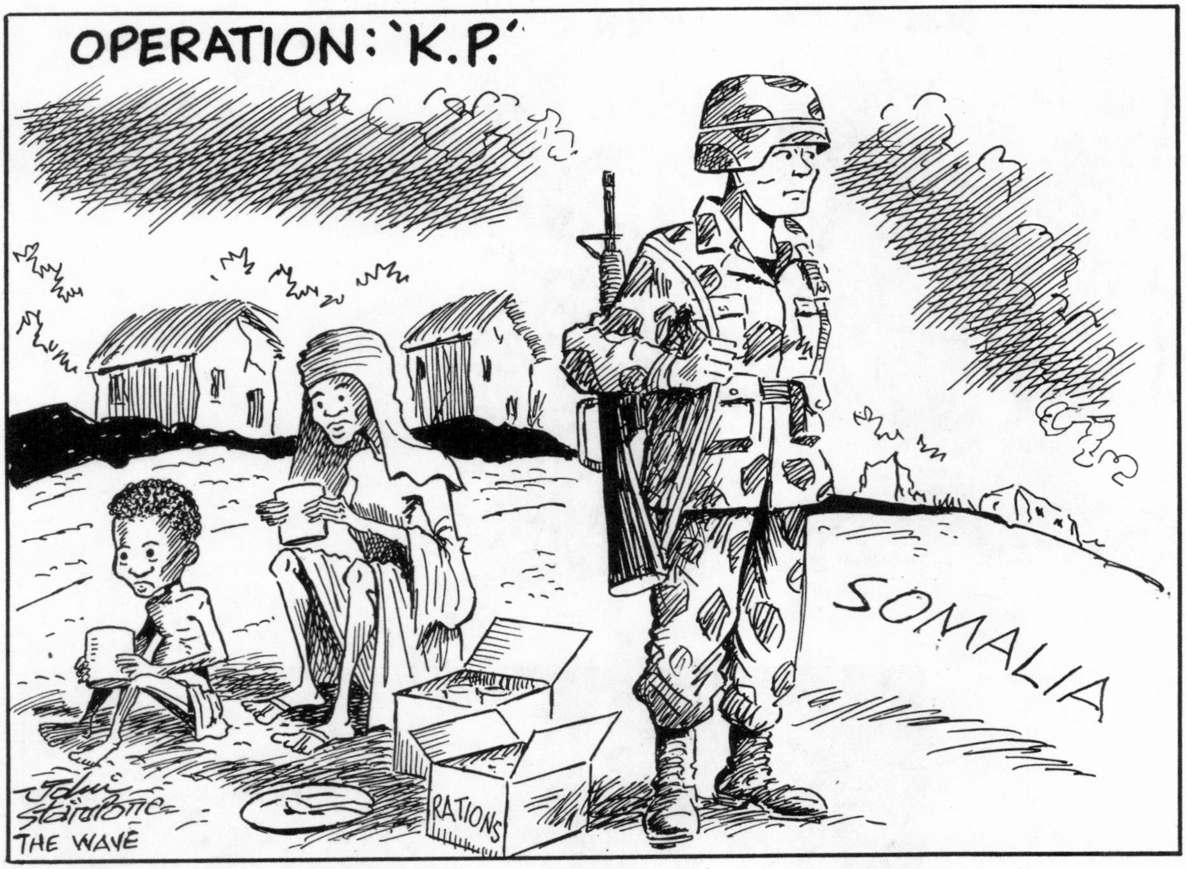
OPERATION: 'K.P.'
SOMALIA
RATIONS
John Stampone
THE WAVE

JOHN STAMPONE
Courtesy The Wave (Del.)

CHIP BECK
Courtesy Northern Virginia Sun
and Associated Features

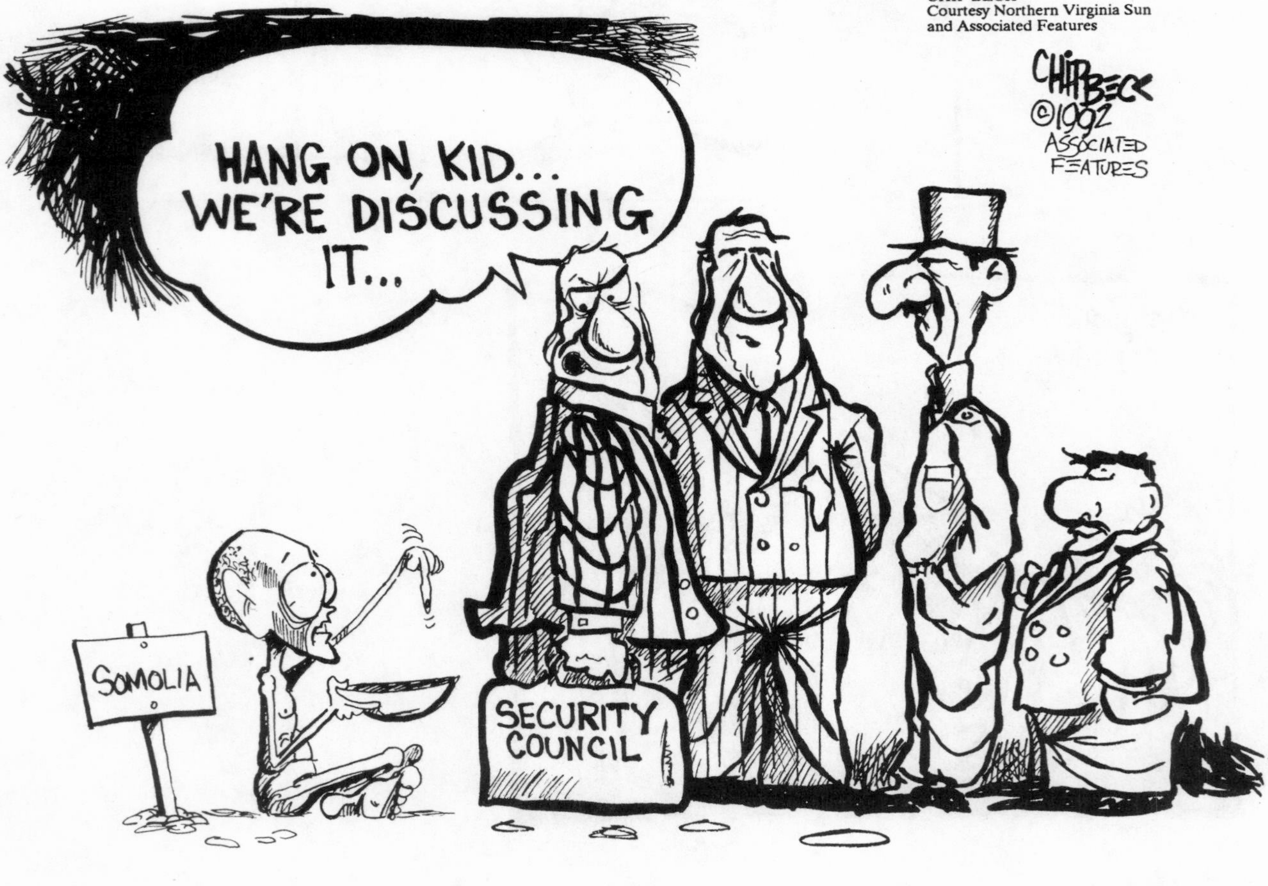
CHIP BECK ©1992 ASSOCIATED FEATURES
HANG ON, KID... WE'RE DISCUSSING IT...
SOMOLIA
SECURITY COUNCIL

CAM CARDOW
Courtesy Regina Leader-Post

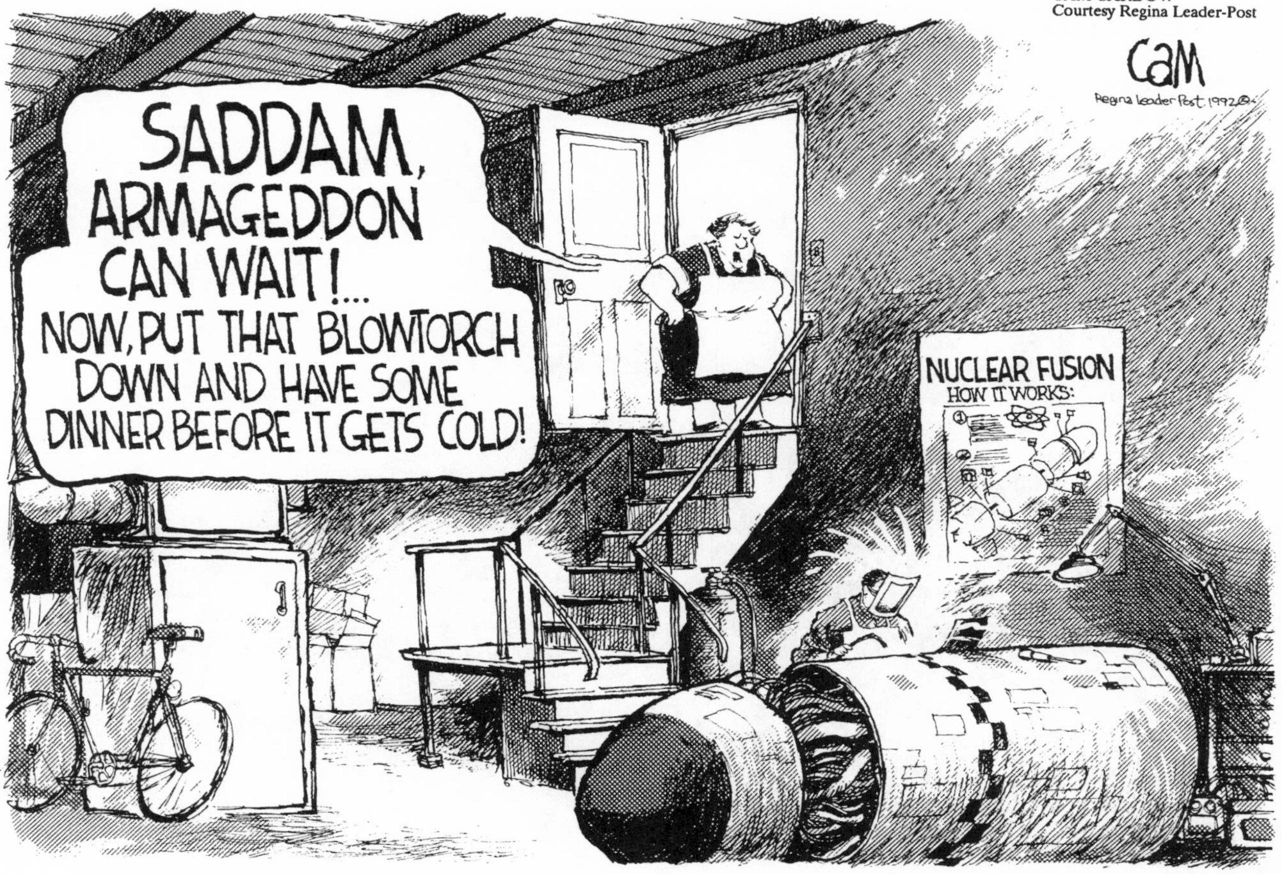
SADDAM, ARMAGEDDON CAN WAIT!.... NOW, PUT THAT BLOWTORCH DOWN AND HAVE SOME DINNER BEFORE IT GETS COLD!
NUCLEAR FUSION
HOW IT WORKS:
CAM
Regina Leader Post 1992

DALE STEPHANOS
Courtesy Haverhill Gazette (Mass.)

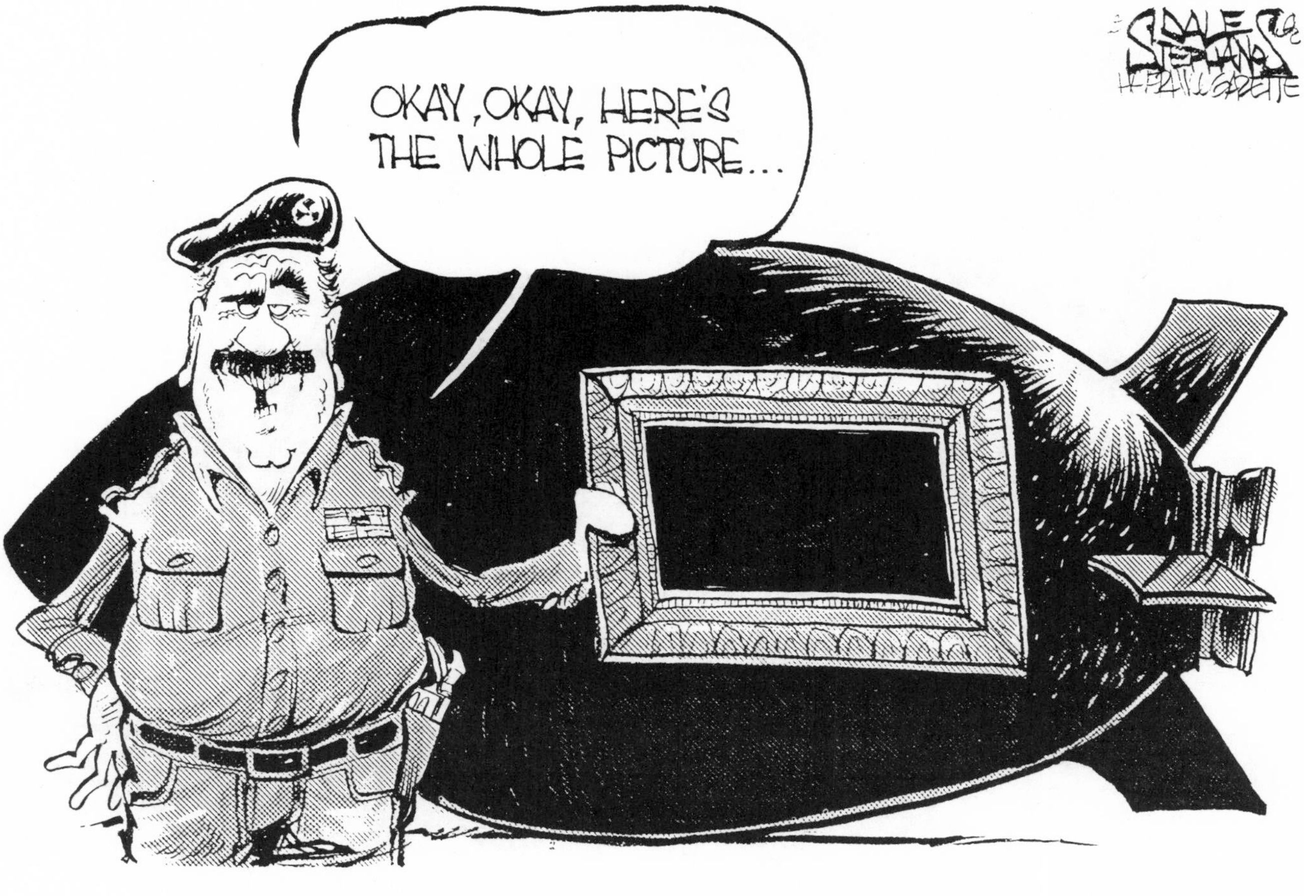
OKAY, OKAY, HERE'S THE WHOLE PICTURE...
DALE STEPHANOS
HAVERHILL GAZETTE

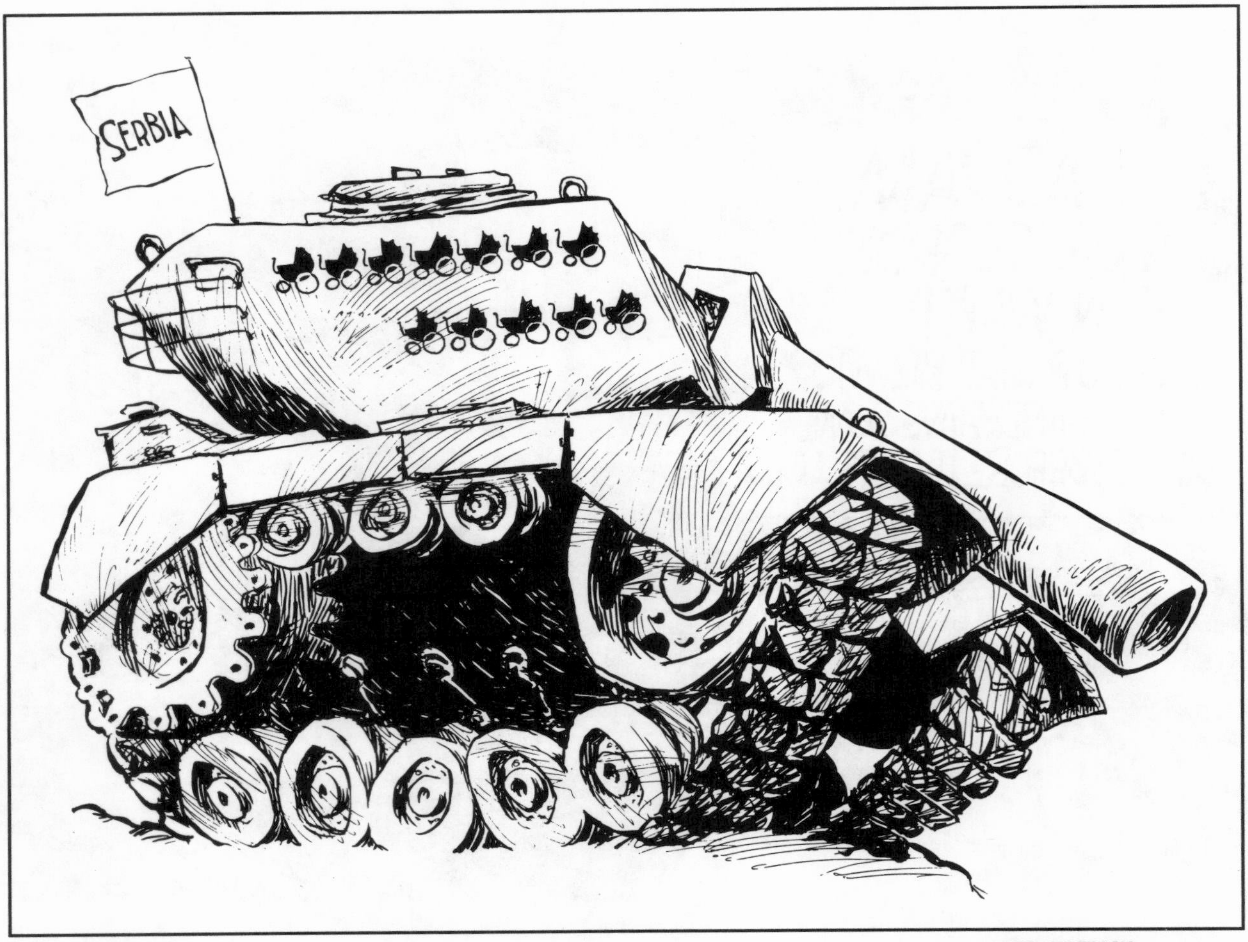
SERBIA

NICK ANDERSON
Courtesy Louisville Courier Journal

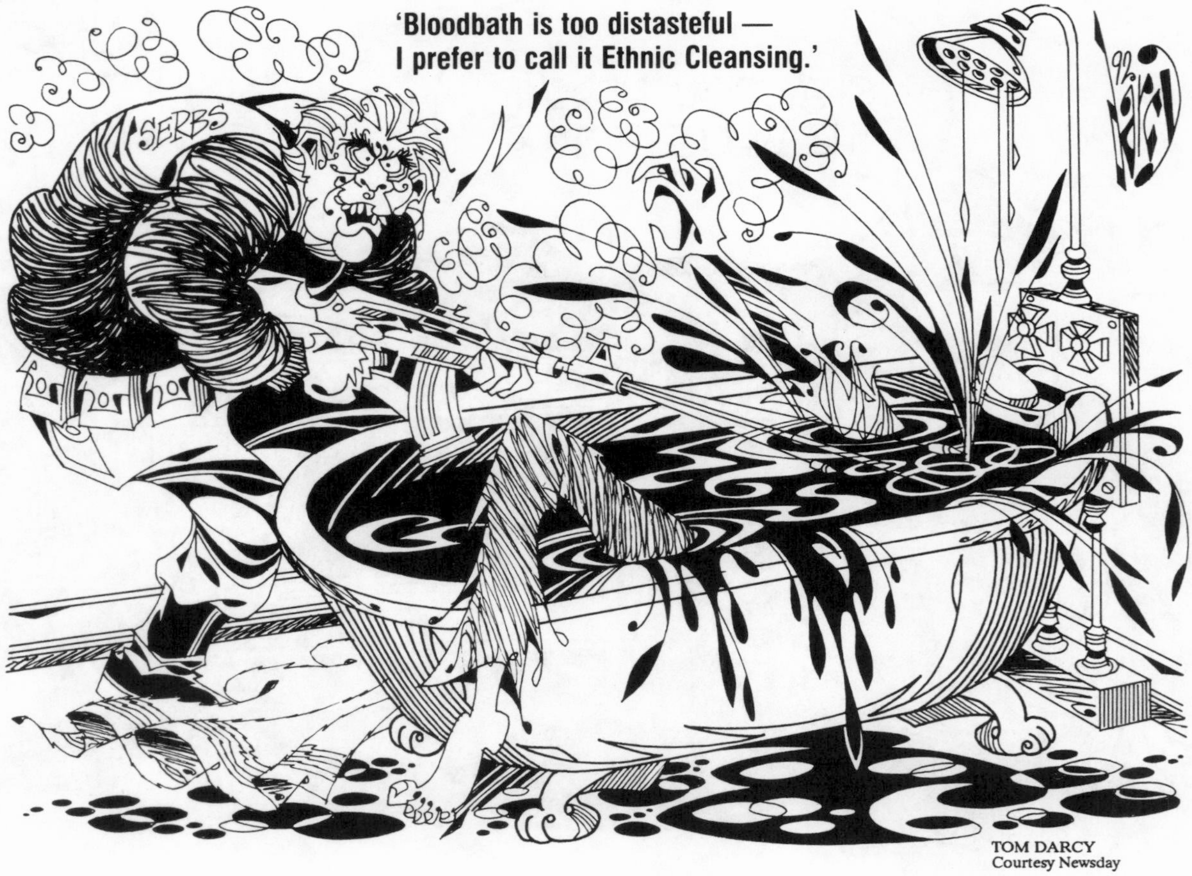
'Bloodbath is too distasteful —
I prefer to call it Ethnic Cleansing.'
SERBS

TOM DARCY
Courtesy Newsday

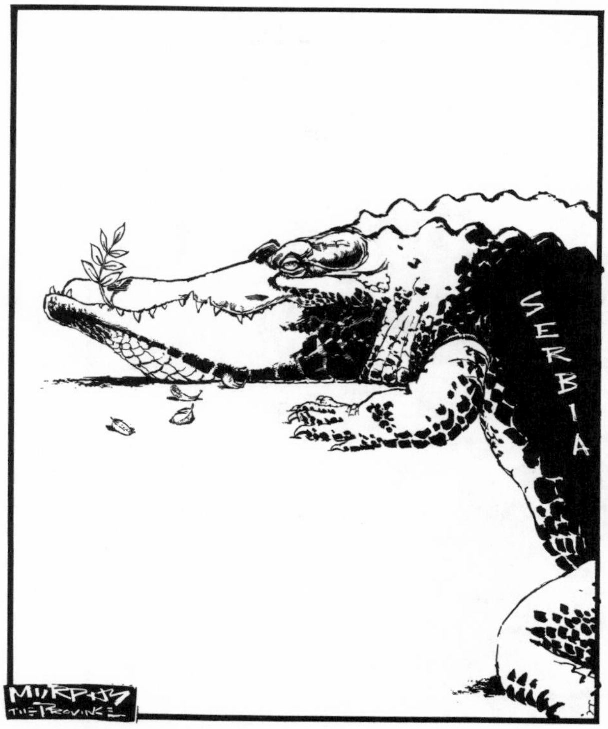
SERBIA
MURPHY
THE PROVINCE

DAN MURPHY
Courtesy Vancouver Province

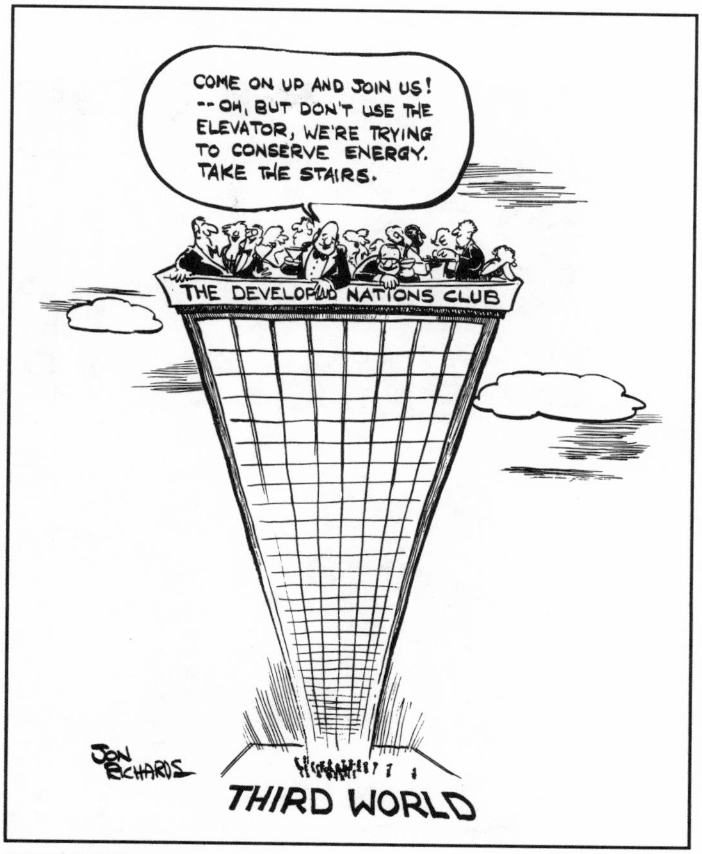
COME ON UP AND JOIN US!
--OH, BUT DON'T USE THE ELEVATOR, WE'RE TRYING TO CONSERVE ENERGY. TAKE THE STAIRS.
THE DEVELOPED NATIONS CLUB
JON RICHARDS
THIRD WORLD

JON RICHARDS
Courtesy Earth Summit Times

REX BABIN
Courtesy Times Union (N.Y.)

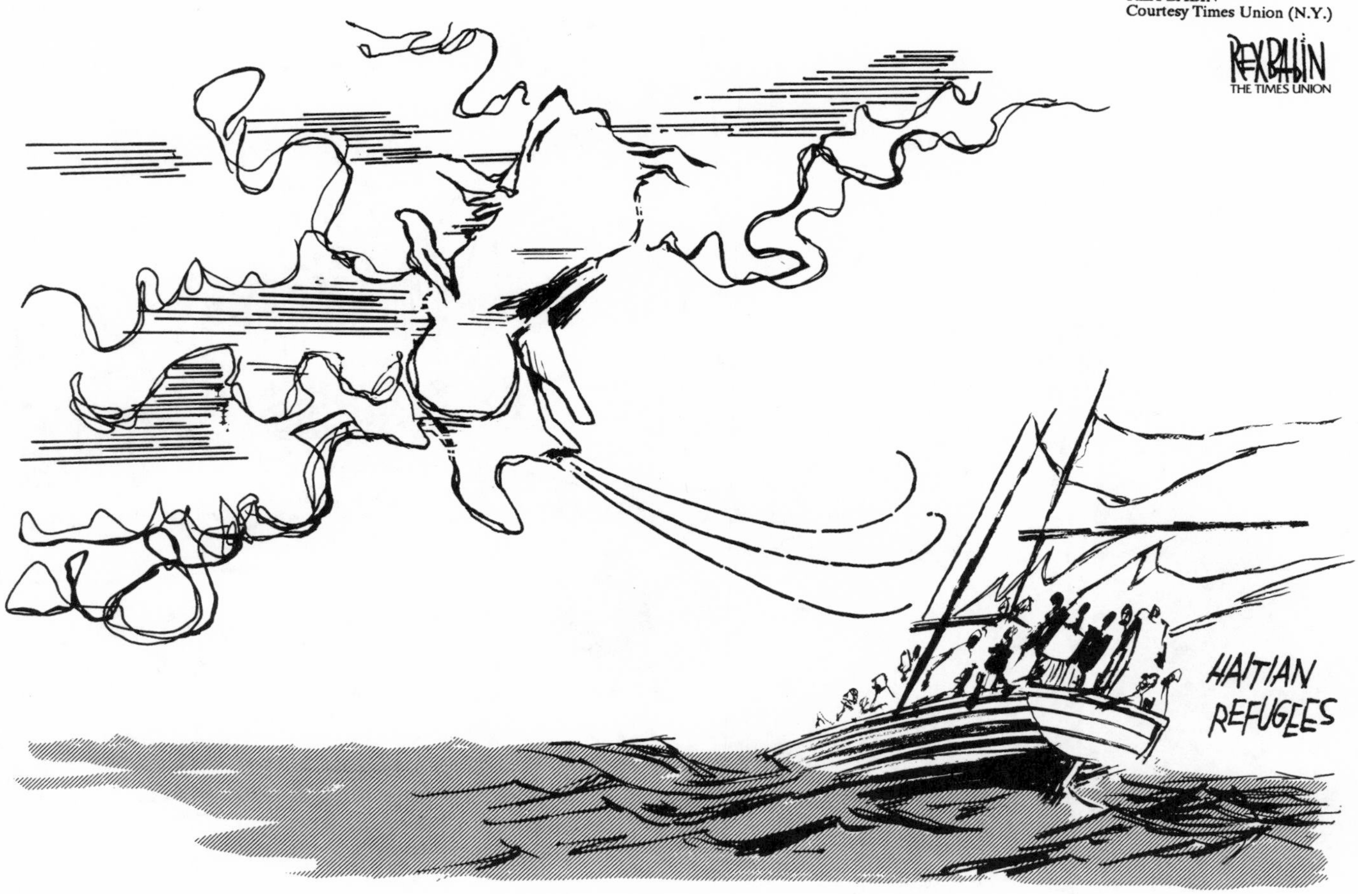
REX BABIN
THE TIMES UNION
HAITIAN REFUGEES

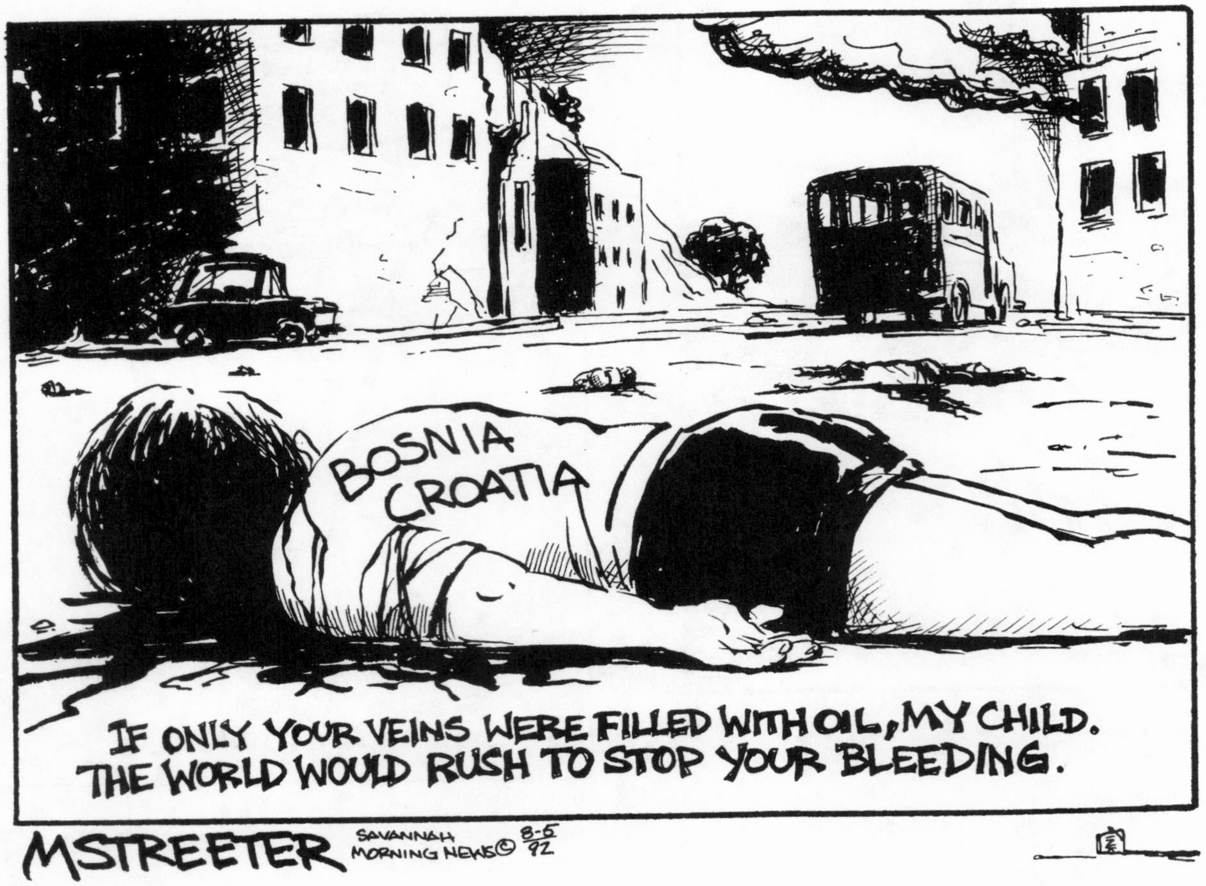
BOSNIA
CROATIA
IF ONLY YOUR VEINS WERE FILLED WITH OIL, MY CHILD.
THE WORLD WOULD RUSH TO STOP YOUR BLEEDING.
MSTREETER
SAVANNAH MORNING NEWS©
8-5 92

MARK STREETER
Courtesy Savannah Morning News

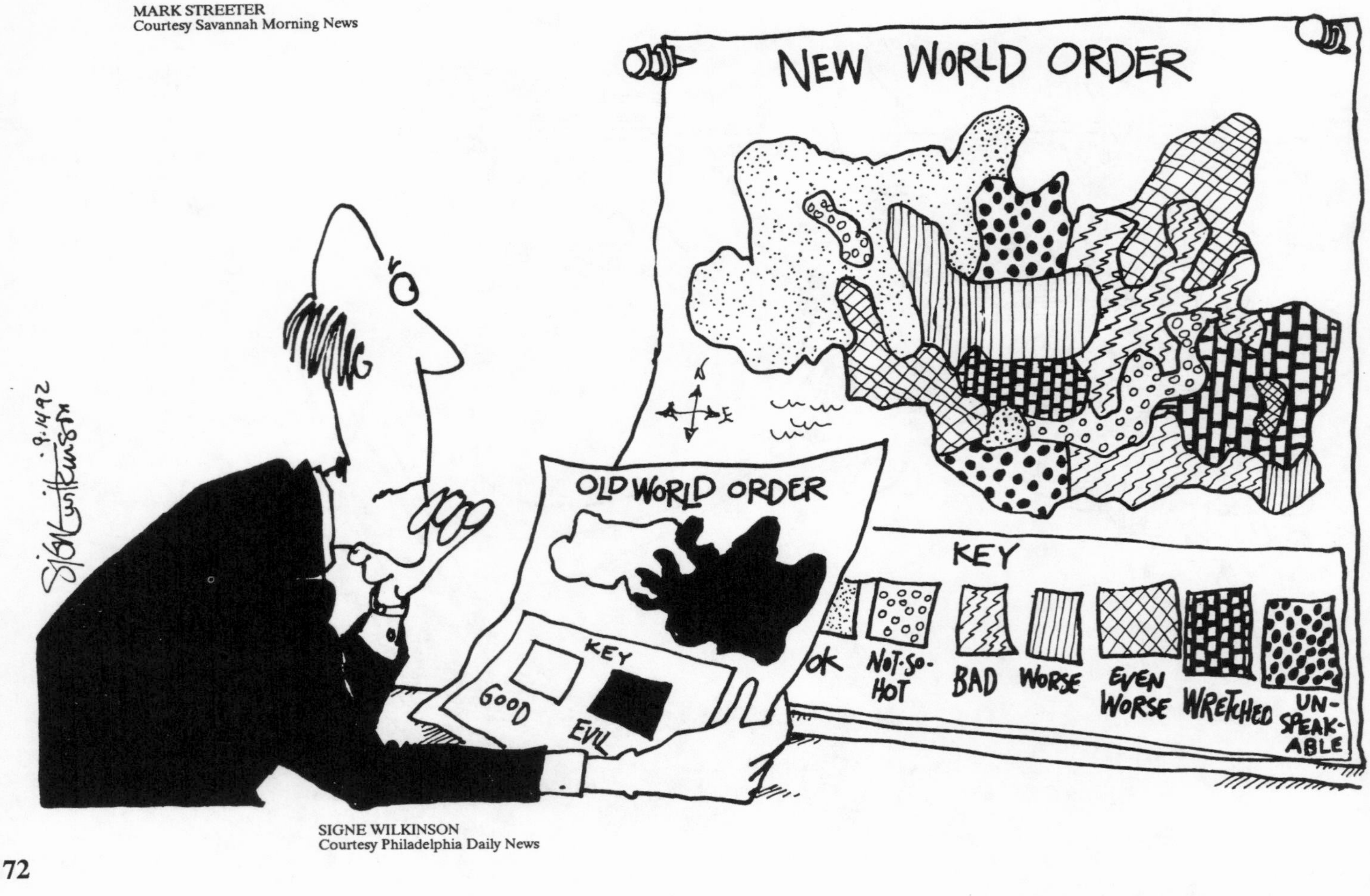
NEW WORLD ORDER
N
E
KEY
OK
NOT-SO-HOT
BAD
WORSE
EVEN WORSE
WRETCHED
UN-SPEAKABLE
OLD WORLD ORDER
KEY
GOOD
EVIL
9.14.92

SIGNE WILKINSON
Courtesy Philadelphia Daily News

REALLY NOW! YOU MUST STOP THAT INCESSANT LIP SMACKING AND STOMACH GROWLING! ...WE'RE TRYING TO SAY OUR GOODBYES!
BRITAIN
HONG KONG
CHINA
©1992 SEATTLE POST-INTELLIGENCER NORTH AMERICA SYNDICATE
HORSEY

DAVID HORSEY
Courtesy Seattle Post-Intelligencer

LAZARO FRESQUET
Courtesy El Nuevo Herald (Miami)

FRESQUET
SENDERO LUMINOSO
PERÚ

YOU SEE, GENTLEMEN, WE ARE MERELY PLANTING SEEDS AT OUR AGRICULTURE MINISTRY BUILDING...
UN
UN
UN
©1992 FLORIDA TODAY
JEFF PARKER

JEFF PARKER
Courtesy Florida Today

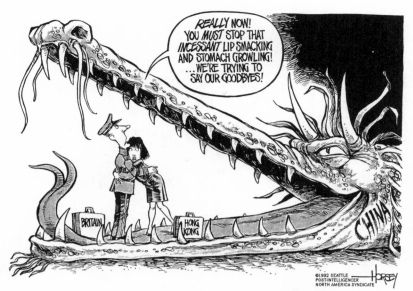

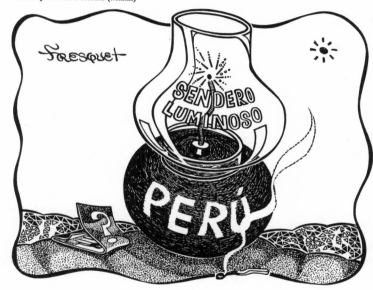

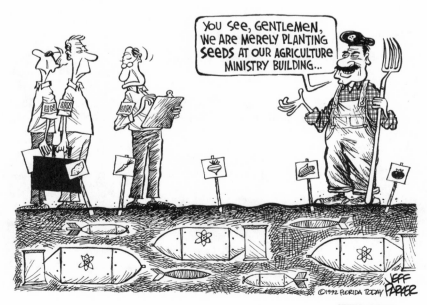

PAUL SZEP
Courtesy Boston Globe

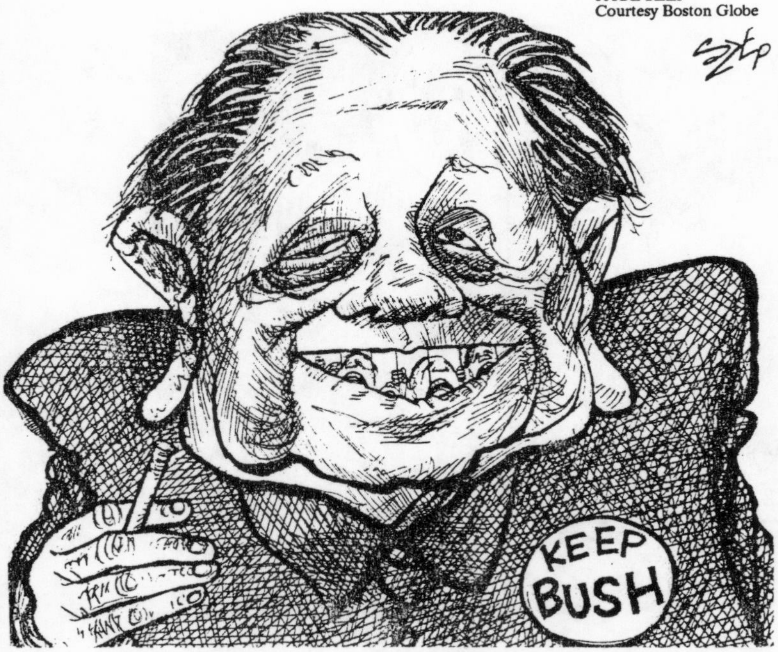
SZEP
KEEP BUSH

DESPITE THE ANNOYING SCREAMS OF ANGUISH AND THE MUFFLED SOUND OF PROTEST, DENG XIAOPING HAS STEADFASTLY MAINTAINED HIS SUPPORT AND FRIENDSHIP FOR HIS OLD FRIEND AND TRADING PARTNER GEORGE BUSH

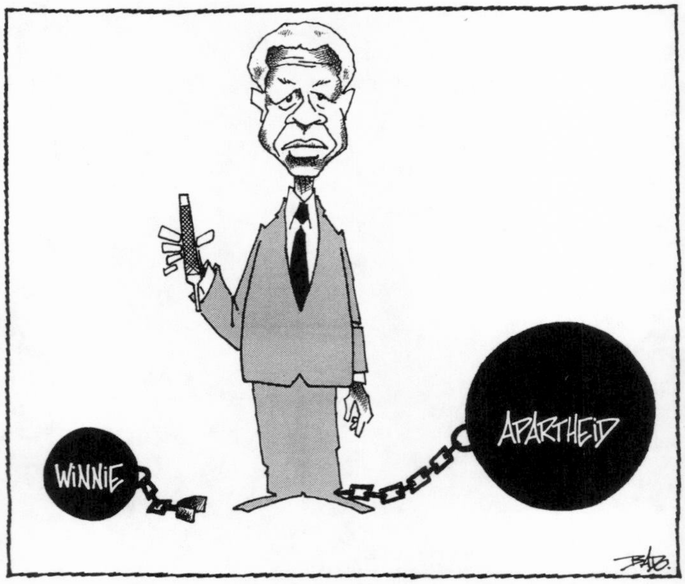
WINNIE
APARTHEID
BAD.

GUY BADEAUX
Courtesy Le Droit (Ottawa)

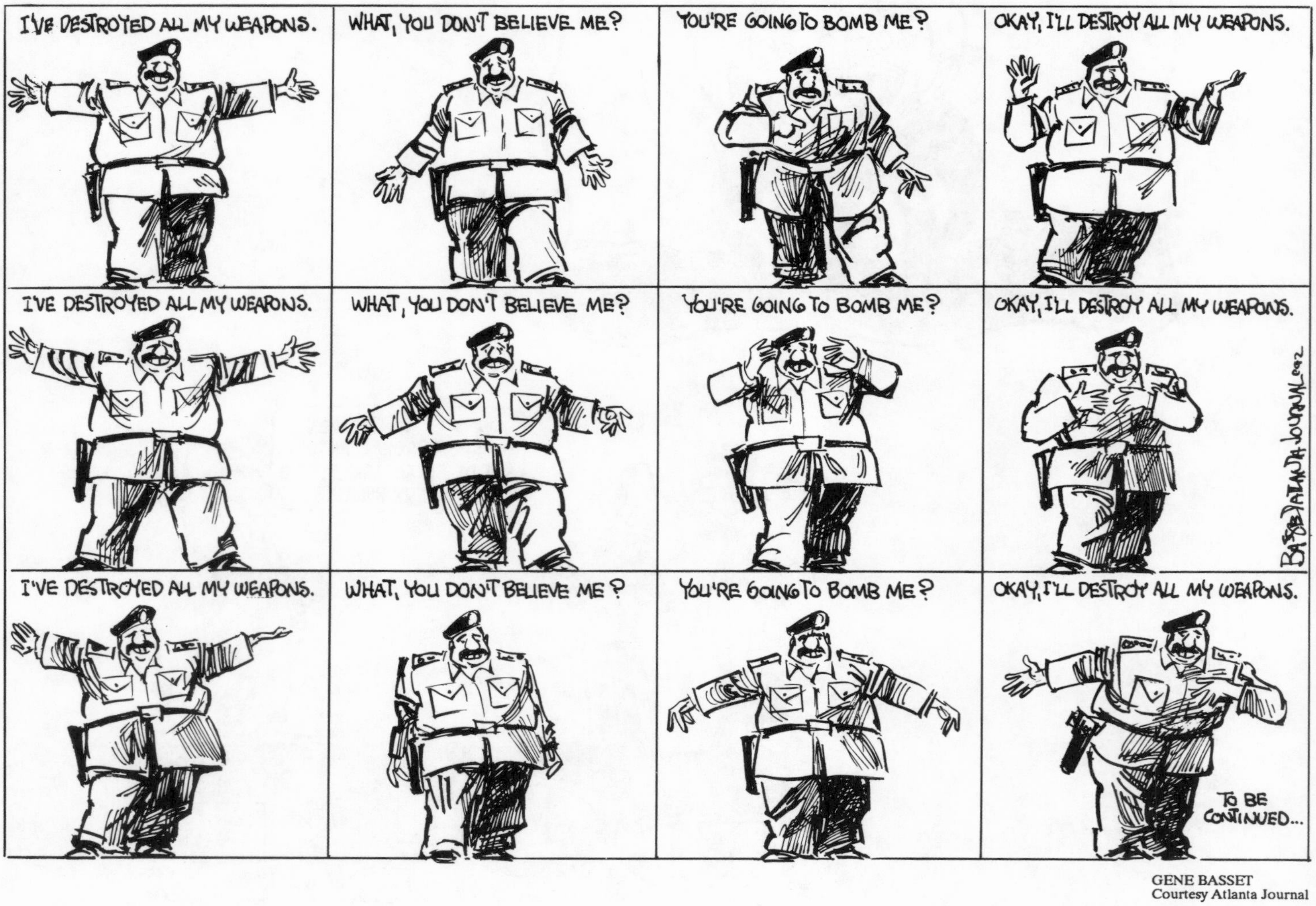
I'VE DESTROYED ALL MY WEAPONS.
WHAT, YOU DON'T BELIEVE ME?
YOU'RE GOING TO BOMB ME?
OKAY, I'LL DESTROY ALL MY WEAPONS.
I'VE DESTROYED ALL MY WEAPONS.
WHAT, YOU DON'T BELIEVE ME?
YOU'RE GOING TO BOMB ME?
OKAY, I'LL DESTROY ALL MY WEAPONS.
I'VE DESTROYED ALL MY WEAPONS.
WHAT, YOU DON'T BELIEVE ME?
YOU'RE GOING TO BOMB ME?
OKAY, I'LL DESTROY ALL MY WEAPONS.
TO BE CONTINUED...

GENE BASSET
Courtesy Atlanta Journal

HUGH HAYNIE
Courtesy Louisville Courier Journal

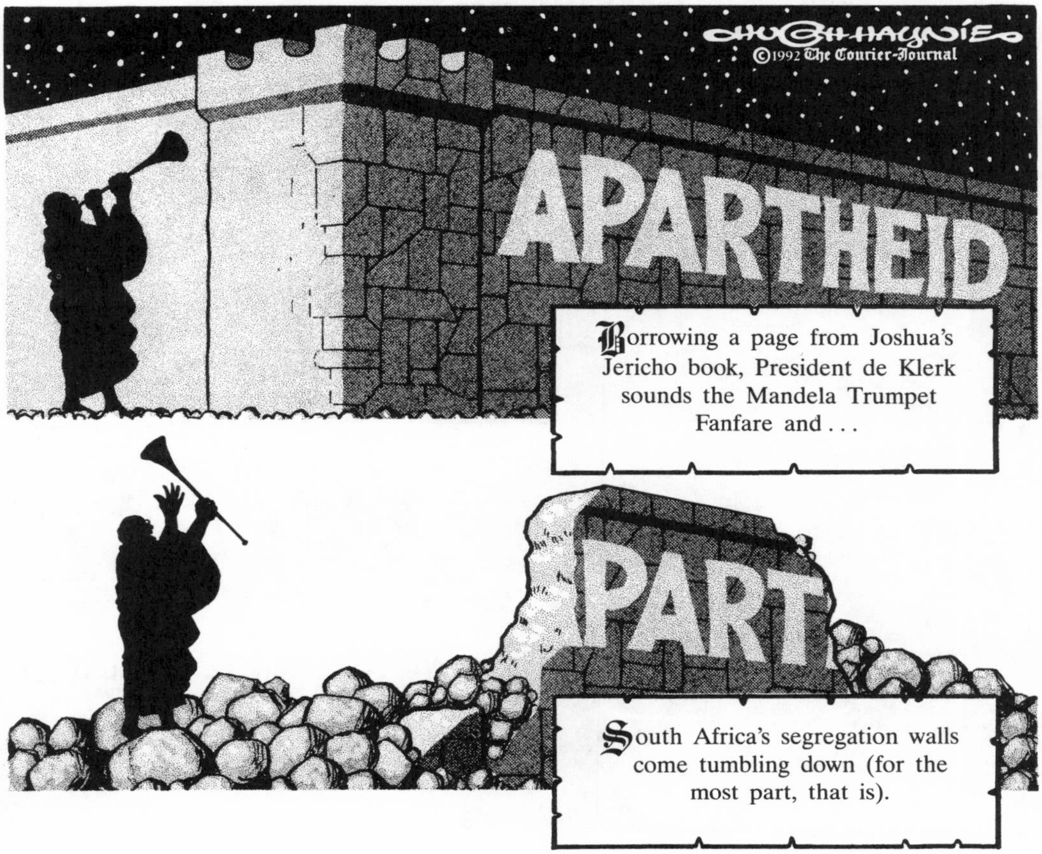
HUGH HAYNIE
©1992 The Courier-Journal
APARTHEID
Borrowing a page from Joshua's Jericho book, President de Klerk sounds the Mandela Trumpet Fanfare and . . .
PART
South Africa's segregation walls come tumbling down (for the most part, that is).

JEFF MACNELLY
Courtesy Chicago Tribune and Tribune Media Services

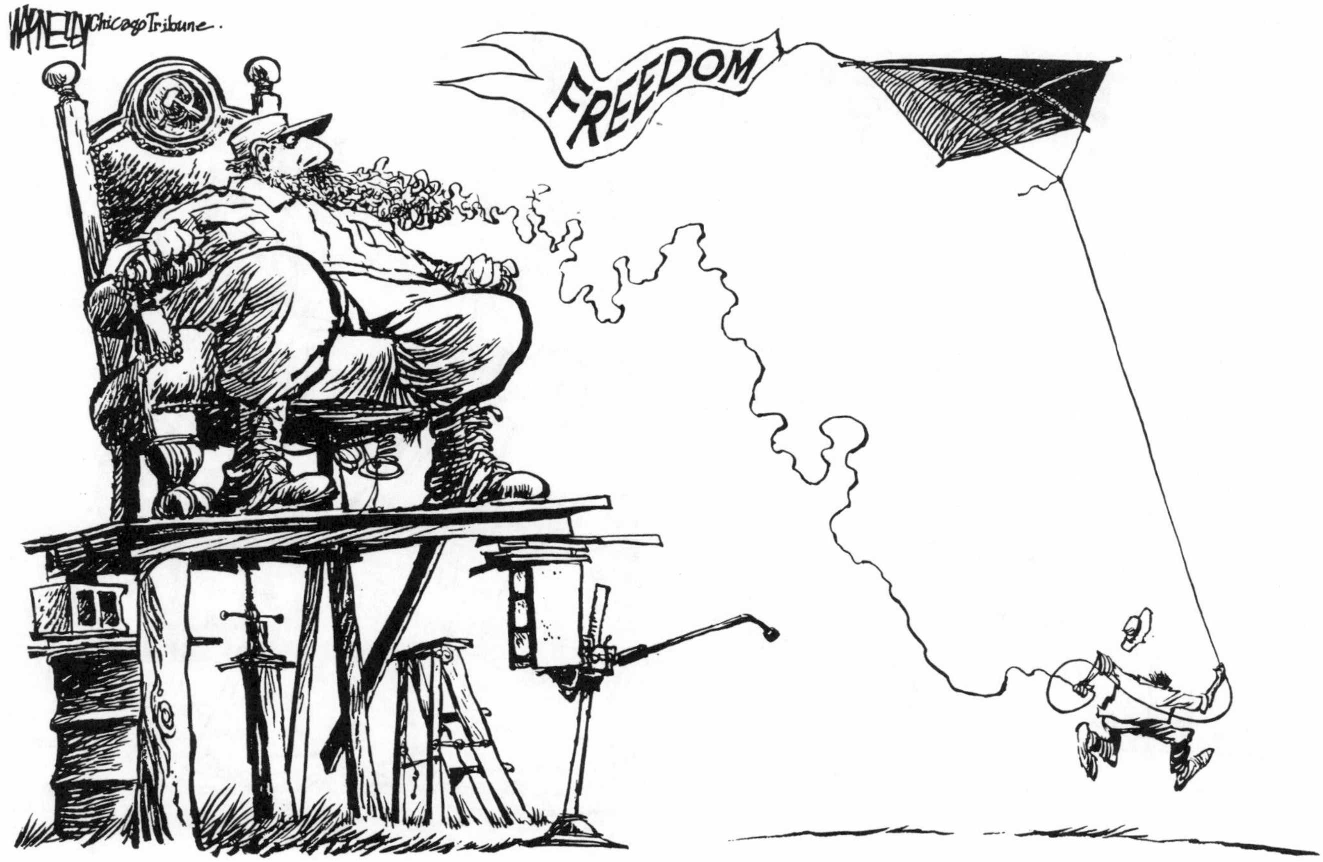
MACNELLY Chicago Tribune
FREEDOM

MARK CULLUM
Courtesy Birmingham News

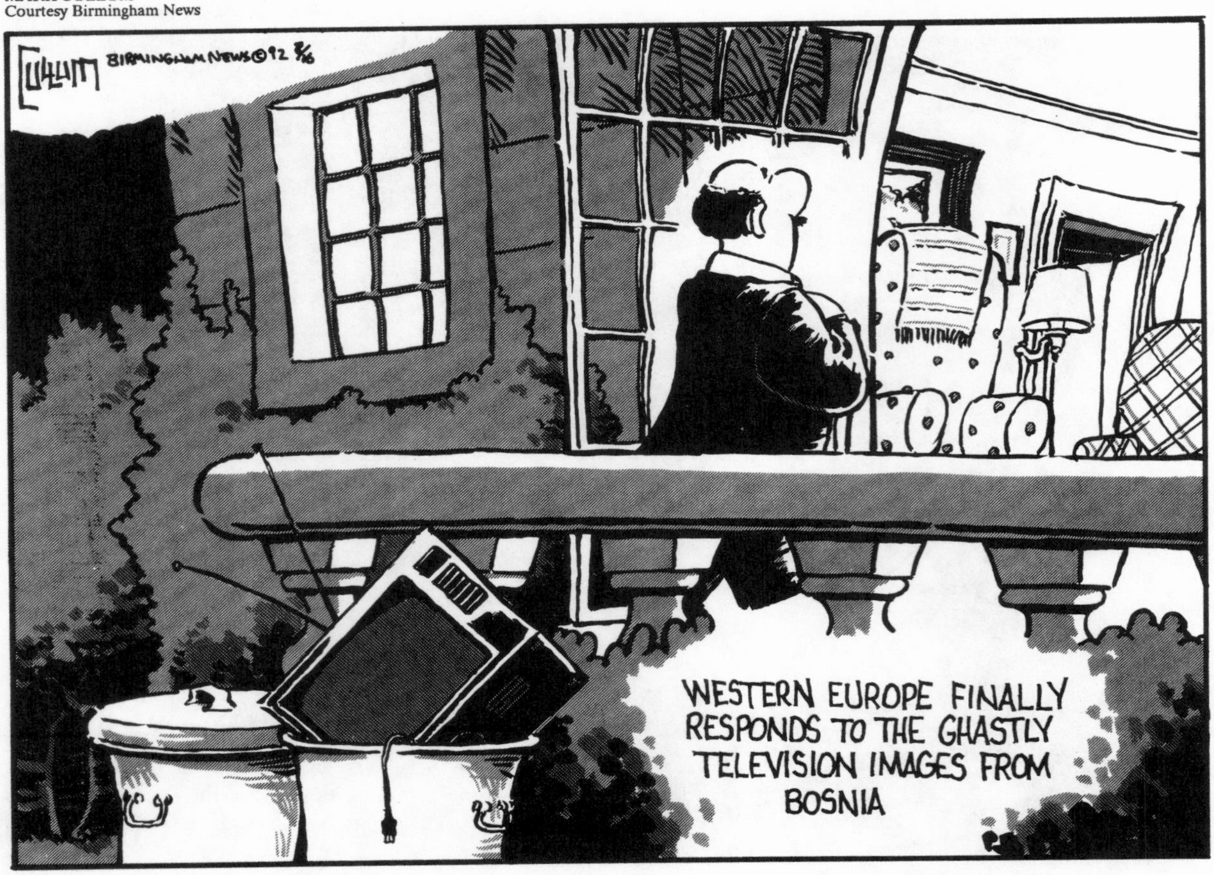
CULLUM BIRMINGHAM NEWS ©92
WESTERN EUROPE FINALLY RESPONDS TO THE GHASTLY TELEVISION IMAGES FROM BOSNIA

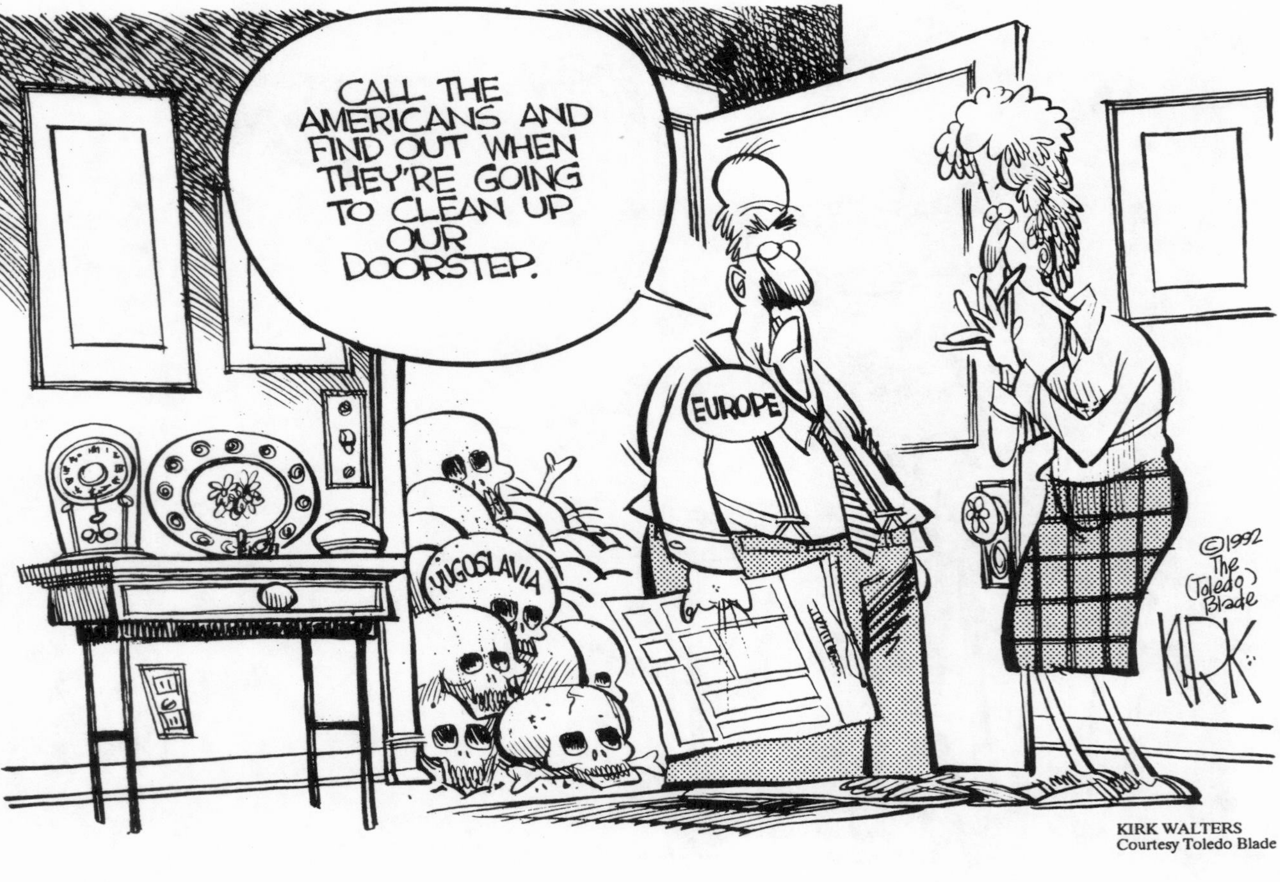
CALL THE AMERICANS AND FIND OUT WHEN THEY'RE GOING TO CLEAN UP OUR DOORSTEP.
EUROPE
YUGOSLAVIA
©1992 The (Toledo) Blade
KIRK

KIRK WALTERS
Courtesy Toledo Blade

ED FISCHER
Courtesy Rochester Post-Bulletin

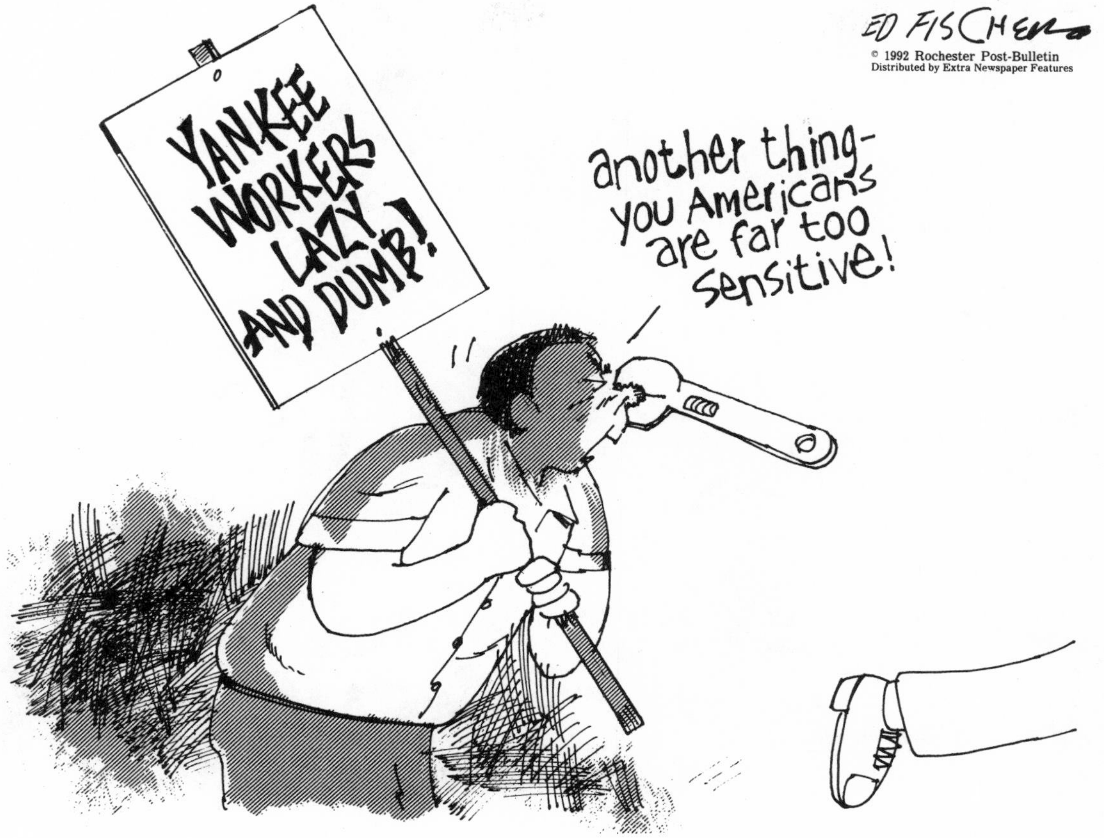
ED FISCHER
© 1992 Rochester Post-Bulletin
Distributed by Extra Newspaper Features
YANKEE WORKERS LAZY AND DUMB!
another thing- you Americans are far too sensitive!

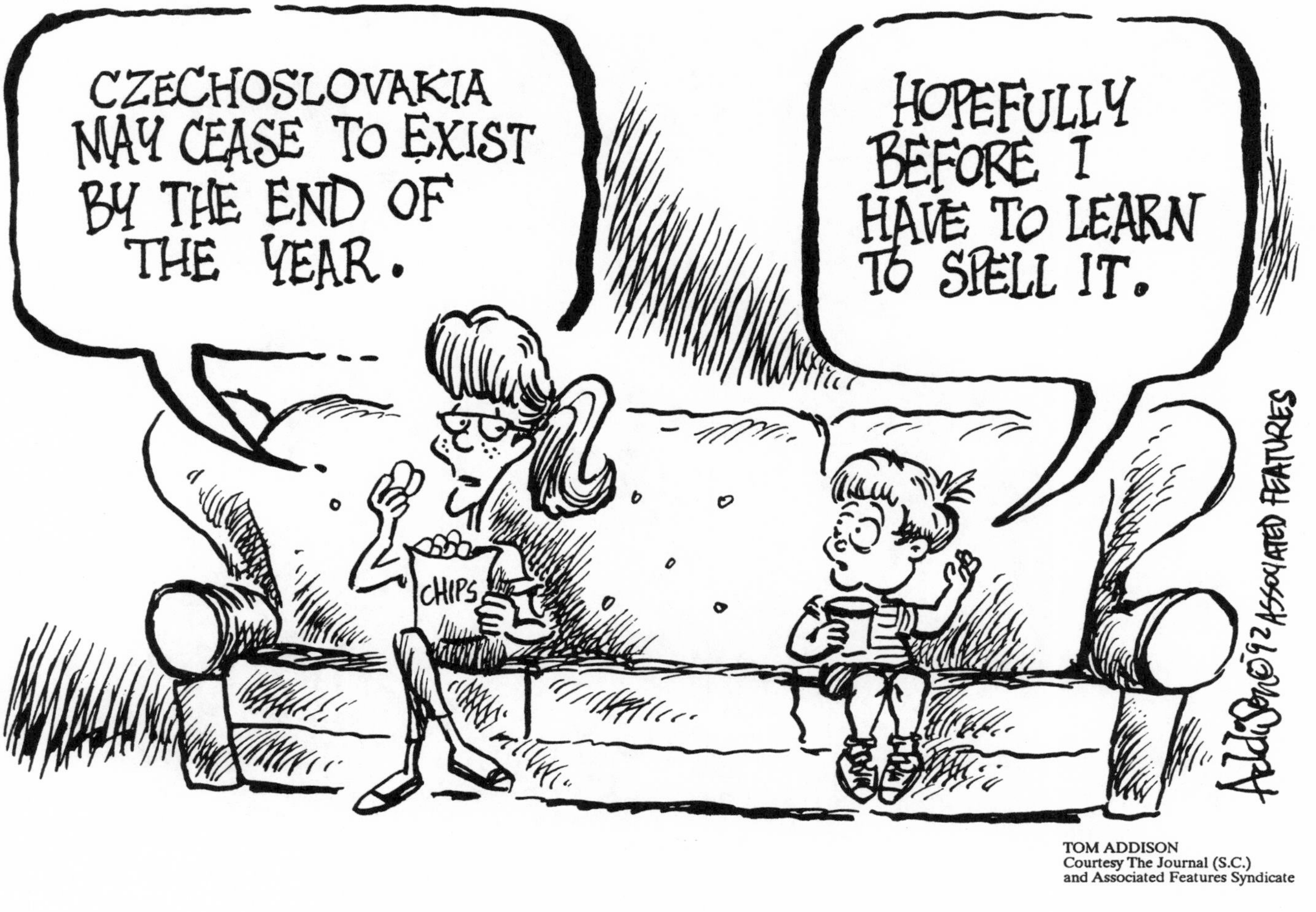
CZECHOSLOVAKIA MAY CEASE TO EXIST BY THE END OF THE YEAR.
HOPEFULLY BEFORE I HAVE TO LEARN TO SPELL IT.
CHIPS
Addison ©'92 ASSOCIATED FEATURES

TOM ADDISON
Courtesy The Journal (S.C.)
and Associated Features Syndicate

RANAN LURIE
Courtesy Cartoonews International

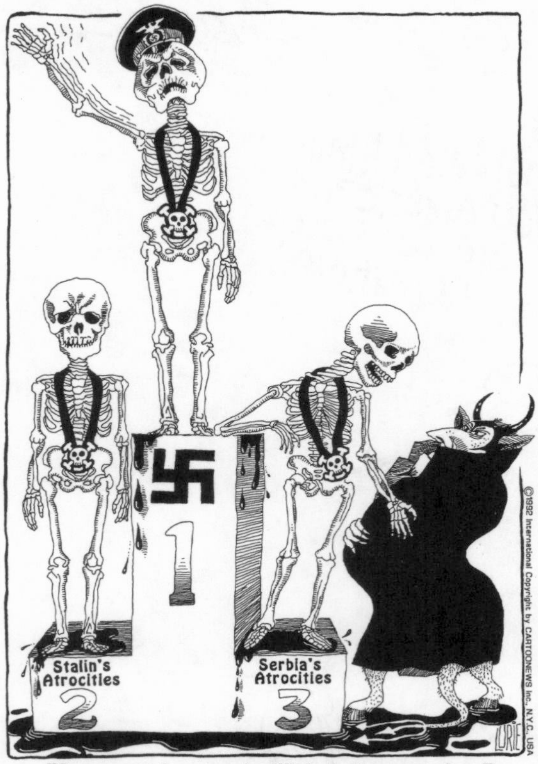
1
Stalin's Atrocities
2
Serbia's Atrocities
3
©1992 International Copyright by CARTOONEWS Inc., N.Y.C., USA
LURIE

"Sorry, coach- - maybe I'll do better next time."

FRED CURATOLO
Courtesy Edmonton Sun

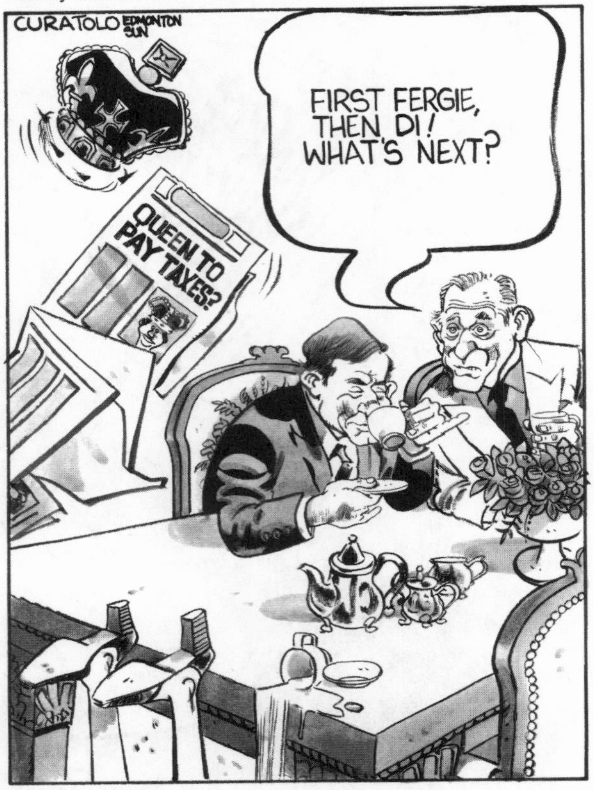
CURATOLO EDMONTON SUN
FIRST FERGIE, THEN DI! WHAT'S NEXT?
QUEEN TO PAY TAXES?

BILL GARNER
Courtesy Washington Times

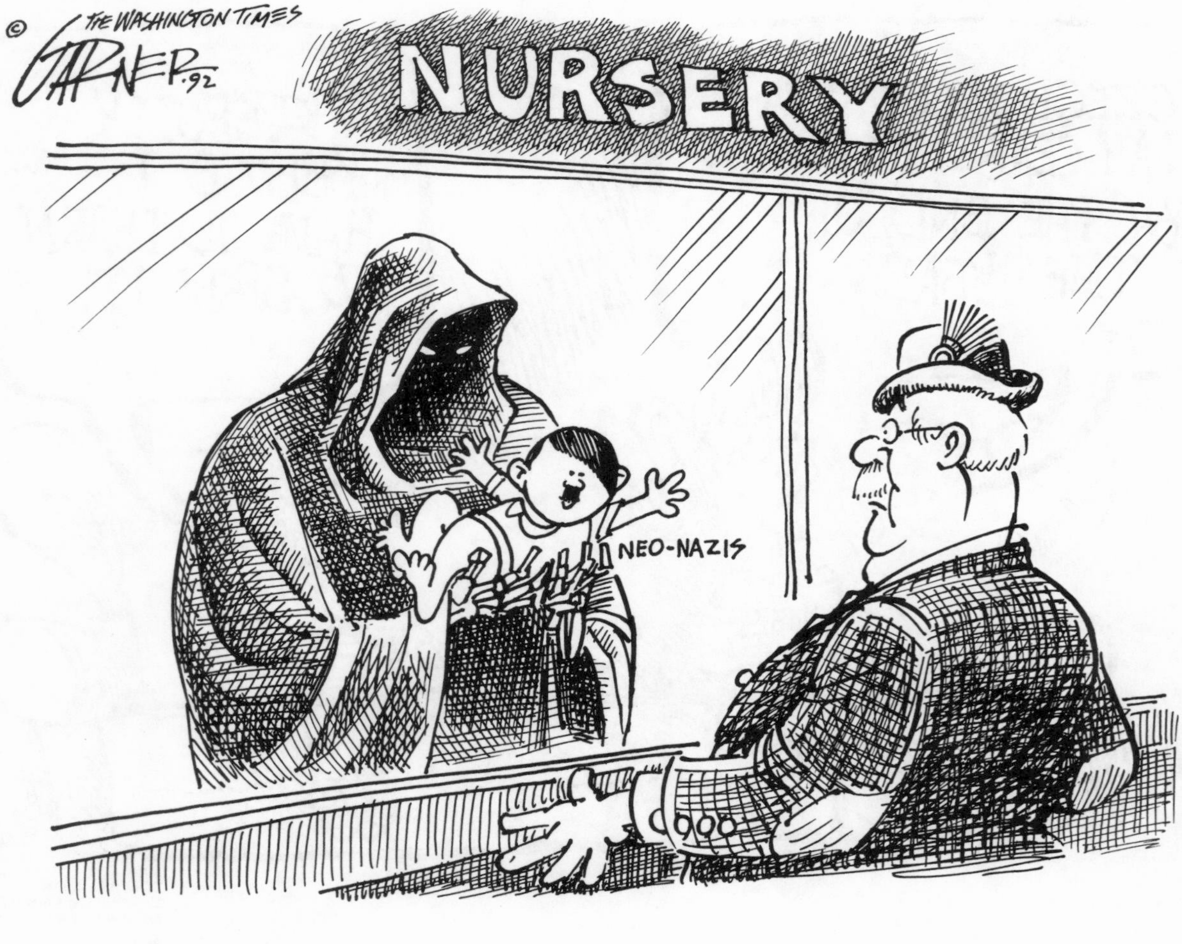
© THE WASHINGTON TIMES
GARNER '92
NURSERY
NEO-NAZIS

The Economy

The world's economies continued to slump during 1992. In the U.S., there was a slight pickup late in the year, and a modest increase of 140,000 jobs in the second half brought the unemployment rate down from 7.8 percent to 7.2 percent. Businesses were learning how to produce more without adding to the workforce.

General Motors reported a record loss of $4.5 billion in 1991, and its market share dropped from 45 percent in 1982 to 33 percent in 1992. In an effort to become lean and competitive again, the company dismissed thousands of employees, closed plants, and announced it would trim production capacity by one-fifth. Over at Chrysler, Lee Iacocca retired after a storied career.

In Japan, corporations watched inventories rise and profits fall. Business confidence in Tokyo sank to a fifteen-year low after three straight years of declining earnings among Japanese manufacturers. Since 1990, Japanese corporations have lost more than $1 trillion in net wealth.

Reunification proved to be an economic albatross for Germany as massive unemployment continued in the former East Germany. In France, the economy stagnated and unemployment reached 10 percent.

In August, the United States, Canada, and Mexico initialed a far-reaching North American Free Trade Agreement.

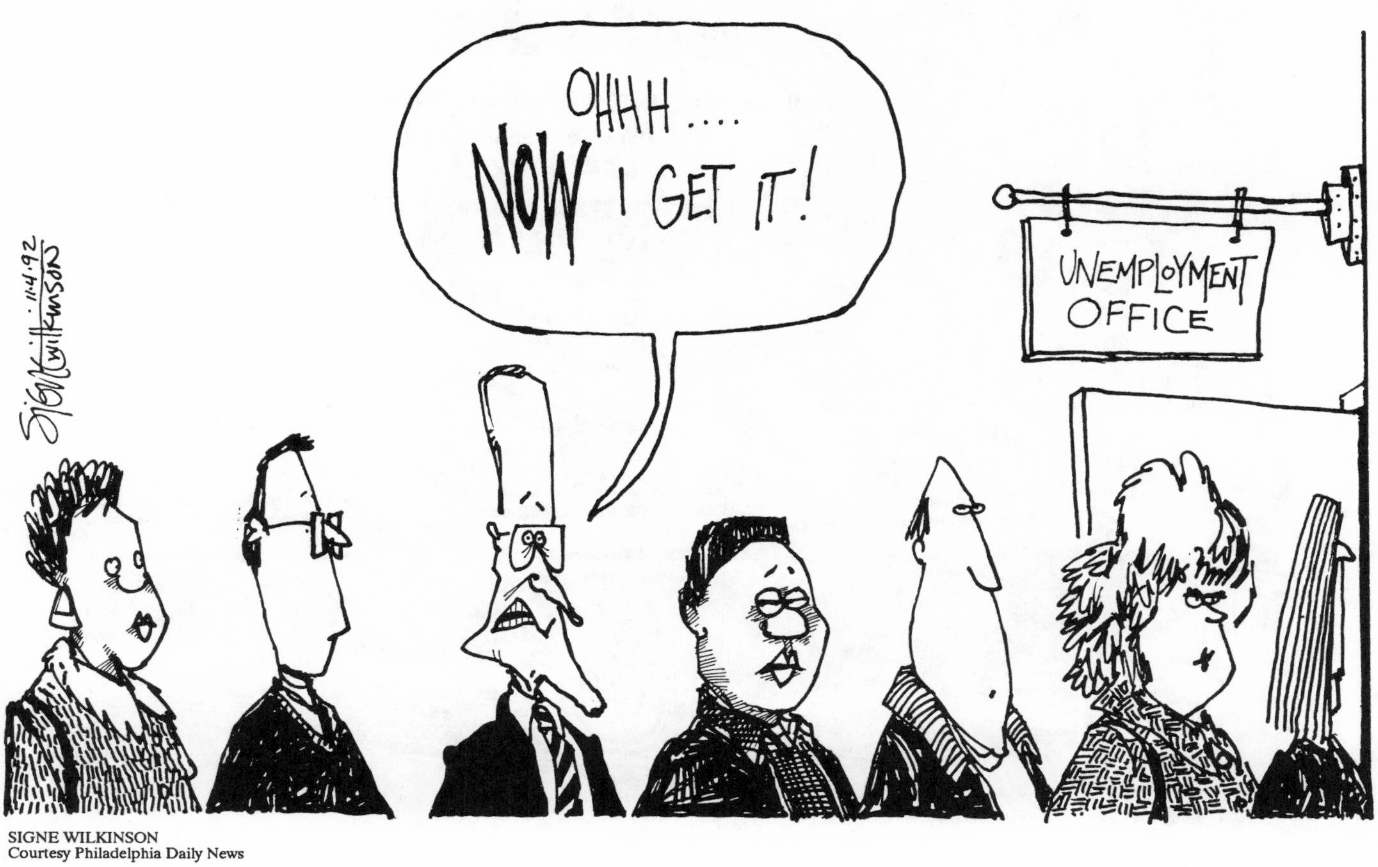
OHHH ....
NOW I GET IT!
UNEMPLOYMENT OFFICE
11.4.92

SIGNE WILKINSON
Courtesy Philadelphia Daily News

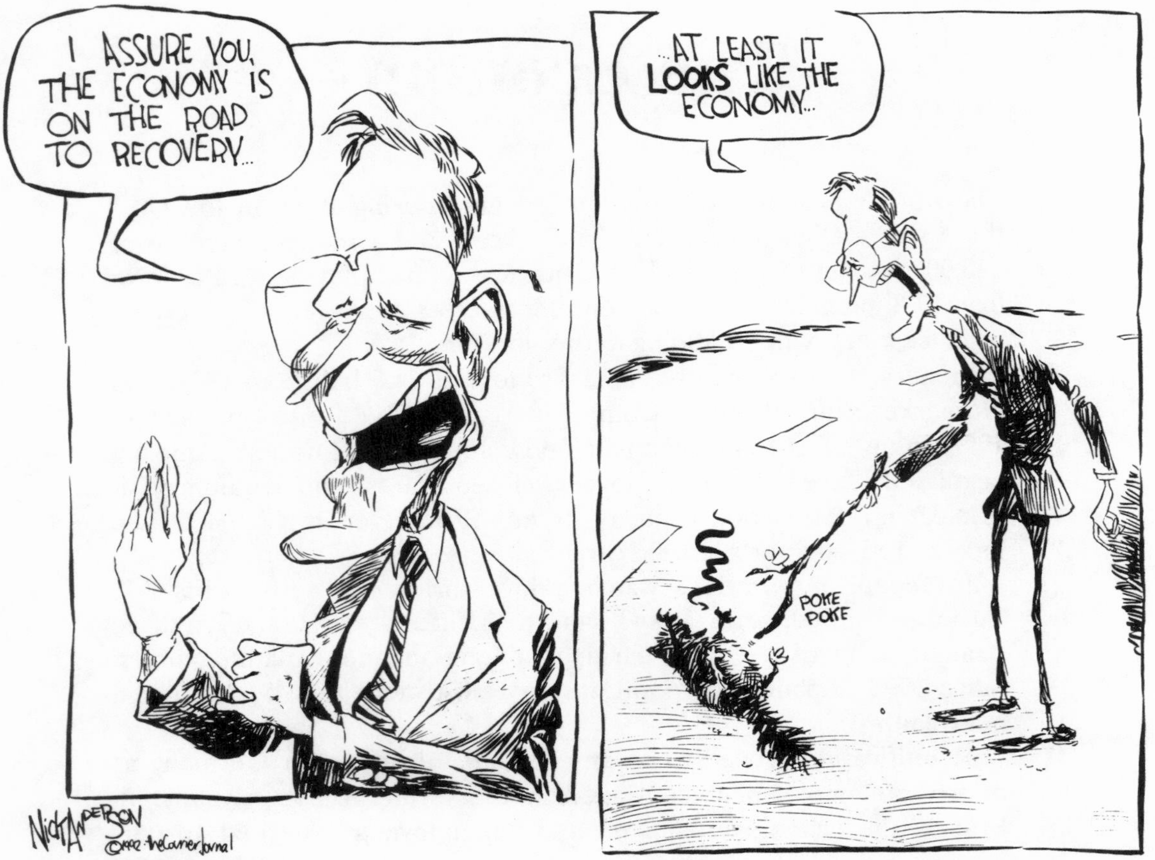
I ASSURE YOU, THE ECONOMY IS ON THE ROAD TO RECOVERY...
...AT LEAST IT LOOKS LIKE THE ECONOMY...
POKE POKE

NICK ANDERSON
Courtesy Louisville Courier Journal

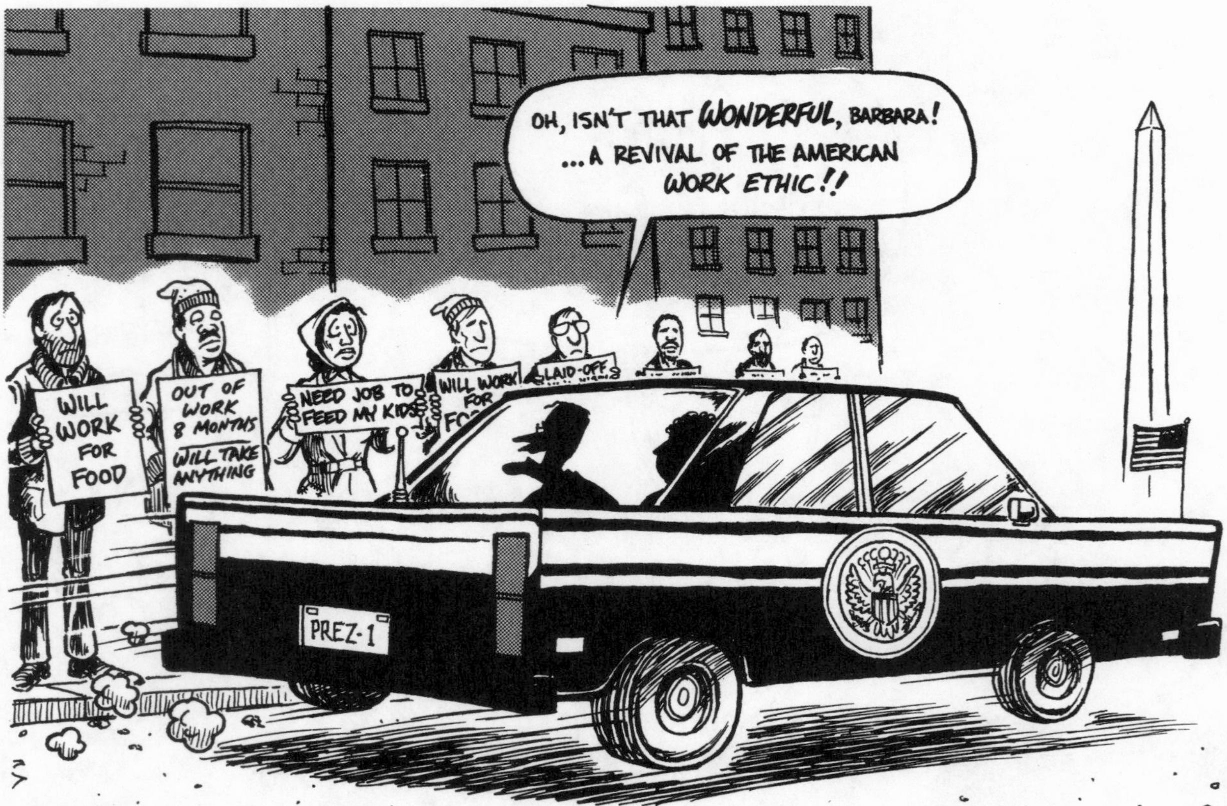
OH, ISN'T THAT WONDERFUL, BARBARA! ...A REVIVAL OF THE AMERICAN WORK ETHIC!!
WILL WORK FOR FOOD
OUT OF WORK 8 MONTHS WILL TAKE ANYTHING
NEED JOB TO FEED MY KIDS
WILL WORK FOR
LAID-OFF
PREZ-1
GREENBERG SEATTLE POST-INTELLIGENCER 1991

STEVE GREENBERG
Courtesy Seattle Post-Intelligencer

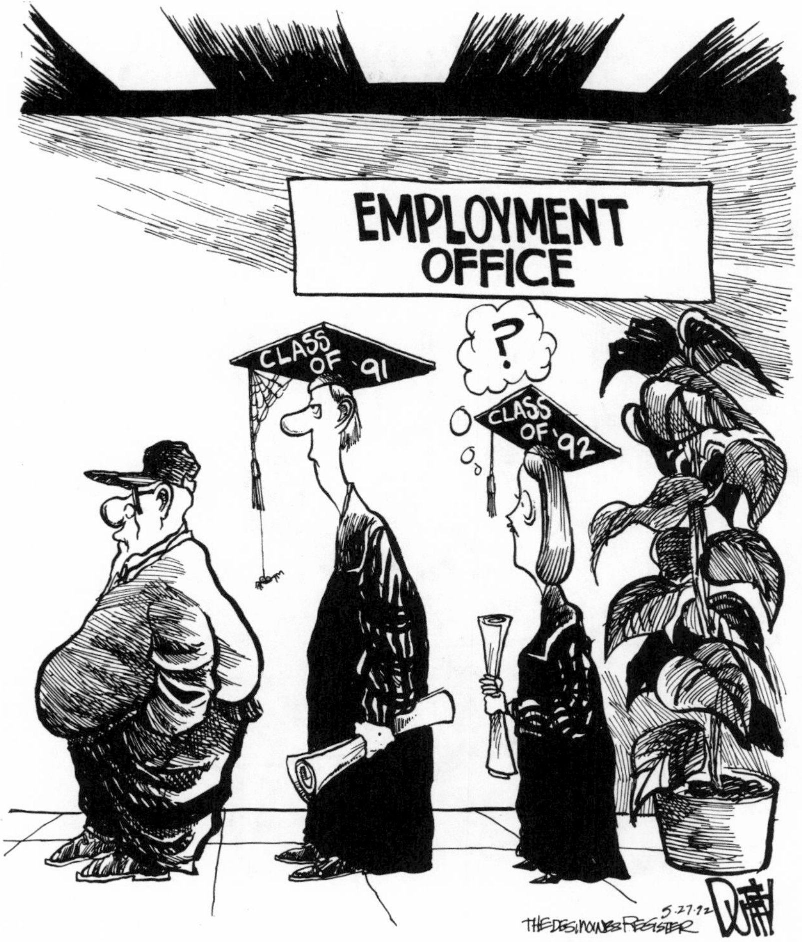
EMPLOYMENT OFFICE
CLASS OF '91
?
CLASS OF '92
5-27-92
THE DES MOINES REGISTER
DUFFY
BRIAN DUFFY
Courtesy Des Moines Register

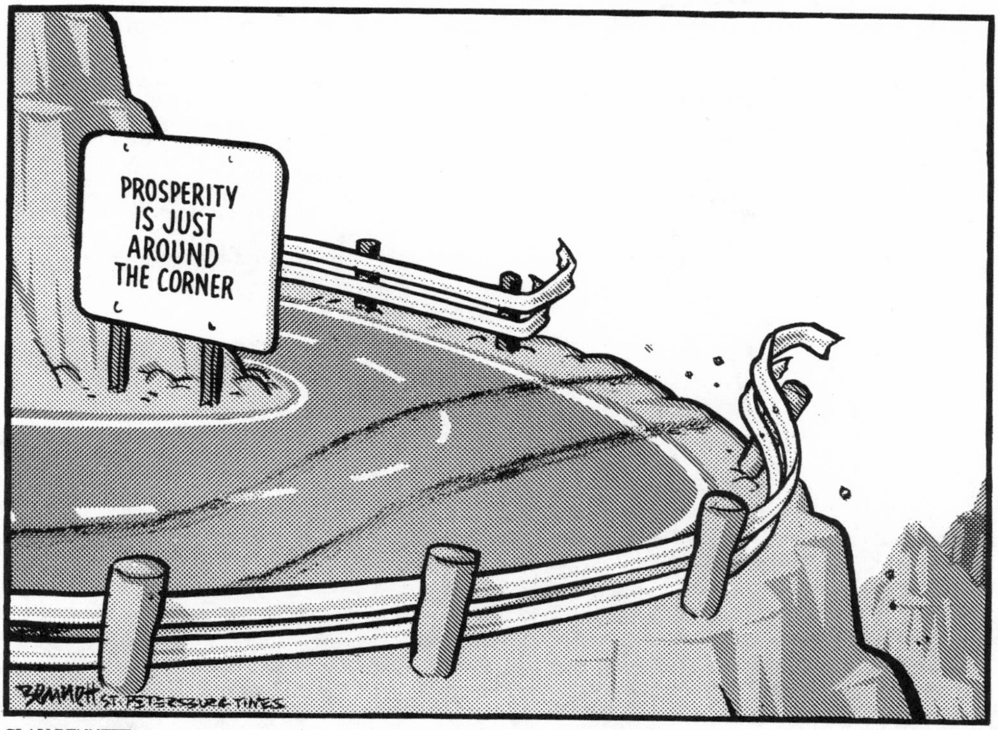
PROSPERITY IS JUST AROUND THE CORNER
BENNETT ST. PETERSBURG TIMES
CLAY BENNETT
Courtesy St. Petersburg Times

STEVE KELLEY
Courtesy San Diego Union

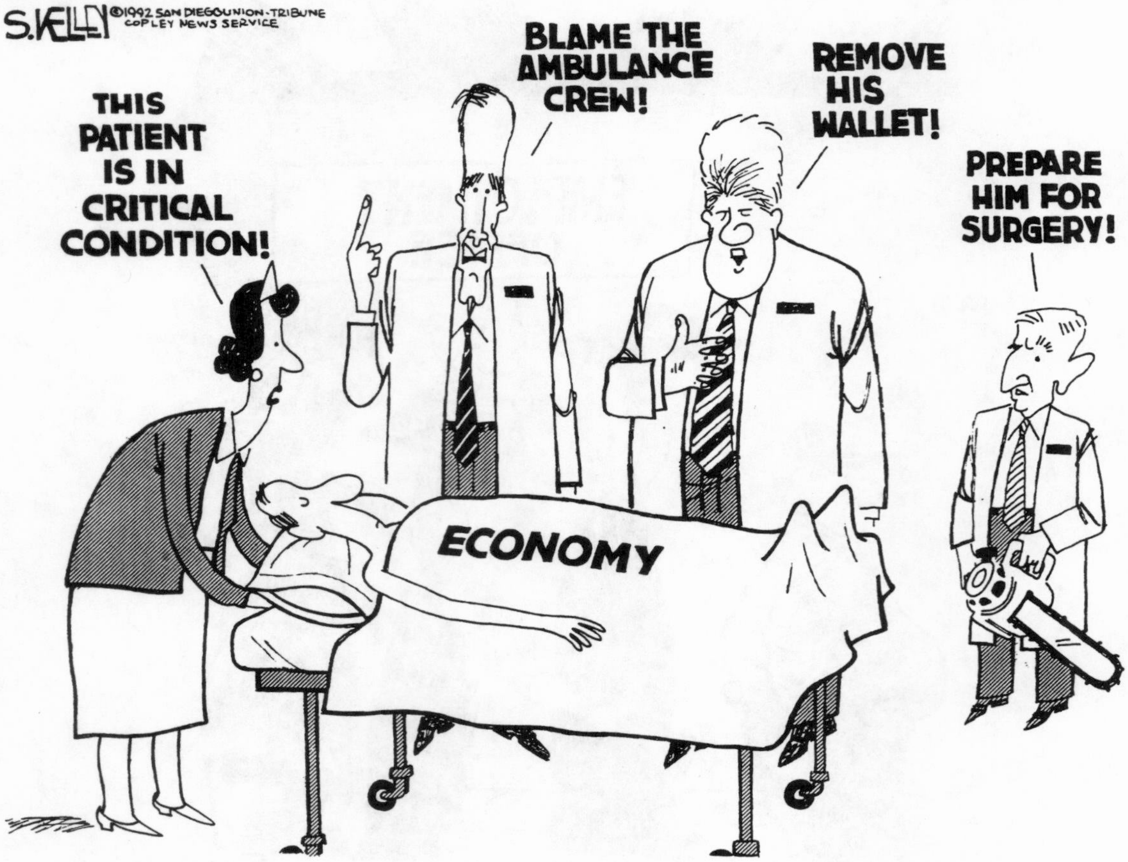
S. KELLEY ©1992 SAN DIEGO UNION-TRIBUNE COPLEY NEWS SERVICE
THIS PATIENT IS IN CRITICAL CONDITION!
BLAME THE AMBULANCE CREW!
REMOVE HIS WALLET!
PREPARE HIM FOR SURGERY!
ECONOMY

ARTHUR BOK
Courtesy Akron Beacon Journal

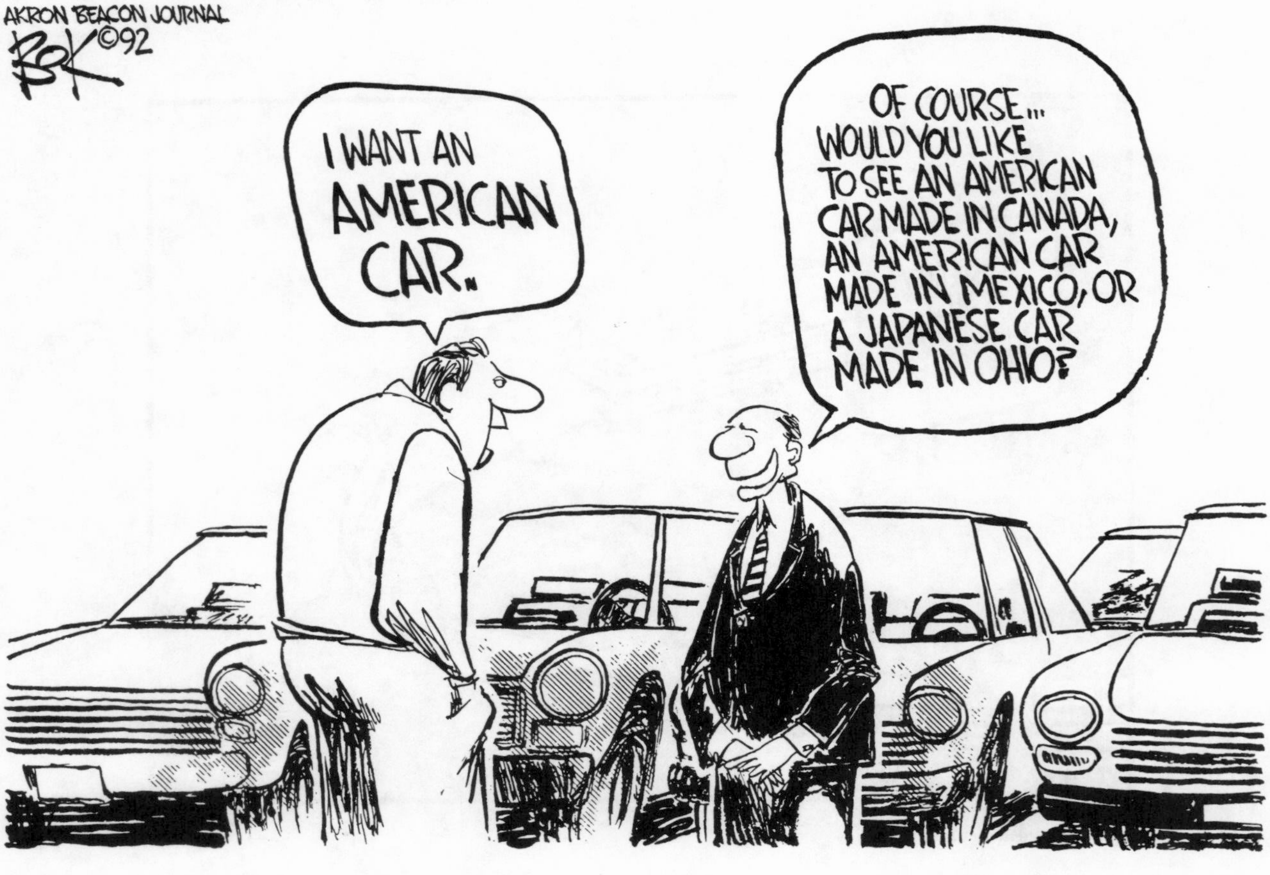
AKRON BEACON JOURNAL BOK ©92
I WANT AN AMERICAN CAR.
OF COURSE... WOULD YOU LIKE TO SEE AN AMERICAN CAR MADE IN CANADA, AN AMERICAN CAR MADE IN MEXICO, OR A JAPANESE CAR MADE IN OHIO?

STEVE NEASE
Courtesy Montreal Gazette

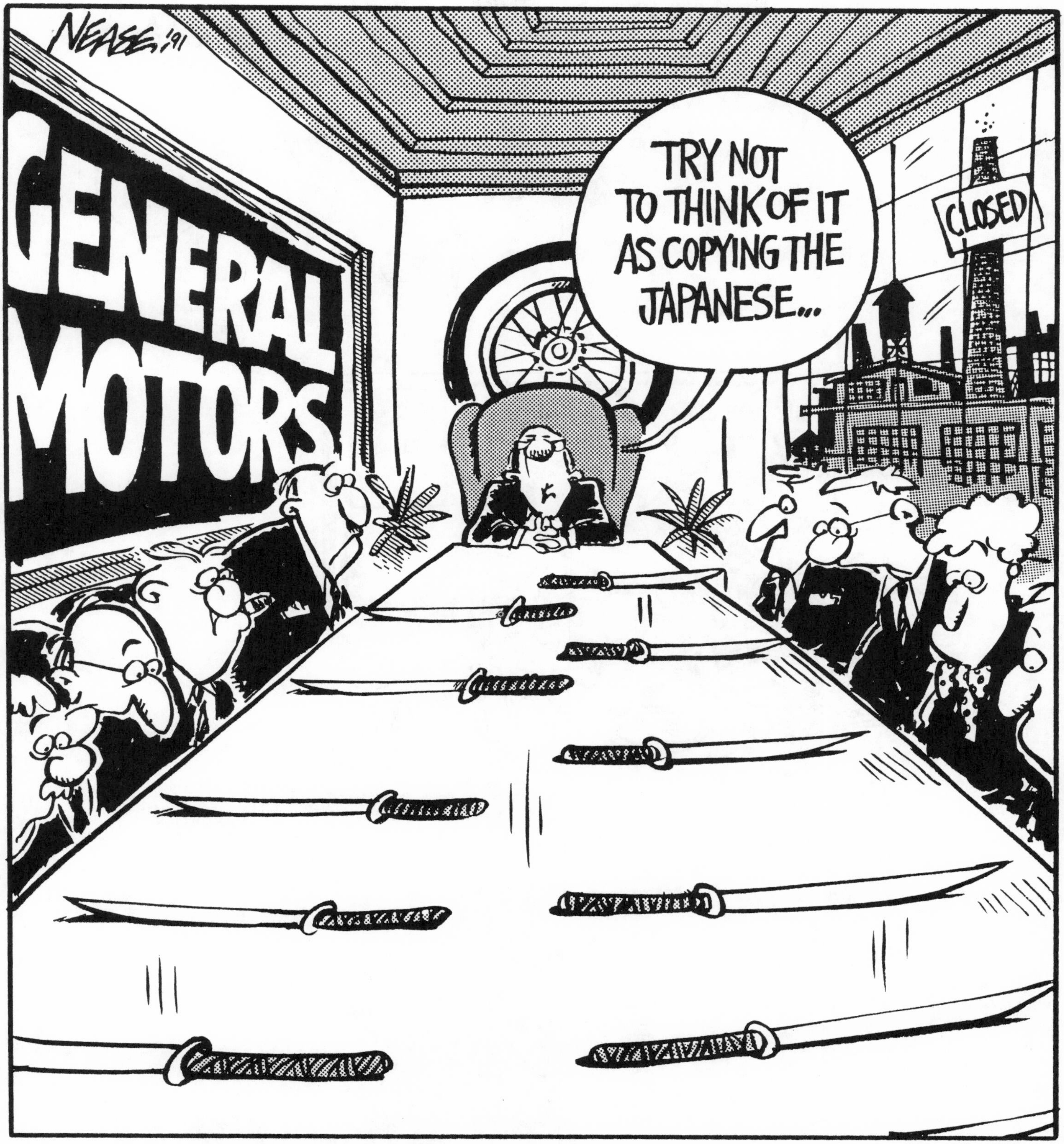
NEASE '91
GENERAL MOTORS
TRY NOT TO THINK OF IT AS COPYING THE JAPANESE...
CLOSED

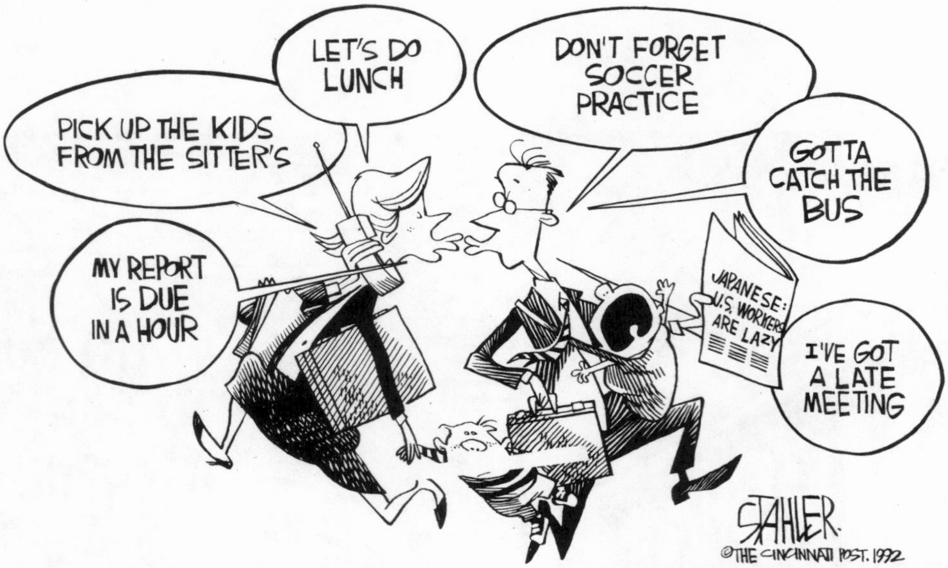
LET'S DO LUNCH
DON'T FORGET SOCCER PRACTICE
PICK UP THE KIDS FROM THE SITTER'S
GOTTA CATCH THE BUS
MY REPORT IS DUE IN A HOUR
JAPANESE: U.S. WORKERS ARE LAZY
I'VE GOT A LATE MEETING
STAHLER
©THE CINCINNATI POST. 1992

JEFF STAHLER
Courtesy Cincinnati Post

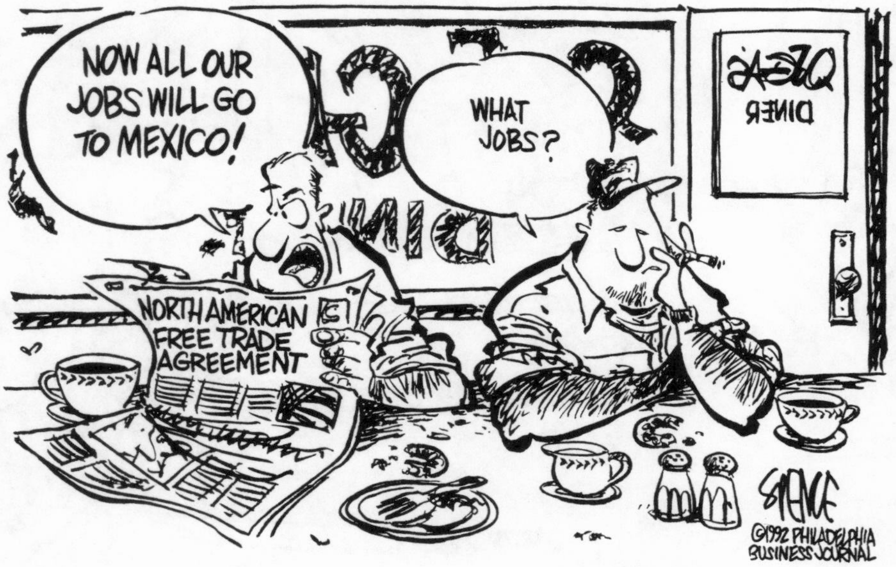
NOW ALL OUR JOBS WILL GO TO MEXICO!
WHAT JOBS?
NORTH AMERICAN FREE TRADE AGREEMENT
SPENCE
©1992 PHILADELPHIA BUSINESS JOURNAL

JOHN SPENCER
Courtesy Philadelphia Business Journal

MIKE SHELTON
Courtesy Orange County Register
and King Features Syndicate

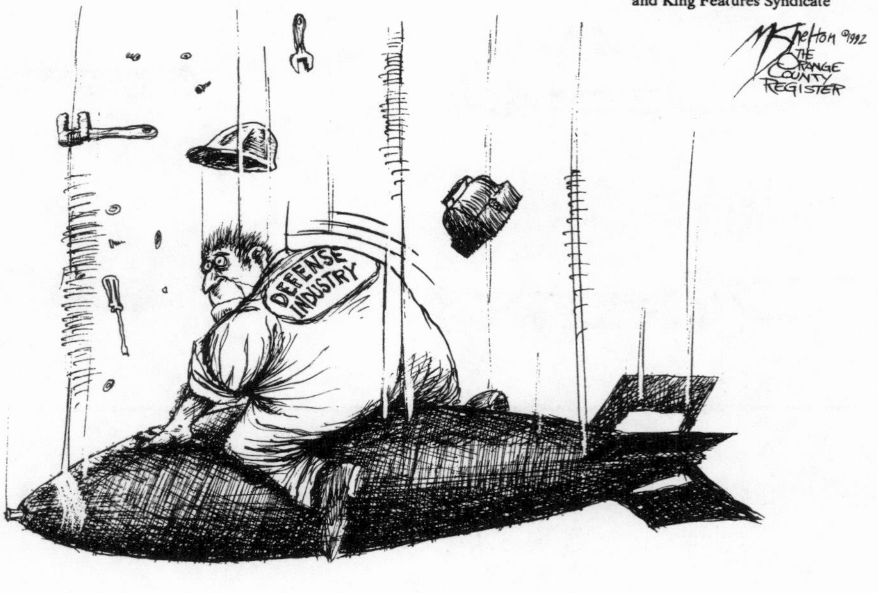
DEFENSE INDUSTRY

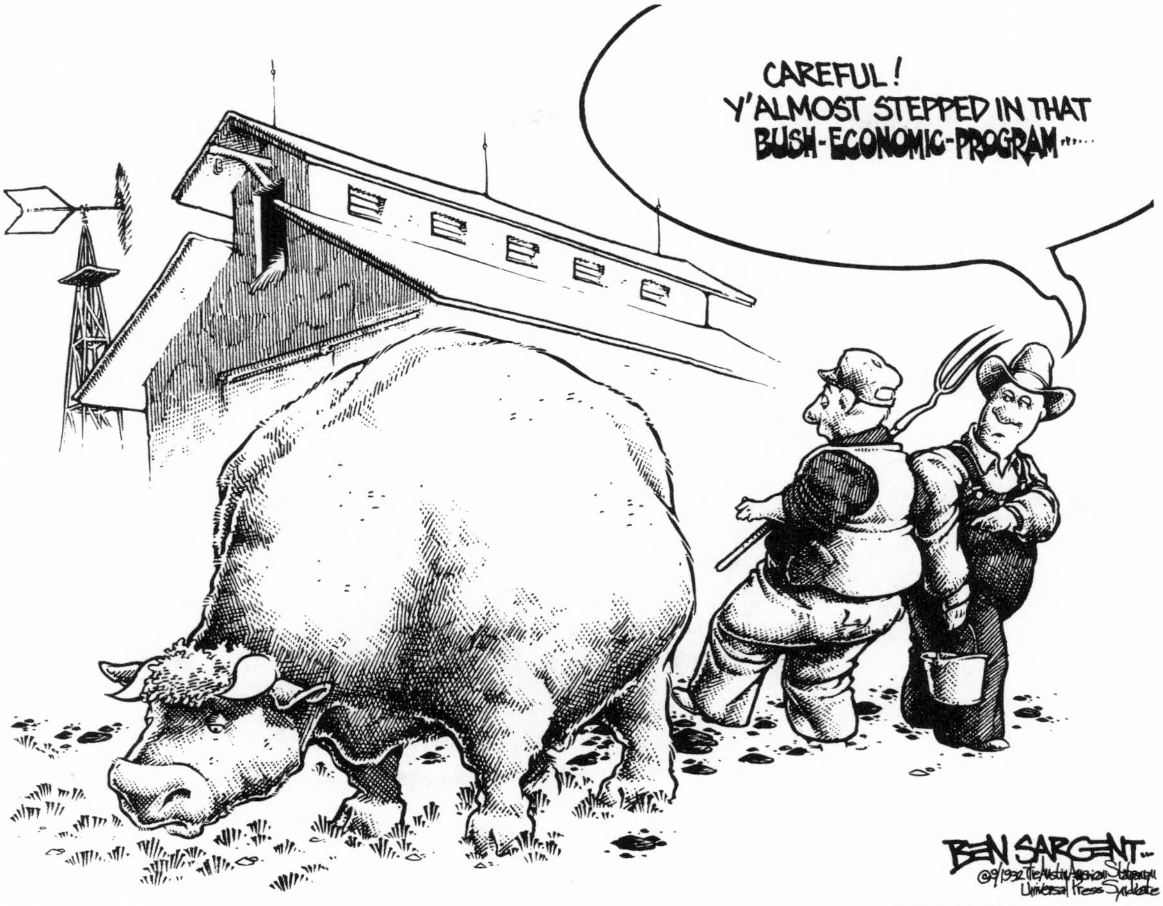
CAREFUL!
Y'ALMOST STEPPED IN THAT
BUSH-ECONOMIC-PROGRAM......
BEN SARGENT

BEN SARGENT
Courtesy Austin American Statesman

ROGER SCHILLERSTROM
Courtesy Crain Communications

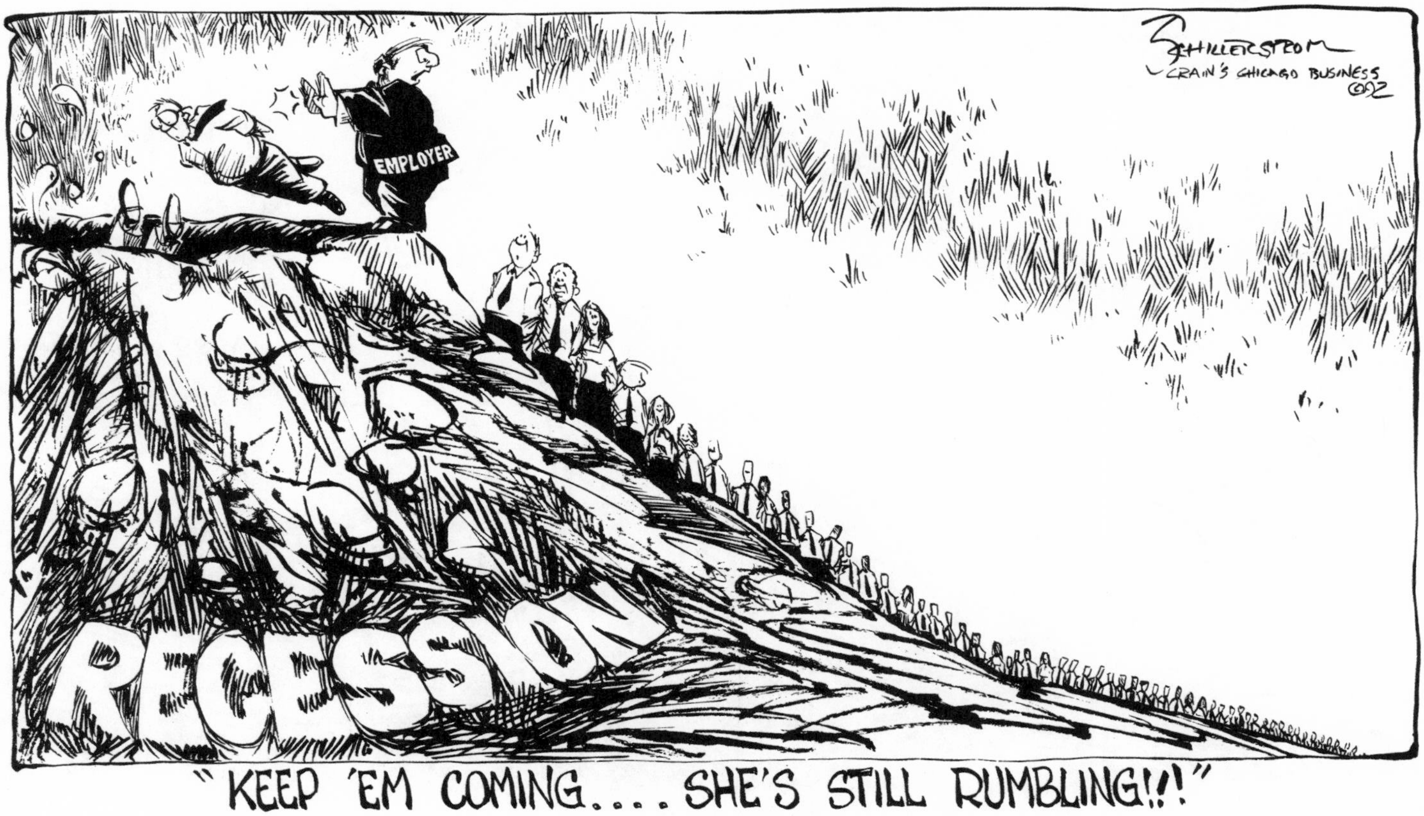
SCHILLERSTROM
CRAIN'S CHICAGO BUSINESS
EMPLOYER
RECESSION

"KEEP 'EM COMING.... SHE'S STILL RUMBLING!!!"

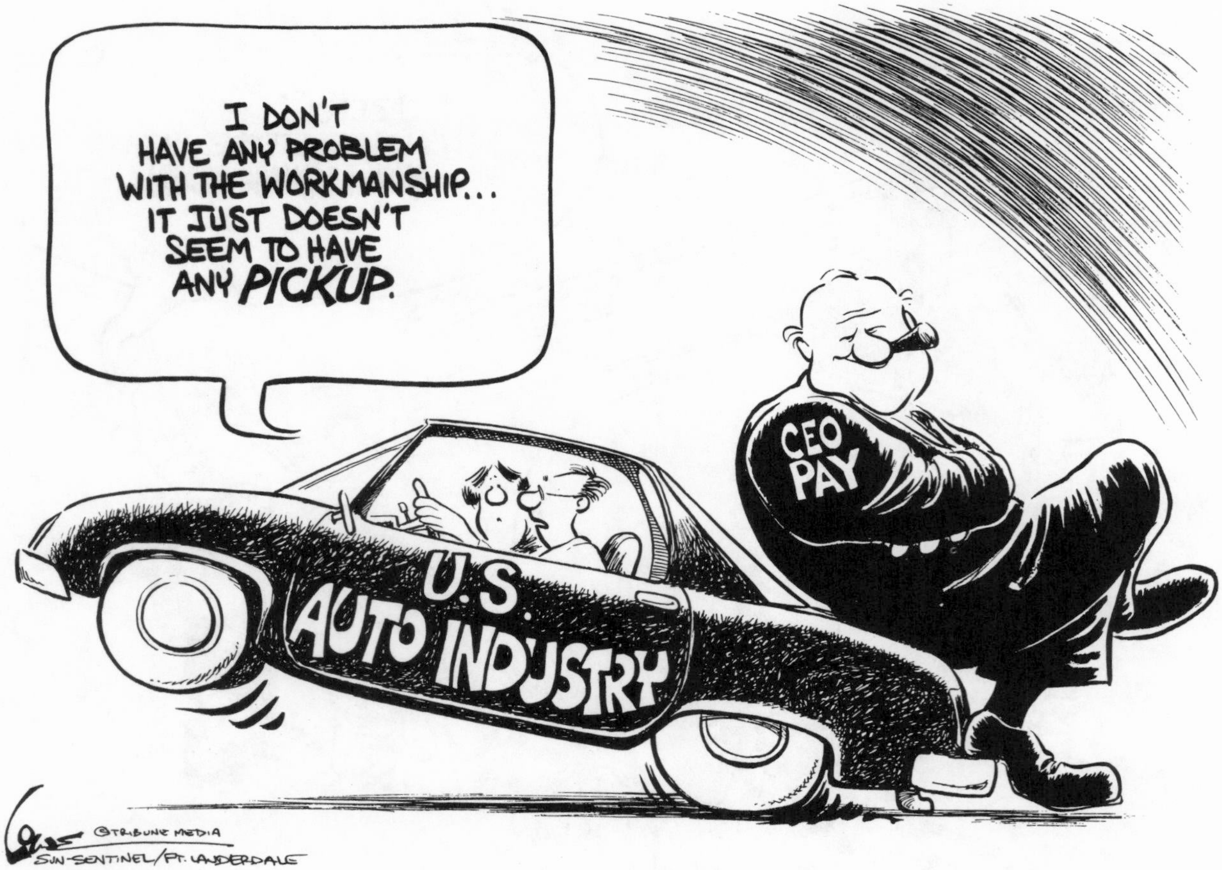
I DON'T HAVE ANY PROBLEM WITH THE WORKMANSHIP... IT JUST DOESN'T SEEM TO HAVE ANY PICKUP.
CEO PAY
U.S. AUTO INDUSTRY
©TRIBUNE MEDIA
SUN-SENTINEL/FT. LAUDERDALE

CHAN LOWE
Courtesy The News/Sun-Sentinel (Fla.)

BRUCE BEATTIE
Courtesy Daytona Beach News-Journal

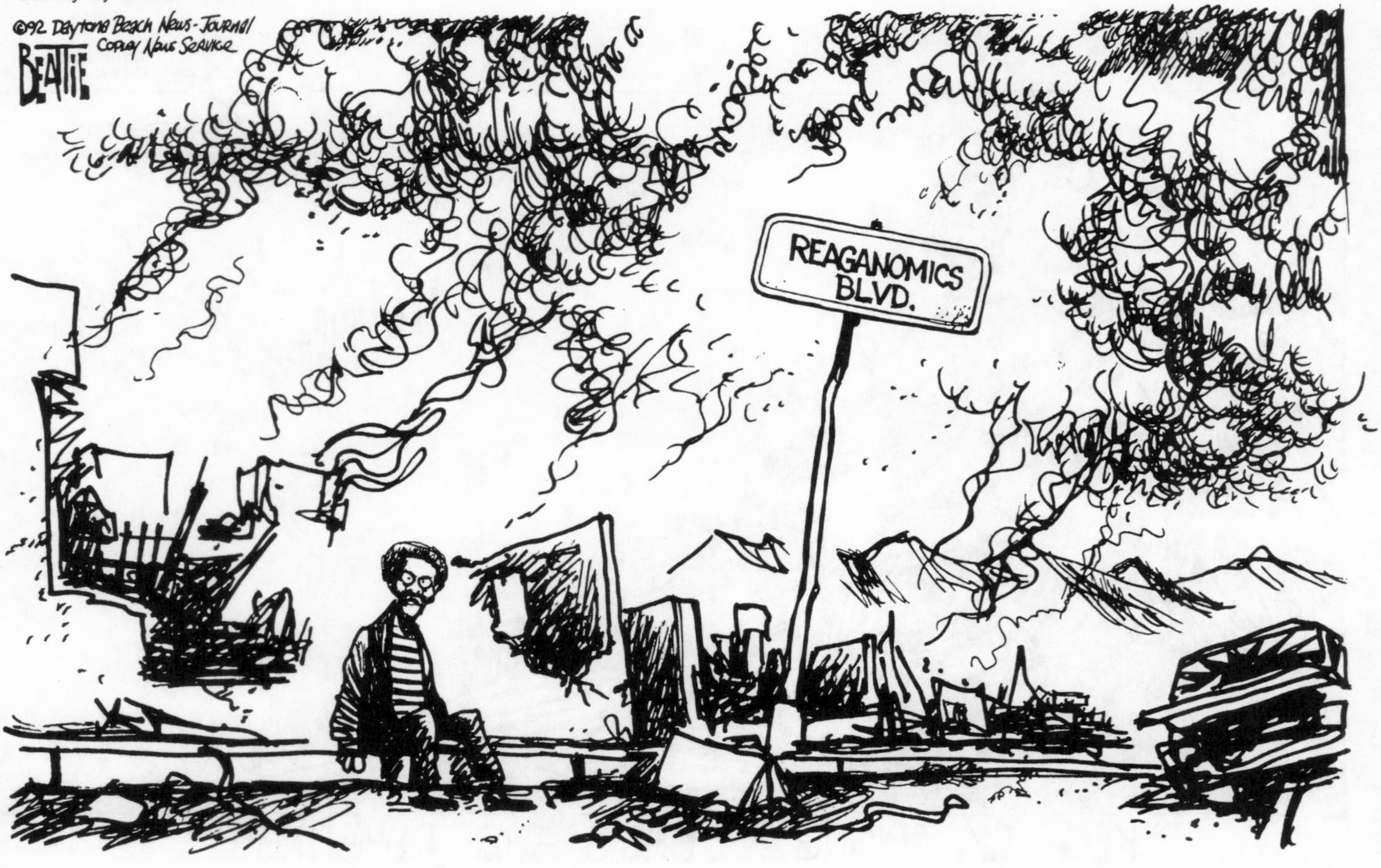
©92 Daytona Beach News-Journal
Copley News Service
BEATTIE
REAGANOMICS BLVD.

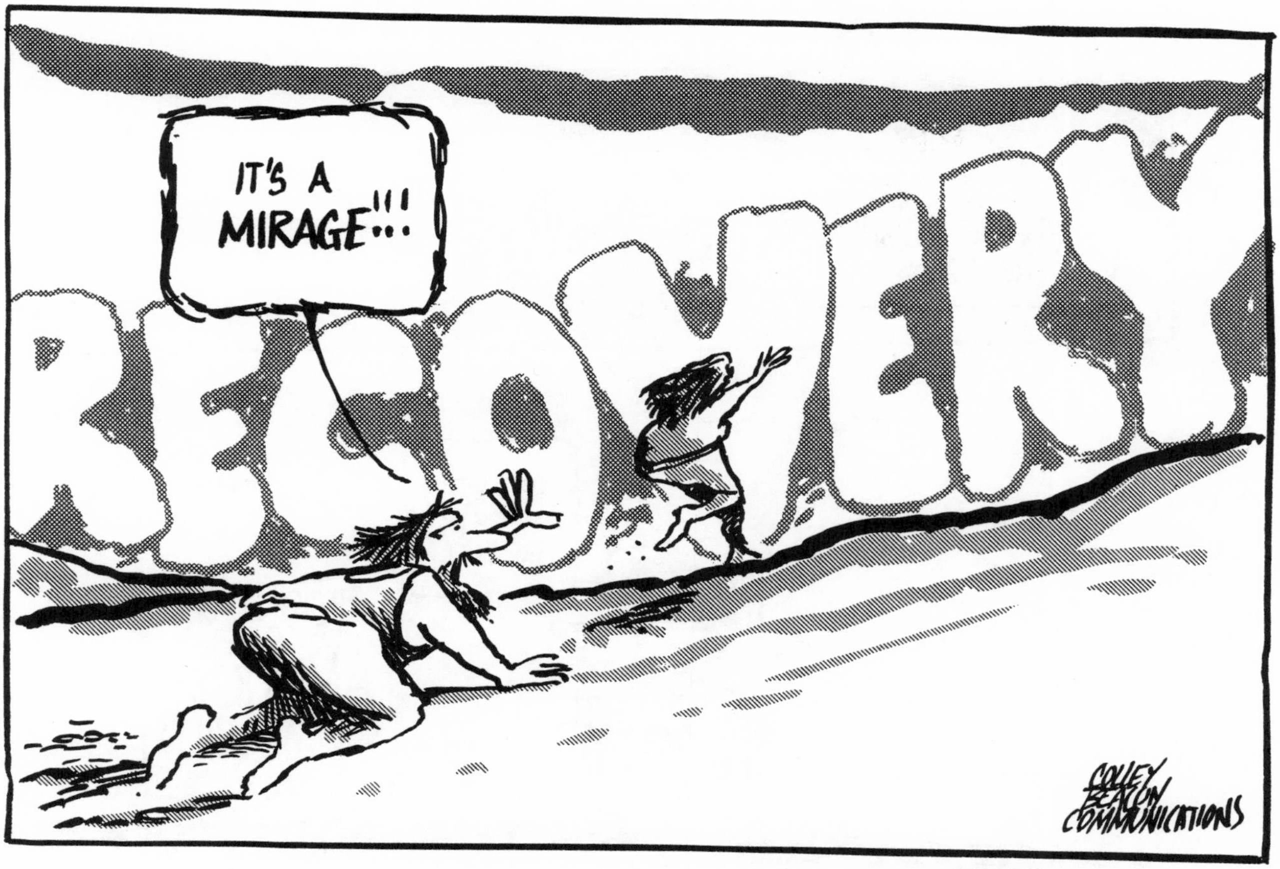
IT'S A MIRAGE!!!
RECOVERY
COLLEY BEACON COMMUNICATIONS

ED COLLEY
Courtesy Beacon Communications

BRUCE BEATTIE
Courtesy Daytona Beach News-Journal

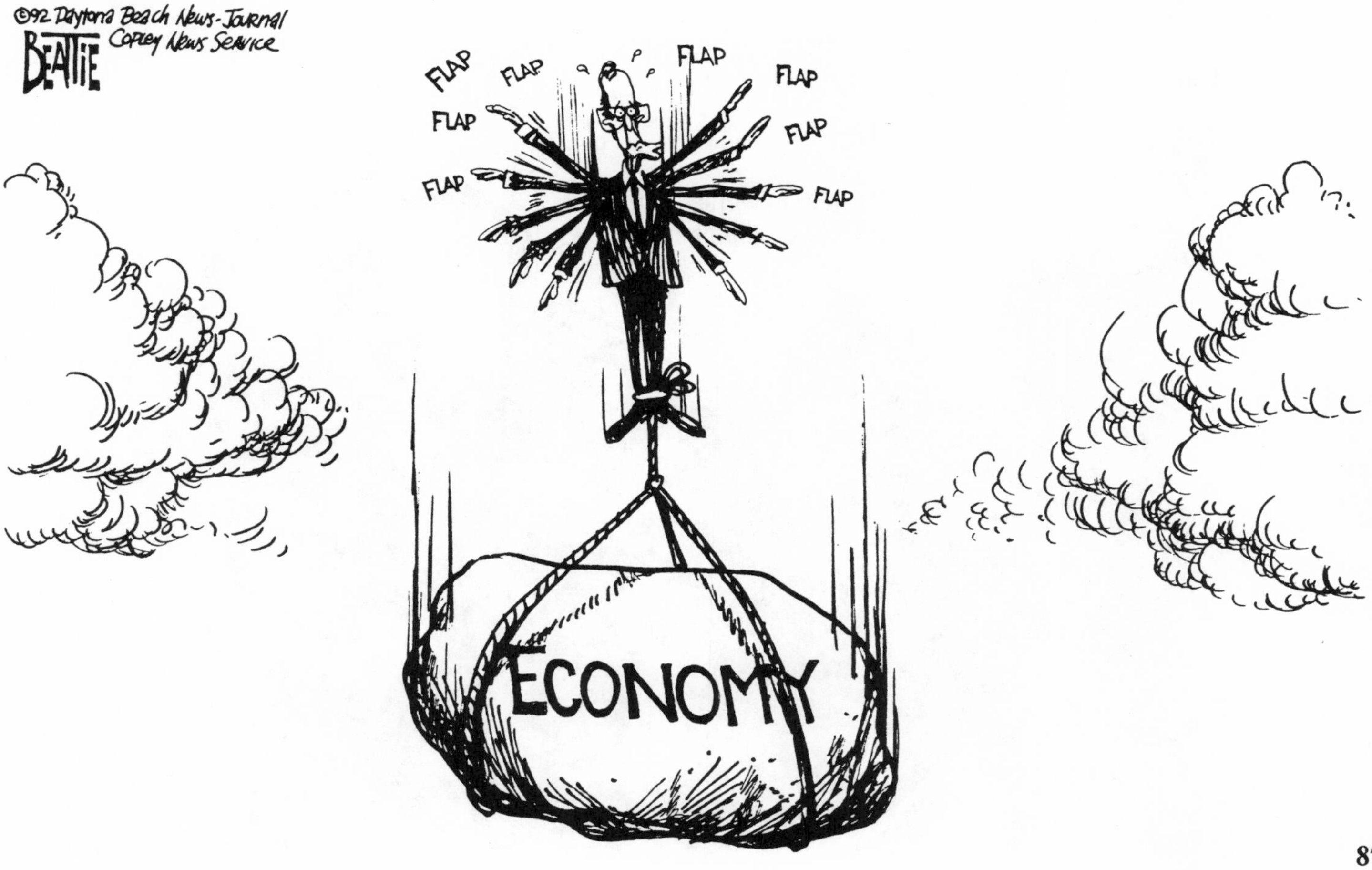
©92 Daytona Beach News-Journal Copley News Service
BEATTIE
FLAP
FLAP
FLAP
FLAP
FLAP
FLAP
FLAP
FLAP
ECONOMY

MIKE SMITH
Courtesy Las Vegas Sun

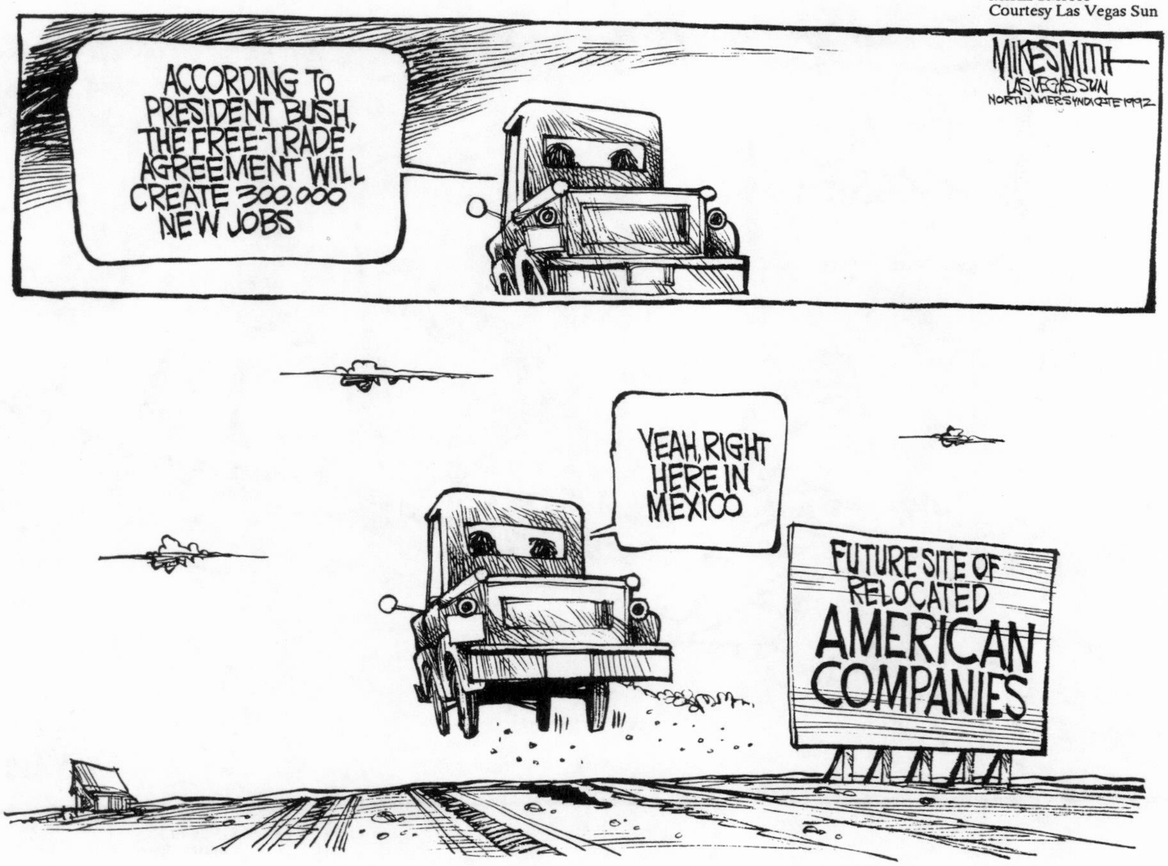
MIKE SMITH
LAS VEGAS SUN
NORTH AMERICA SYNDICATE 1992
ACCORDING TO PRESIDENT BUSH, THE FREE-TRADE AGREEMENT WILL CREATE 300,000 NEW JOBS
YEAH, RIGHT HERE IN MEXICO
FUTURE SITE OF RELOCATED AMERICAN COMPANIES

TOM DARCY
Courtesy Newsday

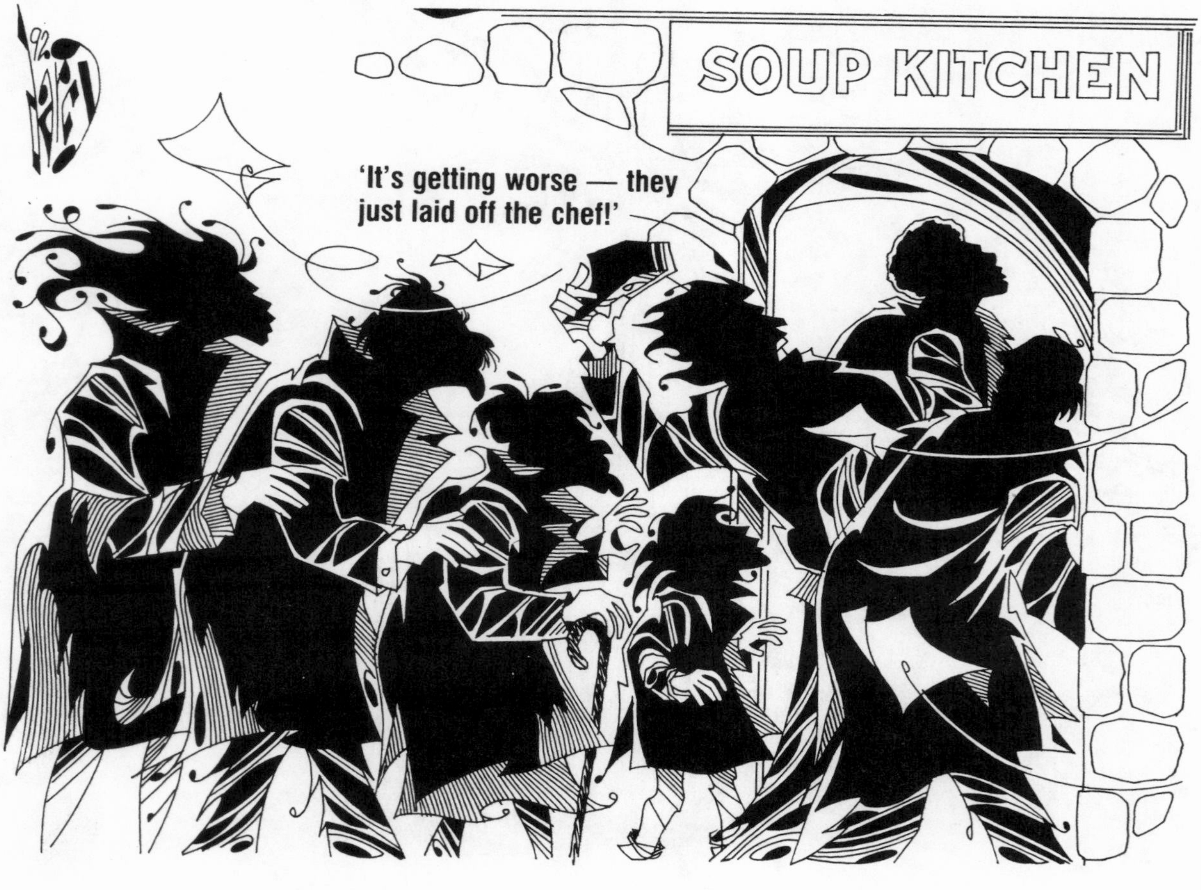
SOUP KITCHEN
'It's getting worse — they just laid off the chef!'

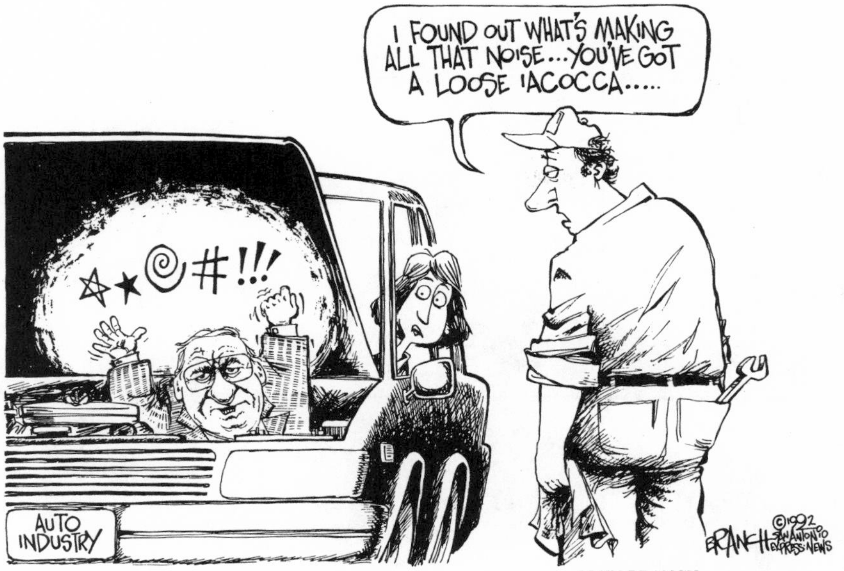
I FOUND OUT WHAT'S MAKING ALL THAT NOISE...YOU'VE GOT A LOOSE 'ACOCCA.....
☆★◎#!!!
AUTO INDUSTRY
BRANCH ©1992 SAN ANTONIO EXPRESS-NEWS

JOHN BRANCH
Courtesy San Antonio Express-News

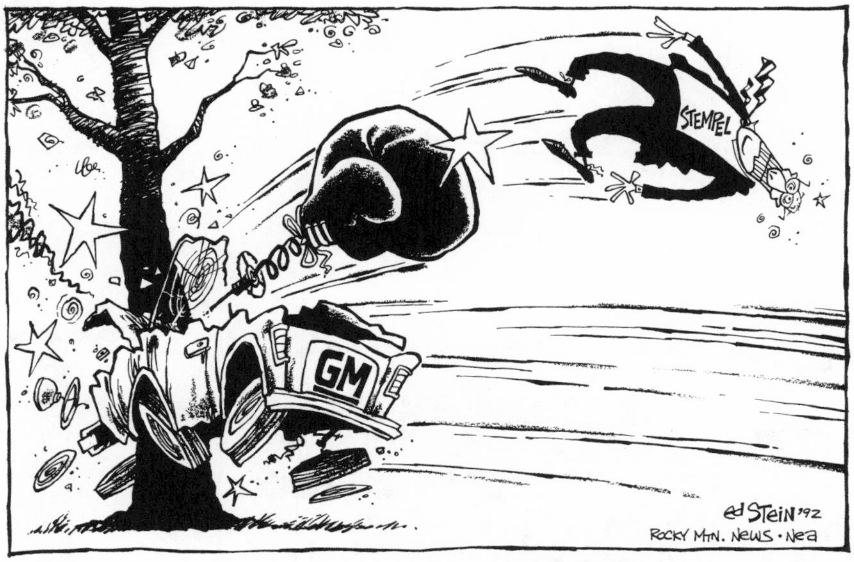
STEMPEL
GM
ed STEIN '92
ROCKY MTN. NEWS • NEA

ED STEIN
Courtesy Rocky Mountain News and NEA

DAVID SWANN
Courtesy Huntsville Times (Ala.)

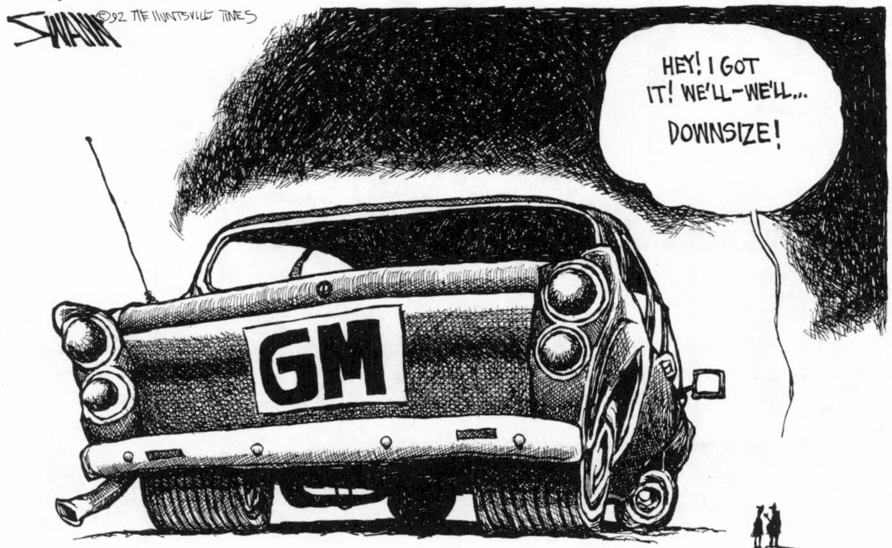
SWANN ©92 THE HUNTSVILLE TIMES
HEY! I GOT IT! WE'LL-WE'LL...
DOWNSIZE!
GM

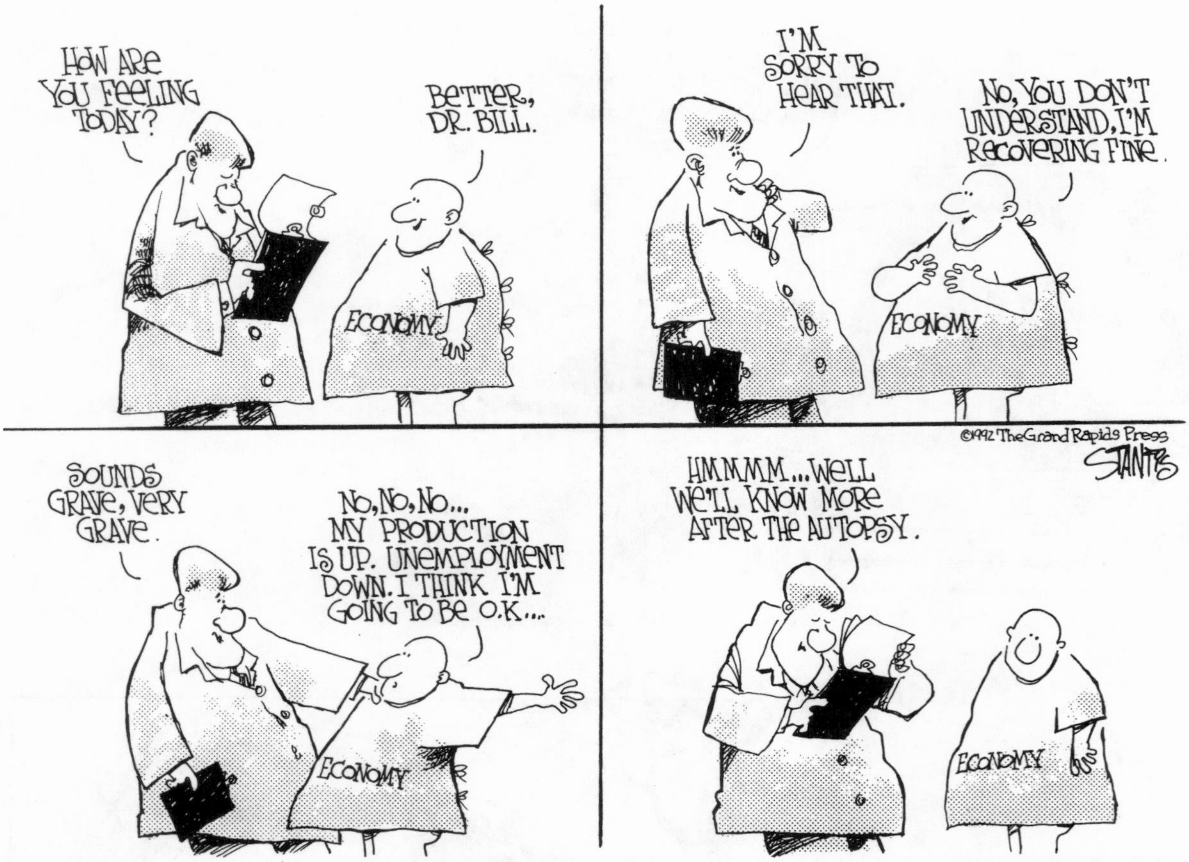
HOW ARE YOU FEELING TODAY?
BETTER, DR. BILL.
ECONOMY
I'M SORRY TO HEAR THAT.
NO, YOU DON'T UNDERSTAND, I'M RECOVERING FINE.
ECONOMY
©1992 The Grand Rapids Press
STANTIS
SOUNDS GRAVE, VERY GRAVE.
NO, NO, NO... MY PRODUCTION IS UP. UNEMPLOYMENT DOWN. I THINK I'M GOING TO BE O.K....
ECONOMY
HMMMM...WELL WE'LL KNOW MORE AFTER THE AUTOPSY.
ECONOMY

SCOTT STANTIS
Courtesy Grand Rapids Press

BOB GORRELL
Courtesy Richmond News Leader

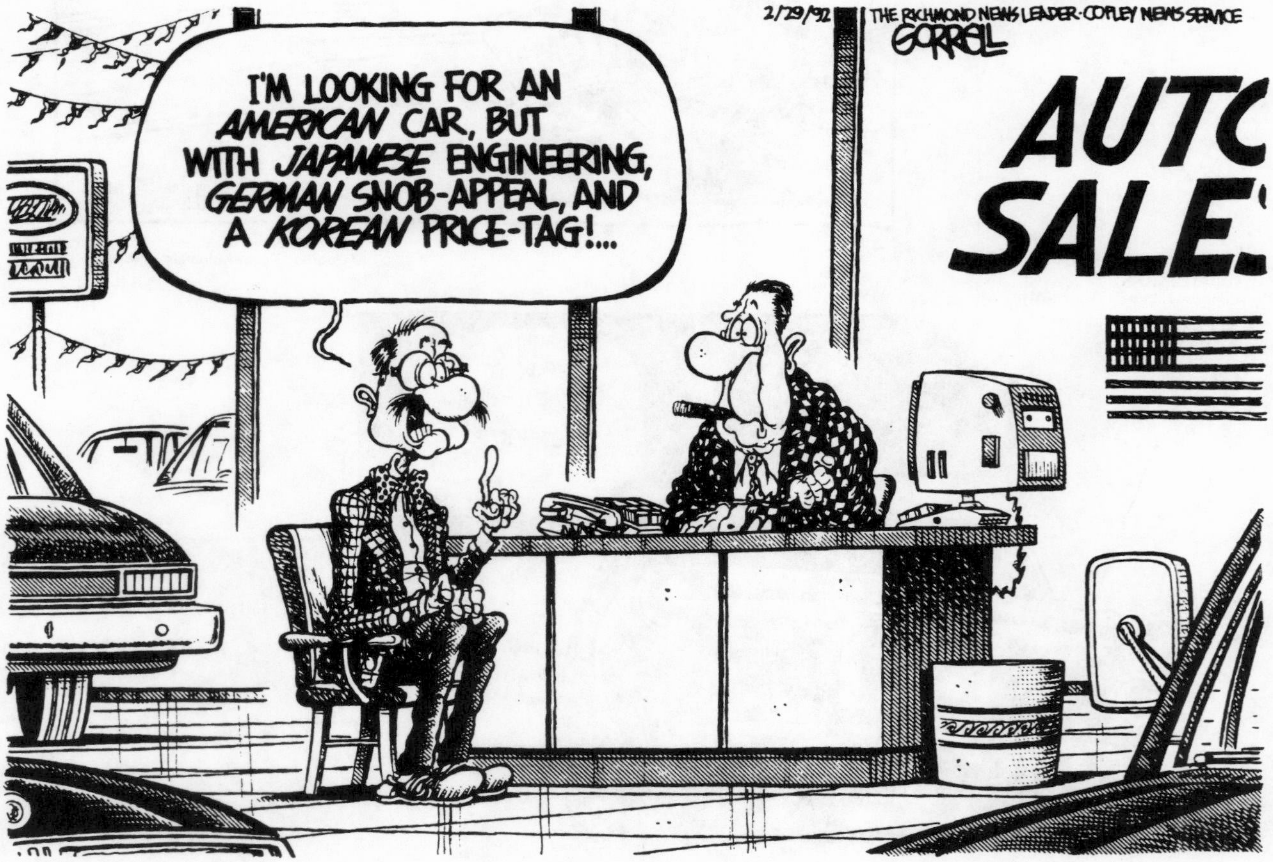
2/29/92 THE RICHMOND NEWS LEADER-COPLEY NEWS SERVICE
GORRELL
I'M LOOKING FOR AN *AMERICAN* CAR, BUT WITH *JAPANESE* ENGINEERING, *GERMAN* SNOB-APPEAL, AND A *KOREAN* PRICE-TAG!...
AUTO
SALE

PAUL SZEP
Courtesy Boston Globe

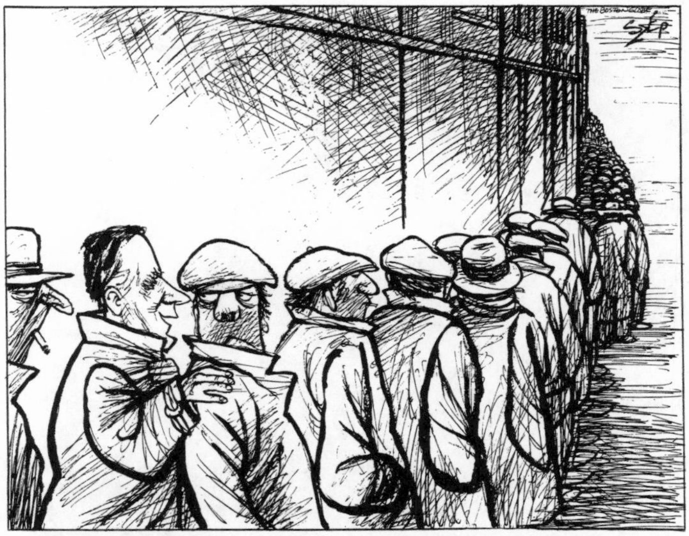

"THE RECESSIONS OVER ... BUSH IS GREAT ... PASS THE WORD ... THE RECESSIONS OVER ... BUSH IS GREAT ... PASS THE WORD"

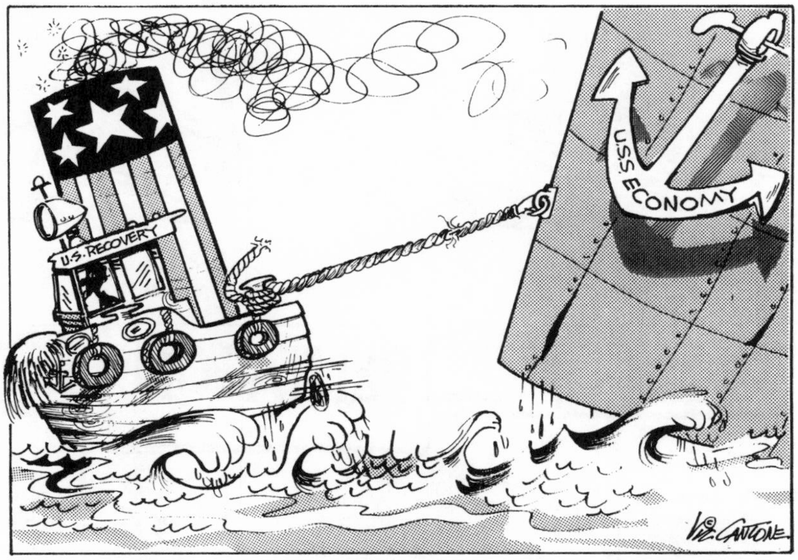
U.S. RECOVERY
U.S.S. ECONOMY
VIC CANTONE

VIC CANTONE
Courtesy N.Y. Daily News

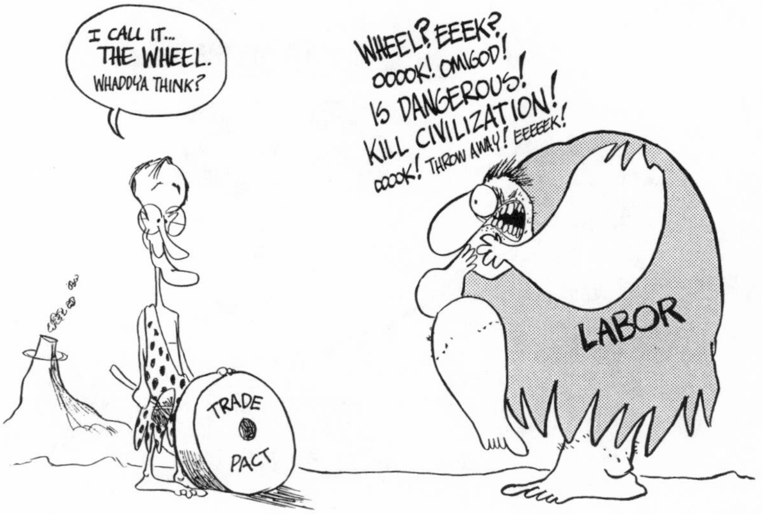
I CALL IT... THE WHEEL. WHADDY'A THINK?
WHEEL? EEEK? OOOOK! OMIGOD! IS DANGEROUS! KILL CIVILIZATION! OOOOK! THROW AWAY! EEEEEK!
TRADE PACT
LABOR

TOM GIBB
Courtesy Altoona Mirror

JEFF MACNELLY
Courtesy Chicago Tribune and
Tribune Media Services

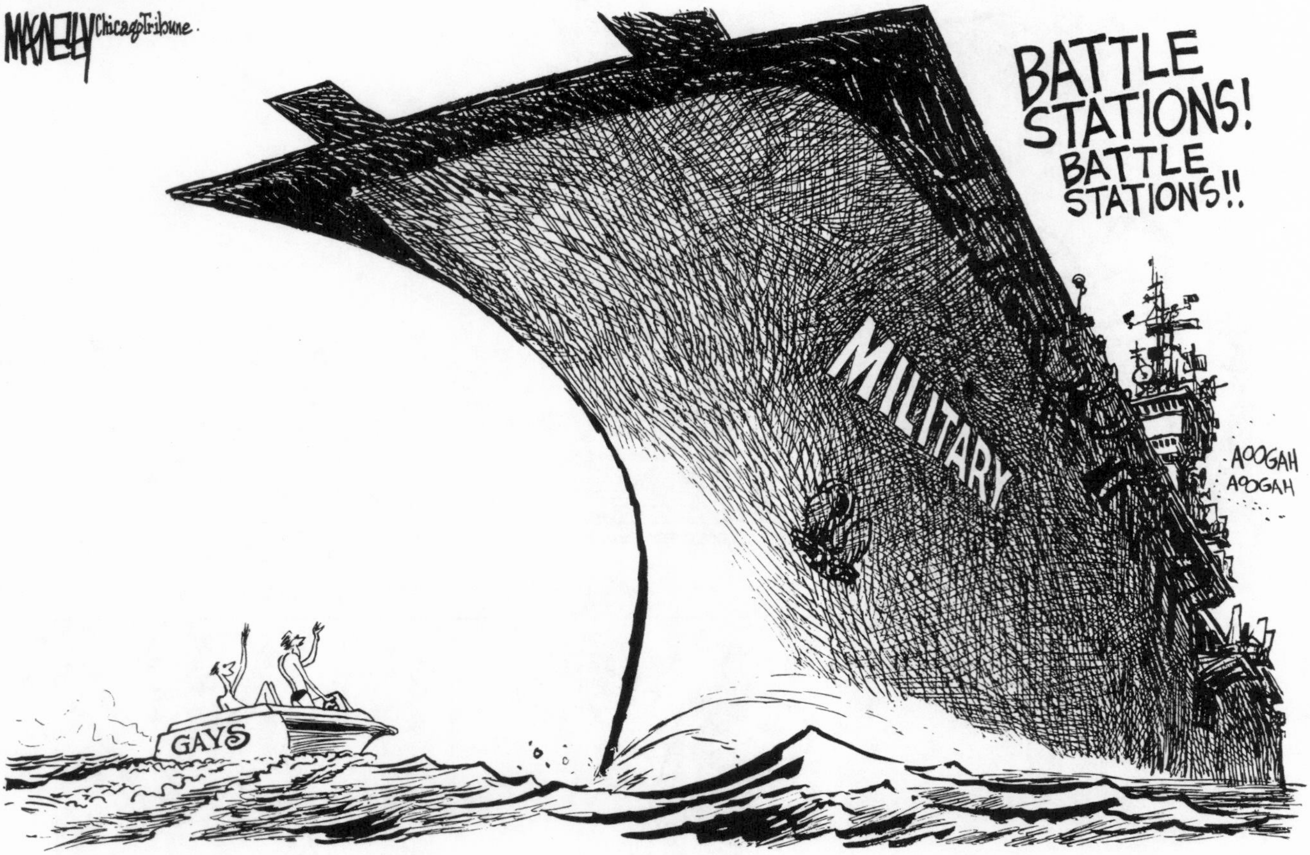
MACNELLY Chicago Tribune
BATTLE STATIONS! BATTLE STATIONS!!
MILITARY
AOOGAH AOOGAH
GAYS

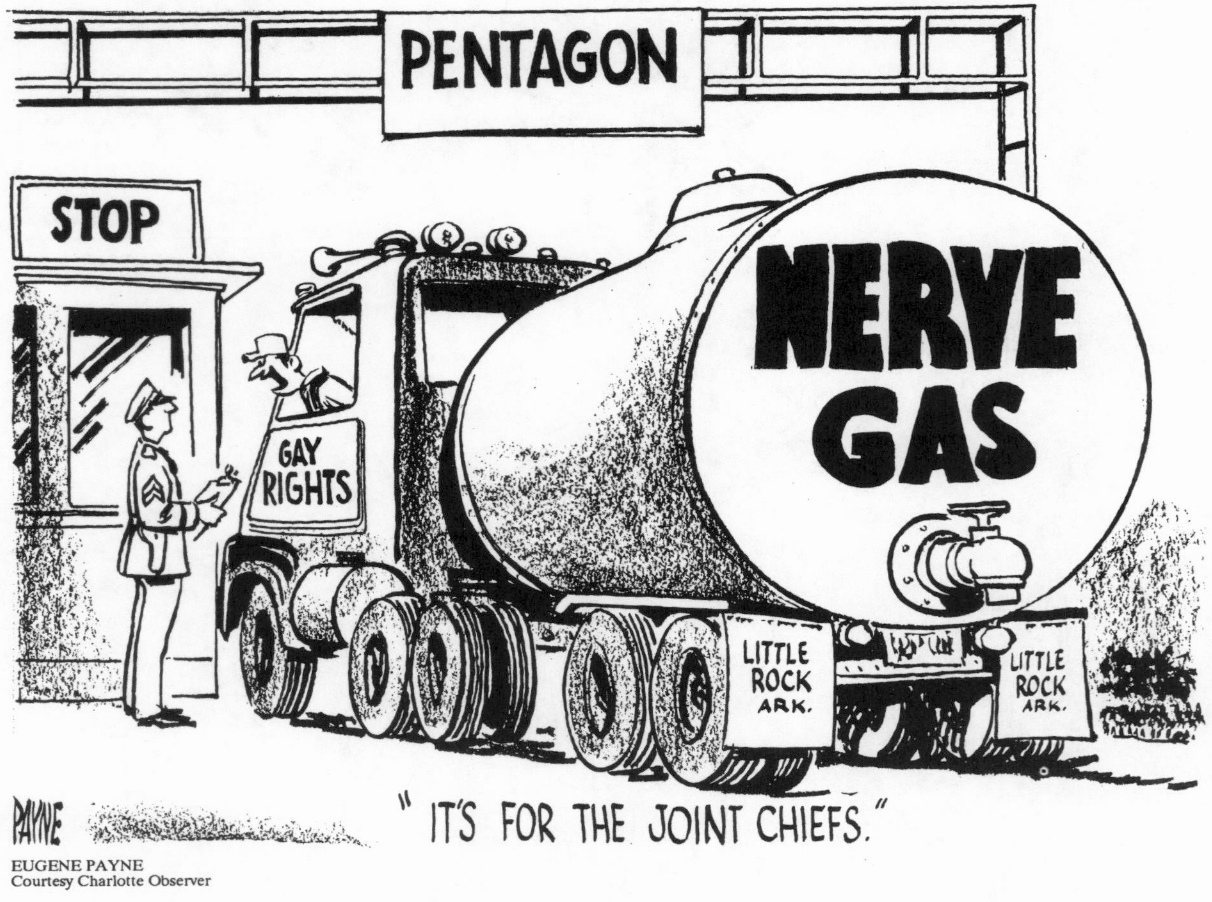
PENTAGON
STOP
NERVE GAS
GAY RIGHTS
LITTLE ROCK ARK.
LITTLE ROCK ARK.
PAYNE

"IT'S FOR THE JOINT CHIEFS."

EUGENE PAYNE
Courtesy Charlotte Observer

The Military

Two admirals left the Navy and another was reassigned in the aftermath of charges that twenty-six women were assaulted by male naval pilots at the national Tailhook convention in Las Vegas. A shake-up of the Naval Investigative Service was ordered as a result of the incident.

There was much conflicting testimony in a Senate hearing over the possibility that many U.S. prisoners of war had been abandoned and left behind in Vietnam. A Senate select committee found that 133 Americans known to have been captured alive still remain unaccounted for. A Russian general and former KGB head claimed that Vietnam held American prisoners as late as the late 1970s.

During the presidential campaign it was disclosed that Bill Clinton had gone to great lengths to avoid serving in the military during the Vietnam War. He admitted that as a Rhodes scholar in England he had organized demonstrations against U.S. participation in the war. A letter surfaced in which Clinton had declared: "I loathe the military."

At year's end, Clinton's campaign pledge to open the military to acknowledged homosexuals had created a firestorm of protest.

Star Wars research dropped sharply on America's list of priorities.

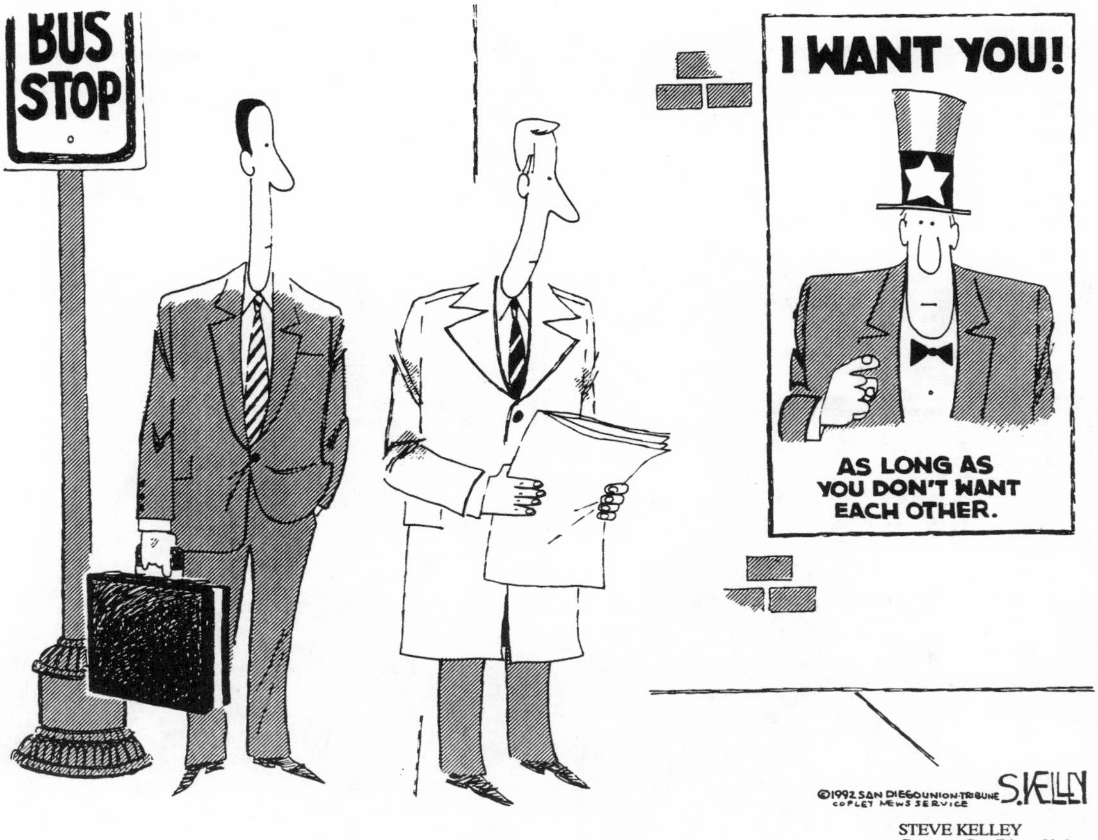
BUS STOP
I WANT YOU!
AS LONG AS YOU DON'T WANT EACH OTHER.
©1992 SAN DIEGO UNION-TRIBUNE COPLEY NEWS SERVICE
S.KELLEY

STEVE KELLEY
Courtesy San Diego Union

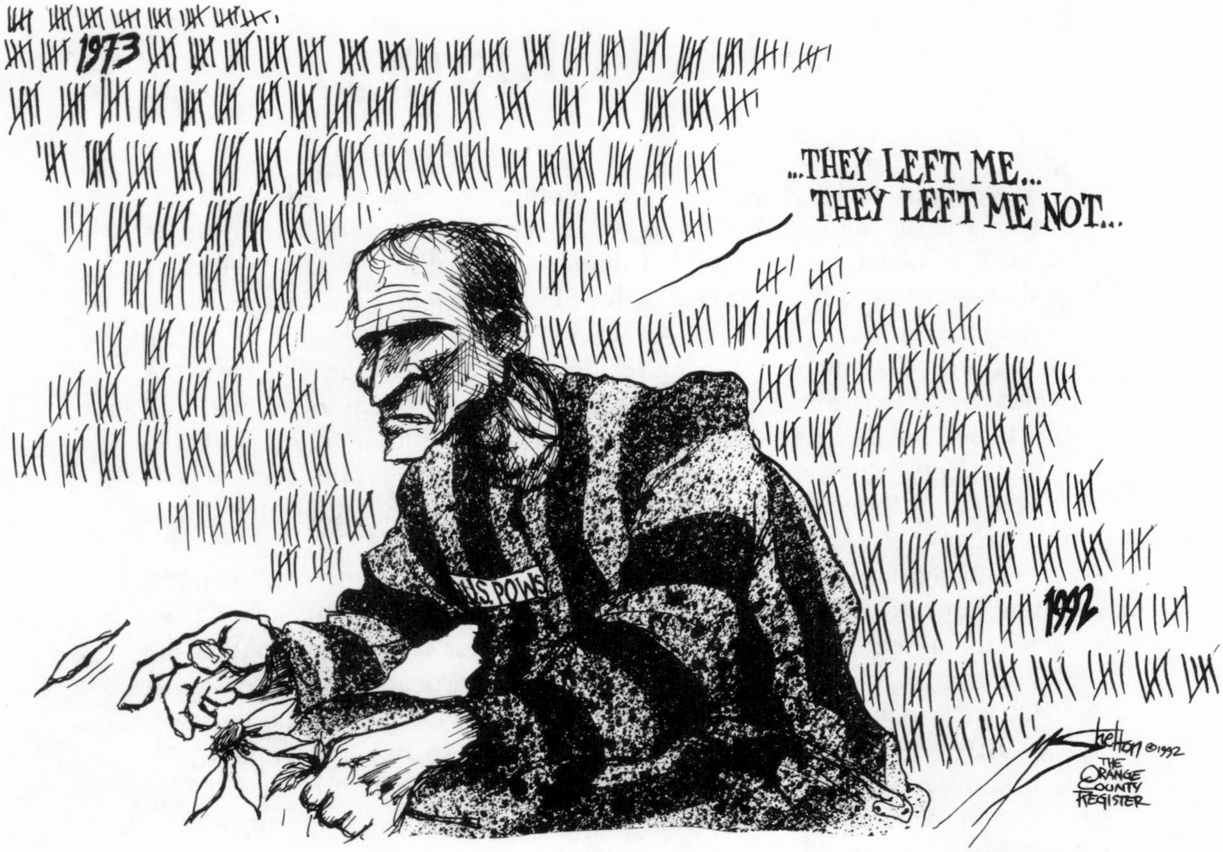
1973
...THEY LEFT ME...
THEY LEFT ME NOT...
U.S. POWS
1992
Shelton ©1992
THE ORANGE COUNTY REGISTER

MIKE SHELTON
Courtesy Orange County Register
and King Features Syndicate

LAMBERT DER
Courtesy Houston Post

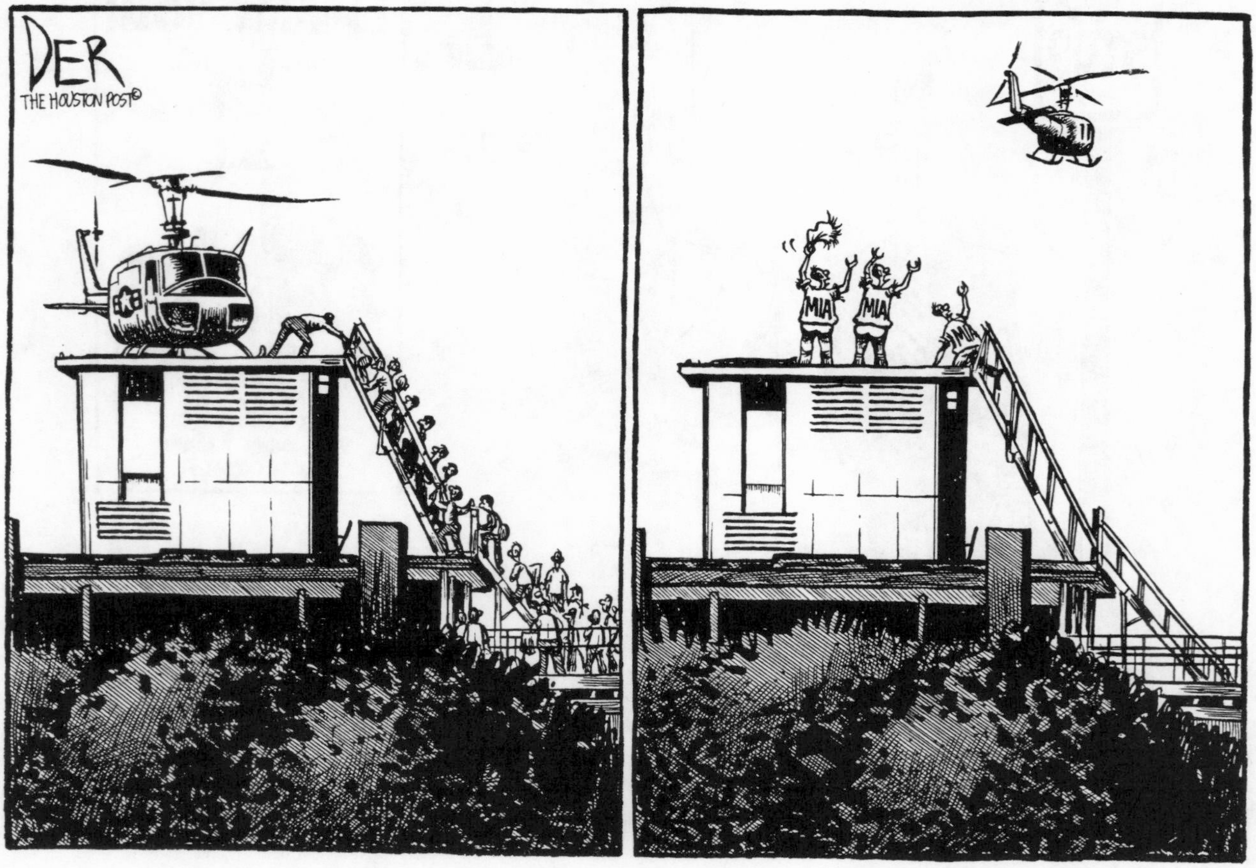
DER
THE HOUSTON POST©
MIA
MIA

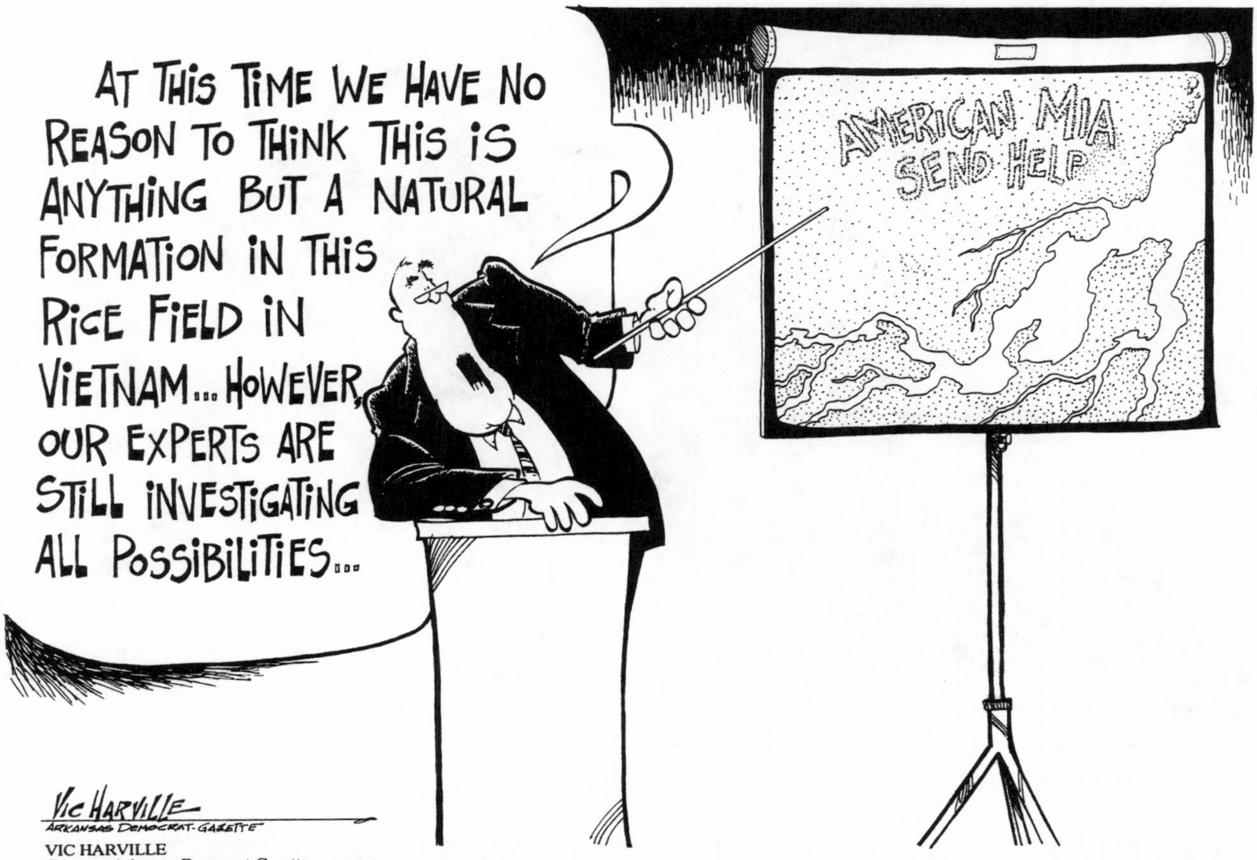
AT THIS TIME WE HAVE NO REASON TO THINK THIS IS ANYTHING BUT A NATURAL FORMATION IN THIS RICE FIELD IN VIETNAM... HOWEVER, OUR EXPERTS ARE STILL INVESTIGATING ALL POSSIBILITIES...
AMERICAN MIA
SEND HELP
VIC HARVILLE
ARKANSAS DEMOCRAT-GAZETTE

VIC HARVILLE
Courtesy Arkansas Democrat-Gazette

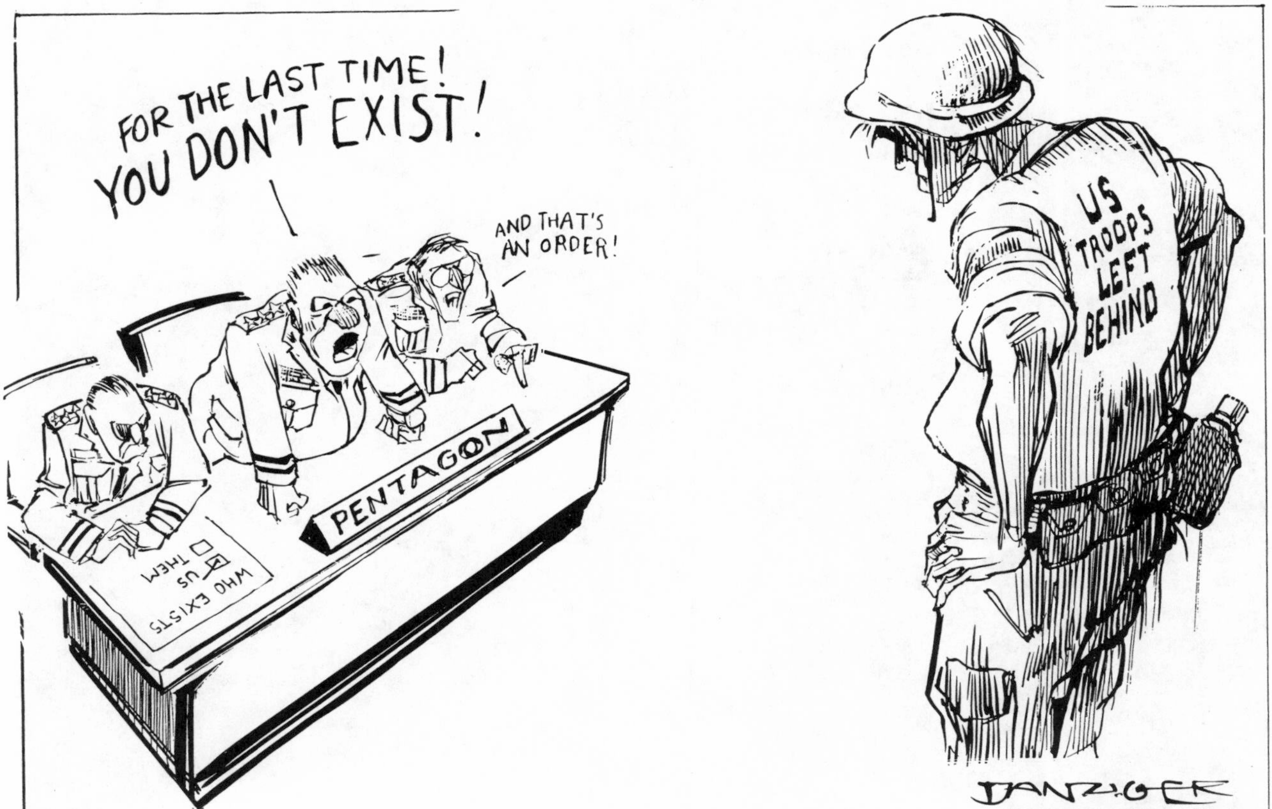
FOR THE LAST TIME! YOU DON'T EXIST!
AND THAT'S AN ORDER!
PENTAGON
WHO EXISTS
US
THEM
US TROOPS LEFT BEHIND
DANZIGER
The Christian Science Monitor
Los Angeles Times Syndicate

JEFF DANZIGER
Courtesy Christian Science Monitor

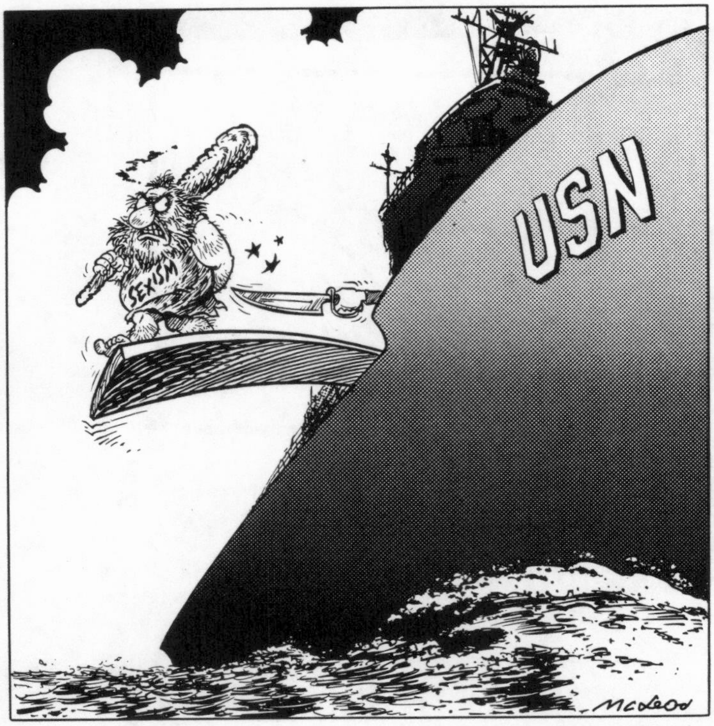
USN
SEXISM
McLeod

JACK MCLEOD
Courtesy Army Times

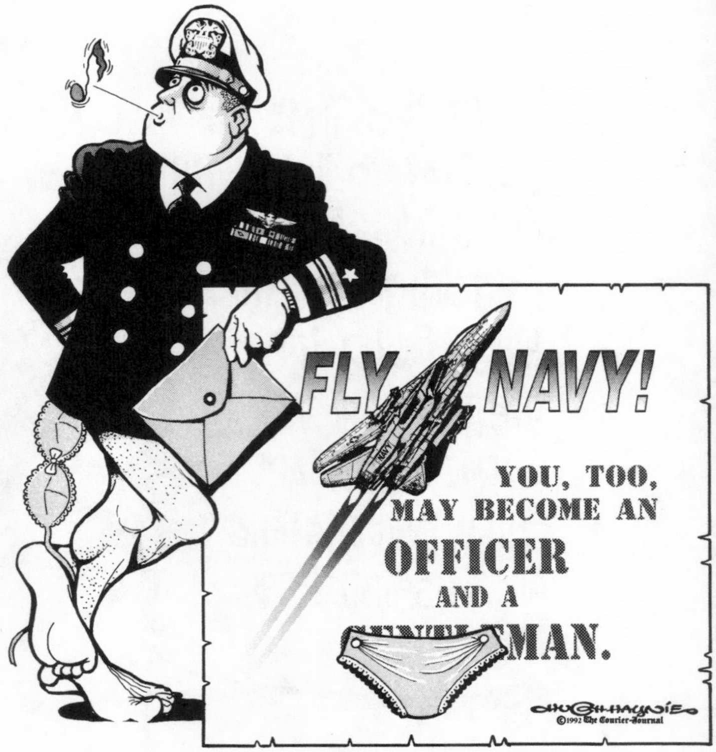
FLY NAVY!
YOU, TOO,
MAY BECOME AN
OFFICER
AND A
MAN.
©1992 The Courier-Journal

HUGH HAYNIE
Courtesy Louisville Courier Journal

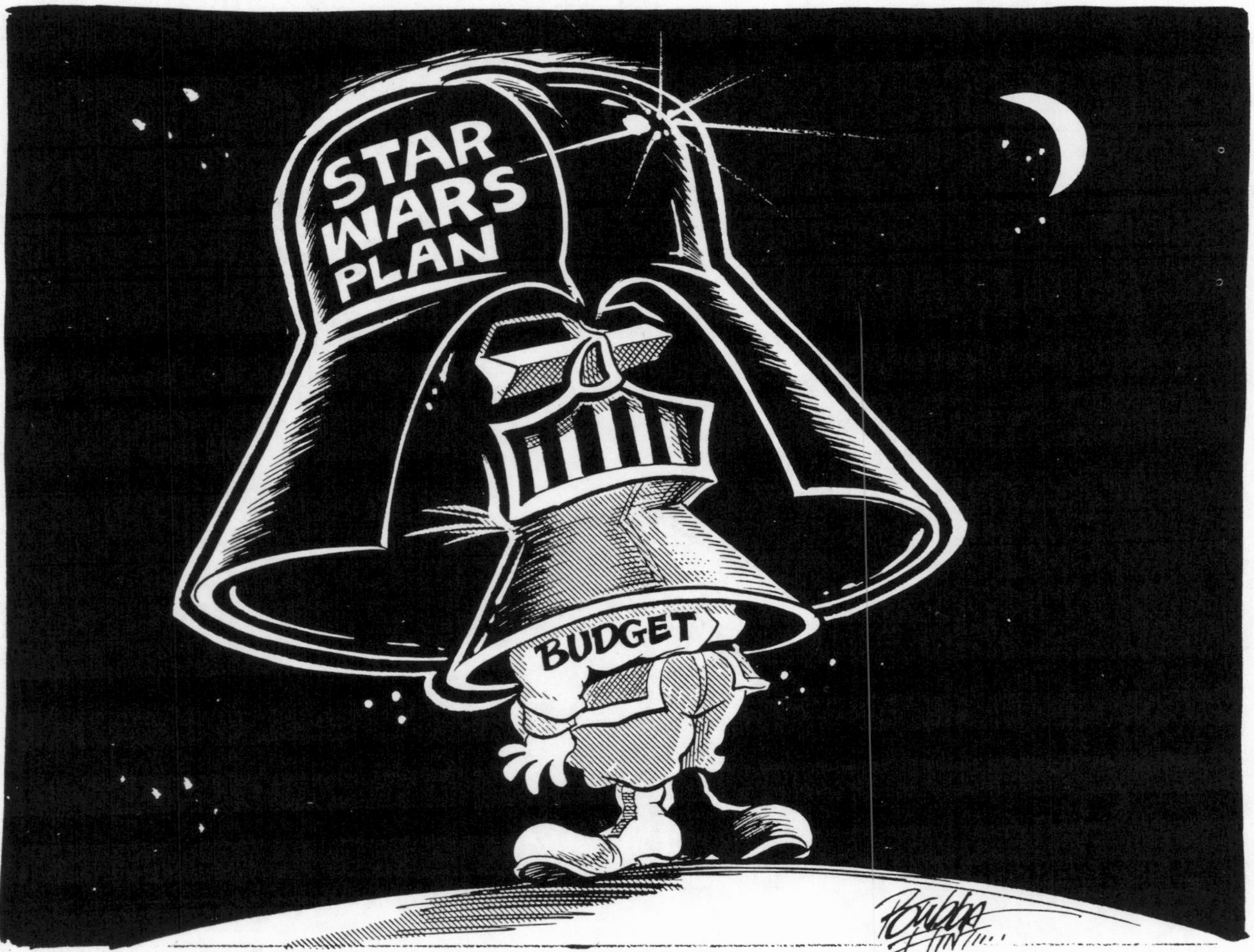
STAR
WARS
PLAN
BUDGET

BUBBA FLINT
Courtesy Ft. Worth Star-Telegram

KEN CATALINO
Courtesy Anchorage Times

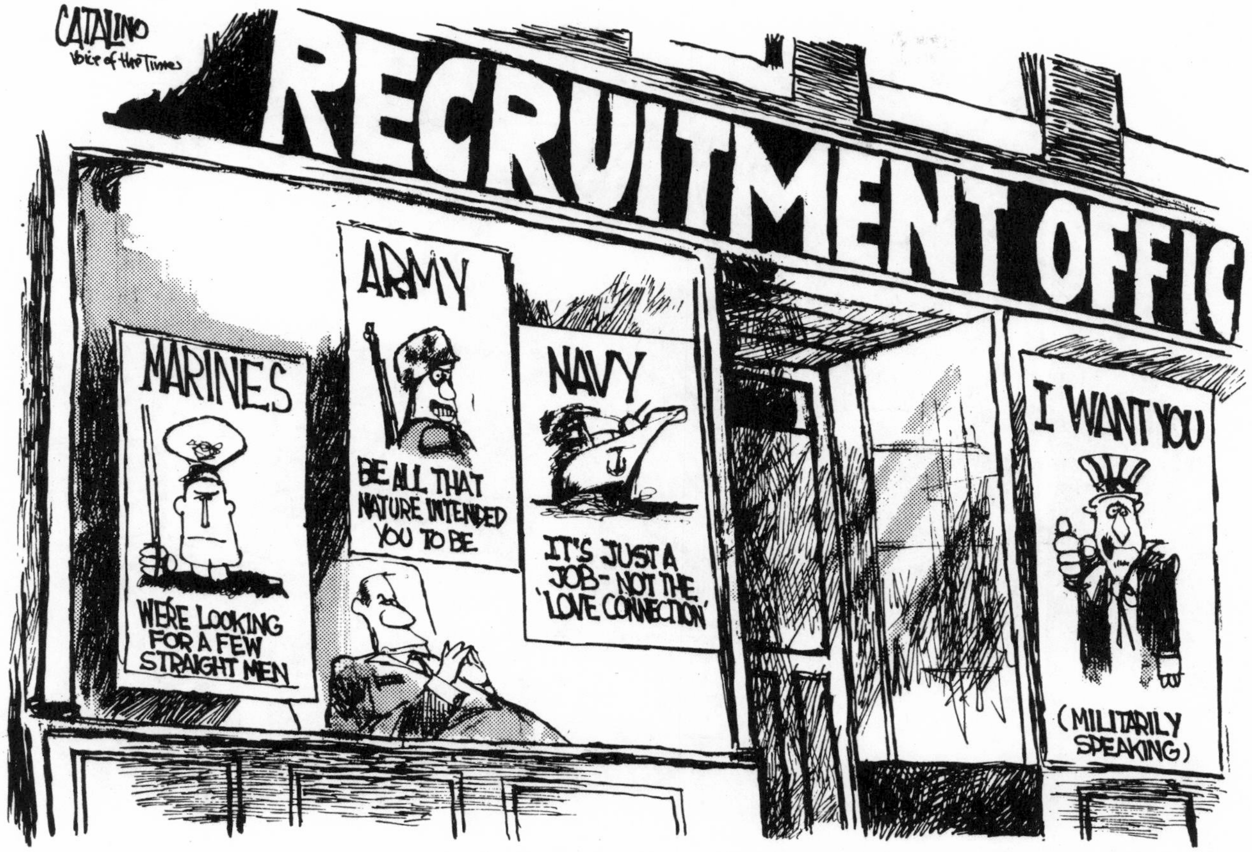
CATALINO
Voice of the Times
RECRUITMENT OFFIC
MARINES
WE'RE LOOKING FOR A FEW STRAIGHT MEN
ARMY
BE ALL THAT NATURE INTENDED YOU TO BE
NAVY
IT'S JUST A JOB- NOT THE 'LOVE CONNECTION'
I WANT YOU
(MILITARILY SPEAKING)

GILL FOX
Courtesy Connecticut Post

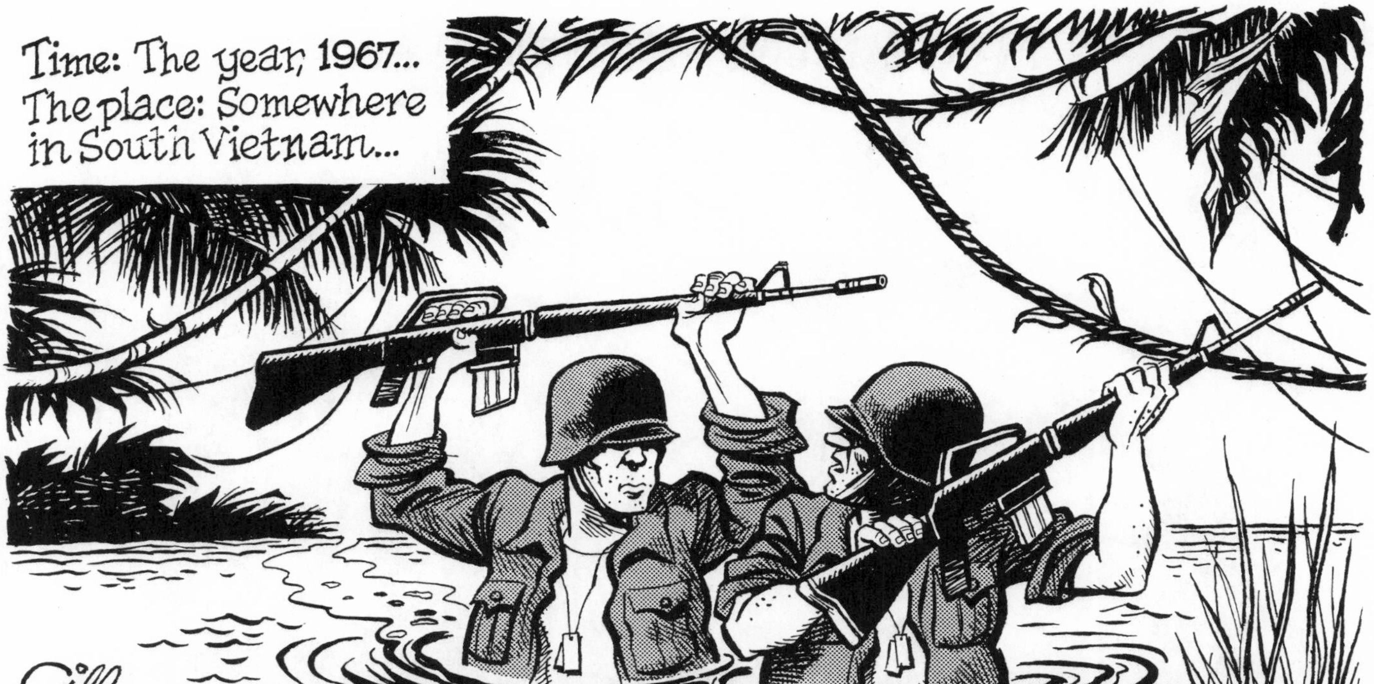
Time: The year, 1967...
The place: Somewhere in South Vietnam...
Gill Fox
CONNECTICUT POST

"JUST HAD A HORRIBLE THOUGHT, IS IT POSSIBLE THAT ONE OF THOSE DRAFT EVADERS COULD BE PRESIDENT OF THE UNITED STATES SOME DAY IN THE FUTURE?"

STEVE MCBRIDE
Courtesy Independence Daily Reporter (Kan.)

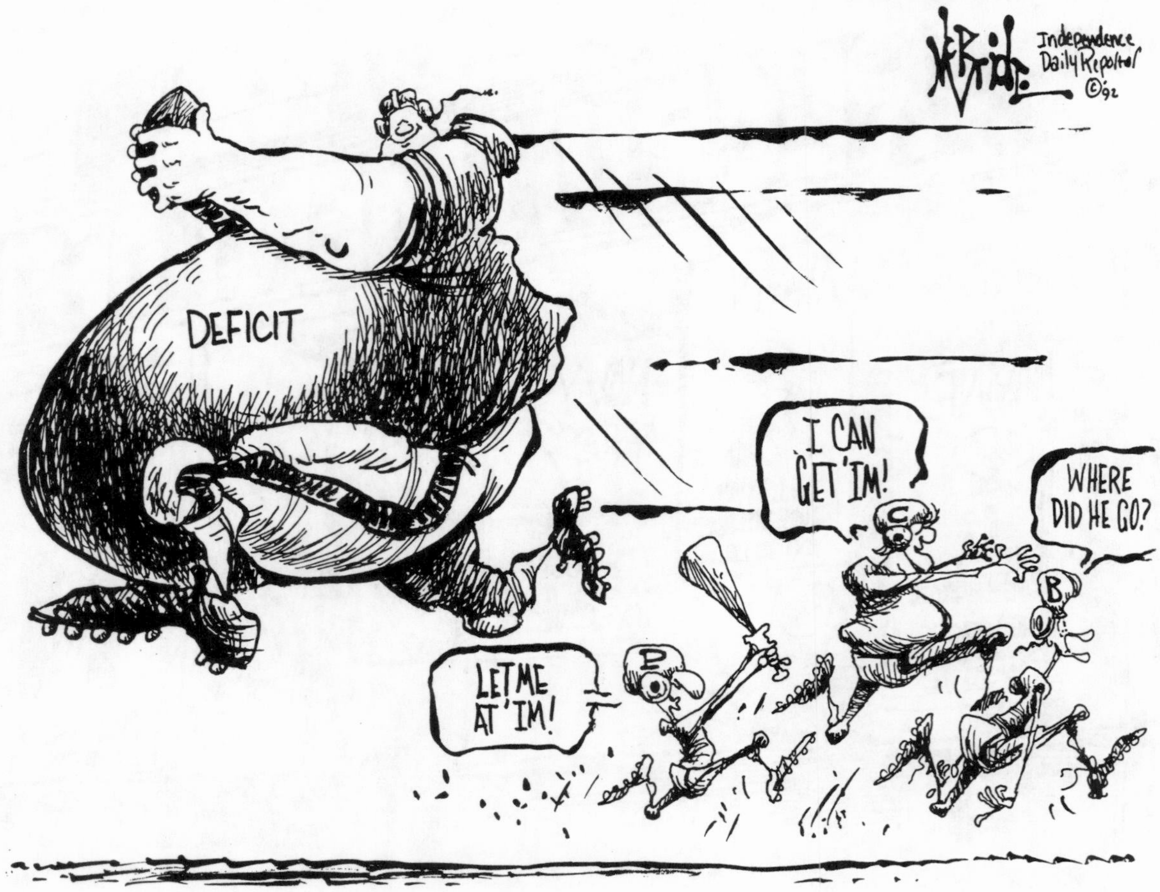
McBride Independence Daily Reporter ©'92
DEFICIT
I CAN GET 'IM!
WHERE DID HE GO?
LET ME AT 'IM!

KEN CATALINO
Courtesy Anchorage Times

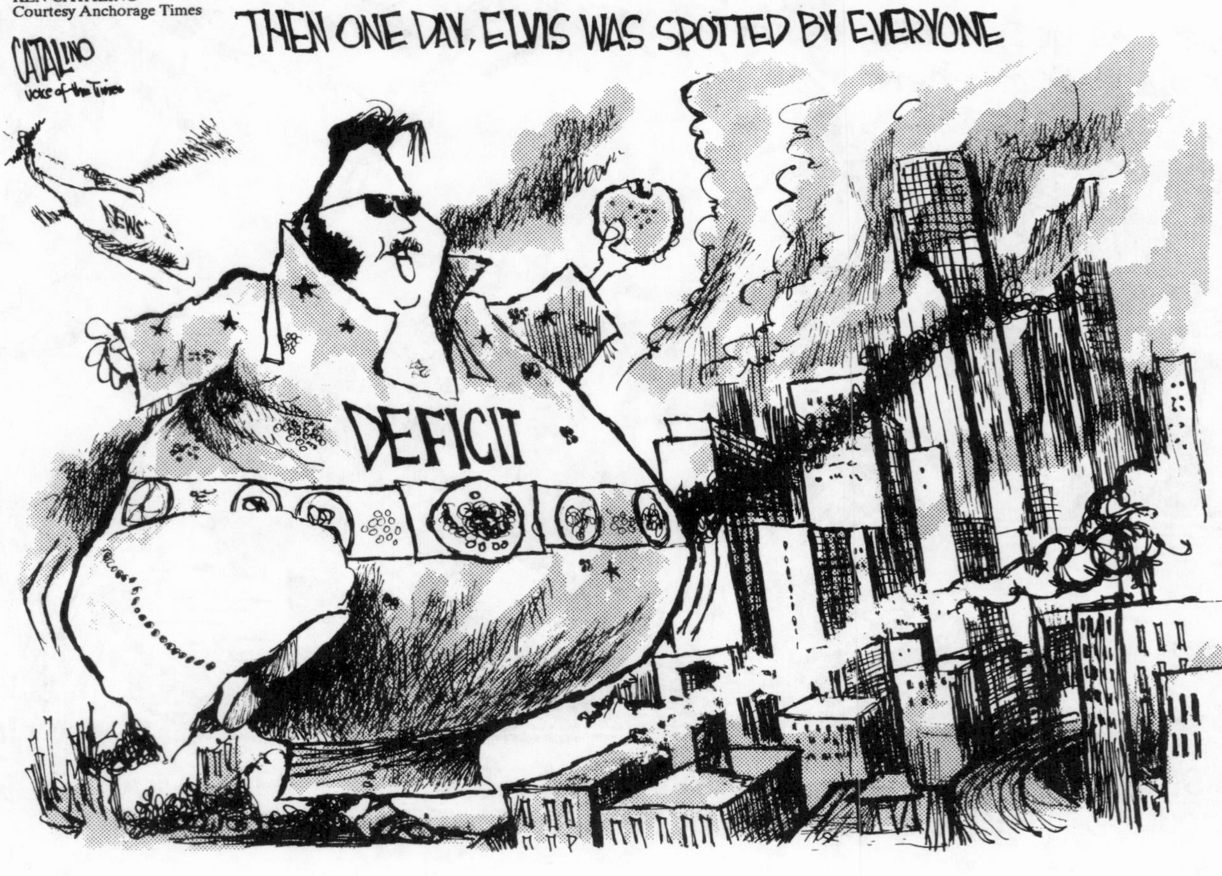
THEN ONE DAY, ELVIS WAS SPOTTED BY EVERYONE
CATALINO
Voice of the Times
NEWS
DEFICIT

Budget Deficits

Economists widely agree that debt is the major impediment to a robust economic recovery in the United States. Throughout 1992 the economy showed signs of upward movement, but the massive national debt kept the economy in recession. Over the past three years, the federal debt soared to $4.1 trillion, while economic growth moved at a snail's pace of 1.1 percent. Four years ago the deficit equaled about 3 percent of the gross domestic product, but by the end of 1992 it had climbed to 7 percent.

For every $4.67 Americans paid in taxes in 1992, they received only $1.81 worth of government. The remainder went to pay off old debts. During the first 175 years as a nation the U.S. balanced the budget or recorded a surplus 60 percent of the time. Since then, with the proliferation of government and expensive programs, the budget has been balanced only 4 percent of the time.

Interest payments on the national debt in 1993 will reach $315 billion, making interest the largest single item in the budget. During the 1992 presidential campaign, only Ross Perot talked seriously about bringing the deficit under control. President Clinton has promised that will be one of his top priorities.

JEFF MACNELLY
Courtesy Chicago Tribune and Tribune Media Services

MACNELLY Chicago Tribune.
WELL, I'M OPEN TO SUGGESTIONS...
BUDGET
POINT B
POINT A

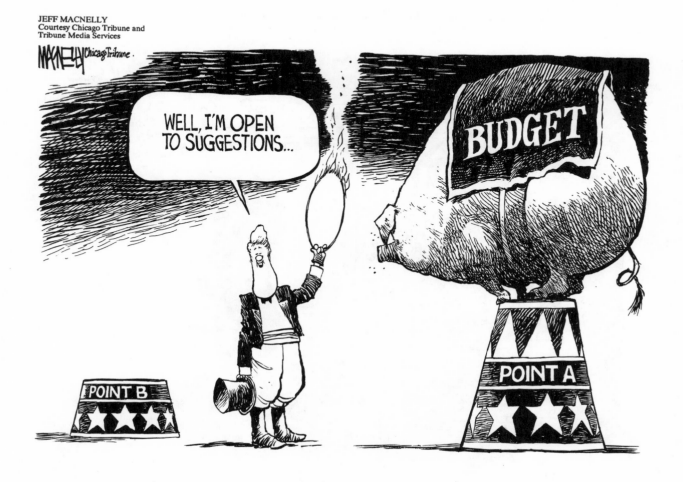

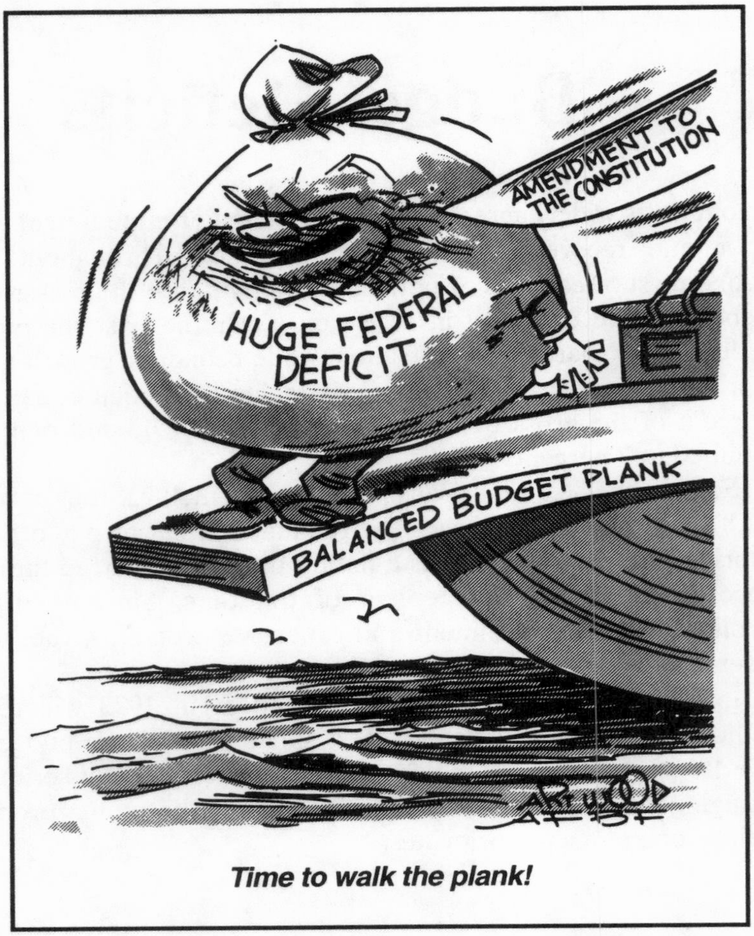
AMENDMENT TO THE CONSTITUTION
HUGE FEDERAL DEFICIT
BALANCED BUDGET PLANK
ART WOOD

Time to walk the plank!

ART WOOD
Courtesy Farm Bureau News

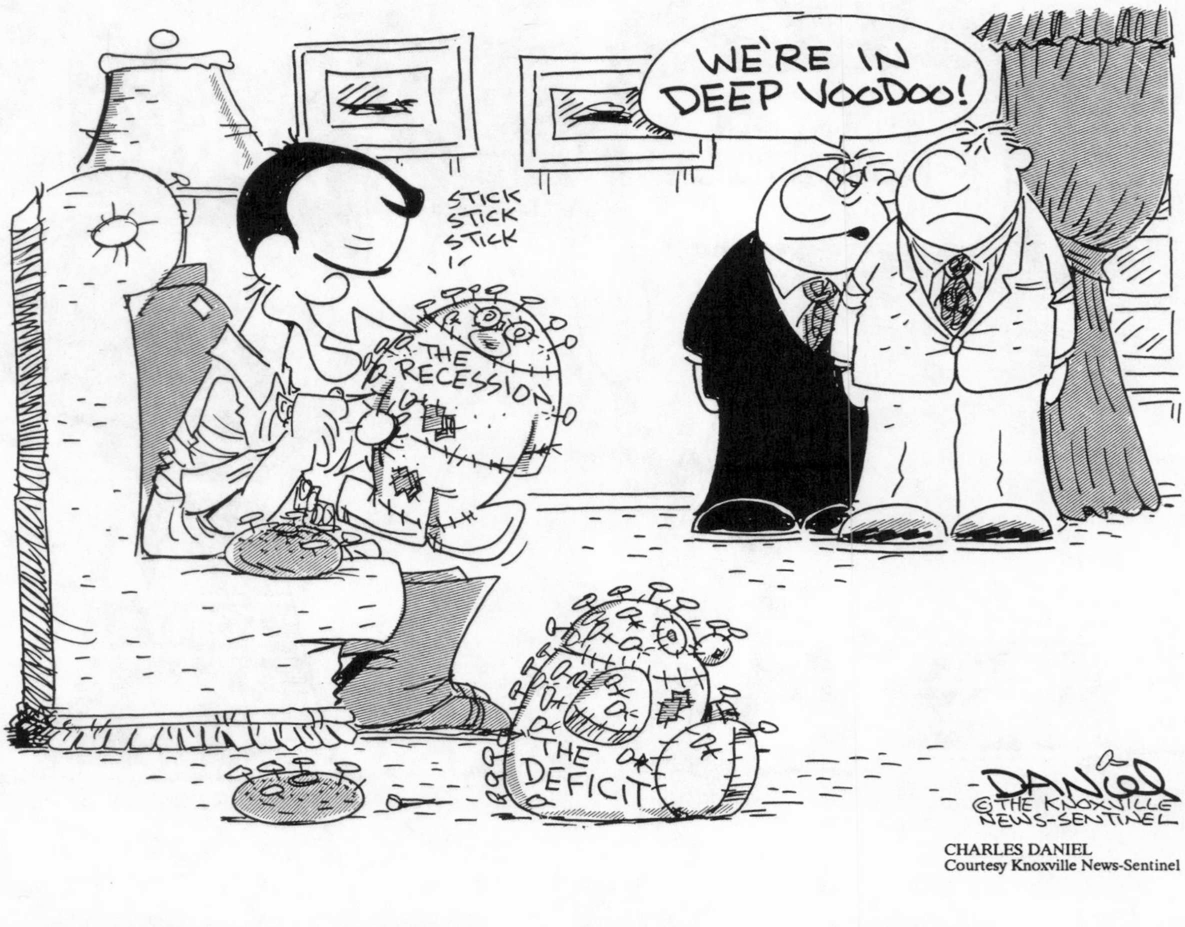
WE'RE IN DEEP VOODOO!
STICK STICK STICK
THE RECESSION
THE DEFICIT
DANIEL
©THE KNOXVILLE NEWS-SENTINEL

CHARLES DANIEL
Courtesy Knoxville News-Sentinel

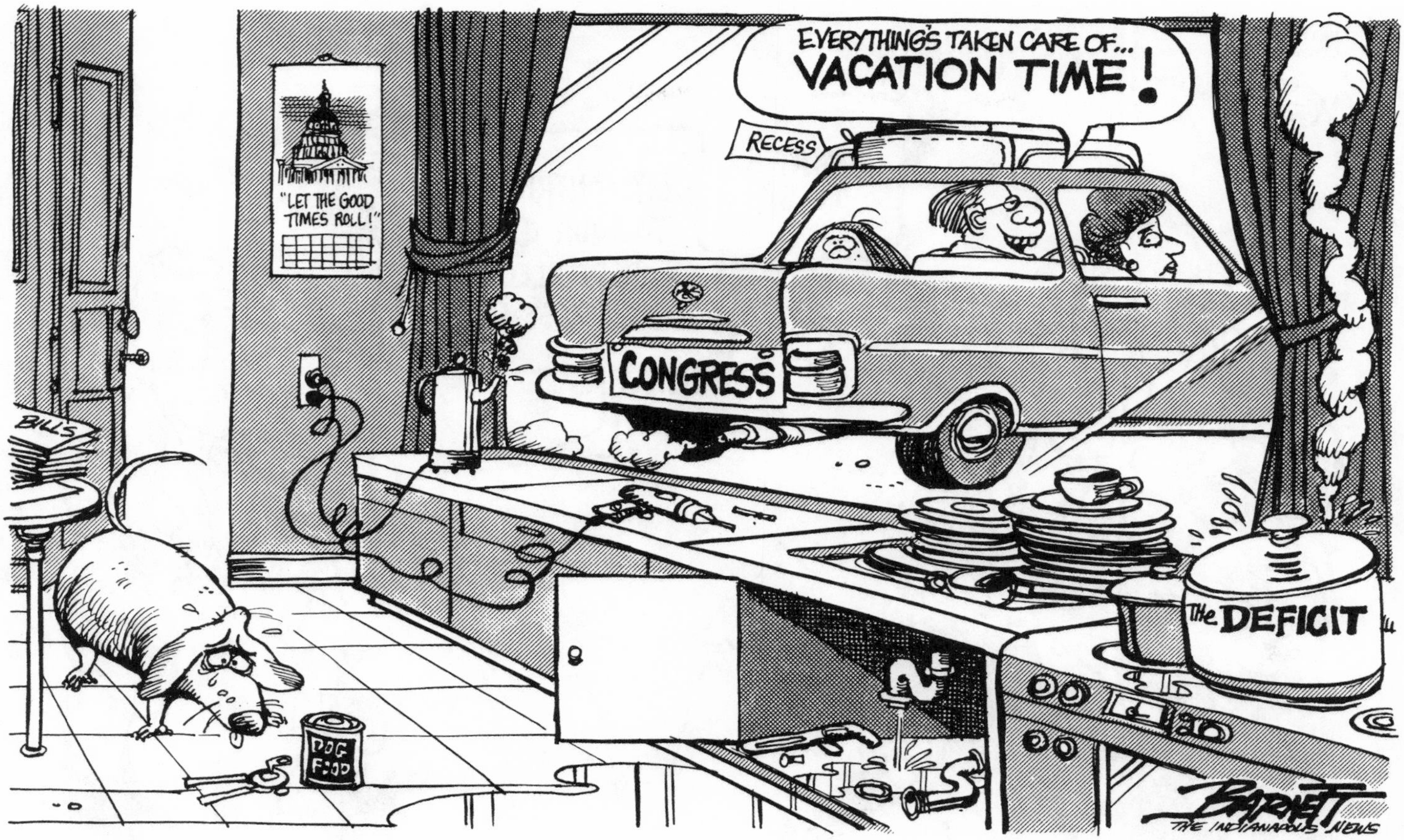
EVERYTHING'S TAKEN CARE OF...
VACATION TIME!
RECESS
CONGRESS
"LET THE GOOD TIMES ROLL!"
BILLS
DOG FOOD
the DEFICIT
BARNETT
THE INDIANAPOLIS NEWS

JERRY BARNETT
Courtesy Indianapolis News

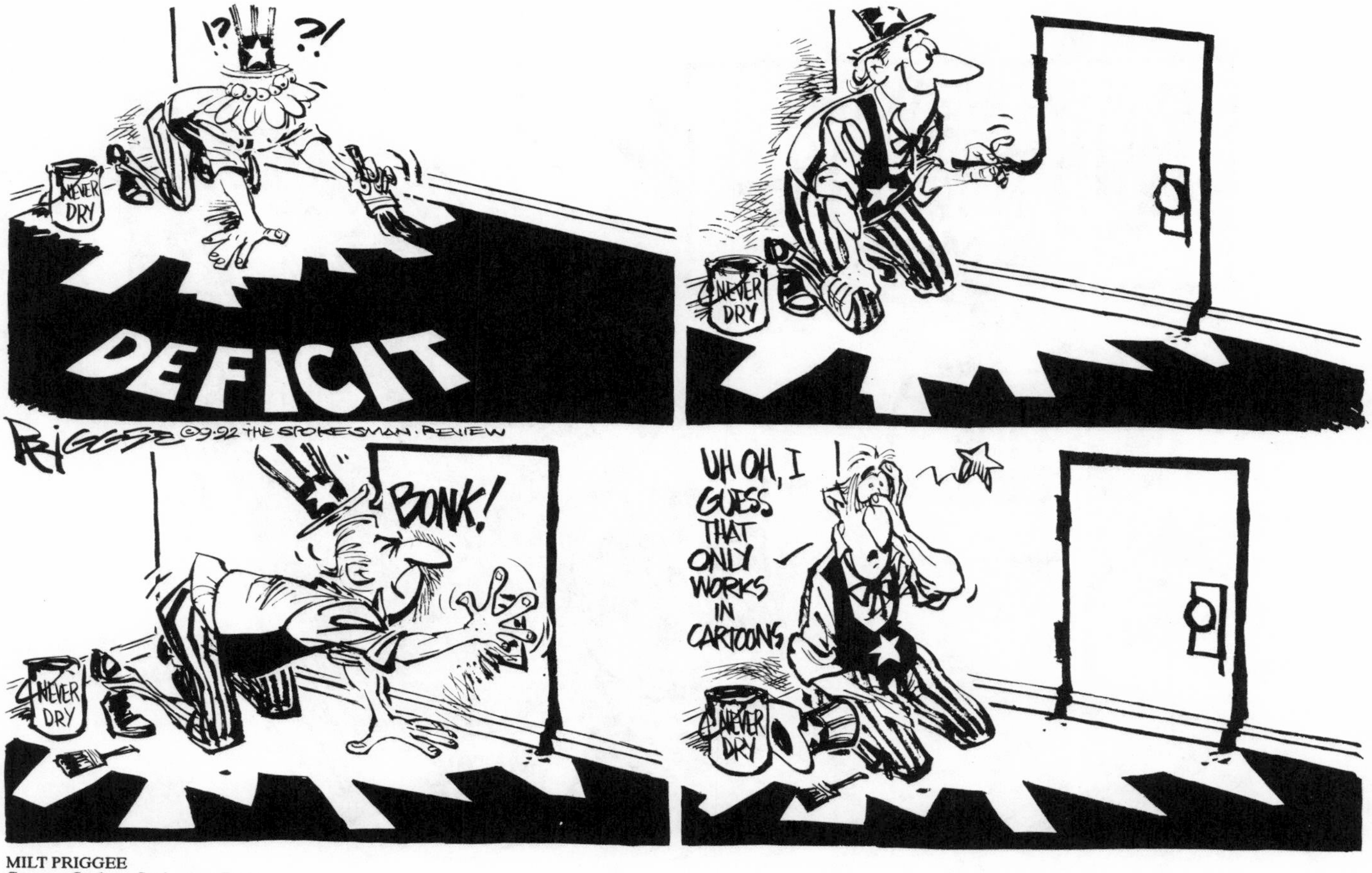
NEVER DRY
DEFICIT
PRIGGEE ©9-92 THE SPOKESMAN-REVIEW
BONK!
UH OH, I GUESS THAT ONLY WORKS IN CARTOONS

MILT PRIGGEE
Courtesy Spokane Spokesman-Review

PATRICK RICE
Courtesy Jupiter Courier

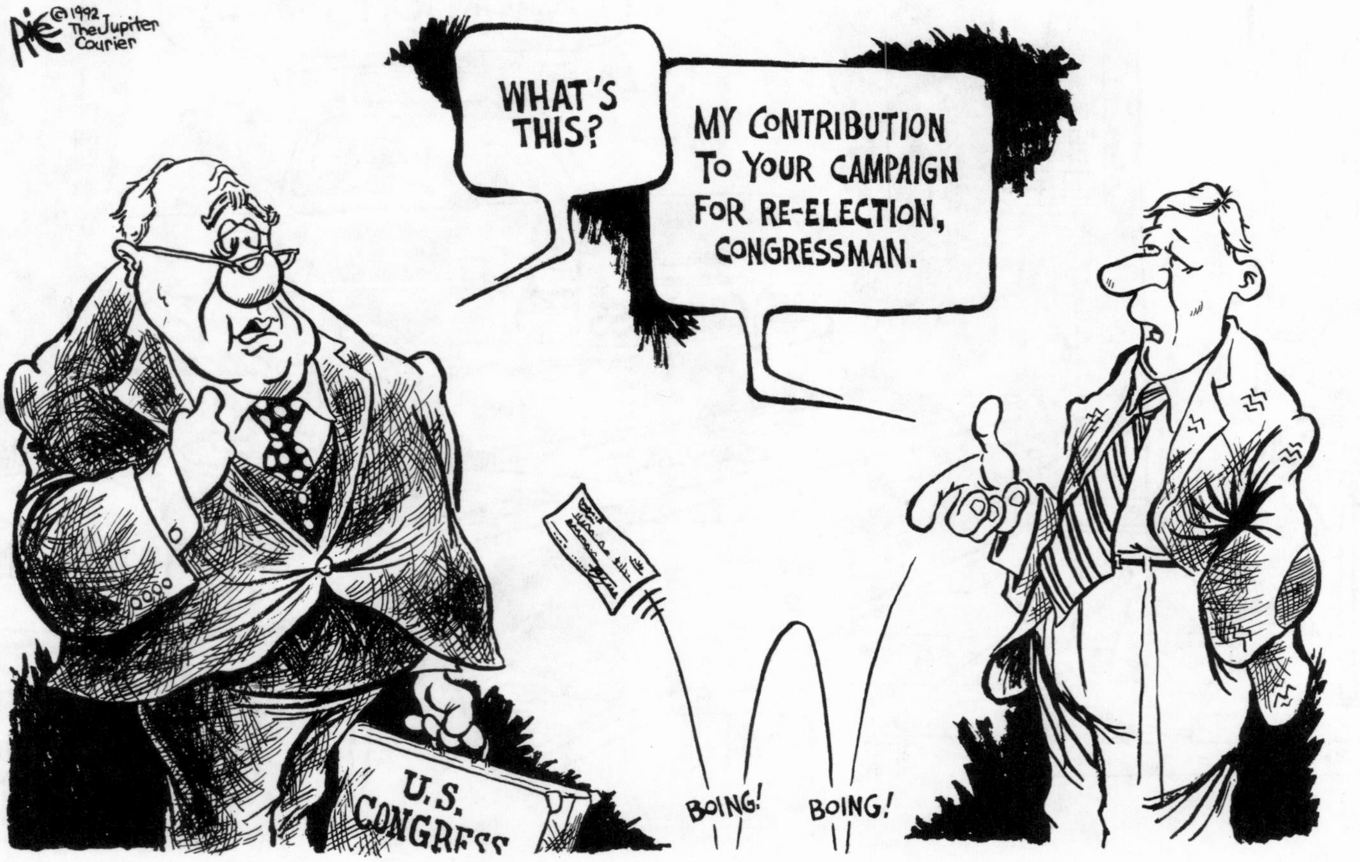
Rice ©1992 The Jupiter Courier
WHAT'S THIS?
MY CONTRIBUTION TO YOUR CAMPAIGN FOR RE-ELECTION, CONGRESSMAN.
U.S.
BOING!
BOING!

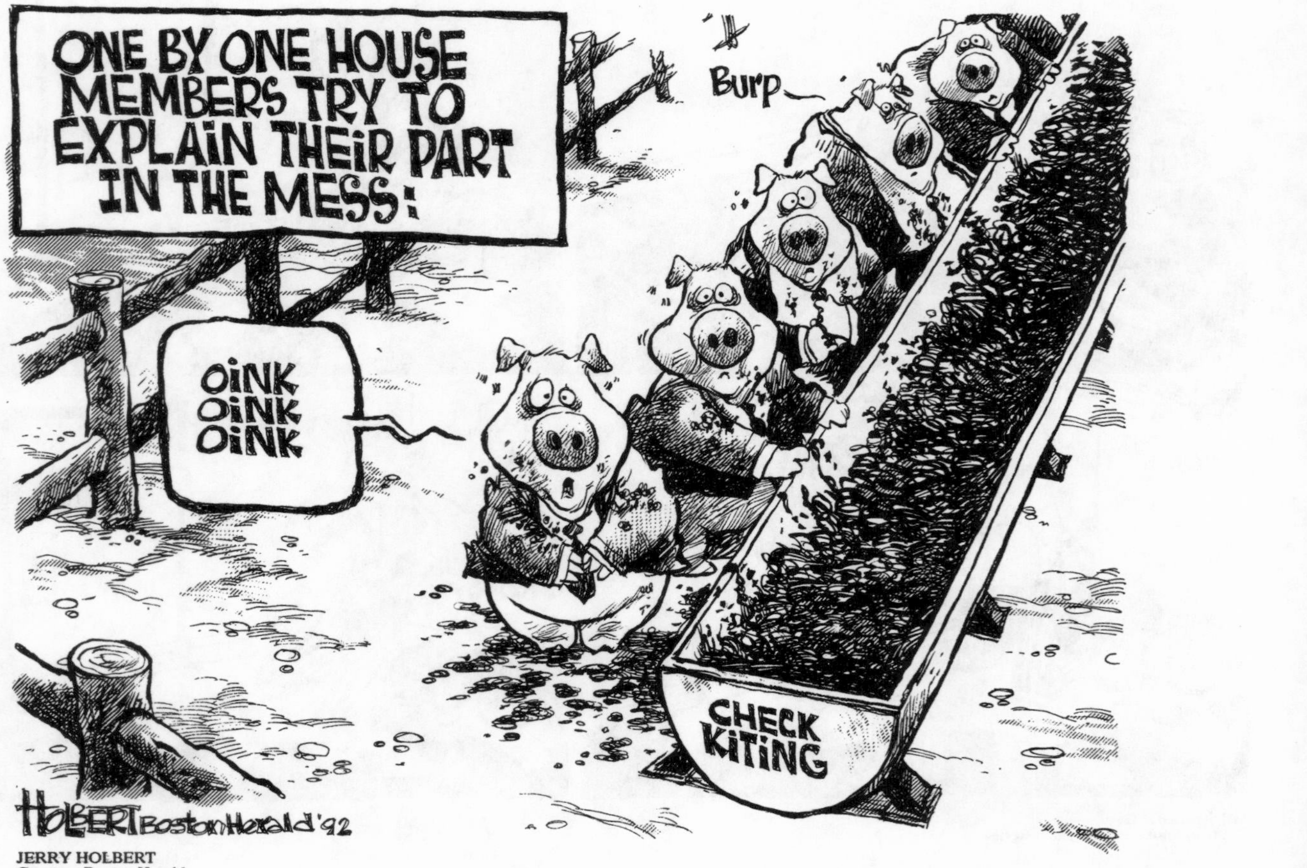
ONE BY ONE HOUSE MEMBERS TRY TO EXPLAIN THEIR PART IN THE MESS:
Burp
OINK OINK OINK
CHECK KITING
HOLBERT Boston Herald '92

JERRY HOLBERT
Courtesy Boston Herald

Congress

The public's regard for Congress, already at a low level, plummeted even further during the year. Thirty-five members of the House and seven members of the Senate announced their retirements, and many of them took their campaign contributions with them. A new law will prohibit this questionable practice after 1992.

The big congressional story, however, was the revelation that 355 members of the House had kited checks through their own private bank. Many gave themselves interest-free loans and advances against their salaries. The twenty-four major abusers wrote bad checks totaling in the millions, and some kept large negative balances for up to three years. In all, the sixty-six worst offenders bounced, or kited, more than 20,000 checks worth more than $10 million.

Names of the wrongdoers were released grudgingly after immense public pressure. The scandal stepped up demands for term limits on a group that somehow had forgotten its responsibilities as public servants.

Once again, there was a hue and cry to throw incumbents out in the November election, but only nine House members suffered that fate. PAC money from special interest groups remains a powerful aid in getting reelected.

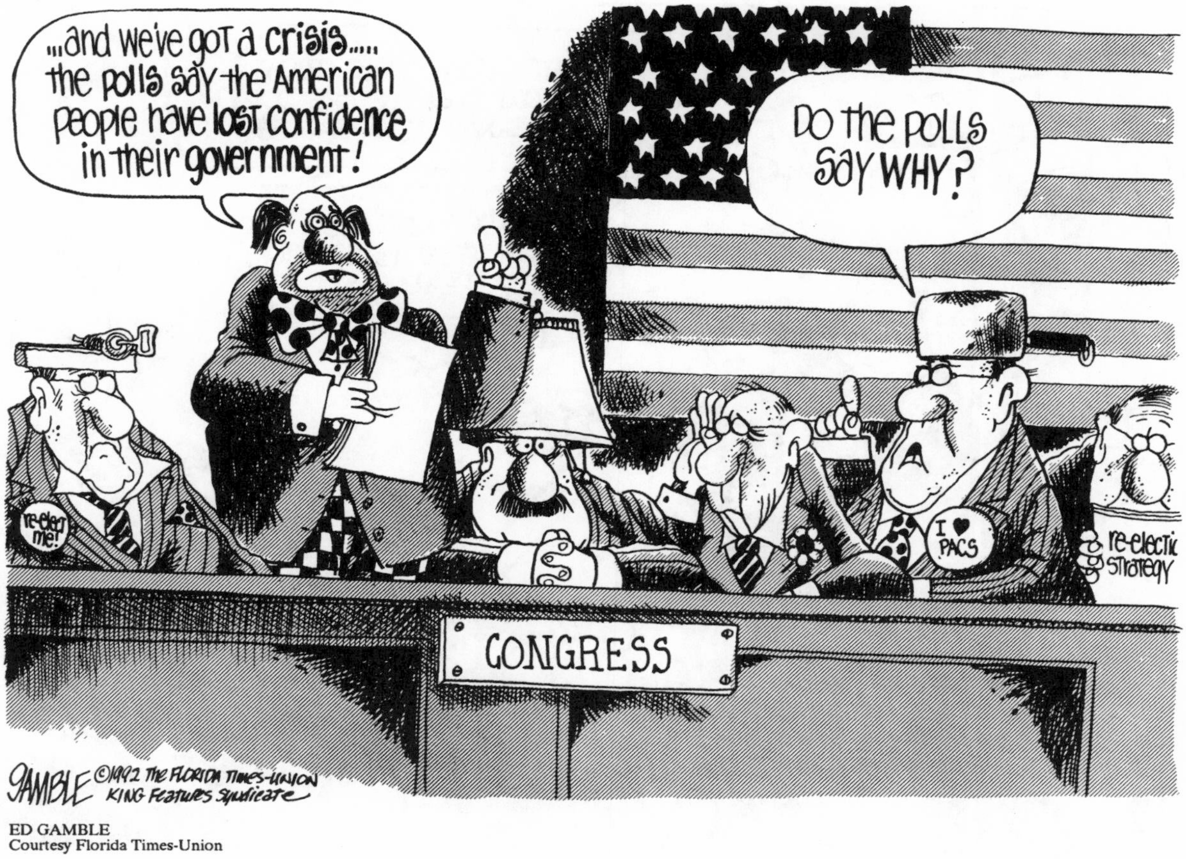
...and we've got a crisis..... the polls say the American people have lost confidence in their government!
Do the polls say WHY?
re-elect me!
I ♥ PACS
CONGRESS
GAMBLE ©1992 The Florida Times-Union King Features Syndicate

ED GAMBLE
Courtesy Florida Times-Union

DAVID HITCH
Courtesy Worcester Telegram & Gazette

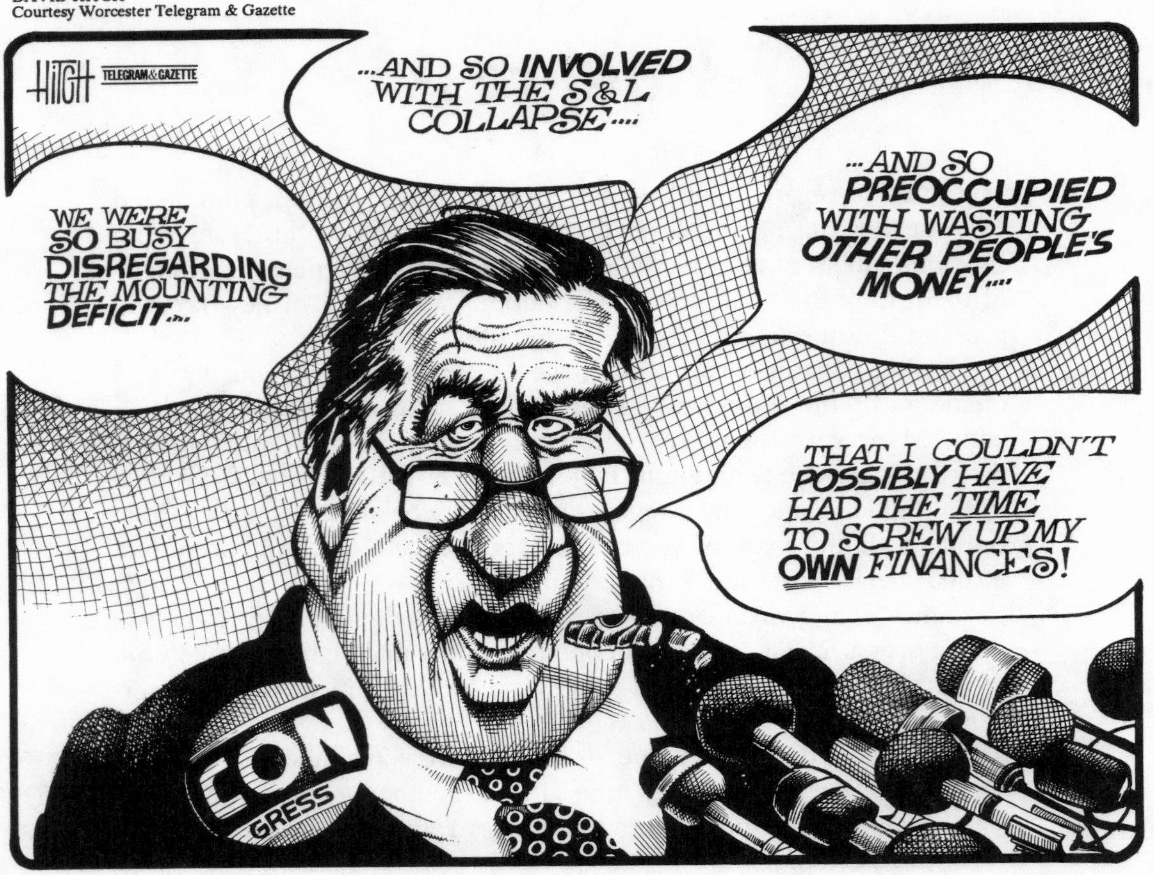
HITCH TELEGRAM & GAZETTE
WE WERE SO BUSY DISREGARDING THE MOUNTING DEFICIT...
...AND SO INVOLVED WITH THE S&L COLLAPSE....
...AND SO PREOCCUPIED WITH WASTING OTHER PEOPLE'S MONEY....
THAT I COULDN'T POSSIBLY HAVE HAD THE TIME TO SCREW UP MY OWN FINANCES!
CON GRESS

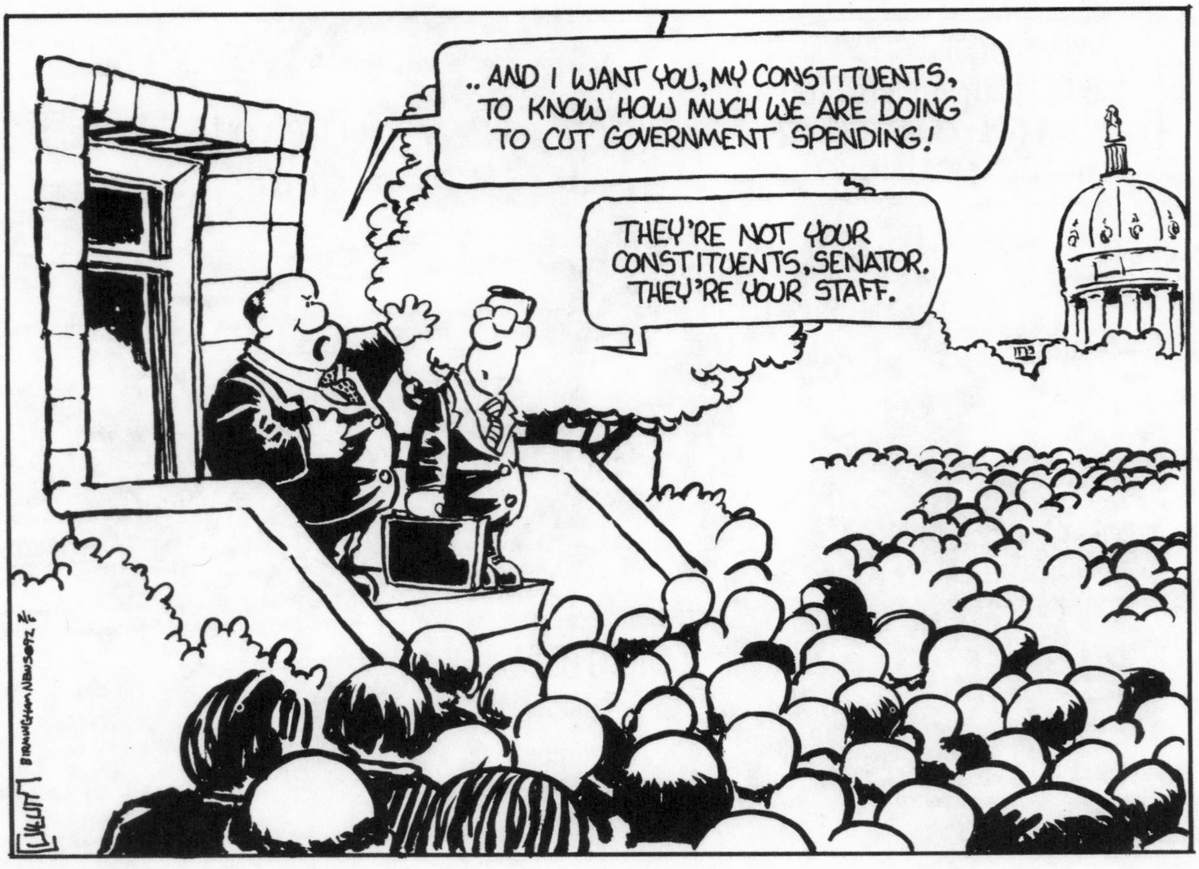
..AND I WANT YOU, MY CONSTITUENTS, TO KNOW HOW MUCH WE ARE DOING TO CUT GOVERNMENT SPENDING!
THEY'RE NOT YOUR CONSTITUENTS, SENATOR. THEY'RE YOUR STAFF.

MARK CULLUM
Courtesy Birmingham News

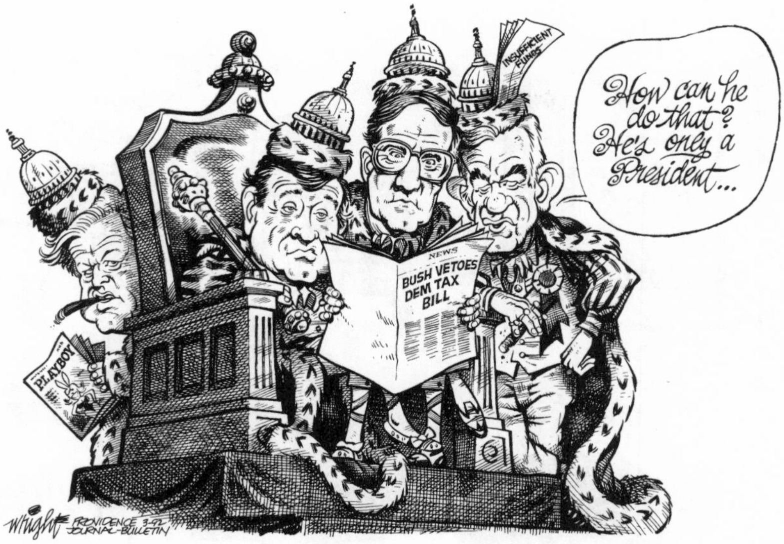

INSUFFICIENT FUNDS
How can he do that? He's only a President...
NEWS
BUSH VETOES DEM TAX BILL
PLAYBOY

DICK WRIGHT
Courtesy Providence Journal-Bulletin

PETER B. WALLACE
Courtesy Boston Herald

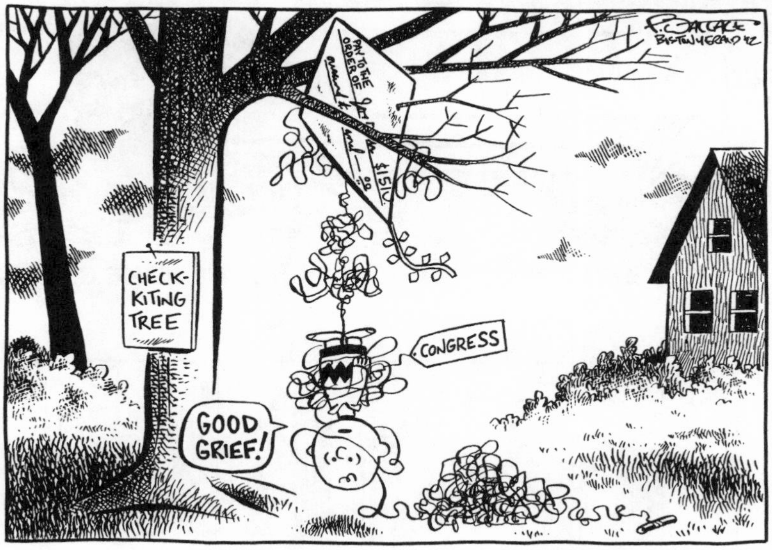

PAY TO THE ORDER OF
$151
CHECK-KITING TREE
CONGRESS
GOOD GRIEF!

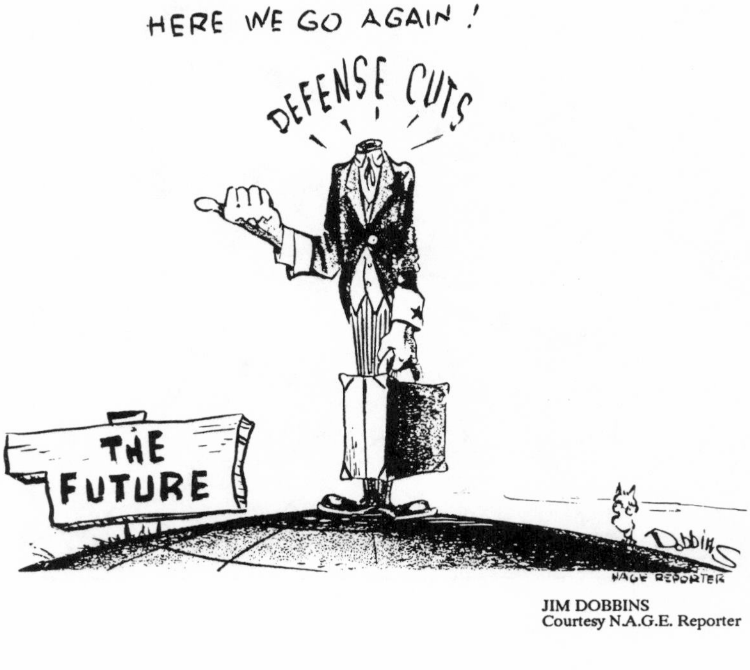

HERE WE GO AGAIN!
DEFENSE CUTS
THE FUTURE

JIM DOBBINS
Courtesy N.A.G.E. Reporter

BOB GORRELL
Courtesy Richmond News Leader

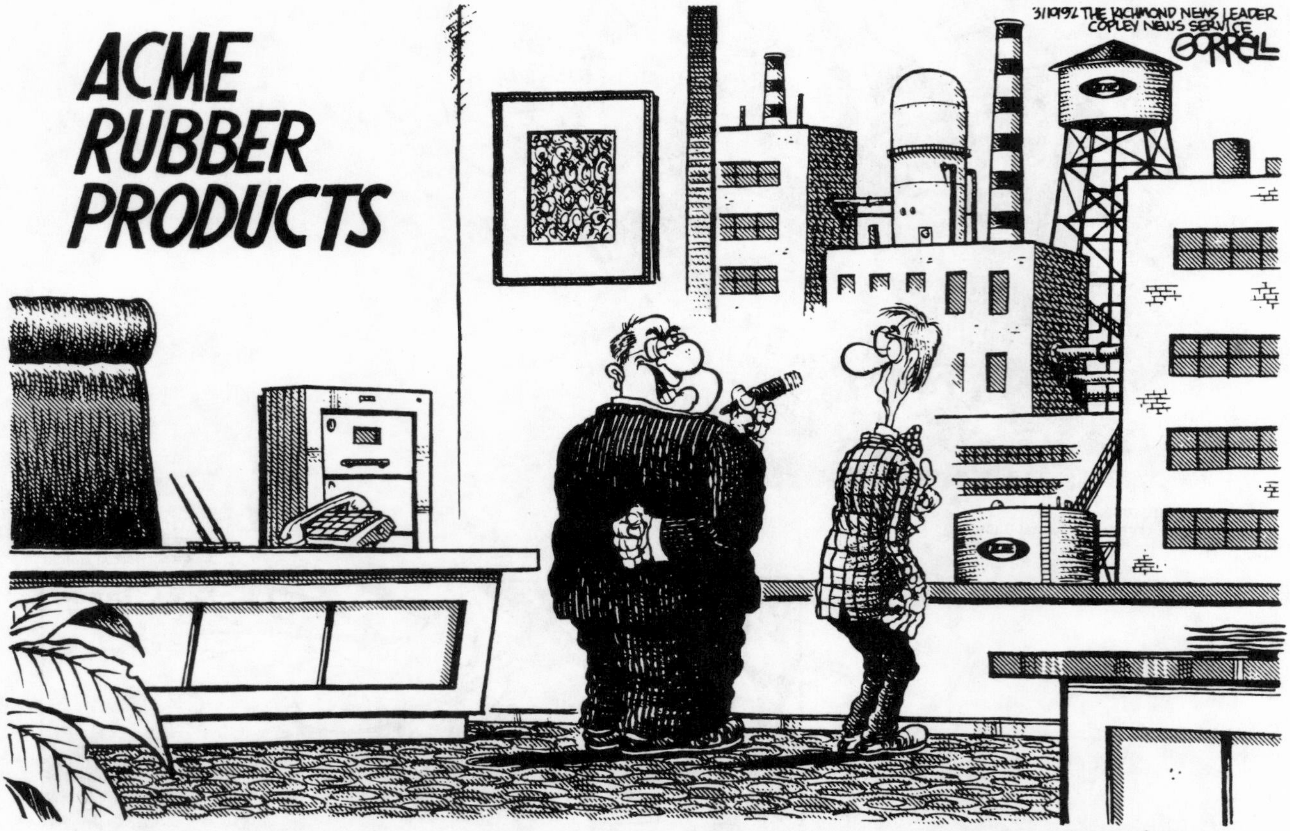
3/10/92 THE RICHMOND NEWS LEADER
COPLEY NEWS SERVICE
GORRELL
ACME
RUBBER
PRODUCTS

"TIRES AND CONDOMS? . . . HECK NO! WE MAKE *CHECKBOOKS FOR CONGRESSMEN!*"

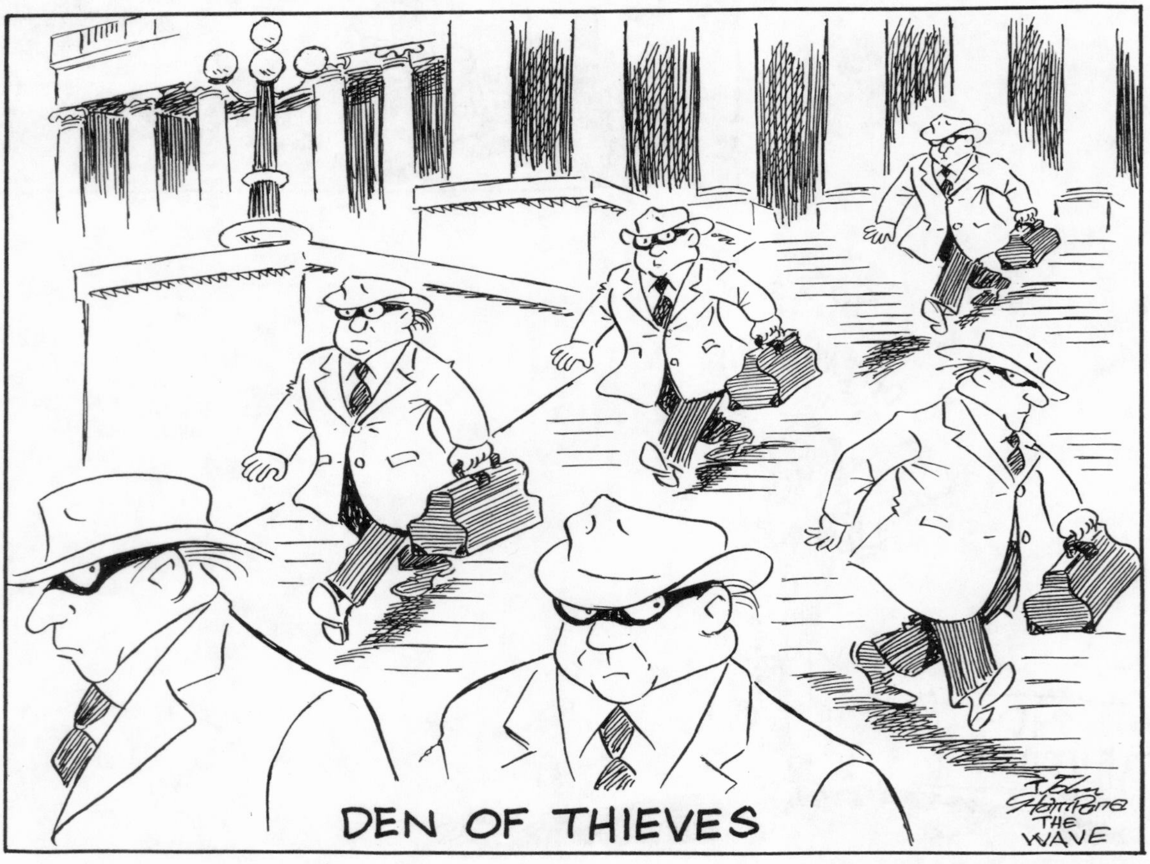
DEN OF THIEVES
THE
WAVE

JOHN STAMPONE
Courtesy The Wave (Del.)

STATE OF THE UNION
SPECIAL INTERESTS
PACS & POLS
DOBBINS
NAGE REPORTER

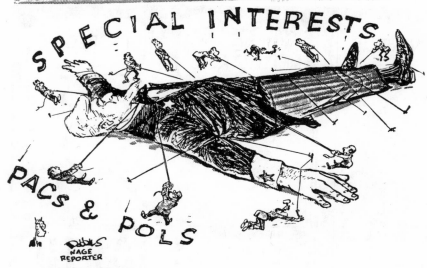

JIM DOBBINS
Courtesy N.A.G.E. Reporter

129 YEARS, ABE, AFTER YOUR EMANCIPATION PROCLAMATION! -- AND SHE'S FROM ILLINOIS TOO!
FIRST BLACK WOMAN ELECTED TO U.S. SENATE
HISTORIC WIN FOR ILLINOIS DEMOCRAT
Carol Moseley Braun
ILLINOIS
DAILY HERALD
ARTHUR HENRIKSON

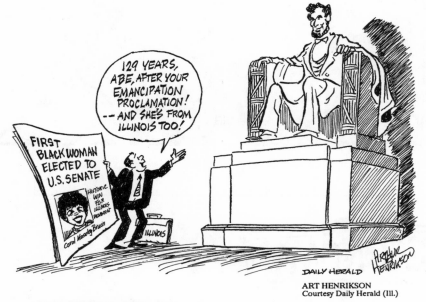

ART HENRIKSON
Courtesy Daily Herald (Ill.)

TAXES
you can tell it's an election year...
...they're using lighter whips
BERTRAM '92

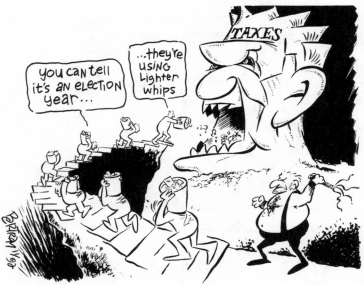

JIM BERTRAM
Courtesy St. Cloud Times

MIKE THOMPSON
Courtesy State Journal-Register (Ill.)

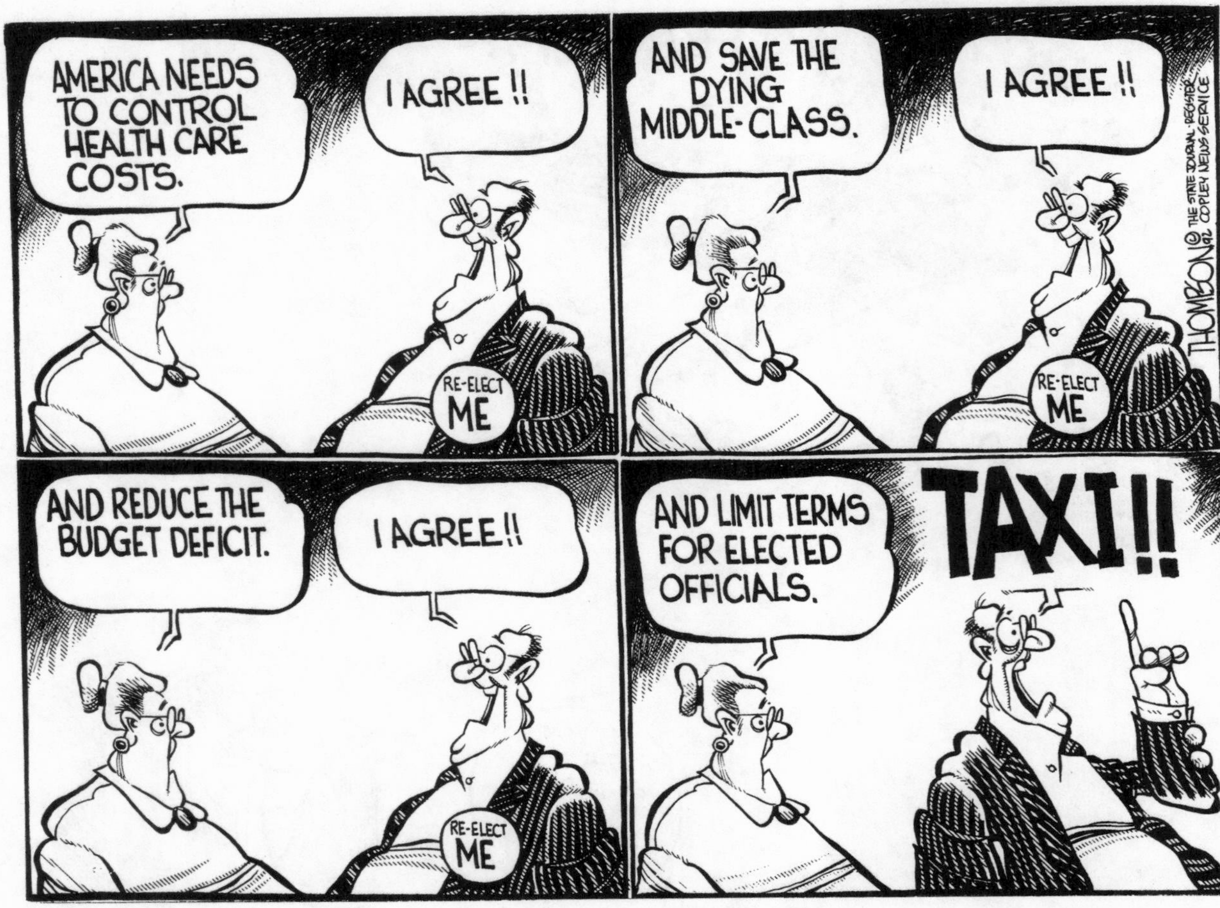
AMERICA NEEDS TO CONTROL HEALTH CARE COSTS.
I AGREE !!
RE-ELECT ME
AND SAVE THE DYING MIDDLE-CLASS.
I AGREE !!
RE-ELECT ME
THOMPSON © '92 THE STATE JOURNAL-REGISTER COPLEY NEWS SERVICE
AND REDUCE THE BUDGET DEFICIT.
I AGREE !!
RE-ELECT ME
AND LIMIT TERMS FOR ELECTED OFFICIALS.
TAXI !!

GARY VARVEL
Courtesy Indianapolis News

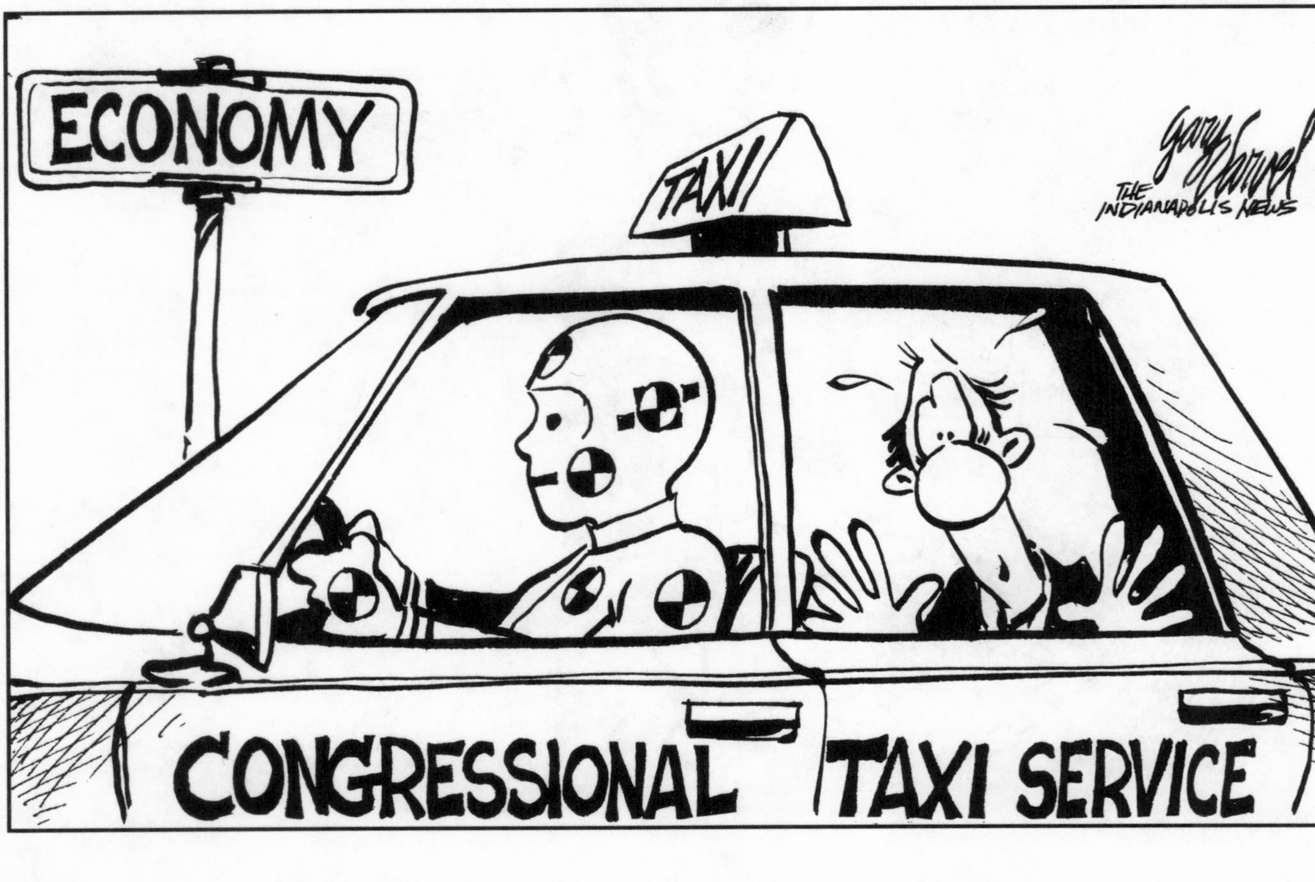
ECONOMY
TAXI
Gary Varvel THE INDIANAPOLIS NEWS
CONGRESSIONAL TAXI SERVICE

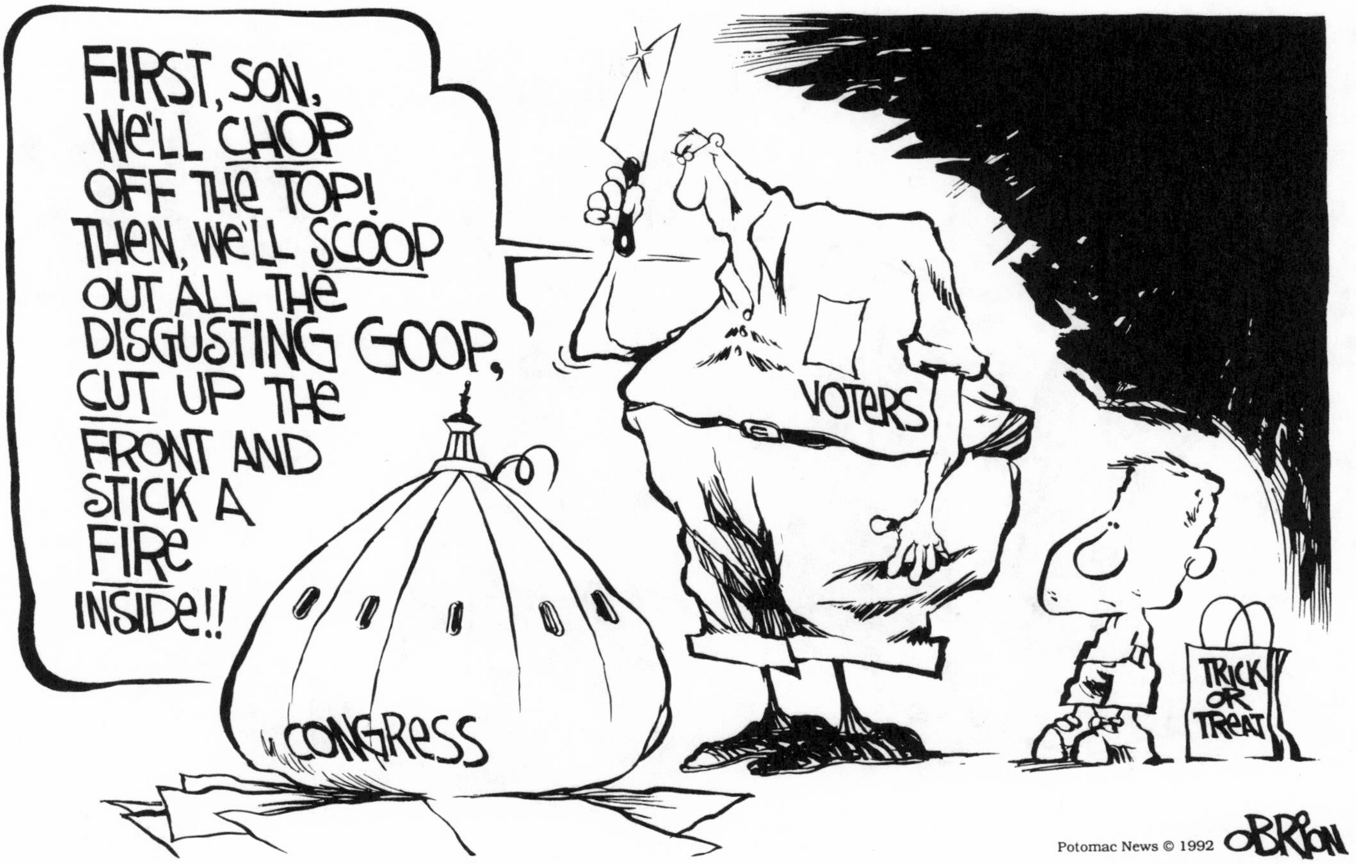
FIRST, SON, WE'LL CHOP OFF THE TOP! THEN, WE'LL SCOOP OUT ALL THE DISGUSTING GOOP, CUT UP THE FRONT AND STICK A FIRE INSIDE!!
VOTERS
CONGRESS
TRICK OR TREAT
Potomac News © 1992 OBRION

CHRIS OBRION
Courtesy Potomac News

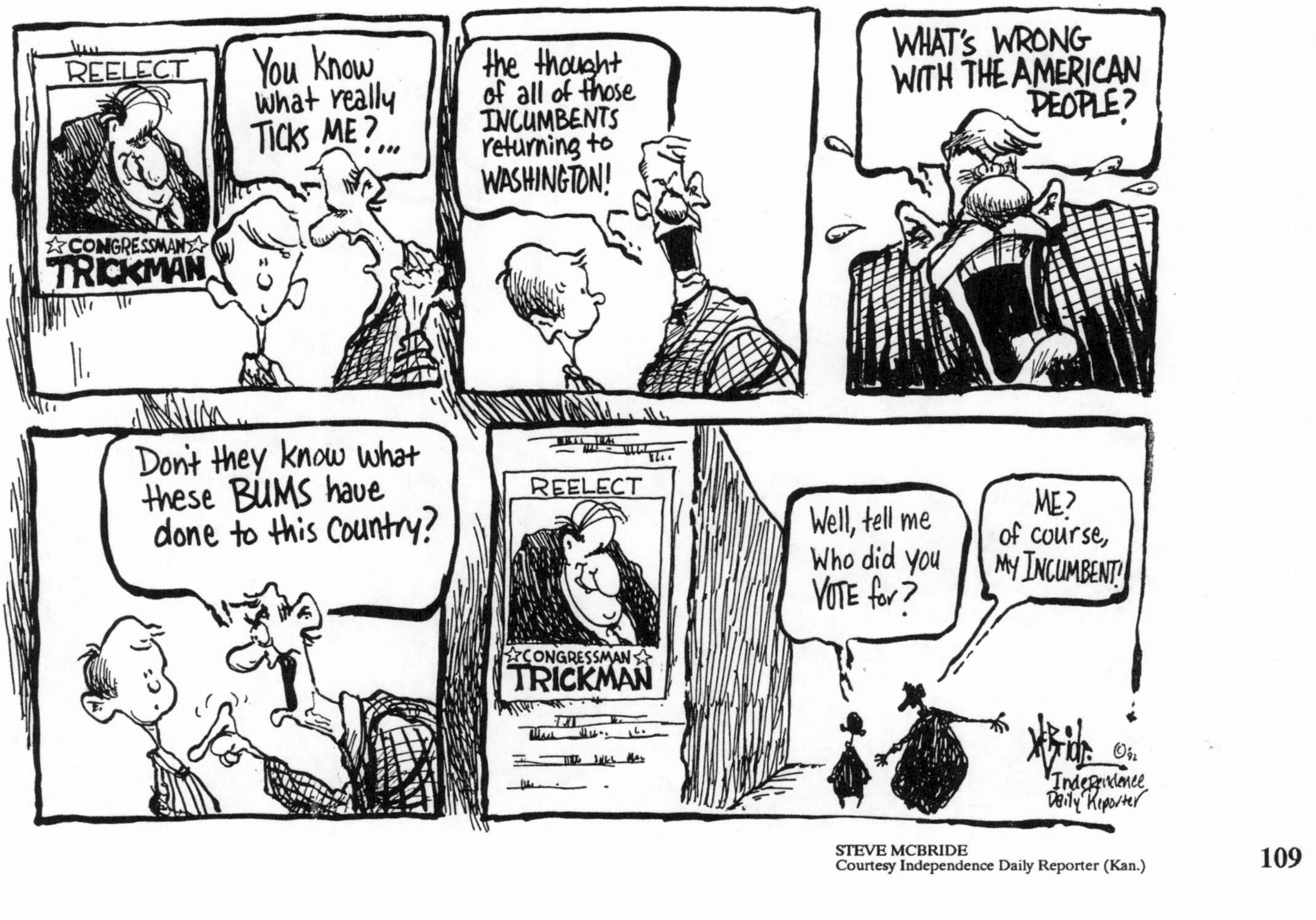
REELECT
☆CONGRESSMAN☆
TRICKMAN
You know what really TICKS ME?....
the thought of all of those INCUMBENTS returning to WASHINGTON!
WHAT'S WRONG WITH THE AMERICAN PEOPLE?
Don't they know what these BUMS have done to this country?
REELECT
☆CONGRESSMAN☆
TRICKMAN
Well, tell me Who did you VOTE for?
ME? of course, MY INCUMBENT!
McBride ©92
Independence Daily Reporter

STEVE MCBRIDE
Courtesy Independence Daily Reporter (Kan.)

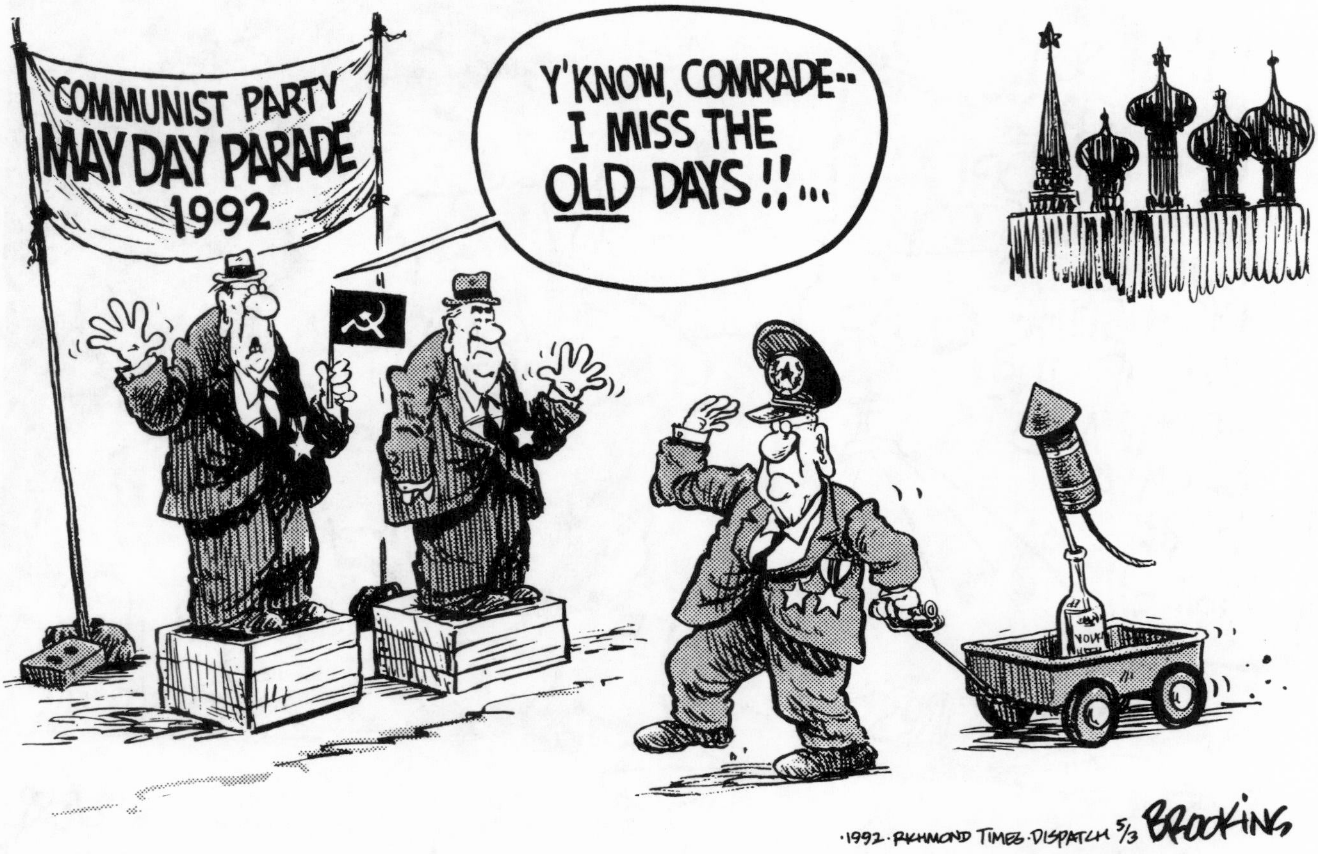
COMMUNIST PARTY
MAY DAY PARADE
1992
Y'KNOW, COMRADE--
I MISS THE
OLD DAYS !!...
·1992· RICHMOND TIMES-DISPATCH 5/3 BROOKINS

GARY BROOKINS
Courtesy Richmond Times-Dispatch

ED GAMBLE
Courtesy Florida Times-Union

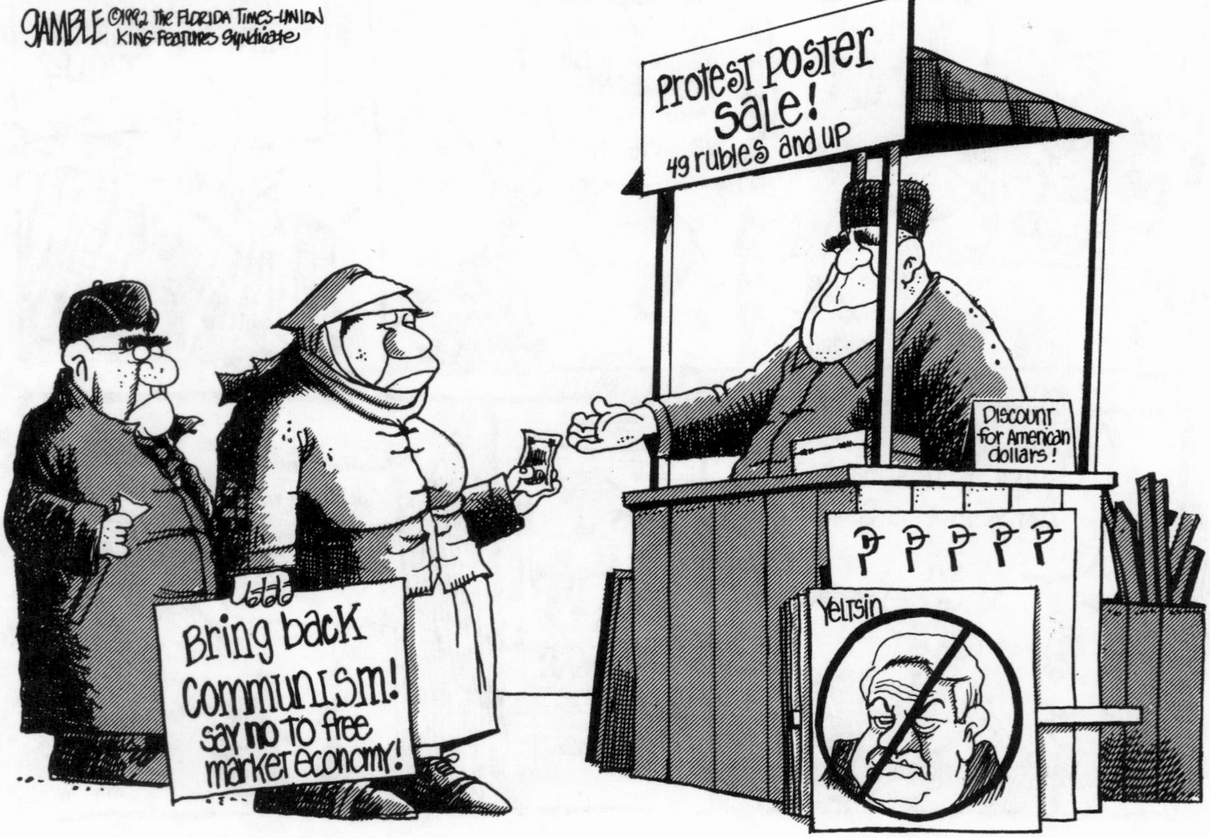
GAMBLE ©1992 The FLORIDA TIMES-UNION
KING FEATURES SYNDICATE
Protest Poster
Sale!
49 rubles and up
Discount
for American
dollars!
Yeltsin
Bring back
communism!
say no to free
market economy!

Russia

Russian President Boris Yeltsin faced growing pressure from hard-liners, nationalists, and military officers to slow his economic reform program and to ease moves to dismantle the huge Soviet nuclear arsenal. Inflation raced upward at 1,300 percent a year as citizens complained bitterly about food shortages and long shopping lines. Tensions escalated between ethnic Russians and the people of Lithuania, Latvia, and Estonia, as well as in other areas of the former Soviet Union.

As was Mikhail Gorbachev, Yeltsin is more popular in the West than at home. He lately has appeared to be retreating from reform while watching carefully for signs of a new coup attempt in the Kremlin. A deadlocked legislature has done little to help Russia throughout a trying period. Unemployment is expected to rise from less than a million in 1992 to seven million in 1993.

It has been only a year since the hammer and sickle was removed from the Kremlin, but time seems to be running out for Yeltsin and democratic reform. A poll showed that 83 percent of the Russian people have diminished confidence in Yeltsin, while 65 percent have little or no trust in the Russian government.

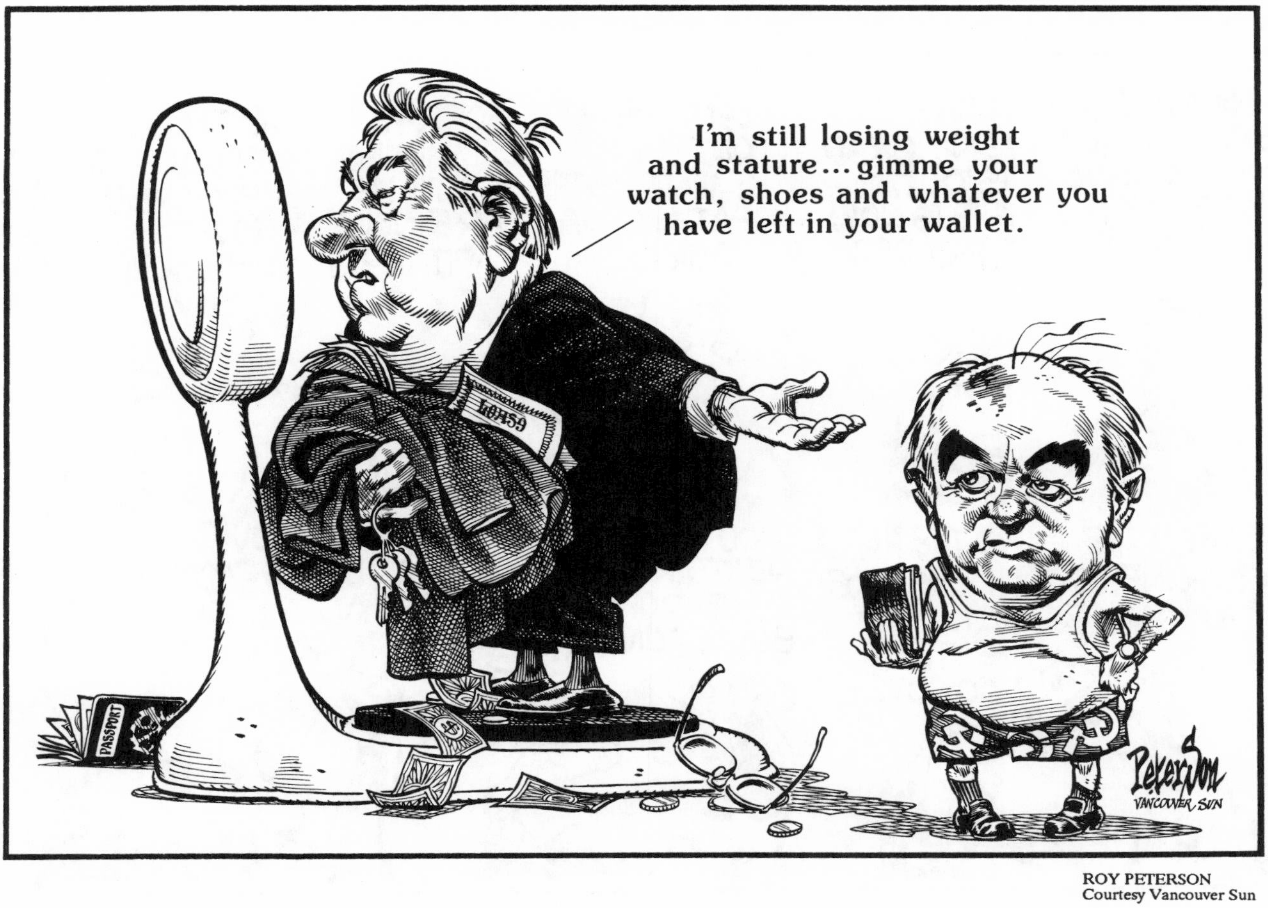
I'm still losing weight and stature... gimme your watch, shoes and whatever you have left in your wallet.
PASSPORT
Peterson
VANCOUVER SUN

ROY PETERSON
Courtesy Vancouver Sun

DICK LOCHER
Courtesy Chicago Tribune

I NEVER SAID IT WOULD HAPPEN OVERNIGHT!
WONDER BREAD
YELTSIN
©1992 CHICAGO TRIBUNE
LOCHER

COMRADE, I'VE BEEN IN SPACE FOR A YEAR. IT'S GOOD TO BE BACK IN LENINGRAD.
SORRY. LENINGRAD IS OUT. THIS IS NOW ST. PETERSBURG.
LENINGRAD OUT? BUT LENIN WAS THE FATHER OF COMMUNISM.
SORRY... COMMUNISM IS OUT. WE ARE NOW CAPITALISTS.
CAPITALISTS?! BUT HOW COULD GORBACHEV ALLOW THIS TO HAPPEN?
SORRY.. GORBACHEV IS OUT. HE WAS OVERTHROWN BY THE HARD-LINERS.
YOU MEAN THE HARD-LINERS ARE IN CHARGE?
NO, THE HARD-LINERS ARE OUT. AND YELTSIN TOOK OVER.
YOU MEAN YELTSIN IS THE HEAD OF THE SOVIET UNION?
NO, THE SOVIET UNION IS OUT TOO.
NO SOVIET UNION?! QUICK ALERT THE WARSAW PACT!
...WE NEED TO TALK.

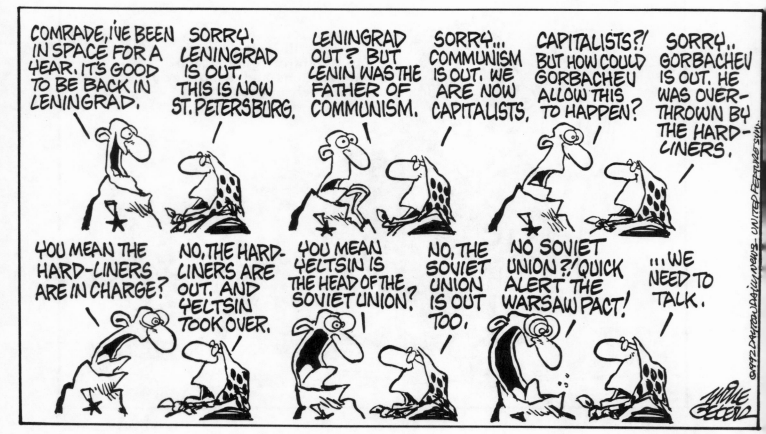

MIKE PETERS
Courtesy Dayton Daily News

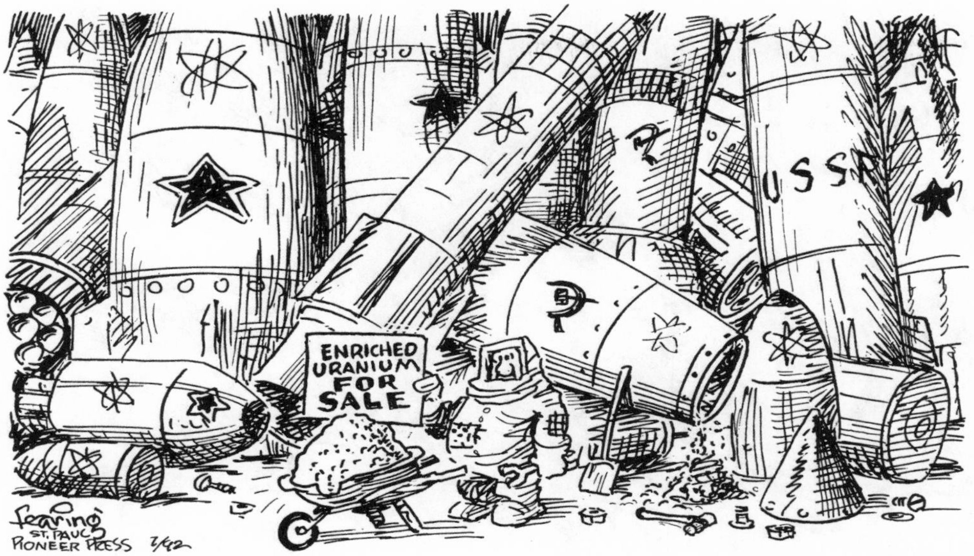
ENRICHED
URANIUM
FOR
SALE
USSR

JERRY FEARING
Courtesy St. Paul Pioneer Press-Dispatch

MALCOLM MAYES
Courtesy Edmonton Journal

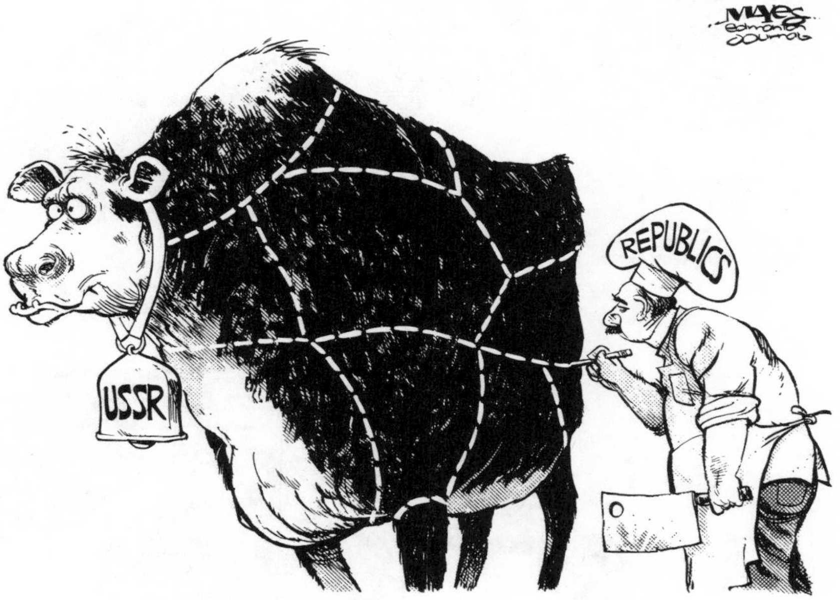
REPUBLICS
USSR

CHARLES BISSELL
Courtesy The Tennessean

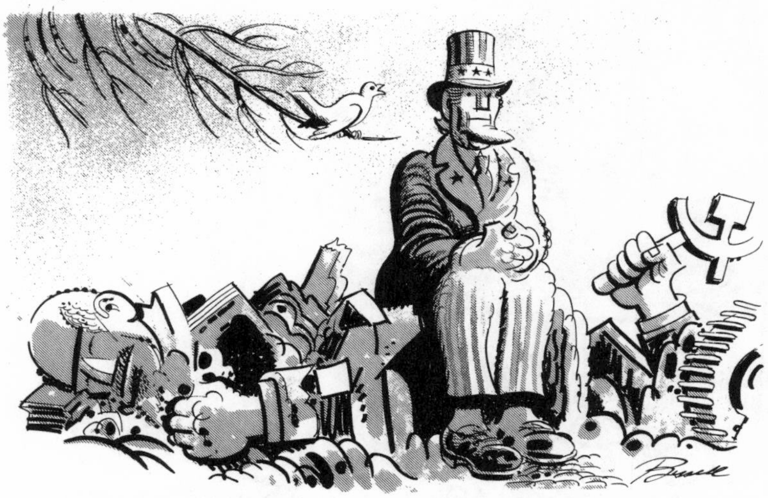

'You've spent trillions to shatter communism ... now do you have a package of inspiration up your sleeve?'

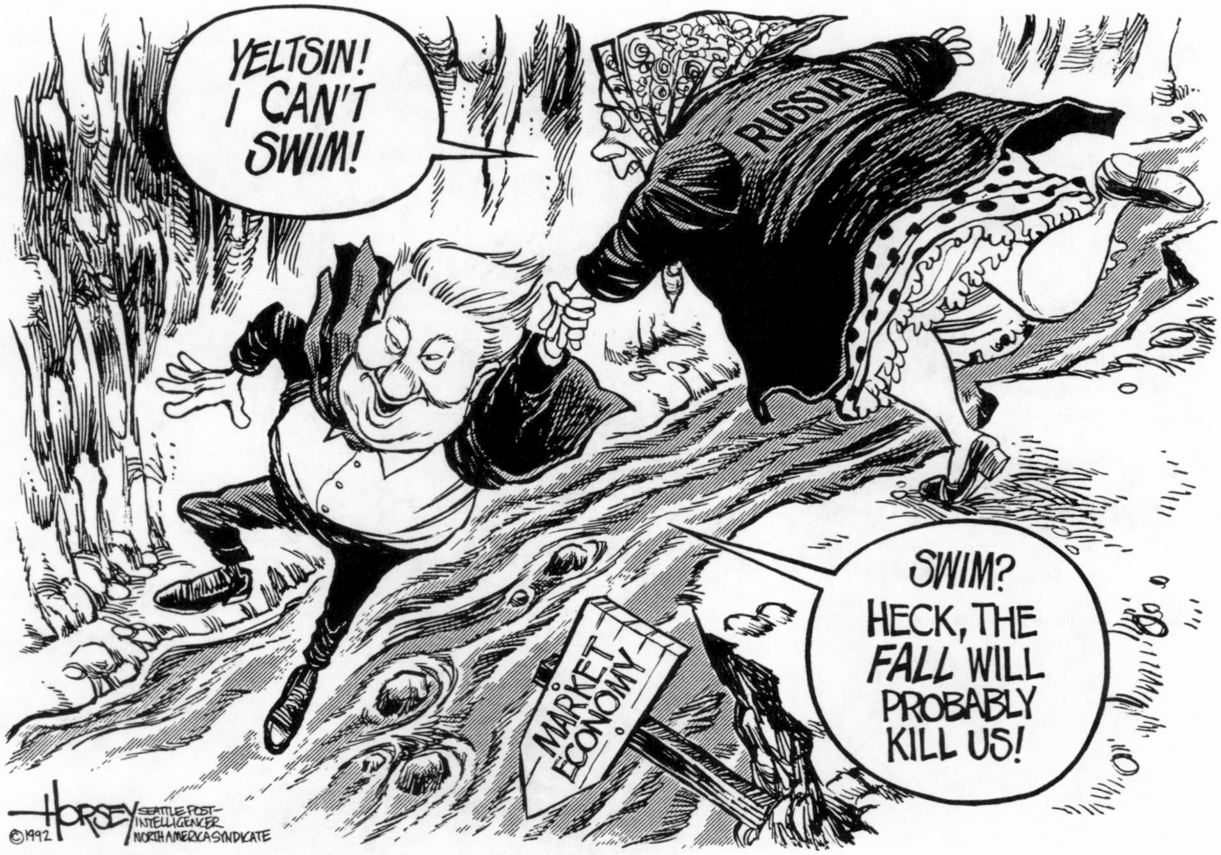
YELTSIN! I CAN'T SWIM!
RUSSIA
MARKET ECONOMY
SWIM? HECK, THE FALL WILL PROBABLY KILL US!
HORSEY SEATTLE POST-INTELLIGENCER NORTH AMERICA SYNDICATE ©1992

DAVID HORSEY
Courtesy Seattle Post-Intelligencer

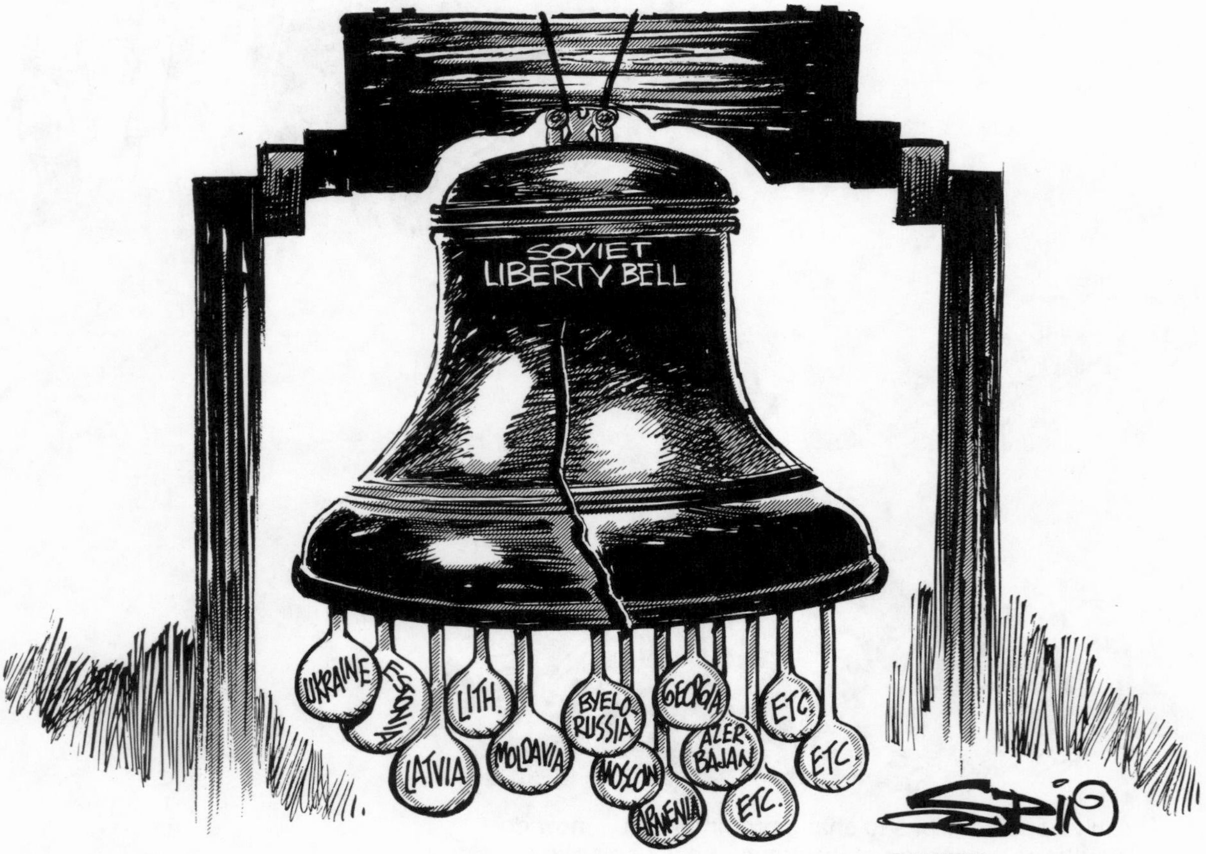
SOVIET LIBERTY BELL
UKRAINE
ESTONIA
LITH.
LATVIA
MOLDAVIA
BYELO RUSSIA
MOSCOW
ARMENIA
GEORGIA
AZER-BAJAN
ETC.
ETC.
ETC
OSRIN

RAY OSRIN
Courtesy Cleveland Plain Dealer

DAVID SWANN
Courtesy Huntsville Times (Ala.)

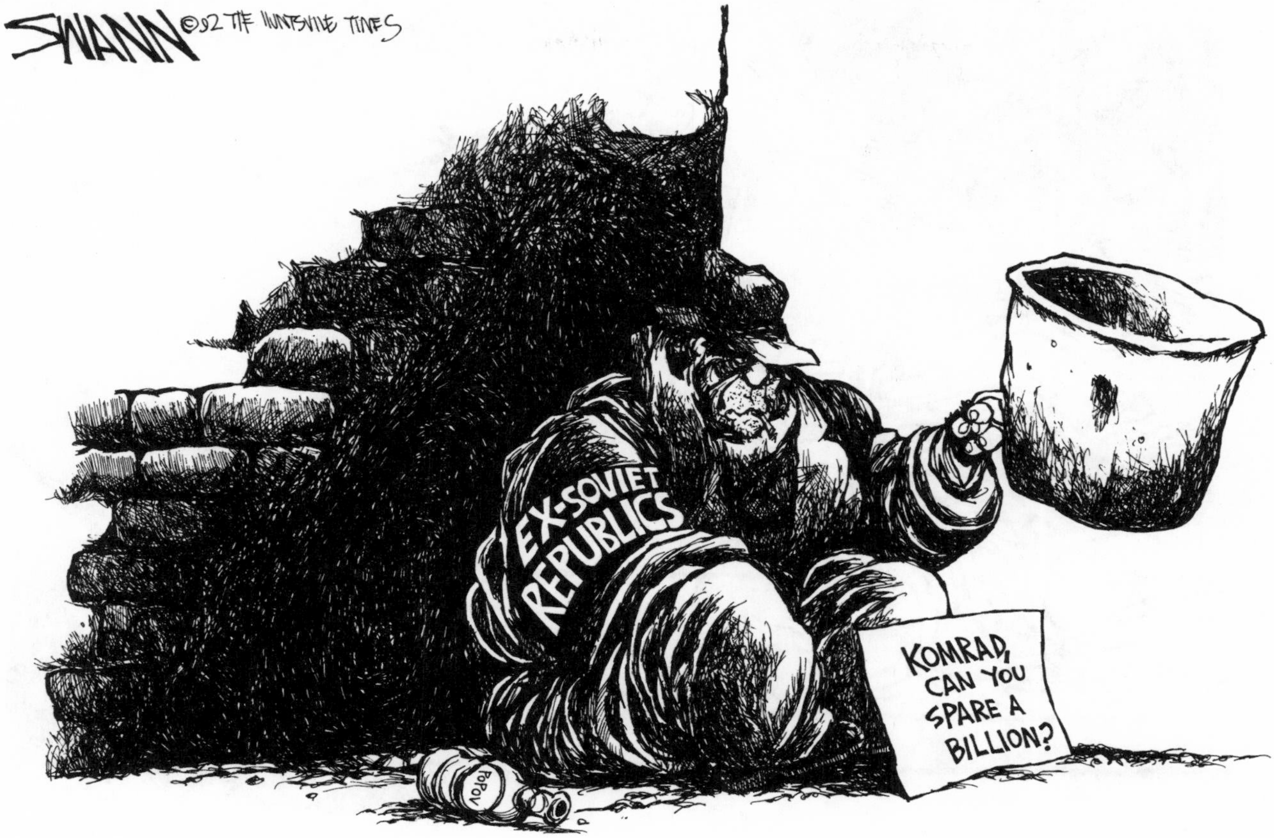
SWANN ©92 THE HUNTSVILLE TIMES
EX-SOVIET REPUBLICS
KOMRAD, CAN YOU SPARE A BILLION?
POPOV

LAMBERT DER
Courtesy Houston Post

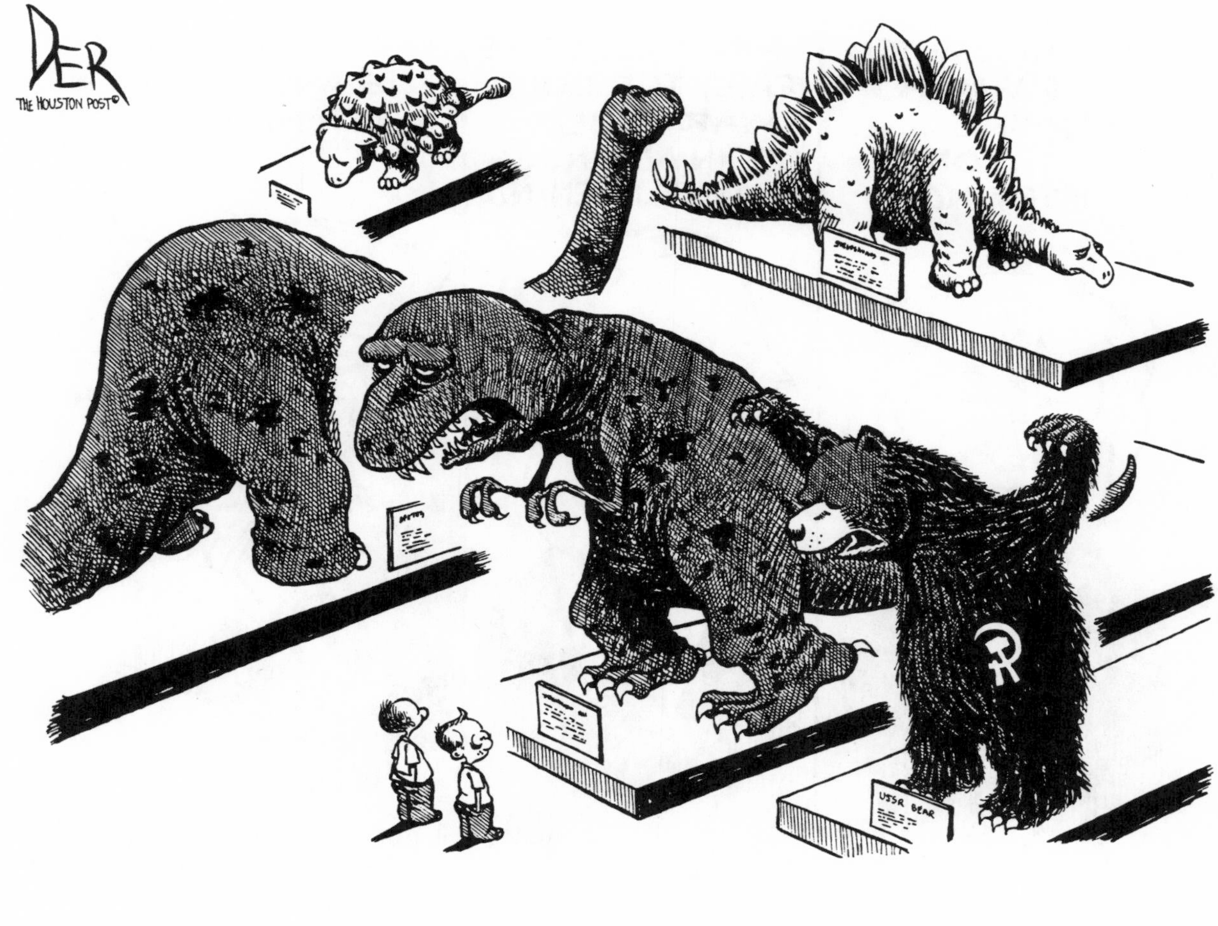
DER
THE HOUSTON POST©
USSR BEAR

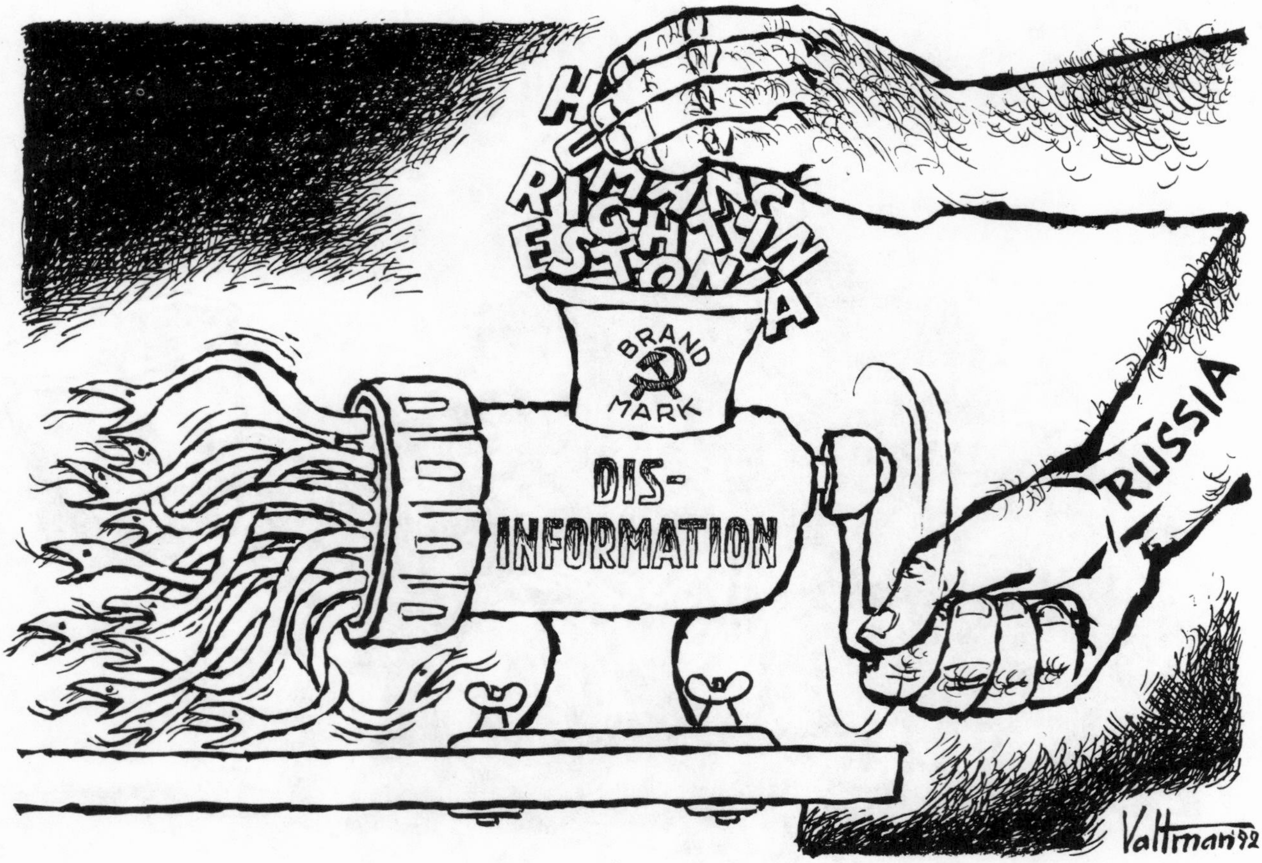
HUMAN RIGHTS IN ESTONIA
BRAND MARK
DIS-INFORMATION
RUSSIA
Valtman 92

EDMUND VALTMAN
Courtesy Chronicle and Middletown Press (Conn.)

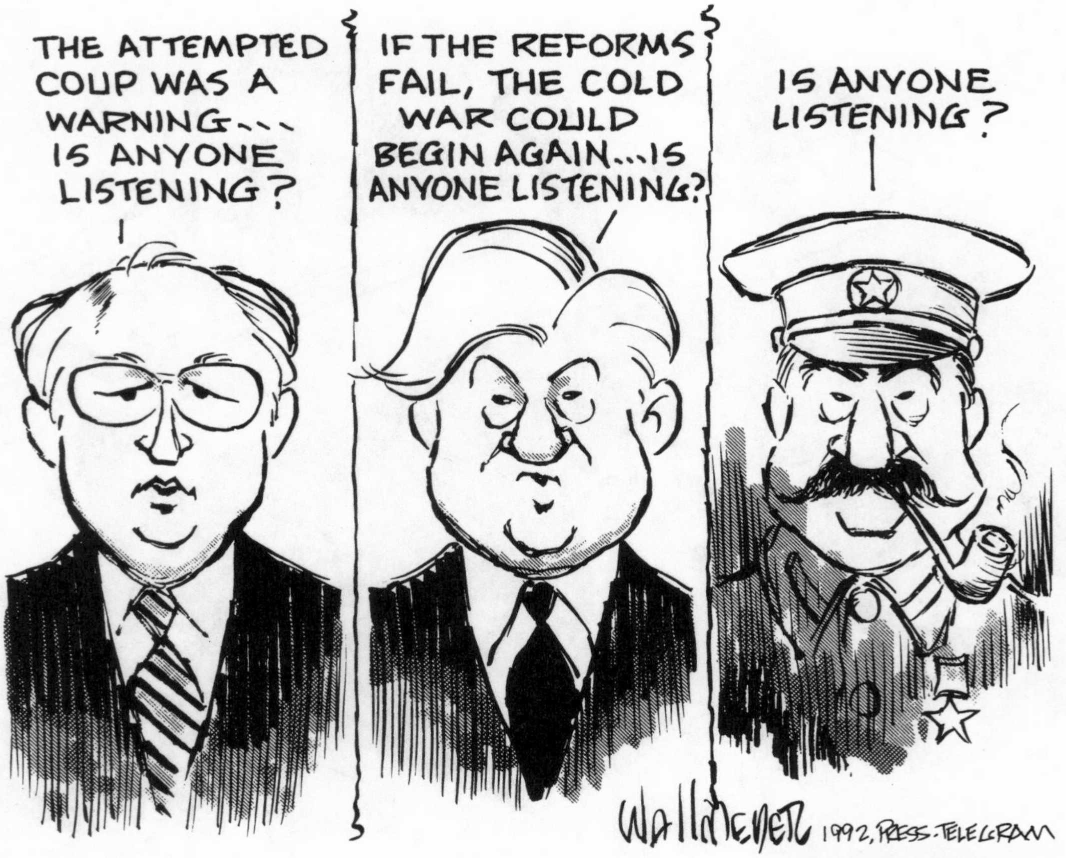
THE ATTEMPTED COUP WAS A WARNING... IS ANYONE LISTENING?
IF THE REFORMS FAIL, THE COLD WAR COULD BEGIN AGAIN...IS ANYONE LISTENING?
IS ANYONE LISTENING?
WALLMEYER 1992, PRESS-TELEGRAM

DICK WALLMEYER
Courtesy Long Beach Press-Telegram

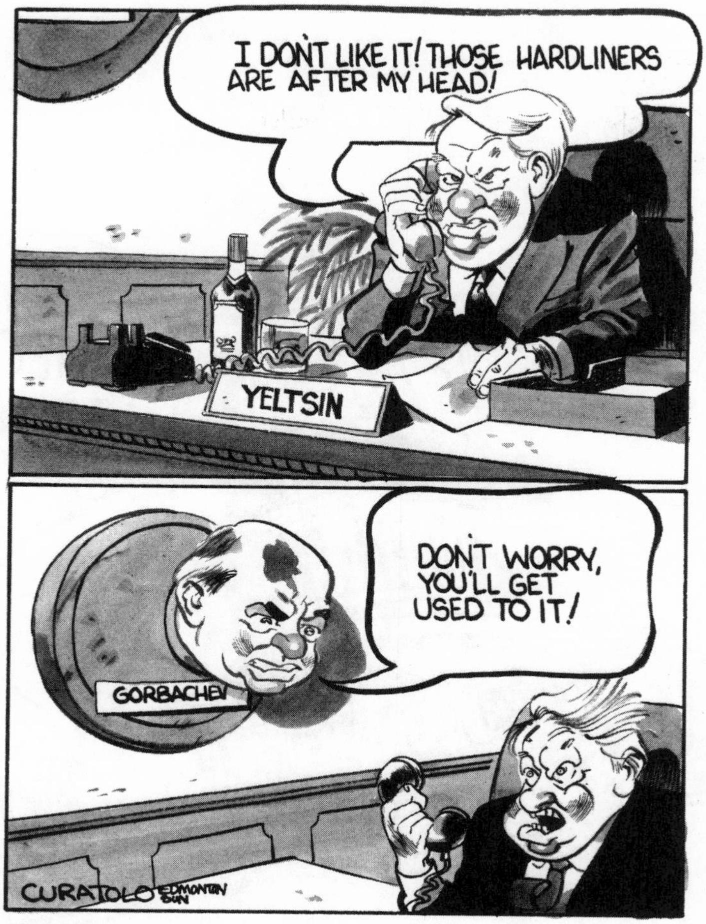
I DON'T LIKE IT! THOSE HARDLINERS ARE AFTER MY HEAD!
YELTSIN
DON'T WORRY, YOU'LL GET USED TO IT!
GORBACHEV
CURATOLO EDMONTON SUN
FRED CURATOLO
Courtesy Edmonton Sun

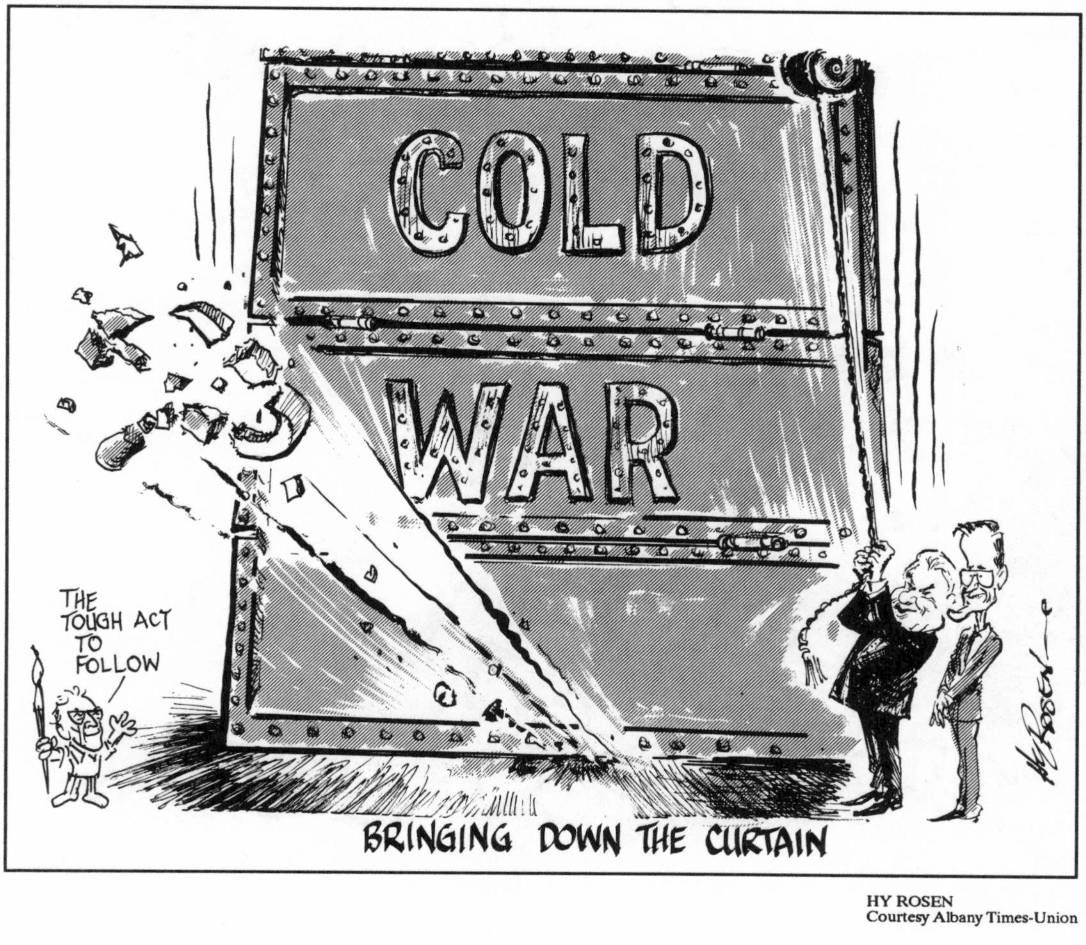
COLD WAR
THE TOUGH ACT TO FOLLOW
BRINGING DOWN THE CURTAIN
HY ROSEN
Courtesy Albany Times-Union

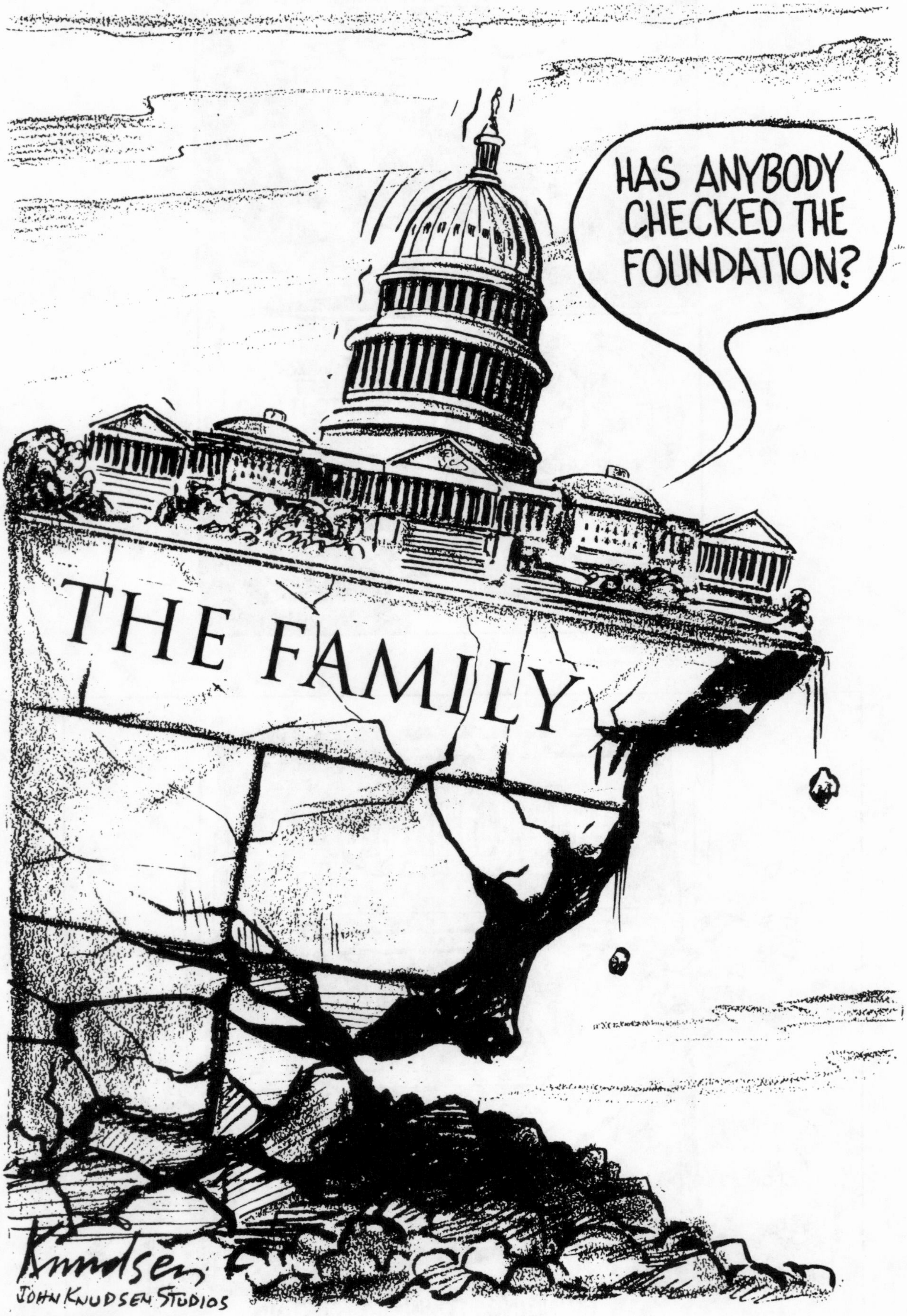
HAS ANYBODY CHECKED THE FOUNDATION?
THE FAMILY
Knudsen
JOHN KNUDSEN STUDIOS

JIM KNUDSEN
Courtesy The Tidings (Calif.)

Family Issues

Vice-President Dan Quayle touched off a rhubarb when he gave a speech criticizing television's portrayal of single motherhood. Quayle emphasized that he was not talking about single mothers who must work to support themselves and their children, but maintained that he thought the father should be present to round out the family. He also argued against having children out of wedlock and said that the highly rated television show "Murphy Brown" did not reflect his idea of upholding family values.

Democrats and Republicans jumped on the "family values" issue, and each sought to win votes with it. With the high divorce rate, the abortion debate, youngsters on drugs, and teenage crime, it seemed a legitimate subject for discussion. Studies have long showed that children who come from a traditional family structure – with both mother and father living in the home and carrying out their parental duties – are less likely to turn to crime or drugs.

Family values, of course, mean different things to different people. And that is where the politicians come in. So far no one has devised a plan that will stem the disintegration of the American family that has been going on since World War II.

A TALE OF TWO CITIES
FANTASY
HY ROSEN
REALITY
UNWED
TEEN
PREGNANT
WELCOME TO PRIME TIME U.S.A.

HY ROSEN
Courtesy Albany Times-Union

AND IN OTHER NEWS DEVELOPMENTS, THE WILLIAM KENNEDY SMITH TRIAL GOES ON... "WELL SHE GRABBED MY BLAH BLAH BLAH AND THEN WE BLAH BLAH, THEN SHE ASKED ME IF BLAH..."
SEX EDUCATION BEGINS AT HOME

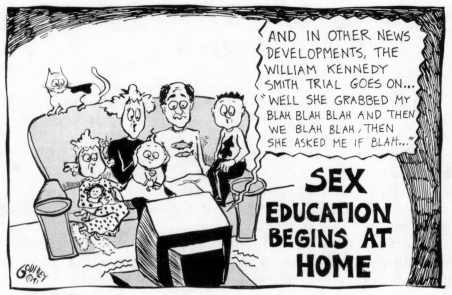

LINDA GODFREY
Courtesy Janesville Gazette
and Walworth County Week (Wis.)

JOHN BRANCH
Courtesy San Antonio Express-News

FIRE
AIR BAG
CONDOMS
ENCOURAGES YOUNG PEOPLE TO PLAY WITH MATCHES
ENCOURAGES YOUNG PEOPLE TO HAVE HEAD-ON COLLISIONS
ENCOURAGES YOUNG PEOPLE TO HAVE SEX

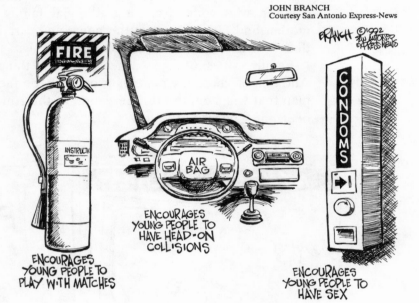

V. CULLUM ROGERS
Courtesy Spectator Magazine

Remember, dear— In spite of everything, she's still OURS!

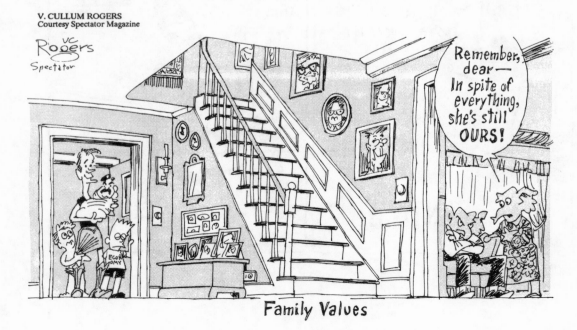

Family Values

STEVE MCBRIDE
Courtesy Independence Daily Reporter (Kan.)

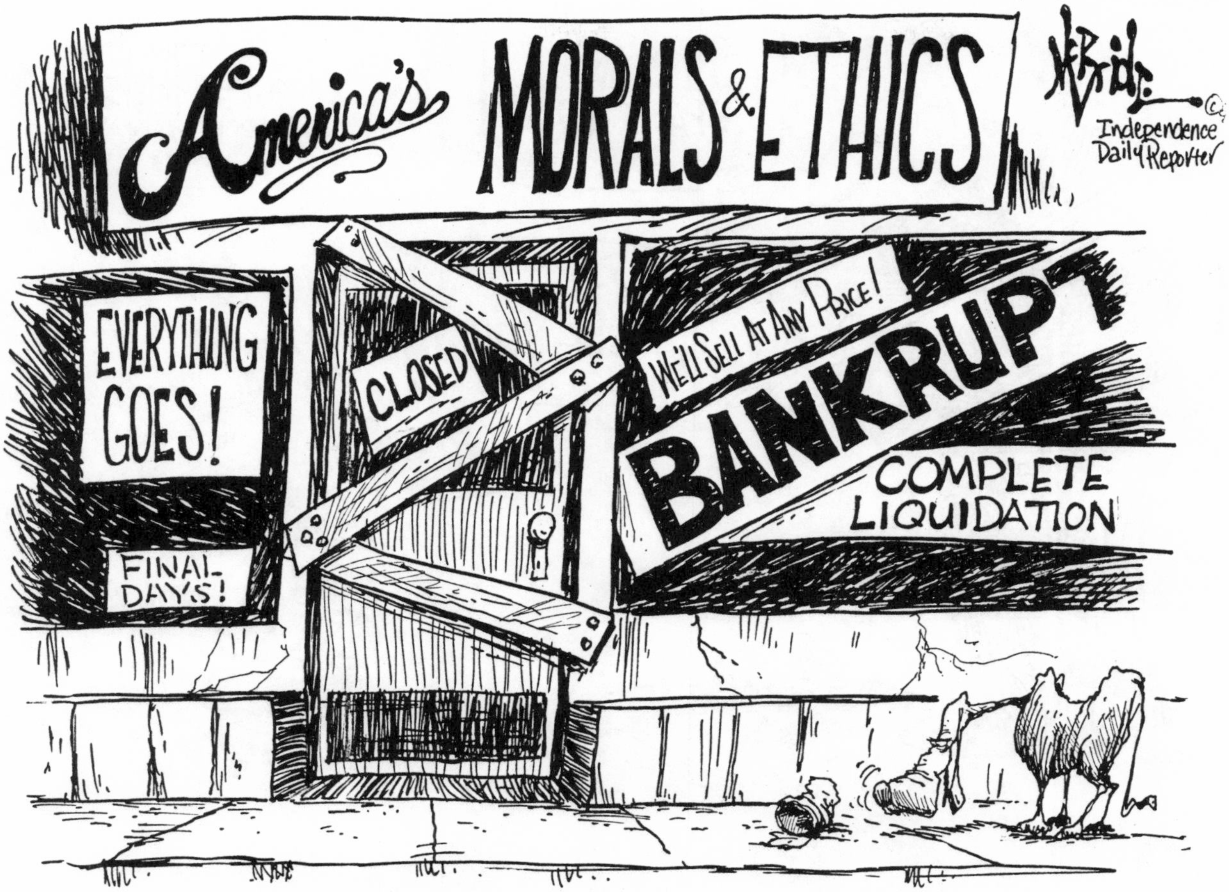
McBride © Independence Daily Reporter
America's MORALS & ETHICS
EVERYTHING GOES!
FINAL DAYS!
CLOSED
WE'LL SELL AT ANY PRICE!
BANKRUPT
COMPLETE LIQUIDATION

JIM BORGMAN
Courtesy Cincinnati Enquirer

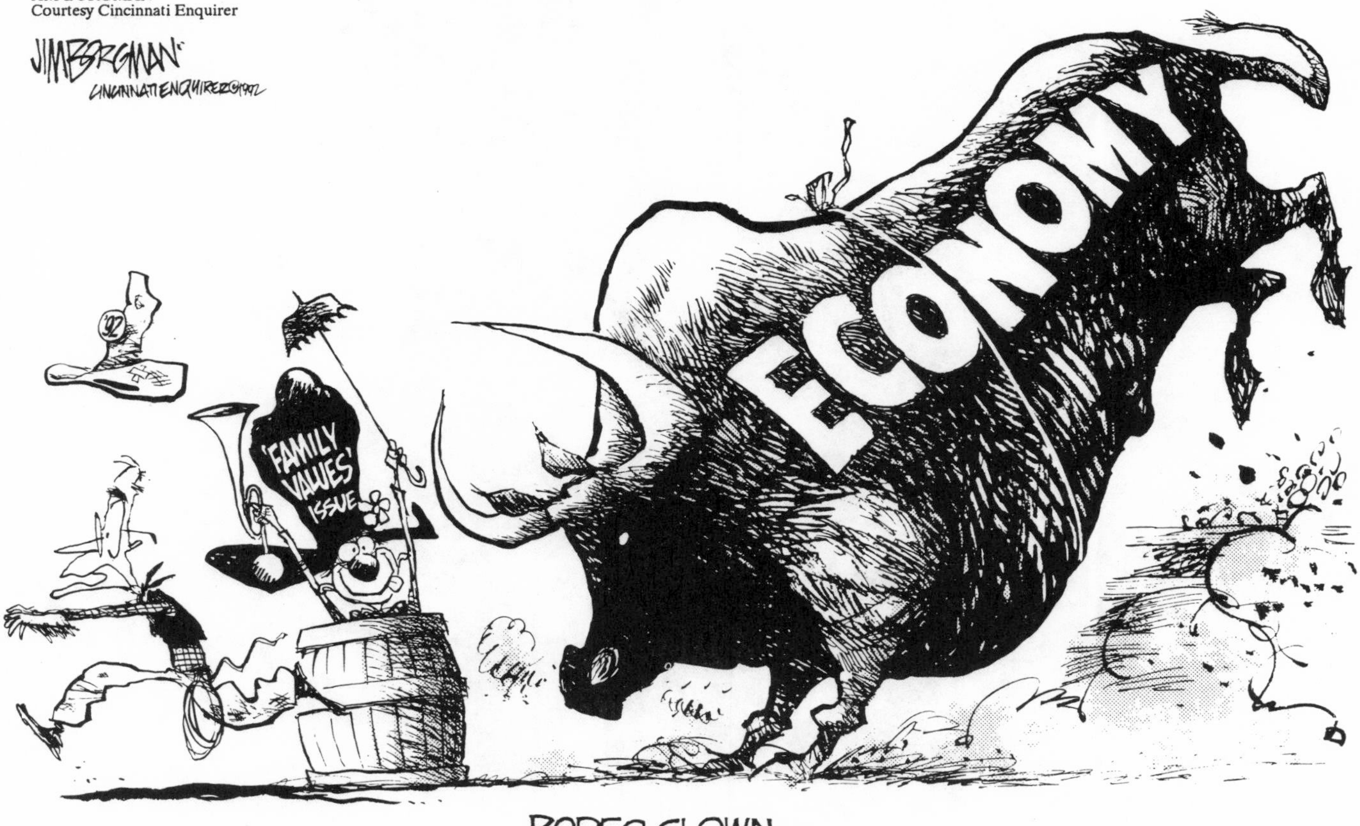
JIM BORGMAN CINCINNATI ENQUIRER ©1992
'FAMILY VALUES' ISSUE
ECONOMY

RODEO CLOWN

JEFF STAHLER
Courtesy Cincinnati Post

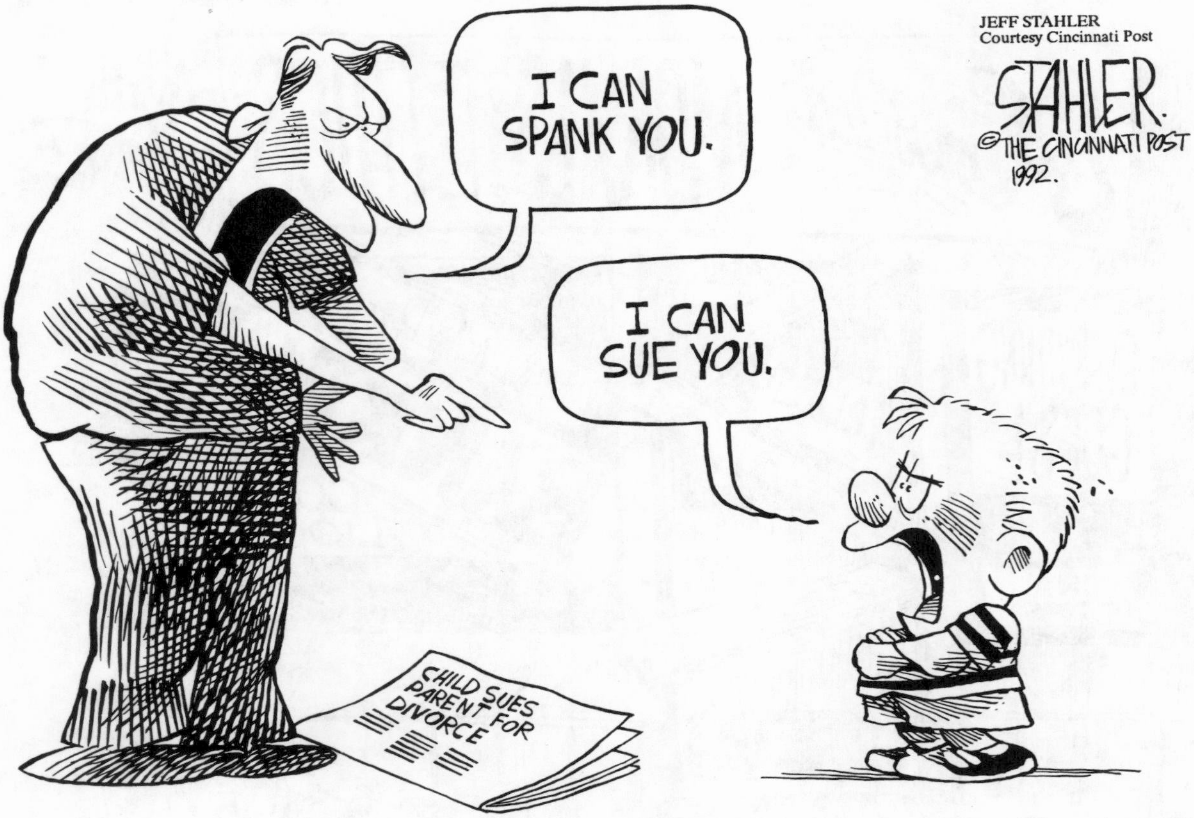
I CAN SPANK YOU.
I CAN SUE YOU.
CHILD SUES PARENT FOR DIVORCE
STAHLER.
© THE CINCINNATI POST 1992.

ALAN KING
Courtesy Ottawa Citizen

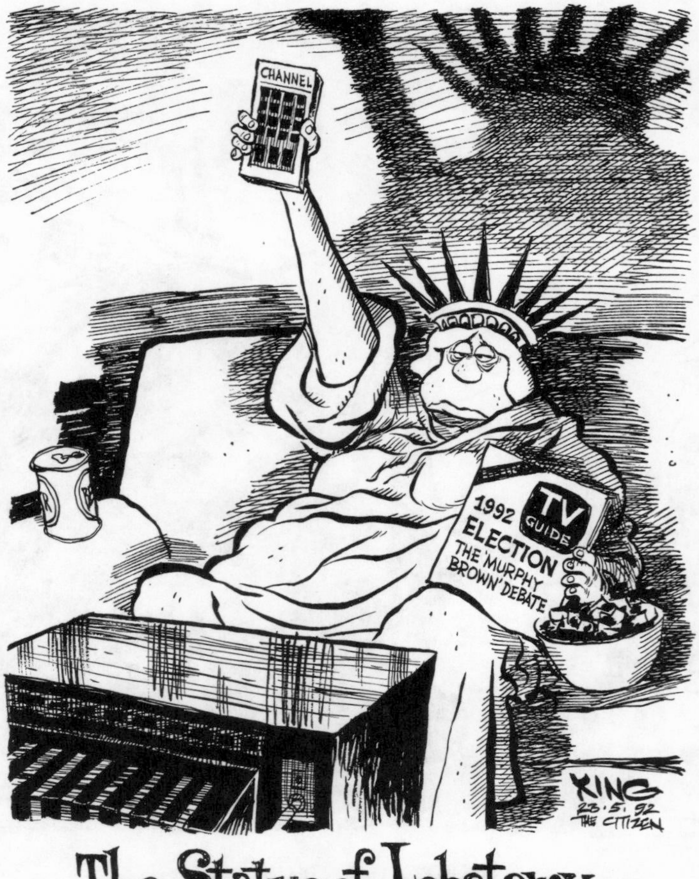
CHANNEL
1992
TV GUIDE
ELECTION
THE 'MURPHY BROWN' DEBATE
KING 23.5.92 THE CITIZEN

The Statue of Lobotomy

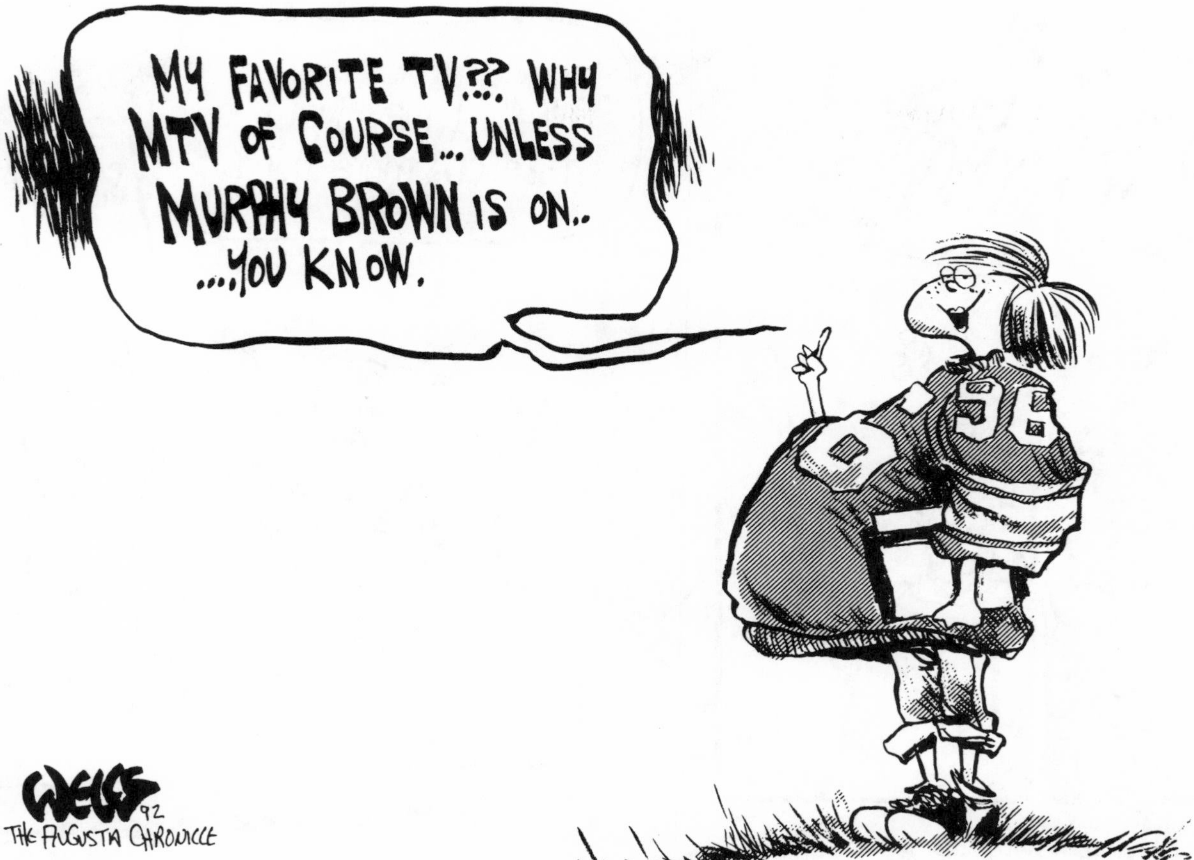
MY FAVORITE TV??? WHY MTV OF COURSE... UNLESS MURPHY BROWN IS ON.. ...YOU KNOW.
WELLS 92
THE AUGUSTA CHRONICLE

CLYDE WELLS
Courtesy Augusta Chronicle

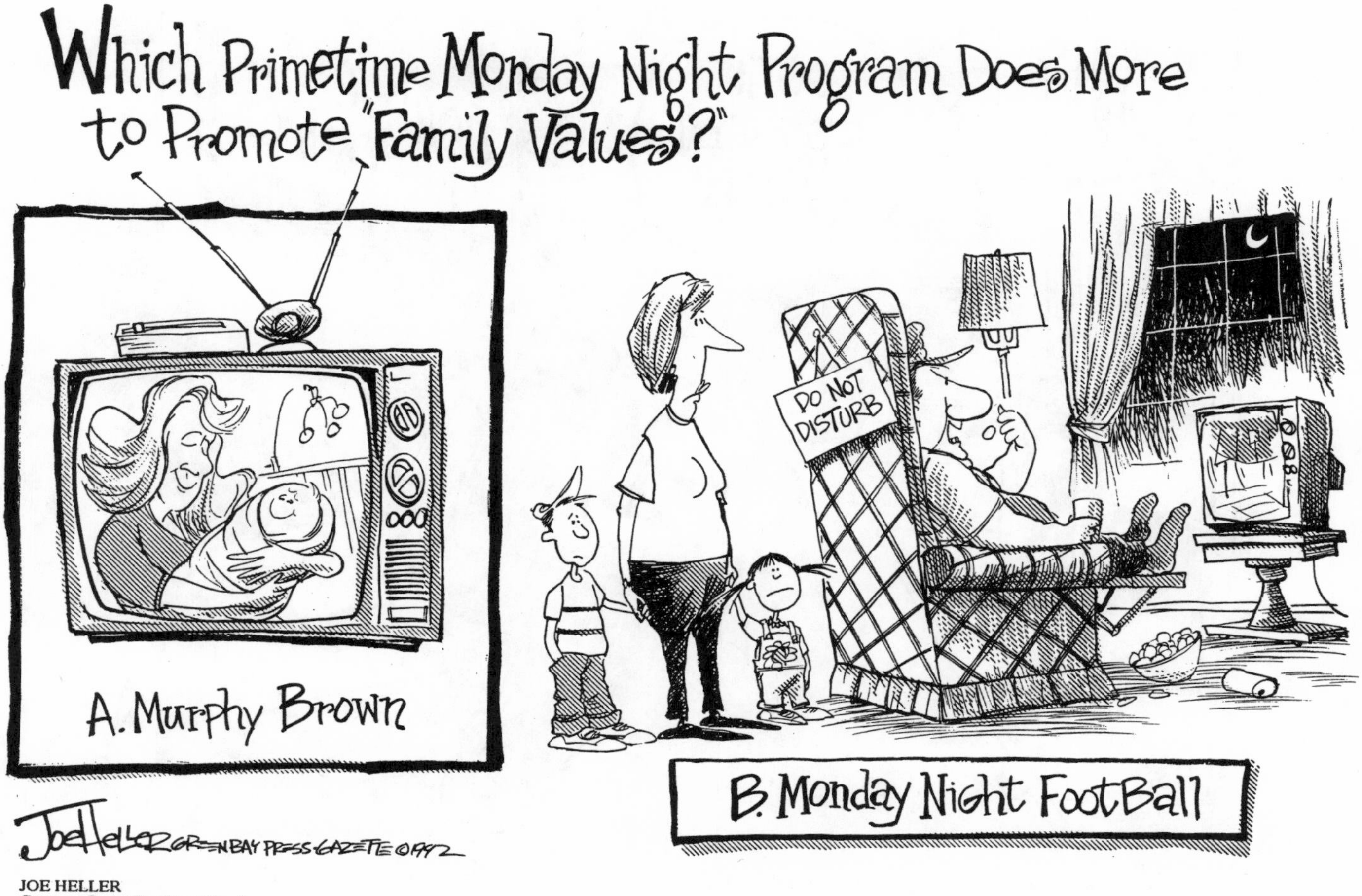
Which Primetime Monday Night Program Does More to Promote "Family Values?"
A. Murphy Brown
DO NOT DISTURB
B. Monday Night FootBall
Joe Heller GREEN BAY PRESS-GAZETTE ©1992

JOE HELLER
Courtesy Green Bay Press-Gazette

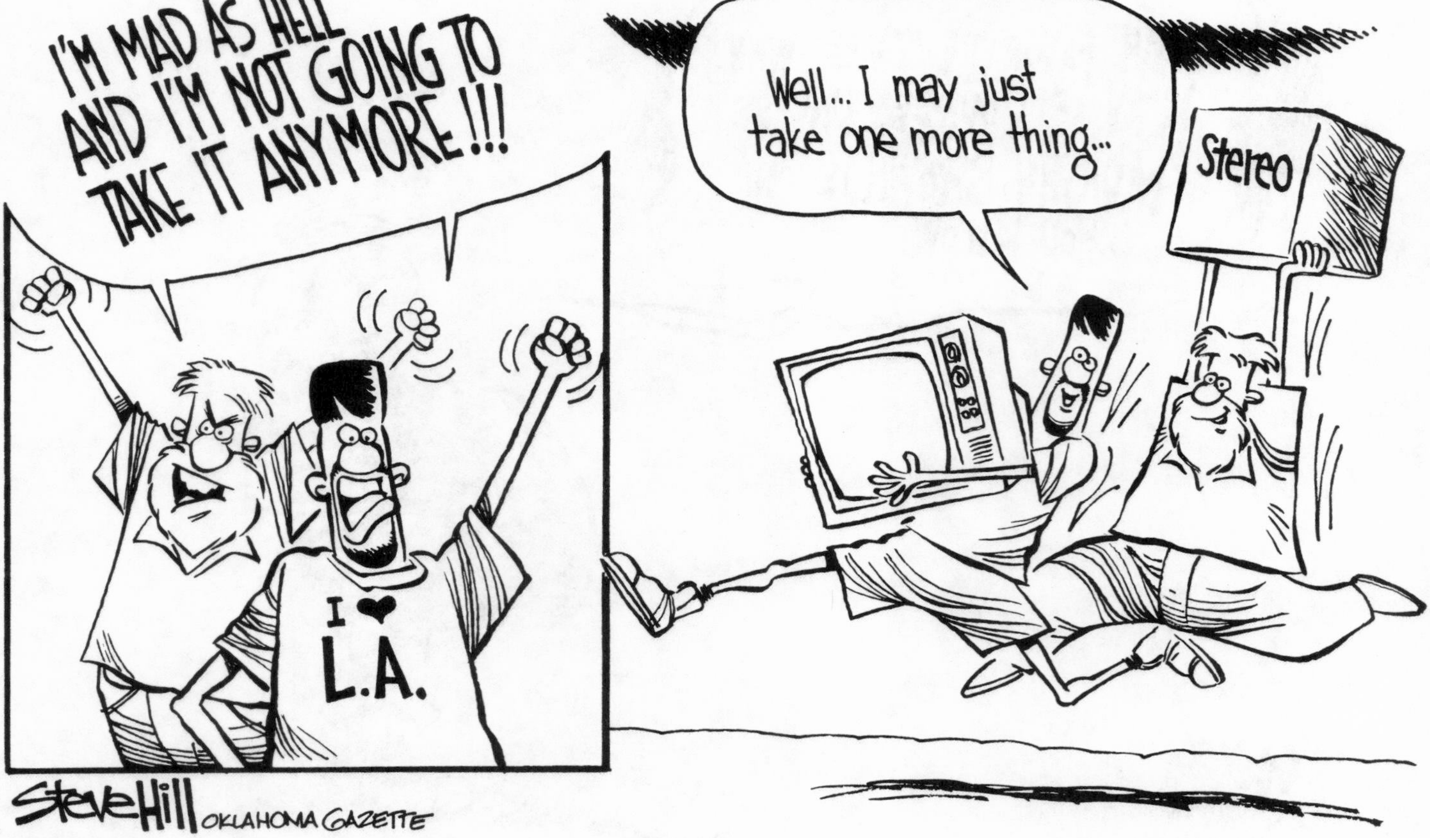
I'M MAD AS HELL AND I'M NOT GOING TO TAKE IT ANYMORE!!!
Well... I may just take one more thing...
Stereo
I ❤ L.A.
SteveHill OKLAHOMA GAZETTE

STEVE HILL
Courtesy Oklahoma Gazette

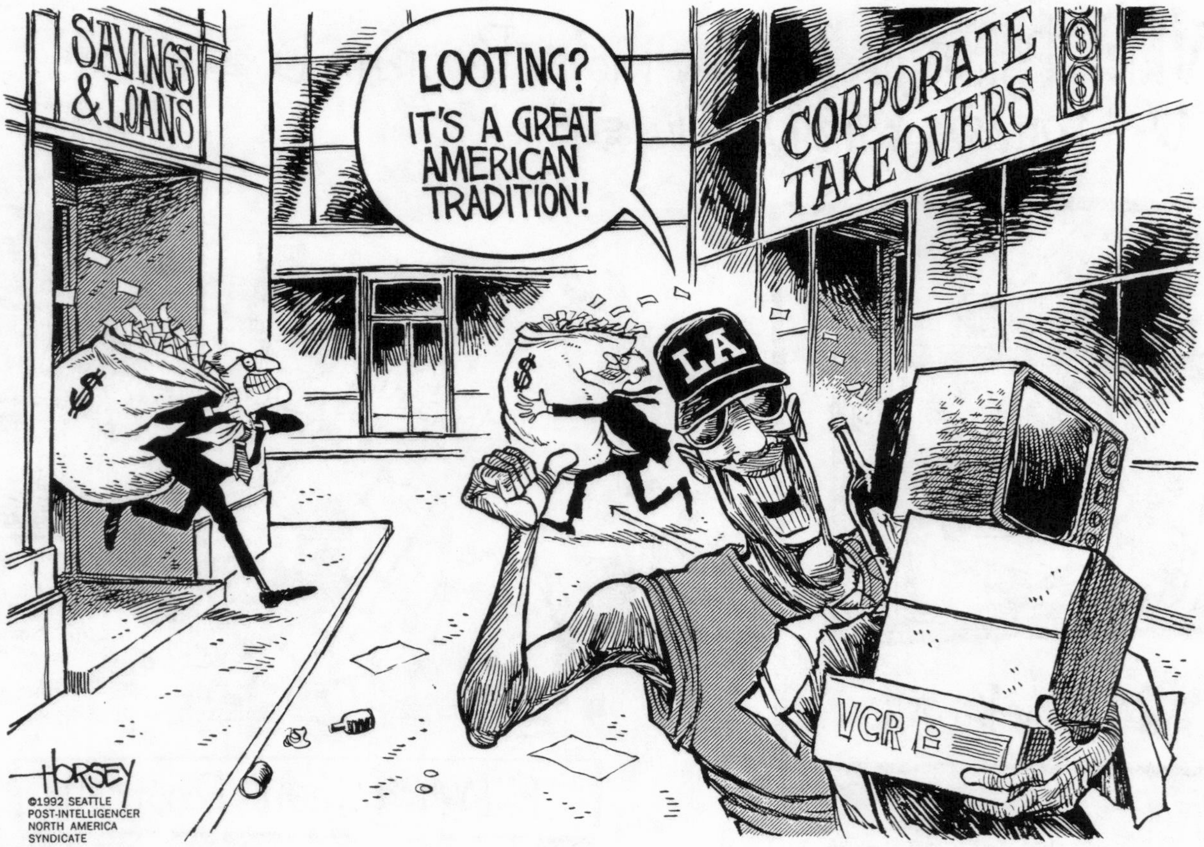
SAVINGS & LOANS
LOOTING? IT'S A GREAT AMERICAN TRADITION!
CORPORATE TAKEOVERS
LA
VCR
HORSEY
©1992 SEATTLE POST-INTELLIGENCER NORTH AMERICA SYNDICATE

DAVID HORSEY
Courtesy Seattle Post-Intelligencer

Crime

In April, one Hispanic, one Asian, and ten white jurors handed down a verdict of "not guilty" in the case of four Los Angeles policemen who were caught on camera clubbing Rodney King while making an arrest. In the wake of the verdict, protesters rampaged through the city, setting 5,000 fires and looting homes and stores of untold millions. Riot-control troops were sent in as fifty-eight people were killed.

A dangerous new craze–carjacking–picked up steam in 1992. During the first ten months of the year, more than 21,000 automobile owners were separated from their vehicles.

Protests mounted against violence portrayed on television and in movies. The lead characters often are portrayed as enjoying violence and killing. Often there is little plot–just car wrecks, brutality, and death. Neither television nor the movie industry seems concerned. Both media focus more and more on depicting alternative lifestyles and a wide range of sexual situations that would not have been shown just a few years ago.

White-collar crimes–insurance scams, health-care fraud, and telemarketing and computer crime–continued to increase. And the savings and loan bailout, made necessary by a wide range of banking fraud, will cost taxpayers at least $160 billion through 1995.

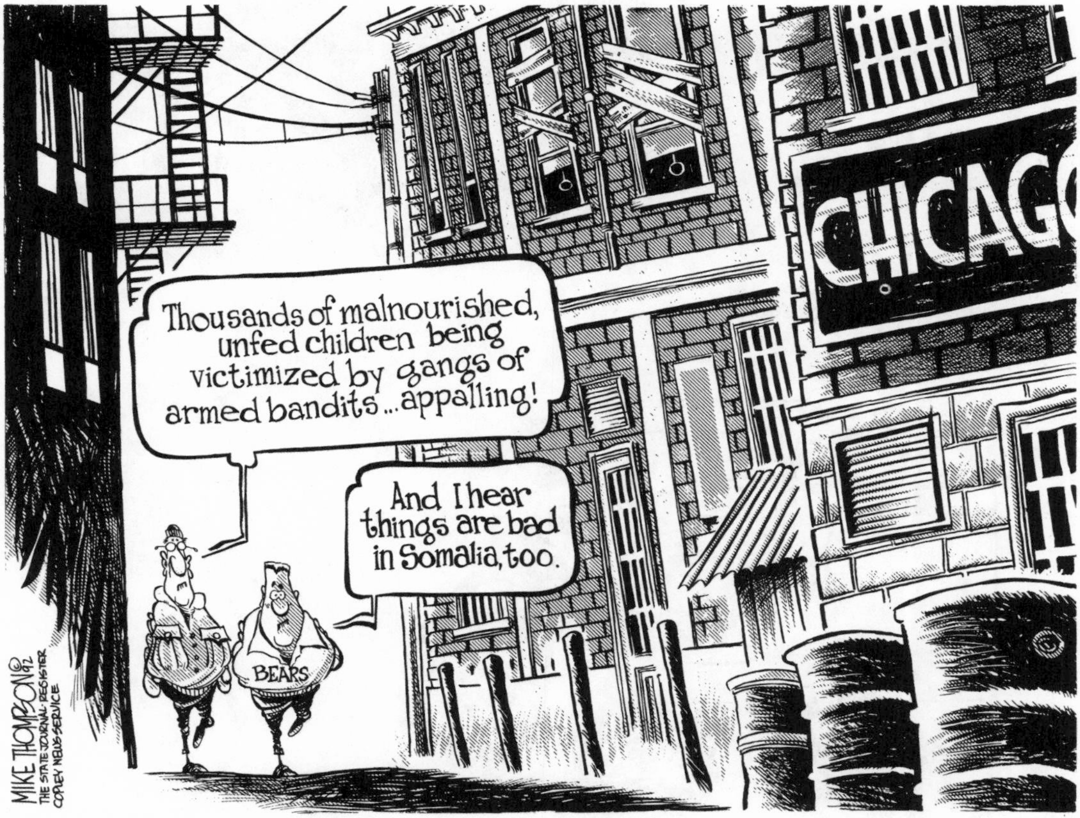
CHICAGO
Thousands of malnourished, unfed children being victimized by gangs of armed bandits...appalling!
And I hear things are bad in Somalia, too.
BEARS
MIKE THOMPSON ©92
THE STATE JOURNAL-REGISTER
COPLEY NEWS SERVICE

MIKE THOMPSON
Courtesy State Journal-Register (Ill.)

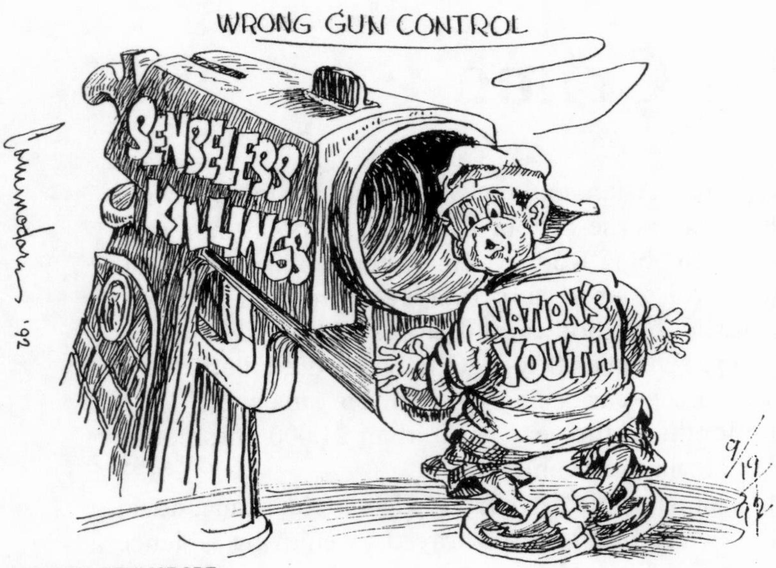
WRONG GUN CONTROL
SENSELESS KILLINGS
NATION'S YOUTH

CHESTER COMMODORE
Courtesy Chicago Defender

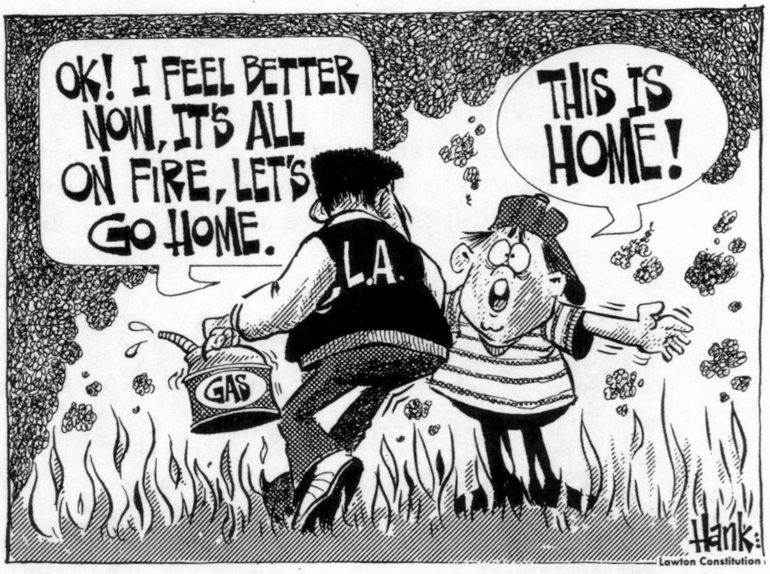
OK! I FEEL BETTER NOW, IT'S ALL ON FIRE, LET'S GO HOME.
THIS IS HOME!
L.A.
GAS
Hank
Lawton Constitution

HANK MCCLURE
Courtesy Lawton Constitution

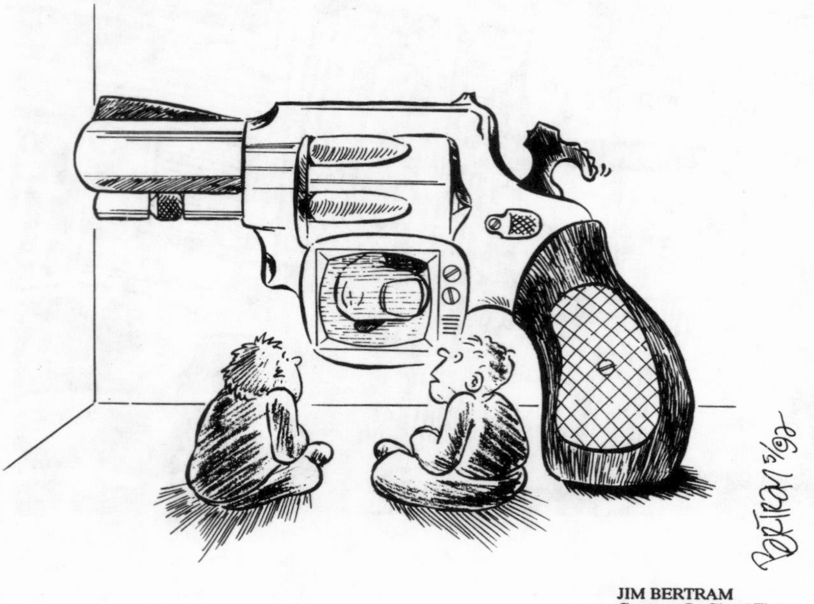

JIM BERTRAM
Courtesy St. Cloud Times

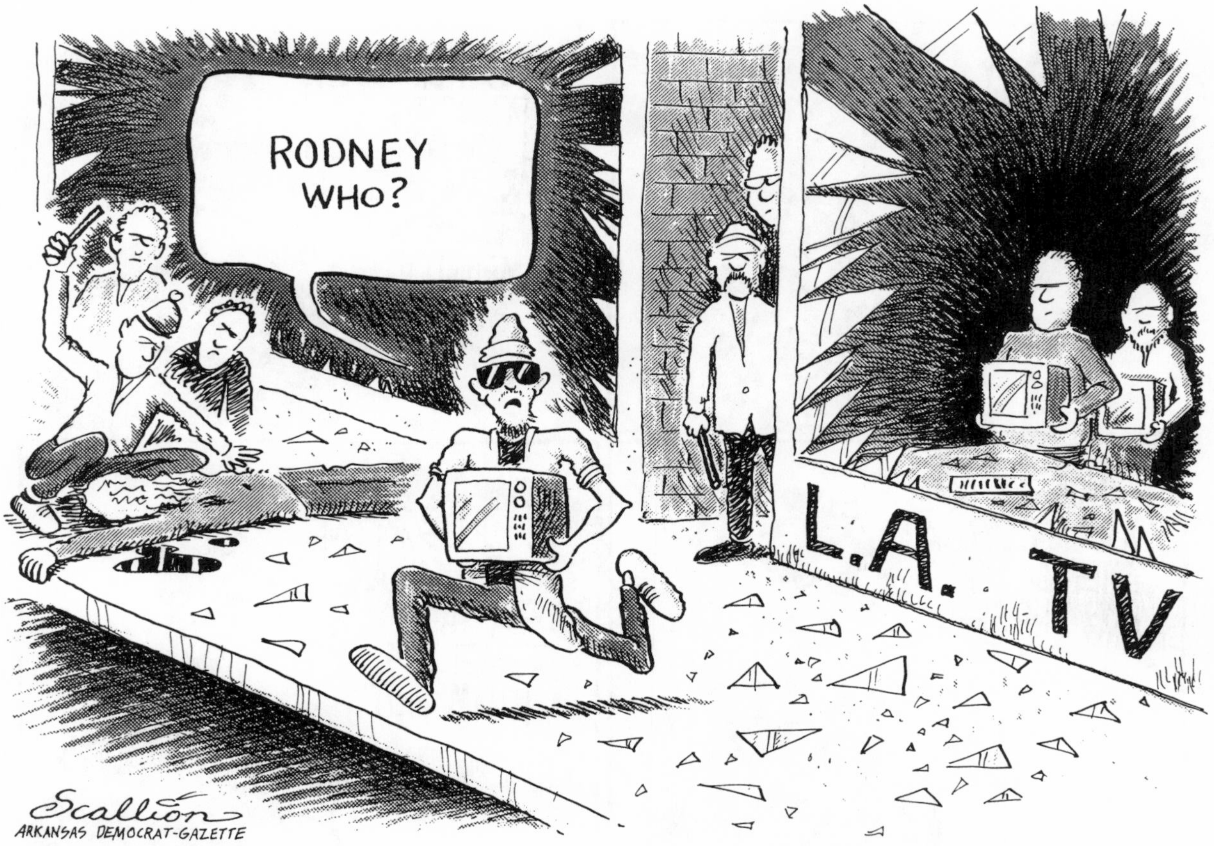
RODNEY WHO?
L.A. TV
Scallion
ARKANSAS DEMOCRAT-GAZETTE

STEVE SCALLION
Courtesy Arkansas Democrat-Gazette

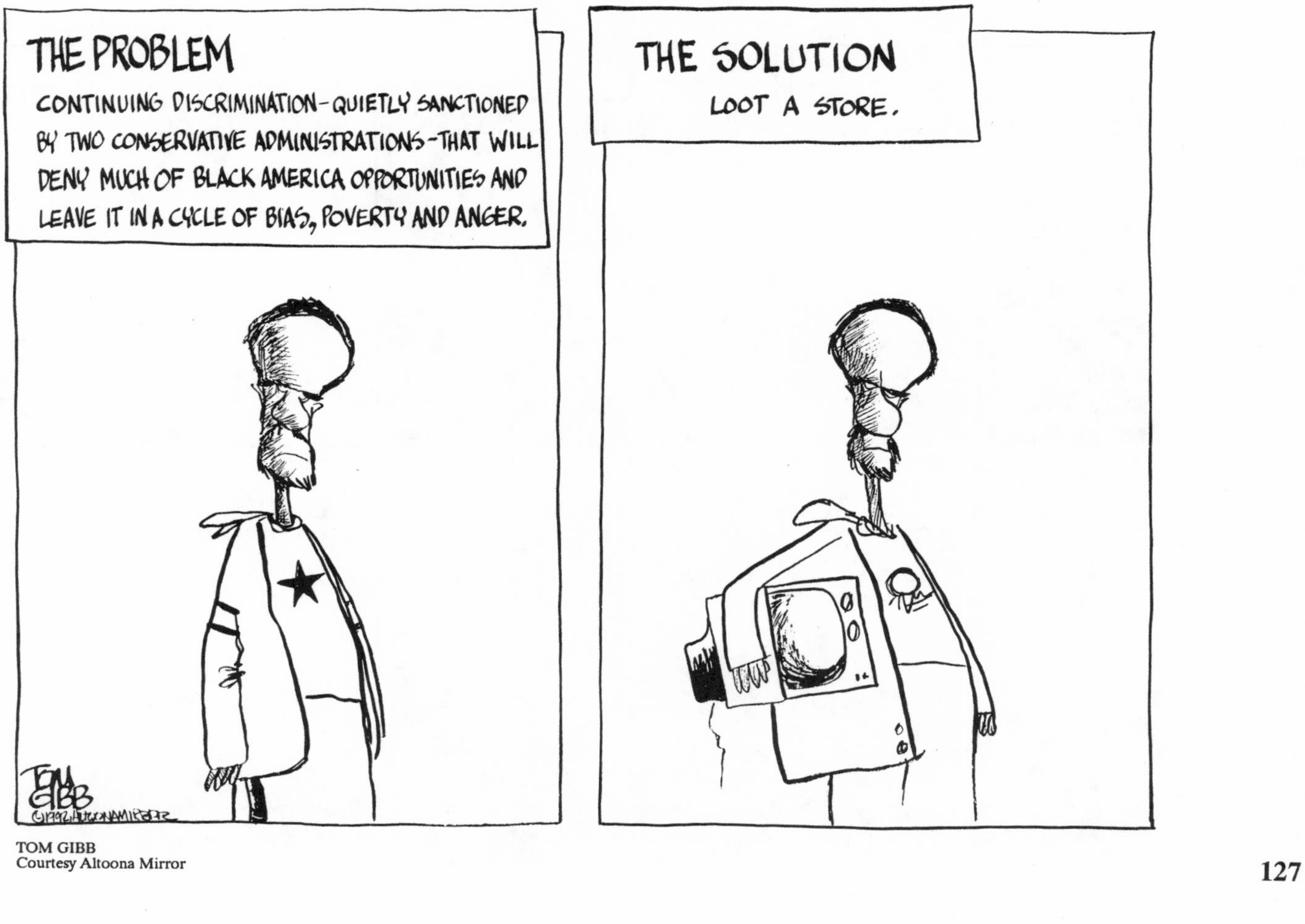
THE PROBLEM
CONTINUING DISCRIMINATION—QUIETLY SANCTIONED BY TWO CONSERVATIVE ADMINISTRATIONS—THAT WILL DENY MUCH OF BLACK AMERICA OPPORTUNITIES AND LEAVE IT IN A CYCLE OF BIAS, POVERTY AND ANGER.
THE SOLUTION
LOOT A STORE.
TOM GIBB

TOM GIBB
Courtesy Altoona Mirror

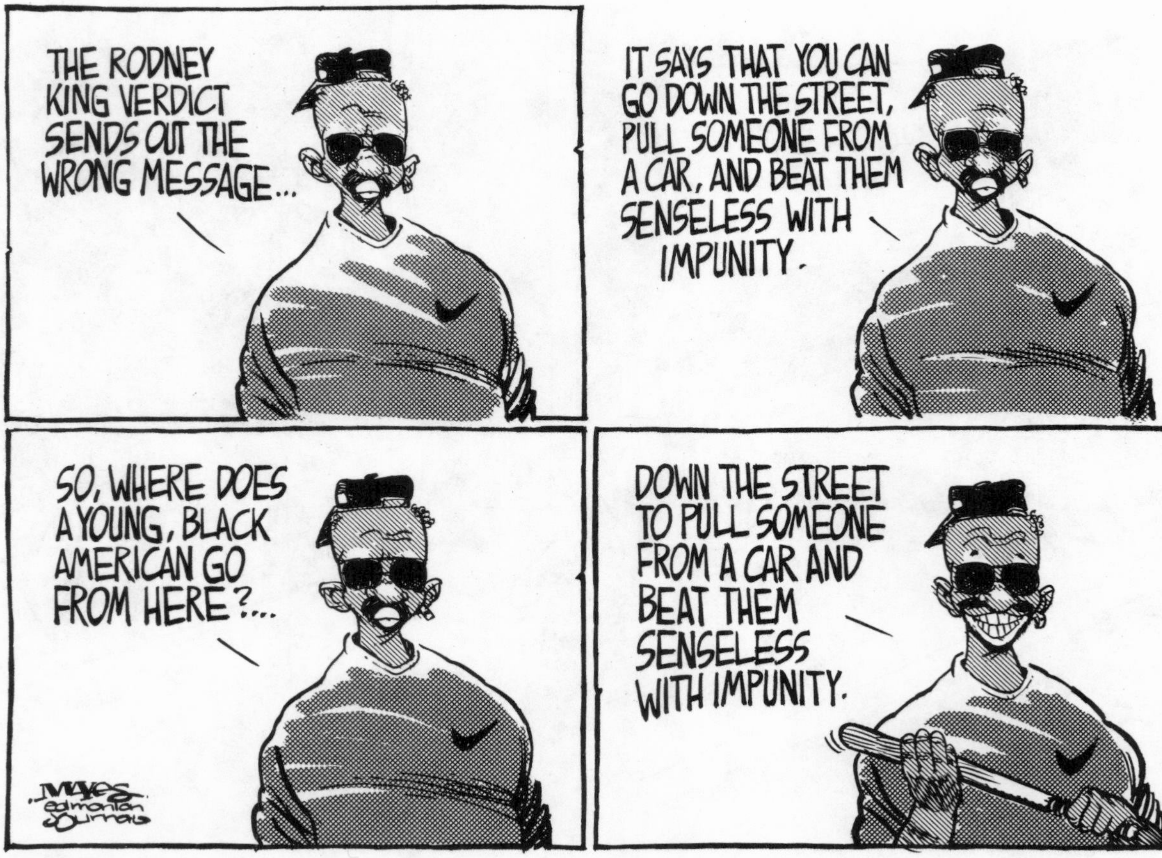
THE RODNEY KING VERDICT SENDS OUT THE WRONG MESSAGE...
IT SAYS THAT YOU CAN GO DOWN THE STREET, PULL SOMEONE FROM A CAR, AND BEAT THEM SENSELESS WITH IMPUNITY.
SO, WHERE DOES A YOUNG, BLACK AMERICAN GO FROM HERE?...
DOWN THE STREET TO PULL SOMEONE FROM A CAR AND BEAT THEM SENSELESS WITH IMPUNITY.
MAYES Edmonton Journal

MALCOLM MAYES
Courtesy Edmonton Journal

KIRK ANDERSON
Courtesy Madison (Wis.) Capital Times

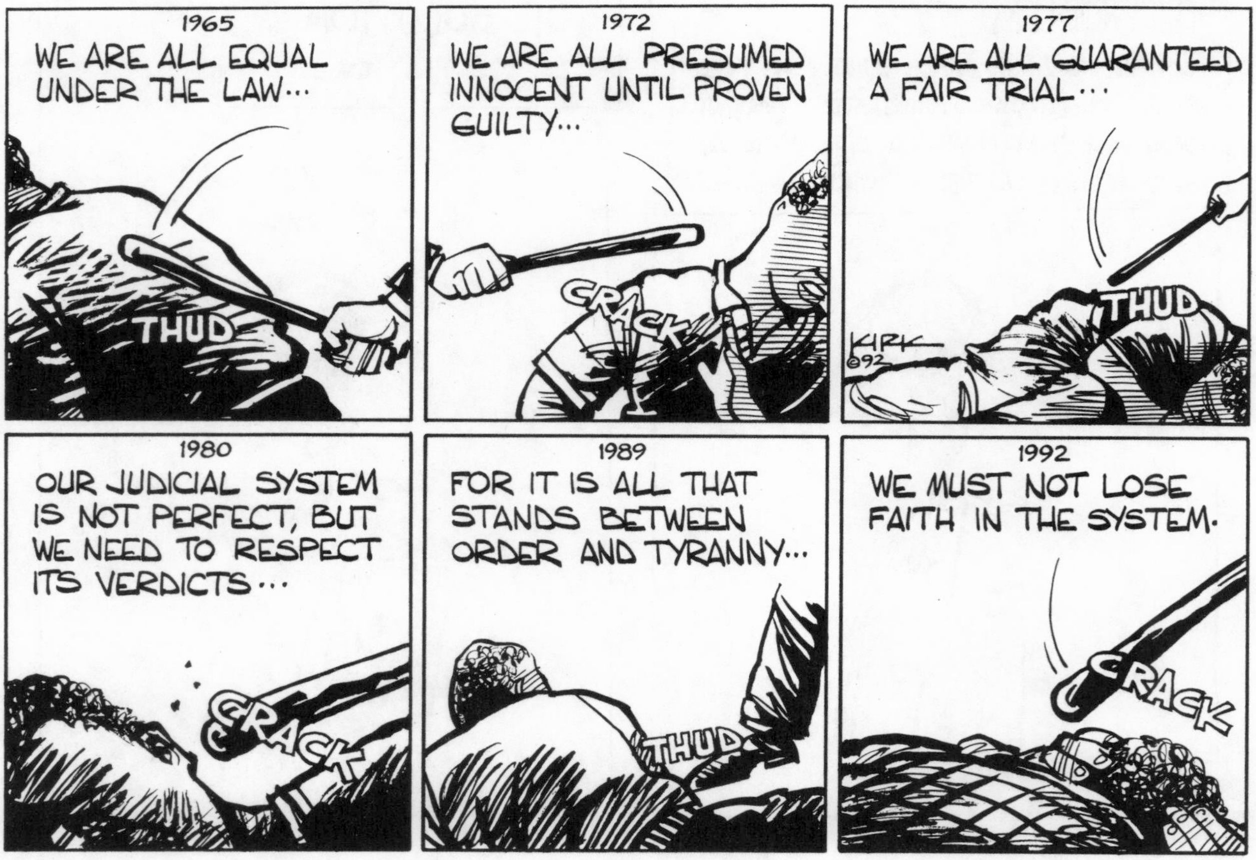
1965
WE ARE ALL EQUAL UNDER THE LAW...
THUD
1972
WE ARE ALL PRESUMED INNOCENT UNTIL PROVEN GUILTY...
CRACK
1977
WE ARE ALL GUARANTEED A FAIR TRIAL...
THUD
KIRK ©92
1980
OUR JUDICIAL SYSTEM IS NOT PERFECT, BUT WE NEED TO RESPECT ITS VERDICTS...
CRACK
1989
FOR IT IS ALL THAT STANDS BETWEEN ORDER AND TYRANNY...
THUD
1992
WE MUST NOT LOSE FAITH IN THE SYSTEM.
CRACK

NOW KEEP A SHARP EYE OUT FOR CAR JACKERS, DEAR! KEEP THE DOORS LOCKED AND WINDOWS UP AT ALL TIMES!
...If anyone approaches the car at a stop light... you scream and I'LL blow the horn... O.K?!
...and please don't point the gun in this direction!!
Stop the car! Let's just stay at home, dear!
good idea... it's safer!
screech!

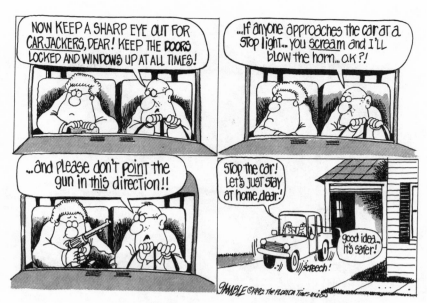

ED GAMBLE
Courtesy Florida Times-Union

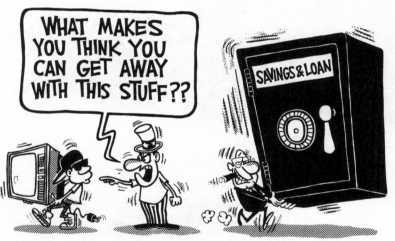

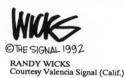

WHAT MAKES YOU THINK YOU CAN GET AWAY WITH THIS STUFF??
SAVINGS & LOAN
WICKS
©THE SIGNAL 1992

RANDY WICKS
Courtesy Valencia Signal (Calif.)

MARK CULLUM
Courtesy Birmingham News

SKYSCRAPERS, MASS TRANSIT, SATELLITE COMMUNICATIONS... DO YOU THINK OUR GREAT GRANDFATHERS WOULD RECOGNIZE OUR MODERN CULTURE?
PARTS OF IT.
VIOLENT CRIME

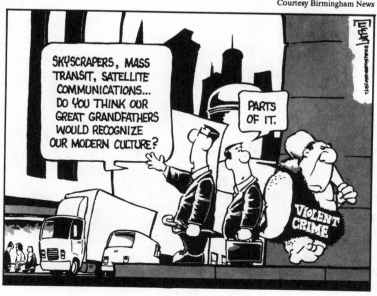

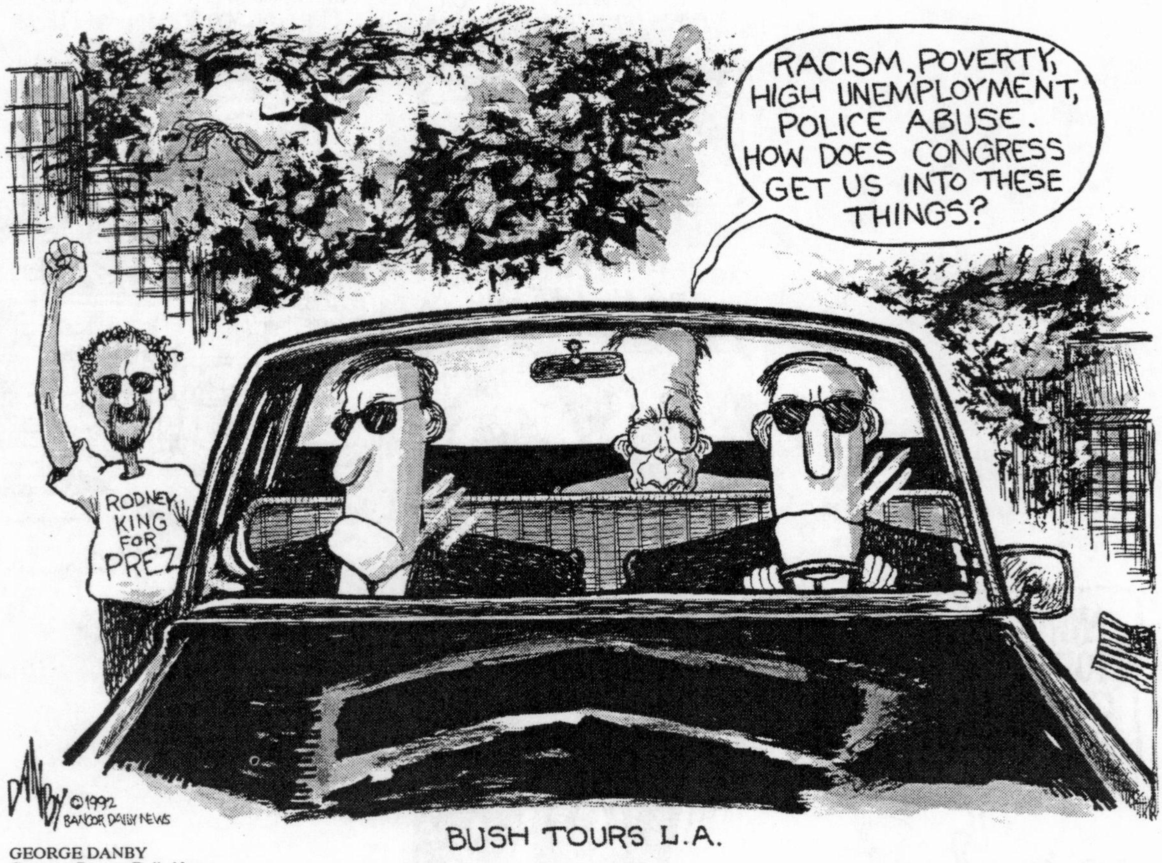
RACISM, POVERTY, HIGH UNEMPLOYMENT, POLICE ABUSE. HOW DOES CONGRESS GET US INTO THESE THINGS?
RODNEY KING FOR PREZ
DANBY ©1992 BANGOR DAILY NEWS
BUSH TOURS L.A.

GEORGE DANBY
Courtesy Bangor Daily News

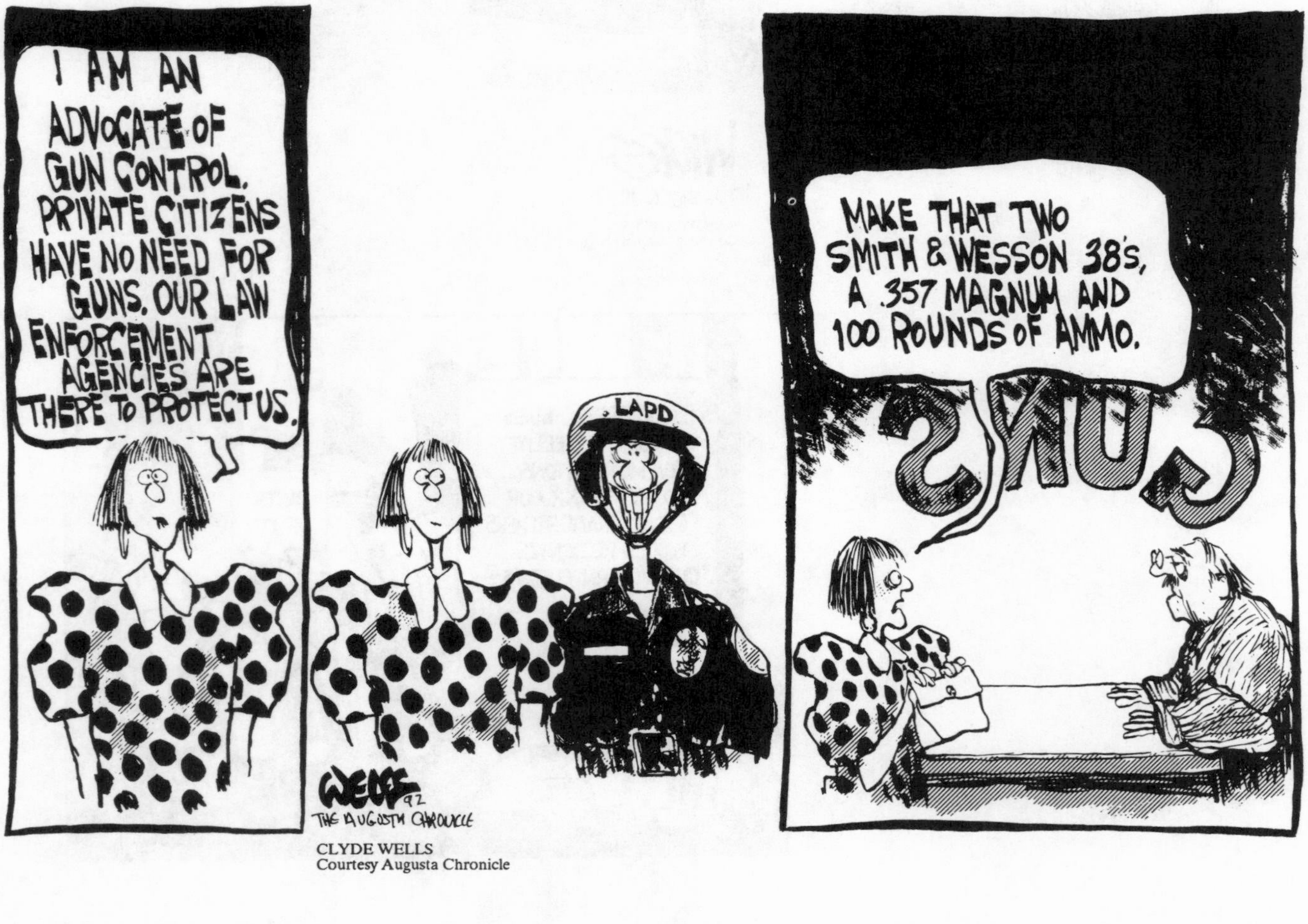
I AM AN ADVOCATE OF GUN CONTROL. PRIVATE CITIZENS HAVE NO NEED FOR GUNS. OUR LAW ENFORCEMENT AGENCIES ARE THERE TO PROTECT US.
LAPD
MAKE THAT TWO SMITH & WESSON 38's, A .357 MAGNUM AND 100 ROUNDS OF AMMO.
GUNS
WELLS 92 THE AUGUSTA CHRONICLE

CLYDE WELLS
Courtesy Augusta Chronicle

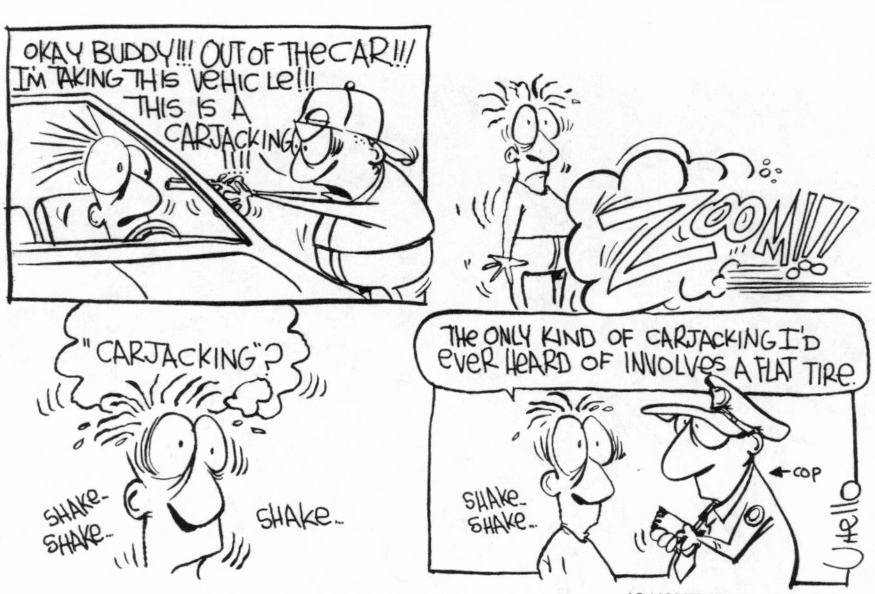
OKAY BUDDY!!! OUT OF THE CAR!!! I'M TAKING THIS VEHICLE!!! THIS IS A CARJACKING!!!!
ZOOM!!!
"CARJACKING"?
SHAKE-SHAKE... SHAKE...
THE ONLY KIND OF CARJACKING I'D EVER HEARD OF INVOLVES A FLAT TIRE.
←COP
SHAKE-SHAKE...
Vitello

ALAN VITELLO
Courtesy Daily Times-Call (Col.)

ROD WARREN
Courtesy Bakersfield Californian

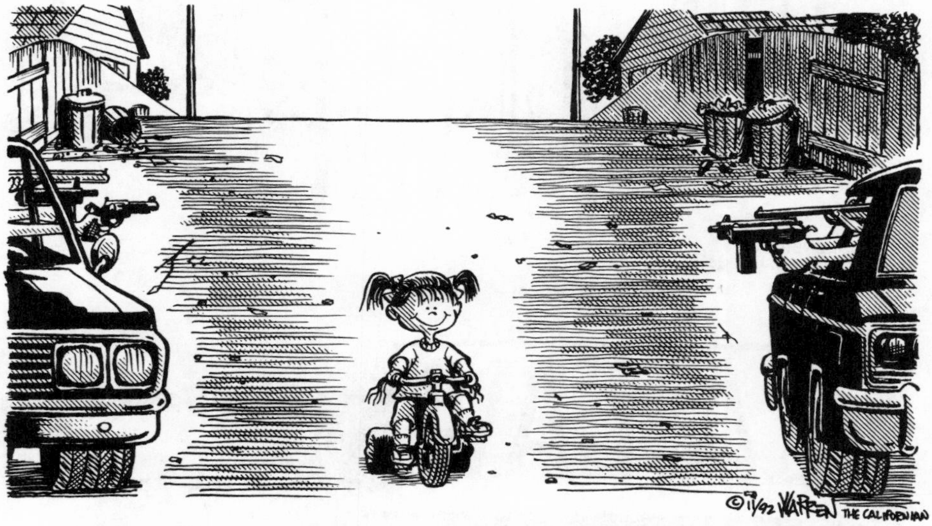
WARREN THE CALIFORNIAN

PARENTS, DO YOU KNOW WHERE YOUR CHILDREN ARE?

MILT PRIGGEE
Courtesy Spokane Spokesman-Review

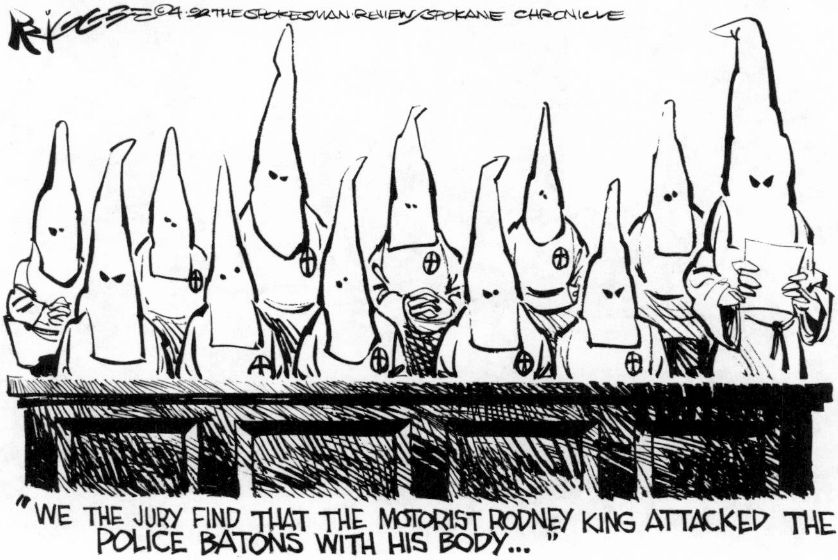
PRIGGEE ©4.92 THE SPOKESMAN-REVIEW/SPOKANE CHRONICLE

"WE THE JURY FIND THAT THE MOTORIST RODNEY KING ATTACKED THE POLICE BATONS WITH HIS BODY..."

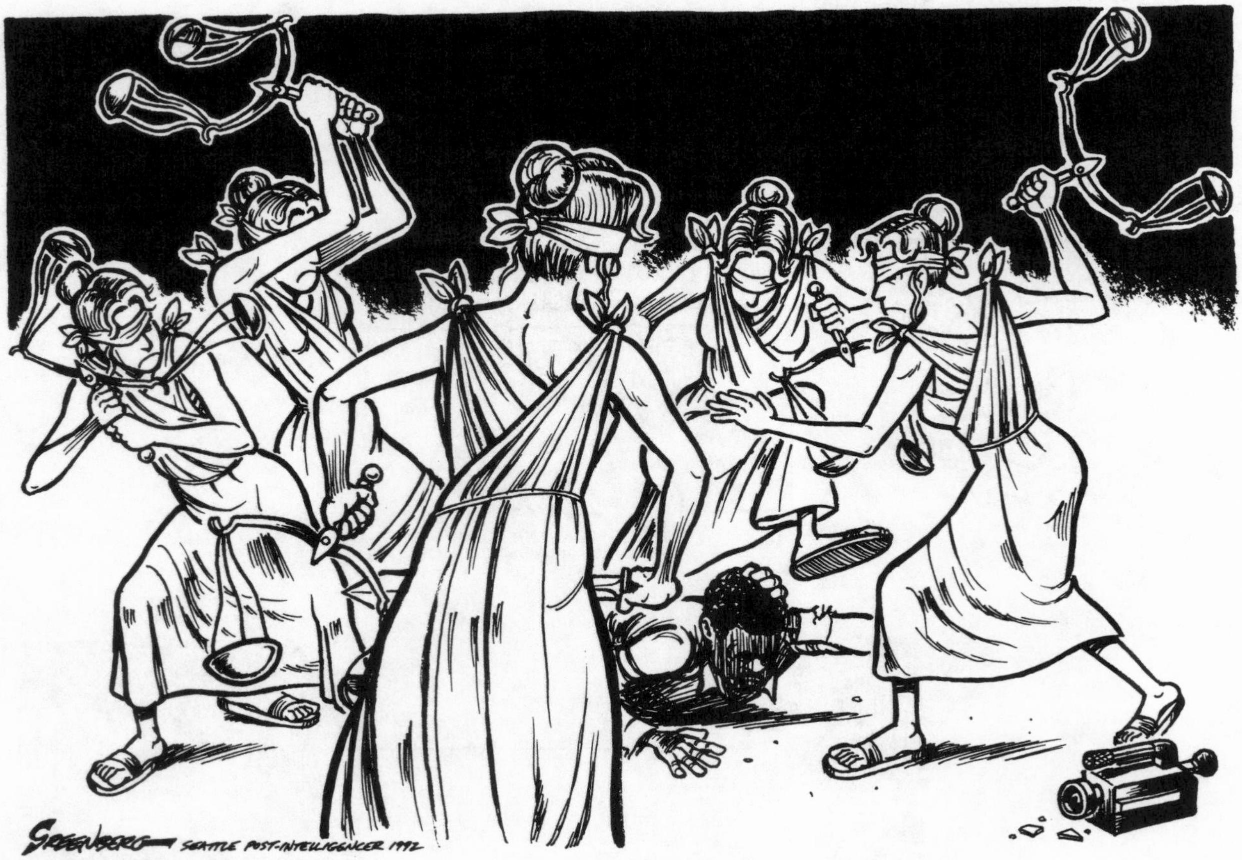
GREENBERG SEATTLE POST-INTELLIGENCER 1992

STEVE GREENBERG
Courtesy Seattle Post-Intelligencer

JERRY HOLBERT
Courtesy Boston Herald

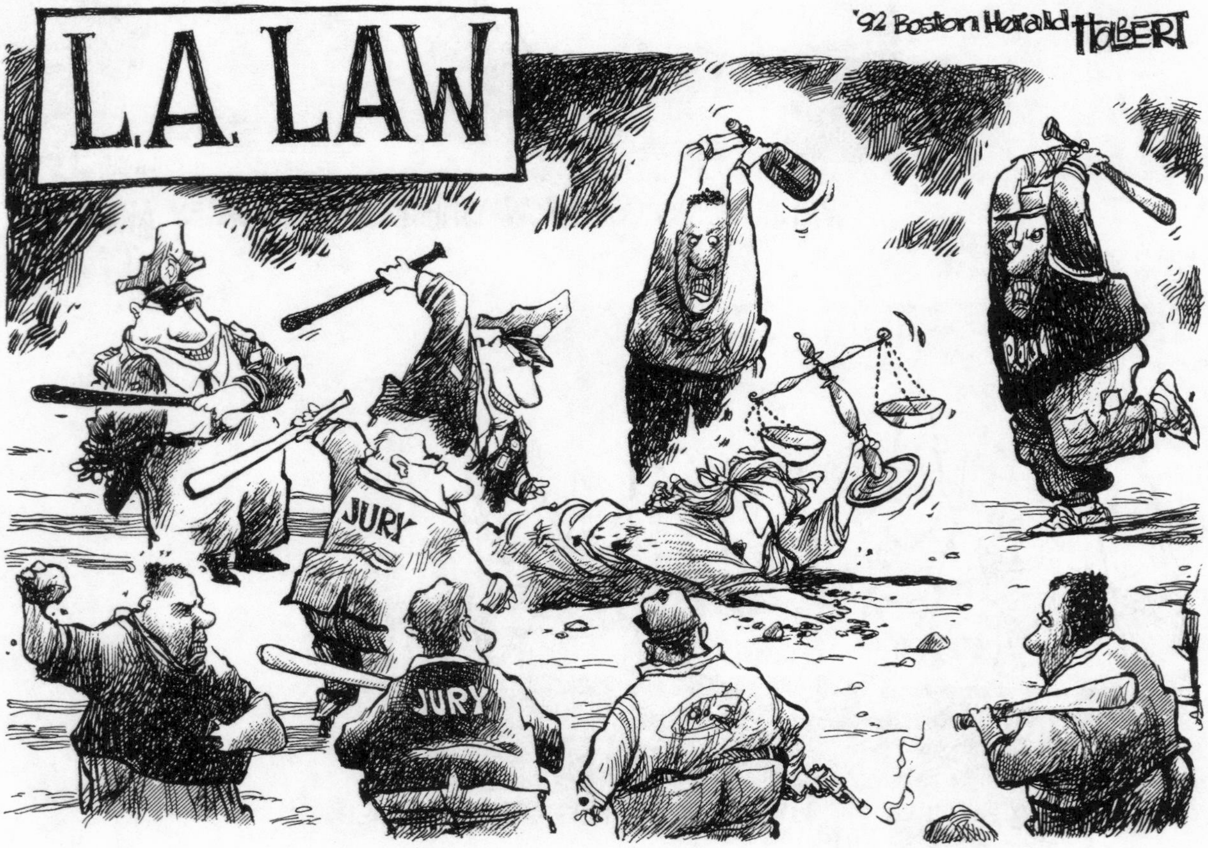
'92 Boston Herald HOLBERT
L.A. LAW
JURY
JURY

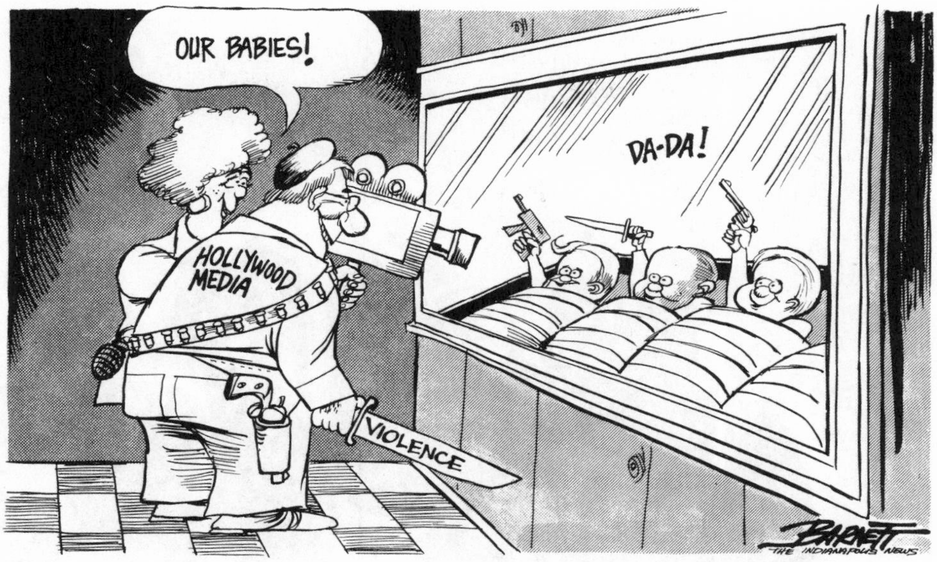
OUR BABIES!
DA-DA!
HOLLYWOOD MEDIA
VIOLENCE
BARNETT
THE INDIANAPOLIS NEWS

JERRY BARNETT
Courtesy Indianapolis News

ROB ROGERS
Courtesy Pittsburgh Press

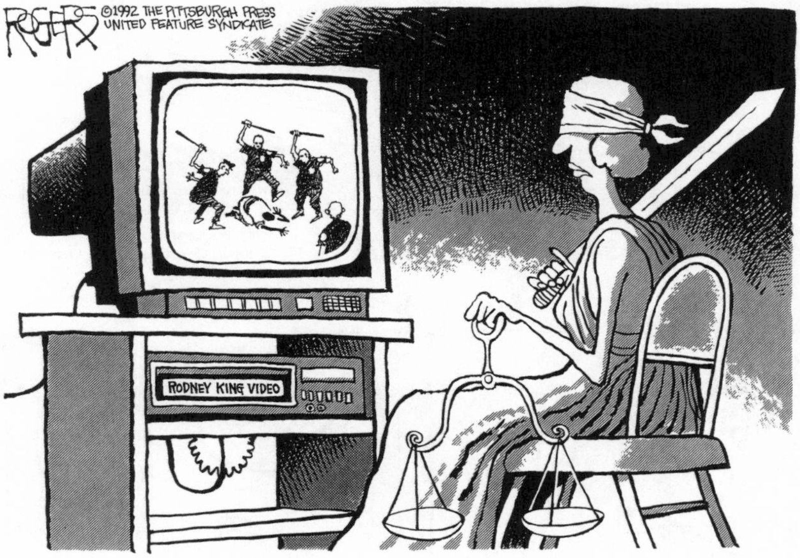
ROGERS ©1992 THE PITTSBURGH PRESS UNITED FEATURE SYNDICATE
RODNEY KING VIDEO

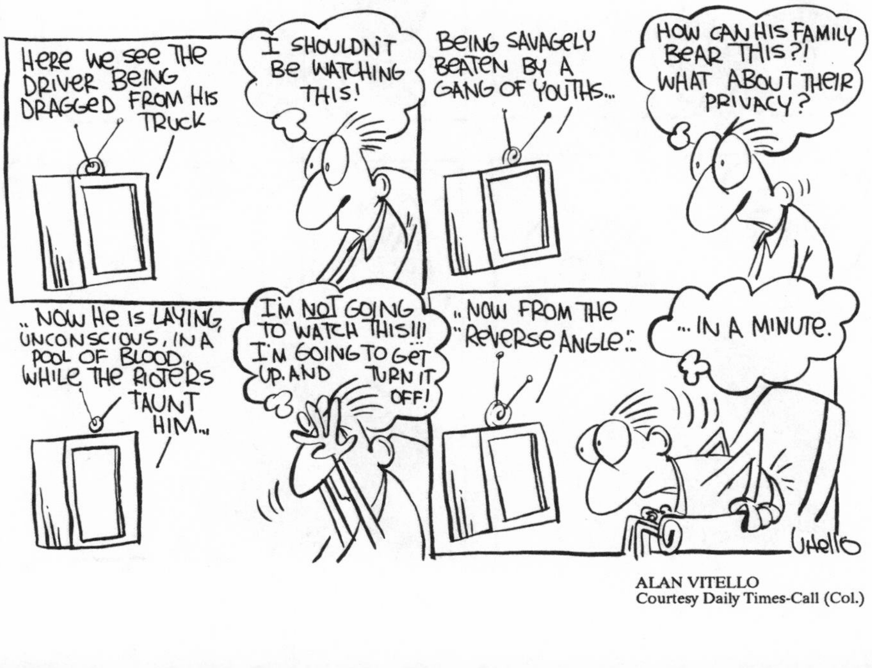
HERE WE SEE THE DRIVER BEING DRAGGED FROM HIS TRUCK
I SHOULDN'T BE WATCHING THIS!
BEING SAVAGELY BEATEN BY A GANG OF YOUTHS...
HOW CAN HIS FAMILY BEAR THIS?! WHAT ABOUT THEIR PRIVACY?
.. NOW HE IS LAYING, UNCONSCIOUS, IN A POOL OF BLOOD, WHILE THE RIOTERS TAUNT HIM...
I'M NOT GOING TO WATCH THIS!!! I'M GOING TO GET UP AND TURN IT OFF!
.. NOW FROM THE "REVERSE ANGLE"..
... IN A MINUTE.
VITELLO

ALAN VITELLO
Courtesy Daily Times-Call (Col.)

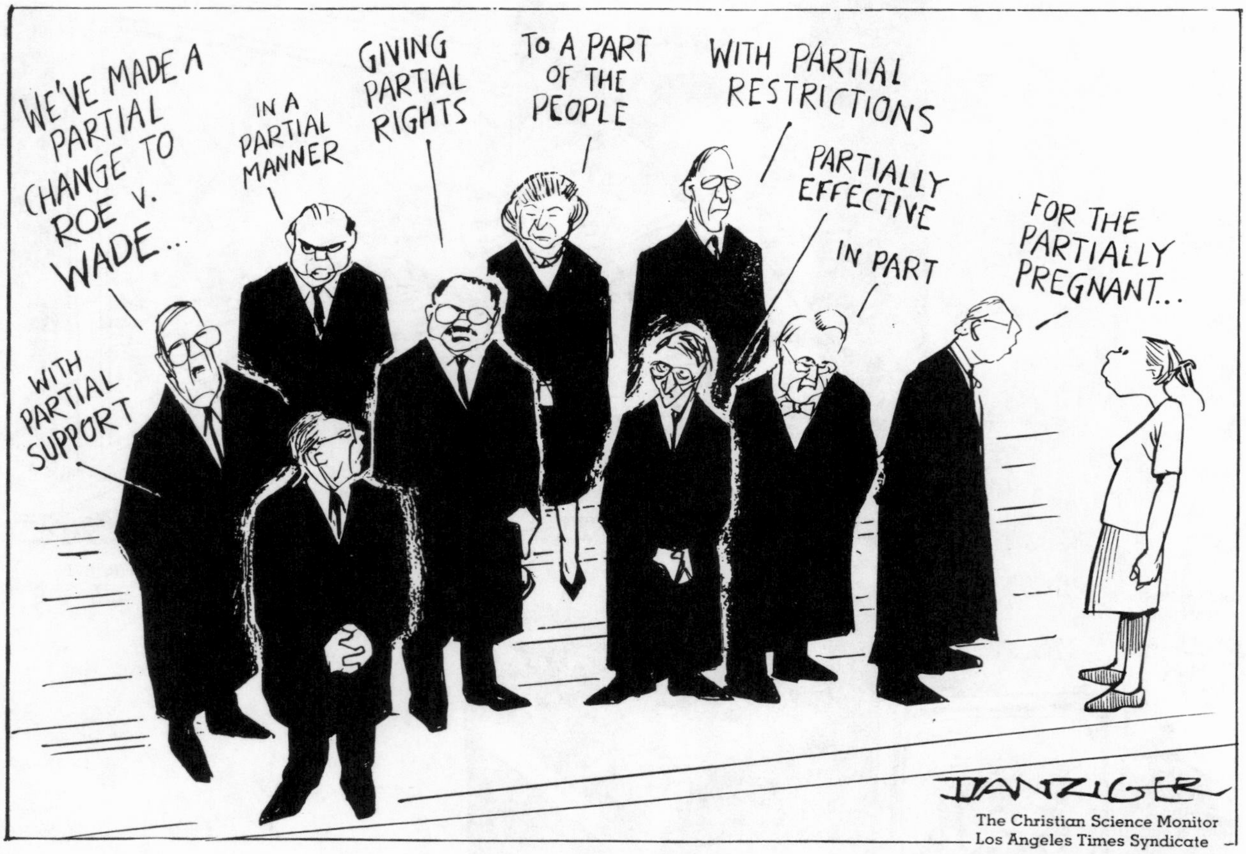

WE'VE MADE A PARTIAL CHANGE TO ROE v. WADE...
WITH PARTIAL SUPPORT
IN A PARTIAL MANNER
GIVING PARTIAL RIGHTS
TO A PART OF THE PEOPLE
WITH PARTIAL RESTRICTIONS
PARTIALLY EFFECTIVE
IN PART
FOR THE PARTIALLY PREGNANT...
DANZIGER
The Christian Science Monitor
Los Angeles Times Syndicate

JEFF DANZIGER
Courtesy Christian Science Monitor

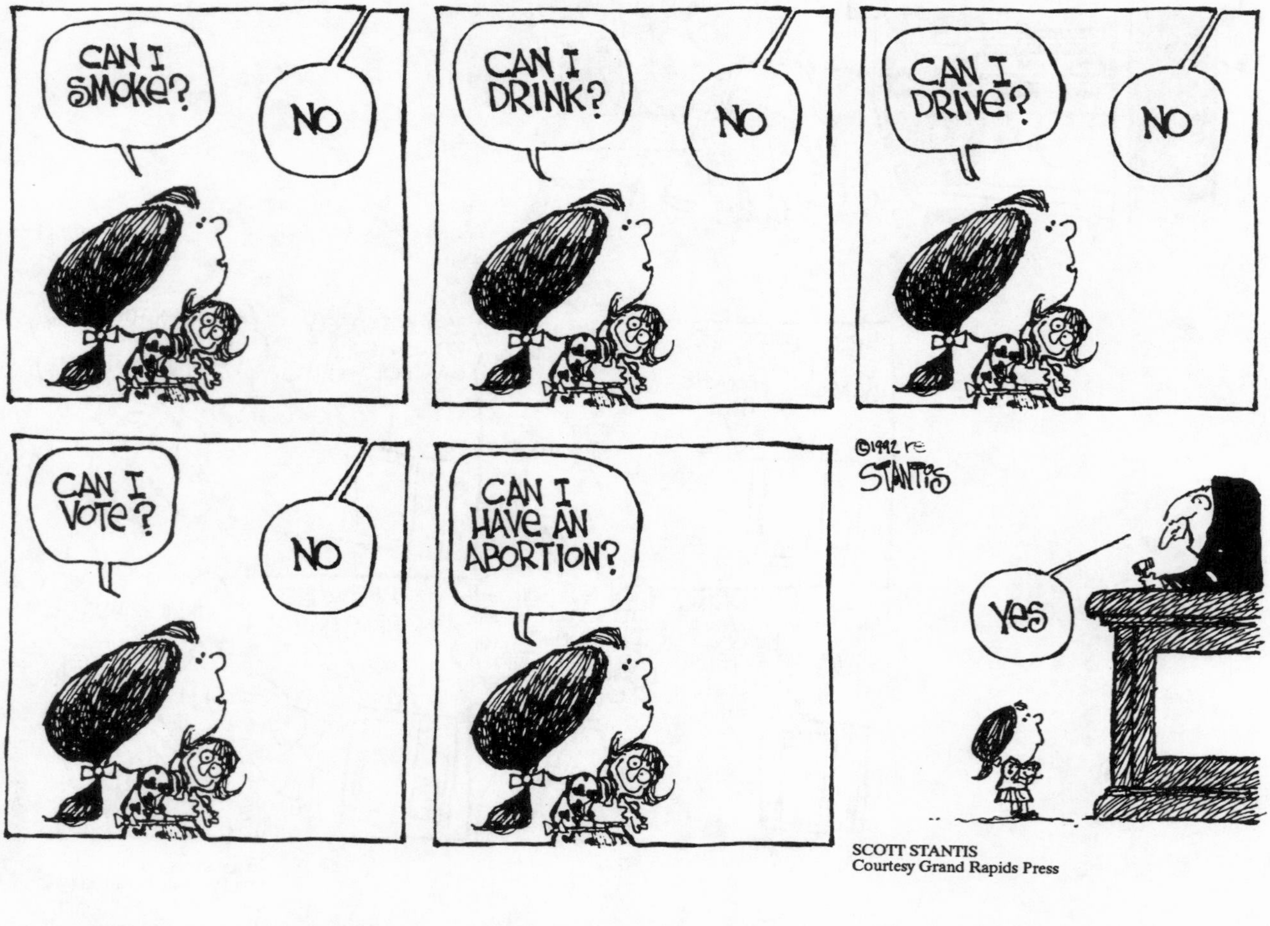

CAN I SMOKE?
NO
CAN I DRINK?
NO
CAN I DRIVE?
NO
CAN I VOTE?
NO
CAN I HAVE AN ABORTION?
©1992
STANTIS
YES

SCOTT STANTIS
Courtesy Grand Rapids Press

Women's Issues

Incidences of breast cancer climbed during the year, and studies indicated that one woman in eight would develop the disease. A new conclusion based on the study of 90,000 nurses, the largest group yet tested, raised doubts that diet is a contributory factor in the disease. Researchers had believed that diet might be partly responsible because they had found fewer cases of breast cancer in countries where the consumption of meat and dairy products was low. The National Institutes of Health is now supporting a fifteen-year, $600 million study on the problem.

Sen. Robert Packwood had been widely regarded as a staunch champion of women's rights, but in 1992 he was accused of sexual harassment by fifteen women. The charges were not made fully public until a few days after his reelection.

Two admirals left the Navy after allegations that twenty-six women had been assaulted by naval officers at the annual Tailhook convention. Women's groups and the media zeroed in on the charges and renewed pressure to safeguard women's rights not only in the armed forces but in the business world as well.

GLEN FODEN
Courtesy Patuxent Pub. Co.

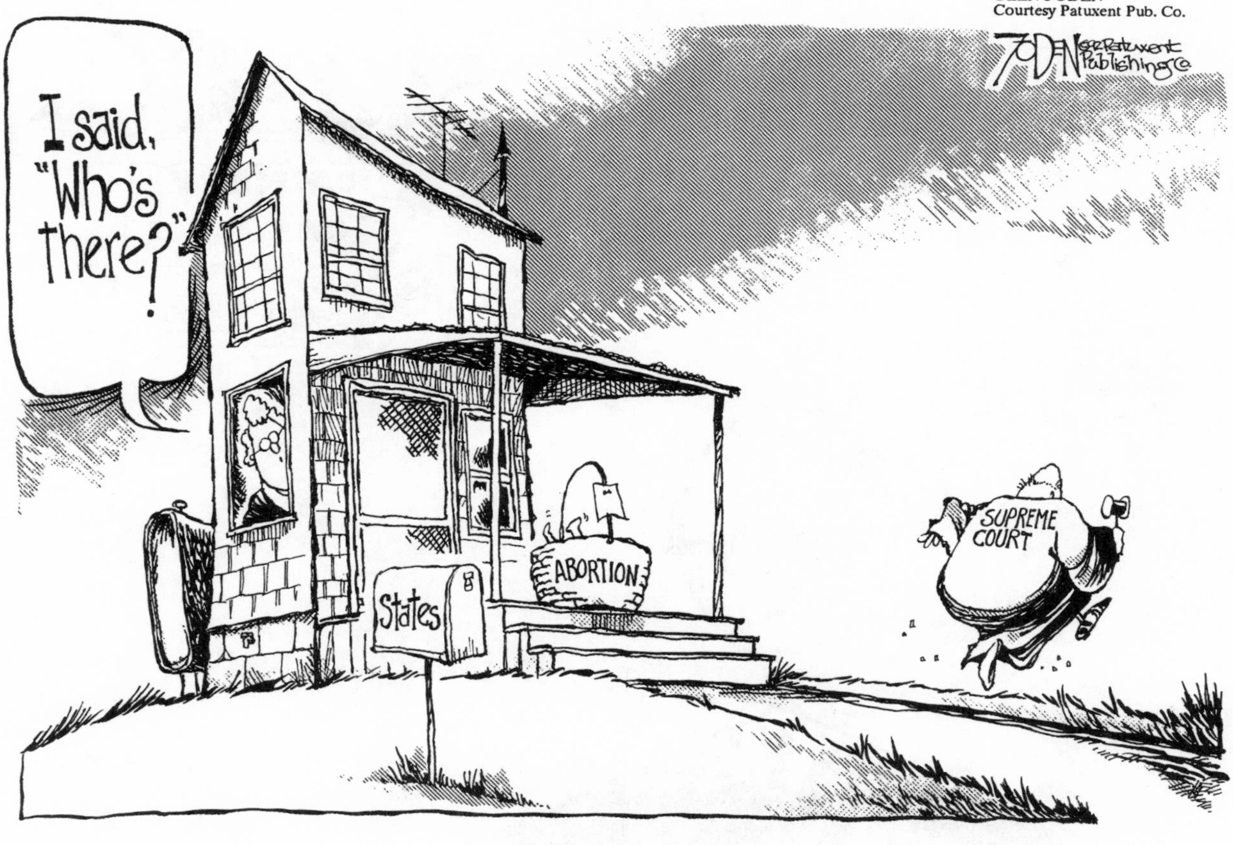
I said, "Who's there?"
States
ABORTION
SUPREME COURT

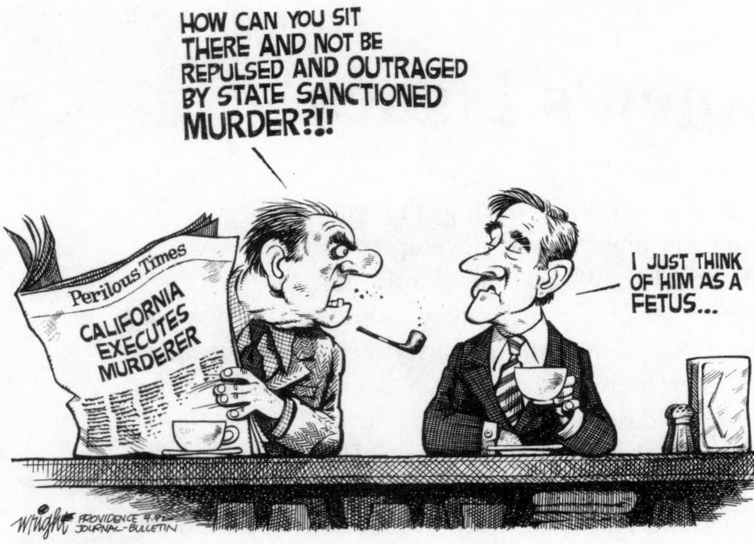

HOW CAN YOU SIT THERE AND NOT BE REPULSED AND OUTRAGED BY STATE SANCTIONED MURDER?!!
I JUST THINK OF HIM AS A FETUS...
Perilous Times
CALIFORNIA EXECUTES MURDERER

DICK WRIGHT
Courtesy Providence Journal-Bulletin

LARRY WRIGHT
Courtesy Detroit News

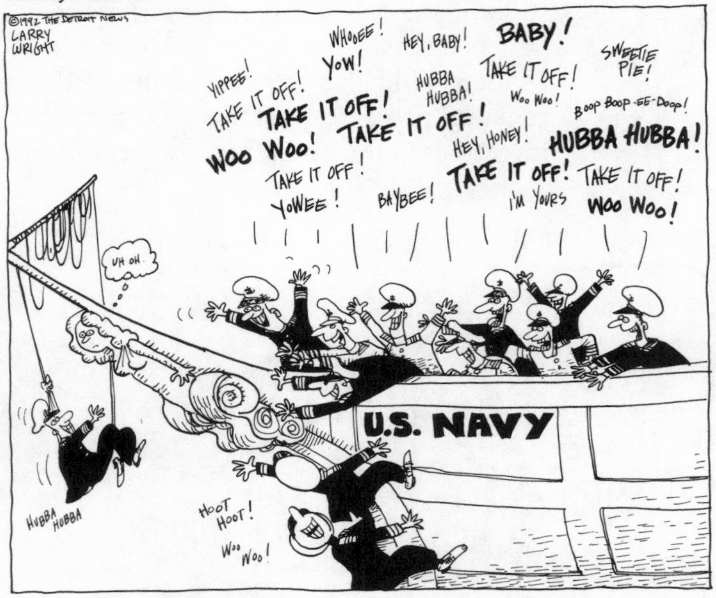

©1992 THE DETROIT NEWS LARRY WRIGHT
YIPPEE!
TAKE IT OFF!
WHOOEE!
YOW!
HEY, BABY!
BABY!
SWEETIE PIE!
HUBBA HUBBA!
TAKE IT OFF!
TAKE IT OFF!
WOO WOO!
TAKE IT OFF!
WOO WOO!
BOOP BOOP-EE-DOOP!
HEY, HONEY!
HUBBA HUBBA!
TAKE IT OFF!
YOWEE!
BAYBEE!
TAKE IT OFF!
I'M YOURS
TAKE IT OFF!
WOO WOO!
UH OH
U.S. NAVY
HUBBA HUBBA
HOOT HOOT!
WOO WOO!

JOHN SHERFFIUS
Courtesy Ventura Star-Free Press

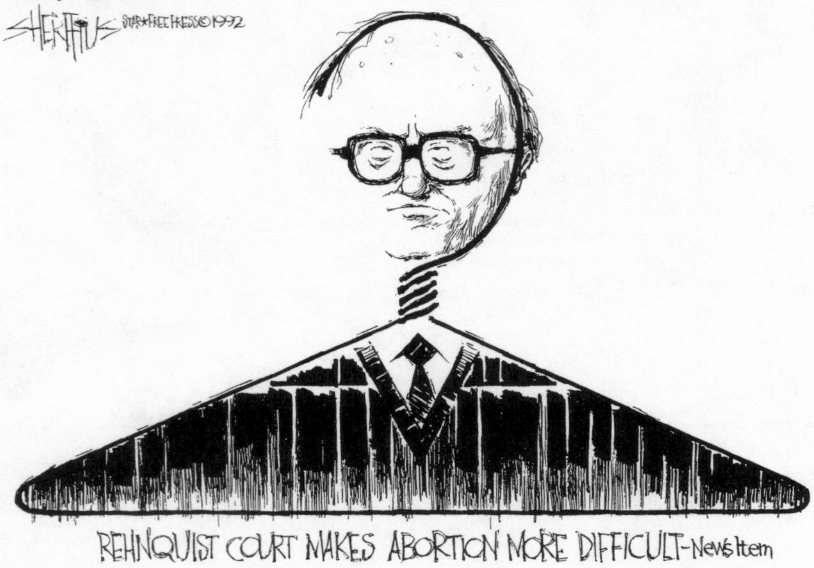

SHERFFIUS STAR★FREE PRESS©1992
REHNQUIST COURT MAKES ABORTION MORE DIFFICULT-News Item

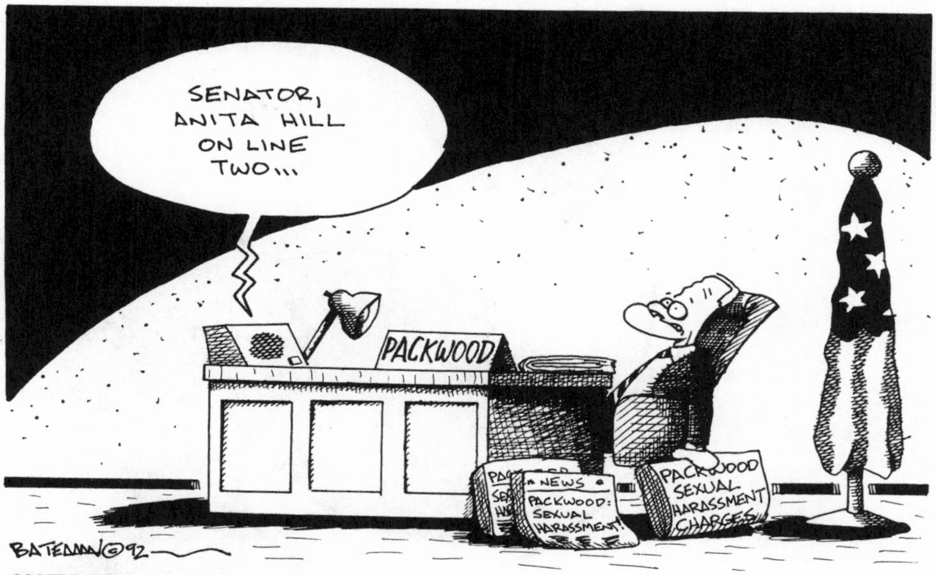
SENATOR, ANITA HILL ON LINE TWO...
PACKWOOD
NEWS
PACKWOOD: SEXUAL HARASSMENT!
PACKWOOD SEXUAL HARASSMENT CHARGES
BATEMAN©92

SCOTT BATEMAN
Courtesy Eugene Register Guard

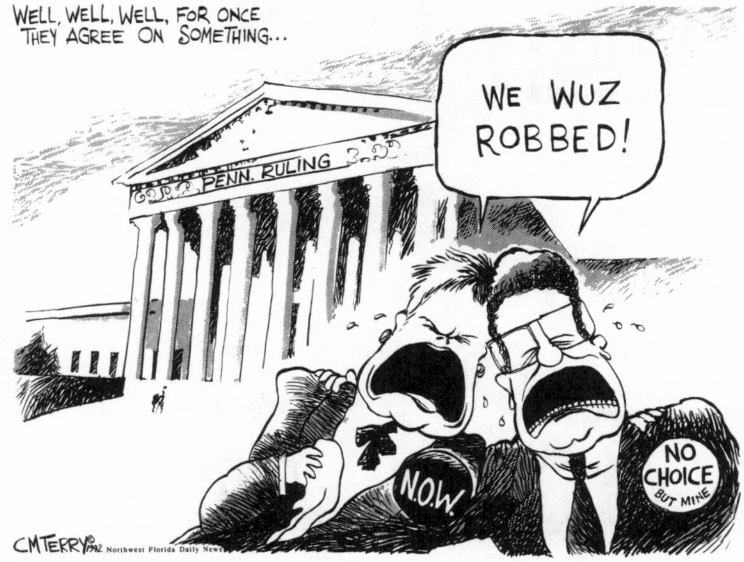
WELL, WELL, WELL, FOR ONCE THEY AGREE ON SOMETHING...
WE WUZ ROBBED!
PENN. RULING
N.O.W.
NO CHOICE BUT MINE
CMTERRY©1992 Northwest Florida Daily News

CRAIG M. TERRY
Courtesy N.W. Florida Daily News

DANA SUMMERS
Courtesy Orlando Sentinel

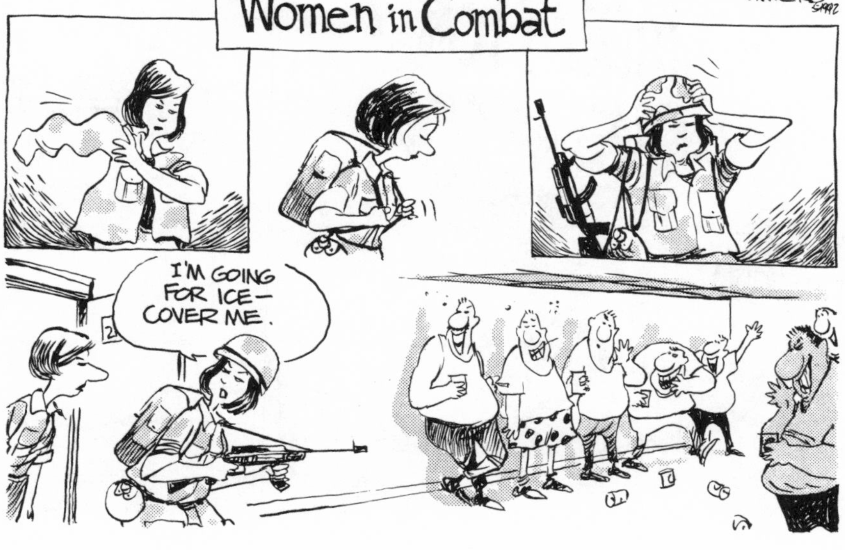
Women in Combat
I'M GOING FOR ICE— COVER ME.

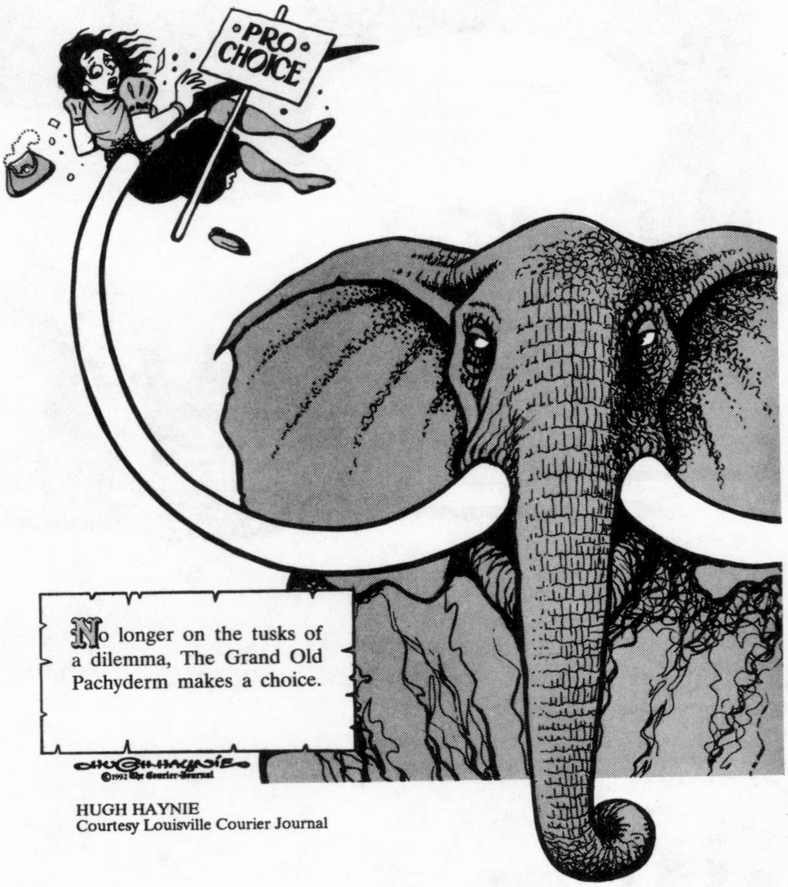
PRO CHOICE
No longer on the tusks of a dilemma, The Grand Old Pachyderm makes a choice.

HUGH HAYNIE
Courtesy Louisville Courier Journal

GARY THOMAS
Courtesy Des Moines Business Record

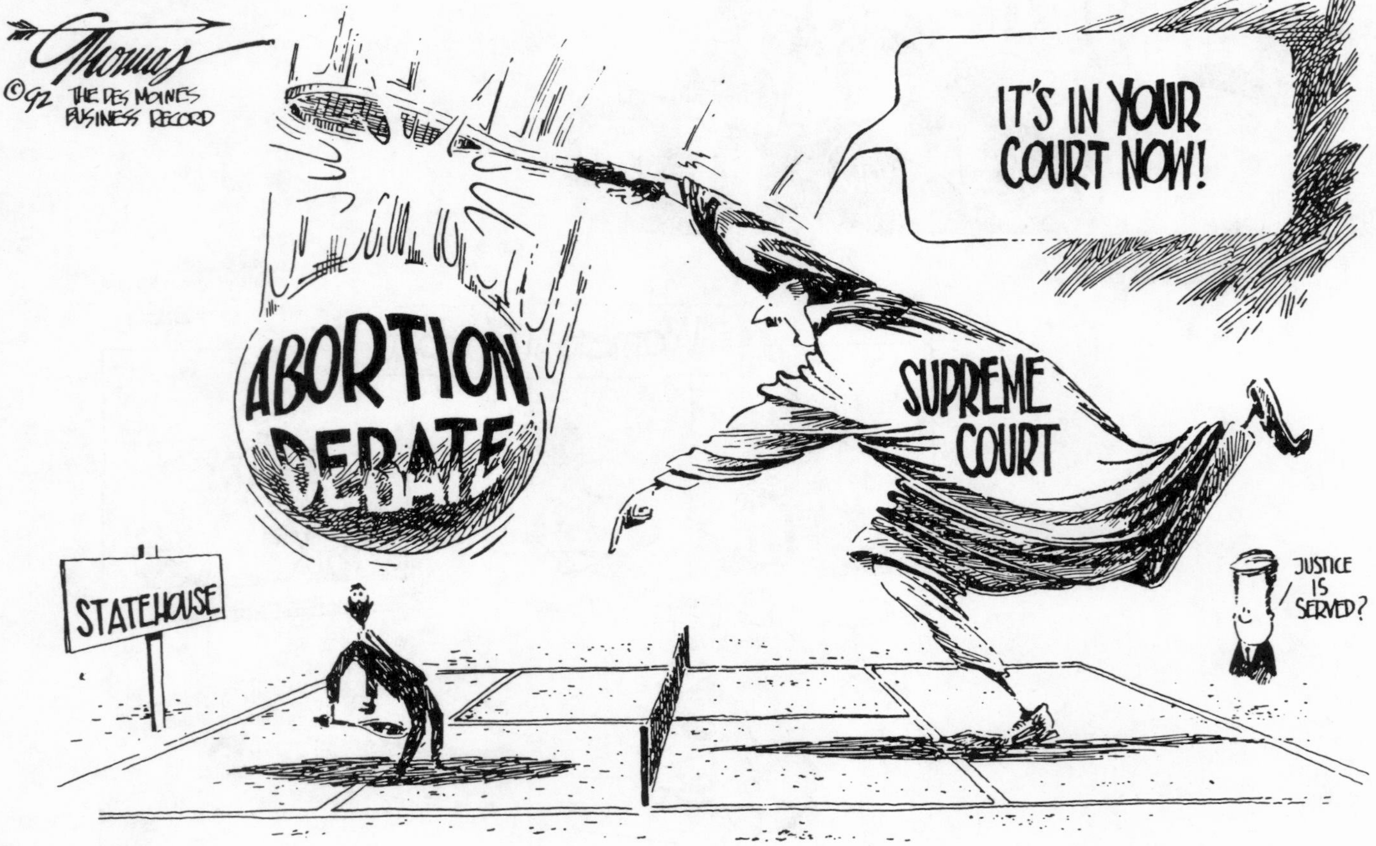
Thomas
©92 THE DES MOINES BUSINESS RECORD
IT'S IN YOUR COURT NOW!
ABORTION DEBATE
SUPREME COURT
STATEHOUSE
JUSTICE IS SERVED?

ROD WARREN
Courtesy Bakersfield Californian

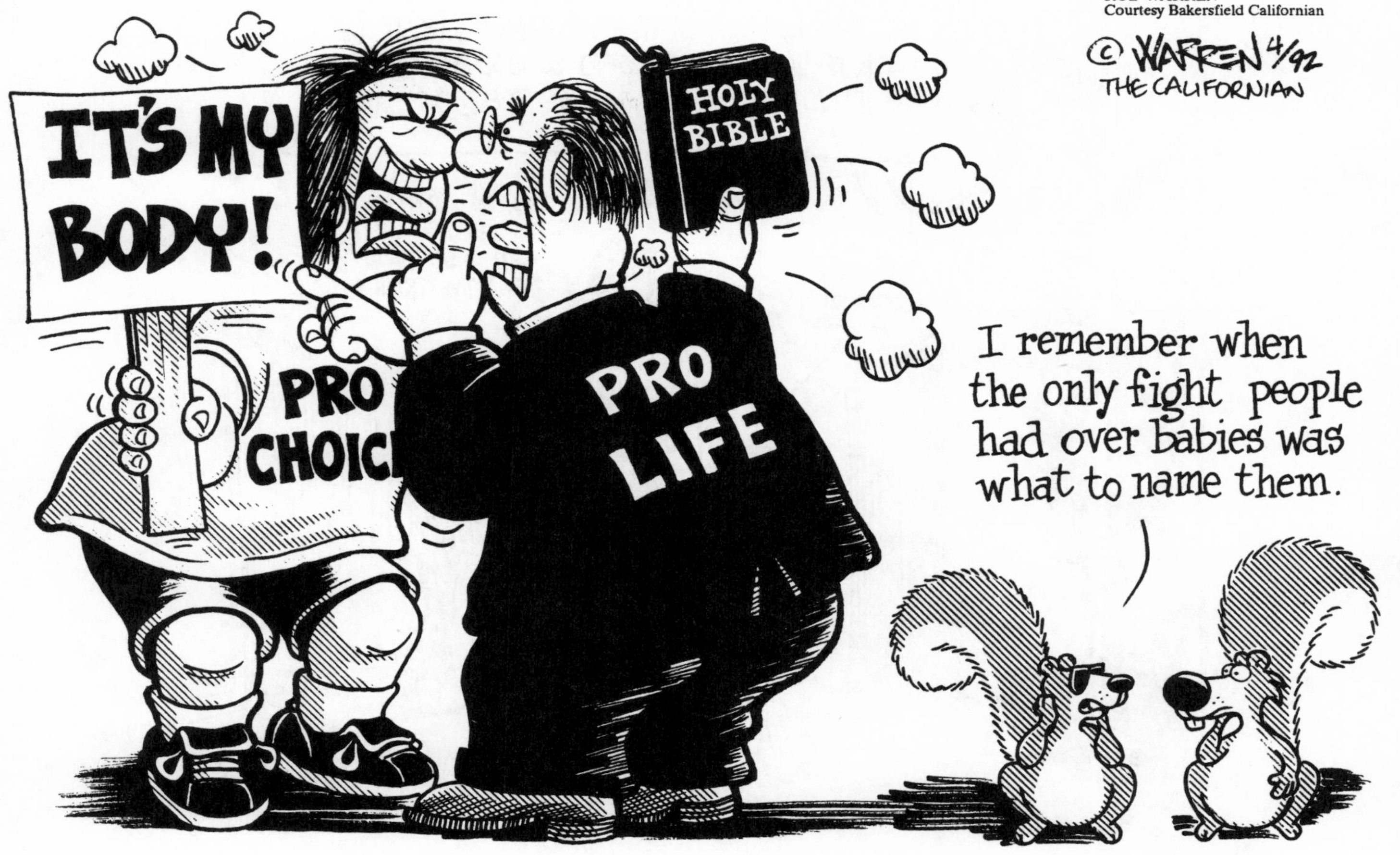
© WARREN 4/92
THE CALIFORNIAN
IT'S MY BODY!
PRO CHOIC
HOLY BIBLE
PRO LIFE
I remember when the only fight people had over babies was what to name them.

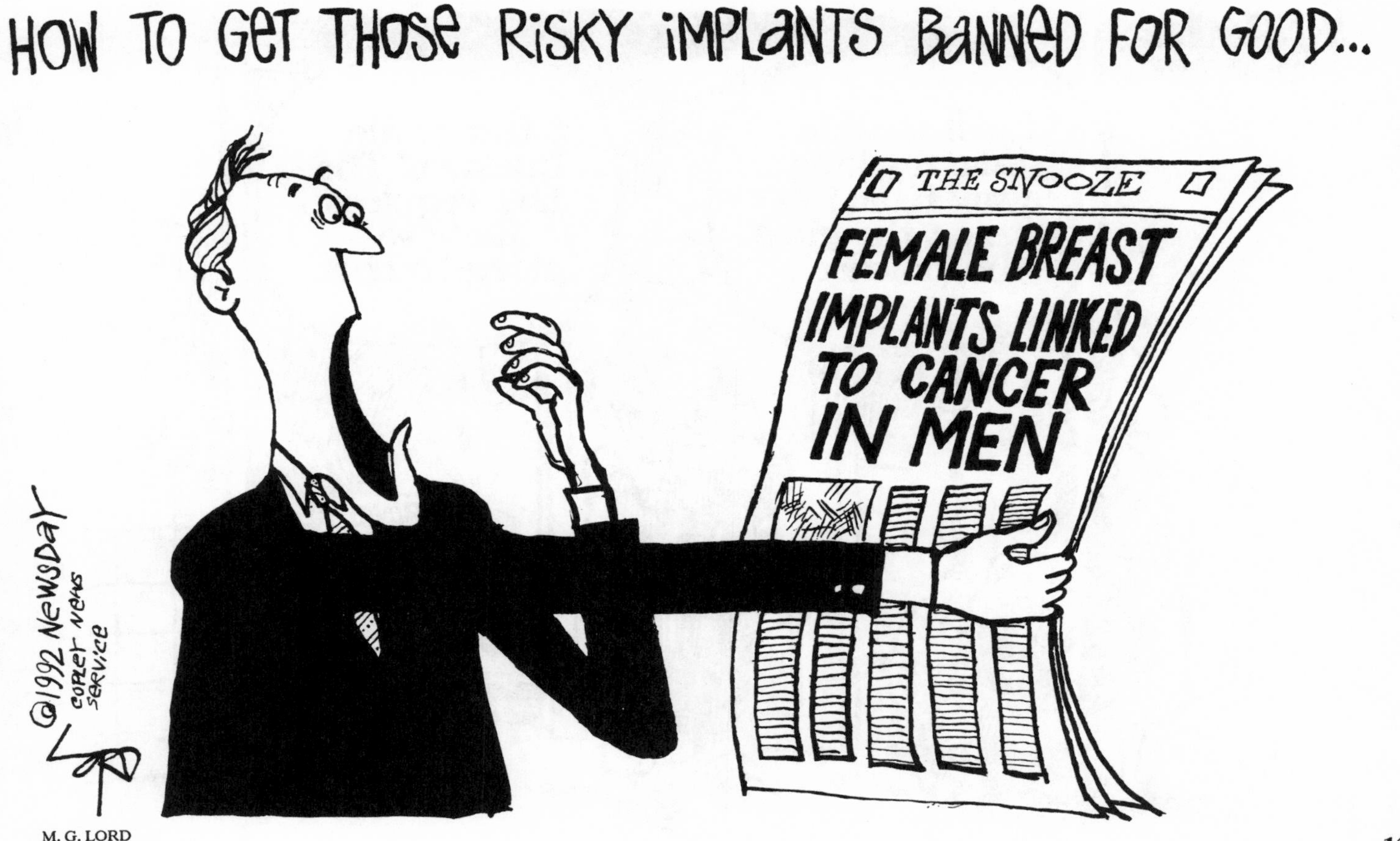
HOW TO GET THOSE RISKY IMPLANTS BANNED FOR GOOD...
THE SNOOZE
FEMALE BREAST IMPLANTS LINKED TO CANCER IN MEN
©1992 NEWSDAY
COPLEY NEWS SERVICE
LORD

M. G. LORD
Courtesy Newsday

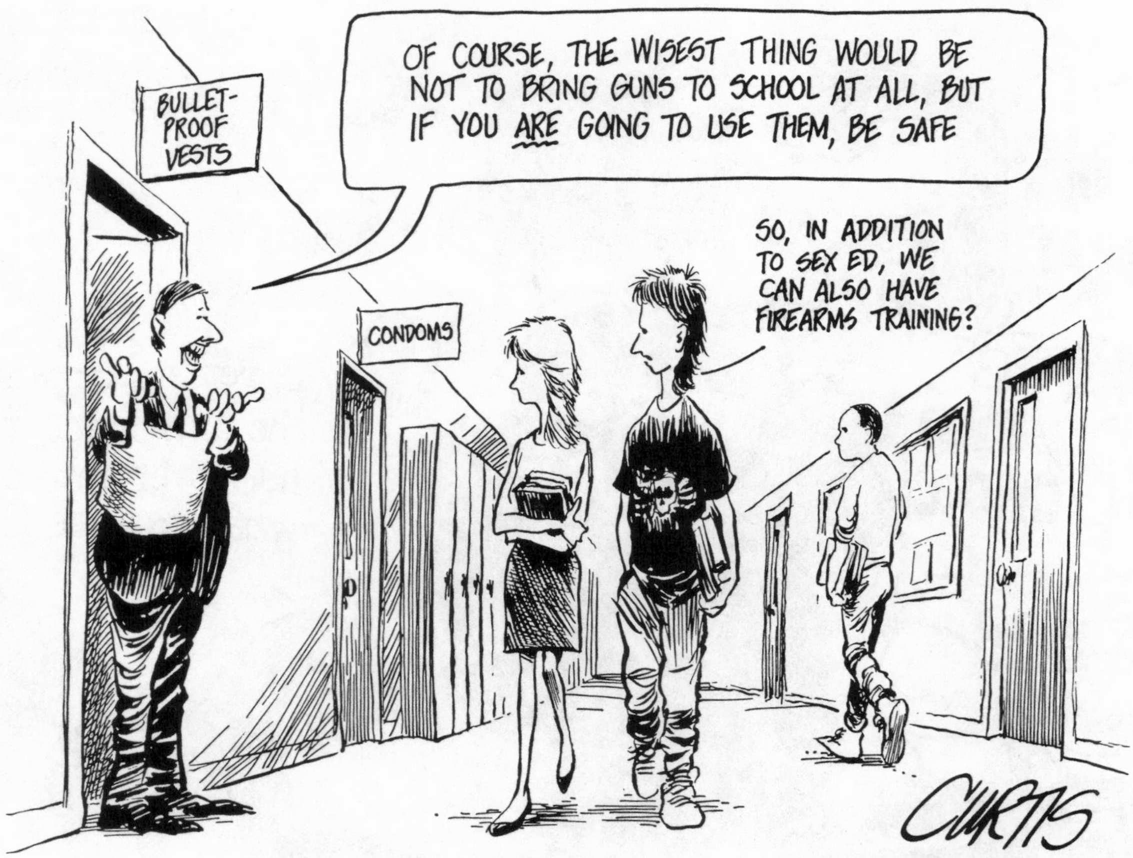
BULLET-PROOF VESTS
OF COURSE, THE WISEST THING WOULD BE NOT TO BRING GUNS TO SCHOOL AT ALL, BUT IF YOU ARE GOING TO USE THEM, BE SAFE
CONDOMS
SO, IN ADDITION TO SEX ED, WE CAN ALSO HAVE FIREARMS TRAINING?
CURTIS

CHRIS CURTIS
Courtesy Alexandria Gazette Packet

JIMMY MARGULIES
Courtesy The Record (N.J.) copyright 1992
North America Syndicate

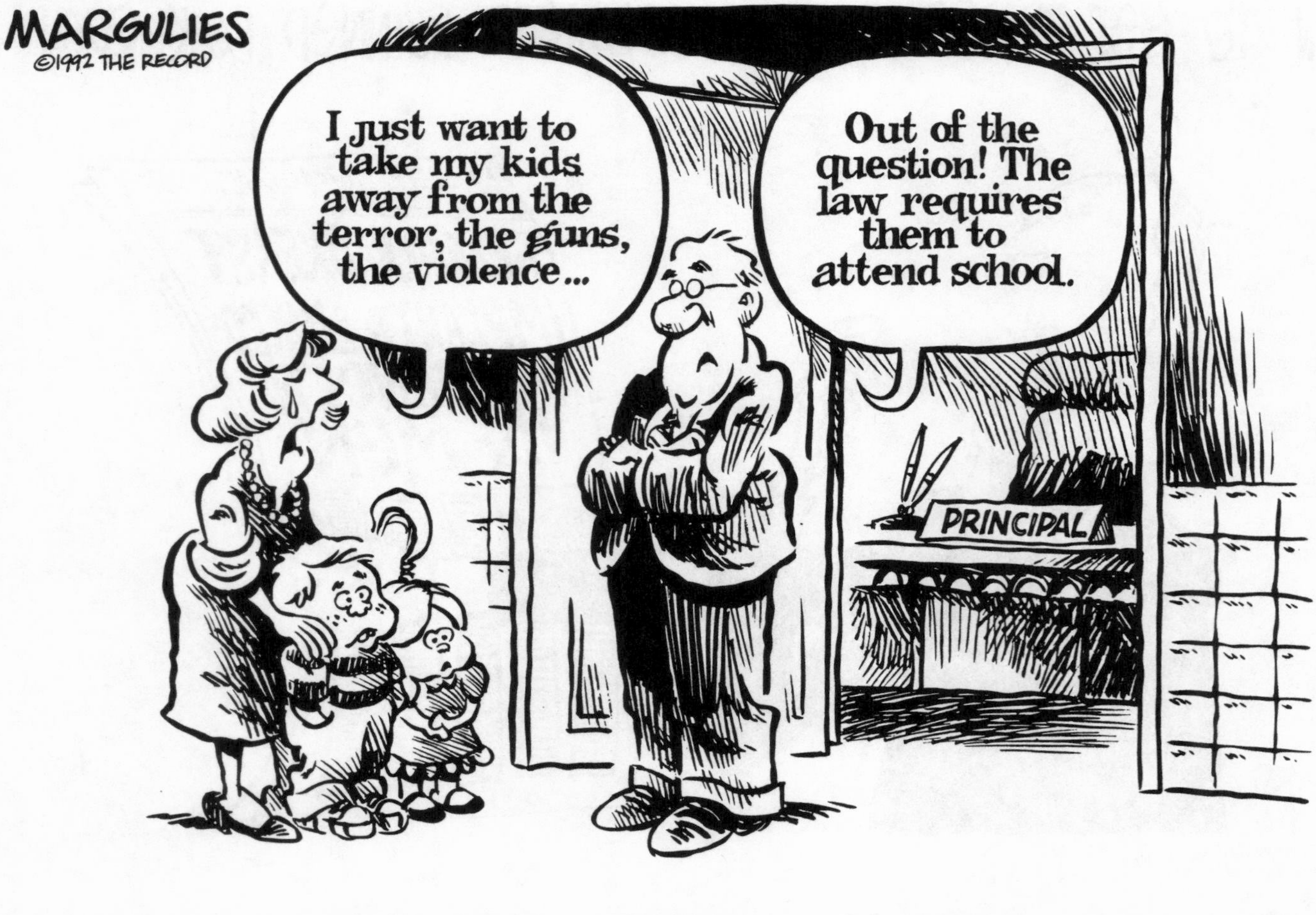
MARGULIES
©1992 THE RECORD
I just want to take my kids away from the terror, the guns, the violence...
Out of the question! The law requires them to attend school.
PRINCIPAL

Education

Some ten years after the landmark report "A Nation at Risk" had warned of "a rising tide of mediocrity" in education, most schools are not meeting the higher standards required today. Many educators are convinced that money alone will not solve the problem, and that drastic reform must flow from the top to the bottom. School curricula must be designed to equip students with the proper tools to be successful in the modern high-tech world.

There was controversy during the year in many school districts over sex education and how best to make students fully aware of the dangers of AIDS. In New York City, condoms were dispensed free of charge to high school students, and condom vending machines were installed on many college campuses. Public schools continued to wrestle with the problems of guns, drugs, and violence.

School dropouts remained at the bottom of the job market, but high school and even college graduates were finding work hard to come by as well. Ten percent of college graduates found themselves in jobs that did not require a college degree. It is estimated that this figure will rise to one in three by the end of the century.

The Supreme Court ruled in 1992 that prayer at high school graduation exercises and football games was not permissible.

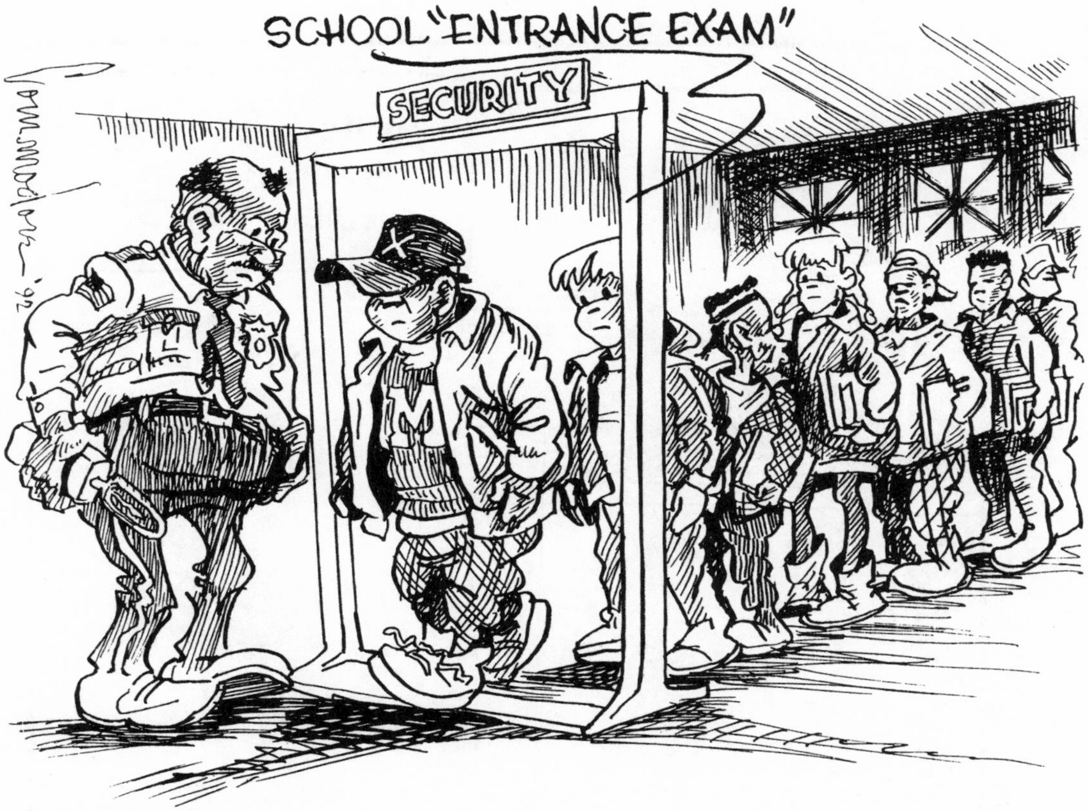
SCHOOL "ENTRANCE EXAM"
SECURITY

CHESTER COMMODORE
Courtesy Chicago Defender

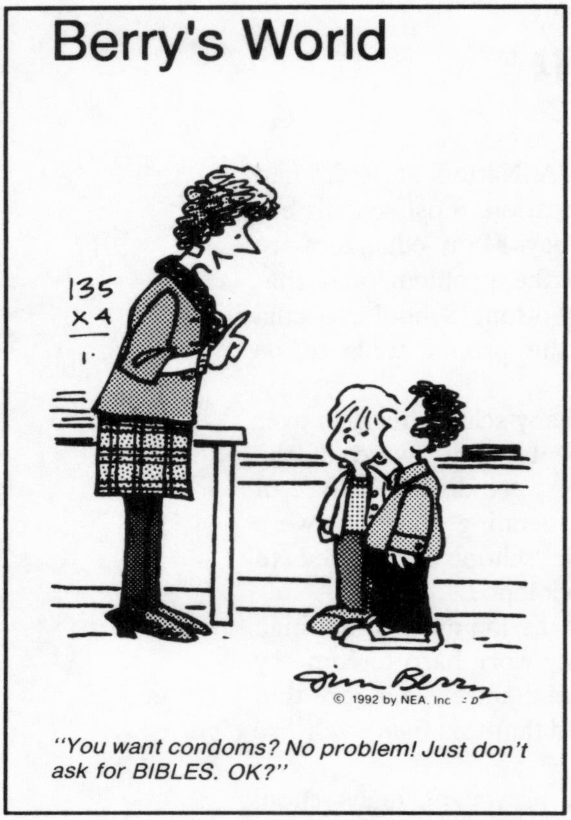
Berry's World
135
x4
1
© 1992 by NEA, Inc
"You want condoms? No problem! Just don't ask for BIBLES. OK?"

JIM BERRY
Courtesy NEA

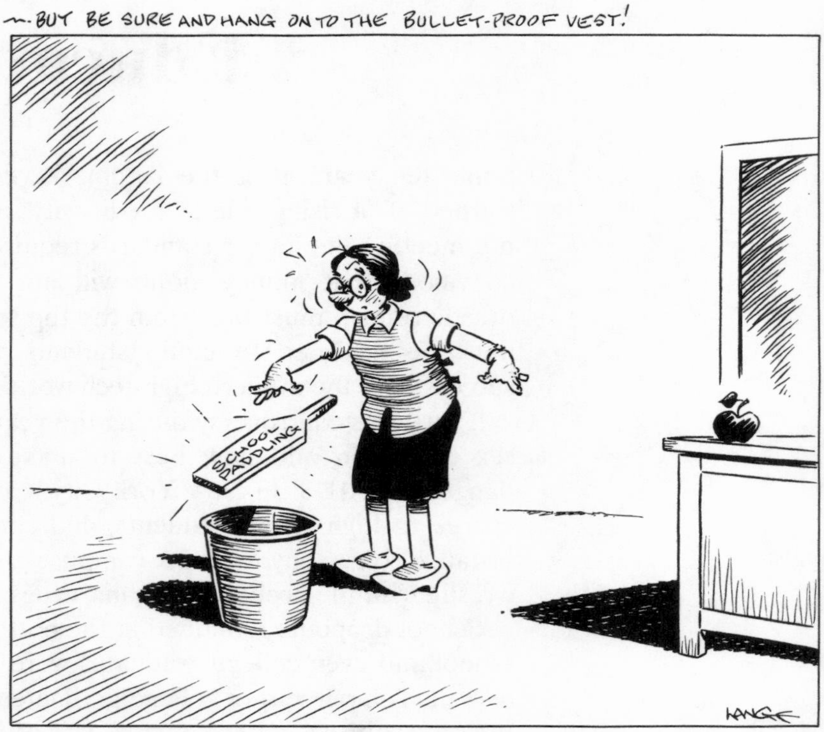
—BUT BE SURE AND HANG ON TO THE BULLET-PROOF VEST!
SCHOOL PADDLING
LANGE
JIM LANGE
Courtesy Daily Oklahoman

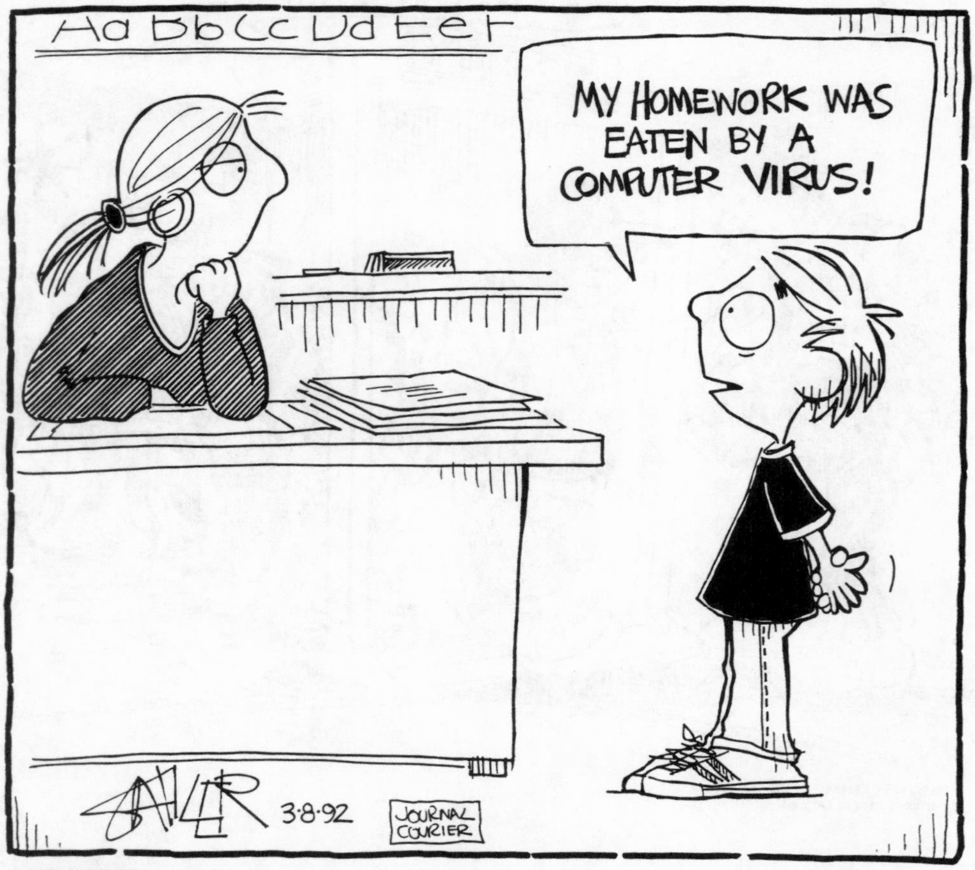
Aa Bb Cc Dd Ee Ff
MY HOMEWORK WAS EATEN BY A COMPUTER VIRUS!
SATTLER 3·8·92
JOURNAL COURIER
DAVE SATTLER
Courtesy Lafayette Journal Courier

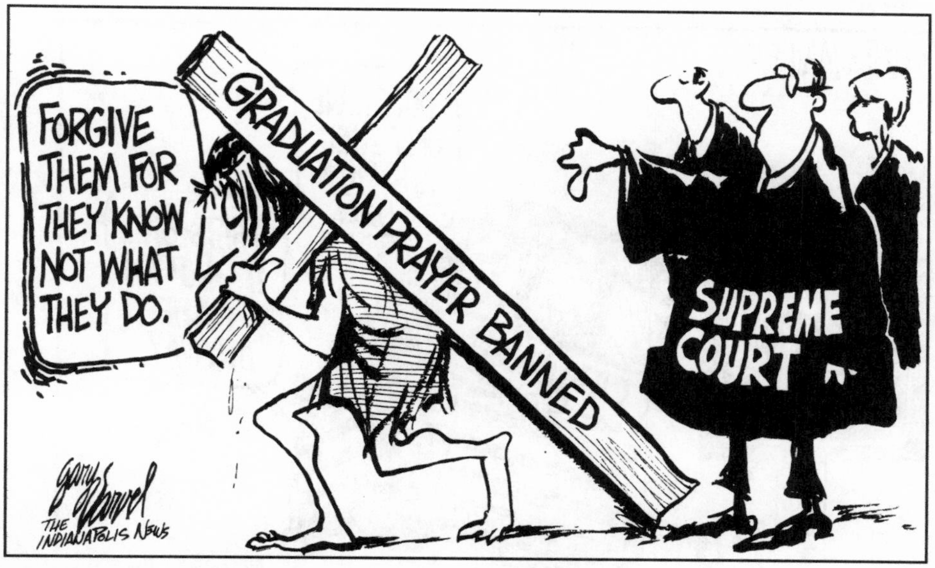
FORGIVE THEM FOR THEY KNOW NOT WHAT THEY DO.
GRADUATION PRAYER BANNED
SUPREME COURT
THE INDIANAPOLIS NEWS

GARY VARVEL
Courtesy Indianapolis News

JOHN SPENCER
Courtesy Philadelphia Business Journal

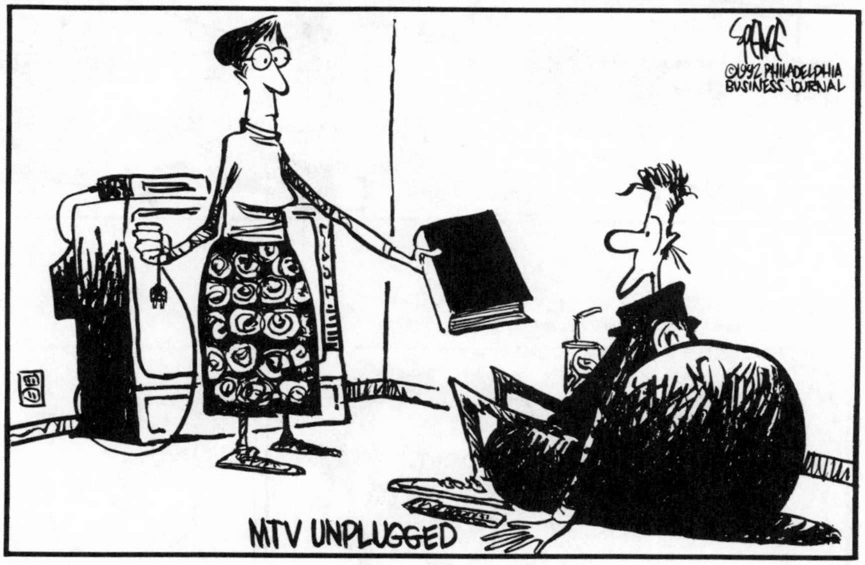
©1992 PHILADELPHIA BUSINESS JOURNAL
MTV UNPLUGGED

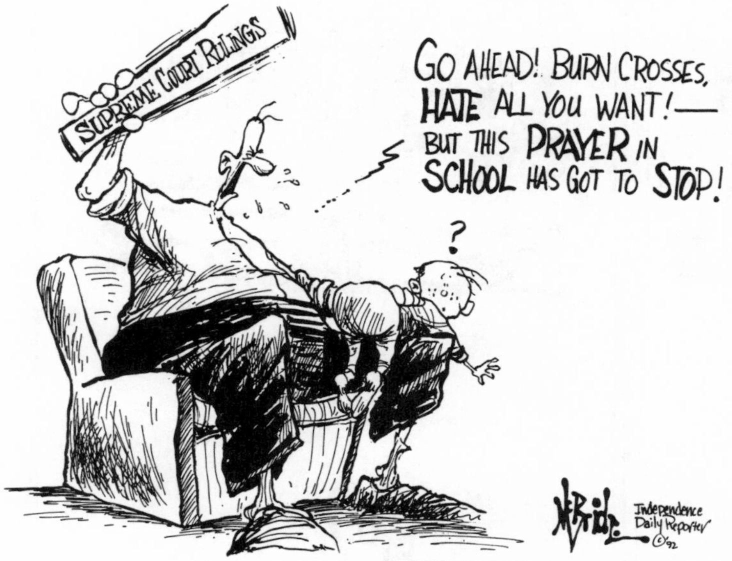
SUPREME COURT RULINGS
GO AHEAD! BURN CROSSES, HATE ALL YOU WANT!— BUT THIS PRAYER IN SCHOOL HAS GOT TO STOP!
?
Independence Daily Reporter

STEVE MCBRIDE
Courtesy Independence Daily Reporter (Kan.)

BOB LANG
Courtesy Columbia City Post & Mail (Ind.)

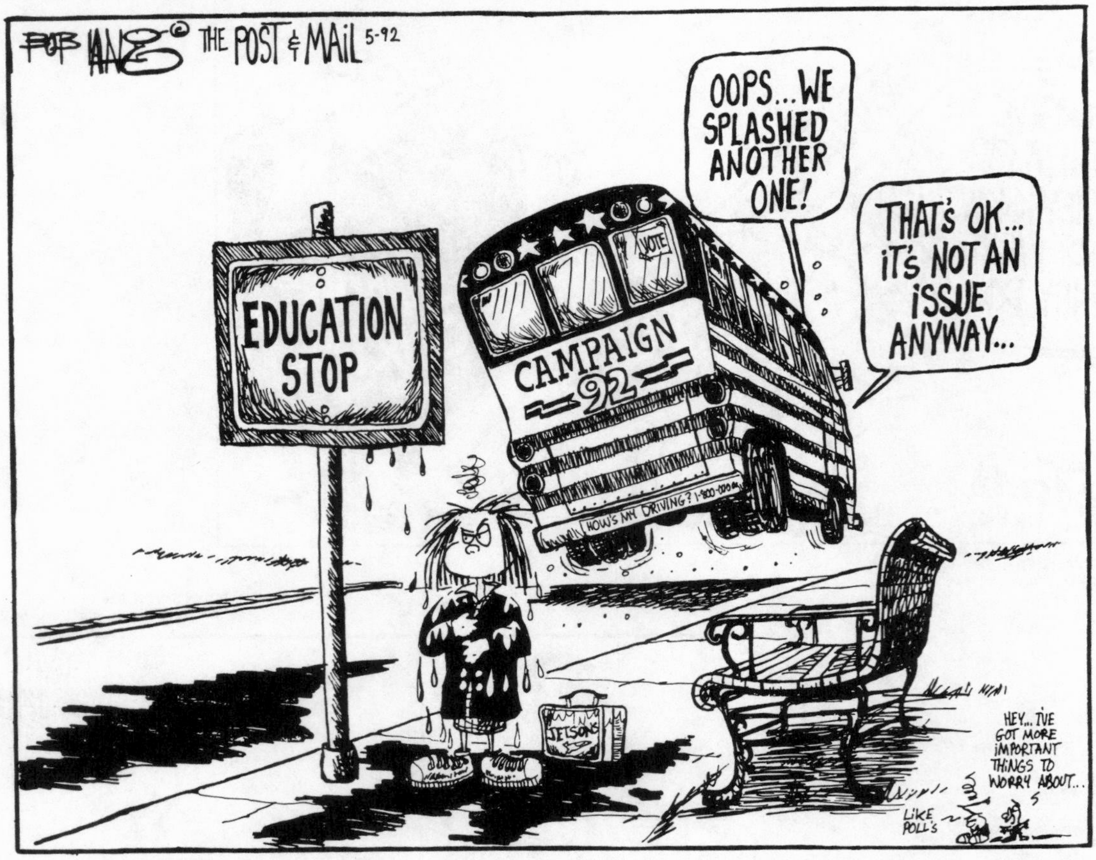
THE POST & MAIL 5-92
OOPS... WE SPLASHED ANOTHER ONE!
THAT'S OK... IT'S NOT AN ISSUE ANYWAY...
EDUCATION STOP
VOTE
CAMPAIGN 92
JETSONS
HEY... I'VE GOT MORE IMPORTANT THINGS TO WORRY ABOUT...
LIKE POLL'S

CLAY JONES
Courtesy Northeast Mississippi Daily Journal

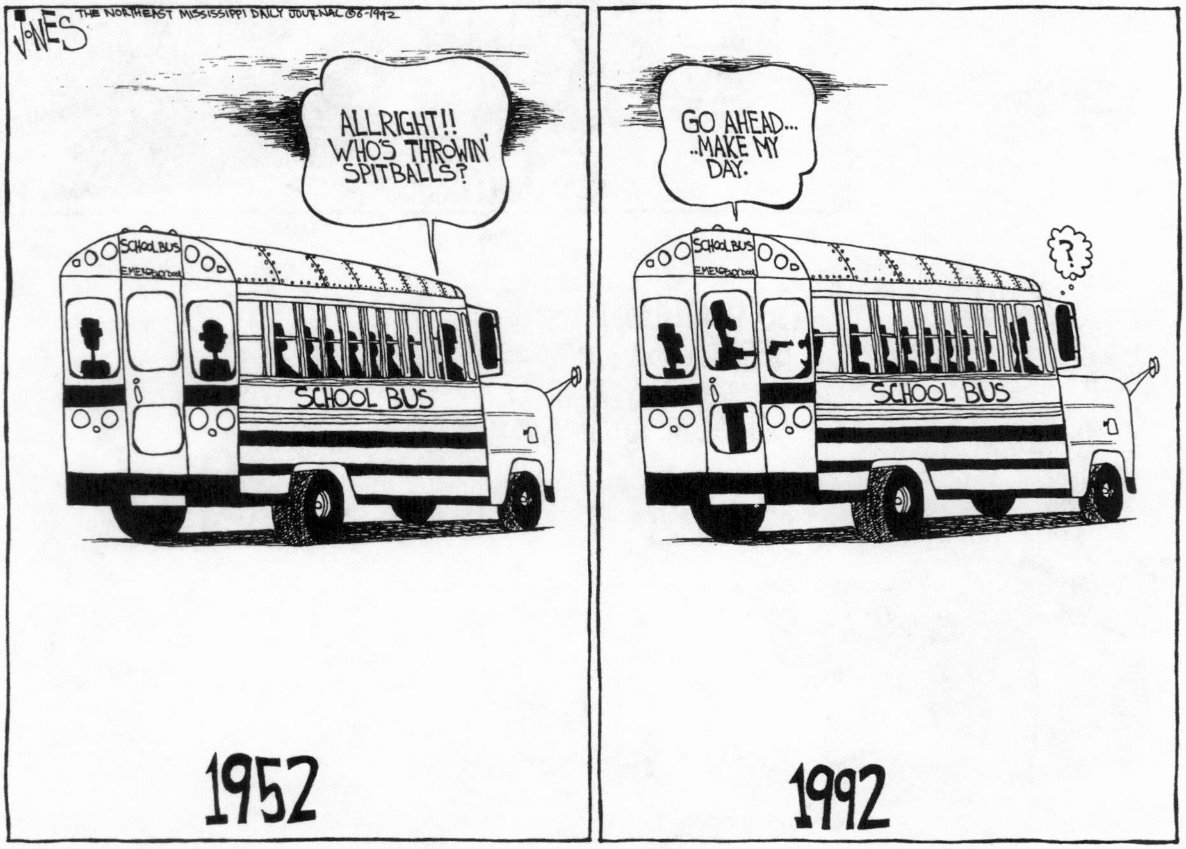
JONES
THE NORTHEAST MISSISSIPPI DAILY JOURNAL ©6-1992
ALLRIGHT!! WHO'S THROWIN' SPITBALLS?
SCHOOL BUS
1952
GO AHEAD... ..MAKE MY DAY.
SCHOOL BUS
?
1992

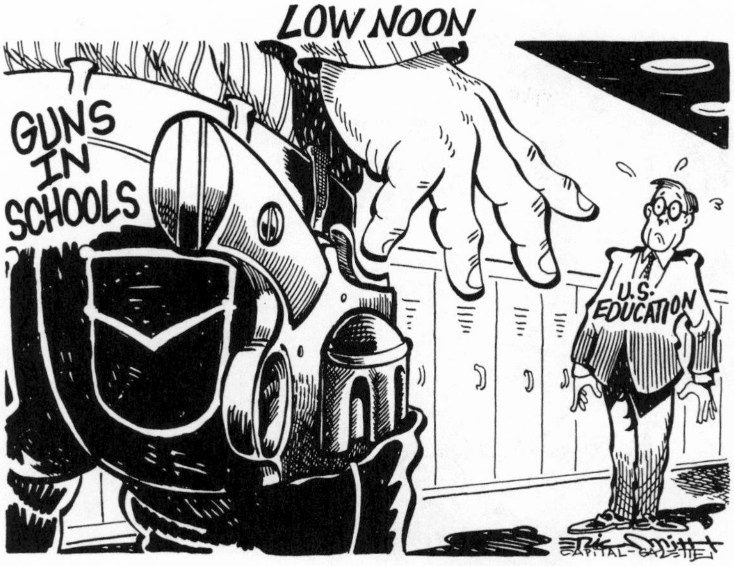
LOW NOON
GUNS IN SCHOOLS
U.S. EDUCATION

ERIC SMITH
Courtesy Capital Gazette Newspapers

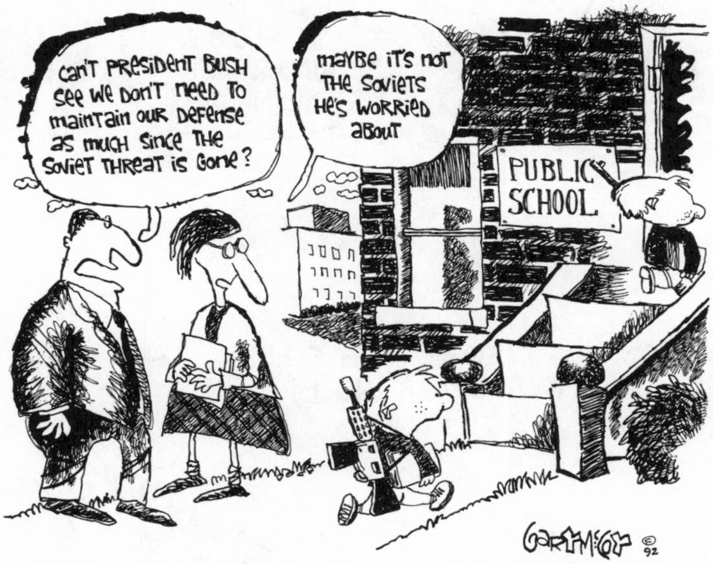
Can't President Bush see we don't need to maintain our defense as much since the Soviet threat is gone?
Maybe it's not the Soviets he's worried about
PUBLIC SCHOOL

GARY MCCOY
Courtesy Suburban Journals

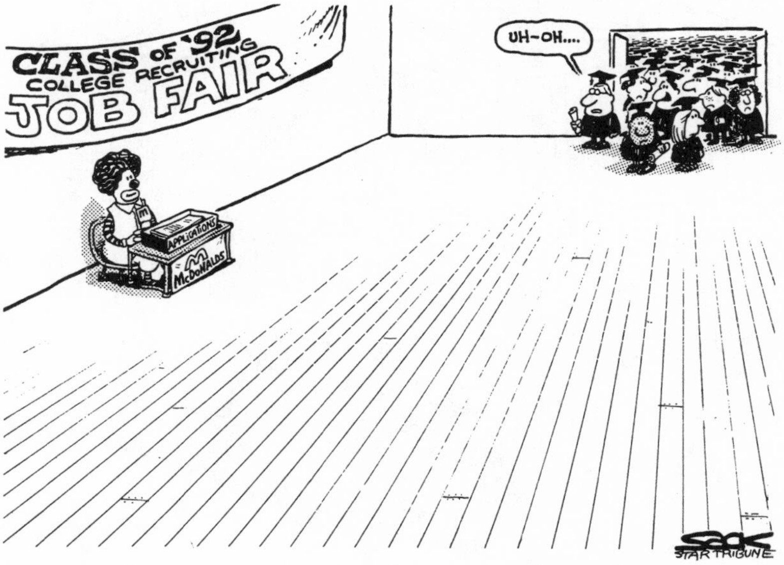
CLASS OF '92
COLLEGE RECRUITING
JOB FAIR
UH-OH....
APPLICATIONS
McDONALDS

STEVE SACK
Courtesy Minneapolis Star-Tribune

RICHARD CROWSON
Courtesy Wichita Eagle

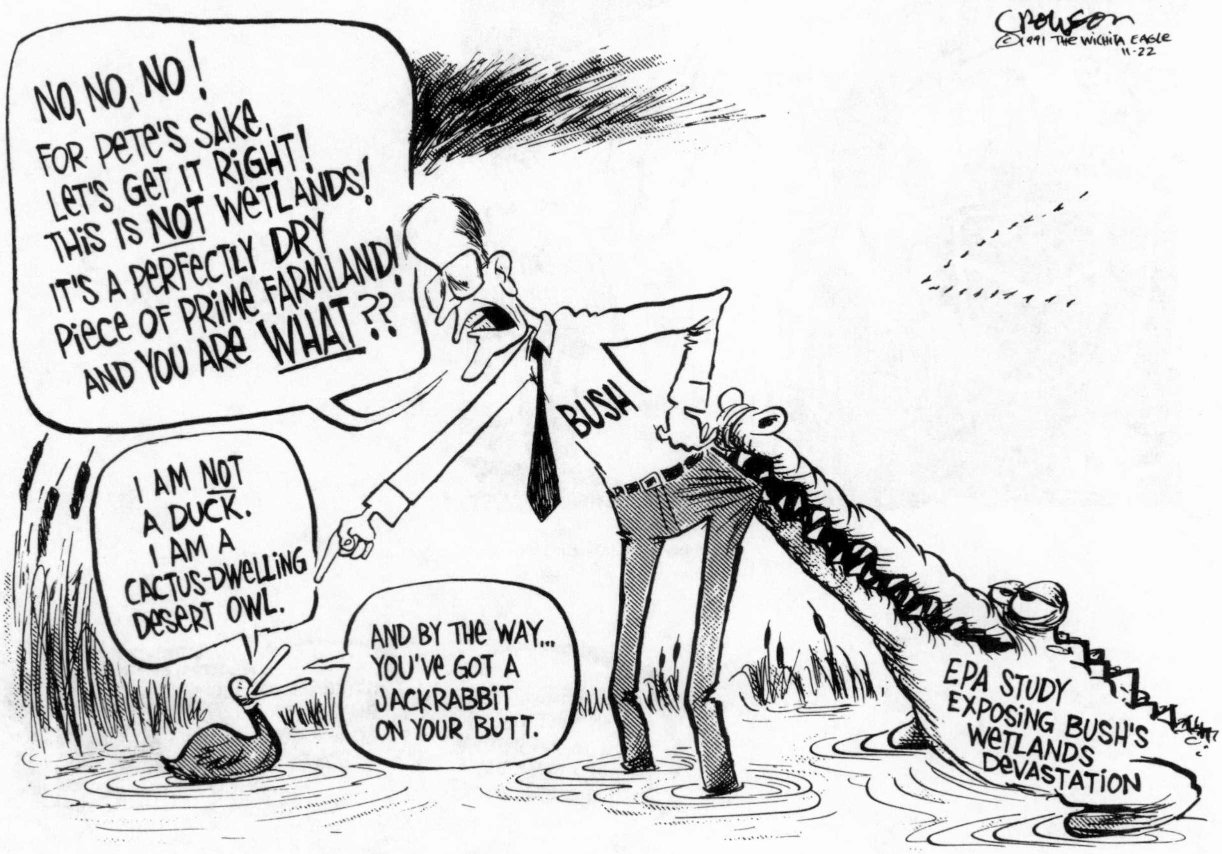
CROWSON ©1991 THE WICHITA EAGLE 11-22
NO, NO, NO! FOR PETE'S SAKE, LET'S GET IT RIGHT! THIS IS NOT WETLANDS! IT'S A PERFECTLY DRY PIECE OF PRIME FARMLAND! AND YOU ARE WHAT??
BUSH
I AM NOT A DUCK. I AM A CACTUS-DWELLING DESERT OWL.
AND BY THE WAY... YOU'VE GOT A JACKRABBIT ON YOUR BUTT.
EPA STUDY EXPOSING BUSH'S WETLANDS DEVASTATION

JACK JURDEN
Courtesy Wilmington News Sentinel

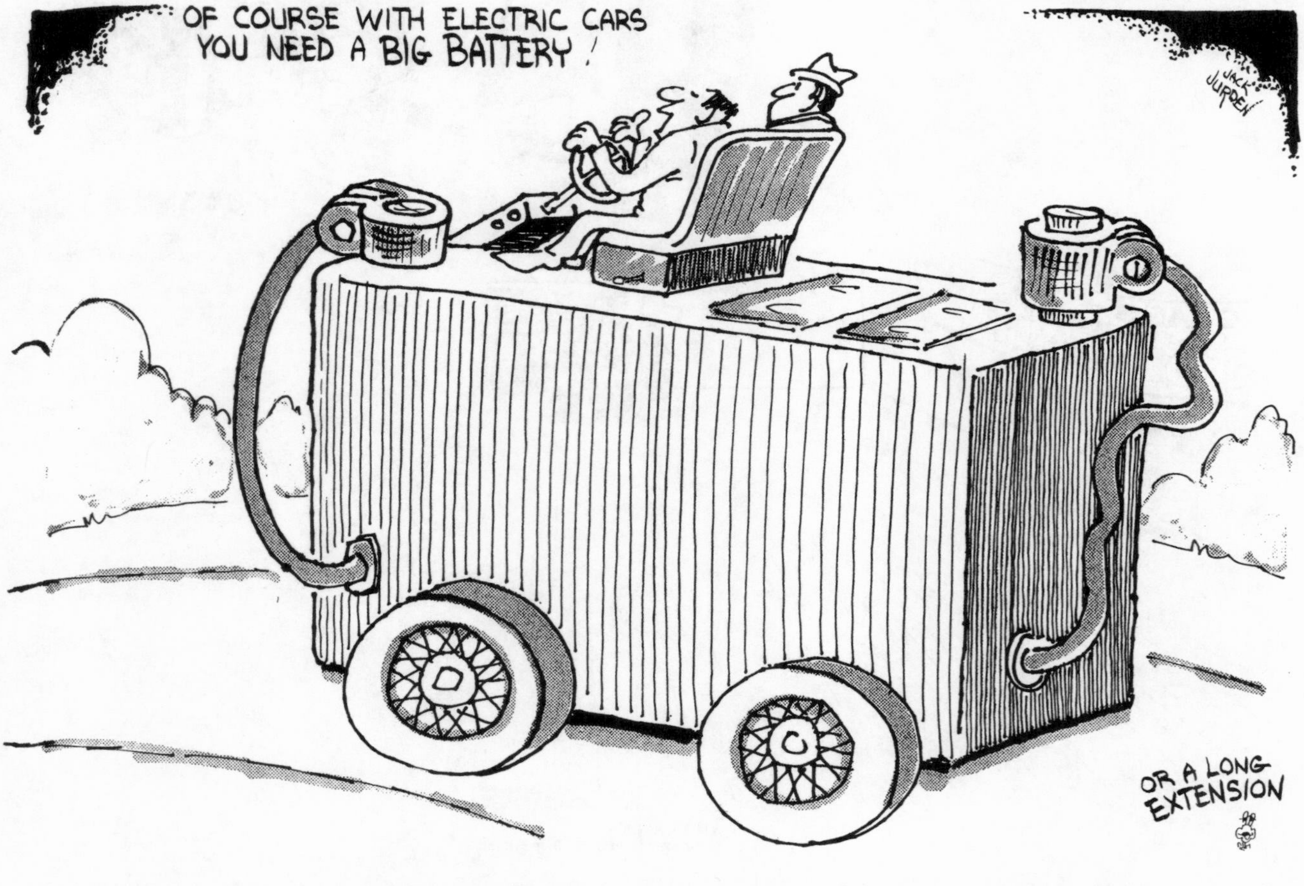
OF COURSE WITH ELECTRIC CARS YOU NEED A BIG BATTERY!
JACK JURDEN
OR A LONG EXTENSION

The Environment

President Bush was reluctant to attend the highly touted Earth Summit in Rio de Janeiro in June, wary that Germany, Japan, and other nations would pressure the U.S. to increase spending on ecological concerns. He noted that the U.S. will spend $1.2 trillion over the next decade to help protect the environment. Bush rejected a sweeping biodiversity treaty intended to protect various species. He did compromise, however, on a long range plan to limit global warming.

Environmentalists expessed disappointment in the Bush Administration's wetlands policy and were working at year's end to substantially expand protected areas. The Environmental Protection Agency signalled a readiness to broaden the definition of wetlands in order to safeguard environmentally sensitive areas throughout the country.

Controversy raged in the Northwest between environmentalists and lumber workers over the spotted owl. The owl is close to extinction, and its only habitat is in areas of the Northwest where lumbering is king. To many workers, it was a matter of animal rights versus job rights.

U.S. automakers continue to experiment with electric cars, but limited battery life remains a problem.

WALT HANDELSMAN
Courtesy Times-Picayune (N.O.)

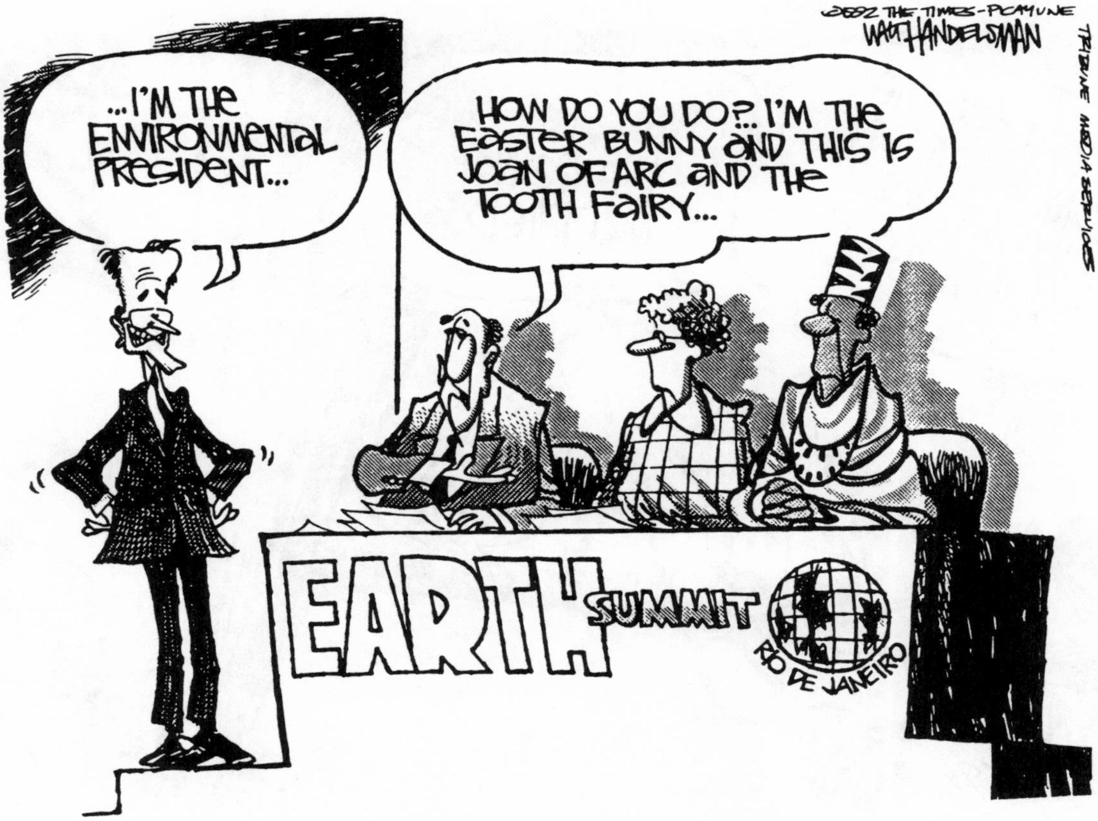
©1992 THE TIMES-PICAYUNE
WALT HANDELSMAN
TRIBUNE MEDIA SERVICES
...I'M THE ENVIRONMENTAL PRESIDENT...
HOW DO YOU DO?... I'M THE EASTER BUNNY AND THIS IS JOAN OF ARC AND THE TOOTH FAIRY...
EARTH SUMMIT
RIO DE JANEIRO

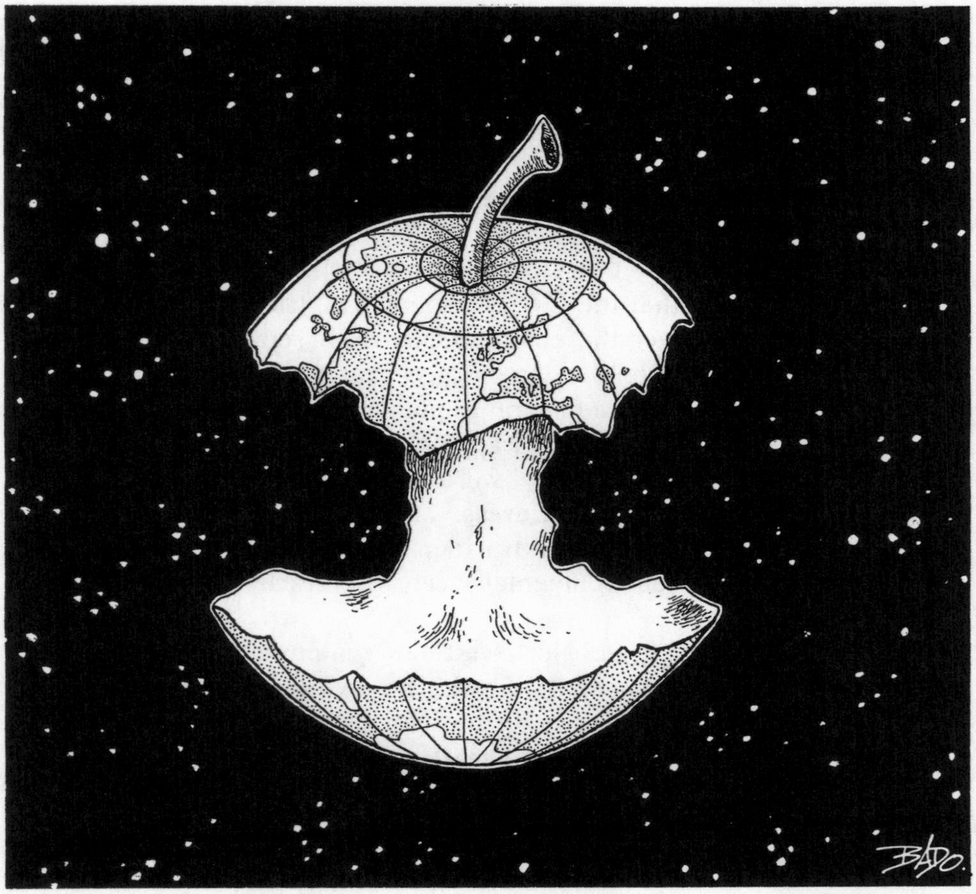

GUY BADEAUX
Courtesy Le Droit (Ottawa)

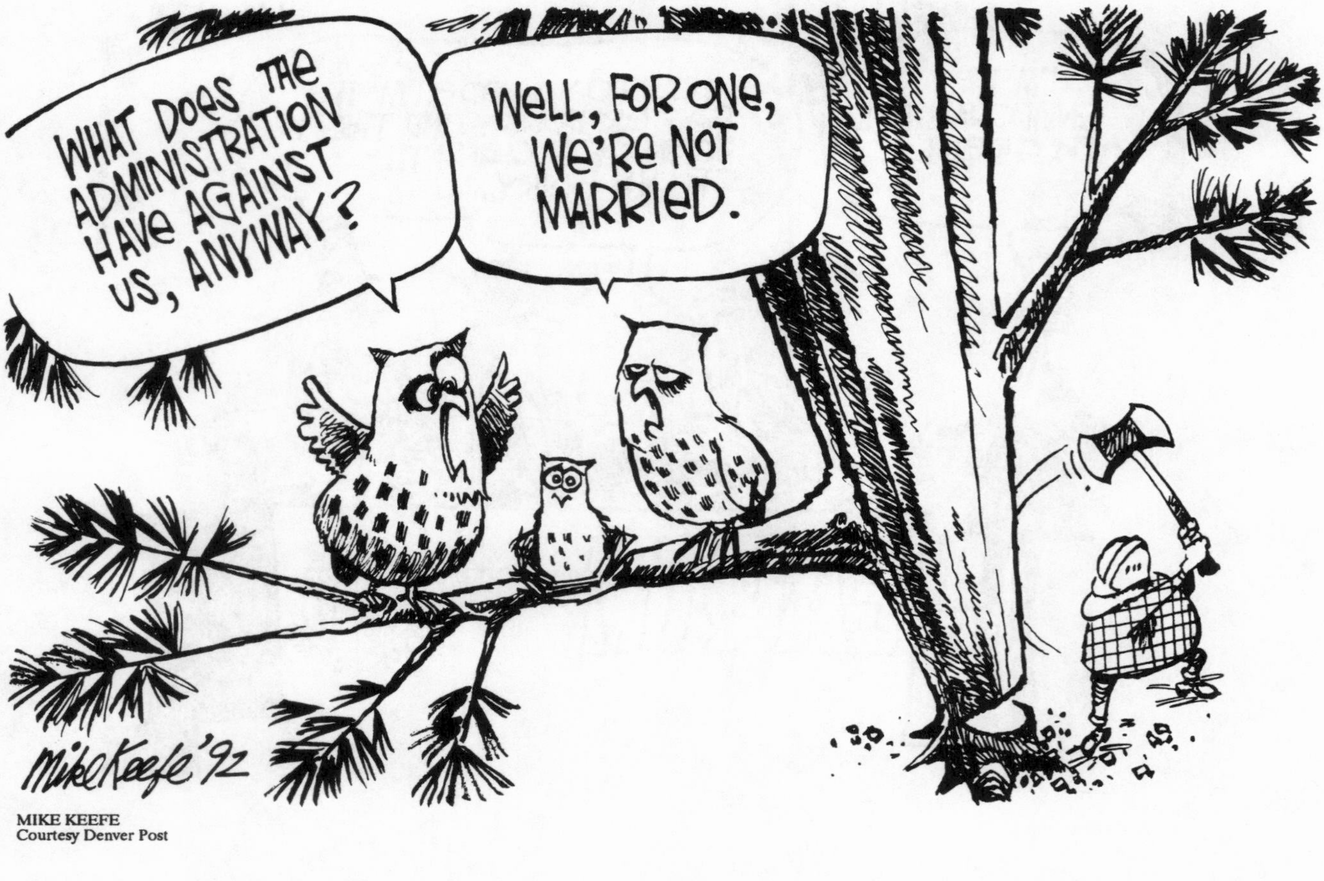
WHAT DOES THE ADMINISTRATION HAVE AGAINST US, ANYWAY?
WELL, FOR ONE, WE'RE NOT MARRIED.

MIKE KEEFE
Courtesy Denver Post

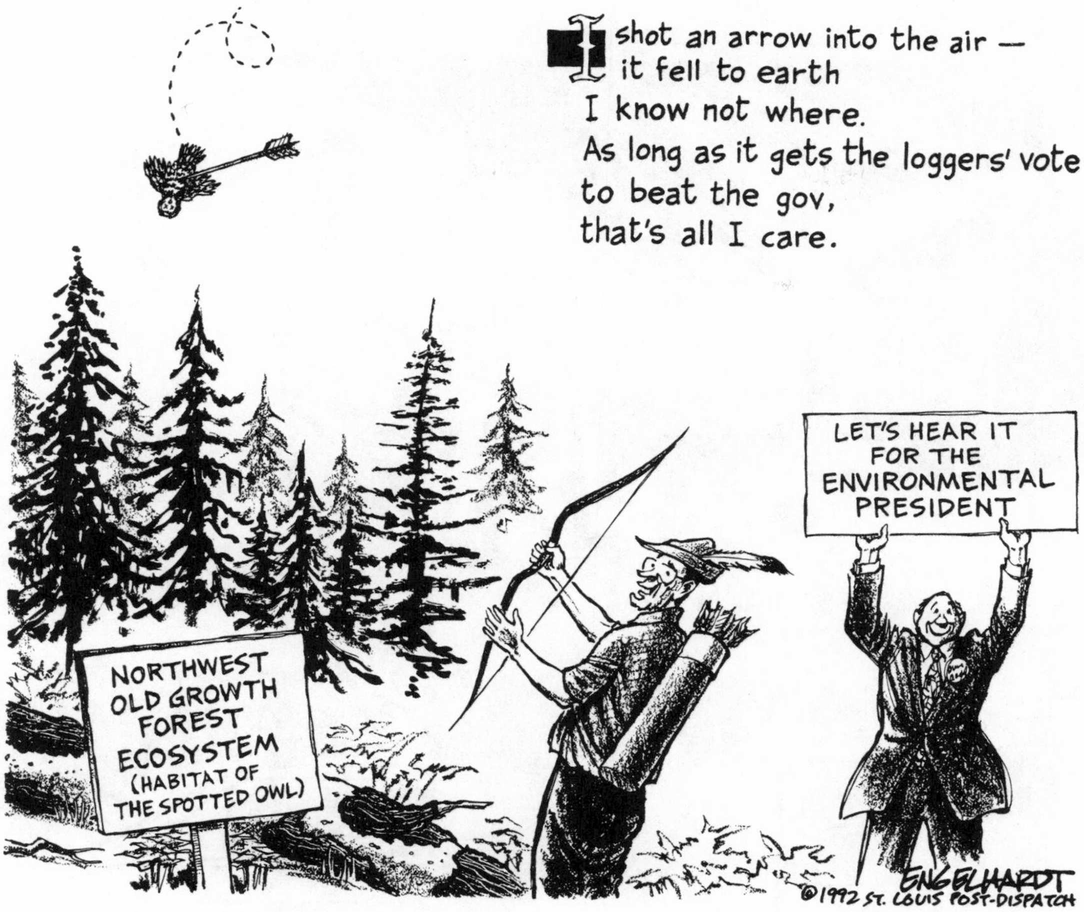
I shot an arrow into the air —
it fell to earth
I know not where.
As long as it gets the loggers' vote
to beat the gov,
that's all I care.
NORTHWEST OLD GROWTH FOREST ECOSYSTEM (HABITAT OF THE SPOTTED OWL)
LET'S HEAR IT FOR THE ENVIRONMENTAL PRESIDENT
ENGELHARDT
©1992 ST. LOUIS POST-DISPATCH

TOM ENGELHARDT
Courtesy St. Louis Post-Dispatch

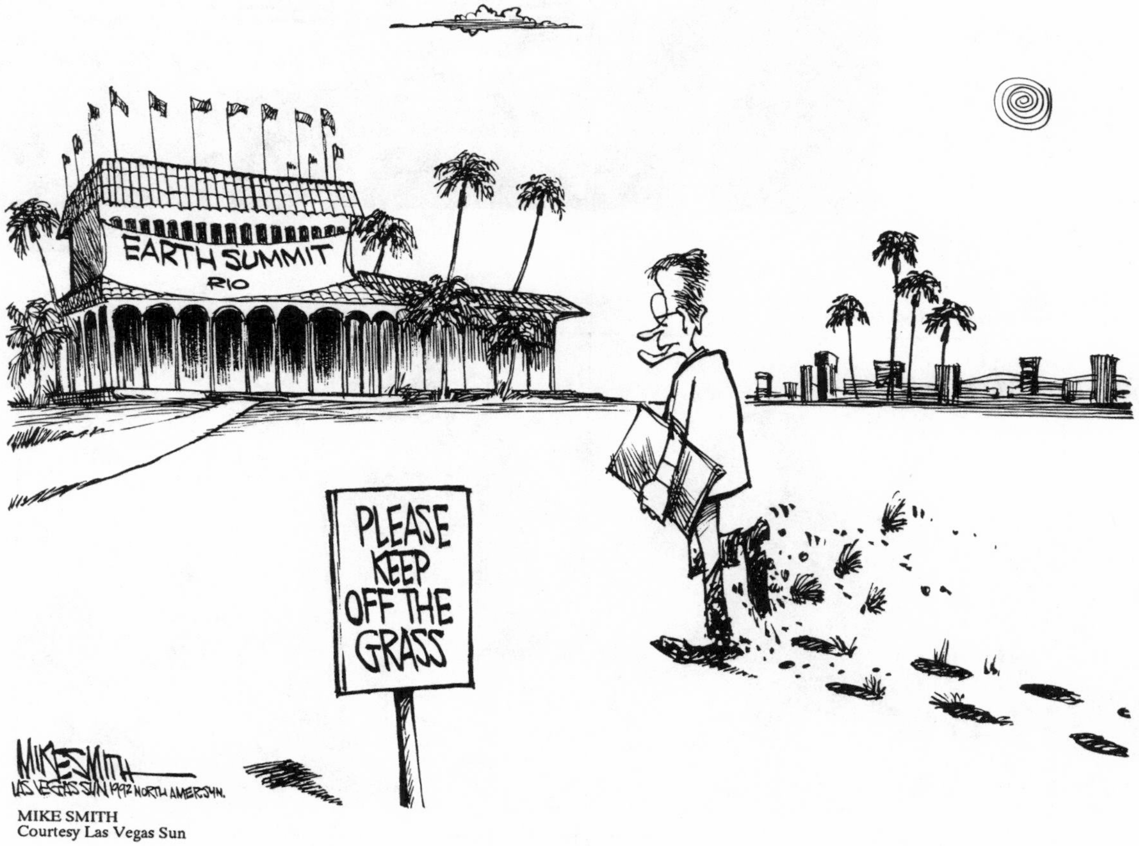
EARTH SUMMIT
RIO
PLEASE KEEP OFF THE GRASS
MIKE SMITH

MIKE SMITH
Courtesy Las Vegas Sun

JIM BORGMAN
Courtesy Cincinnati Enquirer

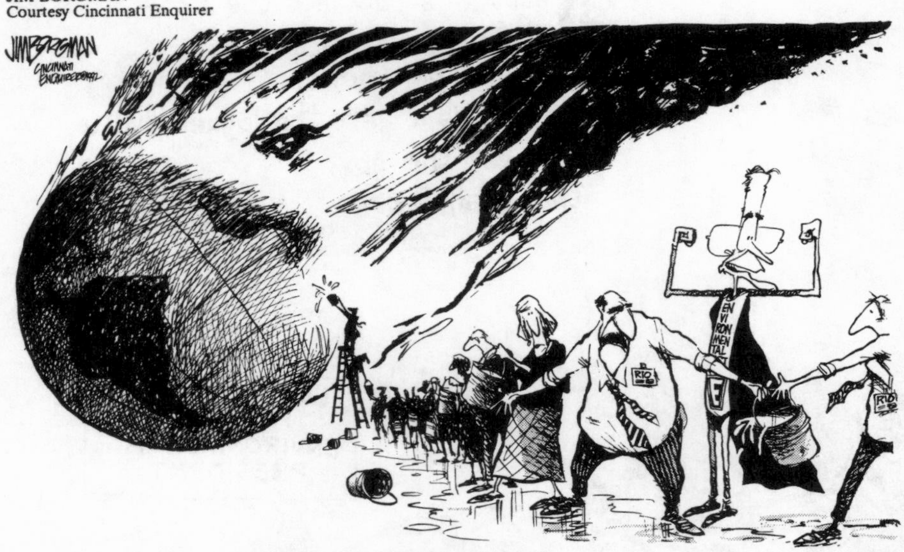
JIM BORGMAN
EN VI RON MEN TAL
RIO

"AM I IN TIME FOR THE PHOTO-OP?"

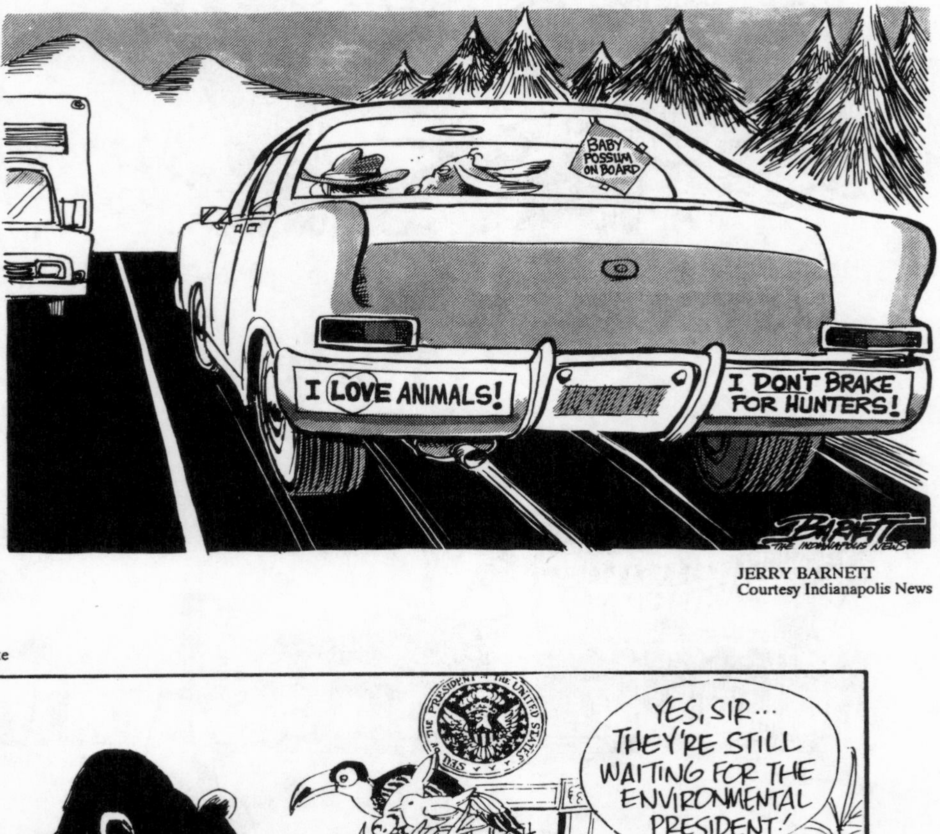
BABY POSSUM ON BOARD
I LOVE ANIMALS!
I DON'T BRAKE FOR HUNTERS!
BARNETT
THE INDIANAPOLIS NEWS

JERRY BARNETT
Courtesy Indianapolis News

JERRY ROBINSON
Courtesy Cartoonists & Writers Syndicate

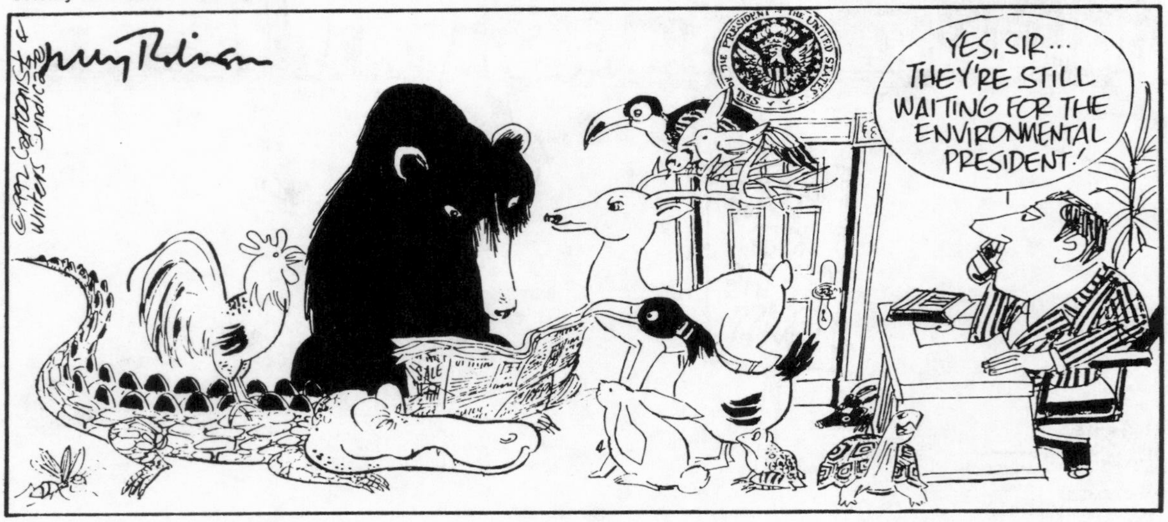
Jerry Robinson
SEAL OF THE PRESIDENT OF THE UNITED STATES
YES, SIR... THEY'RE STILL WAITING FOR THE ENVIRONMENTAL PRESIDENT!

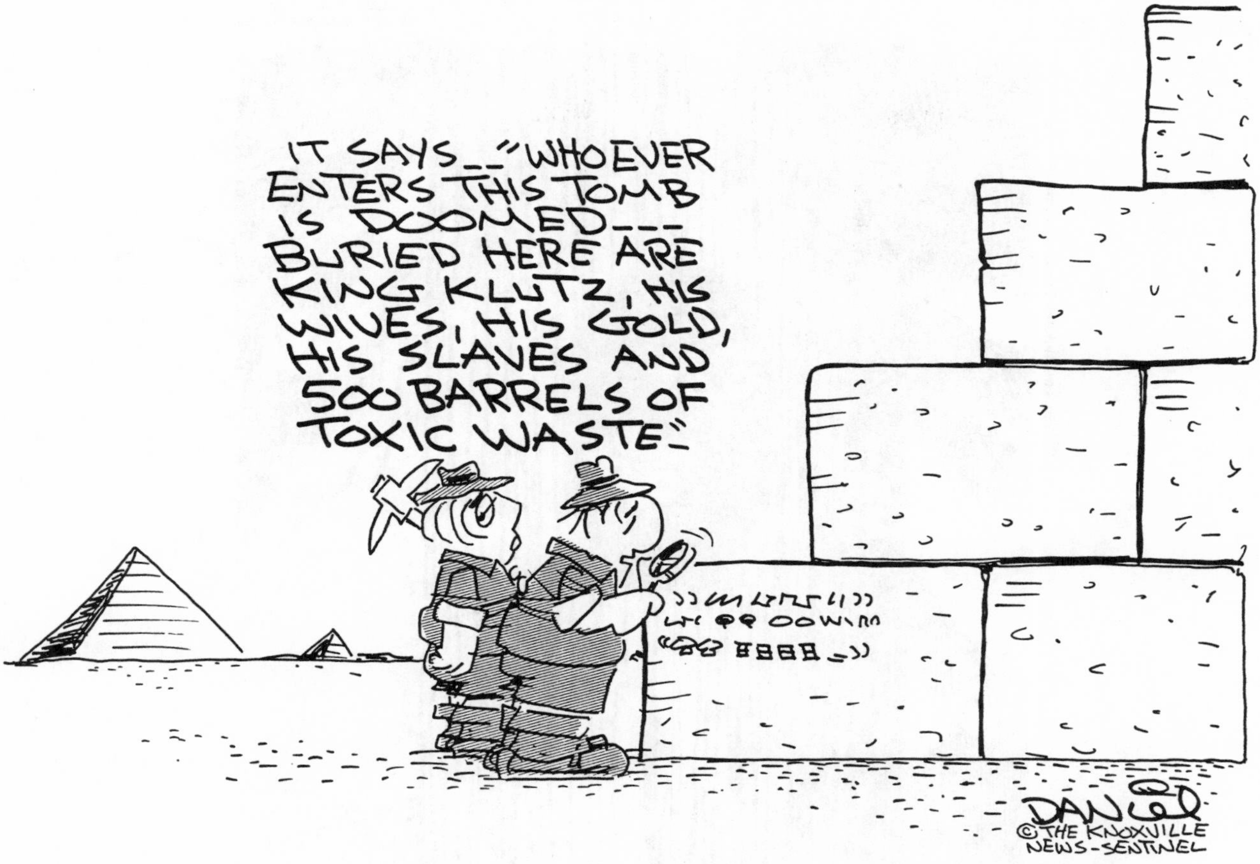
IT SAYS_"WHOEVER ENTERS THIS TOMB IS DOOMED--- BURIED HERE ARE KING KLUTZ, HIS WIVES, HIS GOLD, HIS SLAVES AND 500 BARRELS OF TOXIC WASTE."
DANIEL
© THE KNOXVILLE NEWS-SENTINEL

CHARLES DANIEL
Courtesy Knoxville News-Sentinel

JACK JURDEN
Courtesy Wilmington News Sentinel

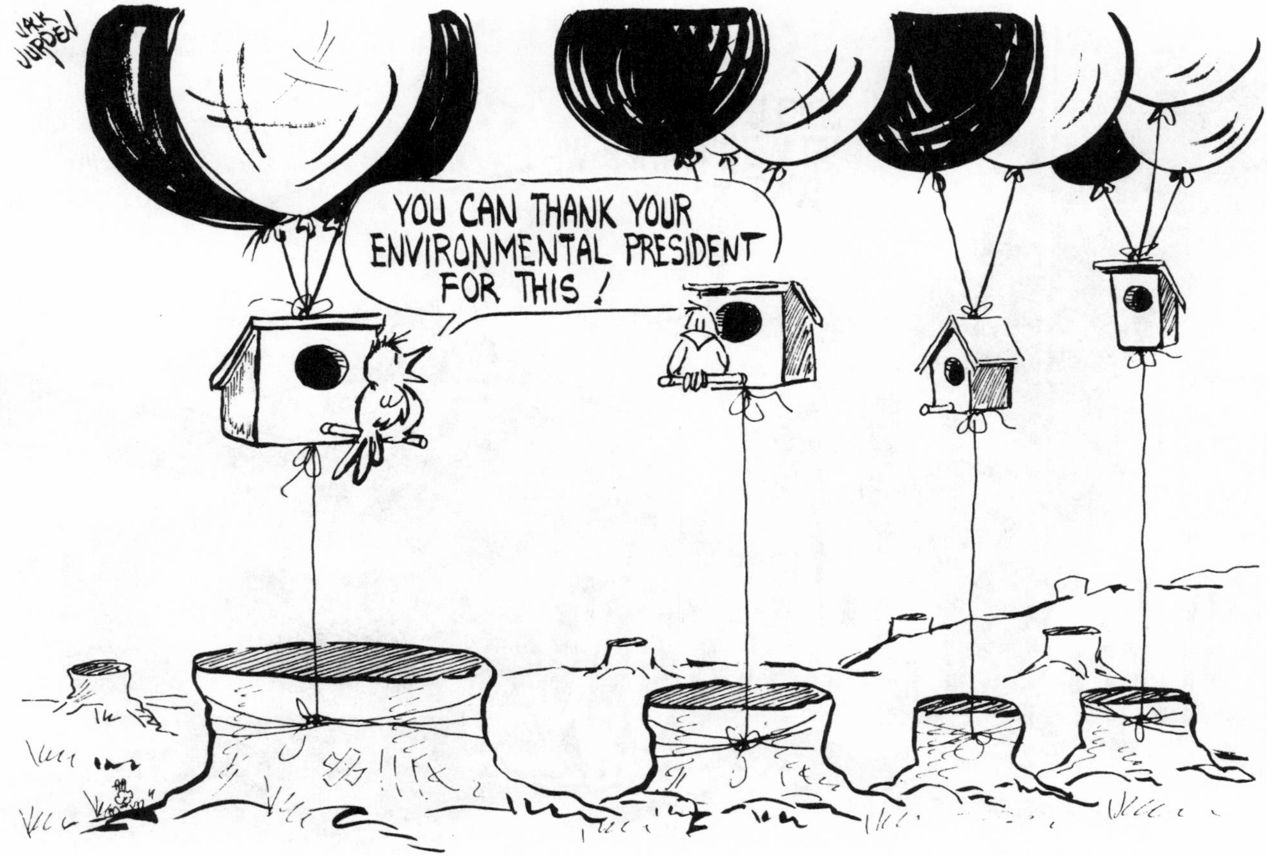
JACK JURDEN
YOU CAN THANK YOUR ENVIRONMENTAL PRESIDENT FOR THIS !

PAUL CONRAD
Courtesy Los Angeles Times

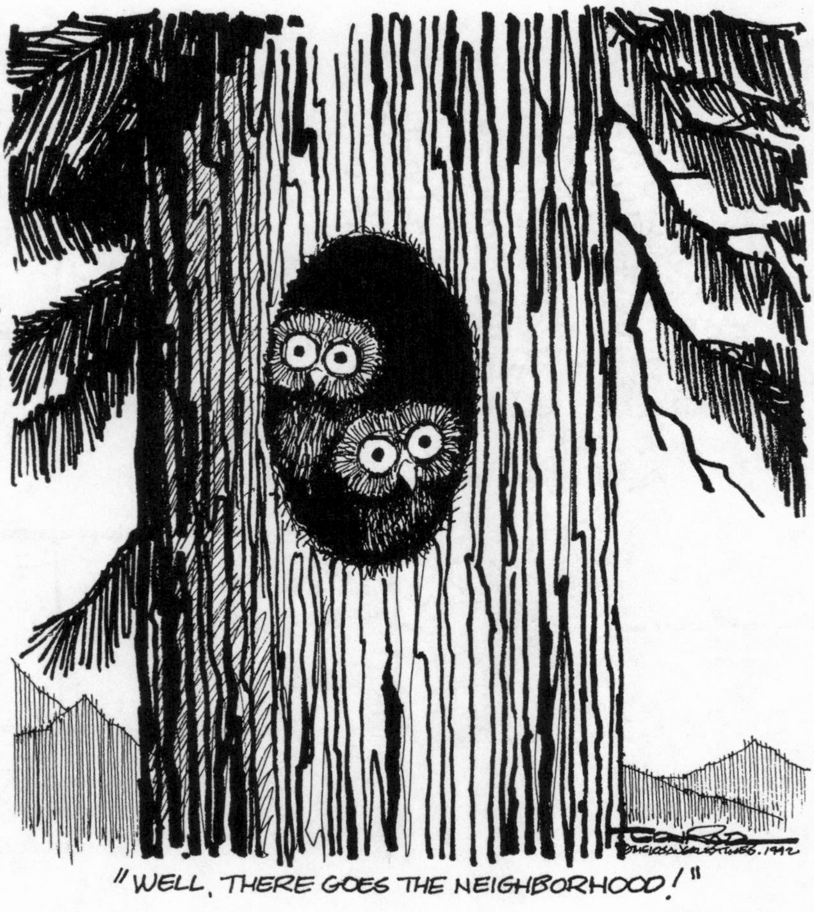
"WELL, THERE GOES THE NEIGHBORHOOD!"

BRUCE MACKINNON
Courtesy Halifax Chronicle-Herald

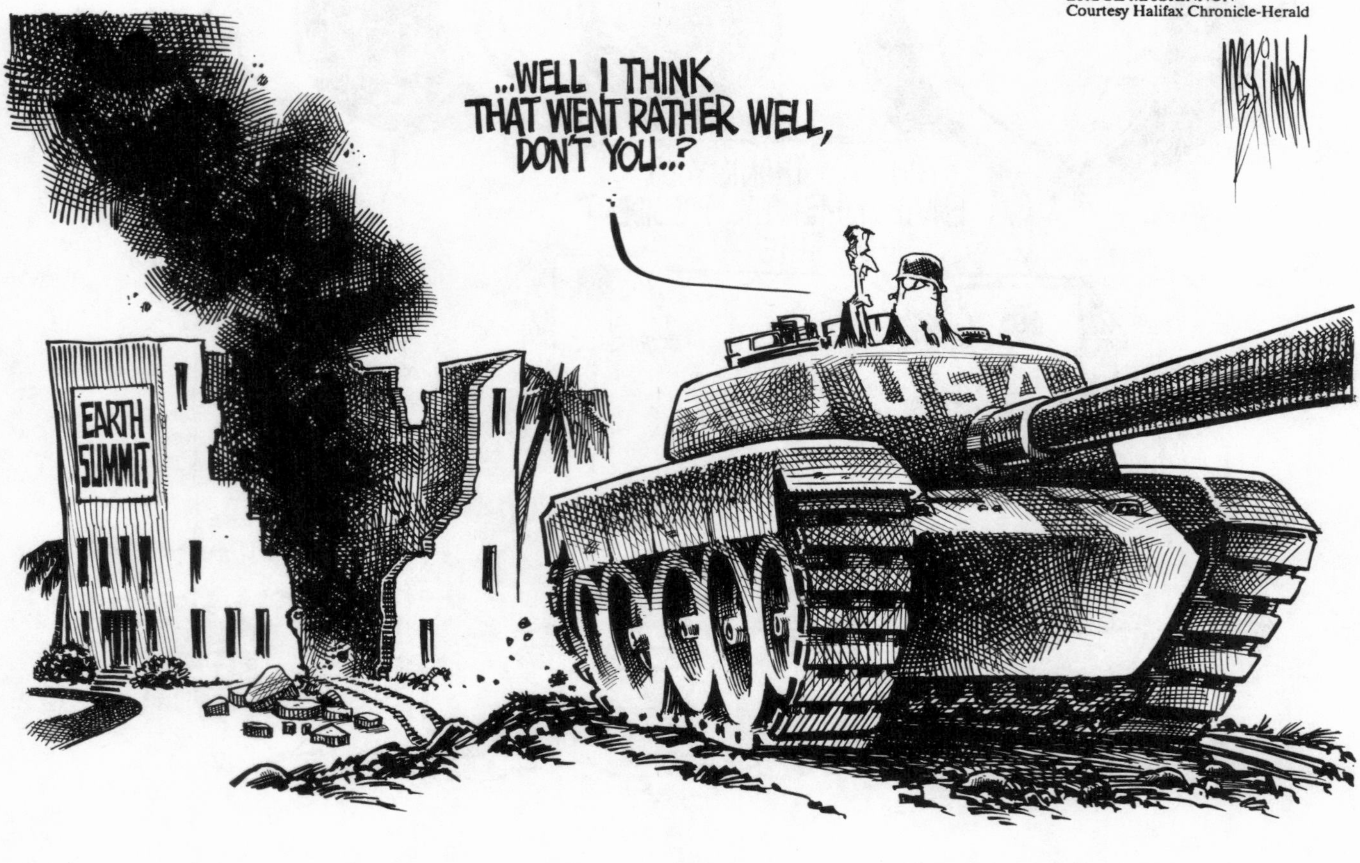
...WELL I THINK THAT WENT RATHER WELL, DON'T YOU..?
EARTH SUMMIT
USA

Canadian Affairs

The Toronto Blue Jays won the 1992 World Series, and that was the good news for Canadians. Other news was not so welcome. The much-publicized November referendum on constitutional reform, which was supposed to offer something to everybody, went down to defeat. French-speaking Quebeckers, as well as native aboriginals, Eskimos, and underrepresented voters in the West, were to be given new rights and powers. With the NO vote, Canada remained divided.

The North American Free Trade Agreement (NAFTA), agreed to in August by the U.S., Canada, and Mexico, is designed to establish a unified market of $6.5 trillion to meet European and Japanese competition. Canada signed a free-trade pact with the U.S. three years ago, and the new agreement added some finishing touches.

Many Canadians, however, felt that large U.S. corporations would come out clear winners in free trade across the border. Others feared Canada would have a net loss of jobs. NAFTA will gradually eliminate the low-tariff barriers that still remain. The popularity of Prime Minister Brian Mulroney has sagged as a result of his embracing the free-trade agreement.

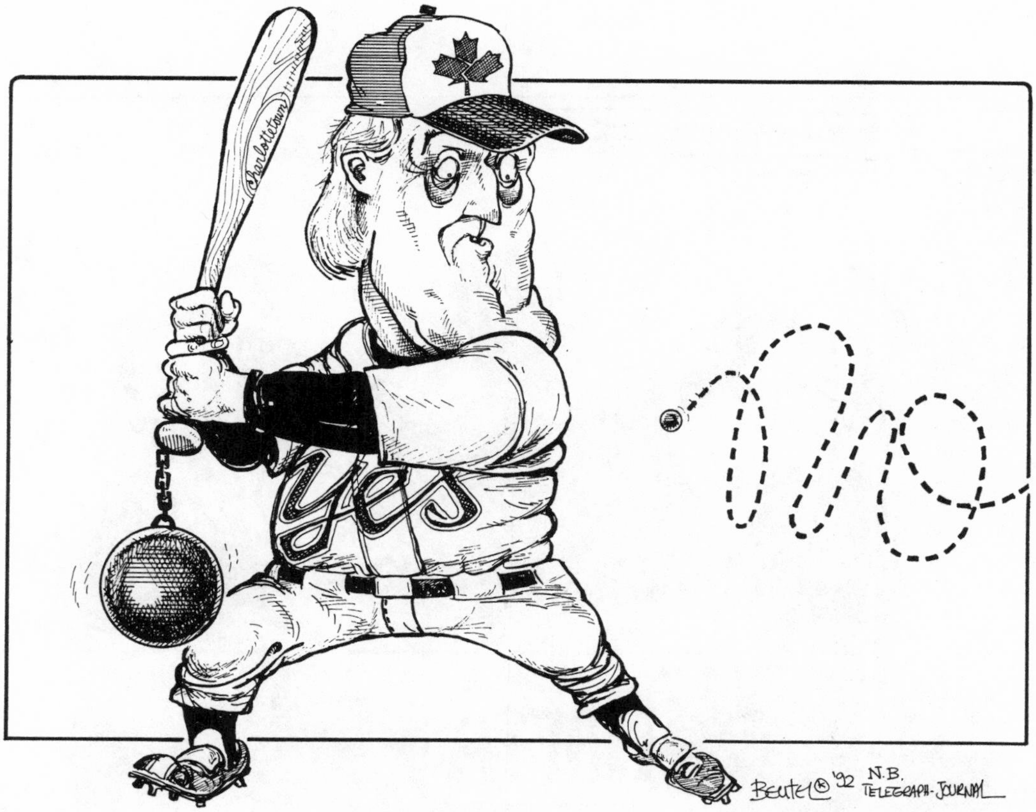
Charlottetown
Yes
NO
Beutel © '92 N.B. Telegraph-Journal

JOSH BEUTEL
Courtesy New Brunswick Telegraph-Journal

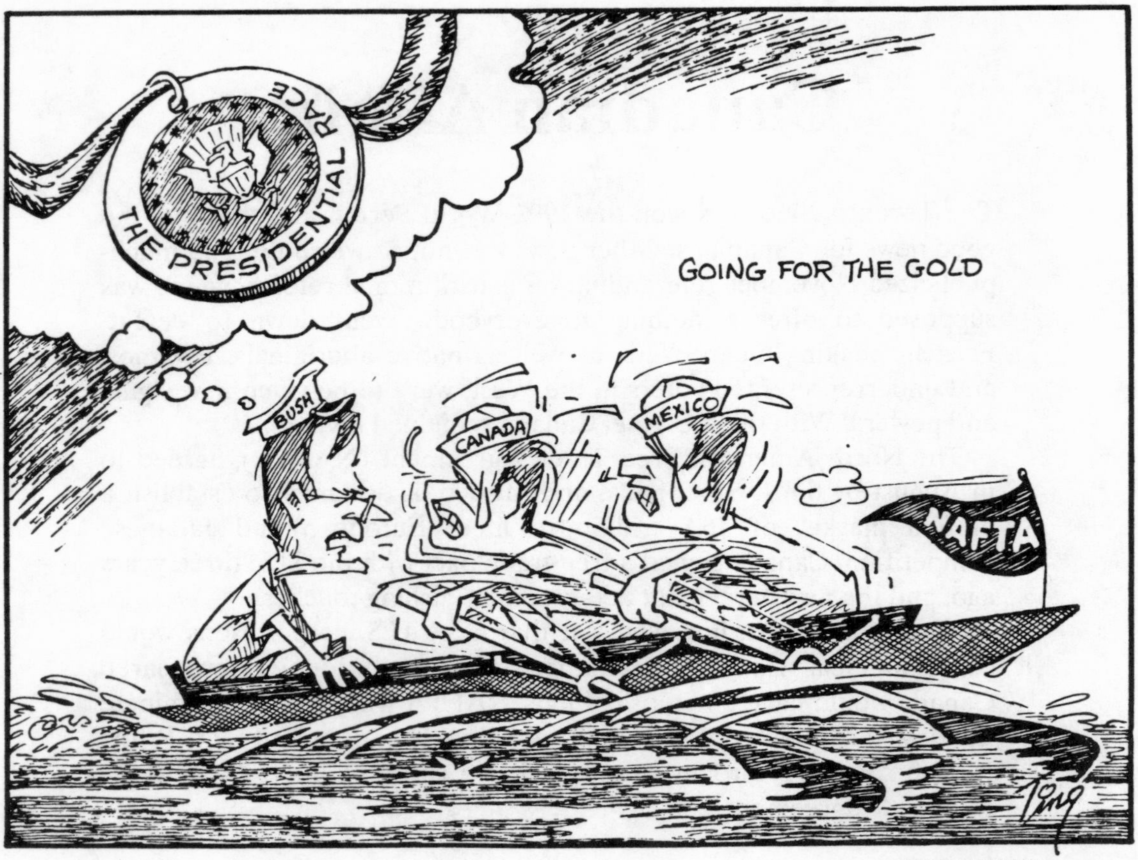
THE PRESIDENTIAL RACE
GOING FOR THE GOLD
BUSH
CANADA
MEXICO
NAFTA

MERLE R. TINGLEY
Courtesy London Free Press (Ont.)

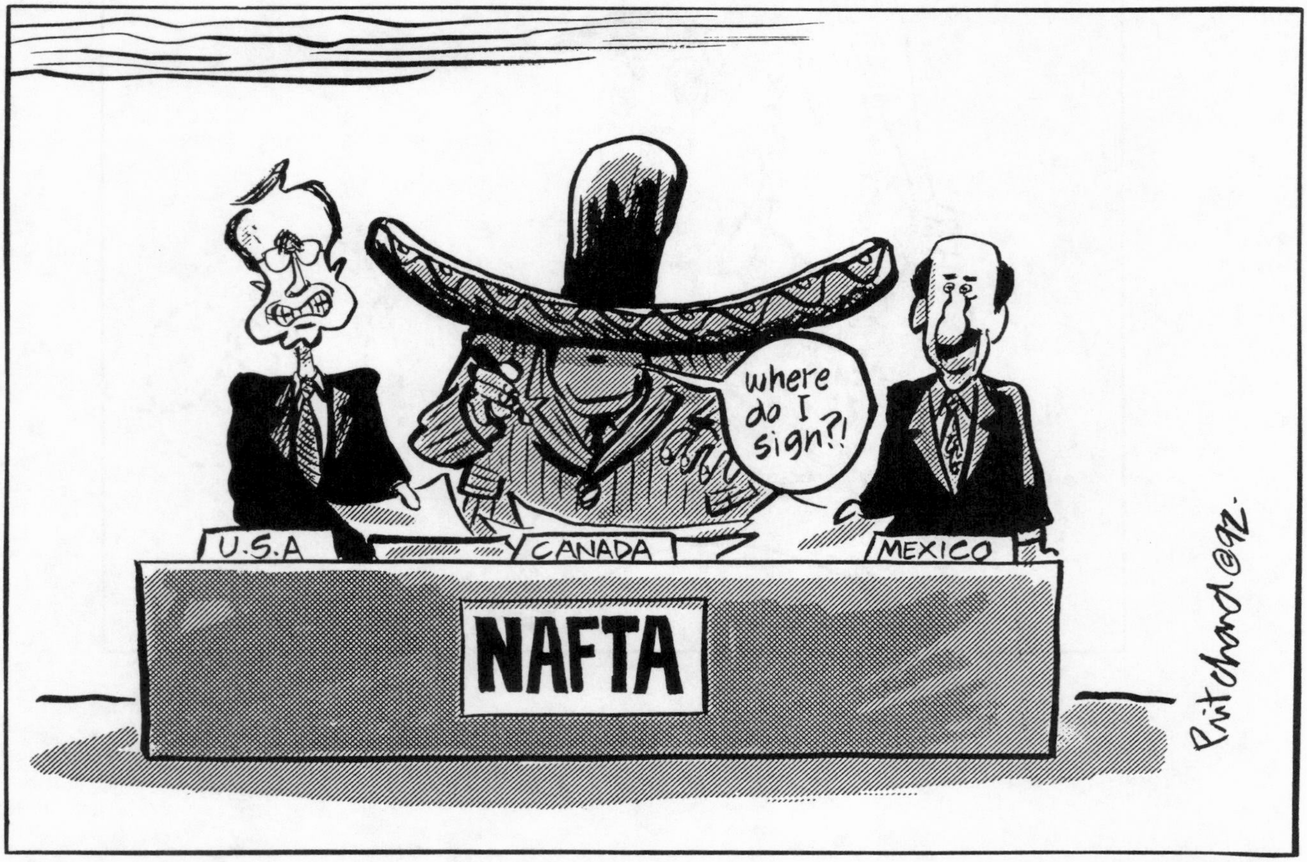
where do I sign?!
U.S.A
CANADA
MEXICO
NAFTA
Pritchard ©92.

DENNY PRITCHARD
Courtesy Ottawa Citizen

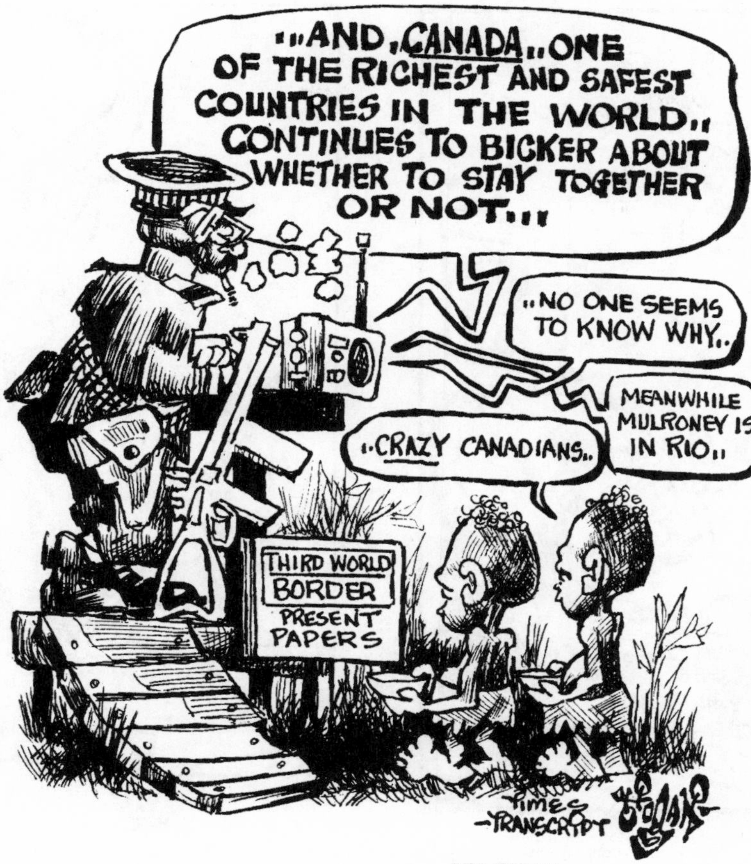
..AND, CANADA.. ONE OF THE RICHEST AND SAFEST COUNTRIES IN THE WORLD.. CONTINUES TO BICKER ABOUT WHETHER TO STAY TOGETHER OR NOT...
..NO ONE SEEMS TO KNOW WHY..
MEANWHILE MULRONEY IS IN RIO..
..CRAZY CANADIANS..
THIRD WORLD BORDER
PRESENT PAPERS
TIMES -TRANSCRIPT
HOGAN

BILL HOGAN
Courtesy Times-Transcript (N. Bruns.)

EDD ULUSCHAK
Courtesy Miller Services

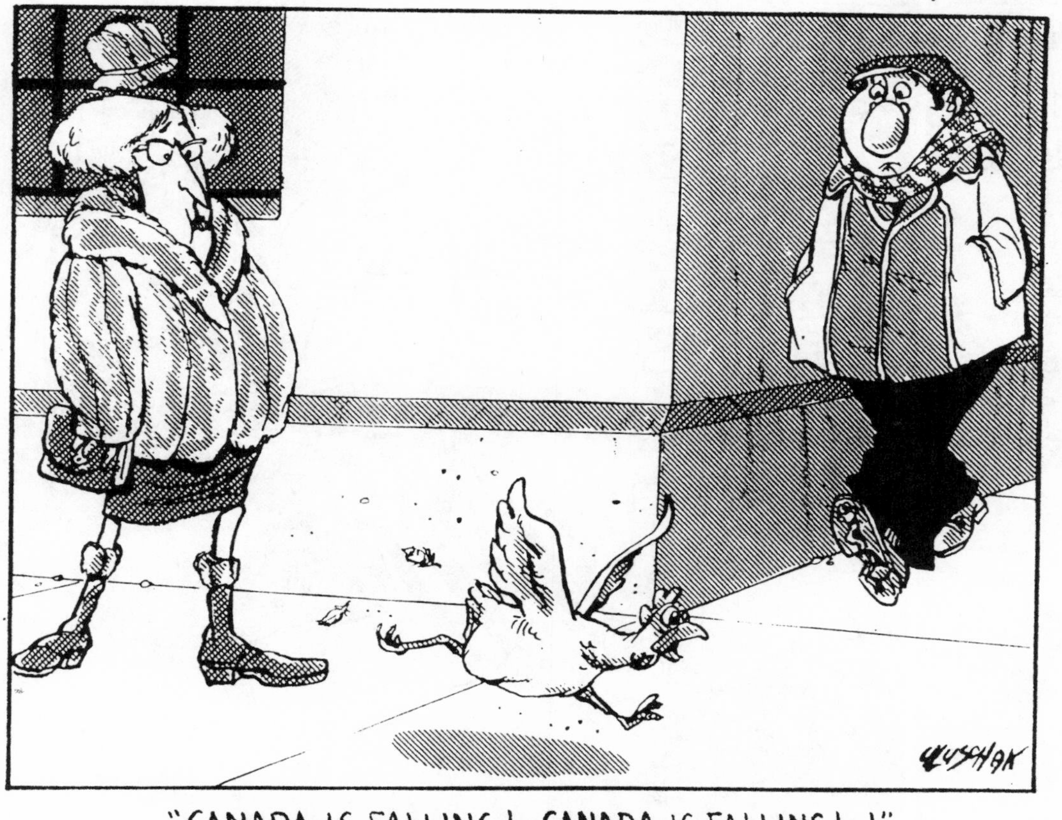
ULUSCHAK

"CANADA IS FALLING! CANADA IS FALLING!..!"

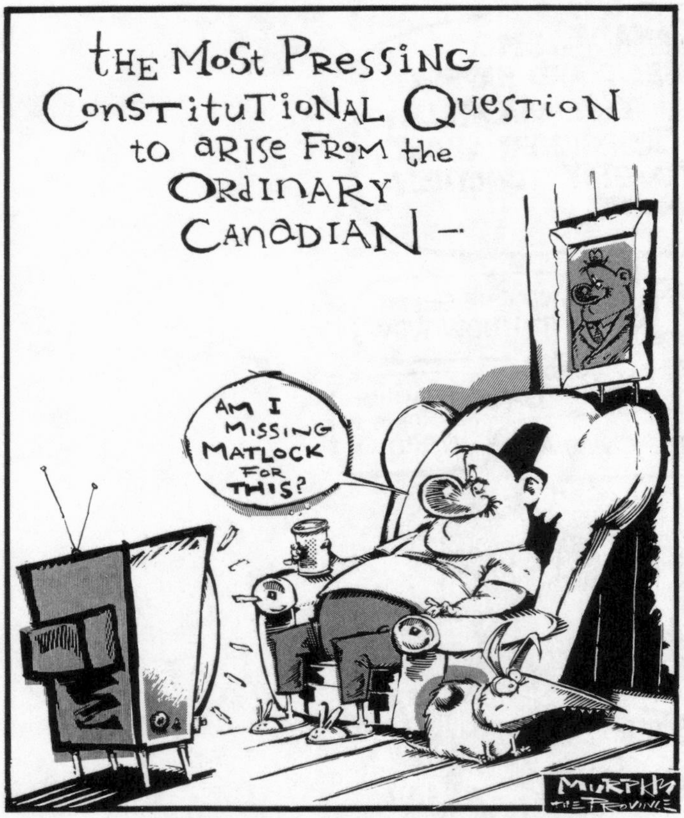
the Most Pressing Constitutional Question to arise from the Ordinary Canadian –
Am I missing Matlock for this?
MURPHY THE PROVINCE

DAN MURPHY
Courtesy Vancouver Province

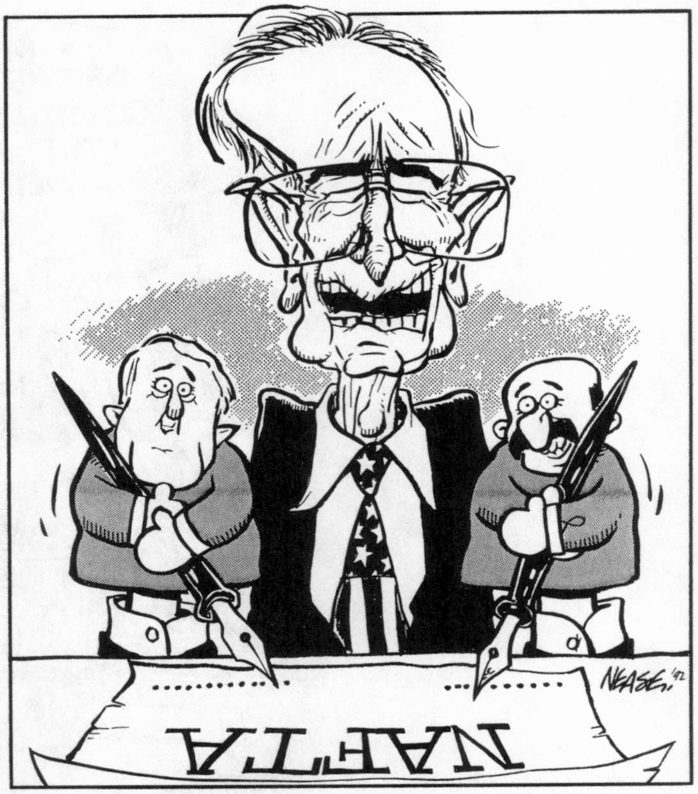
NAFTA
NEASE '92

STEVE NEASE
Courtesy Montreal Gazette

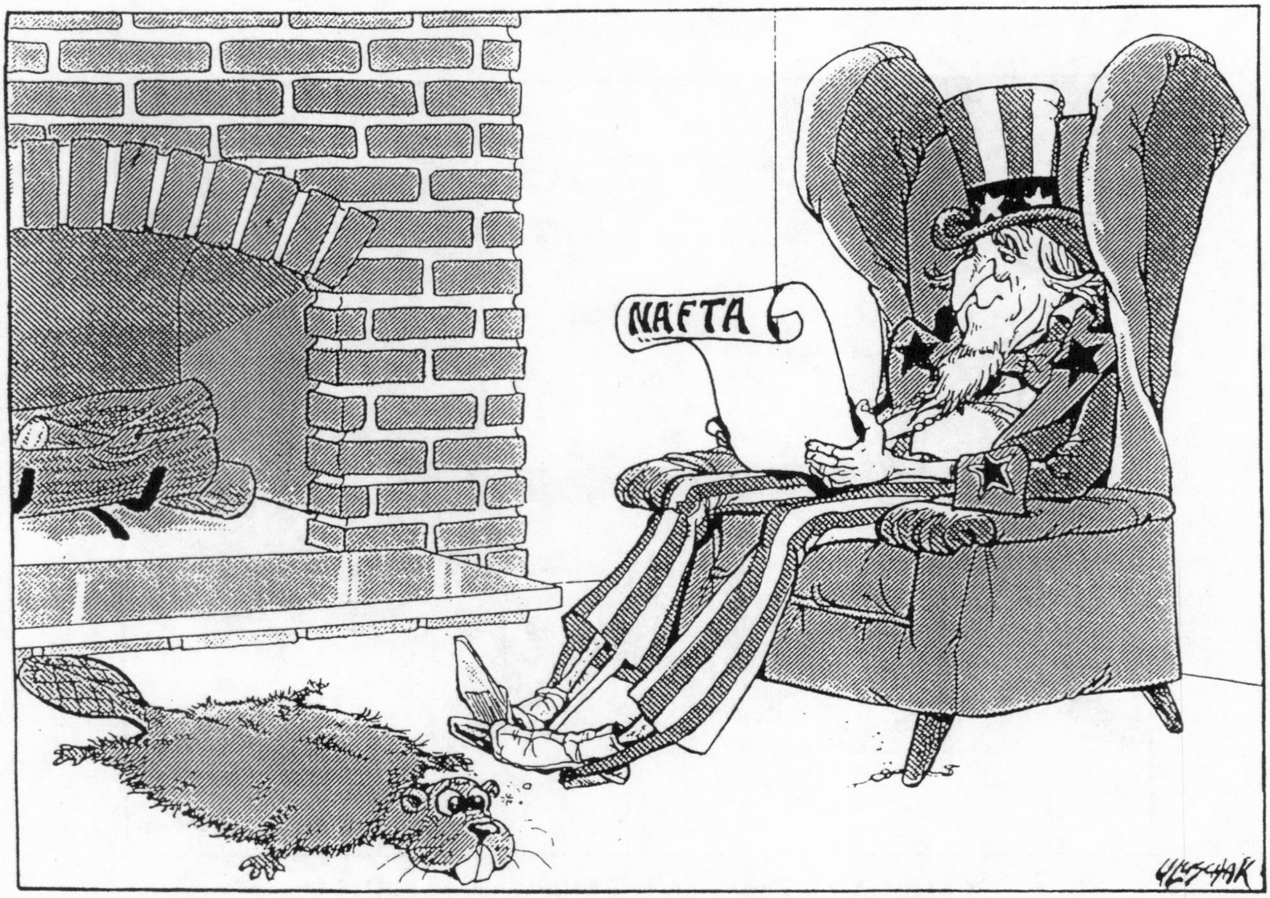
NAFTA
ULUSCHAK

EDD ULUSCHAK
Courtesy Miller Services

CAM CARDOW
Courtesy Regina Leader-Post

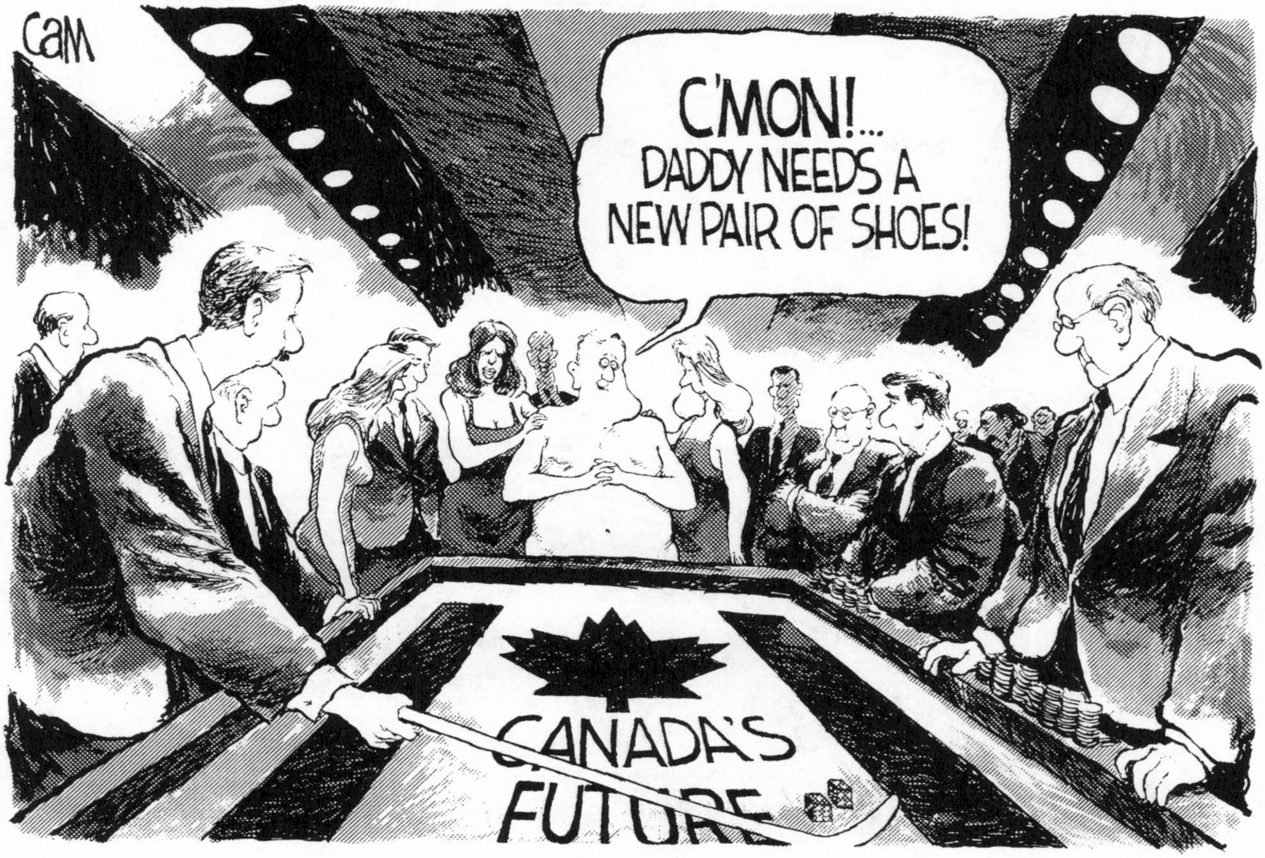
CAM
C'MON!... DADDY NEEDS A NEW PAIR OF SHOES!
CANADA'S FUTURE

EDD ULUSCHAK
Courtesy Miller Services

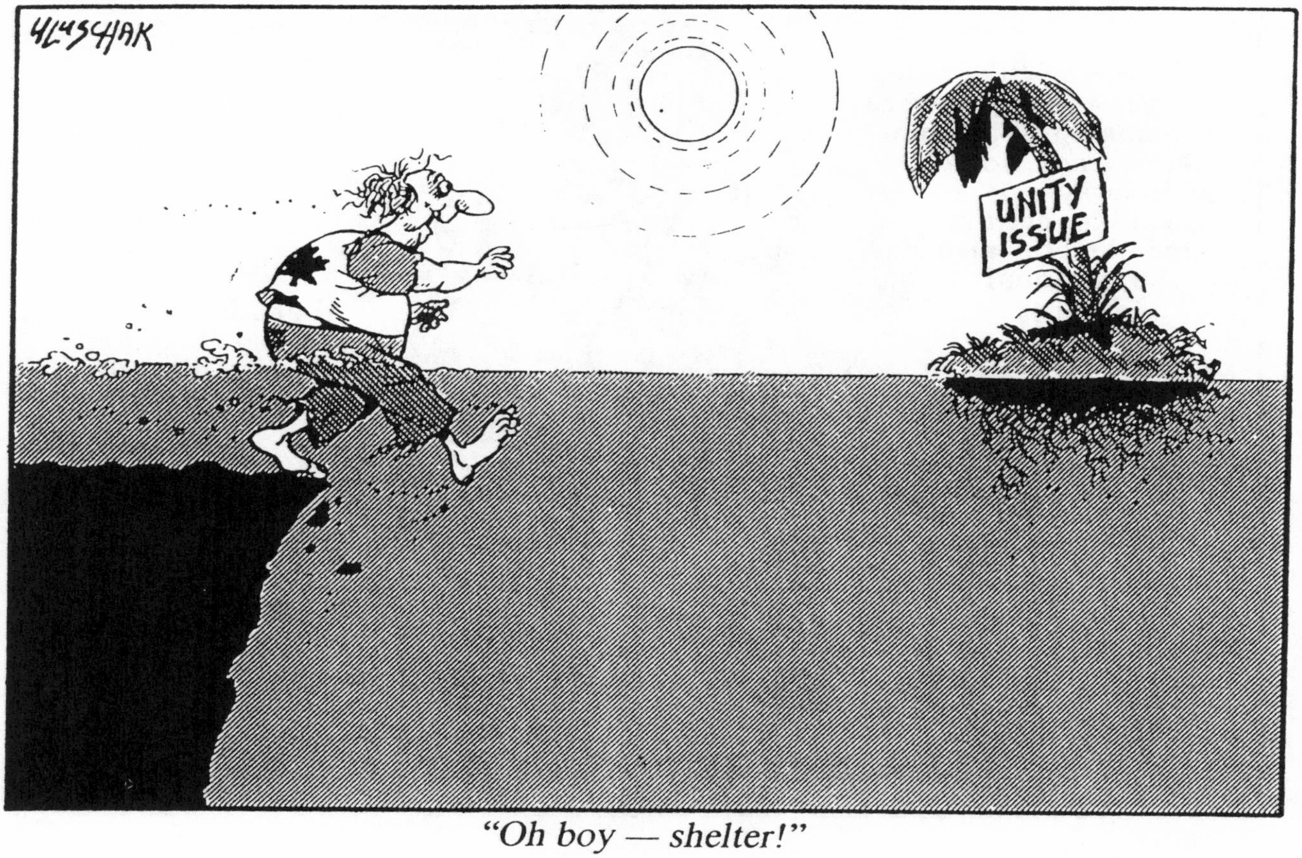
ULUSCHAK
UNITY ISSUE

"Oh boy — shelter!"

JOSH BEUTEL
Courtesy New Brunswick Telegraph-Journal

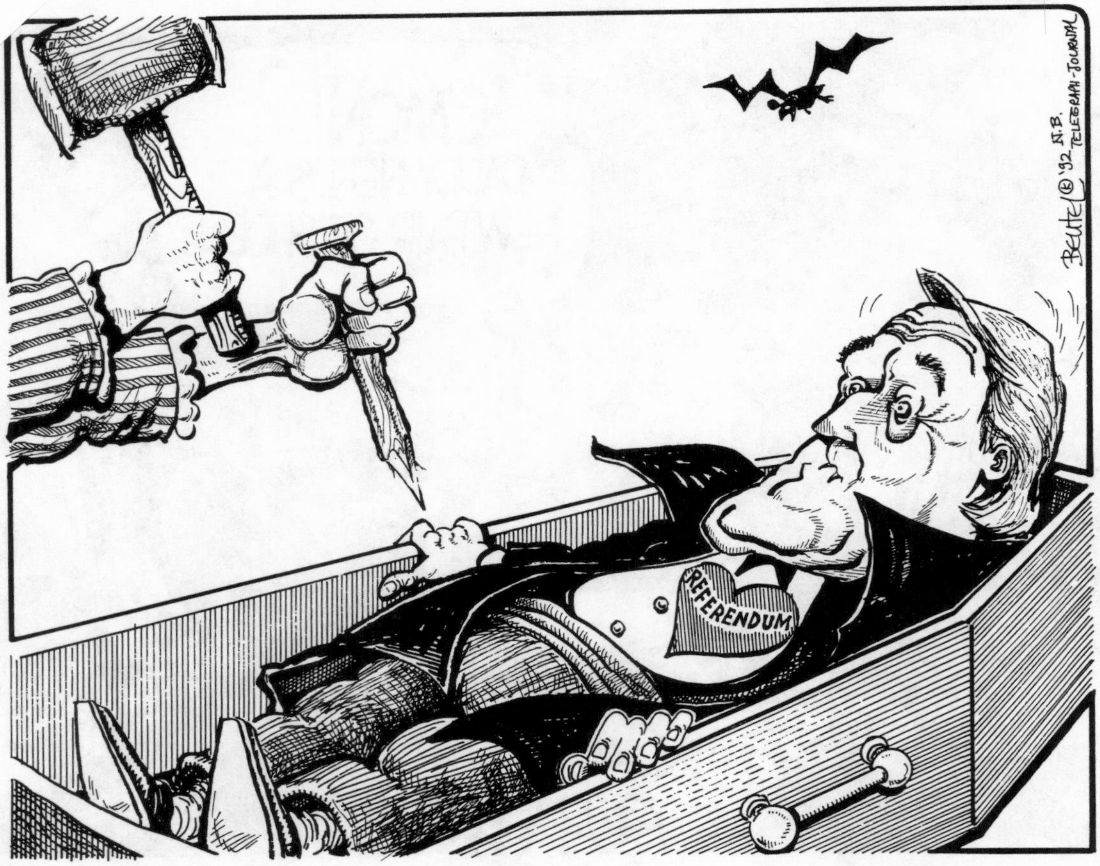
REFERENDUM
BEUTEL © '92 N.B. TELEGRAPH-JOURNAL

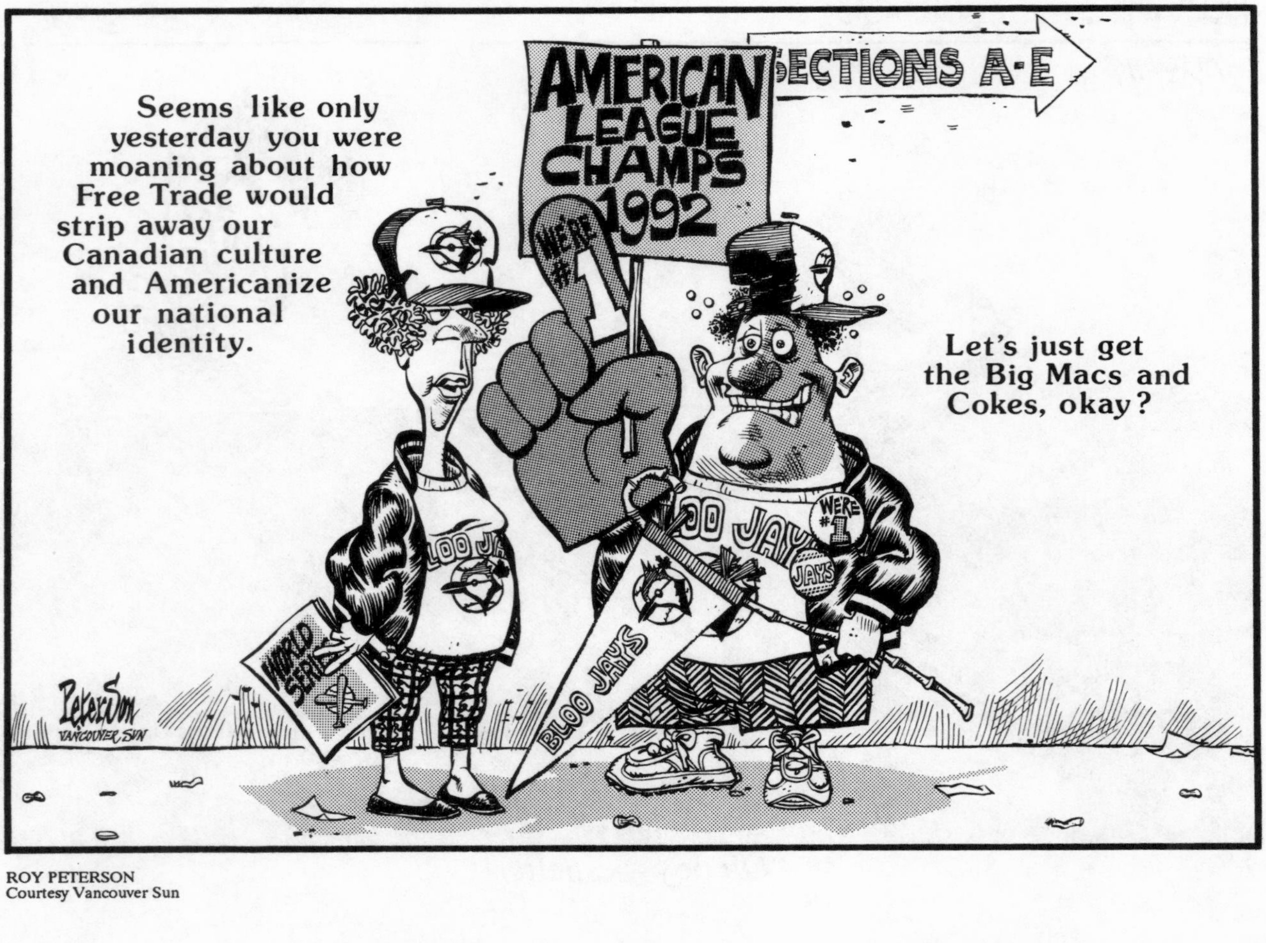
Seems like only yesterday you were moaning about how Free Trade would strip away our Canadian culture and Americanize our national identity.
AMERICAN LEAGUE CHAMPS 1992
SECTIONS A-E
WE'RE #1
Let's just get the Big Macs and Cokes, okay?
BLOO JAYS
BLOO JAYS
WE'RE #1
JAYS
BLOO JAYS
WORLD SERIES
PeterSun VANCOUVER SUN

ROY PETERSON
Courtesy Vancouver Sun

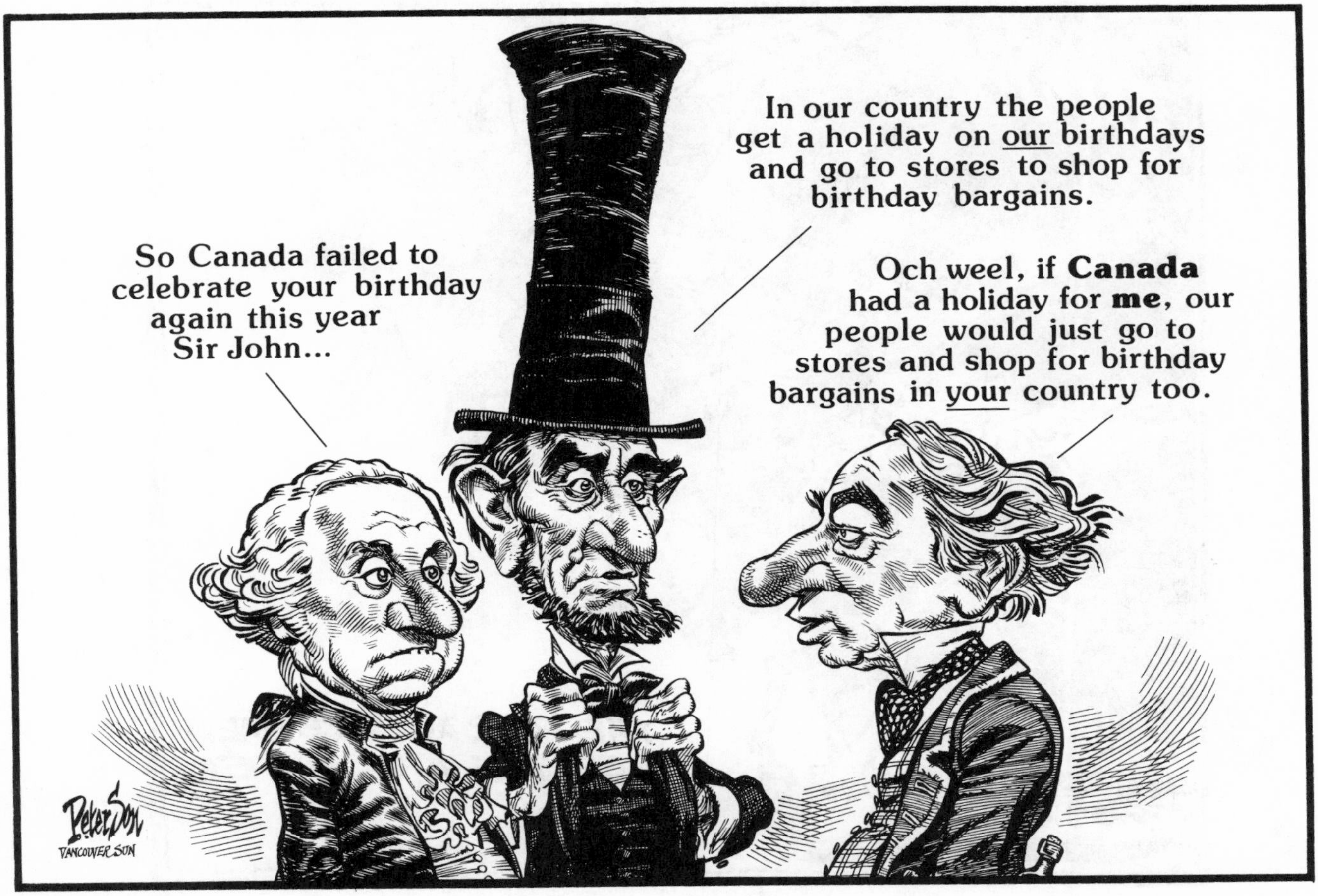
So Canada failed to celebrate your birthday again this year Sir John...
In our country the people get a holiday on our birthdays and go to stores to shop for birthday bargains.
Och weel, if Canada had a holiday for me, our people would just go to stores and shop for birthday bargains in your country too.
Peterson
Vancouver Sun

ROY PETERSON
Courtesy Vancouver Sun

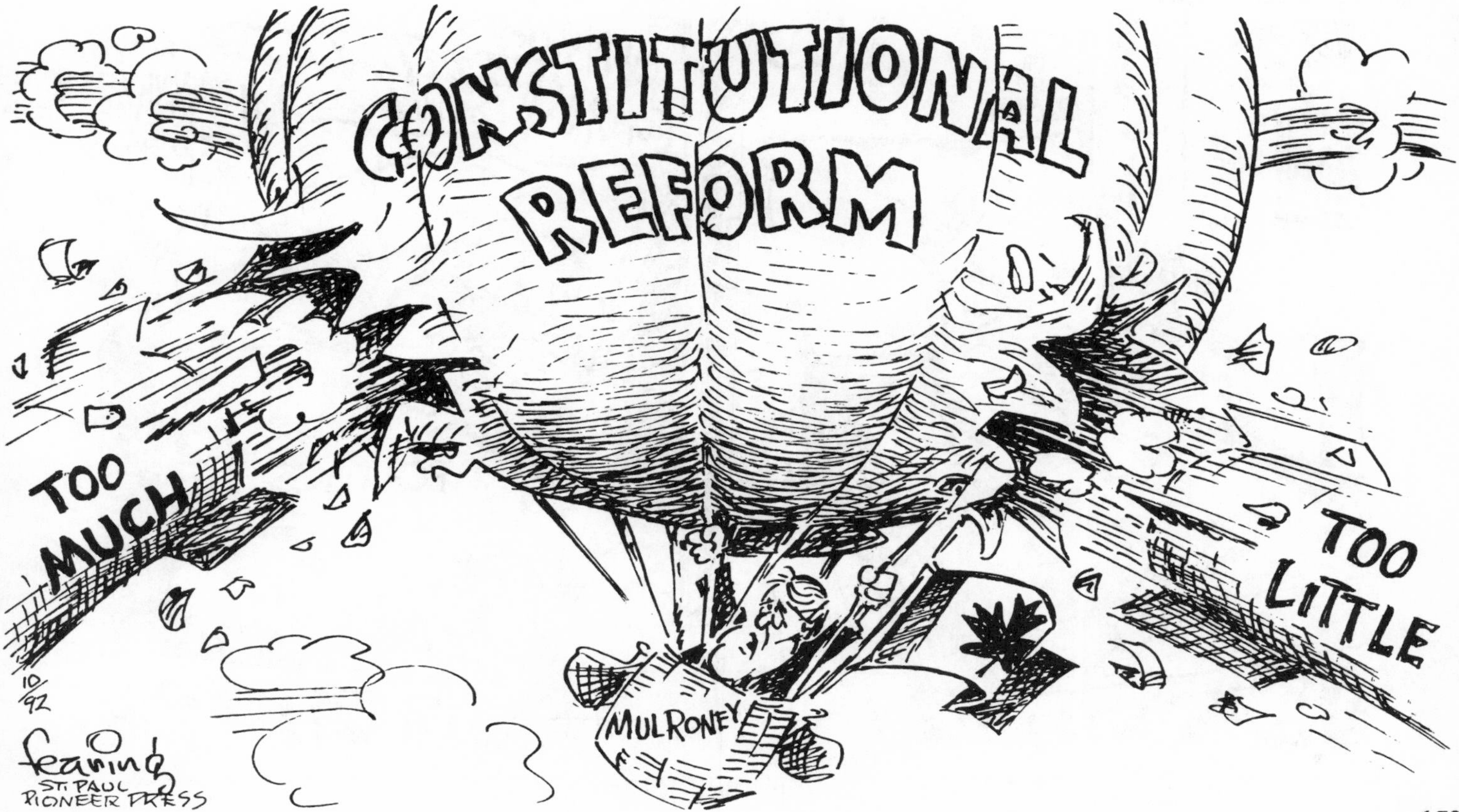
CONSTITUTIONAL REFORM
TOO MUCH
TOO LITTLE
MULRONEY
10/92
Fearing
St. Paul Pioneer Press

JERRY FEARING
Courtesy St. Paul Pioneer Press-Dispatch

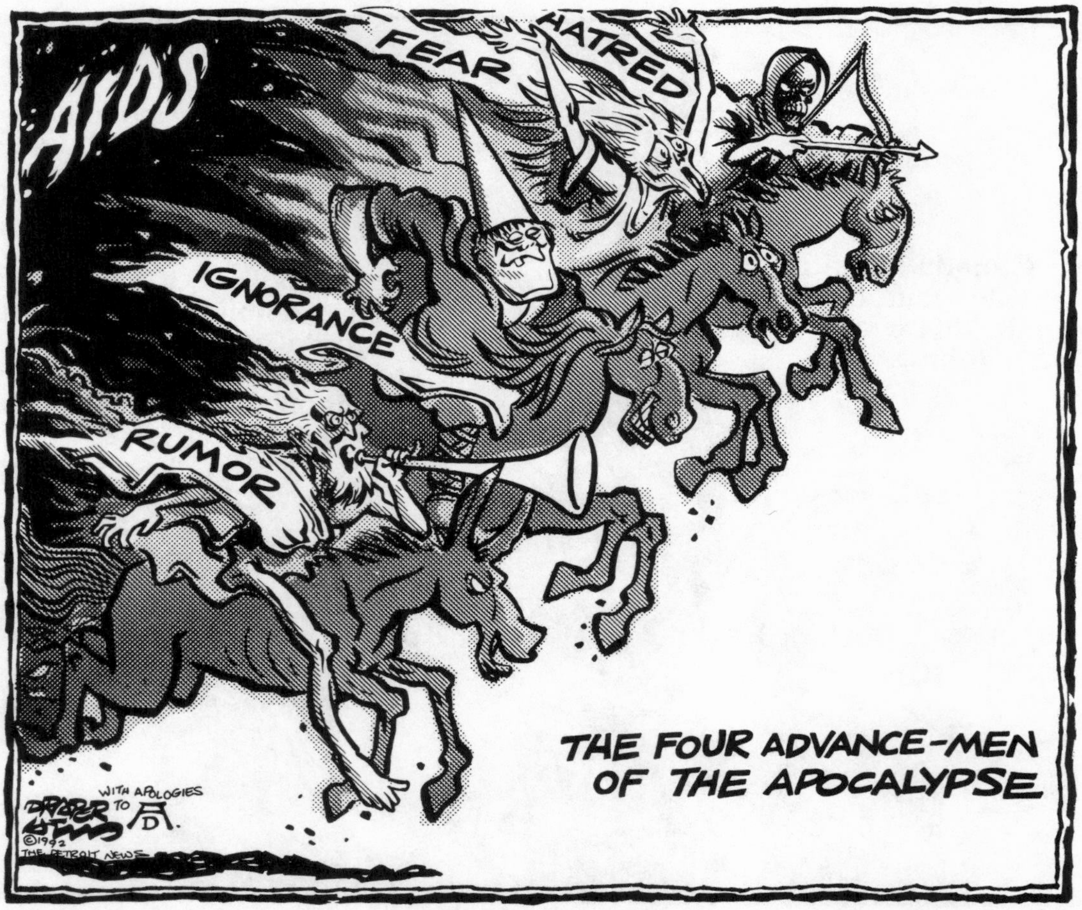

AIDS
FEAR
HATRED
IGNORANCE
RUMOR
THE FOUR ADVANCE-MEN OF THE APOCALYPSE
WITH APOLOGIES TO

DRAPER HILL
Courtesy Detroit News

JIM BORGMAN
Courtesy Cincinnati Enquirer

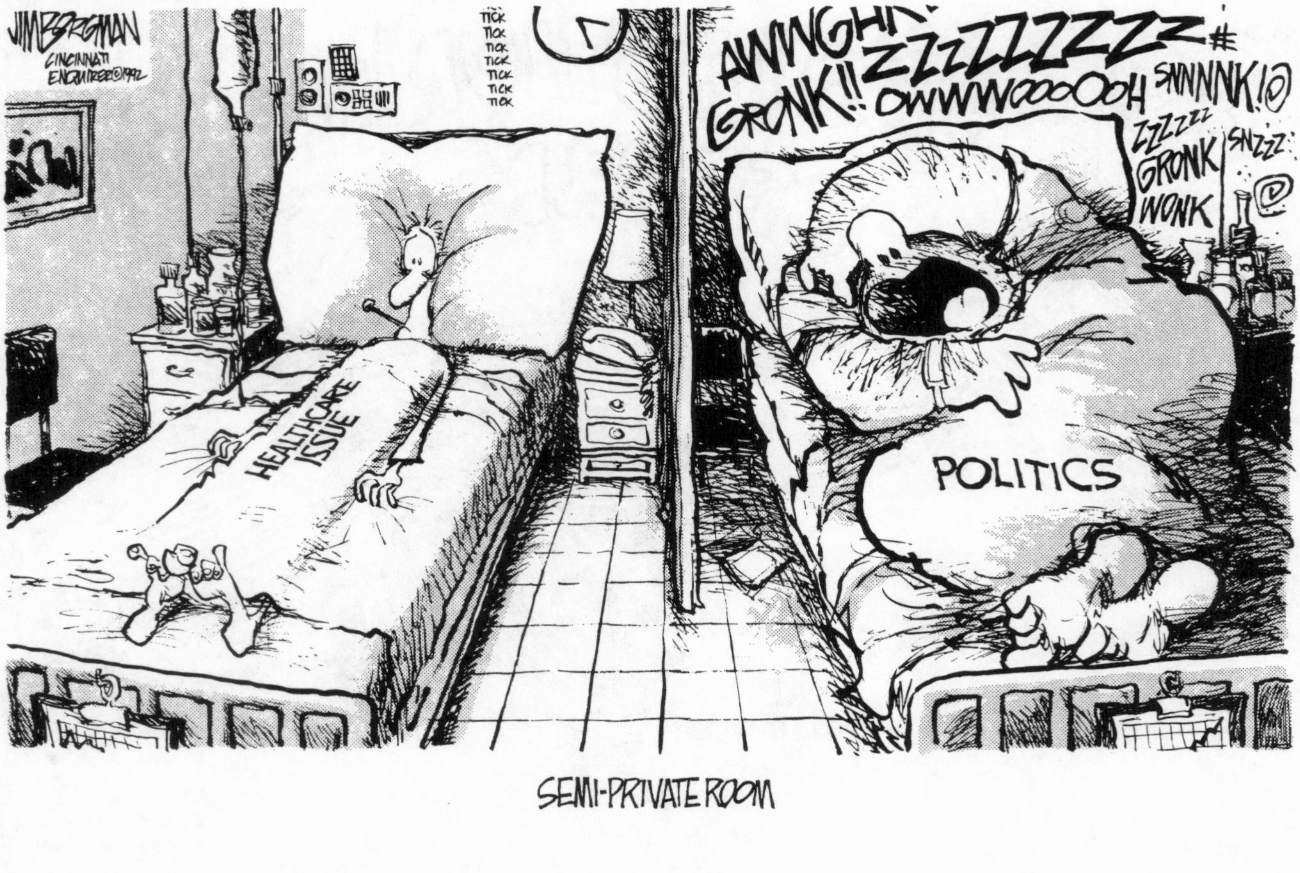

JIM BORGMAN
CINCINNATI ENQUIRER ©1992
TICK
TICK
TICK
TICK
TICK
TICK
TICK
TICK
AWWGH!
ZZZZZZZZZZ
GRONK!!
OWWWOOOOOH
SNNNNK!
ZZZZZZ
GRONK
WONK
SNZZZ
HEALTHCARE ISSUE
POLITICS

SEMI-PRIVATE ROOM

Health

The AIDS epidemic continued to spread during 1992, and there were indications it could soon become the most deadly–and costly–plague in history. The Black Death took about 25 million lives in Europe during the fourteenth century, but health experts believe that by the year 2000 between 30 million and 110 million people will be carrying the HI virus. More than 12 million people were infected with HIV by the end of 1992, and the disease had spread worldwide. Thailand, India, Zambia, and the Dominican Republic have been especially hard hit.

It is expected that 3.7 million children will be orphaned throughout the world by AIDS within three years. Research for a cure continues at a rapid pace, but the outlook is not promising.

Further reports concerning the dangers of secondhand cigarette smoke were made public during the year. It is believed to cause some 3,000 lung cancer deaths each year among nonsmoking adults, and up to a million asthmatic children have their conditions worsened by secondhand smoke annually.

Health care costs continued to rise at a faster rate than inflation. Particularly affected were the elderly, as many companies scaled back retiree health benefits and drug prices continued to spiral.

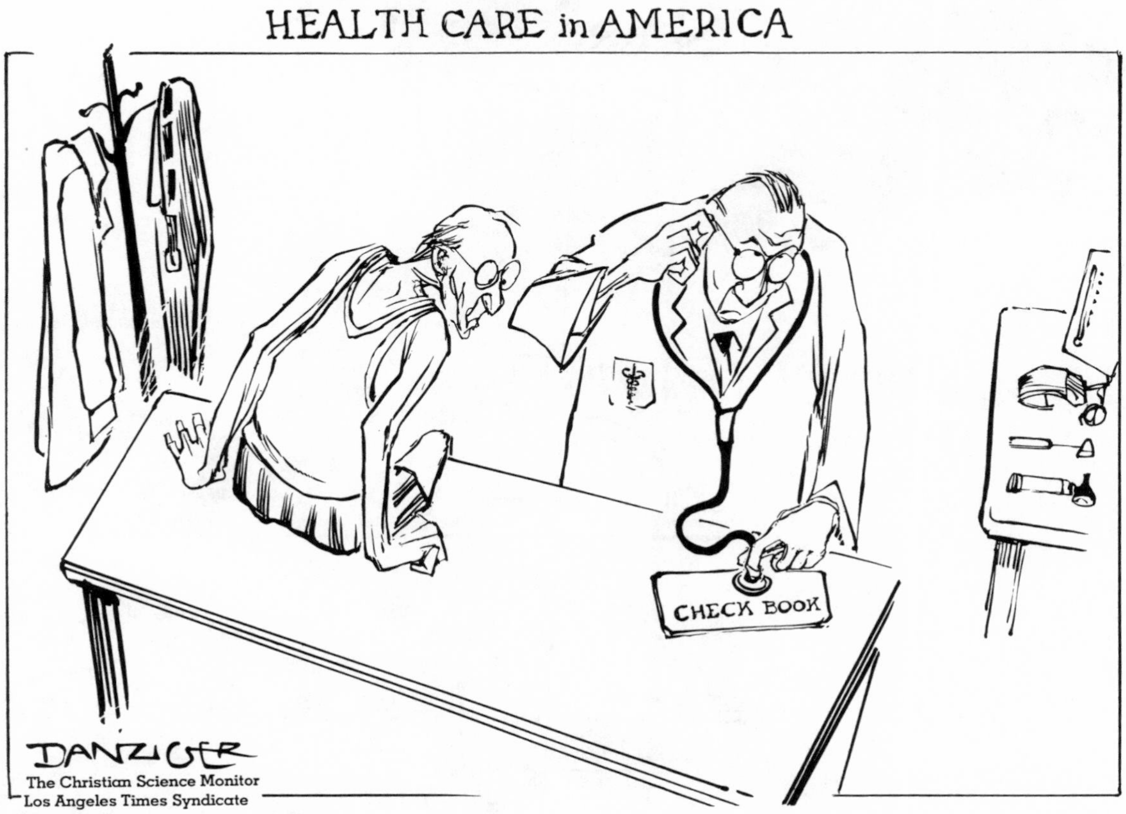
HEALTH CARE in AMERICA
CHECK BOOK
DANZIGER
The Christian Science Monitor
Los Angeles Times Syndicate

JEFF DANZIGER
Courtesy Christian Science Monitor

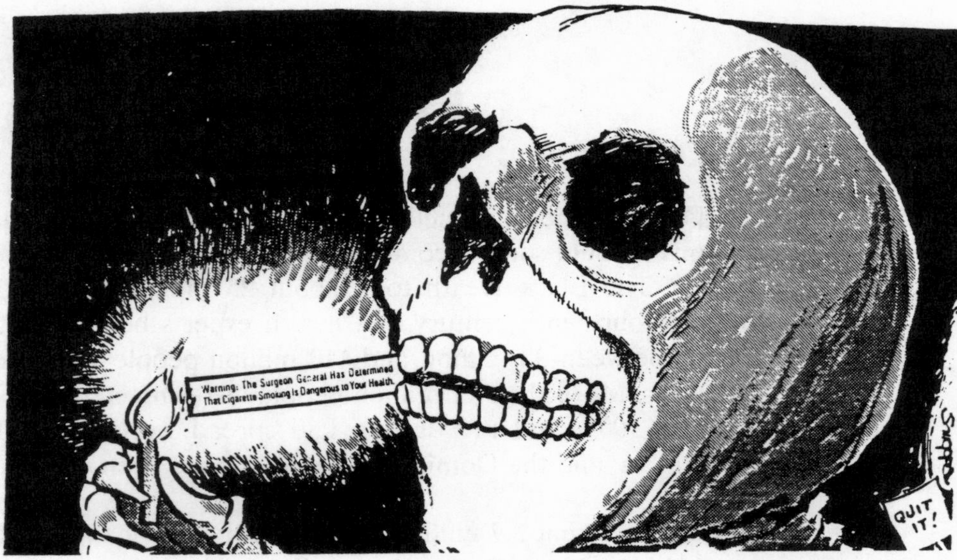
Warning: The Surgeon General Has Determined That Cigarette Smoking Is Dangerous to Your Health.
QUIT IT!

JIM DOBBINS
Courtesy N.A.G.E. Reporter

MIKE LUCKOVICH
Courtesy Atlanta Constitution

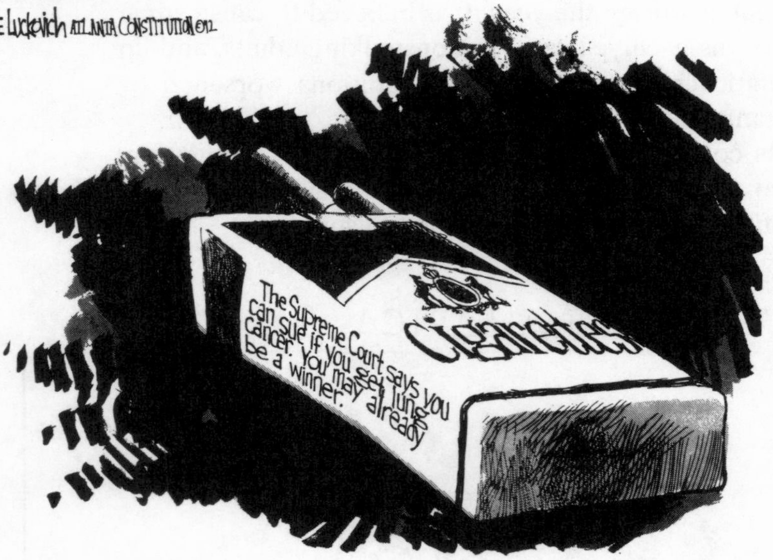
MIKE LUCKOVICH ATLANTA CONSTITUTION
Cigarettes
The Supreme Court says you can sue if you get lung cancer. You may already be a winner.

STEVE SACK
Courtesy Minneapolis Star-Tribune

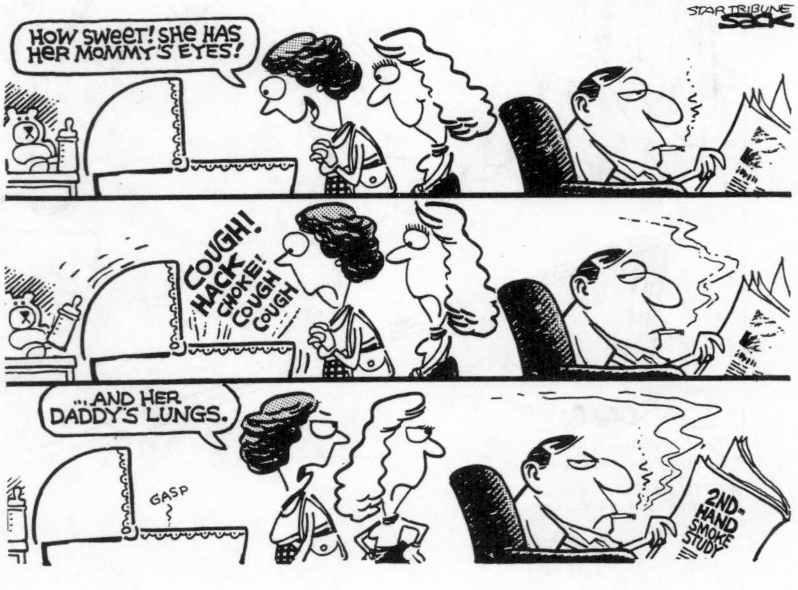
STAR TRIBUNE SACK
HOW SWEET! SHE HAS HER MOMMY'S EYES!
COUGH! HACK CHOKE! COUGH COUGH
...AND HER DADDY'S LUNGS.
GASP
2ND-HAND SMOKE STUDY

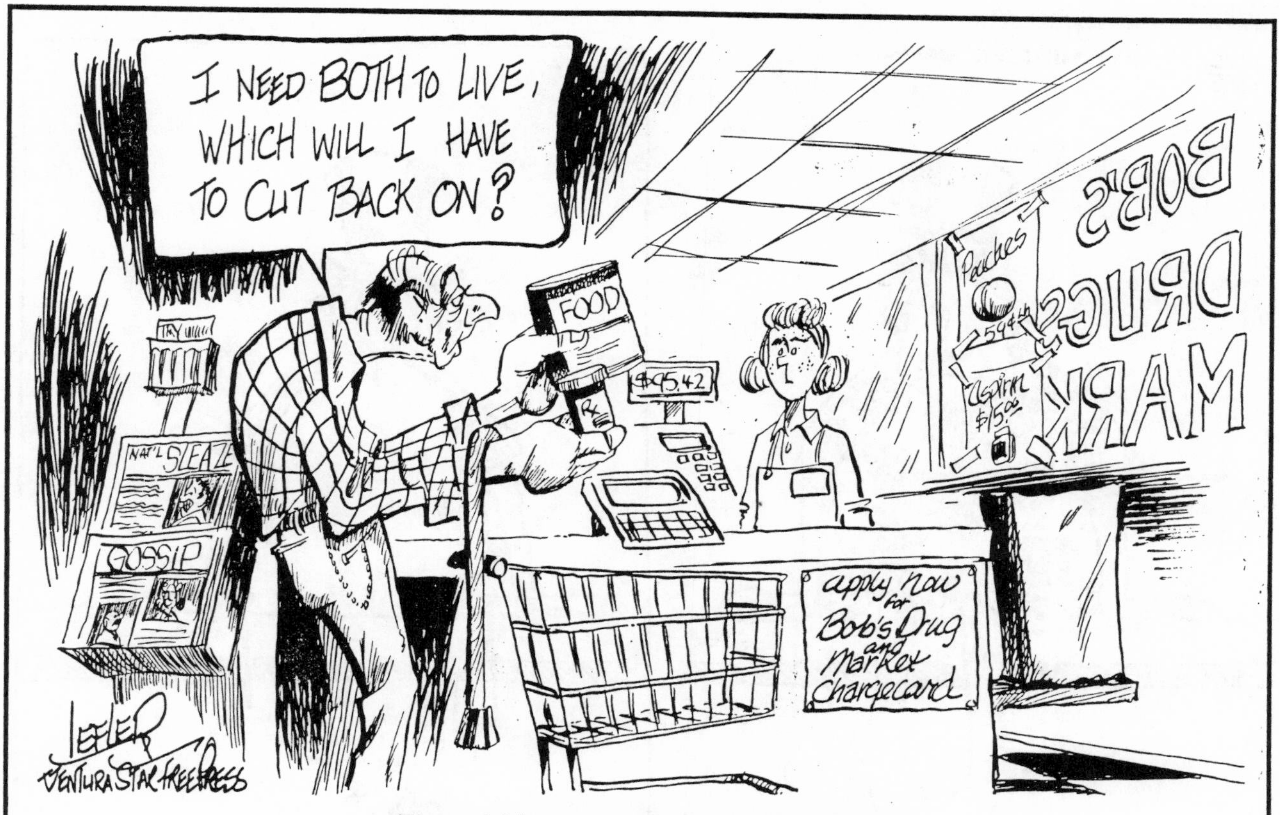
I NEED BOTH TO LIVE, WHICH WILL I HAVE TO CUT BACK ON?
FOOD
NAT'L SLEAZ
GOSSIP
Peaches
apply now for Bob's Drug and Market Chargecard
LEFLER
Ventura Star-Free Press

The orbiting cost of pharmaceuticals

JERRY LEFLER
Courtesy Ventura County Star-Free Press

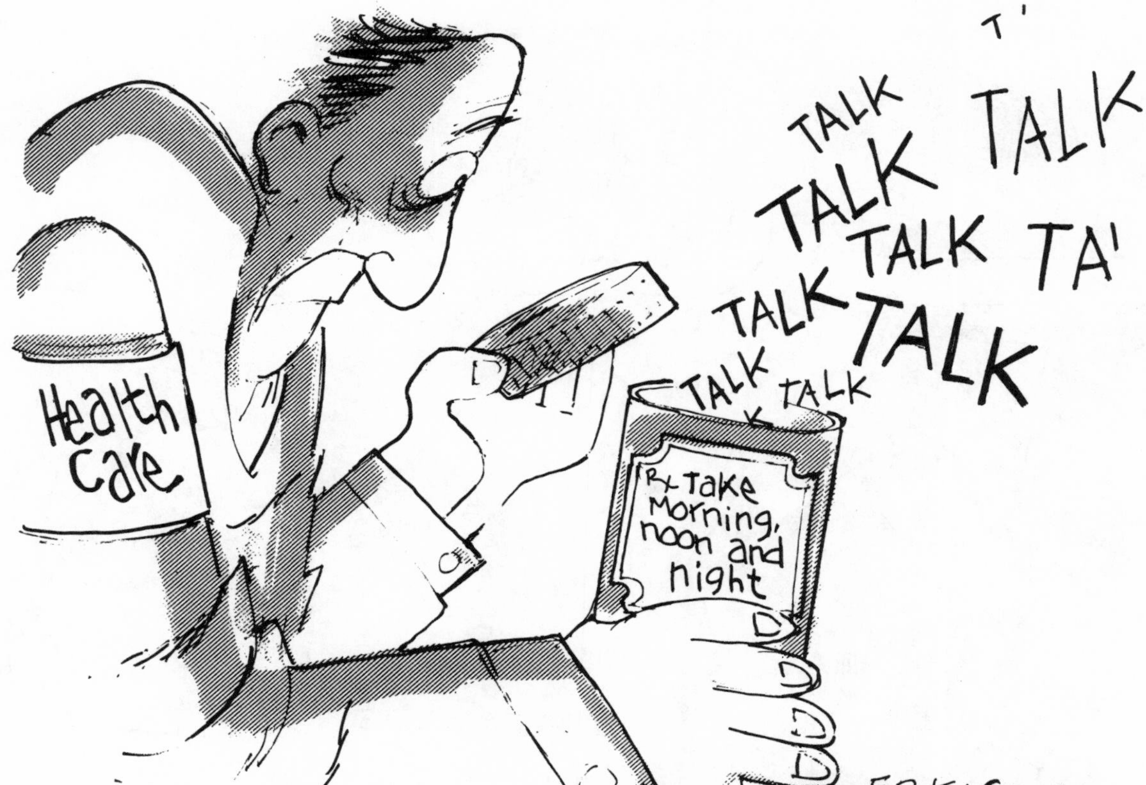
Health care
TALK TALK TALK TALK TALK TA' TALK TALK TALK TALK
℞ Take Morning, noon and night
ED FISCHER

ED FISCHER
Courtesy Rochester Post-Bulletin

ETTA HULME
Courtesy Ft. Worth Star-Telegram

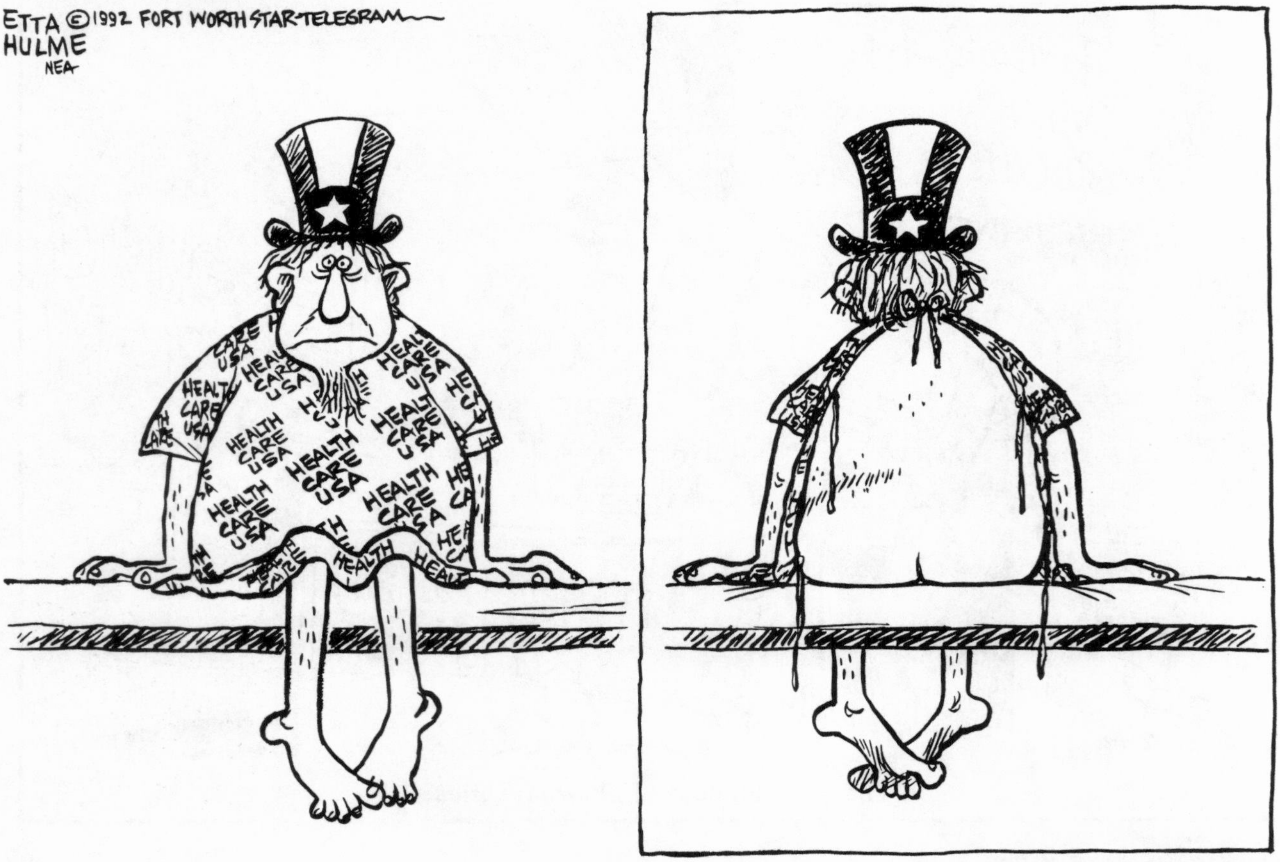
ETTA ©1992 FORT WORTH STAR-TELEGRAM
HULME
NEA
HEALTH CARE USA

CLAY JONES
Courtesy Northeast Mississippi Daily Journal

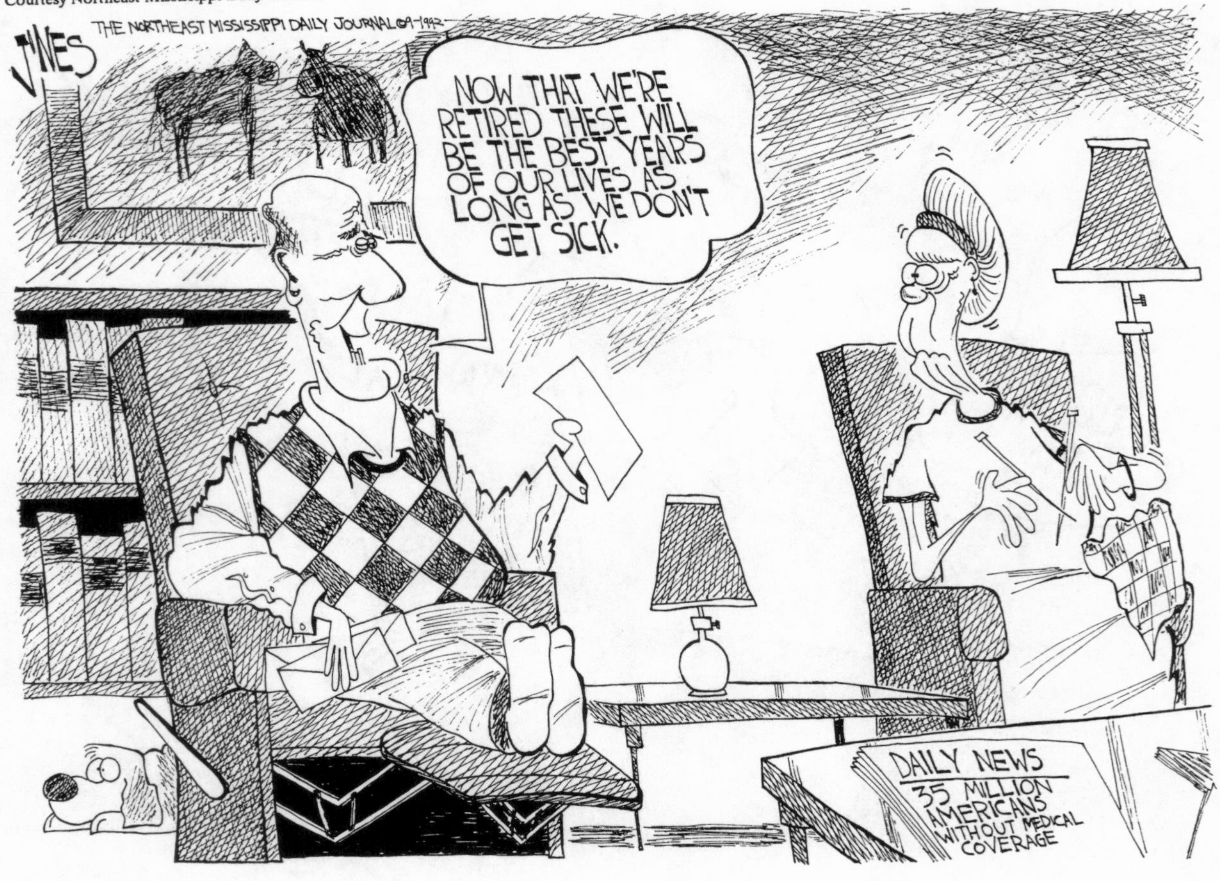
JONES
THE NORTHEAST MISSISSIPPI DAILY JOURNAL ©9-1992
NOW THAT WE'RE RETIRED THESE WILL BE THE BEST YEARS OF OUR LIVES AS LONG AS WE DON'T GET SICK.
DAILY NEWS
35 MILLION AMERICANS WITHOUT MEDICAL COVERAGE

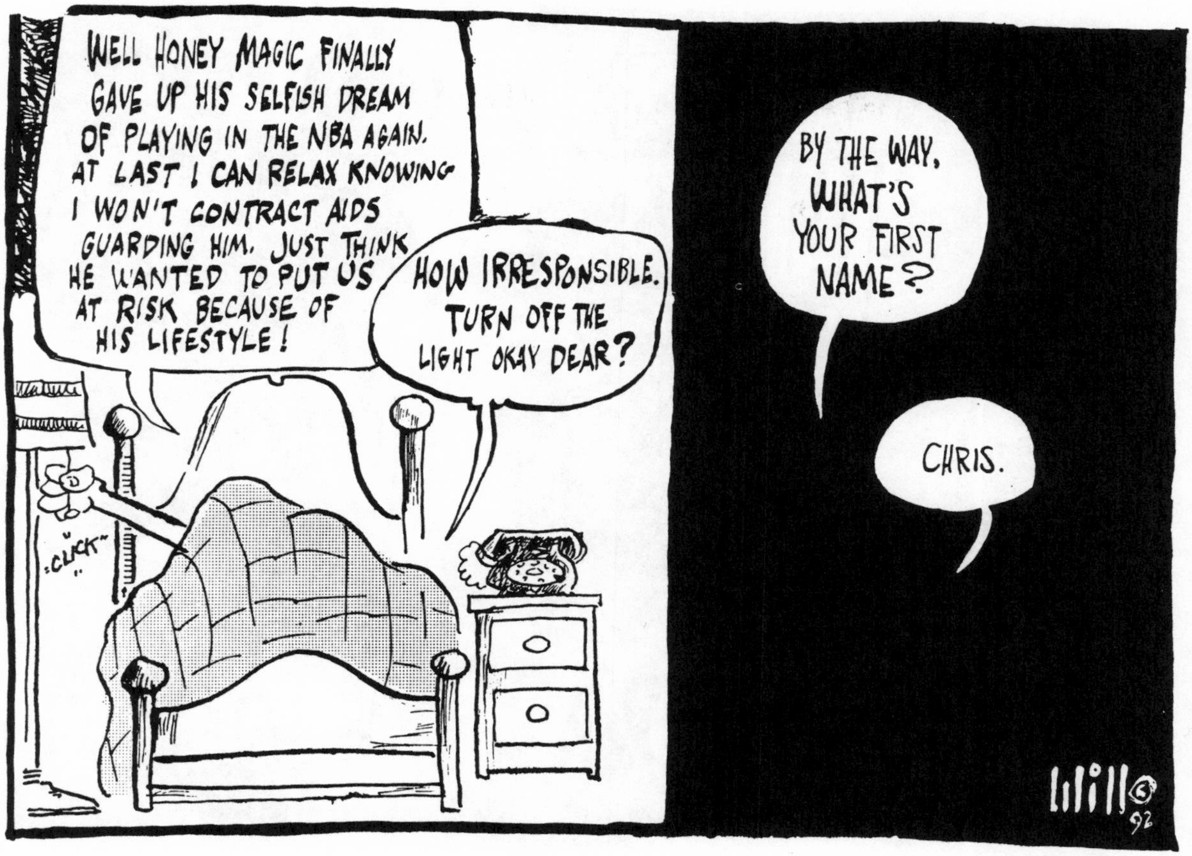
WELL HONEY MAGIC FINALLY GAVE UP HIS SELFISH DREAM OF PLAYING IN THE NBA AGAIN. AT LAST I CAN RELAX KNOWING I WON'T CONTRACT AIDS GUARDING HIM. JUST THINK HE WANTED TO PUT US AT RISK BECAUSE OF HIS LIFESTYLE!
HOW IRRESPONSIBLE. TURN OFF THE LIGHT OKAY DEAR?
"CLICK"
BY THE WAY, WHAT'S YOUR FIRST NAME?
CHRIS.
Will 92

WILL O'TOOLE
Courtesy St. Cloud Times

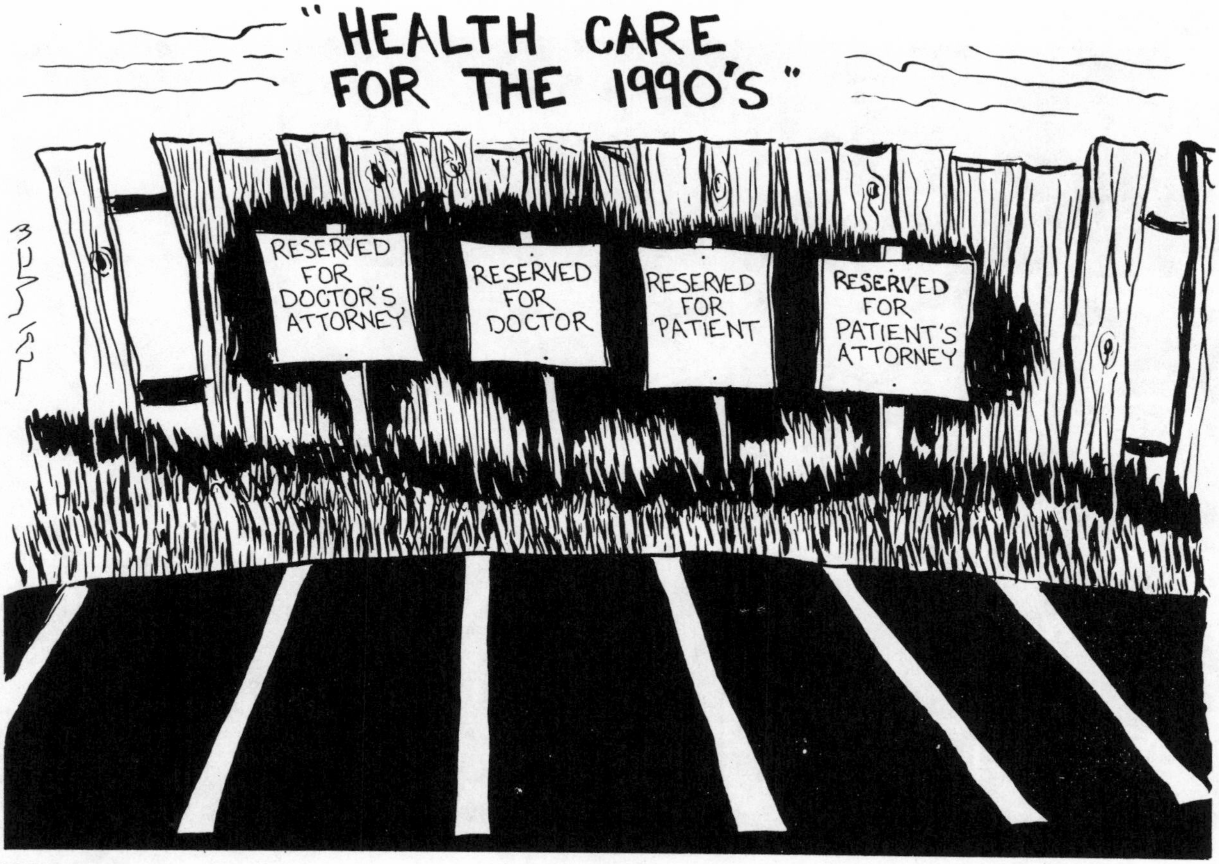
"HEALTH CARE FOR THE 1990'S"
RESERVED FOR DOCTOR'S ATTORNEY
RESERVED FOR DOCTOR
RESERVED FOR PATIENT
RESERVED FOR PATIENT'S ATTORNEY

MICHAEL FURLONG
Courtesy Watertown Press

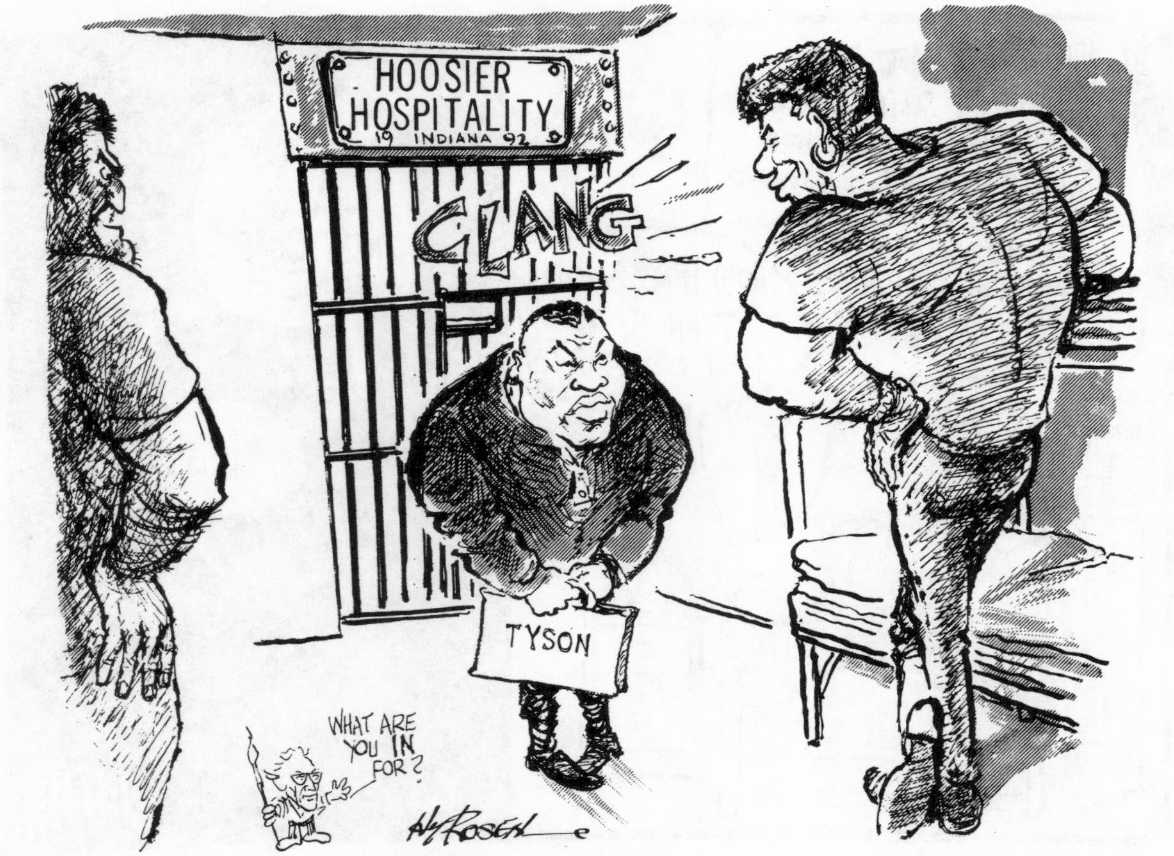
HOOSIER
HOSPITALITY
19 INDIANA 92
CLANG
TYSON
WHAT ARE YOU IN FOR?

HY ROSEN
Courtesy Albany Times-Union

BRUCE MACKINNON
Courtesy Halifax Chronicle-Herald

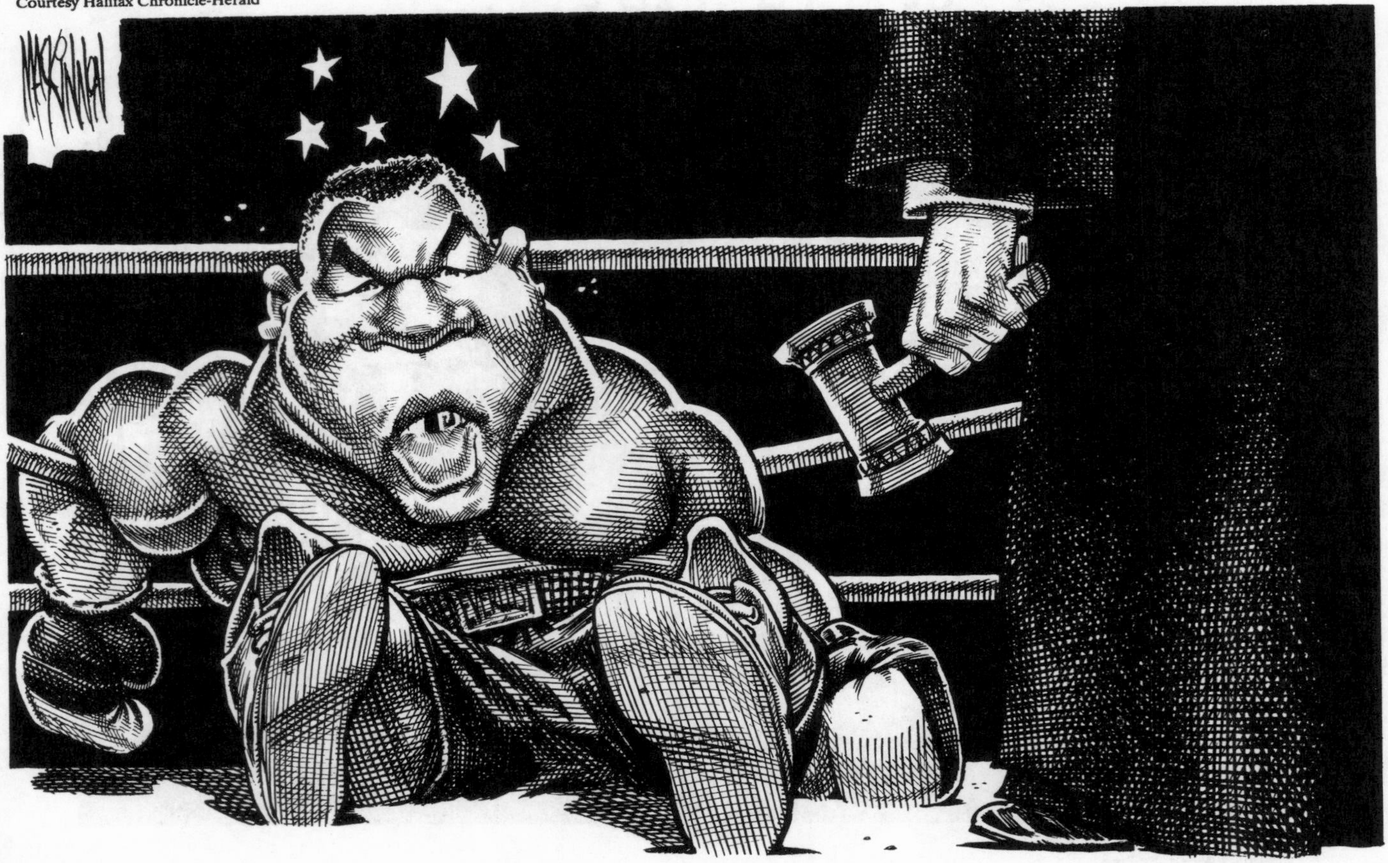

Sports

Former heavyweight boxing champion Mike Tyson was convicted of raping a Black Miss America contestant and was sentenced to a six-year term in prison. Tennis great Arthur Ashe revealed that he had AIDS after he learned that the story was going to be reported on a television news program. Ashe's illness was caused by a blood transfusion in 1983, two years before mandatory screening of blood was begun.

For the Olympics in Barcelona, the U.S. put together what some called the Dream Team, made up of such professional basketball stars as Magic Johnson, Larry Bird, and Michael Jordan. The team trounced the competition to capture the gold medal. Commercialism dominated the 1992 Olympics, with Reebok, Nike, and other companies trying to outdo each other in order to get their names before the public. The Dream Team shunned the official Olympic Village and took accommodations in a swank new hotel.

Greed was the name of the game in major league baseball as team owners fought for the right to pay top stars millions of dollars a year. Marge Schott, majority owner of the Cincinnati Reds, was accused of making racist remarks and was threatened with banishment from baseball.

Stock car racing legend Richard Petty retired in 1992 but lost his final race.

GENE BASSET
Courtesy Atlanta Journal

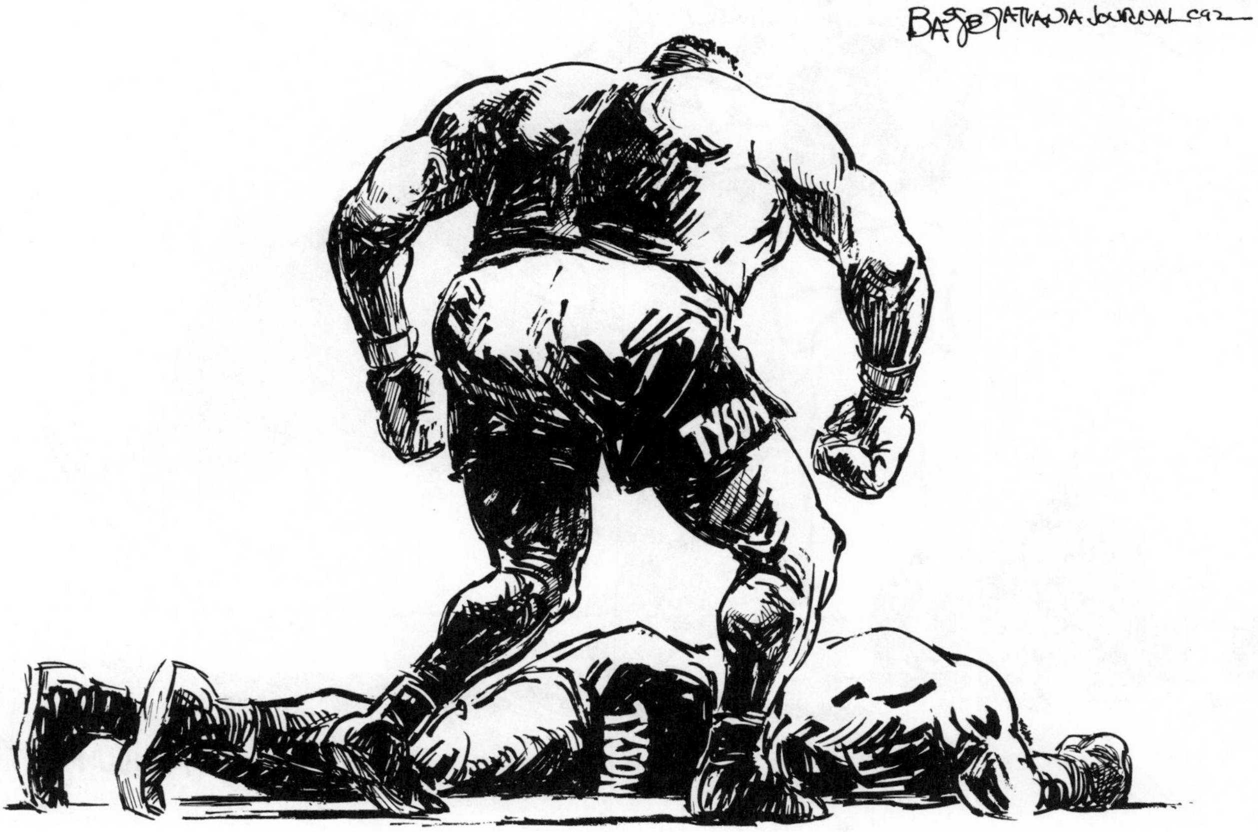
TYSON
TYSON

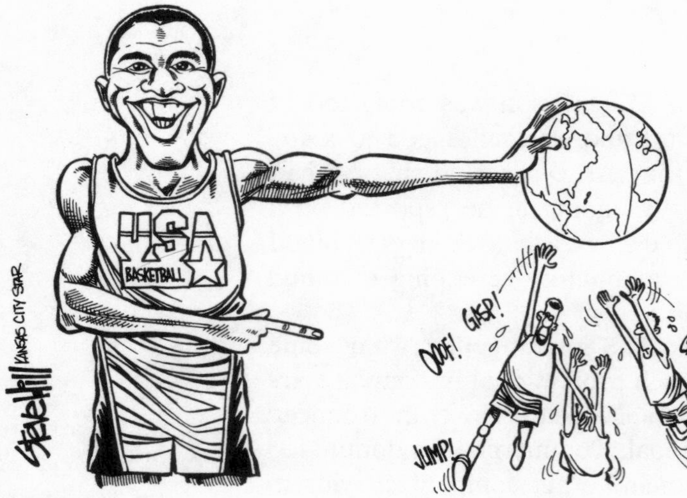
USA
BASKETBALL
OOF!
GASP!
GRUNT!
JUMP!
KANSAS CITY STAR

STEVE HILL
Courtesy Kansas City Star

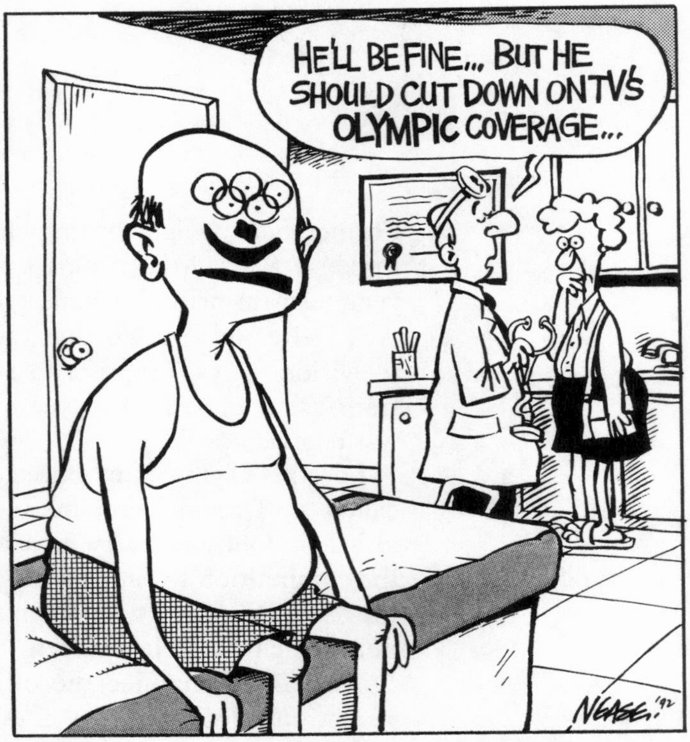
HE'LL BE FINE... BUT HE SHOULD CUT DOWN ON TV'S OLYMPIC COVERAGE...
NEASE '92

STEVE NEASE
Courtesy Calgary Herald

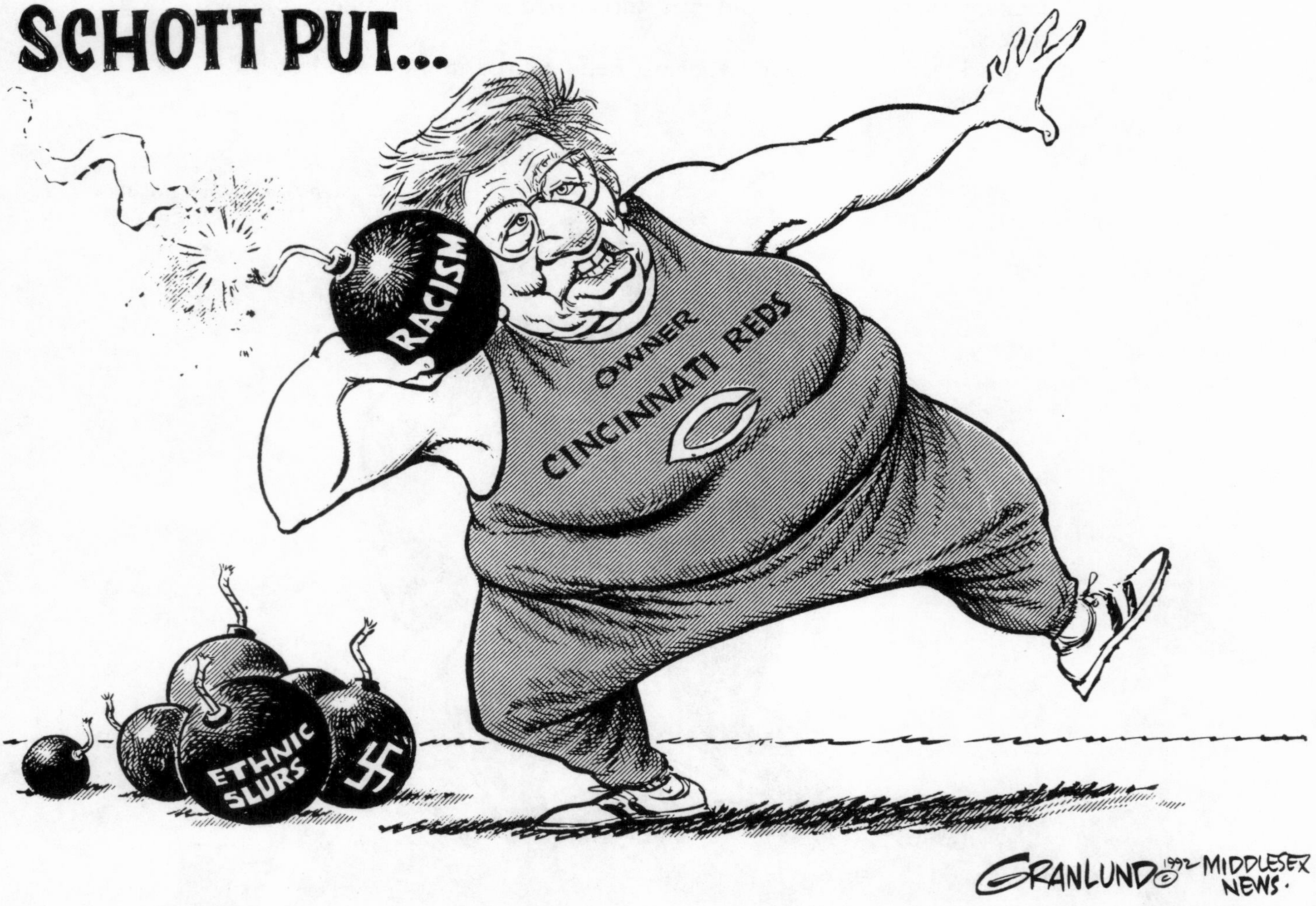
SCHOTT PUT...
RACISM
OWNER
CINCINNATI REDS
ETHNIC SLURS
GRANLUND ©1992 MIDDLESEX NEWS.

DAVID GRANLUND
Courtesy Middlesex News

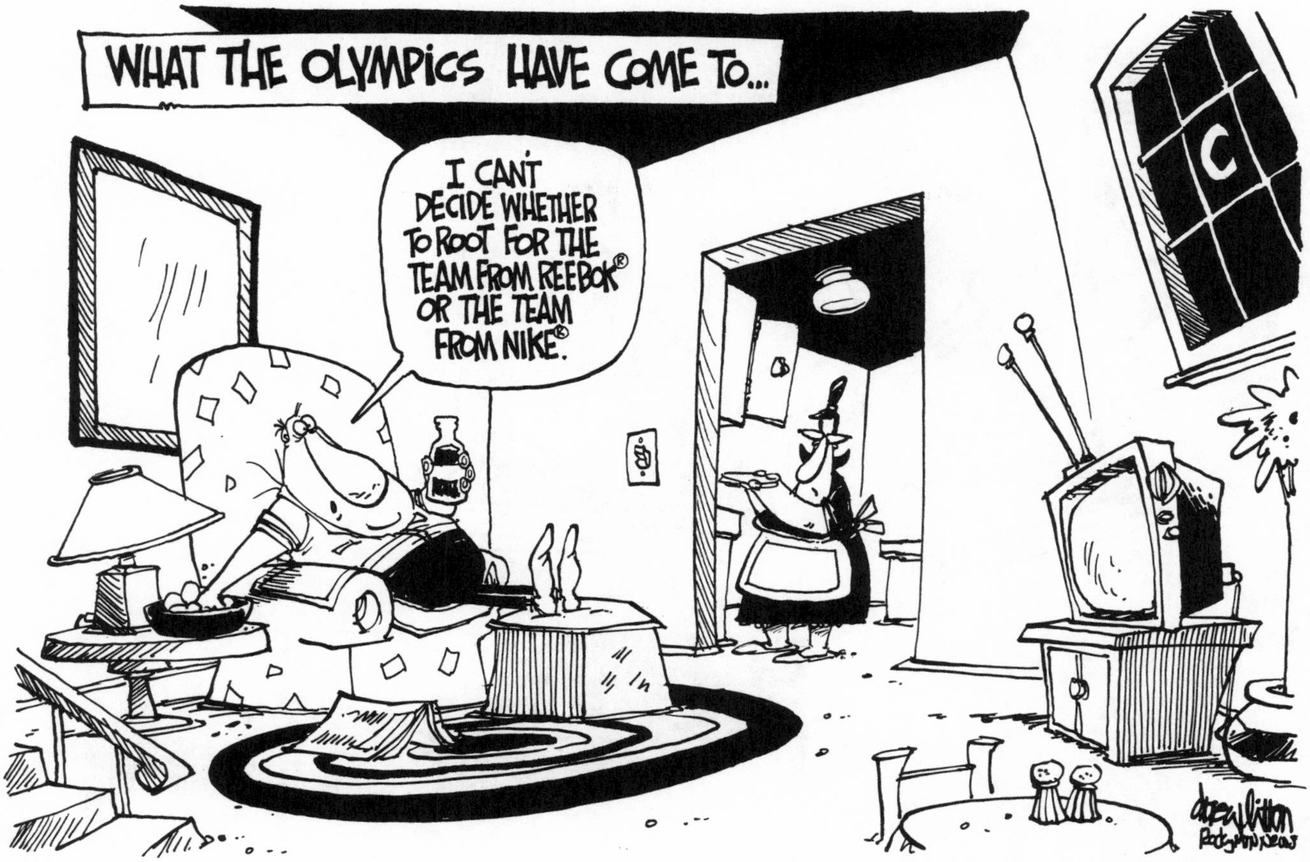
WHAT THE OLYMPICS HAVE COME TO...
I CAN'T DECIDE WHETHER TO ROOT FOR THE TEAM FROM REEBOK® OR THE TEAM FROM NIKE®.
C

DREW LITTON
Courtesy Rocky Mountain News

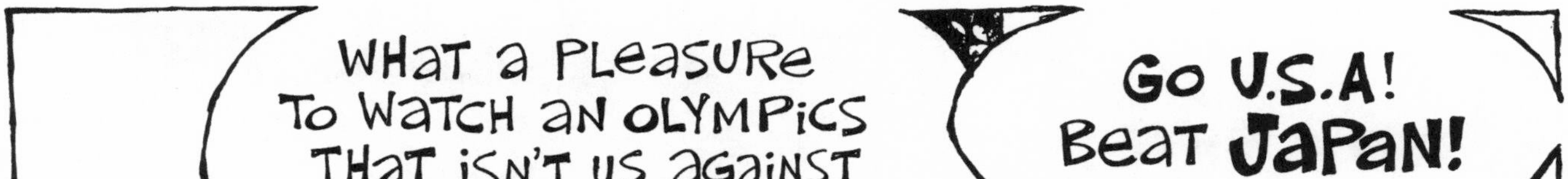
WHAT A PLEASURE TO WATCH AN OLYMPICS THAT ISN'T US AGAINST THE RUSSIANS!
GO U.S.A! BEAT JAPAN!
EDSTEIN'92
ROCKY MTN. NEWS-NEA

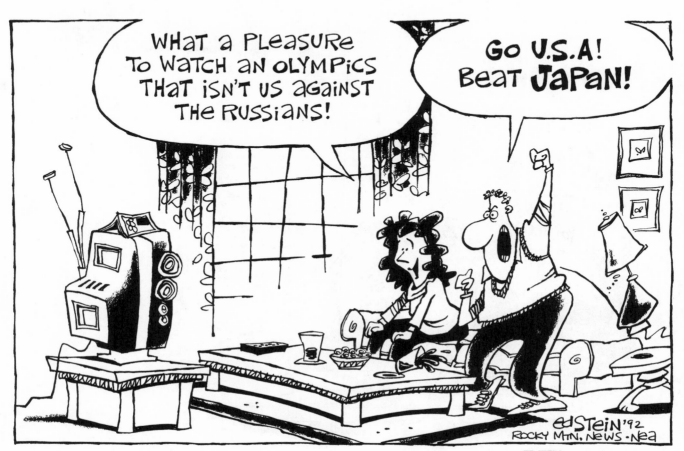

ED STEIN
Courtesy Rocky Mountain News and NEA

KIRK WALTERS
Courtesy Toledo Blade

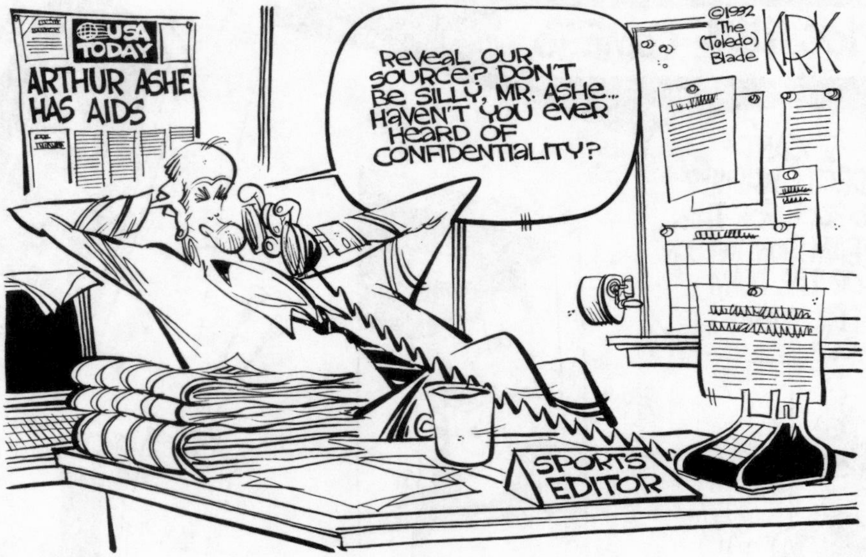
USA TODAY
ARTHUR ASHE HAS AIDS
REVEAL OUR SOURCE? DON'T BE SILLY, MR. ASHE... HAVEN'T YOU EVER HEARD OF CONFIDENTIALITY?
©1992 The (Toledo) Blade
KIRK
SPORTS EDITOR

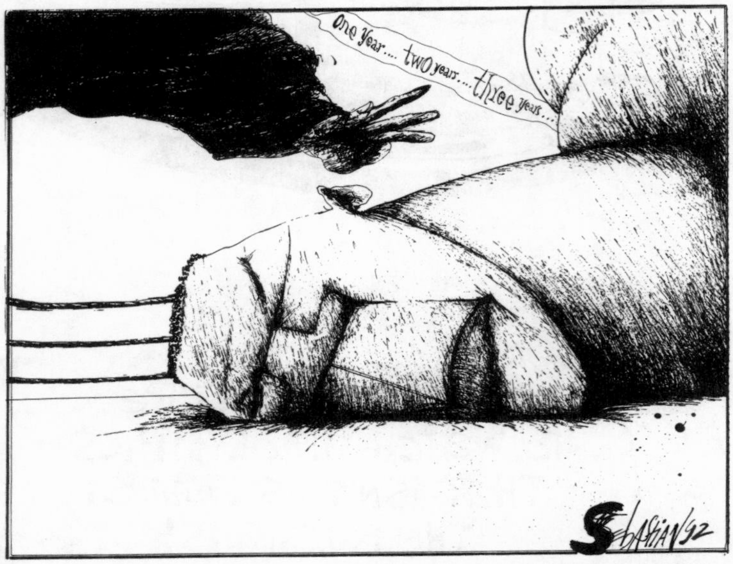
One year.... two years.... three years....
SEBASTIAN '92

FRED SEBASTIAN
Courtesy Ottawa Citizen

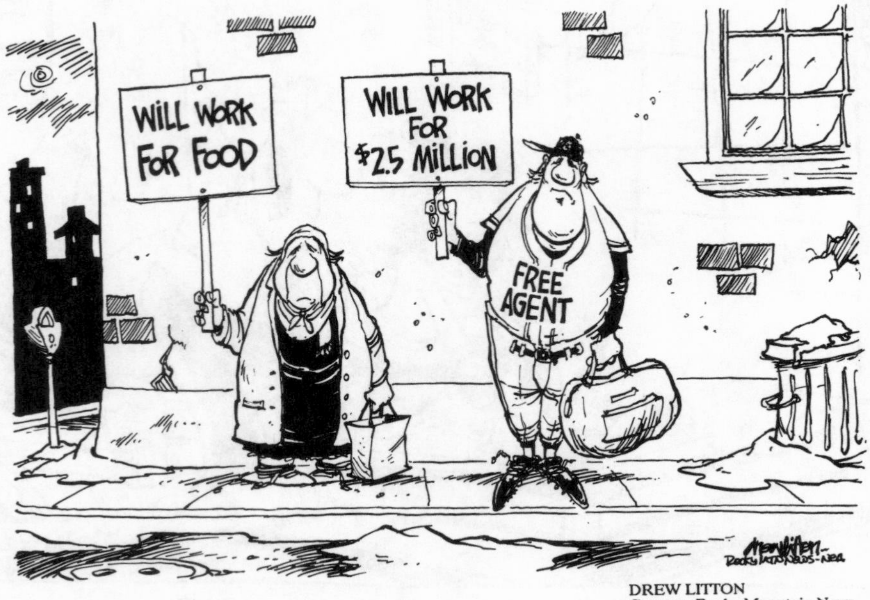
WILL WORK FOR FOOD
WILL WORK FOR $2.5 MILLION
FREE AGENT

DREW LITTON
Courtesy Rocky Mountain News

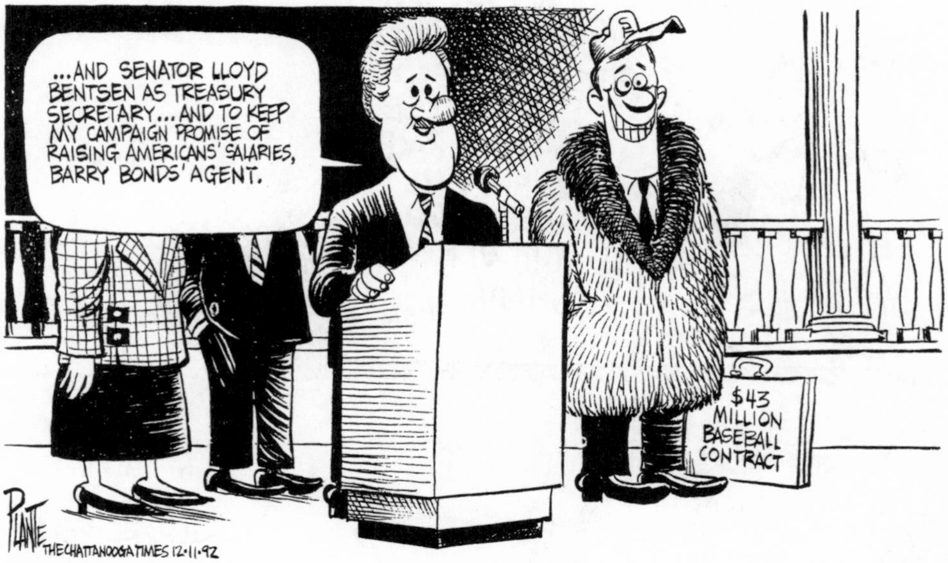
...AND SENATOR LLOYD BENTSEN AS TREASURY SECRETARY...AND TO KEEP MY CAMPAIGN PROMISE OF RAISING AMERICANS' SALARIES, BARRY BONDS' AGENT.
$43 MILLION BASEBALL CONTRACT
PLANTE THE CHATTANOOGA TIMES 12-11-92

BRUCE PLANTE
Courtesy Chattanooga Times and
Extra Newspapers Features

LARRY WRIGHT
Courtesy Detroit News

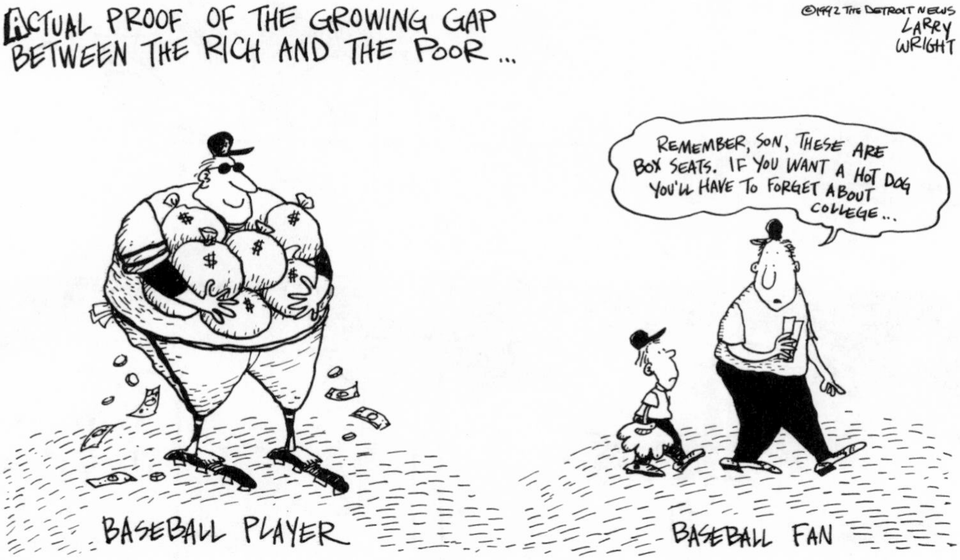
©1992 THE DETROIT NEWS LARRY WRIGHT
ACTUAL PROOF OF THE GROWING GAP BETWEEN THE RICH AND THE POOR...
REMEMBER, SON, THESE ARE BOX SEATS. IF YOU WANT A HOT DOG YOU'LL HAVE TO FORGET ABOUT COLLEGE...
BASEBALL PLAYER
BASEBALL FAN

BOB GORRELL
Courtesy Richmond Times-Dispatch

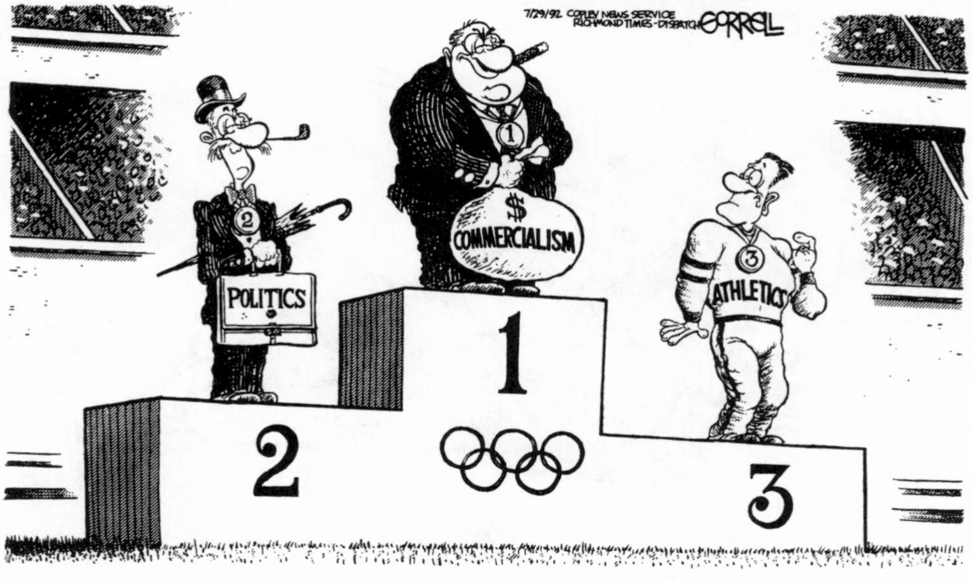
7/29/92 COPLEY NEWS SERVICE RICHMOND TIMES-DISPATCH GORRELL
POLITICS
COMMERCIALISM
ATHLETICS
1
2
3

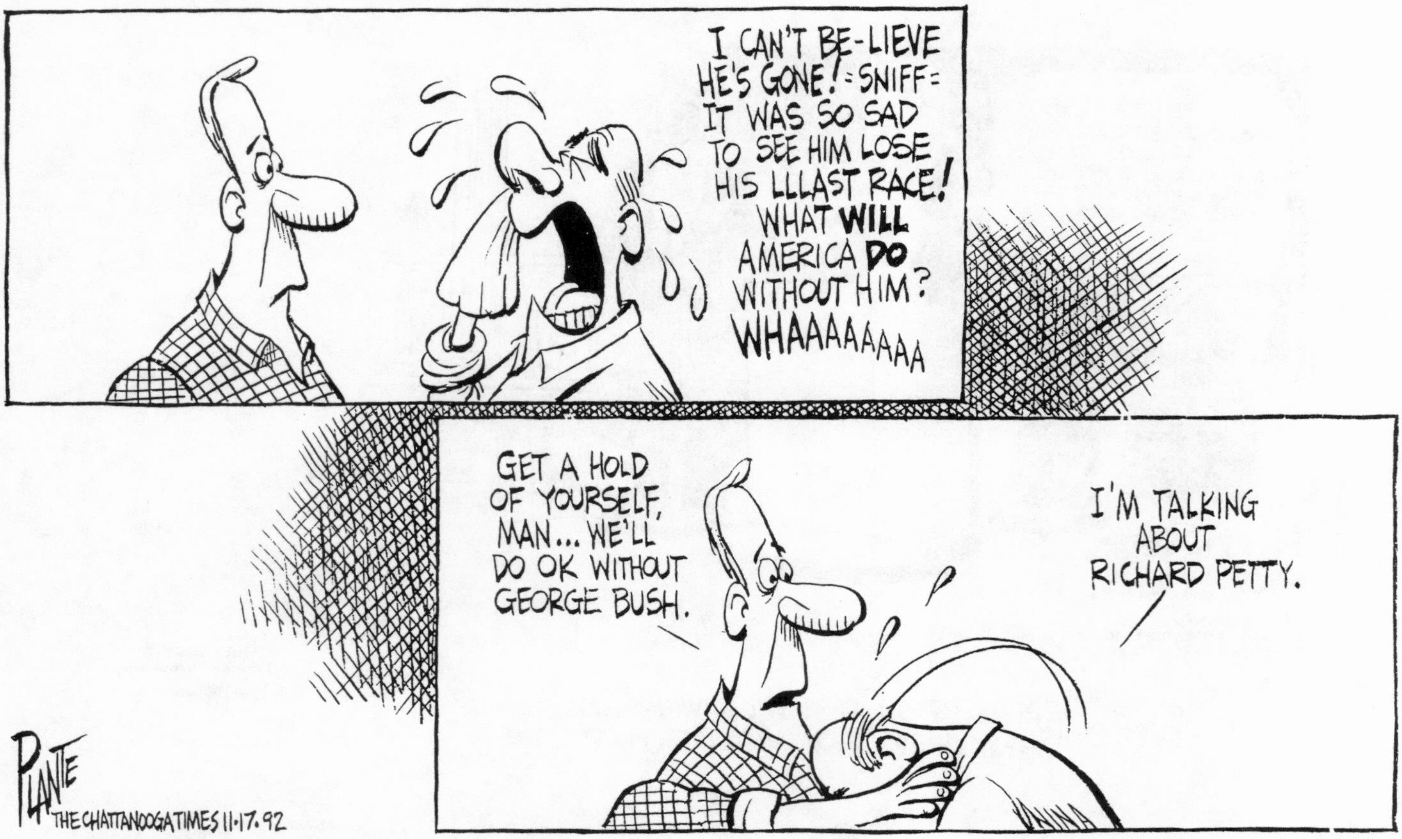
I CAN'T BE-LIEVE HE'S GONE! =SNIFF= IT WAS SO SAD TO SEE HIM LOSE HIS LLLAST RACE! WHAT WILL AMERICA DO WITHOUT HIM? WHAAAAAAAA
GET A HOLD OF YOURSELF, MAN... WE'LL DO OK WITHOUT GEORGE BUSH.
I'M TALKING ABOUT RICHARD PETTY.
PLANTE
THE CHATTANOOGA TIMES 11-17-92

BRUCE PLANTE
Courtesy Chattanooga Times and
Extra Newspapers Features

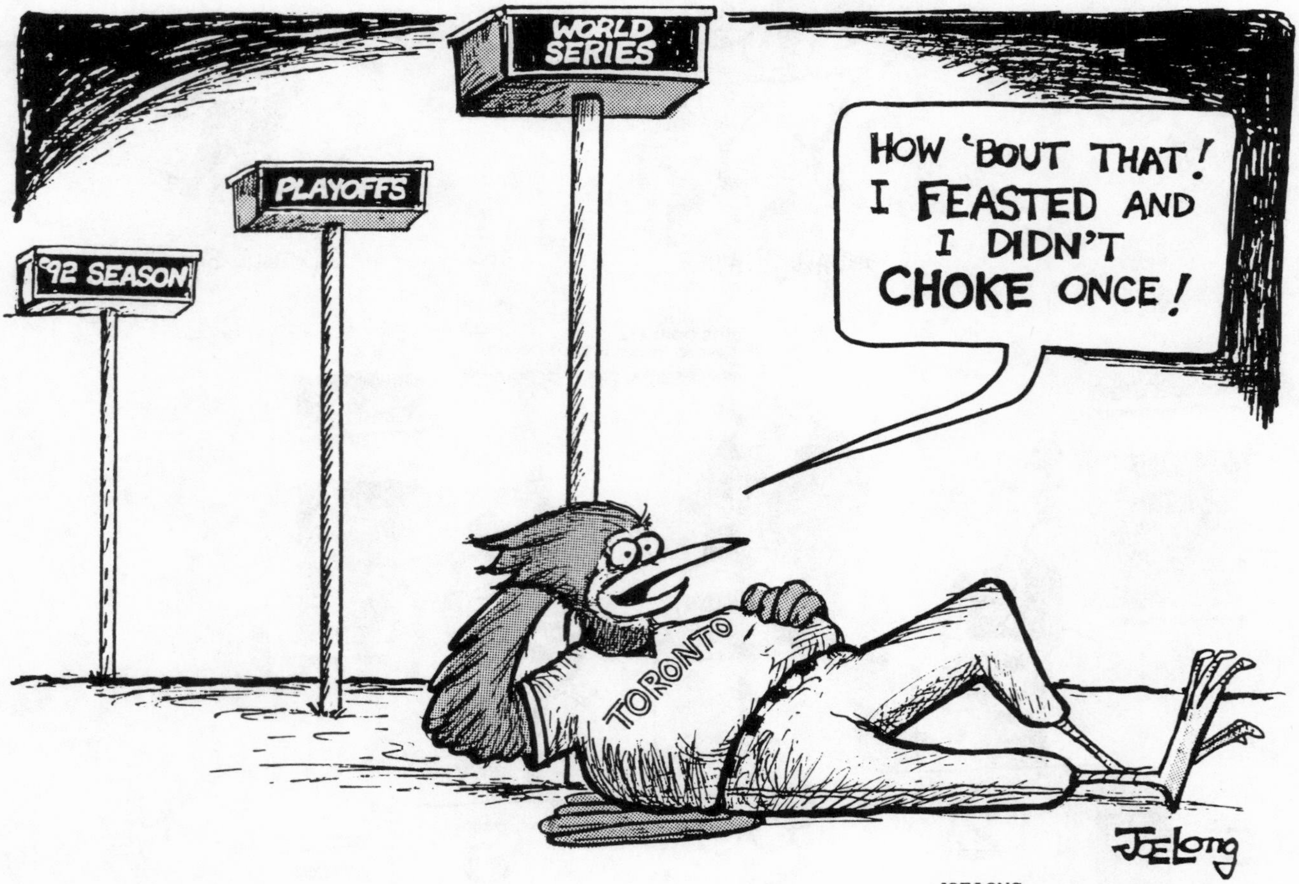
WORLD SERIES
PLAYOFFS
'92 SEASON
HOW 'BOUT THAT! I FEASTED AND I DIDN'T CHOKE ONCE!
TORONTO
TORONTO
JOE LONG

JOE LONG
Courtesy Little Falls Evening Times (N.Y.)

. . . and Other Issues

For more than six years, special prosecutor Lawrence Walsh has been looking for evidence that would tie George Bush and Ronald Reagan to the Iran-Contra affair. After spending $33 million in the quest, he still has come up with little. On Christmas Eve, President Bush pardoned Caspar Weinberger and five other Reagan Administration figures who had been charged with a cover-up by Walsh.

"Malcolmania" swept the country during 1992. Twenty-seven years after his death, black militant Malcolm X, who called himself "the angriest Negro in America," was celebrated on sweatshirts, jackets, and billboards. A movie about his life became an instant hit.

Johnny Carson retired from the "Tonight Show" after thirty years and was replaced by Jay Leno. The 500th anniversary of Columbus's voyage to the New World drew mixed reaction. Many blamed the great discoverer for having opened the doors to slavery and exploitation in the Americas.

Hurricane Andrew savaged Florida and Louisiana, leaving 250,000 people homeless and $20 billion in damages, and Hawaii was rocked by a devastating storm. Buildings in Chicago's Loop were flooded when pilings gave way on the Chicago River.

Well-known figures who died during 1992 included Sam Walton, Jose Ferrer, Alex Haley, Marlene Dietrich, Lawrence Welk, Eric Sevareid, and Red Barber.

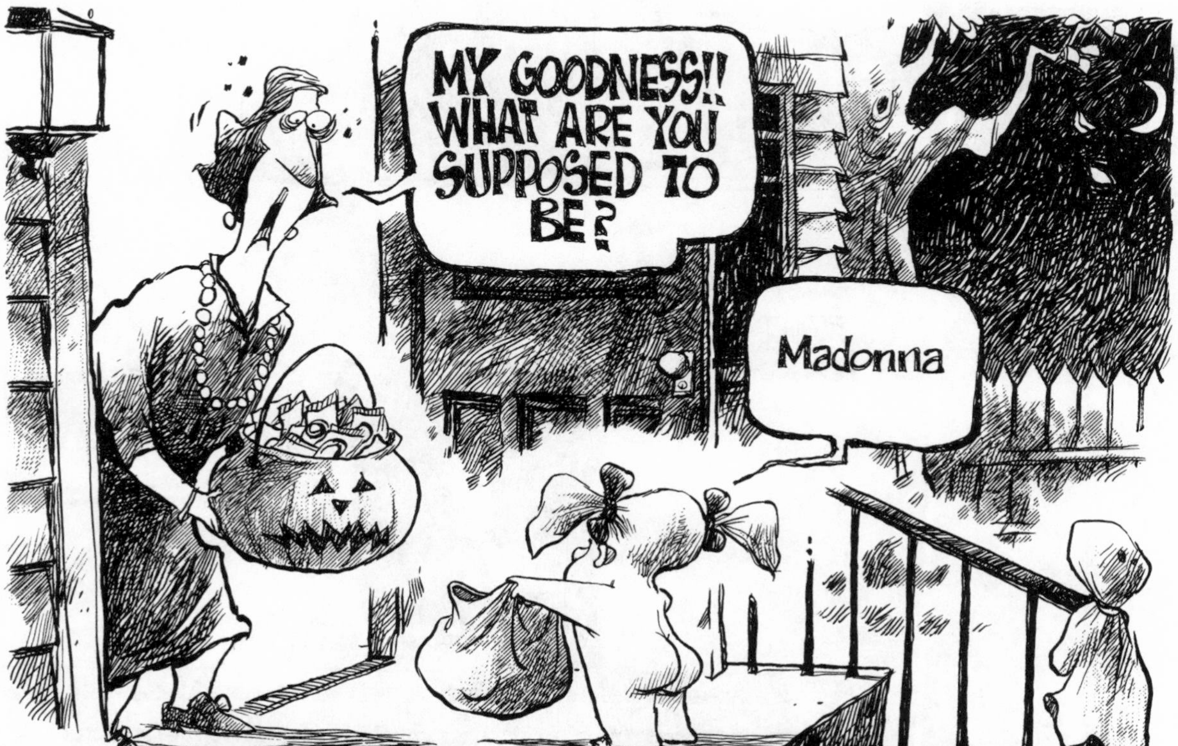
MY GOODNESS!! WHAT ARE YOU SUPPOSED TO BE?
Madonna
HOLBERT BOSTON HERALD '92

JERRY HOLBERT
Courtesy Boston Herald

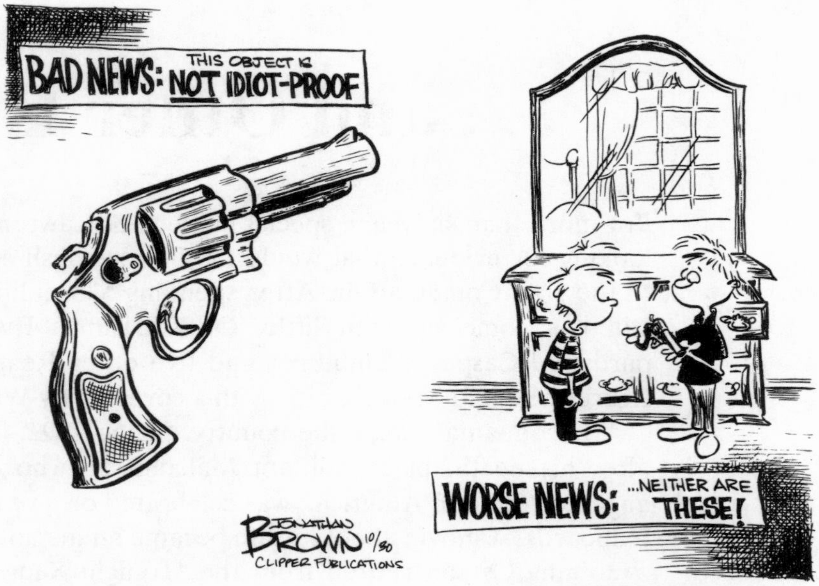
BAD NEWS: THIS OBJECT IS NOT IDIOT-PROOF
WORSE NEWS: ...NEITHER ARE THESE!
JONATHAN BROWN 10/90
CLIPPER PUBLICATIONS

JONATHAN BROWN
Courtesy Davis County Clipper (Utah)

ROGER SCHILLERSTROM
Courtesy Crain Communications

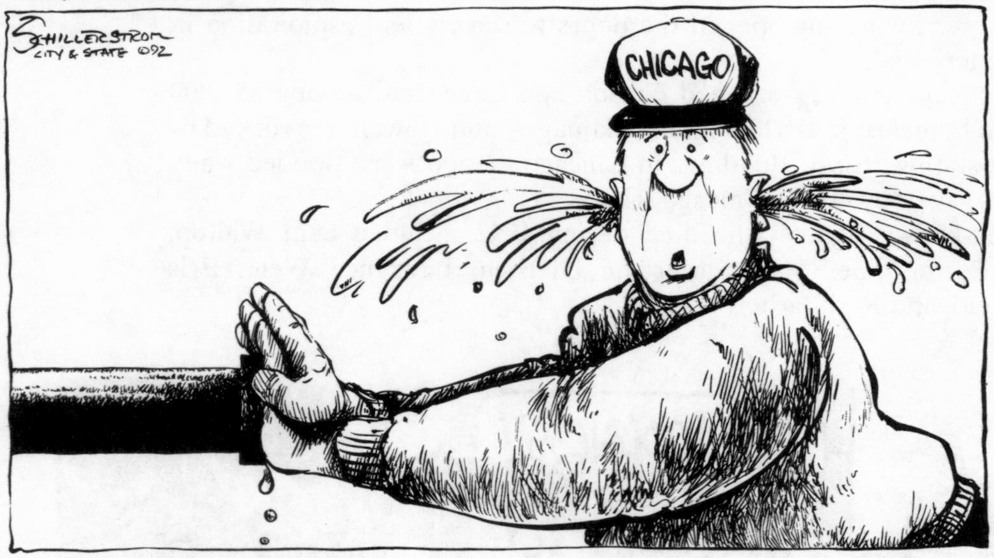
SCHILLERSTROM
CITY & STATE ©92
CHICAGO

JEFF STAHLER
Courtesy Cincinnati Post

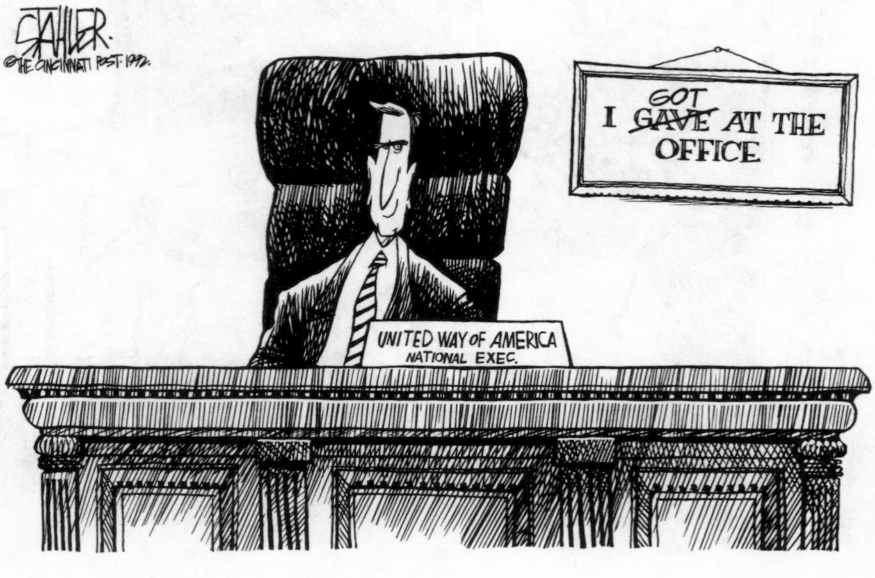
STAHLER
©THE CINCINNATI POST 1992
I ~~GAVE~~ GOT AT THE OFFICE
UNITED WAY OF AMERICA
NATIONAL EXEC.

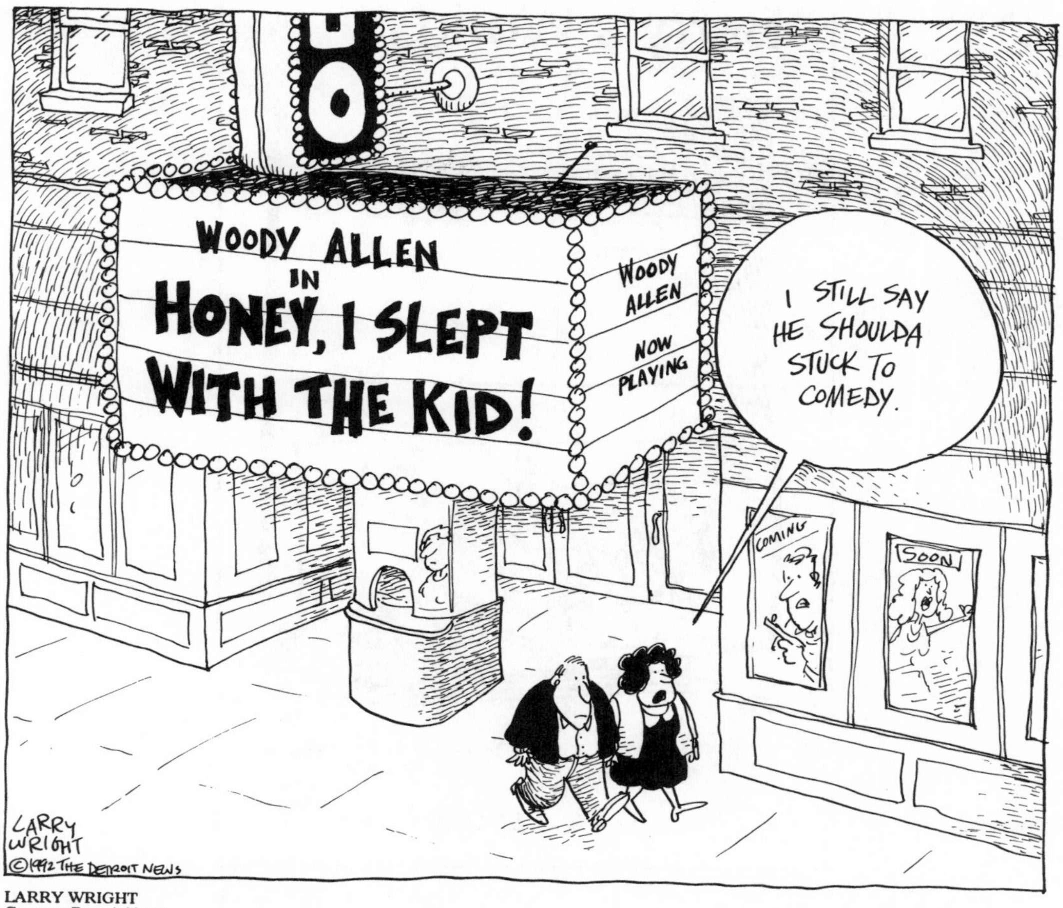
WOODY ALLEN
IN
HONEY, I SLEPT WITH THE KID!
WOODY ALLEN
NOW PLAYING
I STILL SAY HE SHOULDA STUCK TO COMEDY.
COMING
SOON
LARRY WRIGHT
©1992 THE DETROIT NEWS

LARRY WRIGHT
Courtesy Detroit News

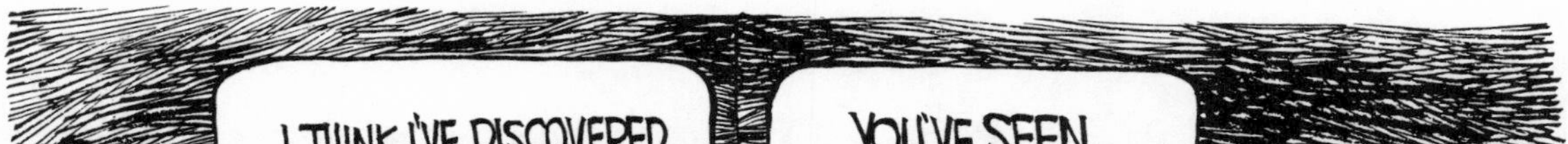
I THINK I'VE DISCOVERED WHY YOUR LIFE IS A MESS...
YOU'VE SEEN TOO MANY WOODY ALLEN MOVIES
MIKE SMITH

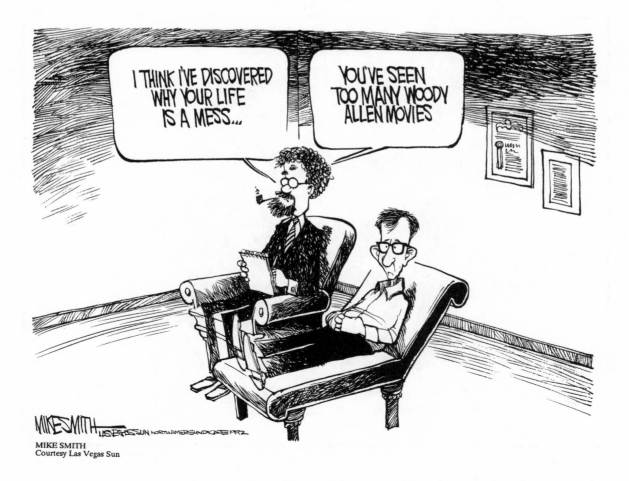

MIKE SMITH
Courtesy Las Vegas Sun

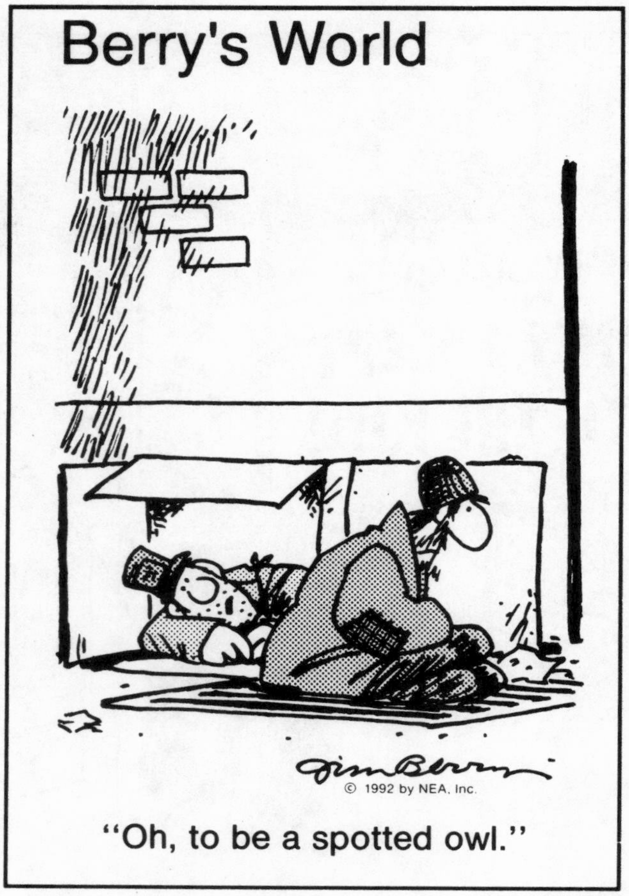
Berry's World
© 1992 by NEA, Inc.
"Oh, to be a spotted owl."

JIM BERRY
Courtesy NEA

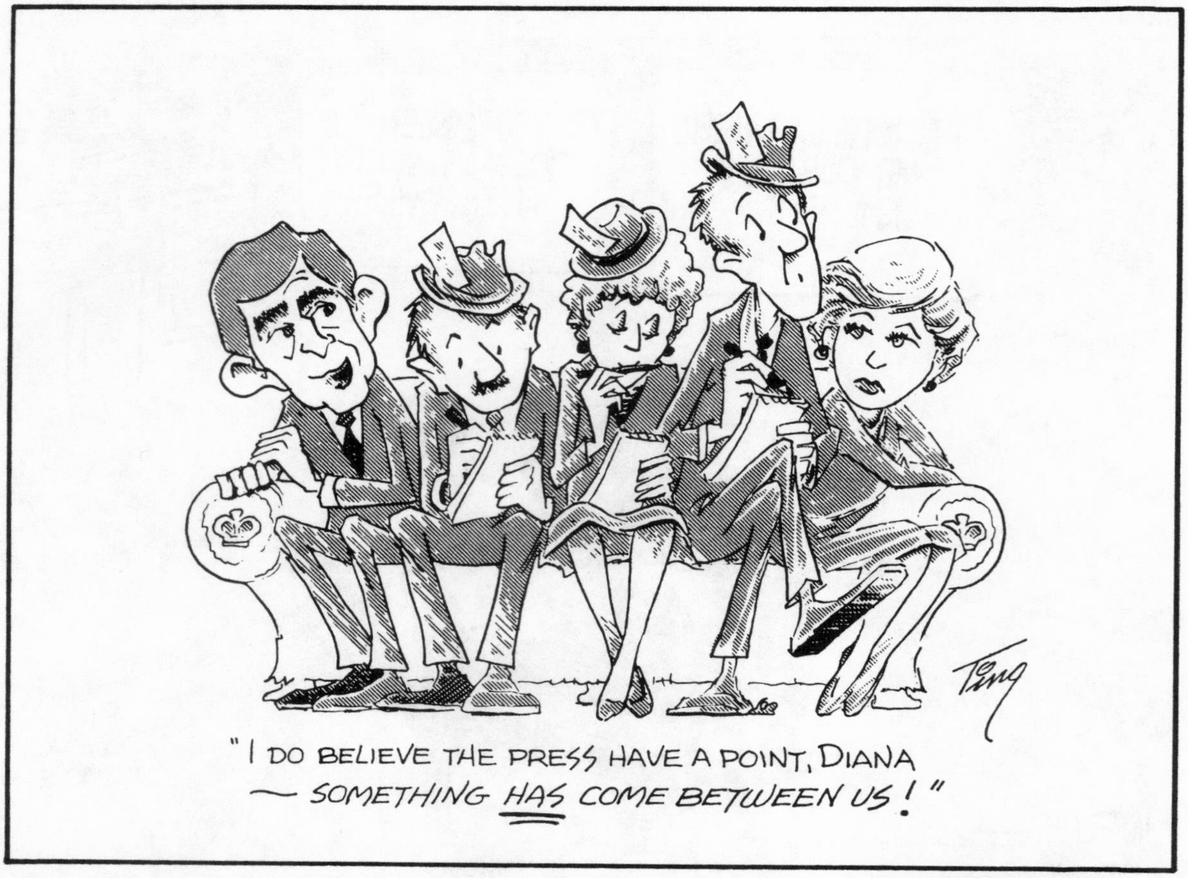
"I DO BELIEVE THE PRESS HAVE A POINT, DIANA
— SOMETHING HAS COME BETWEEN US!"

MERLE R. TINGLEY
Courtesy London Free Press (Ont.)

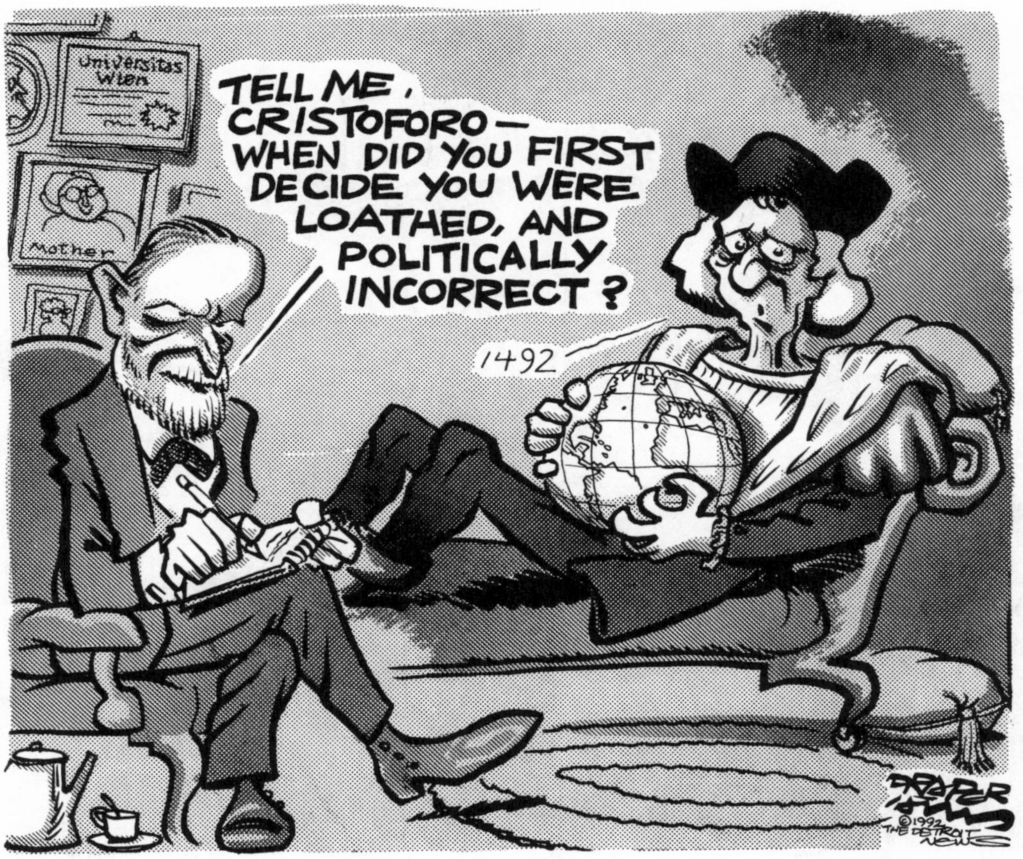
Universitas Wien
Mother
TELL ME, CRISTOFORO— WHEN DID YOU FIRST DECIDE YOU WERE LOATHED, AND POLITICALLY INCORRECT?
1492
DRAPER HILL ©1992 THE DETROIT NEWS

DRAPER HILL
Courtesy Detroit News

DAVID GRANLUND
Courtesy Middlesex News

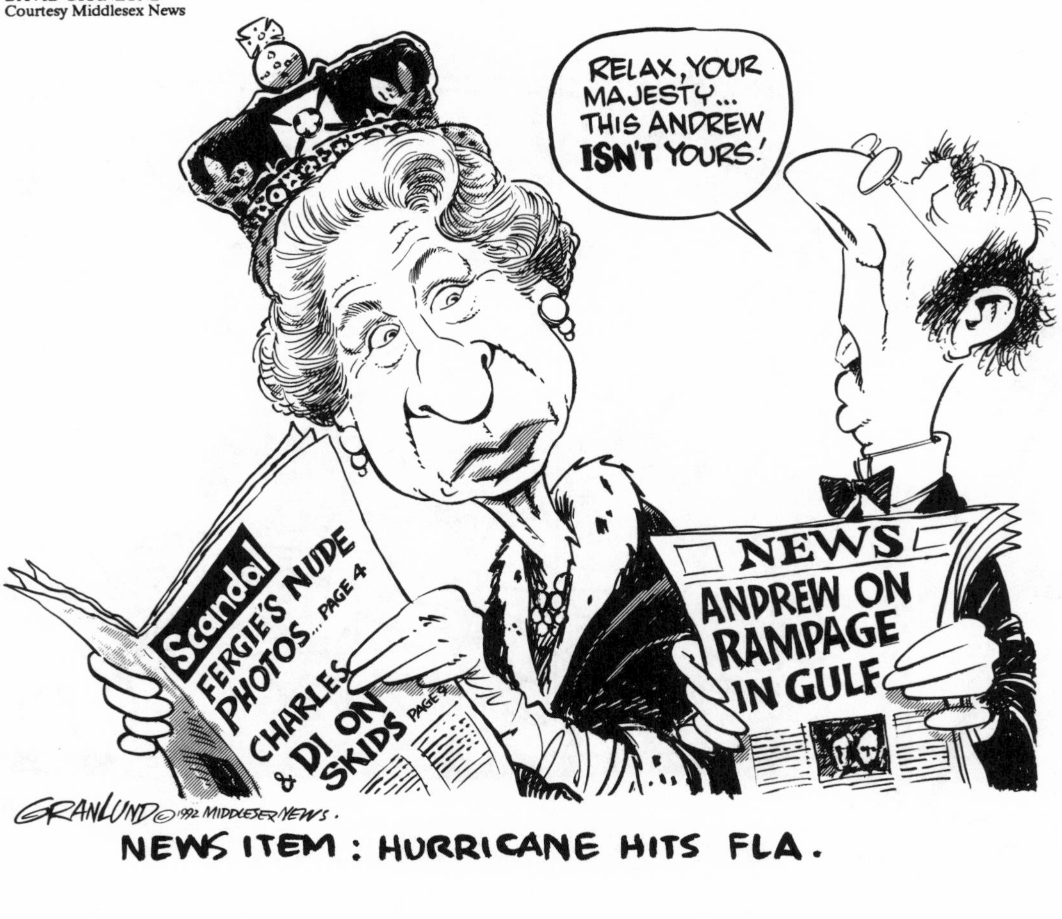
RELAX, YOUR MAJESTY... THIS ANDREW **ISN'T** YOURS!
Scandal
FERGIE'S NUDE PHOTOS... PAGE 4
CHARLES & DI ON SKIDS PAGE 9
NEWS
ANDREW ON RAMPAGE IN GULF
GRANLUND ©1992 MIDDLESEX NEWS.
NEWS ITEM: HURRICANE HITS FLA.

WALT HANDELSMAN
Courtesy Times-Picayune (N.O.)

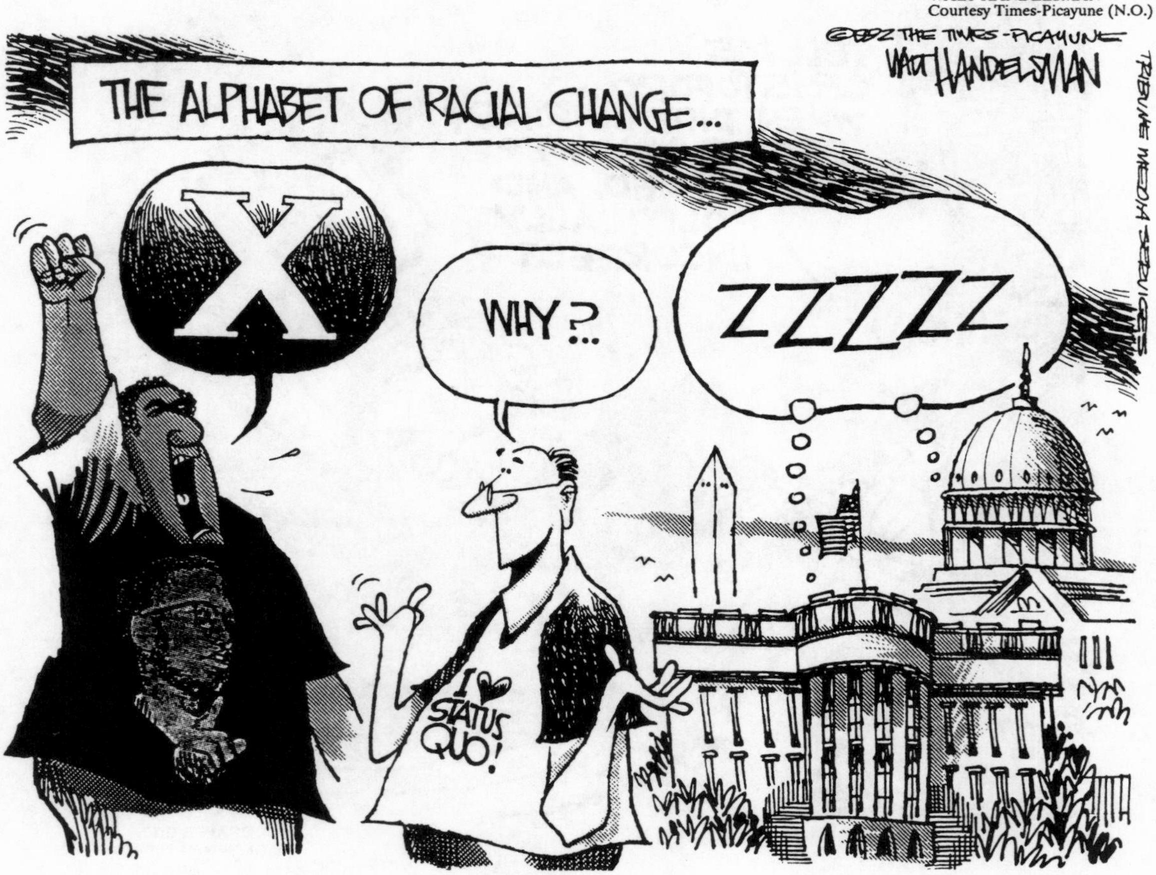
©1992 THE TIMES-PICAYUNE
WALT HANDELSMAN
TRIBUNE MEDIA SERVICES
THE ALPHABET OF RACIAL CHANGE...
X
WHY?...
ZZZZZ
I ♥ STATUS QUO!

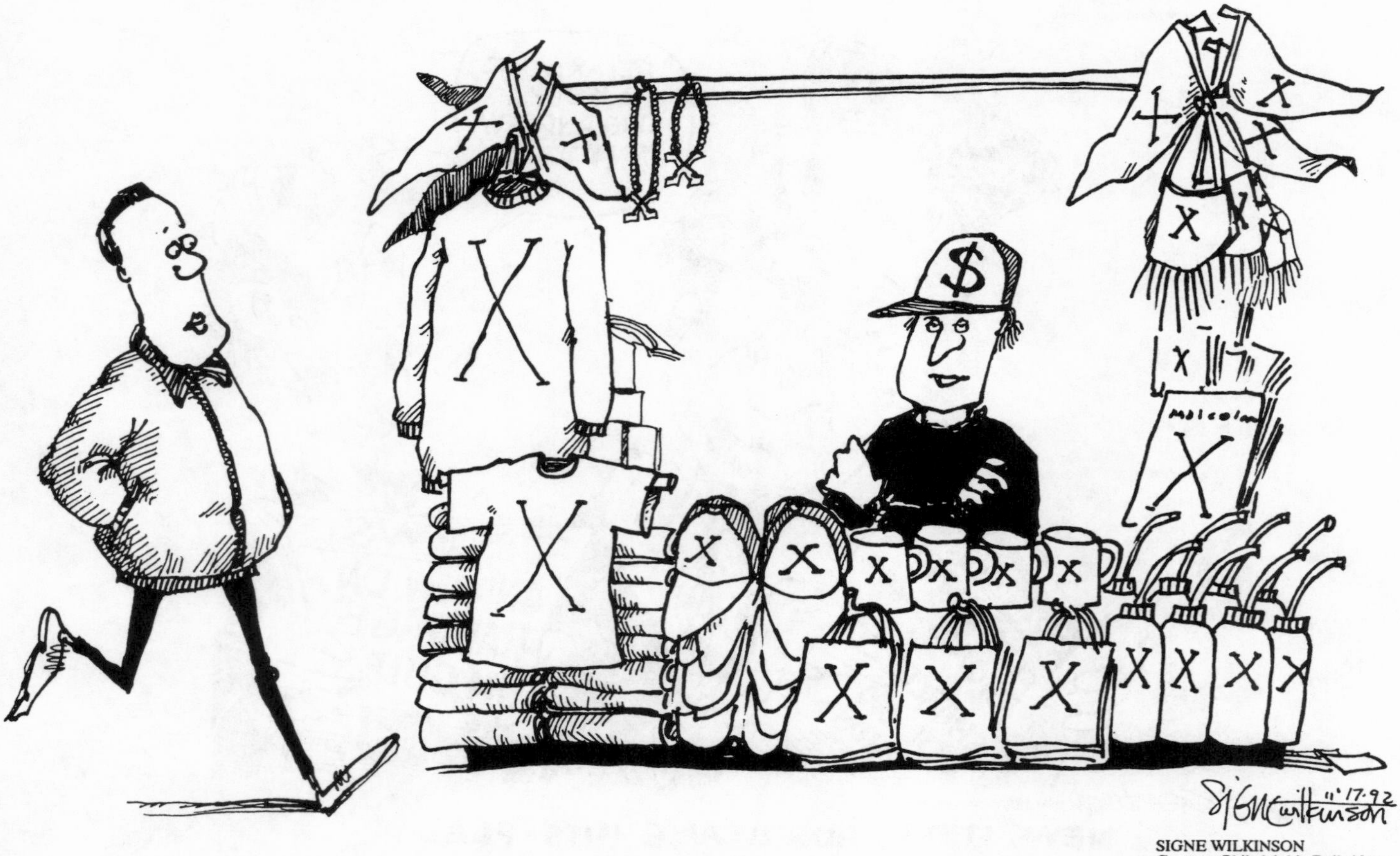
$
X
malcolm X
SIGNE WILKINSON 11·17·92

SIGNE WILKINSON
Courtesy Philadelphia Daily News

Well, It's nice to see things are getting back to normal...
LOANS
BANG! BANG! BANG-BANG! BAM! BAM! POW!
BAR
CRACK
Will work for food
L.A.
For Rent
UNEMPLOYMENT LINE
MIKE LUCKOVICH ATLANTA CONSTITUTION

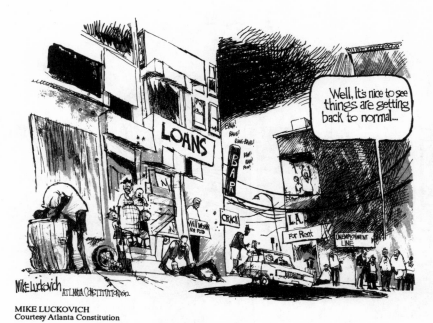

MIKE LUCKOVICH
Courtesy Atlanta Constitution

JEFF KOTERBA
Courtesy Omaha World-Herald

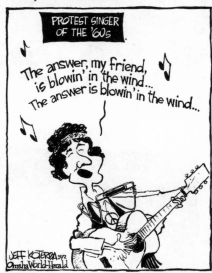

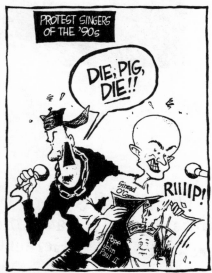

PROTEST SINGER OF THE '60s
The answer, my friend, is blowin' in the wind... The answer is blowin' in the wind...
PROTEST SINGERS OF THE '90s
DIE, PIG, DIE!!
Sinead O'Connor
RIIIIP!
Pope John Paul II
JEFF KOTERBA
Omaha World-Herald
THE TIMES THEY ARE A-CHANGIN'

DICK WRIGHT
Courtesy Providence Journal-Bulletin

WRIGHT PROVIDENCE JOURNAL-BULLETIN 6-92
ME TOLERATE RACISM?!! EVERYBODY KNOWS HOW I DILIGENTLY PREACH LOVE!
I ♥ FARRAKHAN
I ♥ HYMIETOWN
I ♥ SISTER SOULJAH

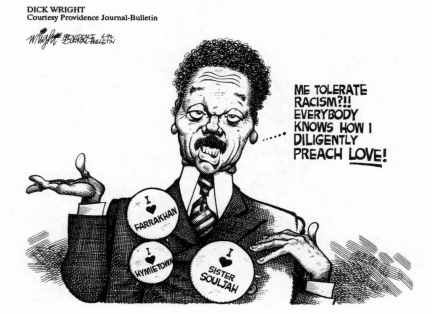

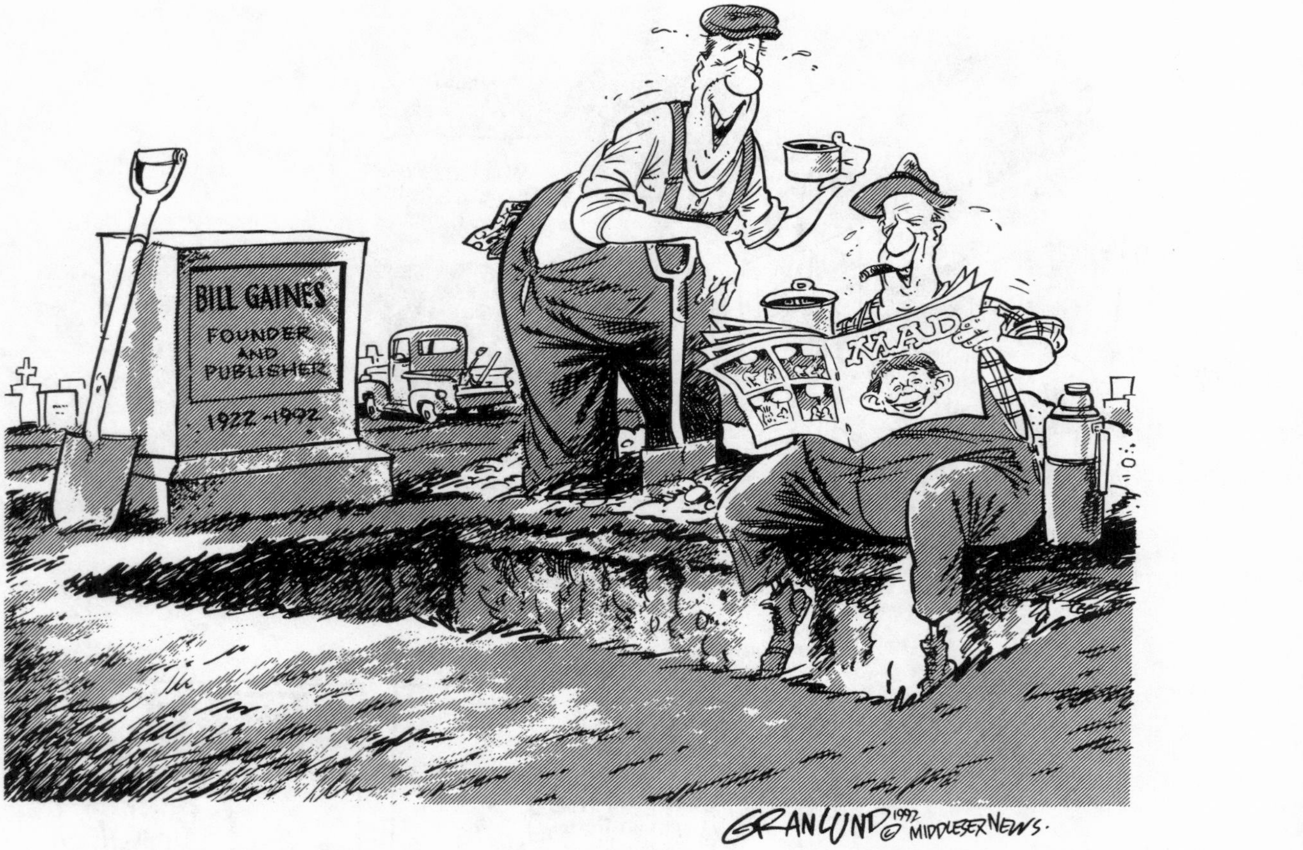
BILL GAINES
FOUNDER AND PUBLISHER
1922–1992
MAD
GRANLUND 1992 © MIDDLESEX NEWS

DAVID GRANLUND
Courtesy Middlesex News

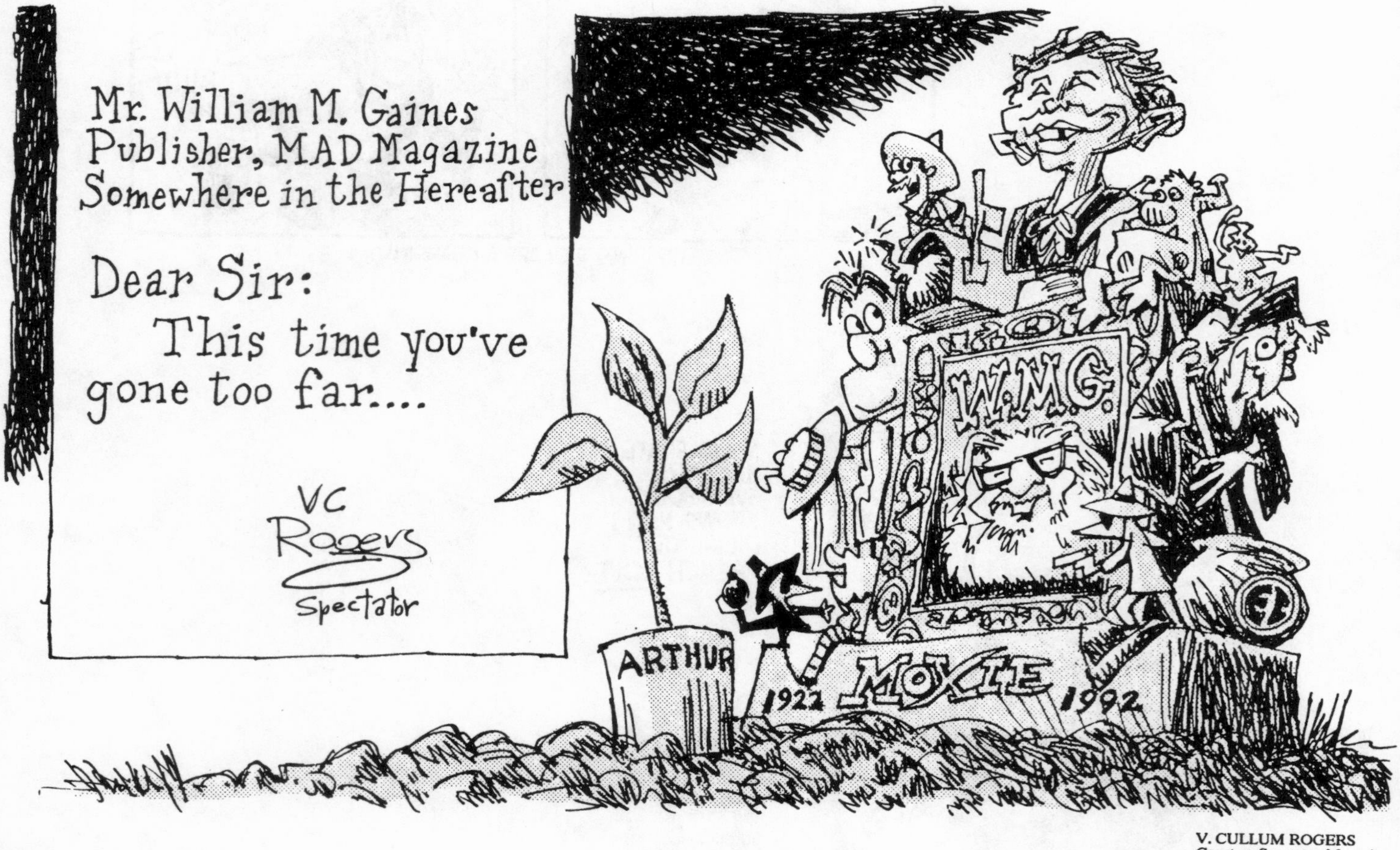
Mr. William M. Gaines
Publisher, MAD Magazine
Somewhere in the Hereafter
Dear Sir:
This time you've gone too far....
VC Rogers
Spectator
W.M.G.
ARTHUR
1922 MOXIE 1992

V. CULLUM ROGERS
Courtesy Spectator Magazine

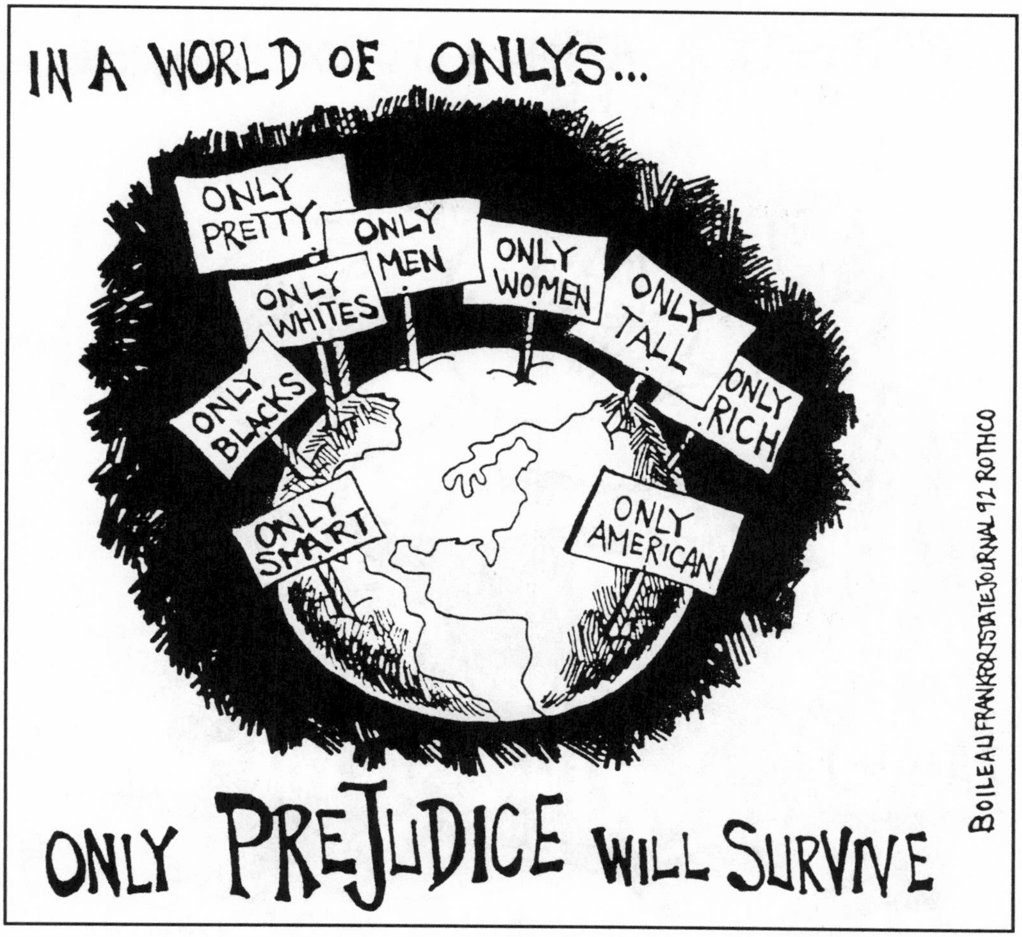
IN A WORLD OF ONLYS...
ONLY PRETTY
ONLY MEN
ONLY WOMEN
ONLY TALL
ONLY WHITES
ONLY BLACKS
ONLY RICH
ONLY SMART
ONLY AMERICAN
ONLY PREJUDICE WILL SURVIVE
BOILEAU FRANKFORT STATE JOURNAL 92 ROTHCO

LINDA BOILEAU
Courtesy Frankfort State Journal

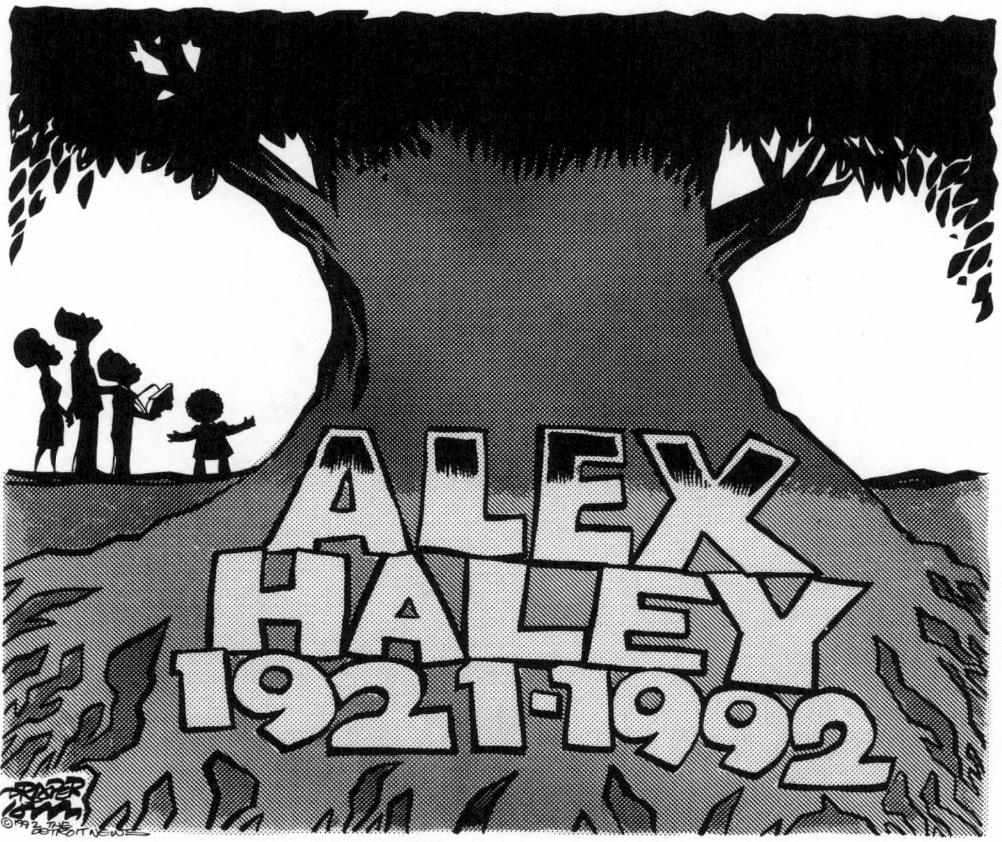
ALEX HALEY 1921-1992
DRAPER HILL

DRAPER HILL
Courtesy Detroit News

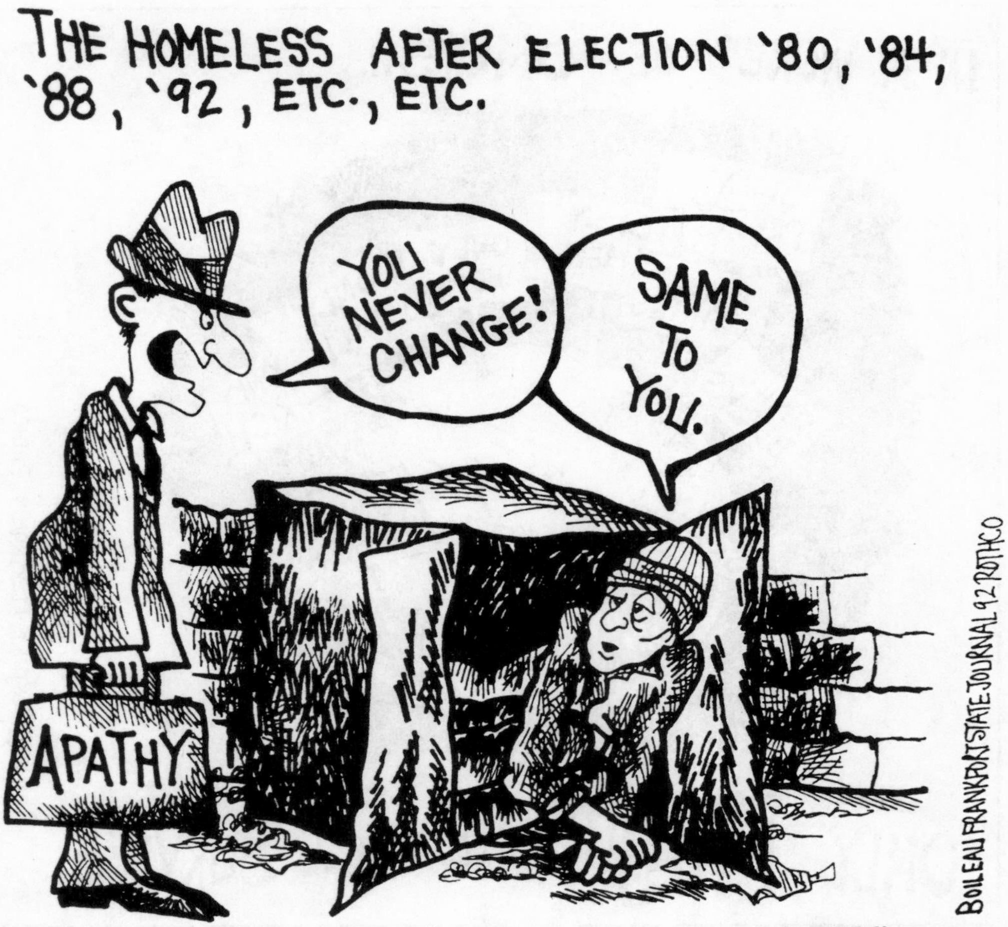
THE HOMELESS AFTER ELECTION '80, '84, '88, '92, ETC., ETC.
YOU NEVER CHANGE!
SAME TO YOU.
APATHY

LINDA BOILEAU
Courtesy Frankfort State Journal

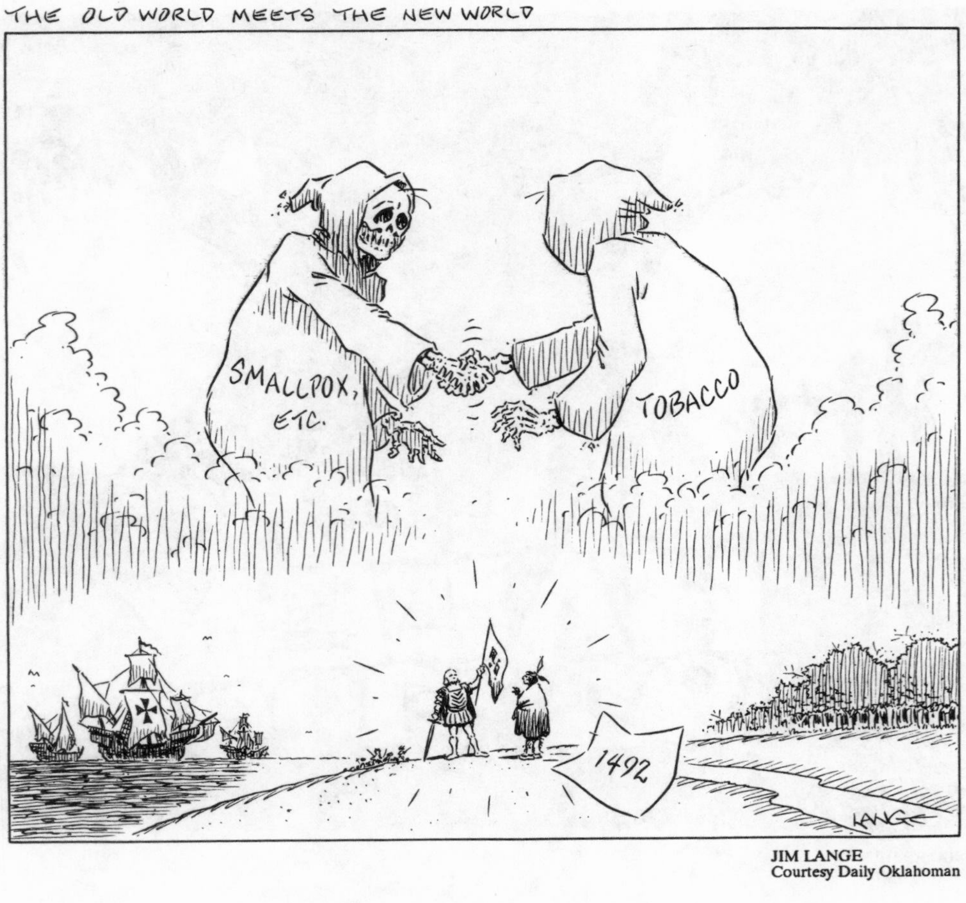
THE OLD WORLD MEETS THE NEW WORLD
SMALLPOX, ETC.
TOBACCO
1492
LANGE

JIM LANGE
Courtesy Daily Oklahoman

MIKE PETERS
Courtesy Dayton Daily News

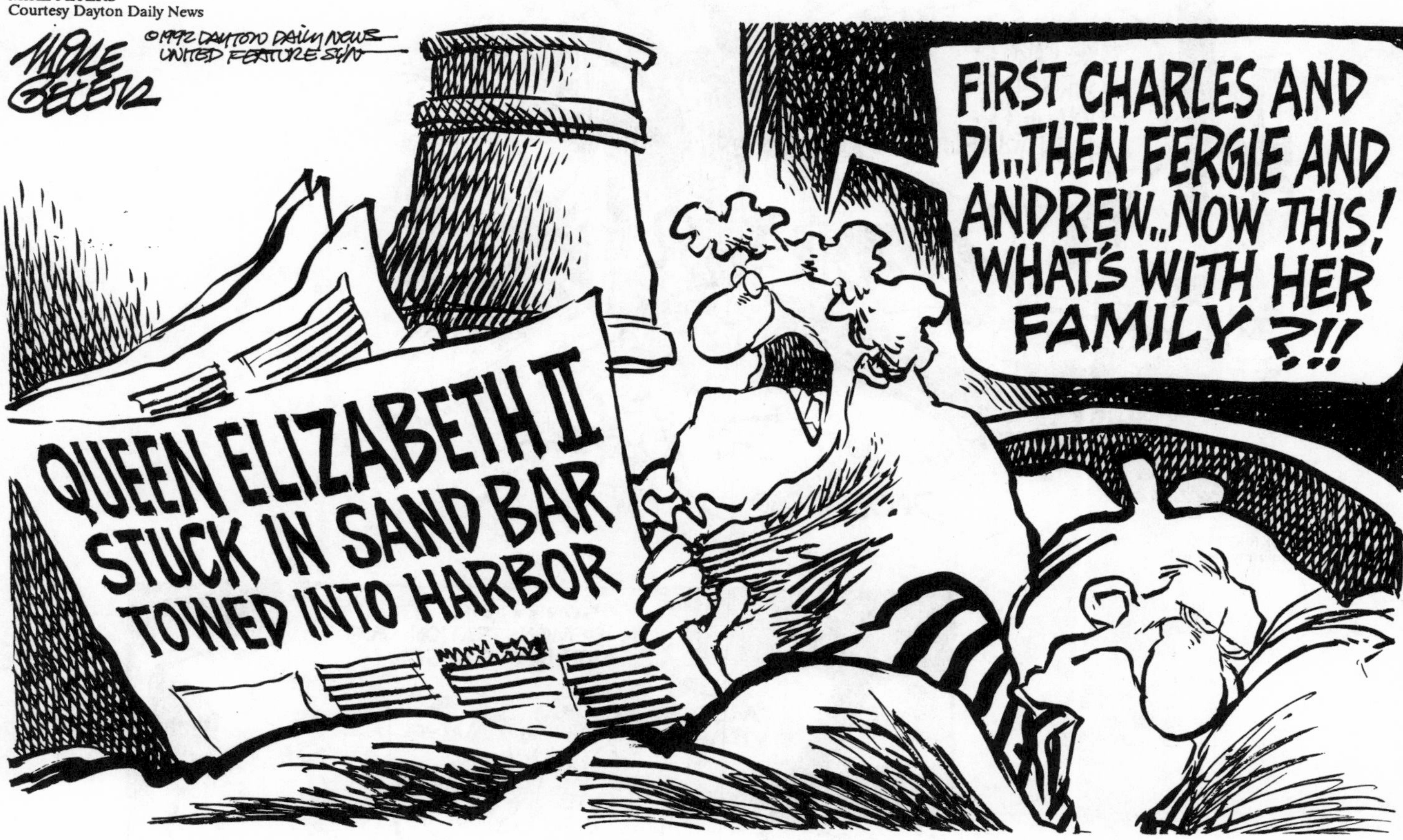
©1992 DAYTON DAILY NEWS UNITED FEATURE SYN
QUEEN ELIZABETH II STUCK IN SAND BAR TOWED INTO HARBOR
FIRST CHARLES AND DI..THEN FERGIE AND ANDREW..NOW THIS! WHAT'S WITH HER FAMILY ?!!

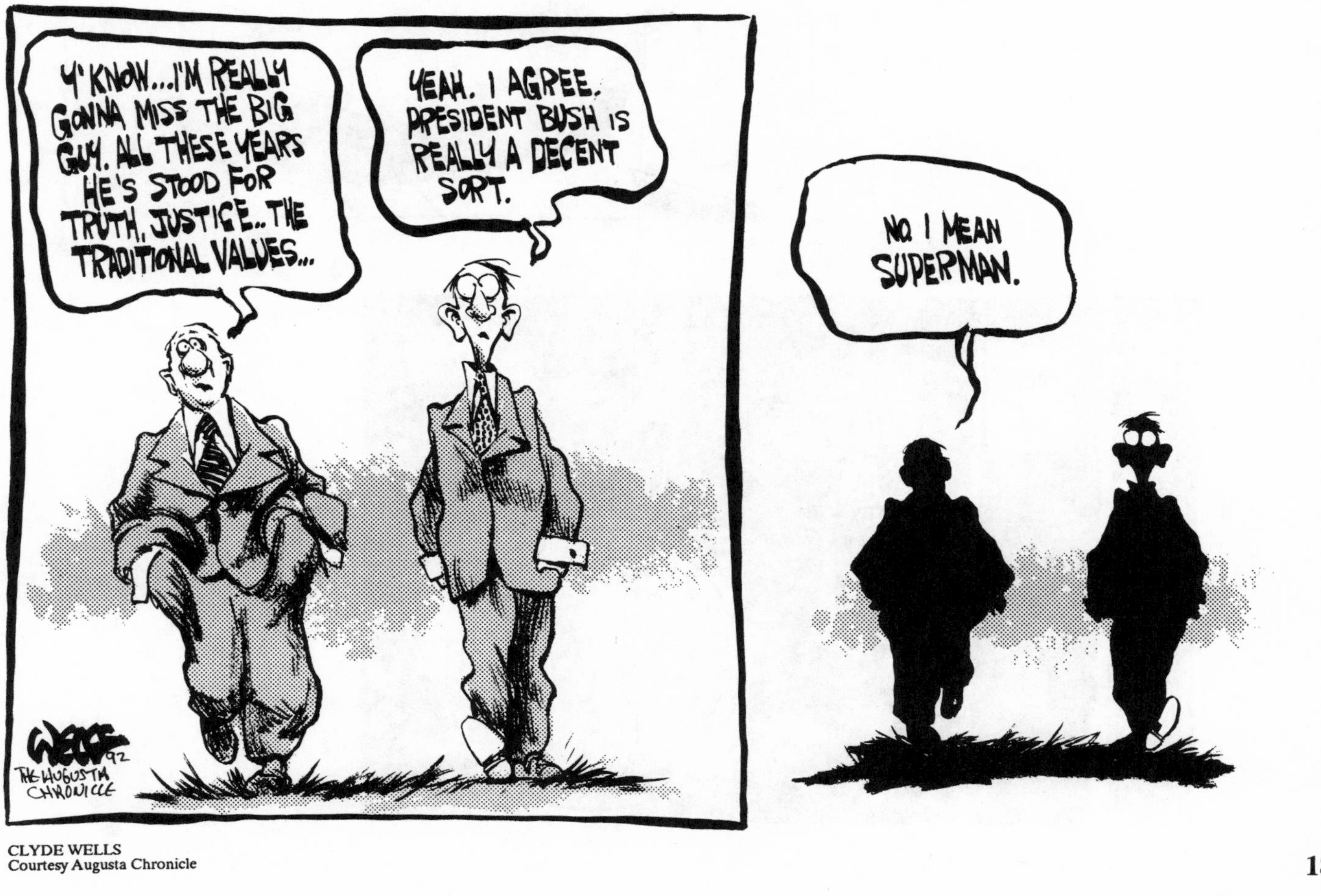
Y' KNOW...I'M REALLY GONNA MISS THE BIG GUY. ALL THESE YEARS HE'S STOOD FOR TRUTH, JUSTICE.. THE TRADITIONAL VALUES...
YEAH. I AGREE. PRESIDENT BUSH IS REALLY A DECENT SORT.
NO. I MEAN SUPERMAN.
'92 THE AUGUSTA CHRONICLE

CLYDE WELLS
Courtesy Augusta Chronicle

TAKE CARE OF YOURSELVES, NOW... I'LL BE IN TOUCH...
CITIES
G.H.W.B.
Mike Keefe '92 THE DENVER POST
DEADBEAT DAD

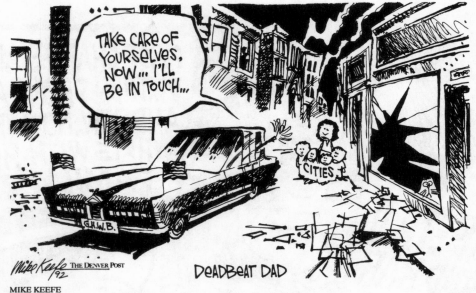

MIKE KEEFE
Courtesy Denver Post

SORRY, SIR. IT'S A DEMONSTRATION FOR JOHNNY CARSON!
FOUR MORE YEARS!
FOUR MORE YEARS
WE ♡ YOU
©lindstrom DULUTH NEWS-TRIBUNE 3-92

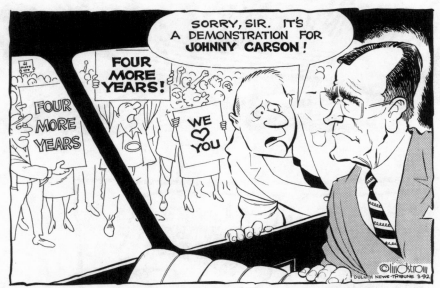

STEVE LINDSTROM
Courtesy Duluth News-Tribune

FOREIGN AID
U.S. TAX PAYERS
Gill Fox
BRIDGEPORT POST

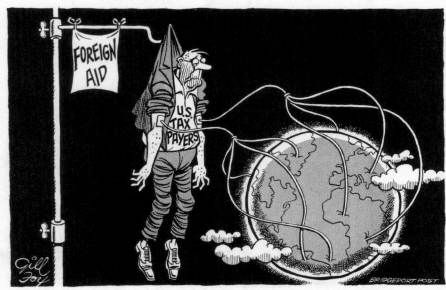

GILL FOX
Courtesy Connecticut Post

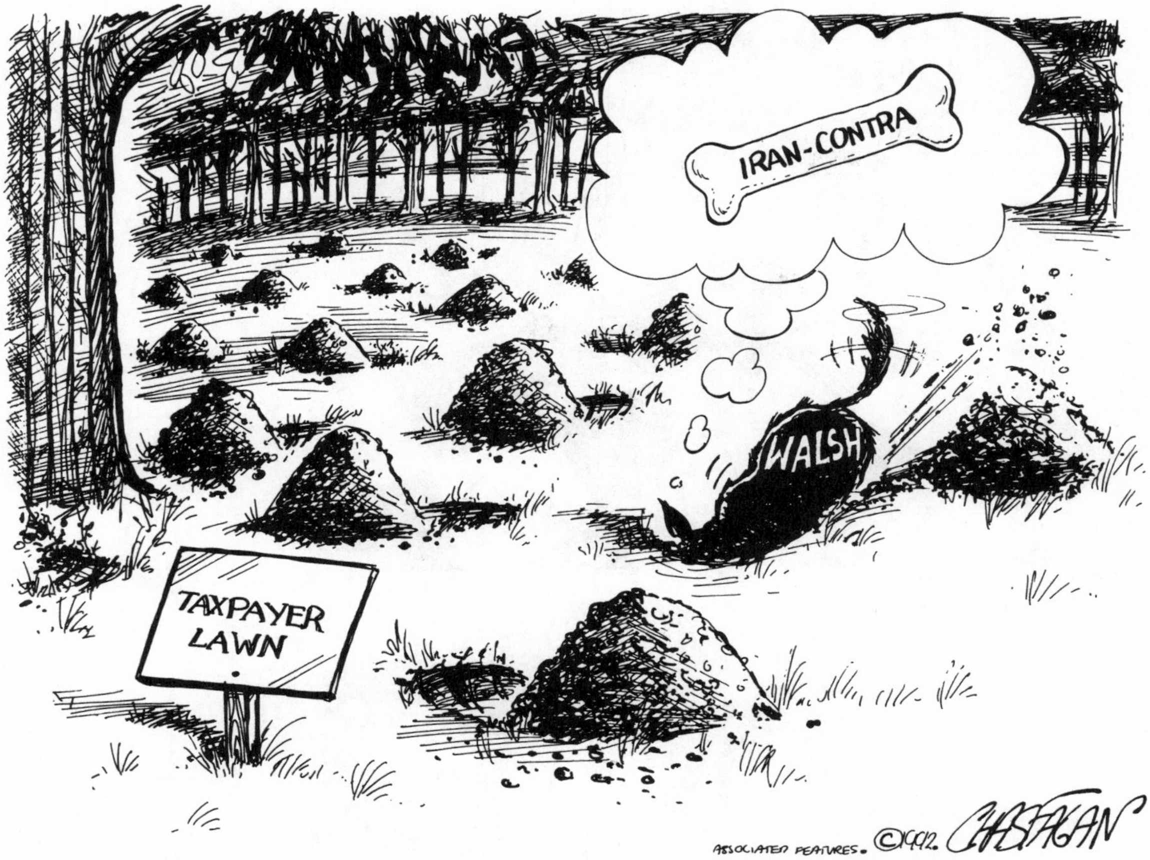

IRAN-CONTRA
WALSH
TAXPAYER LAWN
ASSOCIATED FEATURES. ©1992. CHAS FAGAN

CHARLES FAGAN
Courtesy Associated Features Syndicate

GLEN FODEN
Courtesy Patuxent Pub. Co.

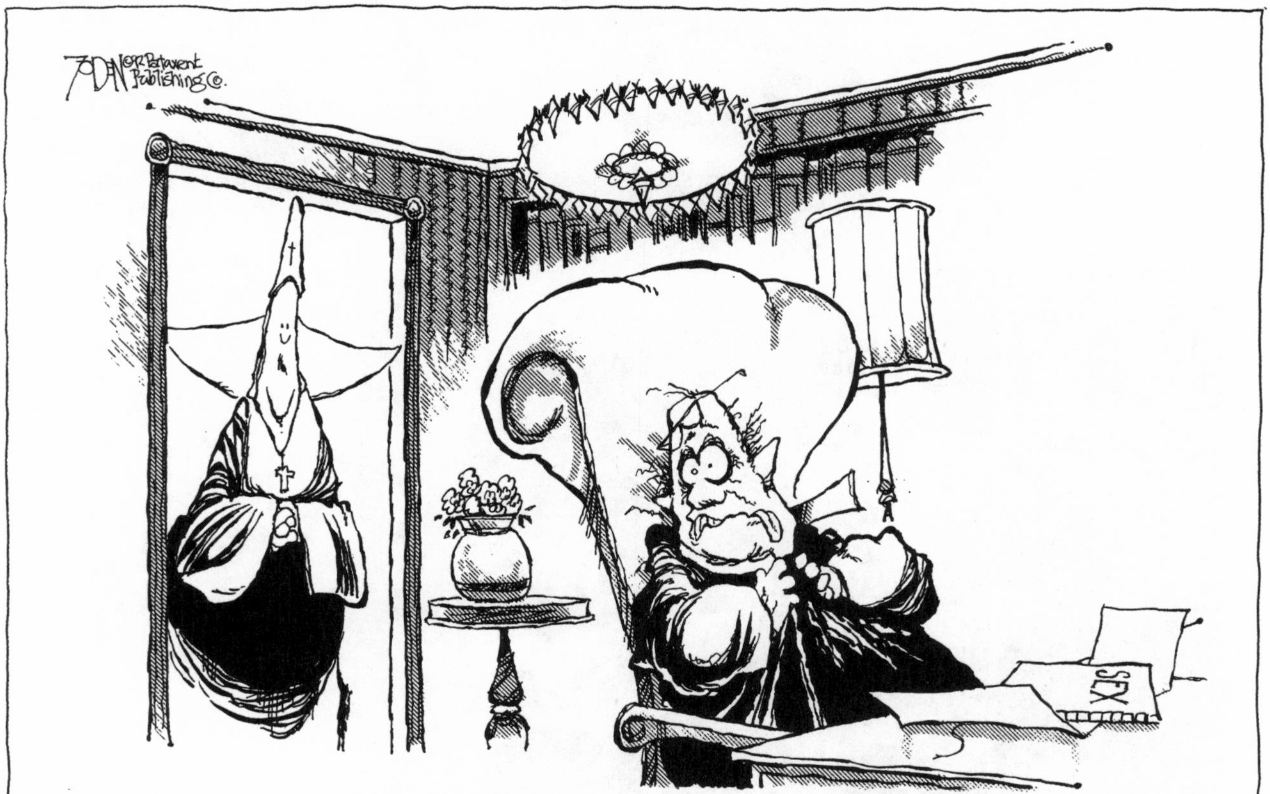

SEX
Father. The reference library called. The book they sent you was on the wrong Madonna... Father?

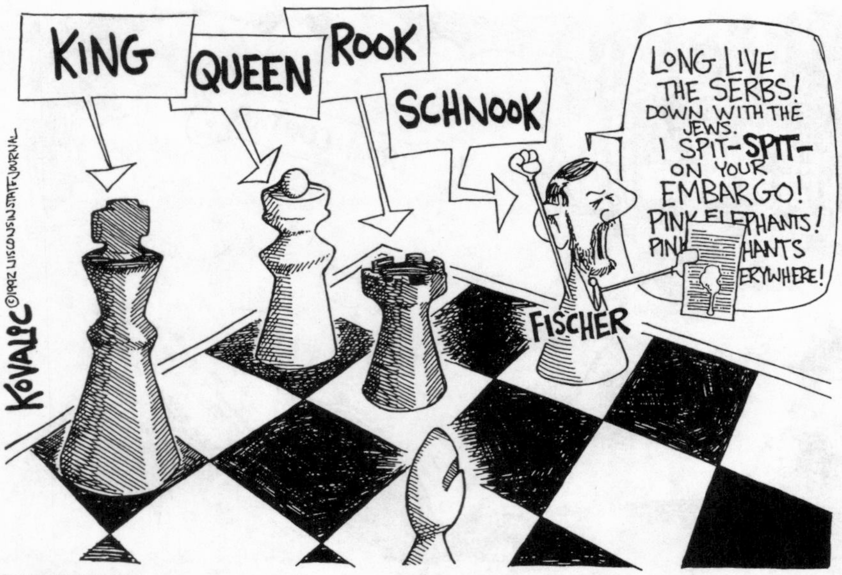
KING
QUEEN
ROOK
SCHNOOK
LONG LIVE THE SERBS! DOWN WITH THE JEWS. I SPIT-SPIT- ON YOUR EMBARGO! PINK ELEPHANTS! PINK ELEPHANTS EVERYWHERE!
FISCHER
KOVALIC ©1992 WISCONSIN STATE JOURNAL

JOHN KOVALIC
Courtesy Wisconsin State Journal

DOUG MACGREGOR
Courtesy Fort Myers News-Press

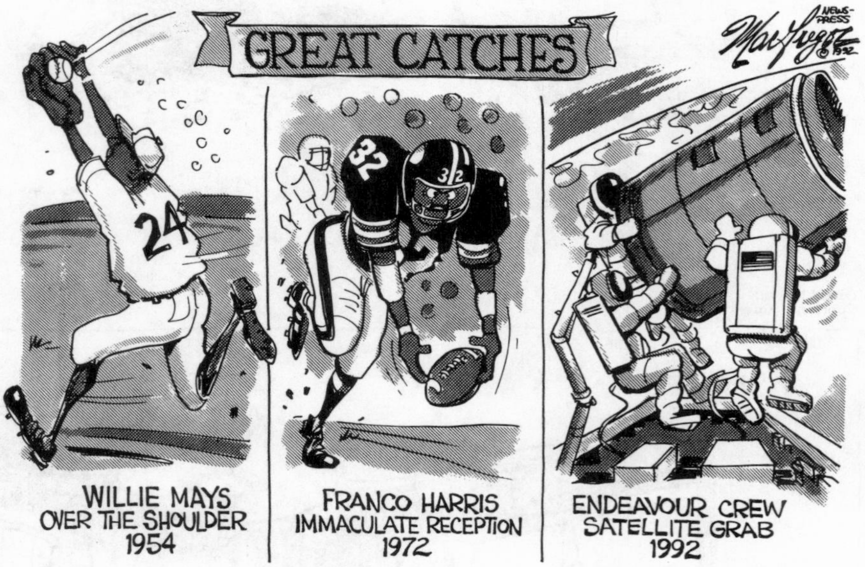
GREAT CATCHES
24
32
WILLIE MAYS
OVER THE SHOULDER
1954
FRANCO HARRIS
IMMACULATE RECEPTION
1972
ENDEAVOUR CREW
SATELLITE GRAB
1992

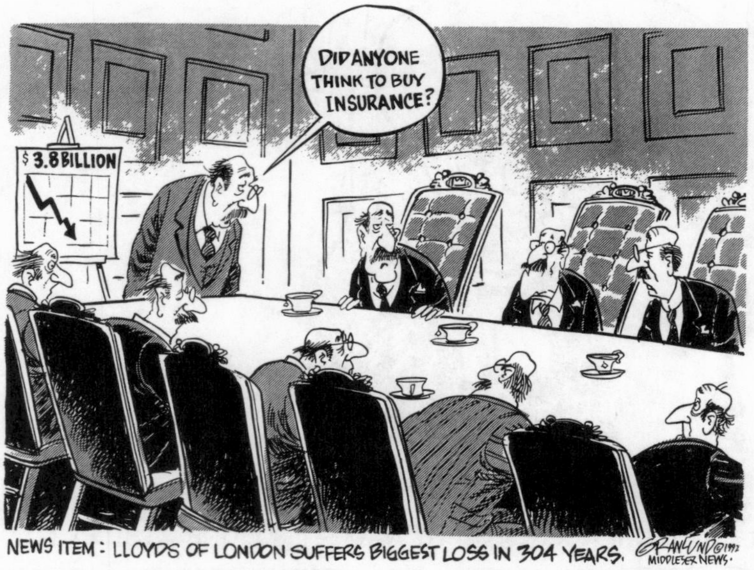
DID ANYONE THINK TO BUY INSURANCE?
$ 3.8 BILLION
NEWS ITEM: LLOYDS OF LONDON SUFFERS BIGGEST LOSS IN 304 YEARS.
GRANLUND ©1992 MIDDLESEX NEWS

DAVID GRANLUND
Courtesy Middlesex News

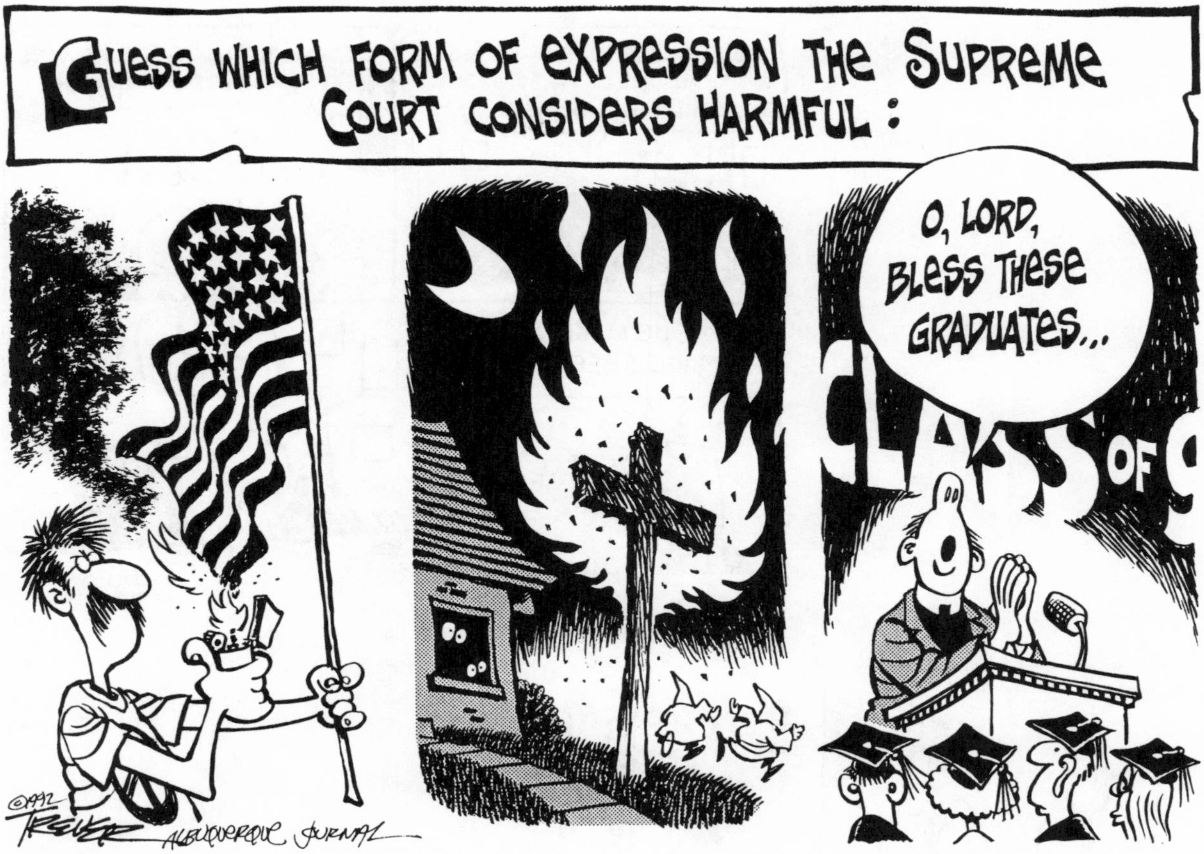
GUESS WHICH FORM OF EXPRESSION THE SUPREME COURT CONSIDERS HARMFUL:
O, LORD, BLESS THESE GRADUATES...
©1992 TREVER ALBUQUERQUE JOURNAL

JOHN TREVER
Courtesy Albuquerque Journal

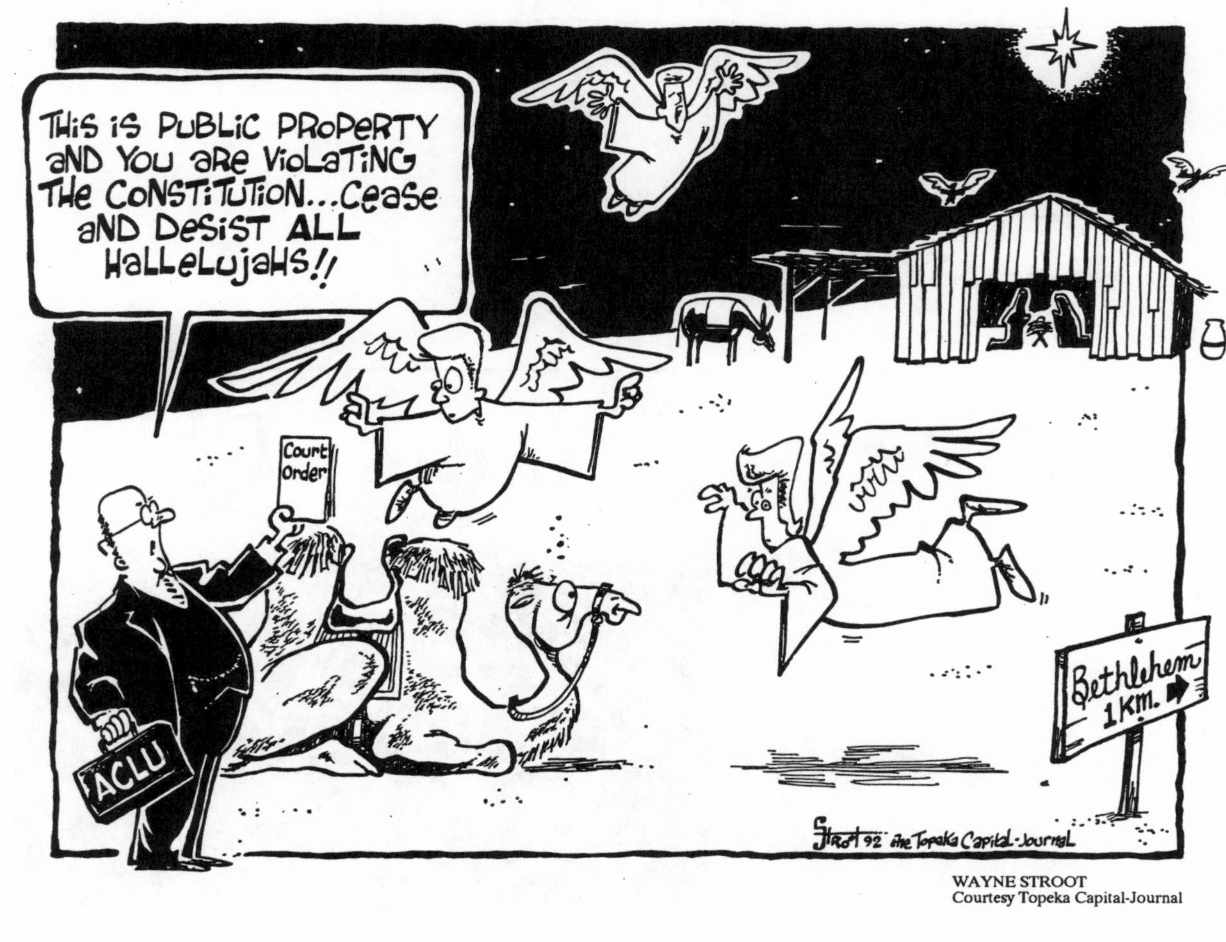
THIS IS PUBLIC PROPERTY AND YOU ARE VIOLATING THE CONSTITUTION...CEASE AND DESIST ALL HALLELUJAHS!!
Court Order
ACLU
Bethlehem 1 Km.
Stroot '92 the Topeka Capital-Journal

WAYNE STROOT
Courtesy Topeka Capital-Journal

THE JAPANESE PRIME MINISTER SAYS AMERICANS ARE LOSING THE DESIRE TO CREATE THINGS OF VALUE!
HE SEEMS TO THINK THE U.S. PRODUCES TOO FEW ENGINEERS AND TOO MANY LAWYERS!
HMPH! HE'LL BE SORRY HE MADE THOSE REMARKS!
YEAH!
WE'LL SUE!

PETER B. WALLACE
Courtesy Boston Herald

GLENN MCCOY
Courtesy Belleville News-Democrat (Ill.)

Belleville News-Democrat
BUS STOP
ACHOO!
GOD BLESS YOU.
SUPREME COURT
WAM

PAUL SZEP
Courtesy Boston Globe

THE BOSTON GLOBE
SZEP
PROCREATION
SCIENTIFIC PANELS WARNS 'WORLD POPULATION GROWING AT RATE OF 100 MILLION A YEAR

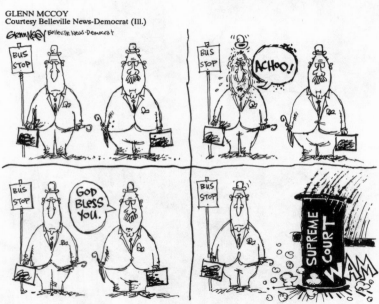

Past Award Winners

NATIONAL SOCIETY OF PROFESSIONAL JOURNALISTS AWARD
(Sigma Delta Chi Award)

1942 – Jacob Burck, Chicago Times
1943 – Charles Werner, Chicago Sun
1944 – Henry Barrow, Associated Press
1945 – Reuben L. Goldberg, New York Sun
1946 – Dorman H. Smith, NEA
1947 – Bruce Russell, Los Angeles Times
1948 – Herbert Block, Washington Post
1949 – Herbert Block, Washington Post
1950 – Bruce Russell, Los Angeles Times
1951 – Herbert Block, Washington Post, and
      Bruce Russell, Los Angeles Times
1952 – Cecil Jensen, Chicago Daily News
1953 – John Fischetti, NEA
1954 – Calvin Alley, Memphis Commercial Appeal
1955 – John Fischetti, NEA
1956 – Herbert Block, Washington Post
1957 – Scott Long, Minneapolis Tribune
1958 – Clifford H. Baldowski, Atlanta Constitution
1959 – Charles G. Brooks, Birmingham News
1960 – Dan Dowling, New York Herald-Tribune
1961 – Frank Interlandi, Des Moines Register
1962 – Paul Conrad, Denver Post
1963 – William Mauldin, Chicago Sun-Times
1964 – Charles Bissell, Nashville Tennessean
1965 – Roy Justus, Minneapolis Star
1966 – Patrick Oliphant, Denver Post
1967 – Eugene Payne, Charlotte Observer
1968 – Paul Conrad, Los Angeles Times
1969 – William Mauldin, Chicago Sun-Times
1970 – Paul Conrad, Los Angeles Times
1971 – Hugh Haynie, Louisville Courier-Journal
1972 – William Mauldin, Chicago Sun-Times
1973 – Paul Szep, Boston Globe
1974 – Mike Peters, Dayton Daily News
1975 – Tony Auth, Philadelphia Enquirer
1976 – Paul Szep, Boston Globe
1977 – Don Wright, Miami News
1978 – Jim Borgman, Cincinnati Enquirer
1979 – John P. Trever, Albuquerque Journal
1980 – Paul Conrad, Los Angeles Times
1981 – Paul Conrad, Los Angeles Times
1982 – Dick Locher, Chicago Tribune
1983 – Rob Lawlor, Philadelphia Daily News
1984 – Mike Lane, Baltimore Evening Sun
1985 – Doug Marlette, Charlotte Observer
1986 – Mike Keefe, Denver Post
1987 – Paul Conrad, Los Angeles Times
1988 – Jack Higgins, Chicago Sun-Times
1989 – Don Wright, Palm Beach Post
1990 – Jeff MacNelly, Chicago Tribune
1991 – Walt Handelsman, Times-Picayune

NATIONAL HEADLINERS CLUB AWARD

1938 – C. D. Batchelor, New York Daily News
1939 – John Knott, Dallas News
1940 – Herbert Block, NEA
1941 – Charles H. Sykes, Philadelphia Evening Ledger
1942 – Jerry Doyle, Philadelphia Record
1943 – Vaughn Shoemaker, Chicago Daily News
1944 – Roy Justus, Sioux City Journal
1945 – F. O. Alexander, Philadelphia Bulletin
1946 – Hank Barrow, Associated Press
1947 – Cy Hungerford, Pittsburgh Post-Gazette
1948 – Tom Little, Nashville Tennessean
1949 – Bruce Russell, Los Angeles Times
1950 – Dorman Smith, NEA
1951 – C. G. Werner, Indianapolis Star
1952 – John Fischetti, NEA
1953 – James T. Berryman and
      Gib Crocket, Washington Star
1954 – Scott Long, Minneapolis Tribune
1955 – Leo Thiele, Los Angeles Mirror-News
1956 – John Milt Morris, Associated Press
1957 – Frank Miller, Des Moines Register
1958 – Burris Jenkins, Jr., New York Journal-American
1959 – Karl Hubenthal, Los Angeles Examiner
1960 – Don Hesse, St. Louis Globe-Democrat
1961 – L. D. Warren, Cincinnati Enquirer
1962 – Franklin Morse, Los Angeles Mirror
1963 – Charles Bissell, Nashville Tennessean
1964 – Lou Grant, Oakland Tribune
1965 – Merle R. Tingley, London (Ont.) Free Press
1966 – Hugh Haynie, Louisville Courier-Journal
1967 – Jim Berry, NEA
1968 – Warren King, New York News
1969 – Larry Barton, Toledo Blade
1970 – Bill Crawford, NEA
1971 – Ray Osrin, Cleveland Plain Dealer
1972 – Jacob Burck, Chicago Sun-Times
1973 – Ranan Lurie, New York Times
1974 – Tom Darcy, Newsday
1975 – Bill Sanders, Milwaukee Journal
1976 – No award given
1977 – Paul Szep, Boston Globe
1978 – Dwane Powell, Raleigh News and Observer
1979 – Pat Oliphant, Washington Star
1980 – Don Wright, Miami News
1981 – Bill Garner, Memphis Commercial Appeal
1982 – Mike Peters, Dayton Daily News
1983 – Doug Marlette, Charlotte Observer
1984 – Steve Benson, Arizona Republic
1985 – Bill Day, Detroit Free Press
1986 – Mike Keefe, Denver Post
1987 – Mike Peters, Dayton Daily News
1988 – Doug Marlette, Charlotte Observer
1989 – Walt Handelsman, Scranton Times
1990 – Robert Ariail, The State
1991 – Jim Borgman, Cincinnati Enquirer
1992 – Mike Luckovich, Atlanta Constitution

PULITZER PRIZE

1922 – Rollin Kirby, New York World
1923 – No award given
1924 – J. N. Darling, New York Herald Tribune
1925 – Rollin Kirby, New York World
1926 – D. R. Fitzpatrick, St. Louis Post-Dispatch
1927 – Nelson Harding, Brooklyn Eagle
1928 – Nelson Harding, Brooklyn Eagle
1929 – Rollin Kirby, New York World
1930 – Charles Macauley, Brooklyn Eagle
1931 – Edmund Duffy, Baltimore Sun
1932 – John T. McCutcheon, Chicago Tribune
1933 – H. M. Talburt, Washington Daily News
1934 – Edmund Duffy, Baltimore Sun
1935 – Ross A. Lewis, Milwaukee Journal
1936 – No award given
1937 – C. D. Batchelor, New York Daily News
1938 – Vaughn Shoemaker, Chicago Daily News
1939 – Charles G. Werner, Daily Oklahoman
1940 – Edmund Duffy, Baltimore Sun
1941 – Jacob Burck, Chicago Times
1942 – Herbert L. Block, NEA
1943 – Jay N. Darling, New York Herald Tribune
1944 – Clifford K. Berryman, Washington Star
1945 – Bill Mauldin, United Features Syndicate
1946 – Bruce Russell, Los Angeles Times
1947 – Vaughn Shoemaker, Chicago Daily News
1948 – Reuben L. ("Rube") Goldberg, New York Sun
1949 – Lute Pease, Newark Evening News
1950 – James T. Berryman, Washington Star
1951 – Reginald W. Manning, Arizona Republic
1952 – Fred L. Packer, New York Mirror
1953 – Edward D. Kuekes, Cleveland Plain Dealer
1954 – Herbert L. Block, Washington Post
1955 – Daniel R. Fitzpatrick, St. Louis Post-Dispatch
1956 – Robert York, Louisville Times
1957 – Tom Little, Nashville Tennessean
1958 – Bruce M. Shanks, Buffalo Evening News
1959 – Bill Mauldin, St. Louis Post-Dispatch
1960 – No award given
1961 – Carey Orr, Chicago Tribune
1962 – Edmund S. Valtman, Hartford Times
1963 – Frank Miller, Des Moines Register
1964 – Paul Conrad, Denver Post
1965 – No award given
1966 – Don Wright, Miami News
1967 – Patrick B. Oliphant, Denver Post
1968 – Eugene Gray Payne, Charlotte Observer
1969 – John Fischetti, Chicago Daily News
1970 – Thomas F. Darcy, Newsday
1971 – Paul Conrad, Los Angeles Times
1972 – Jeffrey K. MacNelly, Richmond News Leader
1973 – No award given
1974 – Paul Szep, Boston Globe
1975 – Garry Trudeau, Universal Press Syndicate
1976 – Tony Auth, Philadelphia Enquirer
1977 – Paul Szep, Boston Globe
1978 – Jeff MacNelly, Richmond News Leader
1979 – Herbert Block, Washington Post
1980 – Don Wright, Miami News
1981 – Mike Peters, Dayton Daily News
1982 – Ben Sargent, Austin American-Statesman
1983 – Dick Locher, Chicago Tribune
1984 – Paul Conrad, Los Angeles Times
1985 – Jeff MacNelly, Chicago Tribune
1986 – Jules Feiffer, Universal Press Syndicate
1987 – Berke Breathed, Washington Post Writers Group
1988 – Doug Marlette, Atlanta Constitution
1989 – Jack Higgins, Chicago Sun-Times
1990 – Tom Toles, Buffalo News
1991 – Jim Borgman, Cincinnati Enquirer
1992 – Signe Wilkinson, Philadelphia Daily News

NATIONAL NEWSPAPER AWARD / CANADA

1949 – Jack Boothe, Toronto Globe and Mail
1950 – James G. Reidford, Montreal Star
1951 – Len Norris, Vancouver Sun
1952 – Robert La Palme, Le Devoir, Montreal
1953 – Robert W. Chambers, Halifax Chronicle-Herald
1954 – John Collins, Montreal Gazette
1955 – Merle R. Tingley, London Free Press
1956 – James G. Reidford, Toronto Globe and Mail
1957 – James G. Reidford, Toronto Globe and Mail
1958 – Raoul Hunter, Le Soleil, Quebec
1959 – Duncan Macpherson, Toronto Star
1960 – Duncan Macpherson, Toronto Star
1961 – Ed McNally, Montreal Star
1962 – Duncan Macpherson, Toronto Star
1963 – Jan Kamienski, Winnipeg Tribune
1964 – Ed McNally, Montreal Star
1965 – Duncan Macpherson, Toronto Star
1966 – Robert W. Chambers, Halifax Chronicle-Herald
1967 – Raoul Hunter, Le Soleil, Quebec
1968 – Roy Peterson, Vancouver Sun
1969 – Edward Uluschak, Edmonton Journal
1970 – Duncan Macpherson, Toronto Daily Star
1971 – Yardley Jones, Toronto Star
1972 – Duncan Macpherson, Toronto Star
1973 – John Collins, Montreal Gazette
1974 – Blaine, Hamilton Spectator
1975 – Roy Peterson, Vancouver Sun
1976 – Andy Donato, Toronto Sun
1977 – Terry Mosher, Montreal Gazette
1978 – Terry Mosher, Montreal Gazette
1979 – Edd Uluschak, Edmonton Journal
1980 – Vic Roschkov, Toronto Star
1981 – Tom Innes, Calgary Herald
1982 – Blaine, Hamilton Spectator
1983 – Dale Cummings, Winnipeg Free Press
1984 – Roy Peterson, Vancouver Sun
1985 – Ed Franklin, Toronto Globe and Mail
1986 – Brian Gable, Regina Leader Post
1987 – Raffi Anderian, Ottawa Citizen
1988 – Vance Rodewalt, Calgary Herald
1989 – Cameron Cardow, Regina Leader-Post
1990 – Roy Peterson, Vancouver Sun
1991 – Guy Badeaux, Le Droit, Ottawa

FISCHETTI AWARD

1982 – Lee Judge, Kansas City Times
1983 – Bill DeOre, Dallas Morning News
1984 – Tom Toles, Buffalo News
1985 – Scott Willis, Dallas Times-Herald
1986 – Doug Marlette, Charlotte Observer
1987 – Dick Locher, Chicago Tribune
1988 – Arthur Bok, Akron Beacon-Journal
1989 – Lambert Der, Greenville News
1990 – Jeff Stahler, Cincinnati Post
1991 – Mike Keefe, Denver Post
1992 – Doug Marlette, New York Newsday

Index

INDEX